Recognition of Commercial Judgments and Awards in the Commonwealth

Commonwealth Law Series

General Editor: Sir William Dale, KCMG, Hon LLD

This volume is one of a series of books published, or to be published, by Butterworths devoted to Commonwealth Law. The titles in the series are intended to serve the needs of law officers and legal practitioners, as well as academic lawyers throughout the Commonwealth. The volumes so far published are as follows:

The Modern Commonwealth by Sir William Dale, KCMG, Hon LLD, Barrister, formerly Legal Adviser to the Commonwealth Office

Recognition of Family Judgments in the Commonwealth by J. D. McClean, BCL, MA, Barrister, Professor of Law, University of Sheffield

Recognition of Commercial Judgments and Awards in the Commonwealth by Keith W. Patchett, LLM, Professor of Law, University of Wales Institute of Science and Technology

England — Butterworth & Co (Publishers) Ltd, 88 Kingsway, **London** WC2B 6AB

Australia — Butterworths Pty Ltd, **Sydney, Melbourne, Brisbane, Adelaide, Perth, Canberra** and **Hobart**

Canada — Butterworth & Co (Canada) Ltd, **Toronto** and **Vancouver**

New Zealand — Butterworths of New Zealand Ltd, **Wellington** and **Auckland**

Singapore — Butterworth & Co (Asia) Pte Ltd, **Singapore**

South Africa — Butterworth Publishers (Pty) Ltd, **Durban** and **Pretoria**

USA — Butterworths Legal Publishers, **St Paul**, Minnesota, **Seattle**, Washington, **Boston**, Massachusetts, **Austin**, Texas
and D & S Publishers, **Clearwater**, Florida

British Library Cataloguing in Publication Data

Patchett, K. W.
Recognition of commercial judgments and awards in the Commonwealth.—(Commonwealth law series, ISSN 0264-8288;3)
1. Commercial law—Commonwealth of Nations
2. International law3. Commonwealth of Nations—Commerce
I. Title
341.7'54[LAW]

ISBN 0 406 40320 1

Printed by Thomson Litho Ltd, East Kilbride, Scotland

Recognition of Commercial Judgments and Awards in the Commonwealth

K. W. Patchett
Professor of Law, University of Wales, UWIST

London
Butterworths
1984

For A. P. and M. T. P-J.

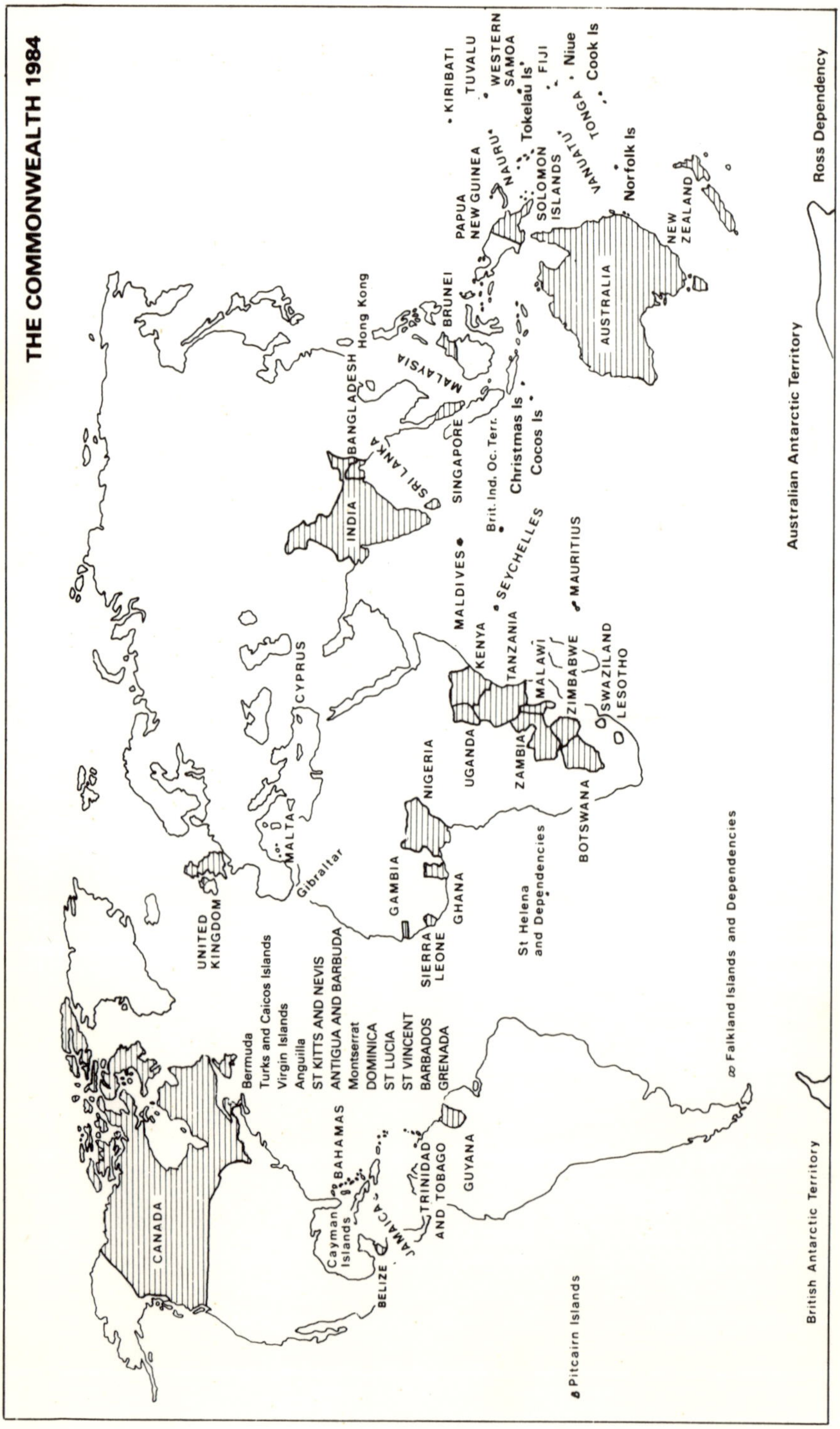
THE COMMONWEALTH 1984
CANADA
Bermuda
Turks and Caicos Islands
Virgin Islands
Anguilla
ST KITTS AND NEVIS
ANTIGUA AND BARBUDA
Montserrat
DOMINICA
ST LUCIA
ST VINCENT
BARBADOS
GRENADA
BAHAMAS
Cayman Islands
JAMAICA
BELIZE
TRINIDAD AND TOBAGO
GUYANA
Falkland Islands and Dependencies
Pitcairn Islands
British Antarctic Territory
UNITED KINGDOM
Gibraltar
MALTA
CYPRUS
GAMBIA
SIERRA LEONE
GHANA
NIGERIA
St Helena and Dependencies
UGANDA
KENYA
TANZANIA
ZAMBIA
MALAWI
ZIMBABWE
BOTSWANA
SWAZILAND
LESOTHO
MALDIVES
SEYCHELLES
MAURITIUS
INDIA
SRI LANKA
BANGLADESH
Brit. Ind. Oc. Terr.
Christmas Is
Cocos Is
SINGAPORE
MALAYSIA
Hong Kong
BRUNEI
AUSTRALIA
Australian Antarctic Territory
PAPUA NEW GUINEA
NAURU
SOLOMON ISLANDS
VANUATU
KIRIBATI
TUVALU
WESTERN SAMOA
Tokelau Is
FIJI
TONGA
Niue
Cook Is
Norfolk Is
NEW ZEALAND
Ross Dependency

Preface

International commerce today necessarily and perhaps increasingly gives rise to the possibility of transnational debts, of the absence of the debtor, or the removal of his assets, from the jurisdiction in which the debt has been incurred, and of the consequent difficulties for the persons entitled to payment in enforcing their rights. For security of commercial transactions, therefore, it must be possible for judgments given where the creditor was required to litigate—whether for procedural, evidentiary or jurisdictional reasons—to be recognised and enforced where the debtor and his assets are to be found. Creditors and debtors need to be certain that once a judgment has been obtained the matter need not be relitigated elsewhere in order to be enforced. By the same token, those who have been unsuccessfully sued or who have satisfied a judgment need the reassurance that they cannot be sued again in another jurisdiction in the same dispute.

National systems of conflict of laws generally make provision for recognition and enforcement of foreign judgments but frequently these involve the institution of fresh proceedings in the requested jurisdiction. What is commonly looked for, therefore, is a rapid, cheap and uncomplicated process whereby the judgment or arbitral award itself can be given direct effect. At the same time, it is only rarely that jurisdictions are prepared to dispense with safeguards for debtors whose interests, for no fault of their own, may not have been adequately protected in the original proceedings. There is, therefore, a widespread international concern to bring about arrangements which balance these interests and to institute them between individual states or among a group of states.

In this book, I have set out to give an account of the considerable experience which has been gained in schemes for the recognition and enforcement of judgments between Commonwealth jurisdictions. It says much about the vitality of Commonwealth legal links that there exist similar facilities for the reciprocal exchange of judgments in 81 jurisdictions in the Commonwealth. Although there are by no means universal reciprocal arrangements amongst these, the legislation almost everywhere follows common patterns, demonstrating forcibly the strength of shared legal traditions. Part of my task has been to describe the origins and development of the various judgment enforcement schemes found in the Commonwealth. Their introduction and their form owe rather more to Commonwealth initiatives than might be suggested by the fact that United Kingdom statutes provide the models upon which most Commonwealth legislation is based. Well before the first Imperial scheme was introduced in 1920, arrangements had operated amongst the Australasian colonies from the middle of the previous century and between dependent African jurisdictions from the early years of this century. The idea of a recognition and enforcement scheme seems to have had particular appeal for individuals. This book gives an opportunity to record the part played by some of these—for example, Craufurd, Piggott, Griffith, Dicey, Nunan, Beckett,

Greer, Gutteridge and Read. We sometimes underestimate the part which individual lawyers of vision and energy have played in the development of Commonwealth law.

The study is also concerned with arbitral awards in which Commonwealth considerations are perhaps less prominent. Although the Commonwealth judgment schemes frequently extend to awards, there is little evidence that they are used in that regard. They are not fully adapted to that end but their availability for award enforcement has, I think, been largely lost sight of. It is more common for reference to be made to one or other of the multilateral treaty schemes in force. Yet the earlier, Geneva scheme provides a good illustration of some of the incidental legal difficulties which have followed upon the emergence of the new Commonwealth and in practical terms its current usefulness may now be limited. It must be hoped that the New York Convention will come to be more widely adopted.

My account of the various schemes currently in force endeavours to bring together the legal experience of the many Commonwealth courts which operate the arrangements, in the hope that this will be helpful to those who may wish to make use of them. I have not made proposals for their modernisation or replacement, although a comparison with other, non-Commonwealth, arrangements indicates the value of some re-examination. A draft model of the revised Commonwealth money judgment scheme is contained in reports on this subject which David McClean and I have put to recent Commonwealth Law Ministers Meetings (see *1980 Meeting Memoranda*, pp 233–276). It will be evidence of the continuing strength of the Commonwealth if developments in this field can be the result of Commonwealth decision and agreement rather than unilateral change and if they can draw upon the wealth of practical knowledge which is available among so many jurisdictions.

This project has lasted many years, has taken me, happily, to several delightful parts of the Commonwealth and has put me in touch with many individuals who have given assistance generously and freely. I am very sensible of the encouragement given to David McClean and myself by the Commonwealth Law Ministers, particularly at their meetings in 1975, 1977 and 1980. I have to thank many individuals for their help, too many to name them all, particularly those in the Chambers of Commonwealth Attornies-General who have answered our questionnaires and queries and sent much-needed documentation, and those Law Officers who took part in the Commonwealth Secretariat's Regional Workshops on this subject in St Kitts (1978), Western Samoa (1979) and Kenya (1980). There are many others who have readily made available their professional skills, at the British Library, the Bodleian Library Oxford, the Foreign and Commonwealth Office, the Institute of Advanced Legal Studies, the Public Records Office, the New South Wales Archives, the School of Oriental and African Studies, University College, Cardiff, UWIST and the University of the West Indies. Access to these resources was greatly facilitated by a much-appreciated grant from the British Academy's Small Grants Research Fund.

My special thanks must be extended to the person who brought me to this subject, Kutlu Fuad, former Director of the Legal Division of the Commonwealth Secretariat, to Jeremy Pope, the present Director, and to Richard Nzerem, Assistant Director, all so resourceful and energetic in their maintenance of Commonwealth legal links, to my friend and associate, David McClean who has set, as ever, a very high standard in his companion volume on Family Judgments, to Butterworths for patience when my University commitments held back the work, to Barbara Lewis, my secretary, for her consistent high quality in word-processing my manuscript, whatever the condition in which it was received and to my wife Audrey, for loving support drawn from her infinite good humour and bottomless teapot.

Keith Patchett
Cardiff
April 1984

Contents

Table of Legislation

This Table also includes Uniform Acts recommended by the Uniform Law Conference of Canada.
References in this Table to *Statutes* are to Halsbury's Statutes of England (Third Edition) showing the volume and page at which the annotated text of the Act will be found.
Paragraph numbers printed in bold type indicate where the section of an Act is set out in part.

Table of Cases

A

B

F

G

Q

R

S

Select Bibliographical References

A. E. Anton: *Private International Law; a treatise from the standpoint of Scots Law* (1967).

J-G. Castel: *Canadian Conflict of Laws* (2 vols, 1975–1977).

G. C. Cheshire and P. M. North: *Private International Law* (10th edn, 1979, by P. M. North).

Committee on British & Foreign Legal Procedure: *Report ... [on] ... the Conduct of Legal Proceedings between Parties in this Country and Parties abroad and the Enforcement of Judgments and Awards,* Cmd 251, 1919 (Sumner Committee).

A. V. Dicey and J. H. C. Morris: *The Conflict of Laws* (10th edn, 1980, by J. H. C. Morris and specialist editors).

Paras Diwan: *Indian and English Private International Law: a comparative study* (1977).

Foreign Judgments (Reciprocal Enforcement) Committee: *Report,* Cmd 4213, 1932 (Greer Committee).

G. Gaja: *International Commercial Arbitration: the New York Convention* (1980).

R. H. Graveson: *Conflict of Laws: Private International Law* (7th edn, 1974).

J. D. M. Lew: *Applicable Law in International Commercial Arbitration* (1978).

Sir Michael Mustill and S. C. Boyd: *Law and Practice of Commercial Arbitration in England* (1982).

K. H. Nadelmann: *Conflict of Laws: International and Interstate* (1972).

P. E. Nygh: *Conflict of Laws in Australia* (3rd edn, 1976).

Sir Francis Piggott: *Foreign Judgments and Jurisdiction* (3rd edn, 3 vols, 1908–1910).

Private International Law Committee: Fifth Report: *Recognition and Enforcement of Foreign Arbitral Awards,* Cmd 1515, 1961.

M. C. Pryles and E. I. Sykes: *Australian Private International Law* (1979).

H. E. Read: *Recognition and Enforcement of Foreign Judgments in the common law units of the British Commonwealth* (1938).

F. Russell: *Law of Arbitration* (20th edn, 1982, by A. Walton and M. Vitoria).

E. I. Sykes: *A Textbook on the Australian Conflict of Laws* (1972).

E. I. Sykes and M. C. Pryles: *International and Interstate Conflict of Laws* (2nd edn, 1981).

UNCITRAL: Report to the Secretary-General: *Study on the application and interpretation of the Convention on the Recognition and Enforcement of Foreign Arbitral Awards (New York, 1958),* A/CN. 9/169, (1979) 10 *Yearbook of the United Nations Commission on International Trade Law,* 100–109.

P. H. R. Webb and J. R. L. Davies: *A Casebook on the Conflict of Laws in New Zealand* (1970).

M. Wolff: *Private International Law* (2nd edn, 1950).

Abbreviations

ABC	Australian Bankruptcy Cases
AC, App Cas	Appeal Cases
ACLD	Australian Current Law Digest
ACT	Australian Capital Territory
AD	Appellate Division
AIR	All India Reporter
AJA	Administration of Justice Act 1920 (UK)
AJIL	American Journal of International Law
Alig LJ	Alighari Law Journal
ALJ	Australian Law Journal
ALJR	Australian Law Journal Reports
All	Allahabad Series (of the All India Reporter)
All ER	All England Reports
All NLR	All Nigeria Law Reports
ALR	African Law Reports
ALR Comm	African Law Reports Commercial Series
ALT	Australian Law Times
Alta	Alberta
Alta LR	Alberta Law Reports
Am Jo Comp L	American Journal of Comparative Law
Andr Pra.	Andhra Pradesh Series (of the All India Reporter)
APR	Atlantic Provinces Reports
AR	Alberta Reports
Aus Bus LR	Australian Business Law Review
B & Ald	Barnewall & Alderson's Reports
B & C	Barnewall & Cresswell's Reports
BC	British Columbia
BCA	British Central Africa
BCLR	British Columbia Law Reports
Bing NC	Bingham's New Cases
Bom	Bombay Series (of the All India Reporter)
Bom LR	Bombay Law Reporter
BT	Board of Trade
Buffalo LR	Buffalo Law Review
BYBIL	British Yearbook of International Law.
C, Cd, Cmd, Cmnd	Command Paper
CA	Court of Appeal
Cal	Calcutta Series (of the All India Reporter)
Cam LJ	Cambridge Law Journal
Camp	Campbell's Reports
Can	Canada
Can BR	Canadian Bar Review
CJJA	Civil Jurisdiction and Judgments Act 1982 (UK)

CLR	Commonwealth Law Reports (Australia) *or* Cyprus Law Reports
CO	Colonial Office
Com LR	Commercial Law Reports (England)
Comm LB	Commonwealth Law Bulletin
Cr App R	Criminal Appeal Reports
DC	Divisional Court
DLR	Dominion Law Reports (Canada)
Doug KB	Douglas' King's Bench Reports
EA	East Africa
East	East's Reports
EG	Estates Gazette
Exch	Exchequer Reports
ExD	Exchequer Division
F	Federal Reporter (US)
Fed Ct	Federal Court
FJREA	Foreign Judgments (Reciprocal Enforcement) Act, 1933 (UK)
FLR	Federal Law Reports (Australia)
FMSLR	Federated Malayan States Law Reports
FO	Foreign Office
FSR	Fleet Street Reports (England)
Hare	Hare's Reports
Harv LR	Harvard Law Review
HC	House of Commons
HCt	High Court
Hem & M	Hemming & Miller's Reports
HK	Hong Kong
HL	House of Lords
HLC	House of Lords Cases
H & N	Hurlstone & Norman's Reports
ICJEA	Inferior Court Judgments Extension Act 1882 (UK)
ICLQ	International and Comparative Law Quarterly
ILQ	International Law Quarterly
ILR	Indian Law Reports
Ind Jo Int Law	Indian Journal of International Law
IR	Irish Reports
J African Law	Journal of African Law
JEA	Judgments Extension Act 1868 (UK)
J Ind Law Inst	Journal of Indian Law Institute
J Int Law Econ	Journal of International Law and Economics
J & K	Jammu and Kashmir Series (of the All India Reporter)
KB	King's Bench
Ken	Kenya
Ker	Kerala Series (of the All India Reporter)
Knox	Knox's Reports (New South Wales)
Law Com	Law Commission (England and Wales)
LC	Lord Chancellor
LCO	Lord Chancellor's Office
Ld Ray	Lord Raymond's Reports
Lloyd's Rep	Lloyd's Reports (UK)
Lloyd's LLR	Lloyd's List Law Reports (UK)

LJEx	Law Journal Reports, Court of Exchequer
LJCP	Law Journal Reports, Common Pleas
LMCLQ	Lloyd's Maritime and Commercial Law Quarterly
LN	League of Nations
LNOJ	League of Nations Official Journal
LQR	Law Quarterly Review
LRCP	Law Reports Common Pleas
LREx	Law Reports Court of Exchequer
LRHL	Law Reports House of Lords
LR(NSW)	Law Reports, New South Wales
LRQB	Law Reports, Queen's Bench
LJ	Law Journal
Macph	Macpherson's Court of Session Cases (Scotland)
Mad	Madras Series (of the All India Reporter)
Man	Manitoba
Man LJ	Manitoba Law Journal
Man R	Manitoba Reports
M & G	Manning & Granger's Reports
MLJ	Malayan Law Journal
MLR	Modern Law Review
MR	Master of the Rolls
M & S	Maule & Selwyn's Reports
M & W	Meeson & Welsby's Reports
Nag	Nagpur Series (of the All India Reporter)
NB	New Brunswick
NBR	New Brunswick Reports
NLJ	New Law Journal
NS	New Series
NSR	Nova Scotia Reports
NSWLR	New South Wales Law Reports
NUC	Notes of Unreported Cases (of the All India Reporter)
NWT	Northwest Territories of Canada
NZ	New Zealand
NZLR	New Zealand Law Reports
NZULR	New Zealand Universities Law Review
OAR	Ontario Appeal Reports
OJ	Official Journal (European Economic Communities)
OLR	Ontario Law Reports
Ont	Ontario
OR	Ontario Reports
Oregon LR	Oregon Law Review
Ottawa LR	Ottawa Law Review
OWN	Ontario Weekly Notes
OWR	Ontario Weekly Reporter
PC	Parliamentary Counsel *or* Privy Council
PEI	Prince Edward Island
PLD	All Pakistan Legal Decisions
PNG	Papua–New Guinea
PNGLR	Papua–New Guinea Law Reports
Pring	Pring's Statutes of Queensland
Punj	Punjab Series (of the All India Reporter)
QB	Queen's Bench

QdR	Queensland Reports
QLJ	Queensland Law Journal
QSCR	Queensland Supreme Court Reports
QWN	Queensland Weekly Notes
Raj	Rajasthan Series (of the All India Reporter)
R Ct of Session	Rettie, Court of Session Cases (Scotland)
Rev du Bar	Revue du Barreau (Quebec)
Roll Abr	Rolle's Abridgment of the Common Law
RPC	Reports of Patent Cases
RPR	Real Property Reports (Canada)
RR	Revised Reports
RSC	Revised Statutes of Canada *or* Rules of the Supreme Court
RSM	Revised Statutes of Manitoba
RSNB	Revised Statutes of New Brunswick
RSS	Revised Statutes of Saskatchewan
SA	South Australia
SASR	South Australia State Reports
Sask	Saskatchewan
Sau	Saurashtra Series (of the All India Reporter)
SC	Session Cases (Scotland) *or* Supreme Court
SCR(NSW)	Supreme Court Reports, New South Wales
Show KB	Shower's King's Bench Reports
SI	Statutory Instrument
Sim	Simons' Reports
SLT	Scots Law Times
SM	Statutes of Manitoba
SNfld	Statutes of Newfoundland
SR(NSW)	State Reports, New South Wales
SRO	Statutory Rules and Orders
SSLR	Straits Settlements Law Reports
State Tr	State Trials
Sup CC	Supreme Court Cases (India)
Syd LR	Sydney Law Review
T	Treasury
Tas	Tasmania
Texas Int LJ	Texas International Law Journal
TLR	Times Law Reports (England)
TS	Treaty Series
Ug	Uganda
UK	United Kingdom
UN	United Nations
UNCITRAL	United Nations Commission on International Trade Law
US	United States
U Tas LR	University of Tasmania Law Review
VC	Vice Chancellor
Ventris	Ventris' Reports
Vern	Vernon's Reports
Ves	Vesey's Reports
Vic	Victoria
VLR	Victoria Law Reports

VR	Victoria Reports
WA	Western Australia
WAR	Western Australia Reports
Washburn LJ	Washburn Law Journal
WIASSC	West Indies Associated States Supreme Court
WIR	West Indian Reports
WLR	Weekly Law Reports
WN	Weekly Notes
WN(NSW)	Weekly Notes, New South Wales
WWR	Western Weekly Reports
Yale LJ	Yale Law Journal
YB Comm Arb	Yearbook of Commercial Arbitration

PART I

Commercial Judgments

CHAPTER 1

Commonwealth Schemes: Origins and Development

The common law origins

1.01 The origins of the present-day schemes for enforcement of money-judgments in Commonwealth countries can be traced to the beginning of the nineteenth century, to a period in which the principles of recognition and enforcement were themselves still in the process of development. In the previous two hundred years, the English courts, having gradually come to accept that foreign cases involving issues of foreign law were best determined by the courts which administered that law, equally gradually came to accept some obligation to give effect to those judgments.[1] Initially, this obligation was seen to arise from the law of nations and was given its clearest effect in relation to foreign Admiralty judgments.[2] As an expanding range of civil matters was brought within the jurisdiction of the common law courts and of Chancery, international comity with its implications of reciprocity, although invoked,[3] came to be seen as an unsatisfactory basis for recognition and enforcement. Instead, the courts accepted the possibility of claims in assumpsit on a simple contract between the parties to the judgment of which the foreign judgment was evidence.[4]

But it was well into the nineteenth century before priority was given to the view that the foreign judgment created a fresh cause of action in the nature of a simple contract which could be sued upon as a debt.[5] It was at the same period that other important law principles became finally established—as for example that the foreign judgment must be final and conclusive,[6] that neither its merits[7] nor the correctness of the law applied by the foreign court may be reviewed,[8] and that the foreign court must have been jurisdictionally competent under the conflict of laws rules of the requested state.[9]

1 A. N. Sack, in *Law—A Century of Progress, 1835–1935* Vol II, pp 384–385; P. E. Nygh, (1964) 2 U Tas LR 28–40.
2 *Wier's Case* (1607) 1 Roll Abr 530, p 1.12; *Jurado v Gregory* (1670) 1 Vent 32; *Hughes v Cornelius* (1683) 2 Show 232; *Ewer v Jones* (1704) 2 Ld Raym 934.
3 *Wright v Simpson* (1802) 6 Ves 714 at 730, per Lord Eldon; *Alves v Bunbury* (1814) 4 Camp 28, per Lord Ellenborough.
4 *Dupleix v De Roven* (1705) 2 Vern 540; *Walker v Witter* (1778) 1 Doug KB 1; *Crawford v Whittal* (1773) 1 Doug KB 4, n.
5 *Russell v Smyth* (1842) 9 M & W 810; *Williams v Jones* (1845) 13 M & W 628. See Piggott, op cit, pp 12–17; Read, op cit, Ch II.
6 *Nouvion v Freeman* (1889) 15 App Cas 1.
7 *Tarleton v Tarleton* (1815) 4 M & S 20; *Martin v Nicholls* (1830) 3 Sim 458.
8 *Godard v Gray* (1870) LR 6 QB 139, 40 LJQB 62.
9 *Copin v Adamson* (1874) LR 9 Ex 345; *Schibsby v Westenholz* (1870) LR 6 QB 155; *Rousillon v Rousillon* (1880) 14 Ch D 351.

The Crown Debts Act 1801

1.02 Coincident with the judicial development of the common law relating to the principles of recognition of external judgments, the first steps were taken to establish statutory schemes to facilitate the inter-jurisdictional enforcement of judgments. These were taken by the United Kingdom Parliament and they were confined to enforcement within different parts of the Kingdom. The first of these schemes was introduced by the Crown Debts Act 1801.[1] It was enacted in the first session of the newly established United Kingdom Parliament after the Act of Union 1800 had declared Great Britain and Northern Ireland to be one Kingdom and appears to have been conceived in consequence of those new legal ties. Its principal purpose was to provide for 'the more speedy and effectual recovery of debts' due to the Crown. It authorised copies of judgments rendered or accounts recorded in the Court of Exchequer in England or Ireland to be exemplified and transmitted to the counterpart court where it had to be enrolled. Process could then be issued against the debtor or his assets in that part of the Kingdom. Monies recovered were then to be remitted via the local Exchequer to its counterpart.[2] The Act, however, also gave rights to certain litigants. Thus exemplified copies of decrees of the English Court of Chancery in cases of 'minors, bankrupts, idiots or lunatics' could be transmitted on application to the Court of Chancery in Ireland for enforcement as if originally pronounced there.[3] Reciprocal facilities were provided, in similar form, in respect of decrees or orders for payment or accounting in suits between party and party issued by the Court of Chancery in England and in Ireland. As a result of a House of Lords amendment, similar arrangements were introduced for suits between party and party in the Courts of Exchequer of the two jurisdictions.[4]

1 41 Geo 3, c 90.
2 Ss 1–4.
3 Ss 5 and 6. Reciprocal arrangements were enacted by the Crown Debts Act 1824.
4 Ss 7 and 8. *Journal of House of Lords* 1801, p 359. There were no equivalent arrangements involving Scotland.

The English and Irish Judgments Bill 1834

1.03 This first measure, therefore, was in the main a device to assist the Crown in its revenue gathering role. The benefits accorded to litigants were secondary and limited. Although certain orders, including orders to pay money, made by the ecclesiastical courts in England and Ireland were made subject to a similar scheme in 1832,[1] judgments in the common law courts of King's Bench and Common Pleas in which the major part of civil litigation occurred were never within this scheme. An attempt was made to meet this shortcoming in 1834 when Lord Wynford (formerly Judge Best) introduced an English and Irish Judgments Bill into the House of Lords, only to see it fail through the obstructiveness of Irish peers suspicious of legislation which seemed likely to have adverse effects upon their interests.[2] The prescience of the Bill's proponent who advocated that reciprocal enforcement facilities might usefully be extended to foreign countries evoked no response.[3]

1 Ecclesiastical Courts (Contempt) Act 1832, 2 & 3 Will 4, c 93, esp ss 2 and 3.
2 22 HC Official Report (3rd series) cols 350–360: the text is in HC Parliamentary Papers 1834, II, 595–599.
3 21 HC Official Report (3rd series) col 1188.

Enforcement of British winding-up orders

1.04 The advantages to the developing mercantile community in the United Kingdom of these uncomplicated methods of enforcing judgments and orders elsewhere in the Kingdom were soon accepted. The major company law reforms effected by Gladstone's Joint Stock Companies legislation in 1844 extended the 1801 Act to all decrees and orders made by the Court of Chancery in England in any suit, proceeding or matter under the new winding-up legislation.[1] In similar terms, provision was made for the registration of this category of judgments in Scotland, the first time that this jurisdiction had been included.[2] Reciprocal arrangements for the transmission to England of similar orders by the Irish Court of Chancery were enacted the following year.[3] Similar provision was made, this time in explicit terms, with respect to English and Irish court orders made under the amending winding-up legislation in 1848.[4] In 1862, full reciprocal arrangements for orders in winding-up proceedings in England, Ireland and Scotland were enacted. Instead of registration, enforcement of an order was authorised on its production before the appropriate court officer.[5] This remains the basis of present-day practice in the United Kingdom.[6]

1 7 & 8 Vic, c 111, s 23.
2 Ibid, s 24.
3 8 & 9 Vic, c 98, s 23.
4 11 & 12 Vic, c 45, ss 115 and 116.
5 25 & 26 Vic, c 89, ss 122 and 123.
6 Companies Act 1948, s 276; Companies Act (Northern Ireland) 1960, s 246.

Money-judgments: Craufurd's first Bill

1.05 But a system of enforcement of orders in Chancery, Exchequer and winding-up proceedings was inadequate to meet the more common needs for enforcing ordinary judgments debts.[1] In 1854, a petition of the Scottish Trade Protection Society of Edinburgh pressed Parliament to enact appropriate legislation for the Kingdom.[2] In response, one E. H. J. Craufurd obtained leave to introduce a Bill which would permit a judgment obtained in both superior and inferior civil courts in any of three United Kingdom jurisdictions to be entered upon the roll of the appropriate court in another part of the Kingdom. This initiative was welcomed by the law officers.[3] But it ran into difficulties in the Second Reading when the Lord Advocate raised doubts about provisions which allowed service of process, where the cause of action arose in one jurisdiction, upon the debtor resident in another.[4] Although substantial improvements appear to have been effected in Committee which enabled the Bill to pass the House of Commons,[5] it did not make progress in the Lords in that session.[6]

1 The Crown Debts Act 1801 with minor amendments and repeals and the Crown Debts Act 1824 remained in force until 1982 when the Civil Jurisdiction and Judgments Act 1982, s 54 and Sch 14 repealed them.
2 131 HC Official Report (3rd series) col 583.
3 Ibid, cols 583–585.
4 Ibid, col 1466; cf vol 144, col 771.
5 Ibid, vol 135, col 1216.
6 Ibid, col 1182.

Craufurd's second Bill

1.06 Craufurd, encouraged by the refinements made to his Bill, re-introduced it into the House of Commons in 1855 where this time it failed to complete its second reading. Irish opposition was particularly strong, being grounded in the belief that the legislation would favour English creditors as against Irish debtors and thus be injurious to Irish trade.[1] Others argued that both English and Irish might be disadvantaged as a result of differences in the law of Scotland which would be applied to the initial proceedings when brought there.[2] Concern was also expressed about the extension of jurisdictional competence which the Bill would entail. Faced with these arguments and a complacent satisfaction with the usual processes of an action on the judgment, Craufurd was obliged to accede to a proposal to defer further debate.[3]

1 137 HC Official Report (3rd series) cols 222–223.
2 Ibid, col 225.
3 Ibid, cols 225–226.

Craufurd's third Bill

1.07 In the following session, Craufurd tried again, seeking leave to introduce an amended version of his Bill, from which certain courts had been excluded and improved procedural features included. Again, support was forthcoming from both law officers and other members who found the principle, if not all the terms, acceptable.[1] Again, powerful Irish backbench opposition was encountered in the Second Reading and in the Select Committee.[2] Considerable play was made with the fear that fraudulent creditors would be able to bring proceedings in England which Irish debtors could not properly defend, enabling automatic enforcement of the judgment against the debtor's Irish properties. On the advice of the Lord Advocate, Craufurd withdrew his Bill, once more.[3]

1 140 HC Official Report (3rd series) cols 182–183.
2 Ibid, cols 207–210, 537, 1002.
3 Ibid, col 1003.

Craufurd's fourth Bill

1.08 Undeterred, Craufurd made a fourth attempt in February 1857, with another revised version of the Bill which again reached the committee stage despite renewed Irish opposition on the now familiar ground that the legislation would work discriminatorily against the Irish amongst whom debtors were more common than creditors.[1] Despite these objections, it is clear that many found the Bill worthwhile and a series of amendments were put at the committee stage which were designed to improve the procedures and provide some safeguards.[2] But the legislation again failed to complete its course in the Commons.

1 144 HC Official Report (3rd series) cols 503–509.
2 Ibid, cols 763–775, 1303–1304.

Craufurd's fifth Bill

1.09 Three months later, Craufurd made his fifth effort to secure parliamentary support for his scheme. Again, he met strong Irish objections, with repetitious emphasis upon the fraudulent advantages allegedly to be gained, particularly in bankruptcy proceedings, by creditors permitted to register default judgments in another part of the Kingdom. Rather more than in the past, however, the Bill encountered a series of technical arguments which indicate that it was still defectively drafted as well as uncertainly understood. Criticisms were made of the principle of automaticity, the absence of any procedure to set aside a registration, the want of notice of registration proceedings, the requirement of a judgment creditor to give security, the possibility of fraud especially in relation to default judgments and the differences in the laws of the parts of the United Kingdom in relation to absent defendants.[1] By the end of the debate on the second reading, it was apparent to Craufurd that he was unlikely to get his Bill through the opposition in the time available and he withdrew it for the last time.[2]

The Government played little part in the preparation of any of the versions of Craufurd's legislation. Although its law officers generally approved in principle, no consultations appear to have taken place with a view to producing a technically defensible draft.[3] Occasional suggestions were made that the legislation should be sponsored by government as an Imperial measure[4] but there appears to have been no thought on the part of the sponsor or of the law officers that a scheme of enforcement should be developed elsewhere than for the United Kingdom.

1 145 HC Official Report (3rd series) cols 227–235, 626; vol 146, col 313.
2 Ibid, vol 146, col 1514.
3 Ibid. It also had the support of the Law Amendment Society and of Lord Brougham, a former Lord Chancellor; ibid, vol 145, col 235.
4 Eg ibid, vol 144, col 509.

Craufurd's Judgments Extension Bill 1868

1.10 Although this scheme for enforcement of judgments came to grief, the principle of mutual recognition of judicial acts in the United Kingdom was gaining momentum in other respects. Thus, from 1857 probates and letters of administration granted in England and Ireland were authorised for resealing in the other jurisdiction[1] and in the following year provision was made for resealing of Scottish confirmations in the other parts of the Kingdom and reciprocally for certification in Scotland of grants made in England and Ireland.[2] In the same year, the Crown Debts Act 1801 was applied to orders made in the Landed Estates Court of Ireland for enforcement in England.[3] In 1859 provision was made for the recovery of debts of record due to the Crown in the Court of Exchequer in England when the debtor was resident elsewhere in the Kingdom, by transmission of an exemplified copy for enrollment in the Court of Exchequer in the appropriate jurisdiction.[4] The acceptance in government legislation of reciprocal enforcement arrangements in these matters no doubt paved the way for Craufurd's final and successful initiative in 1868, when he introduced a freshly drafted and rather verbose Judgments Extension Bill. In sharp contrast with the earlier experience, this legislation passed through both Houses without division and with scarcely any debate or serious opposition,[5] receiving strong support from the Lord Chancellor and the law officers.[6] Craufurd's persistence was rewarded by a statute which remained in force until its repeal by the Civil Judgments and Jurisdiction Act 1982[7] and was used as a model in a number of overseas jurisdictions.[8]

1 Probates and Letters of Administration (Ireland) Act 1857, 20 & 21 Vict, c 79, ss 94 and 95 (repealed by the Administration of Estates Act 1971, s 12(1) and Sch 2, Pt I). The requirement of bonds was introduced by the Court of Probate Act 1858, 21 & 22 Vict, c 95, s 29 and Court of Probate (Ireland) Act 1859, 22 & 23 Vict, c 31, s 25.
2 The Confirmation and Probate Act 1858, 21 & 22 Vict, c 56, ss 12–14, also repealed by the Administration of Estates Act 1971 (see note 1, above).
3 Sale and Transfer of Land (Ireland) Act 1858, 21 & 22 Vict, c 72, s 36.
4 Queen's Remembrancer Act 1859, 22 & 23 Vict, c 21, s 24, repealed by the Civil Judgments and Jurisdiction Act 1982, s 54 and Sch 14. An Extension of Decrees Bill, introduced by

private members in 1863, sought to extend the Crown Debts Act 1801 to resolve what were seen as doubts about the enforceability in England and Ireland of certain categories of judgments following the transfer in 1857 of certain ecclesiastical jurisdiction to the Courts of Probate and Divorce and Matrimonial Causes: HC Parliamentary Papers 1863, vol II, 181–185. The Bill did not proceed beyond the Report stage.

5 The Bill was referred to a Select Committee of the House of Commons which Craufurd chaired.

6 193 HC Official Report (3rd series) col 367.

7 The Judgments Extension Act 1868, 31 & 32 Vict, c 54, repealed by the Civil Judgments and Jurisdiction Act 1982 (see note 4, above). From 1921, the legislation was limited to Northern Ireland: SR & O 1921 No 1804, arts 5 and 7(b) but was applied in the Republic of Ireland: *Gieves v O'Conor* [1924] 2 IR 182.

8 See paras 1.26–1.28 below.

The Judgments Extension Act 1868

1.11 The Act was confined to judgments or decrees for debts, damages or costs of the common law courts of Queens Bench, Common Pleas and Exchequer in England and Ireland and the Court of Session in Scotland. By registration of a certificate of the judgment in due form in the appropriate register, normally within twelve months of the date of judgment, it was possible to enforce the judgment as if locally obtained. As a disincentive to litigation, costs were normally to be withheld if a plaintiff sued on a judgment when it could have been registered. This scheme therefore, embodied near formal procedures for judgment enforcement which accepted without question the jurisdiction of the original courts[1] and the validity of their judgments.[2] As the three systems shared the House of Lords as a common final court of appeal, it is in the final analysis understandable that a full faith and credit approach was followed.[3]

1 *Wotherspoon v Connolly* 1871 9 Macph (Ct of Sess) 510; *English's Coasting and Shipping Co Ltd v British Finance Co Ltd* 1886 14 R (Ct of Sess) 220, 24 Sc LR 167; with the exception of decrees pronounced in absence in an action proceeding on arrestment used to found jurisdiction in Scotland: s 8.

2 *Re Low, Bland v Low* [1894] 1 Ch 147, 63 LJ Ch 60.

3 Anton, op cit, p 596. In respect of inferior court judgments, a rather more cautious approach was adopted: Inferior Courts Judgments Extension Act 1882, 45 & 46 Vict, c 31, s 10 where jurisdiction and process requirements were set out.

Australasian initiatives 1855–1859

1.12 Whilst Craufurd was still finding it necessary to bend to the storms of Irish opposition in the United Kingdom, on the other side of the colonial world a different approach was having greater success. In August 1855, Governor Denison introduced into the New South Wales Legislature a measure which became the Further Remedies to Creditors Act 1855.[1] This legislation appears to have excited no comments at the Colonial Office when it was received. Yet it established the first stage in the first general scheme for judgment enforcement created anywhere in the common law world. Its purpose was to provide simple arrangements under which creditors could enforce their judgment claims against debtors in New South Wales who had removed themselves there from other Australasian colonies. Although no reference was made in the legislation to reciprocal arrangements, the Act appears to have been part of a common design, for almost identical legislation was enacted in South Australia (1856), Western Australia (1856), Tasmania (1857), Victoria (1858) and New Zealand (1858).[2] The New South Wales statute itself was continued as part of the law of Queensland on its separation into a separate colony in 1859.[3]

1 19 Vict, No 12, CO 201/486, Desp No 147/1855. The Act was also known as the Intercolonial Judgments Act.

2 1855–56, No 9 (SA); 19 Vict, No 13 (WA); 21 Vict, No 20 (Tas); 21 Vict, No 48 (Vict); 21 & 22 Vict, No 21 (NZ).

3 1 Pring 264.

The first Australasian scheme

1.13 The scheme applied in relation to any money judgment obtained in the Supreme Court of any of the seven Australasian colonies listed above. The judgment creditor was permitted by the legislation of each colony to file in the Supreme Court of that colony a memorial in the prescribed form of the original judgment, authenticated by the seal of the original court. This memorial thereupon became a record of the judgment upon which local execution could issue. A judge of the Supreme Court was authorised, on the application of the judgment creditor, to issue a summons for personal or other service, as prescribed by the judge, upon the debtor to show cause within a time also prescribed by the judge why execution should not issue. If the debtor failed to show cause or defaulted in making an appearance, the judge on proof of service could direct execution subject to terms or conditions. The creditor was entitled 'to all such process and to all such remedies for the enforcement' of the judgment and the debtor 'to all such protective rights and advantages' to which they would have been entitled had the judgment been that of the local Supreme Court.

On its face, the scheme seems to have been devised as a simple procedural arrangement which would obviate the need to sue on the original judgment. The courts, however, were not prepared to treat it as a scheme of formal operation in which the debtor had no safeguards against automatic execution. They declined to issue leave to execute as a matter of course merely on the filing in appropriate form of the memorial of the judgment.[1] Further, they ruled that it was open to the debtor to show cause against execution by raising any defence which he could have invoked in a common law action on the judgment.[2] Thus objections were allowed on the grounds of absence of jurisdictional competence in the original court,[3] want of due notice of the proceedings[4] and fraud or manifest injustice,[5] although the statutes were silent on these matters. In addition, the summons to show cause against execution could not be served upon a debtor outside the jurisdiction.[6] Unlike the United Kingdom Judgment Extension scheme, therefore, this scheme treated the money judgments to which it applied as foreign judgments. The judges read into it, from the common law, requirements which became central statutory characteristics of the later Commonwealth arrangements.

1 *Johnson v Dickson* (1870) 1 VR (L) 159; *Morrow v Bellamy* (1873) 3 QSCR 190.

2 *Barker v Johnson* (1861) 1 QSCR 28; *Warner v Fischer* (1875) 13 SCR (NSW) 346; *Hogan v Moore* (1884) 6 ALT 156 (Vic).

3 *Brisbane Oyster Fishery Co v Emerson* (1877) Knox 80 (NSW); *Berry v Shead* (1886) 7 LR (NSW) 39; *Victorian Phillip-Stephan Photo Litho etc Co v Davis* (1890) 11 LR (NSW) 257; *Seegner v Marks* (1895) 21 VLR 491; *Permanent Building and Investment Association v Hudson* (1896) 7 QLJ 23; *Bank of New Zealand v Lloyd* (1898) 14 WN (NSW) 160.

4 *Warner v Fischer,* above.

5 *Hogan v Moore,* above; *Ruby Extended Tin Mining Co Ltd v Woolcott* (1880) 6 VLR (L) 301.

6 *Clarke v Clarke* (1893) 5 QLJ 82; *London Chartered Bank of Australia v McEdward* (1894) 10 WN (NSW) 195.

Developments in the Australasian scheme

1.14 The apparent utility of these arrangements encouraged further activity in the Australasian jurisdictions, usually in the form of re-enactment of the money judgment legislation, sometimes with clarifying amendments.[1] But notable extensions were also effected. Thus similar legislation was enacted in the newly acquired colony of Fiji[2] although the other colonies did not reciprocally extend their provisions. The South Australian statute was made applicable beyond Australasia, in respect of Canada and its Provinces, Cape Hope, Natal and Mauritius, with power in the Governor to extend it by proclamation elsewhere.[3] The re-enacted New Zealand Act of 1882 went even further by making the scheme available with respect of money judgments from 'any court in any of Her Majesty's dominions',[4] thereby becoming the first enforcement scheme with Empire-wide application. Alternative arrangements, however, also began to be contemplated. In 1878, Tasmania, after inter-colony discussions in which agreement to introduce new uniform legislation appears to have been reached, enacted fresh legislation, the Inter-Colonial Judgments Act.[5] From the similarity in provision, it was clearly influenced by the United Kingdom Judgments Extension legislation. Registration of other Australasian Supreme Court money judgments thereafter was possible in Tasmania, without notice of registration to the debtor and without power in the receiving court to question the original judgment.

1 Victoria: Common Law Procedure Statute 1865, 28 Vict, No 274, ss 307–308; Queensland: Supreme Court (Common Law Practice) Act 1867, 31 Vict, No 17, ss 20–22.
2 Memorial of Judgment Ordinance 1875, 39 Vict, No 12, itself subsequently extended to embrace New Zealand judgments.
3 Creditors Remedies Act 1880, No 181.
4 New Zealand: Supreme Court Act 1882, 46 Vict, No 29, ss 27–29: re-enacted as Judicature Act 1908, No 89, s 56; para 2.41 below.
5 42 Vict, No 8: see Proceedings of the Colonial Conference, 1887, C. 5091, p 54 for an account, albeit with uncertain references to dates.

Australia: federal initiatives

1.15 As the federal movement in Australasia gained momentum, it is hardly surprising that this subject and the analagous subject of service of process were given prominence as matters upon which common arrangements were desirable. The Sydney Convention of Australasian Colonies in December 1883 favoured the inclusion of these subjects in the powers of the proposed Federal Council[1] and this recommendation was accepted when the Imperial Parliament enacted the Federal Council of Australasia Act 1885.[2] Despite the refusal of New Zealand and New South Wales to participate in the new federal arrangements, the Council under the directing hand of the Premier, Samuel Griffith, later Chief Justice of Queensland and of Australia, proceeded to enact legislation on civil process and judgments for the remaining five jurisdictions[3] which accepted the Council's legislative authority. The judgments legislation[4] was expressly stated to have effect in addition to the existing colonial statutes. It marked certain significant departures both from the original Intercolonial Judgments statutes and from the Tasmanian replacement.[5] It was to have effect only in relation to judgments from any Supreme Court in the Federation but these comprised not only money judgments but any judgment 'whereby the doing of or the forebearing to do any act ... is required or enjoyed'[6] and extended to actions for the possession or delivery of possession of property or declaration of status or to any matrimonial, bankruptcy or insolvency proceedings or actions before a Vice-Admiralty Court.[7] The scheme was only to apply if appropriate jurisdictional tests had been met in the original case. Thus the defendant must be shown to have been duly served under the law of that originating colony or out of that jurisdiction in accordance with the Australasia Civil Process Act 1886 or to have submitted to the jurisdiction.[8] The procedural steps also differed. Registration within twelve months of a certificate in due form and under court seal of the original judgment in a local register was a formality[9] but execution could not issue unless the judgment creditor or some other person cognisant with the facts filed an affidavit that the judgment remained unsatisfied.[10] But no requirement was made for service of notice of the registration upon the judgment debtor, as the debtor had received notice of the original proceedings but the debtor was expressly permitted to apply for a stay of execution.[11] The receiving court was not vested, expressly or by implication, with powers on any such application to examine any matters relating to the original judgment, other than the jurisdictional issues prescribed by the statute.[12] The Act contemplated that other matters were to be challenged in the original jurisdiction:[13] the local courts' powers were to be exercised with respect to questions relating to execution of the judgment locally. This scheme co-existed, however, with existing inter-colonial legislation in all the colonies to which it applied,[14] except Tasmania which appears to have relied entirely upon this statute from 1886.

1 C.4397 (1884). Discussions took place at earlier inter-colonial conferences on the question of uniform legislation, notably in 1878 and 1881.
2 48 & 49 Vict, c 30, s 15(d) and (e).
3 Fiji, Queensland, Tasmania, Victoria, Western Australia: South Australia did not participate.
4 The Australasian Judgments Act 1886, 49 Vic, No 4. The civil process legislation was the Australasian Civil Process Act 1886, 49 Vic, No 3.
5 This was a cause of considerable concern to the Tasmania representatives: see Committee Debate, C.4841 (1886), pp 147–150. The conflict was shortly resolved by the local repeal in 1886 of the Tasmania Act by 50 Vict, No 4.
6 S 2. The first draft applied to judgments of inferior courts and 'the Imperial Court'.
7 Ibid.
8 S 3.
9 Ss 4 and 5.
10 S 6.
11 S 8.
12 *Donald v Donald* (1899) 9 QLJ 211.
13 S 8, which provided for stay of execution pending an application to the original court.
14 Indeed, the original legislation continued for many years, in some cases to date. NSW: Interstate Debt Recovery Act 1901, No 48, Part II, consolidating Inter-colonial Debts Act 1889, 52 Vict, No 23 (re-enacted), repealed by Administration of Justice Act 1924, No 42; Queensland: 31 Vict, No 17 (re-enacted), still in force; South Australia: 1880 Act repealed by Administration of Justice Act 1921, No 1461; Victoria: Supreme Court Act 1915, No 2733, ss 185–186 (re-enacting 54 Vict, No 1142, ss 182–183 itself a re-enactment), repealed by Judgments Reciprocity Act 1925, No 3395, s 5; Western Australia: 19 Vict, No 13; New Zealand: Judicature Act 1908, No 89, s 56 (re-enactment, still in force); Fiji: repealed by Memorial of Judgment (Repeal) Ordinance 1929.

Pressure for an Imperial scheme

1.16 Other initiatives were being taken in Australasia at this time. Following the United Kingdom model, Victoria made provision for the resealing there of grants of probate and letters of administration made in the United Kingdom or in any other Australasian colony, when the deceased had left property in Victoria.[1] The legislation was sanctioned by the Colonial Office which appears to have seen its potential for general colonial application despite some opposition from the law officers,[2] when it was drawn to their attention by a firm of London solicitors.[3] This incident seems to have added conviction to the Colonial Office's thinking that the subject of judgment enforcement generally was one suitable for the Imperial Conference proposed for 1887.

A number of events had contributed to this belief. At a meeting of the International Law Association in Milan in 1883,[4] the value of international arrangements to facilitate judgment enforcement was recognised and preliminary work was undertaken by the Association. This encouraged the Italian Foreign Minister, Mancini, to invite the major powers to a conference to discuss a multilateral convention on the subject. The conference was never held, due to the 'sanitary condition' of Italy at the time[5] but as a preliminary step towards future multilateral discussions, Italy and the United Kingdom entered into negotiations in 1887 for a bilateral treaty.[6] A draft was agreed but never signed.[7]

1 Probates Act 1886, 50 Vict 902. Similar legislation appears to have been enacted at this time in South Australia, Tasmania, Western Australia and New Zealand. See also the Australasian Testamentary Process Act 1897 of the Federal Council.
2 CO 309/131, Doc No 6851/87 (CO).
3 Barber and Sladen Wing, see Appendix to *Proceedings of the Colonial Conference 1887*, C5091, Appendix, No 8, encls, 8–10.
4 The Association was then known as the Association for the Reform and Codification of International Law: see *Report of Proceedings of 11th Meeting, 1883*; Chairman, Sir Travers Twiss.
5 HC Official Report (3rd series) vol 292 (1884), col 99; vol 294 (1885), cols 1597–8.
6 CO 323/369, Doc No 22458/87 (FO); no treaties were in existence on the matter. Sir F. T. Piggott, (1922) 38 LQR at 339 records that Sir Julian Paunceforte, then Under-Secretary at the Foreign Office, invited Piggott to draft a 'projet de convention'.
7 '... owing to the divergencies in the laws of the two states and to absence of a Code in this country': CO 167/718, Doc No 21769/98 (FO).

Piggott's intervention

1.17 The importance of the proposals had not been lost upon one of the United Kingdom negotiators, Mr F. T. Piggott, who then and for the next thirty years was to play a gadfly role in the process of bringing about an Imperial scheme. Piggott, then in practice at the bar in London, had already taken an academic interest in the subject, having achieved some success with the first edition of his *Foreign Judgments: their effect in English Courts*, published in 1879–1881. Encouraged by the apparent interest of the United Kingdom in international arrangements, Piggott wrote to the Secretary of State for the Colonies in October 1885[1] suggesting that action on judgment enforcement with respect to the colonies deserved attention, as these jurisdictions had much in common, not least in usually having similar procedures for service upon absent defendants which derived from United Kingdom legislation.[2] He enclosed a draft Bill,[3] drawn up by himself which he claimed drew in part upon the New Zealand legislation but mainly upon United Kingdom arrangements including recent provisions on bankruptcy,[4] and the earlier legislation concerned with companies and probates.[5] This was referred by the Colonial Office to the Law Officers.

1 *Proceedings of Colonial Conference, 1887* C.5091 Appendix, No 8, encl 1.
2 Eg Common Law Procedure Act 1852 and Order XI as contained in the Rules of the Supreme Court of 1875 and 1883.
3 C.5091, Appendix, pp 24–26.

4 The Bankruptcy Act 1883, s 117, making court orders in bankruptcy matters enforceable in any of the Kingdom, and s 118, requiring UK courts and British courts elsewhere to act in aid of and auxiliary to each other in bankruptcy and insolvency matters.

5 Paras 1.04 and 1.11 above.

The Imperial Conference 1887

1.18 At much the same time, the Colonial Office received a proposal from the Board of Trade following on the recent changes in United Kingdom law, raising the possibility of including enforcement provisions in a proposed Indian Bankruptcy Bill.[1] The Colonial Office sent Piggott's draft for the consideration of the Board of Trade with certain reservations[2] but the Board for want of funds to pay counsel deferred consideration until the Law Officers had reported.[3] The Law Officers for their part generally supported the Bill, except for its application to inferior courts and to grants of probate[4]. They became reconciled to the latter after considering the effects of the Victoria legislation,[5] although doubts were raised about potential savings and simplification. The Secretary of State, Sir Henry Holland, expressed opposition to Piggott's Bill[6] and the Lord Chancellor, Lord Halsbury, registered a number of objections, stressing in particular the importance of reciprocity.[7] Piggott, on receiving the latter, wrote back suggesting that the forthcoming Colonial Conference would be an appropriate place for the issues to be examined. The matter was put on the agenda of the Conference which met in London in April 1887[8] and Piggott's request to be permitted to participate was agreed to. The subject engaged the attention of the Conference for three days and Piggott's draft legislation was used as the initial basis of the discussion.[9] It was evident, however, that improved legislation would be required. Much labour by Parliamentary Counsel, Jenkyns and Ilbert, produced new drafts in which bankruptcy and winding-up were treated in separate Bills from other judgments, and matrimonial proceedings and grants of administration excluded altogether, largely, it appears, in the latter case, because they could be dealt with by legislation modelled on statutes already in use.[10]

1 CO 323/364, Doc No 18342/85 (BT); C.5091, Appendix, No 8, encl 2.

2 CO 323/364, Doc No 6937/86 (CO); C.5091, Appendix, No 8, encl 3.

3 CO 323/364, Doc No 8689/86 (BT).

4 CO 323/365, Doc No 9047/86 (LO). Reassurances were later given to the Board of Trade on the bankruptcy provisions: CO 323/365, Doc No 13790/86 (LO); C.5091, Appendix, No 8, encl 4 and 5.

5 Para 1.16 above; CO 309/131, Doc No 6851/87 (LO).

6 C.5091, Appendix, No 8, encl 6.

7 Ibid, encl 11.

8 South Australia proposed that the Conference should discuss the question of absconding debtors: ibid, Appendix, No 5.

9 *Proceedings of the Colonial Conference* 1887, Vol I, C.5091, pp 51–75; 124–141; 446–460.

10 Ibid, Appendix, No 9–11 (Enforcement of Colonial Judgments Bill); No 15 and 16 (Bankruptcy and Winding-up of Companies Bill).

The Conference debate

1.19 The debate on the judgments legislation reflected concerns which had already become evident in earlier Australasian discussions. Was the scheme to follow the United Kingdom legislation with its largely formal process, as Piggott proposed, or was the registering court to have authority to examine the jurisdictional basis upon which the original judgment was given, as was the case in Australasian legislation? Piggott argued that the jurisdictional rules in the United Kingdom and the colonies were so similar that no injustice would be done if there was an obligation to recognise and enforce all colonial judgments.[1] An alternative solution would be to provide a common code for assumed jurisdiction.[2] Sir Samuel Griffith of Queensland forcefully emphasised that the receiving state must retain the right to determine whether to recognise that the original court had properly assumed jurisdiction. For the possibility of exorbitant jurisdictional rules, as a result of each jurisdiction developing its own service rules, could not be ignored.[3] These concerns were widely shared.

Further and related anxiety was expressed with respect to the notice to be given of the registration to the judgment debtor. Was it enough that he had received notice of the original proceedings or should there be an additional requirement of notice in the receiving state which would provide the debtor with a further opportunity to seek a stay of execution? Piggott's Bill, in following the United Kingdom Act of 1868, had favoured the former approach but Australasian experience suggested that safeguards were necessary if the debtor was not to be subject to unexpected execution of judgments, especially if he had no actual knowledge of the original judgment or if it had been reached in excess of jurisdiction.[4]

1 C.5091, Vol I, pp 67, 130–131, 450.
2 Ibid, Appendix, No 14 (Piggott's proposals).
3 Ibid, Vol I, pp 448–449.
4 Ibid. p 59.

Draft legislation of 1887

1.20 The solutions to these problems were embodied in the second of Henry Jenkyn's Heads of Bills, which partook more of the recent Australian federal legislation than that of the United Kingdom.[1] This Bill provided that:

(a) any judgment recovered in a British possession could be registered on production of a certificate of the judgment after which it could be enforced as if a local judgment;
(b) the certificate of the judgment must state, inter alia,[2] that the process was served on the defendant according to the local law (whether personally or otherwise or whether in the jurisdiction or by proper service ex juris) or that the defendant submitted to the jurisdiction of the court;[3]
(c) the debtor could seek a stay of execution on the grounds that he was not personally served in the jurisdiction and that he was not amenable to the jurisdiction of the original court under its law: in such case the debtor must seek within a reasonable time to set aside the judgment in the original court;[4]
(d) the scheme would depend upon the enactment of reciprocal statutory provisions in all jurisdictions and would be applied in respect of particular jurisdictions by local Order-in-Council or proclamation.[5]

Not surprisingly in view of the basic differences of principle, final agreement on these matters was not received at the Conference but there was support for the proposal that Parliamentary Counsel produce further versions of the Bills which had been prepared for the Conference[6] and also a Colonial Probates Bill. The Conference had, however, identified major issues of principle which were to face those in later generations who were to be called upon to prepare schemes of enforcement for the Commonwealth.

1 C.5091, Appendix II. It also extended to judgments or orders not requiring payment of money (cl 10) and could be applied to inferior courts (cl 11).

2 It must also state that the judgment could be executed in the possession and that there was a specified and substantial reason for its execution in the requested jurisdiction: cl 3(a), (b).
3 Cl 3(c).
4 Cl 5. It could also be stayed if an appeal was intended and, possibly, if there was already a local judgment on the matter.
5 Cl 1.
6 Bankruptcy also ran into some difficulties: *Proceedings of Colonial Conference 1887*, Vol I, pp 68–74; 142–146.

Dicey takes a look

1.21 New drafts were quickly prepared based upon the Heads of Bills and circulated amongst interested government departments.[1] They were also shown to Piggott whose numerous and critical comments were not wholly acceded to by Parliamentary Counsel.[2] Ilbert, therefore, suggested that the drafts should be shown to A. V. Dicey, who was coming to be recognised as an authority on the Conflict of Laws. Dicey was generally supportive of the whole initiative, although he concluded that the legislation attempted too much and should be simplified. It would be best to concentrate upon money judgments which were the most common case and on colonial probates. His conclusion was farsighted:

'the practical gain and the political advantage of strengthening the legal ties which bind the different parts of the British Empire together might be very considerable.'

Bankruptcy gave rise to too many problems in the current state of private international law and should be excluded.[3]

The Secretary of State too favoured this less ambitious approach and asked Parliamentary Counsel to prepare revised drafts for circulation to the colonies.[4]

The matter of probates presented little difficulty and a circular with a draft Bill which drew substantially upon the United Kingdom legislation was sent out in April 1888.[5] In due course, replies from the colonies gave evidence of general support. In March 1890, the Colonial Office informed Parliamentary Counsel that the matter was in good shape and requested preparation of a final draft, without waiting for progress on the other subjects.[6] The Colonial Probates Act 1892 was enacted virtually without debate and was quickly followed by reciprocal legislation throughout the Empire.

1 CO 328/368, Doc No 11511/87 (PC).
2 Ibid, Docs No 13726/87 (CO); 17372/87 (PC); 22342/87 (PC).
3 CO 323/373, Doc No 2351/88 (PC). He also made detailed comments upon the drafts and Piggott's criticisms.
4 Ibid, Doc No 4675/88 (T).
5 CO 323/372, Docs No 3081/88 (LC); 4420/88 (PC); 5096/88 (PC); 7226/88 (PC).
6 CO 323/380, Doc No 4409/88 (PC).

The draft money judgment scheme 1888

1.22 The Colonial Judgments legislation proved to be more controversial. Dicey's comments caused Parliamentary Counsel to rethink many features. If the legislation was to have value, it must in his view be speedier and simpler than a summary judgment obtained under Order XIV in an action upon the original judgment. Parliamentary Counsel doubted whether this could be achieved. Dicey also stressed that greater reliance could be placed upon judgments of colonial courts than those of foreign systems: 'every assumption ought to be made in favour of the validity of the colonial judgment'. Thus the United Kingdom and the Australian federal statutes should be relied upon but a body of rules of service be provided in the legislation. Initially at least, Parliamentary Counsel felt constrained by the Conference discussions which had favoured some power in the receiving court to question the jurisdictional competence of the original court.[1] The new drafts were completed at the end of 1888[2] and were circulated to the colonies in January 1889 with explanatory documentation, pointing out Dicey's contribution.[3]

The new version was not confined to money judgments, as Dicey had suggested, though certain types of judgment were expressly excluded.[4] It was to be applied to any British possession by Order-in-Council if two statutory conditions were met. First, the possession must have made adequate provision for giving effect to Supreme Court judgments of the United Kingdom and 'to the provisions of this Act so far as respects that possession'. Secondly, the rules observed in that possession with respect to ex juris service must be 'in substantial accordance' with the rules observed in 'some part of the United Kingdom'.[5] This provision was thought likely to produce, indirectly, uniformity of practice on service out of the jurisdiction, Parliamentary Counsel considering Dicey's proposal for a uniform code to be impracticable. The Bill went on to provide that the certificate of judgment must state that the debtor had submitted to the jurisdiction or had been duly served with notice of the original proceedings, in the latter case stating the details of the service process.[6] No duty was imposed to serve notice of registration upon the debtor although an affidavit from the judgment creditor that the judgment had not been satisfied was required. As previously, the debtor was to have power to apply for a stay of execution on the grounds that the original process was not served upon him within the jurisdiction of the original possession and that he was not by the law of that place 'amenable to the jurisdiction of the original court'.[7] It is clear that in other respects the validity of the colonial judgment could not be questioned by the receiving court.

1 CO 323/373, Doc No 2351/88 (PC).
2 Piggott's comments were sought but in most cases they were rejected. The memorandum prepared to accompany the Bill originally contained references to Piggott by name but these were deleted in the final document, indicating a growing impatience with his contributions. CO 323/372, Doc No 23511/88 (LO).
3 CO 323/373, Doc No 2351/88 (PC).
4 Bankruptcy, winding-up, matrimonial orders, grants of administration, relating to land in the United Kingdom or restraining local court proceedings (cl 12). It applied to British courts in foreign countries (cl 9) and could be extended to inferior courts (cl 10).
5 Cl 1.
6 Cl 3.
7 Cl 6. A stay of execution could also be sought if the defendant established that the judgment had been satisfied in whole or part (cl 4(2)), or had already been recovered in the receiving jurisdiction (cl 5), that execution could not issue in the original court (cl 6(b)) or that an appeal was intended (cl 6(c)). Third party applications for stay were also permitted (cl 7).

Disappearance of the 1888 proposals

1.23 During the course of 1889 detailed responses were received from the colonies, almost all favourable, although several respondents questioned whether the scheme would be much utilised as far as their colony was concerned. Numerous detailed amendments were also proposed for consideration.[1] Responses were not received, despite reminders, from two important areas, New South Wales and Canada (the matter there having been referred to the Provinces in whose legislative competence the matter fell). Nonetheless, the Colonial Office were satisfied that there was sufficient colonial support to proceed with legislation and Parliamentary Counsel were instructed in December 1889 to finalise the draft.[2]

There progress ceased. Although reminders were sent to Parliamentary Counsel in the ensuing years until 1894, a final draft was never completed.[3] The formal explanation given in the Colonial Office records was the continuing absence of replies from Canada and New South Wales but there are suggestions of some lack of interest by Parliamentary Counsel.[4] A resolution of the Colonial Conference held in Ottawa in 1894 drawing particular attention to the matter of bankruptcy and winding-up orders and generally asking for renewed activity excited no response[5] and in 1895, the Colonial Office concluded that the matter was 'practically dead'.[6] But at the turn of the century Piggott injected a little life in a curious episode.

1 Summary of replies is appended to CO 323/373, Doc No 23511/88 (CO). The Government of India replied a little later and favourably: CO 232/380, Doc No 3598/90 (CO).
2 CO 323/376, Doc No 22311/89 (T).
3 CO 323/515, Doc No 11015/97 (CO); Doc No 29711/06 (CO).
4 Ibid which contains a Colonial Office memorandum of the history of the legislation.
5 C.7753, pp 256–257.
6 See references in note 3.

The Mauritius episode

1.24 A letter was received in the Colonial Office in 1897[1] from one W. Newton QC of Mauritius drawing attention to a serious problem of enforcement of a foreign judgment which had arisen from a notorious local decision, *Sangerhausen Machinery Factory v de Chazal*, in which a Mauritius citizen, having been awarded heavy costs against a German company which had sued him unsuccessfully, had been unable to rely upon that judgment in proceedings in Germany for apparent want of reciprocal enforcement facilities. The ability to bring proceedings at common law by way of an action on the judgment was, in German eyes, insufficient. A statutory procedure was called for. The Colonial Office response was to enquire after the fate of the earlier legislation, the papers for which had remained with Parliamentary Counsel, albeit that the scheme had no application to foreign jurisdictions. A proposal to approach again the colonies whose replies to the original 1889 circular were outstanding was given effect.

This would not meet the Mauritius needs. To fill that gap, Piggott, now the Procureur and Advocate General in Mauritius, persuaded the local Legislature to enact its own legislation which he prepared. It was a general measure applicable to both foreign and colonial judgments received into Mauritius.[2] It drew upon Piggott's experience not only of the Colonial Conference exercise but from the abortive UK-Italy treaty negotiations of 1877. He conceded that it was 'slightly in advance of what is supposed to be the law of England'. The statute caused deep concern in the Colonial Office. It was said to be 'clumsily expressed and clumsily arranged and will create many more difficulties than it proposed to remove' and to involve 'a step far bolder' than the draft legislation which has circulated through the Empire. Parliamentary Counsel, the Law Officers and A. V. Dicey, once more consulted on the matter, all opposed the Ordinance and it was disallowed on the grounds that it was impolitic in good international relations to allow, as the Ordinance did, for the Governor-in-Executive Council to exclude judgments of particular foreign countries and thereby to affix a stigma to them. The Law Officers thought that the matter should be dealt with by some simpler and shorter version capable of general application, whilst Dicey asked whether it was not possible 'to turn the present state of public feeling to account' by a scheme of direct enforcement of colonial judgments. Parliamentary Counsel still favoured summary judgments under Order XIV on actions on a judgment and preferred to see a general extension of that practice throughout the colonies.

1 The events are recounted in CO 167/718, Doc No 11015/97 (CO); CO 167/722, Desp Nos 245/99 (CO); CO 167/724, Desp Nos 379/98; 507/99; 514/99 (CO). See also Piggott, (1922) 38 LQR 339 at p 340.
2 The Foreign Judgments Ordinance 1899, No 42, reprinted in Piggott's *Foreign Judgments and Jurisdiction* Appendix, pp 35–44.

Piggott tries again: 1907

1.25 It was perhaps for the latter reason that no further action is recorded as having been taken, despite the revived interest in the Colonial Office.[1] As far as the needs of the United Kingdom were concerned—and this seems to have been the principal consideration—the availability of actions on colonial judgments and the Order XIV procedure for summary judgments was seen to be adequate. In 1903, it was again noted that some replies to the original circular were still outstanding. Moreover the question had not turned up at the Colonial Conference of 1902. Accordingly, instructions were given to put the papers away without further action 'until the Colonies ask us again to take the matter up'.[2] There was one person in the colonies who was not prepared to allow the scheme to die. In 1906, Sir Francis Piggott, now Chief Justice of Hong Kong, wrote to the Colonial Office suggesting that the subject was an appropriate one for the Colonial Conference scheduled for 1907.[3] The Colonial Office did not treat this as a formal request from a colony but as that of an individual pursuing his 'pet hobby'. A memorandum of the history of the exercise to date was prepared in case the matter was formally requested but in the event it was not. Piggott was told that time would not allow of the question being discussed at the Conference and the papers were again put by.

1 CO 96/453, Doc D/15296/06 reiterates this view of the reasons.
2 CO 323/373, Doc No 20243/94 (CO).
3 CO 323/515, Doc No 29711/06 (CO).

East African developments, 1902–3

1.26 Yet for some time new initiatives on this matter had been under way in African territories under United Kingdom authority, although initially these, as protectorates, fell under the jurisdiction of the Foreign Office. In 1902, the Chief Judicial Officer, J. Nunan, in the British Central Africa Protectorate (later Nyasaland) pressed for the introduction of a Judgment Extension scheme amongst the neighbouring protectorates. He submitted draft legislation modelled closely upon the United Kingdom Act of 1868 but designed for British Central Africa and North Eastern Rhodesia (later Northern Rhodesia)[1]. It was forwarded by the Commissioner Sharpe 'more as a suggestion than as a Draft Ordinance for approval'. The Foreign Office proposed that a copy be sent to the other protectorates in East Africa, Uganda and Zanzibar for a report by the judicial authorities there as to the need for its enactment. Before replies could be received, the Commissioner was writing to the Foreign Office stating that the need for the legislation had become imperative through a series of local cases. Nunan provided a revised draft. The Administrator for

North Eastern Rhodesia indicated local willingness to enact reciprocal legislation,[2] only to withdraw his consent temporarily unless the scheme was to be limited to final judgments for debts, damages and costs.[3] Meanwhile both East Africa and Uganda replied favourably,[4] encouraging the Foreign Office to produce a revised draft which included a power of extension to other protectorates by proclamation. This was circulated in July 1903. The consequence was the enactment of the British Central Africa Judgments Extension Ordinance 1903 which permitted North Eastern Rhodesia money judgments to be registered in the High Court of British Central Africa, normally within twelve months. A power was given to extend the scheme to other superior court judgments of any colony or protectorate in Africa.[5] Reciprocal provision was made in North Eastern Rhodesia.[6] Two years later, the protectorate passed another Judgments Extension Ordinance which applied to the High Court and courts subordinate thereto of East Africa and Uganda, the decrees of which 'may be transferred to the Protectorate'.[7] Copies of the latter statute were sent by the Colonial Office (now responsible for these territories) to the Commissioners of East Africa and Uganda requesting reciprocal steps.[8]

1 FO 2/608, Desp No 301/02 (BCA).
2 FO/746, Desp No 34/03 (BCA).
3 Ibid, Desp No 60/03 (BCA). Suggestions that the Africa Order-in-Council 1889, s 23 (allowing claims for mutual assistance to be acceded to) could be utilised for judgment enforcement were not accepted: ibid, Desp No 87/03 (BCA).
4 Ibid, Desp No 104/03 (EA); 91/03 (Ug); according to present practice in Uganda, judgments of East African Protectorates were filed in Uganda under the Code of Civil Procedure, cl 9, leading to the suggestion that this Indian Code procedure might be followed in the Ordinance for these jurisdictions. The Foreign Office suggested that a draft be on these lines. Similar arrangements were made by the draft East African Judicature Ordinance, cl 39: FO 2/856, Desp No 37/04 (EA).
5 Ordinance 1903, No 6, s 5. Reciprocal legislation was enacted by N. E. Rhodesia, Regulations 1904, No 1.
6 Administrator's Regulations, 1 January 1904.
7 Ordinance 1905, No 4: power of application to any British protectorate or possession was given (s 4).
8 CO 525/8, Doc No 30618/05.

Further African developments, 1907–12

1.27 In the meantime, Uganda had enacted a Judgments Extension Ordinance in relation to East Africa, on the lines originally suggested by the Foreign Office, which applied relevant provisions of the Indian Code of Civil Procedure. [1] Reciprocal legislation was introduced at the same period by the East Africa Protectorate.[2] In 1907, steps were taken to bring the British courts in Zanzibar into these arrangements.[3] In 1908, Uganda replaced its legislation which thereafter applied to East Africa, British Central Africa and British courts in Zanzibar, still utilising the Indian Civil Procedure Code provisions.[4] Similar replacement provisions were made by East Africa.[5] In 1912, the British Central African Protectorate also replaced its two statutes by a single Extension Ordinance, applicable to the other territories in East and Central Africa.[6] These statutes, although differing in the mechanisms for transmission and registration or filing of the original judgments, constituted a set of reciprocal arrangements in this part of Africa. Each statute also contained reciprocal provision for the execution of warrants of arrest for absconding debtors from another territory in the scheme.

1 Ordinance 1905, No 6, s 2: this included a power of extension to British protectorates and possessions (s 4).
2 Judgments Extension Ordinance 1905, No 5.
3 Judgments Extensions Regulations 1907 of Zanzibar, CO 533/35, Docs No 9488/07; 14405/07 (FO). Attempts were made to permit arrest in Zanzibar of debtors who had absconded from the other two jurisdictions. In the absence of reciprocal legislation, which was suggested, the Secretary of State doubted the propriety of this provision. Uganda in due course made such provision; Ordinance 1908, No 3, ss 3 and 4, which was adopted elsewhere.
4 Judgments Extension Ordinance 1908, No 3.
5 Judgments Extension Ordinance 1908, No 2.
6 Judgments Extension Ordinance 1912, No 7 The scheme was adopted by Tanganyika in 1921, Ordinance 1921, No 13 and applied to Kenya Colony, Uganda, Nyasaland and Zanzibar: CO 525/95, Doc No 16526/21.

West Africa moves: 1906–1908

1.28 Developments were also taking place in British territories in West Africa about the same period. The trigger was a letter from a trading company in the Gold Coast to the District Commissioner complaining of debtors who absconded to the Ivory Coast, a French jurisdiction. The company suggested that extradition arrangements should be instituted.[1] The Colonial Secretary replied that as the fault lay with the traders who allowed credit indiscriminately, the law as it stood provided sufficiently for the ordinary usages of trade. The company, incensed by the tone of this response, wrote directly to the Secretary of State, stating that extradition facilities to deal with frauds would be to the benefit of all the European territories in West Africa. They added that the problem was equally serious as between one British colony and another. The Colonial Office, initially inclined to reiterate their earlier position, took a second look at the matter. Recognising that in most cases the proper remedy was to seek enforcement of a civil judgment, the legal adviser suggested that a registration system for money judgments based upon the United Kingdom legislation should be considered for these colonies. This advice was followed and copies of the 1905 Ordinance of British Central Africa were sent in 1906 to Gambia, Gold Coast, Northern and Southern Nigeria and Sierra Leone with the suggestion that similar provision should be enacted to apply to the nearest colonial neighbours with discretion to extend beyond.

Prompt response came from Gambia, where a draft was prepared on the lines proposed by the Colonial Office and, after approval there, was enacted in late 1906.[2] Equivalent legislation was introduced into Northern Nigeria[3] and Sierra Leone[4] in the following year. Meanwhile, Gold Coast legislation was passed which, though similar in approach, differed in certain important details.[5] It did not apply to subordinate courts nor could it be used in respect of judgments 'obtained by default in the absence, other than wilful, of the defendant from the jurisdiction' of the original court.[6] These changes were considered by the Colonial Office to be improvements and other West African jurisdictions were asked to replace or introduce equivalent statutory provisions, with the minimum of divergence. This request was carried out in each of the territories during the course of 1908.[7] Although in each case, the short title referred to 'foreign judgments', the scheme was confined to British jurisdictions. Circumstances of the kind which had actually initiated the activity were not affected.

1 The correspondence is contained in CO 96/453, Doc D/15293/06 (Gold Coast).
2 Judgments Extension Ordinance 1906, No 13. CO 87/176 Doc No 35175/06 and 1746/06–07.

3 Judgments Extension Proclamation 1907, No 3.
4 Judgments Extension Ordinance 1907, No 17.
5 Foreign Judgments Extension Ordinance 1907, No 4. Correspondence is contained in CO 96/458, Doc No 25730/07. These changes were made as a result of objections in the Gold Coast Legislature.
6 Ss 2 and 3(2).
7 Gambia: Foreign Judgments Extension Ordinance 1908, No 5; Northern Nigeria: Foreign Judgments Extension Proclamation 1908, No 21; Southern Nigeria: Foreign Judgments Extension Ordinance 1908, No IV; Sierra Leone: Foreign Judgments Extension Ordinance 1908, No 4. The Gambia Ordinance, s 5, allowed registered judgments to be enforced by sale of land in Gambia under the Registration Ordinance 1880, s 10: CO 87/189, Doc No 17377/08.

Empire judgment schemes as at 1910

1.29 By 1910, therefore, judgment enforcement schemes in relation to civil money judgments were in operation in several parts of the British Empire, in the main as regional schemes: Australasia,[1] Central and East Africa, West Africa and in the United Kingdom itself. Each scheme was designed essentially for a particular group of neighbouring jurisdictions to which individual statutes applied expressly and although most made provision for extension to other British jurisdictions, presumably, though not explicitly, on the intended basis of reciprocity, in practice, such extensions were not negotiated. Alone, the New Zealand statute gave full recognition to judgments obtained anywhere in His Majesty's dominions without reciprocity.[2] In the main, the schemes allowed for automatic acceptance of superior court judgments for local enforcement, in the majority of schemes without power in the receiving court to enquire into the competence of the original court or to question the judgment in any respect. Although these arrangements suggest greater interest in enforcement facilities in the Empire than the Colonial Office was prepared to acknowledge, large areas of the Empire were not affected, notably Canada, Southern Africa,[3] India and the West Indies. In those places proceedings had to be brought by local actions on the judgment normally governed by the common law,[4] in some instances subject to limited statutory modifications.[5]

1 The Service and Execution of Process Act 1901, No 11 of the Commonwealth introduced the present full faith and credit system of enforcement for judgments of the Australian states, replacing the 1886 statute in those states in which it had force of law.
2 Judicature Act 1908, No 89, s 56.
3 Provincial Division judgments of the Supreme Court were enforceable in other such divisions: South Africa Act 1909, s 112.
4 A Code of Civil Procedure (1897), arts 210–212, governed the position in Quebec. W. J. Johnson (1957) 35 Can Bar Rev 911, gives the history of these provisions. In India, the Code of Civil Procedure 1908, ss 13 and 14 also provided statutory rules for recognition of foreign judgments: these were based upon earlier provisions in the Civil Procedure Code of 1877, ss 13 and 14.
5 A summary of these is contained in the Report of the British and Foreign Legal Procedure Committee, 1918 ('Sumner Committee'), paras 24–27.

International activity

1.30 If little interest in civil judgments enforcement was being evinced in the Colonial Office, the same was not true elsewhere. A number of international bodies, notably the International Law Association,[1] the Hague Conference on Private International Law,[2] the International Congress of Chambers of Commerce[3] and the Congress of the Chambers of Commerce of the British Empire began to concern themselves with these matters. A number of bilateral treaties involving European countries had begun to prove their worth.[4] In addition, strong interest in the enforcement of foreign arbitral awards emerged in the mercantile community.[5] The latter led to a survey by the Board of Trade of Empire and foreign country experience and to consideration by the Imperial Conference of 1911.[6] The committee which examined this matter shared the sentiment of their Chairman, Sir Rufus Isaacs, that discussion should not be confined to arbitral awards.[7] At the plenary meeting, therefore, Isaacs proposed that the final resolution should concern itself also with the more important issue of judgment enforcement. In consequence the Conference itself resolved that the Imperial Government should consider, with the dominion governments, the making of mutual arrangements for enforcement of judgments and orders, including those for the reinforcement of arbitration awards.[8]

1 The matter had been discussed substantially at the 17th meeting (Brussels, 1895), 18th meeting (Buffalo, 1899), 19th Meeting (Rouen, 1900), 20th meeting (Glasgow, 1901—a draft General Convention) and 21st meeting (Antwerp, 1903—a draft Anglo-Belgian Treaty).
2 Discussed at the Hague Conference in 1893, a Hague Convention, 14 November 1896, was produced, to which 15 states were party.
3 A resolution favouring bilateral treaties was passed in 1910: Cd 5746–I, p 129.
4 Eg France–Switzerland, 1869; Austria–Serbia, 1881; France–Belgium, 1899.
5 See para 5.01, below.
6 Cd 5745, pp 160–162, 326–332, 424–425; Papers laid before the Conference (V), Cd 5746–I, pp 129–137.
7 Ibid, pp 330–332.
8 Ibid, pp 425. In separate debates, the Conference supported the principle of reciprocal action on deserted wives and children which led ultimately to the Maintenance Orders (Facilities for Enforcement) Act 1920; ibid, pp 206–212.

Renewed Imperial interest

1.31 This development was received with little enthusiasm in the Colonial Office. In answering, after the Conference, the inevitable pre-conference suggestion from Piggott in Hong Kong that the matter should be put on the Conference agenda, it was noted that the question of judgment enforcement had been discussed at the Conference and that it would receive further consideration. But the memorandum notes that the Conference resolution 'will not in practice mean anything substantial but . . . might well be used to dispose of Sir F. Piggott'.[1] The Board of Trade, however, did not allow the matter to fall into abeyance. Copies of the resolution were sent out in 1911 for consideration by the dominion governments and appear to have elicited widespread support over the next year.[2] Other support was forthcoming in the evidence given to the Dominions Royal Commission,[3] though many commercial interests now favoured giving priority to the question of arbitration award enforcement.[4] It was nevertheless evident from evidence submitted that the principle of judgment extension was widely seen as capable of making a desirable contribution to the development of trade within the Empire. This was a view with which the Board of Trade strongly concurred. In due course, therefore, when the replies from the dominions were at last with it, the Board of Trade, with the Lord Chancellor, arranged for fresh legislation to be prepared on the matter of civil judgments.[5]

1 CO 129/378, Doc No 20633/11 (HK), written by A. B. Keith.
2 Reservations appear in certain of the provincial Canadian responses set out in the Sumner Committee Report, Cd 251, p 8: British Columbia, Manitoba and Quebec were opposed, p 10.
3 The Commission was on natural resources, trade and legislation of the dominions, in particular upon the extent to which the mutual trade of the several parts of the Empire was affected beneficially or otherwise by the laws in force: 1st Interim Report 1912, Cd 6515, Final Report 1917, Cd 8462.

4 Minutes of Evidence in London, 1912, Cd 6517: Sir Albert Rollitt, Chairman of London Court of Arbitration at pp 72–76; W. R. Bisschop, pp 80–82; Charles Charleton, pp 84–87; G. H. Wright, pp 290–291. As the Royal Commission took evidence in the Empire, support for legislation was also found in New Zealand (1914, Cd 7170, pp 209–10 (A. E. Mabin)), in Australia (1914, Cd 7171, pp 307, 315 and 318 (F. W. (later Sir Frank) Eggleston)), in South Africa (1915, Cd 7707, p 164 (A. Buchanan and W. Butcher)) and in Canada (1917, Cd 8459, p 429 (Board of Trade of City of Toronto)). The Commission itself made no proposals.

5 CO 532/73, Doc No 27939/14 (BT); CO 323/766, Doc No P/53162/17.

The Judgments Extension Bill 1914–1916

1.32 The new Bill, although clearly having its origins in the earlier drafts, was in a simpler and more direct form.[1] The scheme would apply to money judgments only of superior courts of any part of HM dominions with reciprocal legislation and to arbitration awards enforceable as judgments of a court. Certificates of the judgment were to be registered in a manner determined by local law, normally within twelve months, on application. No provisions were made concerning jurisdictional requirements, notice of registration to the debtor or power in the receiving court to stay execution. But the original court could not issue a certificate of the judgment unless it was shown that the debtor was resident in a reciprocating part of the Empire. The receiving court was to have control over the registered judgment 'only so far as relates to the execution under the Act'. It is apparent that concerns expressed in earlier discussions were brushed aside in favour of a scheme which gave full and automatic recognition to money judgments as having equal status and equal currency wherever given, once reciprocity was granted. The Colonial Office when asked to comment—a condition of its agreement to the drafting of the statute—merely requested the inclusion of protectorates in the categories of those jurisdictions to which the legislation could be extended. For almost two years thereafter, in the emergencies of World War I, nothing further was done. In April 1916, however, an unamended version of the draft was circulated to the dominions and colonies for their comments. During the following two years usually favourable replies to the circular were received, from the Commonwealth of Australia, all the states, except Queensland, from New Zealand and South Africa but, in Canada, only from Quebec and New Brunswick,[2] whilst Newfoundland in an excess of loyalty enacted legislation based upon the circulated draft.[3]

In this period of relative inactivity, Piggott, now retired and back in London from Hong Kong,[4] wrote in 1917 to the Colonial Office repeating his interest and asking to be consulted on proposed legislation. A month later, he wrote again, expressing astonishment that he had not been consulted on the draft and pointing out that the proposed legislation, in following the 1868 approach, was in conflict with the 1887 Conference discussions. The Colonial Office record, noting its own lack of present involvement with the matter, expressed great distaste for Piggott's interventions of the past, dismissing his criticism in a biting memorandum setting out the history of the matter.[5] Once more the conclusion was reached that there was insufficient interest in the Empire, 'Dominion Governments being so slow to take up projects which have been blessed by their representatives at Colonial or Imperial Conferences'.[6] It is clear that the Colonial Office itself wished no active role.

1 The Bill is printed in Cmd 251, Appendix A.

2 Some criticisms were offered: Quebec was opposed: Cmd 251, p 10.

3 Judgments Extension Act 1917, No 23, which did not have effect as no reciprocal legislation, other than that of New Zealand, existed.
4 Piggott appears to have been sued in Hong Kong, and ironically, when he failed to satisfy his judgment debtor, the Colonial Office had to threaten to deduct the sum from his pension. The age of retirement of Chief Justices was reduced to relieve him of his office. He also irritated the Foreign Office when after retirement he went to practise in Peking and had sought to become legal adviser to the Chinese Government: CO 323/766, Doc No P/53162/17.
5 Ibid.
6 Ibid.

The Sumner Committee, 1918

1.33 The conclusion of the World War, however, brought an early revival of interest outside the civil service amongst commercial communities. In 1918, a petition was presented to the United Kingdom by 'eminent gentlemen in the City' representing the London Court of Arbitration and the London Chamber of Commerce and 'other important interests', drawing attention to the resolution of the Imperial Conference of 1911 which had supported extension of the 1868 scheme to the Empire.[1] The Lord Chancellor responded by appointing a committee under the Chairmanship of Lord Sumner which took evidence from persons of commercial and legal standing.[2] Its report, delivered in 1919, concluded that the time was 'fully ripe' for the introduction of a scheme for the British Empire 'with as little further delay as possible'.[3] The existence of workable schemes already in many parts of the Empire, the acceptance in principle of an Imperial scheme by the self-governing dominions and the utility to colonies with important commercial business of such a scheme were at last officially recognised as powerful justifications for arrangements based upon reciprocity. At the same time, the Report accepted certain criticisms which had been directed against the Judgment Extension statute as the model for Imperial use. These exhibited, in the Committee's view, a common desire for caution and common solicitude for the protection of debtors from exorbitant jurisdiction. In the interests of acceptance by territories with differences in history, race, institutions and traditions, and often geographically distant, proposals based on the 1868 model were deemed to be premature, though favourable experience of a more cautious scheme might permit later amendments in that direction.[4] It was proposed, therefore, that enforcement should not be the result of a ministerial act but should involve a decision in the discretion of the receiving court when satisfied that it was 'just and convenient'. This would permit questions of competence[5] in the original court or issues of fraud to be raised in the receiving court. The debtor should be given a proper opportunity of showing cause before execution was issued.[6] Accordingly specific amendments to the 1916 draft were recommended on those lines. The long-standing Australian reservations had prevailed. The Committee also proposed that arbitration awards should be included only where an order had been made in the original jurisdiction giving effect to the award as a judgment.[7]

The Committee also examined the question of judgments emanating from countries outside the Empire.[8] In their view, it was not a favourable time for setting in motion the negotiation of the international agreements which would be needed before the present law could be changed. A 'considerable legal equipment' would be needed for ensuring that negotiators of the bilateral arrangements were well informed both on the legal systems involved and the practicalities. Uniformity between foreign countries would be difficult to secure and invidious discrimination would be unavoidable. Not only was the present law in respect of foreign judgments seen as satisfactory by lawyers and laymen as far as enforcement in England was concerned but there was little evidence that different arrangements were needed abroad, as 'England has hitherto been a creditor country'. It was moreover sensible to await the benefits of the experience gained from working the new Empire scheme. These considerations were said to apply with even greater force to arbitration awards.[9]

1 Report, para 1.
2 Its terms of reference required a report upon 'what steps, if any, are feasible and are to be recommended to facilitate the enforcement of judgments, decrees and awards elsewhere than in the country in which they have been made'. The original petitioners refused to give evidence as no representative of the Court of Arbitration was appointed to the Committee: ibid, para 2.
3 Ibid, para 34. Detailed consideration was given to amendments to English jurisdiction rules, paras 4–23.
4 Ibid, paras 31 and 32.
5 The Committee seems to have envisaged the possibility of recognition of certain judgments where there had been service out of the jurisdiction, especially in actions on bills of exchange and ordinary mercantile transactions but even in cases where no personal service was achieved, recognition might be 'sparingly accorded': ibid, para 33.
6 Ibid, para 33. It was not intended that examination of the merits 'should be obligatory' but quaere whether it was to be discretionary?
7 Ibid, para 35: see para 5.03 below.
8 Ibid, paras 36–42.
9 Ibid, para 47. The Committee did make proposals for improvements in relation to the commencement of legal proceedings against absent debtors and serving documents and securing evidence abroad: ibid, paras 43–47.

The Administration of Justice Act 1920, Part II

1.34 The strong recommendations produced early response. The Report was circularised to the dominions and the colonies for information.[1] At the same time, provisions were drafted for inclusion in the Administration of Justice Bill, already scheduled for Parliament. These followed closely the Committee's detailed proposals and were enacted by Parliament in 1920 for application to the United Kingdom, with little detailed comment.[2] In due course, rules of court were made which inter alia required notice of registration to be given to the debtor with execution suspended until the debtor had had time to apply to set the registration aside.[3] This legislation was made available throughout the Empire[4] and in the ensuing years the great preponderance of jurisdictions enacted their own statutes modelled, with little modification, upon it and orders bringing reciprocal arrangements into force took effect extensively.[5] Only two parts of the Empire were not substantially involved with this development, India and Canada.[6]

1 CO 323/810, Doc No 47684 (CO).
2 Administration of Justice Act 1920, Pt II. See paras 2.18–2.22 below for fuller discussion.
3 1922 SR & O 824.
4 General Circular, 15 February 1921 which especially advised the East and West African dependencies to substitute the new legislation for their Judgments Extension legislation which did not apply to the United Kingdom. The East African statutes remained in force.
5 By 1932, extensions had been made by the UK in respect of 62 jurisdictions, 52 of these having been made between 1921–1924: SR & O 1948, XI, pp 139–162. Extension orders elsewhere applied to far smaller numbers of territories.
6 Legislation based directly on this model and applicable to other parts of the Empire was enacted by Newfoundland (S Nfld, 1922, c 14), then not a part of Canada.

Canada and judgments schemes

1.35 Canada had, however, been concerned about the question of judgment enforcement for some years, principally as it affected judgments of other provinces. The British North America Act 1867 had not dealt with the matter and provincial legislation had merely regulated certain aspects of actions on judgments which in some jurisdictions were open to re-examination in the requested court. From its establishment in 1914, the Canadian Bar Association took an active interest[1] leading in 1918 to the reference to the Committee on Uniform Legislation of a draft Bill. The newly formed Commissioners on Uniformity of Legislation in Canada took charge of the matter. At their request the Commissioners for Prince Edward Island produced in 1921 a model Act, which drew heavily upon the 1920 statute. The Commissioners however, favoured its initial application only at the provincial level.[2] When, therefore, in 1924, the Conference of Commissioners approved a model Reciprocal Enforcement of Judgments Act which followed the Empire scheme but with modifications[3] the model applied only to those provinces making reciprocal provision. Legislation based upon it was enacted in several provinces in the following years.[4] Saskatchewan, however, also enacted in 1927 legislation which allowed it to have reciprocal arrangements under the Empire scheme.[5]

1 Dominions Royal Commission, Minutes of Evidence in Canada, 1917, Cd 8459, pp 430–1 (Sir James Askins).
2 See the account in K. Nadelmann, (1960) 38 Can Bar Rev 68 at pp 71–72.
3 In particular, it was provided that no registration could take place if the debtor would have a good defence if an action were brought on the original judgment.
4 Alberta (1925), British Columbia (1925), New Brunswick (1925), Ontario (1929), Saskatchewan (1924): Nadelmann, loc cit, p 72.
5 Ss 1927, c 12 (still in force). Nadelmann, loc cit, pp 74–75 points out that as the model Canadian Act allowed the registering court to apply its own rules of recognition, the scheme was not reciprocal.

Demand for an extra-Empire scheme

1.36 The new Empire arrangements[1] appear to have given general satisfaction as having worked well, although in 1932 registrations in the United Kingdom, and presumably elsewhere too, were said not to have been numerous.[2] Much less satisfaction was felt in so far as foreign jurisdictions were concerned.

In June 1926, at the instigation of Sir Hubert Llewellyn Smith, British representative at the League of Nations, the agenda of the World Economic Conference included the question of executing judgments and arbitral awards in foreign countries.[3] This unsolicited reference to judgments caused some irritation to the British ministries. Sir Thomas Willes Chitty, a Senior Master of the Supreme Court, in a memorandum prepared for the Foreign Office contended that summary judgments in actions on foreign judgments were quite sufficient and satisfactory and that any registration system on the Imperial model would require so many safeguards that enforcement would be as protracted as through litigation. This parochial view overlooked an important consideration. The Foreign Office had been constantly pressed through the 1920s by the United Kingdom business community with their difficulties in enforcing their judgments abroad in contrast with the ease of enforcement at common law of foreign judgments in the English courts. The want of a statutory code governing the English practice led foreign courts to assume an absence of reciprocity, a normal pre-requisite for allowing English judgments to be enforced by them. The Sumner Committee's complacency in this respect began to appear to be misplaced.[4]

In the following three years, the Lord Chancellor's Department, the Board of Trade and the Foreign Office came to accept that the question of bilateral conventions should be looked into, but that an expert examination should first be conducted.[5] In March 1929, the Foreign Secretary, Sir Austin Chamberlain, drew the matter to the attention of the Lord Chancellor, Lord Hailsham, who appointed a small preliminary committee under Lord Justice Greer.[6] Their report in June 1929 favoured prompt action through the negotiation of bilateral treaties within a framework set by legislation, which might adopt the 1920 Act's procedures but should not depart from the common law on the matter.[7] Following the report, informal discussions with the Belgian, French and German Governments were instituted through an expert committee, in which draft conventions were drawn up.[8] At this committee's suggestion, the Lord Chancellor created the Foreign Judgments (Reciprocal Enforcement) Committee under Lord Justice Greer to report upon the nature of conventions required and of implementing legislation. The Committee reported in 1932 with the recommended legislation, rules of court and conventions in draft.[9]

The scheme was seen by the Committee as fully consistent with the general principles of existing law,[10] although alterations from the 1920 scheme were put forward as necessary to secure the agreement of foreign countries.[11] The Committee were strongly of the view that conventions should be negotiated within the limits set by the legislation. Provided substantial reciprocity of treatment was assured, individual Orders-in-Council could accommodate small differences of detail arising for differences in particular foreign law systems.[12]

1 The Maintenance Orders (Facilities for Enforcement) Act 1920, the model widely followed in the Empire, was enacted at this time: 132 HC Official Report (5th series) col 2159: H. C. Gutteridge, (1948) 2 ILQ 155–172.
2 Greer Committee Report, p 13: see below.
3 LCO/2, Doc No 1687: see para 5.07 below, in relation to awards.
4 Above, para 1.33. Moreover progress in relation to enforcement of arbitral awards had provided a marked contrast: see para 5.07 below. Representations had also been made by foreign countries seeking to negotiate conventions with the UK on the matter but these had been declined: LCO/2, Doc No 1687.
5 LCO/2, Doc No 1687.
6 The other members were W. E. Beckett, Assistant Legal Adviser, FO, and Sir Thomas Barnes (Board of Trade Solicitor).
7 LCO/2, Doc No 1688 contains this Report and a draft Bill, prepared by Beckett.
8 Initially, Barnes, Beckett and Sir Maurice Gwyer (Treasury Solicitor): LCO/2; Doc No 1688 contains the printed, confidential report of the committee, now Gwyer and Beckett: Greer Report, pp 15–17.
9 Report, Cmd 4213: Minutes are in LCO/2, Doc No 1690.
10 Ibid, para 24.
11 Ibid, para 18 and Annex V.
12 Ibid, paras 19–21.

The Greer Committee proposals

1.37 For our purposes, the most important proposal was that the new legislation could be applied also to dominion and colonial judgments. The draft was preferred as 'on the whole less tentative and more complete'[1] than the 1920 Act. As one system was thought to suffice, the Committee foresaw agreed extensions substituted under the new statute in relation to parts of the Empire already within the earlier scheme. But once the new legislation had been made applicable to the Empire, they advocated that no new extensions would be possible under the earlier Act for territories outside that scheme. Moreover, if dominions[2] or colonies were to be beneficiaries of the conventions with foreign countries, similar new legislation modelled on the 1933 Act would also need to be enacted by them.[3] Whilst inconveniently two systems were likely to co-exist for a time, it is apparent that the Committee hoped that the new statute would become the sole scheme.

1 Report, Annex V, para 12.
2 It was intended that the dominions would have a right to accede to the conventions, whilst the UK would have power to apply the conventions to dependencies.
3 Report, Annex V, para 12, commenting on the proposed cl 5.

The Foreign Judgments (Reciprocal Enforcement) Act 1933

1.38 The United Kingdom Parliament enacted the Foreign Judgments (Reciprocal Enforcement) Act 1933 with little debate and with but one drafting amendment made to the text prepared by the Greer Committee.[1] Shortly afterwards, the Act was made to apply to HM dominions, mandated territories and those under Crown protection,[2] thereby precluding new extensions by the United Kingdom under the 1920 scheme.[3] The immediate use of the Act by the United Kingdom was to conclude the bilateral arrangements in 1934 with two of the European countries with which it had already reached preliminary agreement.[4] In 1938, following the enactment of reciprocal provisions in British India and British Burma, an extension order was made for those jurisdictions.[5] Thereafter for seventeen years, no further extensions were made of any kind by the United Kingdom.

The legislation was circulated throughout the Empire and led to a variety of responses. In most cases, no action was taken to adopt the new legislation; in others, the new legislation was enacted to replace the earlier, whilst in others the two sets of legislation were put into operation.[6] The necessity for the new legislation, if treaties negotiated by the United Kingdom were to be extended to dependencies or, in the case of a full member of the Commonwealth, to be acceded to, seems to have carried little weight. For only New Zealand acceded to the two treaties put into force at this time,[7] having passed the replacing legislation,[8] whilst no dependent jurisdiction was at that time brought within their purview. The impression is gained that the 1933 legislation in many cases was enacted because it was the modernised legislation of the mother Parliament and not because it was seen as having any marked utility.

1 276 HC Official Report (5th series) cols 2333–5 removing superfluous words from cl 5(1).
2 1933 SR & O No 1073.
3 FJREA, s 7(1).
4 Belgium: 1936 SR & O No 1169; France: 1936 SR & O No 609.
5 1938 SR & O No 1363.
6 The present position is set out in Chapter 2, Annex I.
7 Accession: France (1937) and Belgium (1938): [1938] NZ Statutory Regulations, Nos 176–177.
8 Act 1934, No 11.

Repercussions in India and Canada

1.39 The enactment of the 1933 scheme, however, had important consequences for the development of the law of reciprocal enforcement in two parts of the Commonwealth which had not been significantly involved previously. In 1937 British India added new provisions to the Code of Civil Procedure, principally to permit reciprocal arrangements to be put into effect with the United Kingdom,[1] although there is no limitation to Commonwealth jurisdictions; they must merely be 'reciprocating territories'. The provisions do not follow the terms of the 1933 Act but were designed to interlink with existing provisions in the Code. They merely provide that enforcement is secured by filing an application for execution but the court must refuse execution if the judgment fails to satisfy the general conditions laid down in the Code for recognition and enforcement of any foreign judgment.[2]

The United Kingdom developments were of particular interest to the Conference of Commissioners on Uniformity of Legislation in Canada which between 1935 and 1939 looked into the question of international arrangements for judgment enforcement. In 1939 the Conference received a report commending adoption of a new Uniform Act based upon the 1933 statute, to replace the earlier model which had followed the 1920 Act.[3] The need for a common policy amongst the provinces was evident but its realisation was made more difficult by the special position of Quebec. In the post-World War II period, a number of initiatives were taken by the Conference to overcome provincial reservations, culminating in 1952 in a new draft Uniform Act which drew in the main upon its predecessor, rather than the 1933 Act, but with application to extra-Canadian judgments.[4] With minor modifications this became in 1958 the new Uniform Reciprocal Enforcement of Judgments Act.[5] As in the early model Act, this version did not lay down any common rules for the recognition of judgments and in that respect it did not fulfil the requirements which foreign countries were looking for before reciprocal treatment was granted.[6] By no means all provinces adopted this version of the legislation thereby restricting the capacity of the Federal Government to enter into treaty arrangements with foreign countries. In consequence, extensions beyond Canada both within the Commonwealth and outside were necessarily exceptional.[7] Even after the 1933 Act, therefore, Canadian arrangements remained essentially for intra-Canadian use in the matter of money judgments.

1 Code of Civil Procedure (Amendment) Act 1937, No 8, inserting s 44A. The reciprocal arrangements were put into effect in 1938.
2 Ibid, s 13, which applies also to actions upon foreign judgments.
3 K. H. Nadelmann, (1960) 38 Can Bar Rev 68 at p 77.
4 Ibid, pp 78–79.
5 Some of the delay was the consequence of awaiting the challenge to the constitutionality of related provisions in the Reciprocal Enforcement of Maintenance Orders Act before the Supreme Court: *A-G of Ontario v Scott* (1956) 1 DLR (2d) 433.
6 Newfoundland, however, had of its own initiative enacted legislation following the 1933 Act: S Nfld, 1938, No 20, now repealed by Act 1960, No 12.
7 See Chapter 2, Annex III for the present position.

Renewed international activity

1.40 The enactment of the 1933 scheme and its rather inconsistent implementation around the Commonwealth represented the last major consideration of the question anywhere in the Commonwealth for almost forty years.[1] The change-over from the 1920 to the 1933 scheme did not occur as widely as had been expected. Even after the enactment in 1956 of modifications, largely to deal with transitional matters which appear to have presented problems in effecting the alteration,[2] the United Kingdom still depends principally upon 1920 arrangements. In this period, however, considerable general activity took place at the international level, in some of which Commonwealth jurisdictions were represented. The general wave of interest, which in the 1920s and 1930s had produced not only proposals for legal arrangements[3] but a series of bilateral agreements[4] and two multilateral conventions[5], was more than matched by a fresh round of activity in the 1950s and 1960s. The International Law Association returned to the field and between 1958 and 1964 prepared a model Act. The Asian-African Legal Consultative Committee examined the matter in 1965[6] whilst the Hague Conference worked on a draft convention in sessions in 1964, 1966 and 1968, which resulted in a convention and additional protocol of 1 February 1971.[7] Bilateral agreements were frequently negotiated, particularly amongst European nations[8] and multilateral arrangements resulted from the Reciprocal Enforcement of Judgments Agreement of the Arab League in 1953, and the Benelux Convention of 24 November 1961 between Belgium, Netherlands and Luxembourg, replaced by the Brussels Convention on Jurisdiction and the Enforcement of Judgments in Civil and Commercial Matters negotiated by the six original members of the European Communities in 1968 and put in force in 1973. During this period too, the Commissioners on Uniformity of State Laws in the United States produced two influential models, the Uniform Foreign Money Judgments Recognition Act (1962) and the Uniform Enforcement of Foreign Judgments Act (1948) and a revised version (1964).[9] Although individual Commonwealth jurisdictions were involved in some of these exercises, it was invariably the result of their non-Commonwealth links, often with other international organisations. Thus, for example, Cyprus adopted the Hague Convention as an additional set of obligations[10] whilst Quebec modelled the relevant parts of its revised draft Civil Code upon the same document.[11] In the main, however, such positive action as resulted was supplementary to Commonwealth arrangements[12] or at the most in the form of updating existing statutes with minor modifications and some revision of the extension orders.[13] Only South Australia has enacted legislation which represents any substantial divergence from the earlier patterns.[14] By the 1970s however, it was becoming clear some re-examination of the existing Commonwealth arrangements would be necessitated by developments in this area of the conflict of laws which were taking place elsewhere. In particular, the accession of the United Kingdom to the Brussels Convention following her entry in the European Communities would require such a reappraisal.

1 Work has continued in Canada with further modifications to the Uniform Model: para 2.30, note 1, below.

2 Administration of Justice Act 1956, s 51. The United Kingdom, however, made considerable use of the 1933 scheme with respect to judgments under specialist treaty schemes: see para 3.08 below.

3 International Law Association: *Draft Rules for the Enforcement of Foreign Judgments* (1924); Hague Conference on Private International Law: *Draft Convention on Recognition and Enforcement of Foreign Judgments* (1928).

4 Particularly amongst European countries: Council of Europe *The Practical Guide to the recognition and enforcement of foreign judicial decisions in civil and commercial law* 1975, Part II, pp 218–322.

5 Bustamante Code of Private International Law (6th International Conference of American States, 1928); Nordic Convention regarding Recognition and Enforcement of Judgments (1932).

6 Asian–African Legal Consultative Committee *Reciprocal Recognition and Enforcement of Judgments* (nd).

7 Convention on the recognition and execution of foreign judgment in civil and commercial matters, 1 February 1971.

8 Council of Europe, loc cit n 4 above, pp 323–500. The United Kingdom entered into treaties with Germany, SI 1961/1199; Norway, SI 1962/636; Austria, SI 1962/1339; Netherlands, SI 1969/1063; Israel, SI 1971/1039; Italy, SI 1973/1894; Tonga, SI 1980/153; Surinam, SI 1981/735; the power of extension to dependent territories of the UK contained in the treaties has been exercised in a number of cases: para 3.08 below.
9 For a short historical survey, see R. J. Fowks, (1972) 11 Washburn LJ 372–389.
10 Law No 11 of 1976, in force between Cyprus and the Netherlands.
11 Civil Code Revision Office Report on the Quebec Civil Code, (1977) Draft Code, C.IV.
12 Eg Sierra Leone–Guinea Relations Act 1964, No 55: para 3.10 below.
13 This has been the case in Australia, in particular.
14 Foreign Judgments Act 1971, No 72; a Bill more closely modelled upon the 1933 Act was not endorsed by the South Australian Law Reform Committee, *8th Report* (1969): see paras 2.42–2.47 below.

The Commonwealth Law Ministers initiative, 1973–1980

1.41 The matter arose at the Meeting of Law Ministers of the Commonwealth in 1973, with special reference to maintenance orders. The Bangladesh Minister of Law suggested that a report be prepared to provide an up-to-date picture of reciprocal arrangements in force. A preliminary report was presented to the next meeting in 1975[1] and a fuller study to the following meeting in 1977.[2] The Law Ministers then concluded that

'the legal heritage of the Commonwealth made it both practical and justifiable for its independent members to continue special procedures and rules in their relationships *inter se* which might differ from those ordinarily in force between sovereign states. These special arrangements fashioned for intra-Commonwealth cooperation did not preclude adherence to more universally applicable rules, nor did they prevent non-Commonwealth participation. [The Minsters] were conscious of the need to develop these rules in a way compatible both with activity in the international sphere and with existing obligations of Commonwealth countries.'[3]

The Ministers favoured regular review of the existing arrangements with a view to bringing them up to date and improving them, particularly by a regional approach. In consequence, a series of regional workshops were conducted under the auspices of the Commonwealth Secretariat for these purposes.[4] A model Bill which incorporated a number of modifications to existing Commonwealth legislation suggested by international developments was evolved in the course of these discussions.[5]

These meetings were revealing.[6] There was widespread acceptance of the principle of providing international mechanisms which reduced the cost and delays which a creditor seeking to enforce his judgment abroad encounters and general recognition that in the long term it was advantageous to states with developing economies to have reliable and expeditious reciprocal arrangements at least with their main trading partners. The existing Commonwealth schemes were generally seen as uncomplicated in their operation and giving rise to few practical difficulties. At the same time, shortcomings were evident, not least in the limited and apparently haphazard way in which extensions to other jurisdictions, both in the Commonwealth and outside, had come about. Whilst developments were usually seen as desirable, both in the jurisdictions and the range of judgments to be covered, extensive change was seen as unlikely to constitute a high priority, particularly amongst those jurisidictions with small economies. There were some fears that improved facilities would be principally to the advantage of the Commonwealth countries with advanced economies.

1 J. D. McClean and K. W. Patchett *The Reciprocal Enforcement of Judgments within the Commonwealth: A Preliminary Report* (1975) (money judgments, maintenance orders, arbitration awards).
2 J. D. McClean and K. W. Patchett *The Recognition and Enforcement of Judgments and Orders and the Service of Process within the Commonwealth: A Further Report* (1979) (with wider coverage both of jurisdictions and subjects—service of process, bankruptcy, dissolution and winding-up, grants of administration).
3 Final Communiqué of Meeting of Commonwealth Law Ministers, 1977.
4 *Report of a Working Meeting held at Basseterre, St. Kitts, 1978* (Canada and the Caribbean); *Report of a Second Working Meeting held at Apia, Western Samoa, 1979* (Australasia, Far East and Pacific); *A Report of a Working Meeting held in Nairobi, Kenya, 1980* (Africa, Asia and Europe), published by the Commonwealth Secretariat.
5 The final version is contained in *1980 Meeting of Commonwealth Law Ministers: Memoranda* pp 265–275.
6 A summary is contained in ibid, pp 238–9.

Impact of international agreements upon Commonwealth schemes

1.42 It was also evident to the Law Ministers that the Commonwealth schemes could not remain immune to changes in practice which were taking place through the adhesion of member states to other schemes. Problems which had become evident in the work on the Hague Convention and more importantly the results of negotiations for adhesion of the United Kingdom to the Brussels Convention and for a UK/US Judgments Convention[1] were likely to lead to alterations in existing domestic legislation of the Commonwealth states affected, in relation to such matters as the jurisdictional bases of the original court which would be recognised, the currency in which judgments were payable[2] and judgments for multiple damages,[3] especially under antitrust legislation. The desirability of consistent treatment in Commonwealth countries of such matters as these was evident since the schemes were predicated upon substantial reciprocity. At the same time, it was generally conceded that any fundamental alterations to the existing schemes, either unilaterally or collectively, would be premature given the extent of international activity then taking place.

1 The draft was published in 1977, Cmnd 6771, a further version appeared in a *Third Consultative Paper*, March 1979. P. Hay and R. J. Walker, (1976) 11 Texas Int LJ 421–451; I. Mather, (1977) NLJ 777–779, 819–821; P. M. North, (1978) NLJ 315–318; S. Marshall, ibid, 1199–1200.
2 Administration of Justice Act 1977, s 4 (UK).
3 Foreign Antitrust Judgments (Restriction of Enforcement) Act 1979 (Aust); Protection of Trading Interests Act 1980 (UK).

The Brussels Convention and Civil Jurisdiction and Judgments Act 1982

1.43 The development outside the Commonwealth schemes which is likely to have far-reaching consequences is the adhesion of the United Kingdom to the Brussels Convention.[1] Unlike the Commonwealth schemes, this Convention provides for a common body of direct jurisdictional rules governing the circumstances in which courts in a Community country may hear civil and commercial matters. A judgment on this matter handed down in a contracting country must in consequence be presumed to be that of a competent court and be recognised and enforceable without any special procedure in any other contracting state. This represents a substantial difference of approach from existing Commonwealth arrangements which utilise indirect jurisdictional rules, that is to say, the receiving state applies its own conflict of laws rules (which under the 1933 system are contained in the governing Act) to determine whether the original court was competent.[2] What may be of considerable long-term significance is that the bases of jurisdiction set out in the Convention are more extensive than those upon which judgments are normally recognised within the Commonwealth.[3] It remains to be seen whether any extension of the acceptable bases of jurisdiction will follow in Commonwealth practice.[4]

Effect has been given to the Brussels Convention in the United Kingdom by the Civil Jurisdiction and Judgments Act 1982. The opportunity was also taken to make a series of amendments to existing private international law and to the United Kingdom legislation relating to the Commonwealth schemes. The principal developments affecting those schemes which this Act initiates may be summarised as follows:

(i) the replacement of the United Kingdom Judgment Extension legislation by modern provisions;[5]
(ii) fresh provision authorising refusal of recognition where the original court took jurisdiction in breach of an agreement for settlement of disputes;[6]
(iii) clarifying provision on what does not constitute submission to the jurisdiction of the original court;[7]
(iv) abolition of the rule that the original cause of action did not merge into the foreign judgment;[8]
(v) fresh provision in relation to foreign judgments given against states;[9]
(vi) power to extend the 1933 scheme to any courts or tribunals, in addition to superior courts;[10]
(vii) extension of the 1933 scheme to judgments providing for interim payments;[10]
(viii) extension of the 1933 scheme to any arbitral award which under the law of the place it was made has become enforceable in the same manner as a judgment;[11]
(ix) fresh provision for the issue of certificates of judgments;[12]
(x) power to make provision corresponding to that made in the Brussels Convention to regulate jurisdiction and recognition and enforcement of judgments between the United Kingdom on the one had and the Isle of Man, the Channel Islands, Gibraltar and the sovereign base areas on Cyprus on the other.[13]

Generally, these changes are consistent with the underlying principles of the Commonwealth scheme. Although they are generally welcome in total effect, they constitute a considerable unilateral development, which has not been the subject of any discussion with other Commonwealth states.[14] It remains to be seen how far other jurisdictions adopt similar rearrangements.

1 The negotiations for a UK/US Judgments Convention appear to have foundered: *Economist* 15–21 September 1979. A LAWASIA Convention is currently under discussion: (1984) Comm LB 392–393.

2 A considerable literature relating to the Brussels Convention now exists, particularly since the signing of the Convention of Accession by the United Kingdom on 9 October 1978. In this context, see I. F. Fletcher *Conflict of Laws and European Community Law* (1982); L. Collins *The Civil Jurisdiction and Judgments Act 1982* (1983).

3 Convention, Title II, arts 2–23.

4 By virtue of CJJA 1982, Pt III, these rules have largely become the basis of Scottish jurisdiction. They may be put into effect for the European territories of the United Kingdom, ibid, s 39.

5 CJJA 1982, ss 18, 19 and Schs 5, 6. For criticisms of the earlier provisions, see Scottish Law Commission, Memorandum No 12 (1980) and in relation to new arrangements, Report of the Scottish Committee on Jurisdiction and Enforcement (1980).
6 CJJA 1982, s 32, replacing FJREA 1933, s 4(3)(b).
7 Ibid, s 33, replacing FJREA 1933, s 4(2)(a)(i), and *Henry v Geoprosco International* [1976] 2 QB 726, [1975] 2 All ER 702.
8 Ibid, s 34.
9 Ibid, s 31.
10 Ibid, s 35, Sch 10.
11 Ibid, replacing the Administration of Justice Act 1956, s 51(a) which was confined to Commonwealth countries.
12 Ibid, replacing AJA 1920, s 10 and FJREA 1933, s 10.
13 CJJA 1982, s 39.
14 The United Kingdom did not participate in the Commonwealth Secretariat Working Meetings.

Commonwealth implications of the Brussels Convention

1.44 One further feature of the Convention calls for notice as having Commonwealth implications. Judgments may be obtained in any part of the Community against defendants who are not domiciled in the Community not only on the basis of jurisdictional links prescribed in the Convention but also on other jurisdictional bases prescribed in the lex fori, even though the latter are excluded as exorbitant insofar as Community domiciliaries are concerned. In both cases, the judgment against the debtor is subject to automatic enforcement anywhere in the Community.[1] Accordingly, contracting states are permitted to enter into an appropriate judgments convention with third states not to recognise and enforce judgments against domiciliaries or habitual residents of the latter which have been given exorbitantly by another contracting state.[2] The implication of this is that if any Commonwealth country wishes to avoid this consequence as far as enforcement in the United Kingdom is concerned, it will be necessary to enter into a judgments treaty in which such a provision is included. In future, therefore, it seems probable that inter-Commonwealth links involving the United Kingdom will necessarily involve the negotiation of a treaty, not merely the existence of reciprocal legislation. Such considerations have been prominent in the recent negotiations for a UK/Canada convention.[3] The relative ease of extension which the earlier mechanism provided has been unfortunately impaired.

It is perhaps too early to determine whether the approaches established by the Brussels Convention are the first step in a process which will have radical consequences for the Commonwealth schemes. If this kind of multilateral agreement with its developed rules on jurisdictional competence and an automatic enforcement process is seen to be successful amongst states with diverse legal systems, a case may be pressed for a similar approach amongst nations which share a common legal tradition. The shortcomings of existing arrangements which will be apparent in discussions in later chapters may not yet be perceived as sufficiently strong to undermine support for the existing schemes. But with the increasing sophistication in this area of law in the practice of developed countries with strong commercial interests, there is always a risk that unilateral changes may be effected which will weaken the claim that reciprocal treatment is afforded. It is improbable that reconsideration of the schemes will be undertaken in many of the developing Commonwealth states where reliance upon them is a rare event. On the other hand, if unilateral changes are made by developed countries protective of their citizens' interests, withdrawal by individual developing states may result. If these schemes are to be maintained—and the past recognition of their worth seems to justify that course of action—amendment should be the consequence of Commonwealth discussion in which the interests of litigants throughout the Commonwealth and the commercial implications of any change have been fully explored.

1 Art 4: see M. Pryles and F. A. Trindade, (1974) 48 ALJ 185 on the Australian implications.

2 Art 59. Certain types of exorbitant jurisdiction based upon presence of assets or seize of property cannot be exempted.

3 The draft Canada–United Kingdom Convention on the Recognition and Enforcement of Judgments 1982 is set out in The Proceedings of the Uniform Law Conference, 64th Annual Meeting, 1982, pp 64–85, with a Uniform Act. The draft deals also with the general matters covered in the reciprocal legislation of the United Kingdom and the provinces. Reconsideration of the latter is currently being undertaken to reflect these developments. The convention between the UK and Tonga of 28 June 1979 (SI 1980/1523) does not contain provisions in terms of art 59.

CHAPTER 2

Enforcement Schemes in the Commonwealth

I SCHEMES WITHIN A SINGLE STATE

2.01 This study is principally concerned with the schemes of judgment enforcement which are capable of application to more than one sovereign state within the Commonwealth. As a preliminary, however, it may be useful to describe shortly a number of domestic schemes devised by Commonwealth countries for judgment enforcement between jurisdictions comprised in the same sovereign state. These schemes make a marked contrast with the principal Commonwealth arrangements. For they seek to minimise the separate nature of the individual legal systems by requiring judgments handed down in any part to be treated with full faith and credit in any other part. The considerations of private international law which reflect a cautious acceptance of the judgments of external law systems and insist upon safeguards generally carry less weight in relation to the other jurisdictions which make up a federal or unitary state. Where a court is asked to enforce judgments from other parts of the same state, it may be possible to dispense with any power in that court to question the competence of the trial court, in particular the basis upon which jurisdiction was assumed, or the judgment itself and the circumstances in which it was obtained. In the interests of integrating the commercial and economic life of the single state, differences in the law, the procedure and the policies of the parts may have to be accepted or at least tolerated. As a result the interests of the union are made to transcend those of the parts by demanding that the judicial actions in any part must be given effect automatically through the enforcement facilities of any other part in which the judgment debtor or his assets may be found.

2.02 In contrast with the Commonwealth schemes, these arrangements are usually drafted in order to provide an essentially administrative scheme in which the judgment creditor is able, with the minimum of formalities, to secure enforcement of his judgment. Even here, however, differences exist. In some instances, production of evidence of the judgment is sufficient to permit enforcing action to be taken: in other cases, the judgment has to be registered, a step which in most cases cannot be challenged by the judgment debtor on jurisdictional or other grounds found in the conflict of laws. The following short accounts are designed to emphasise the main characteristics of this kind of arrangement.

(1) Australia

2.03 The Service and Execution of Process Act 1901 creates a system of direct enforcement of judgments for Australian jurisdictions.[1] It applies to the six states and two territories in the mainland of Australia and to Christmas

Island, the Cocos (Keeling) Islands and Norfolk Island.[2] It extends to judgments, decrees, rules or orders given by any court of record (which includes Supreme Courts, District Courts and magistrates courts[3]) whereby a sum of money is payable or a person is required to do or not to do an act or thing.[4] It must, however, be given in 'a suit', which is so defined as to mean actions inter partes and to include proceedings for maintenance and affiliation[5] and in rem but to exclude orders in criminal proceedings.[6] The Act sets an uncomplicated procedure. The judgment creditor may obtain from the registrar or appropriate officer of the court where the judgment was given a certificate in the prescribed form. This provides quite basic information about the parties and the nature and terms of the judgment. By producing the certificate to the appropriate officer of a court of like jurisdiction[7] in another state or territory, the judgment creditor may secure its entry into the Australian Register of Judgments of the executing court.[8] The certificate is a record of the registering court. From the date of registration 'the like proceedings (including proceedings in bankruptcy and insolvency) may be taken upon the certificate as if the judgment had been a judgment of that court'.[9] Thus the laws and practice of that jurisdiction will govern enforcement. In respect of execution upon the certificate and enforcement of the judgment, the registering court has the same control and jurisdiction over the judgment as if the judgment were a judgment of that court.[10]

The legislation gives the registering court power to stay proceedings on the application of the judgment debtor and to set aside the registration.[11] The latter power is given in the court's discretion with no legislative indication of the circumstances in which it should be exercised.[12] Moreover, there is no definitive judicial guidance whether the judgment debtor can successfully raise issues as to the jurisdiction of the original court or as to want of notice or of fraud in order to have the registration set aside.

The better view seems to be that challenges to the judgment should be taken before the original court and if there are good grounds for that course of action a stay of proceedings should be granted by the registration court until that is done.[13] The basis of the challenge would then be found in the law of the trial jurisdiction[14] and the common law rules relating to the enforcement of foreign judgments would have no place.[15] On this view, the registrar's function is essentially administrative and the registering court's power of review will be limited to the grounds for challenging a domestic judgment as unenforceable.[16]

On principle and on a literal construction of the statute, the intention appears to have been to create a full faith and credit arrangement, under which judgments which satisfy the statutory description must be given automatic effect. It does not seem open to a court to reject a judgment because it was based upon a cause of action unknown to the receiving state,[17] or comprised a revenue judgment,[18] or because jurisdiction was found on ex juris process to another state[19] or in any way exorbitantly.

1 Part IV. This is a statute of the Commonwealth Parliament. For a helpful account, see M. Pryles and P. Hanks *Federal Conflict of Laws* (1974) especially ch 2. The subject is currently under review by the Australian Law Reform Commission: (1983) Comm LB 943.

2 Until 1975, this system also included Papua-New Guinea.

3 S 20: *Fallshaw Bros v Ryan* (1902) 28 VLR 279.

4 S 3. A liberal construction has been placed upon this: *Re E and B Chemicals and Wool Treatment Pty Ltd (No 2)* [1940] SASR 267.

5 Now governed by the Family Law Act 1975 (Com).

6 S 3. But see Service and Execution of Process Act, Pt IVA.

7 This term has also been liberally construed: *Good and Borchers v Johnson* [1958] QWN 26.
8 S 20: the certificate is set out in the Third Schedule. Leave of the court is required where the judgment is more than twelve months old: s 21(b).
9 S 21(2): interest is payable. The judgment remains that of the rendering court: *Re Abrahamson, ex p Crisp & Gunn Ltd* (1978) 34 FLR 217.
10 S 24.
11 S 25. The stay may be granted on terms as to security or to making an application to the rendering court.
12 Except with respect to a judgment already satisfied: s 26(2).
13 Pryles and Hanks, op cit, pp 24–25; Nygh, op cit, p 108; Sykes and Pryles, op cit, pp 82–83, where the contrary view is also examined.
14 *Remilton v City Mutual Life Assurance Soc Ltd* (1907) 24 WN (NSW) 177; *Smith v Cotton* (1926) 27 SR (NSW) 41 at 63; *Re E and B Chemicals and Wool Treatment Pty Ltd*, above, at 274.
15 *Ex p Penglase* (1903) 3 SR (NSW) 680; *R v White and Noonan, ex p TA Field Pty Ltd* (1975) 133 CLR 113.
16 Nygh, op cit, p 110; Sykes and Pryles, op cit, p 82. *Re E and B Chemicals and Wool Treatment Pty Ltd (No 1)* [1939] SASR 441.
17 Nygh, op cit, p 114.
18 *R v White and Noonan, ex p TA Field Pty Ltd*, above; *Chief Collector of Taxes v Bayliss* (1976) 31 FLR 490.
19 Jurisdiction acquired by the issue of a writ ex juris under Part II of the Service and Execution of Process Act must be recognised by all courts.

(2) India

2.04 The Constitution of India expressly provides that full faith and credit are to be accorded throughout the territory of India to judicial proceedings of the Union and the states.[1] Further, it states:

> 'Final judgments or orders delivered or passed by civil courts in any part of the territory of India shall be capable of execution anywhere within that territory according to law.'[2]

This rule is confined to judgments in civil matters.[3] It does not extend to criminal proceedings nor does it require the courts of a state to enforce the penal laws of another jurisdiction.[4] The judgment, however, must be final under the law where it was handed down. A judgment of this kind is capable of being executed in any part of India[5] in accordance with the procedural law in force there.[6] Under the Code of Civil Procedure which now has general application,[7] this is done largely administratively and with the minimum of formalism.[8] The courts in the receiving jurisdiction may not re-open the matter decided nor may they examine the basis upon which jurisdiction was assumed or the way in which it was exercised by the original court.[9]

1 Art 261(1). Generally, see D. V. Chitaley *The Constitution of India* (2nd edn, 1973) vol IV, pp 611–621.
2 Art 261(3). For the position of eg courts established by the Central Government outside India: see Code of Civil Procedure 1908, ss 43, 45: *Kishendas v Indo-Carnatic Bank Ltd* AIR 1958 Andh Pra 407.
3 It applies also to decrees (as formal expressions of adjudication are referred to under the Code of Civil Procedure, s 2(5)); *Maloji Nar Singh Rao v Shankar Saran* AIR 1958 All 775; affd AIR 1962 SC 1737.
4 V. N. Shukla *The Constitution of India* (6th edn, 1975) p 443.
5 Defined by art 1(3) of the Constitution.
6 *Dwarkadas Jethabhai v Golkaldas Naranji* AIR 1952 Sau 90; *Kishendas v Indo-Carnatic Bank Ltd*, above.
7 Following the Code of Civil Procedure (Amendment) Act 1951, No 2.
8 Code of Civil Procedure 1908, ss 40–42.
9 *Murari Lal Saraf v Firm Bhagwan Das Gurdyal* AIR 1955 J & K 5; *Maloji Nar Singh Rao v Shankar Saran*, above; *Pannalal Umediram v Narahari Shivram Shet Narvekar* AIR 1968 Goa 1; (1973) 3 Sup CC 203.

(3) Malaysia

2.05 Similar provision is to be found in the Constitution of Malaysia:

'Subject to any limitations imposed by or under federal law, any order, decree, judgment or process of the courts referred to in Clause (1) or of any judge thereof shall (so far as its nature permits) have full force and effect according to its tenor throughout the Federation, and may be executed or enforced in any part of the Federation accordingly . . .'[1]

The courts referred to are the High Courts in Malaya and Borneo and the inferior courts established by federal law.[2]

1 Art 121(3).
2 Art 121(1).

(4) New Zealand

2.06 Bilateral enforcement arrangements have been instituted between New Zealand on the one hand and the Cook Islands and Niue on the other.[1] Money judgments of the Supreme Court of New Zealand or her Magistrates' Courts in civil proceedings may be enforced in either territory and the equivalent kinds of judgments of the High Court of the Cook Islands and Niue may be enforced in the New Zealand Supreme Court. The judgment creditor may cause a memorial of the judgment in the prescribed form and duly sealed to be filed in the appropriate superior court: it thereafter constitutes a record of the judgment. Execution is issued in the same manner as in the case of a local judgment, though the appropriate High Court or the Supreme Court, as the case may be, may impose such conditions as it sees fit. But in every case leave to issue must first be given by the court on an application by the person filing the memorial. The court may, in its discretion, grant leave ex parte or on notice to the judgment debtor.[2]

In relation to High Court judgments from the two territories the legislation indicates factors which must be taken into account in granting leave. Indeed, leave cannot be given unless there is affidavit evidence that the judgment debtor was resident or present in the Cook Islands or Niue, as the case may be, when the original proceedings were begun or unless the cause of action or some material part of it was in the dependency.[3] What other factors may be taken into account is not clear from the legislation but it appears unlikely that the courts may introduce defences under common law such as public policy and fraud, in its discretion. There is no equivalent provision with respect to granting leave to execute New Zealand judgments in either territory. It seems improbable that the High Courts will enter into jurisdictional questions, in the absence of explicit rules. A judgment of the Supreme Court will be treated as enforceable, whatever the actual basis of jurisdiction exercised. Other judgments of the Supreme Court, ordering a person to do or abstain from doing any act in the appropriate dependency, may be registered by filing a memorial under seal. Disobedience constitutes contempt of the relevant High Court.[4]

1 Although the New Zealand Supreme Court and the High Court of Niue may exercise jurisdiction in civil matters in respect of Tokelau (Tokelau Amendment Act 1970, No 41, ss 4–5), no express provision is made for the enforcement of their judgments outside Tokelau, although the judgments of the former at least by implication can be enforced in New Zealand itself.
2 Cook Islands Act 1915, (NZS 1976, vol 4, p 3074), ss 142, 173; Niue Act 1966 (ibid, vol 5, p 3958), ss 95–126.
3 Cook Islands Act 1915, s 142(6), (7); Niue Act 1966, s 95(6), (7).
4 Cook Islands Act 1915, s 174; Niue Act 1966, s 127.

(5) Nigeria

2.07 The Constitution of the Federal Republic enacted in 1979, after making provision for the enforcement of the judgments of the Supreme Court and Federal Court of Appeal throughout the Federation, provides:

> 'The decisions of a High Court and of all other courts established by this Constitution shall be enforced in any part of the Federation by all authorities and persons and by other courts of law with subordinate jurisdiction to that of the High Court and those other courts, respectively.'[1]

The Constitution provides for a High Court for each of the nineteen states and a Sharia Court of Appeal and a Customary Court of Appeal for any state requiring it.[2] It is evident that this full faith and credit clause does not extend to judgments of courts subordinate to these.

The section does not state explicitly that one High Court is under a duty to enforce the decisions of another. It is arguable that such courts do not come within the term 'authorities'[3]: in such a case the matter falls to be determined by legislation. Under the Sheriffs and Civil Process Ordinance, a certificate of a judgment recovered can be required from the appropriate Registrar by the judgment creditor. Such a certificate may then be registered in any state by the local Registrar in a Register of Judgments and thereafter has full force and effect and may be enforced as if it were a judgment of the court in which it is registered.[4]

1 S 251(3). 'Decisions' is defined to include 'judgment, decree, order, conviction, sentence or recommendation': s 277(1).
2 Ss 234, 240, 245.
3 Defined to include 'governments': s 277(1).
4 Sheriffs and Civil Process Ordinance, Cap 189, Part VII, especially ss 104–105.

(6) Tanzania

2.08 The Constitution of the United Republic of Tanzania contains provisions which may be intended to deal with this matter, although as expressed they are concerned with 'warrants and orders issued by the Courts'. Section 70(1) states:

> 'Orders issued by the Courts of Mainland Tanzania and the Courts of the Tanzania Islands[1] in civil proceedings of any kind and in criminal proceedings of any kind (including warrants of arrest) may be sent to any place within Tanzania and these orders may be executed at any place within Tanzania . . .'

The section goes on to provide that execution will be in accordance with the law prevailing in the place to which the order is sent: this may include compliance with any requirement of endorsement before execution. The terms used suggest that this section is not designed principally for the enforcement of judgments. This matter is in any case dealt with by the Civil Procedure Code 1966 which makes provision for the transfer of judgments of the High Court and of the resident magistrates and district courts by administrative procedures.[2]

1 The term is now used to refer to Zanzibar (s 94(1)) although the High Court of Zanzibar and its subordinate courts are retained (s 66).
2 Civil Procedure Code 1966, Act No 49 of 1966, Part II, especially ss 33–36.

(7) United Kingdom

Coverage of new scheme

2.09 The Civil Jurisdiction and Judgments Act 1982 replaced the Judgments Extension Scheme which, for over a hundred years, governed the enforcement in the United Kingdom of money judgments handed down in other parts of the Kingdom.[1] The new system is more sophisticated in its form, though retaining the same approach as its predecessor, and it is more extensive in its application than its forerunner. The scheme now extends with limited exceptions to all categories of judgments or orders in civil proceedings, and is not confined to money judgments.[2] Thus it appears to extend to equity judgments, injunctions and similar orders which were excluded from the earlier scheme.[3] Like the old, the new arrangements apply to judgments of the superior courts of the United Kingdom and to those of the inferior courts, other than the magistrates' courts in England and Northern Ireland.[4] But unlike the earlier, it also applies to awards by arbitral tribunals which have become enforceable in one part of the United Kingdom and to enforceable awards or orders of other types of tribunal[5] in any part of the Kingdom.[6] There are, however, certain exceptions relating to matters which in the main are governed by other legislation or enforcement schemes:

- (i) judgments given in bankruptcy proceedings;
- (ii) judgments given in winding-up proceedings;
- (iii) judgments given in proceedings relating to the obtaining of title to administer the estate of a deceased person;[7]
- (iv) maintenance orders enforceable under Part II of the Maintenance Orders Act 1950;
- (v) judgments insofar as they concern the status or legal capacity of an individual (which includes decrees of divorce or nullity or judicial separation, decrees of separation and provisions relating to guardianship or custody[8]);
- (vi) judgments insofar as they concern the management of persons lacking full capacity to manage their own affairs;
- (vii) provisional and protective measures,[9] other than those for interim payments;[10]
- (viii) foreign judgments which have been registered in a part of the Kingdom under one of the statutory enforcement schemes.[11]

1 Sch 14, which also repeals the principal parts of the Crown Debts Act 1801 and the Crown Debts Act 1824, which applied to certain judgments of English or Irish origin.
2 'debts, damages and costs' in JEA 1868, s 1. See now CJJA, s 18(2), (3)(b).
3 See Dicey and Morris, op cit, pp 1099, 1100: *Re Howe Machine Co, Fontaine's Case* (1889) 41 Ch D 118, 6 LT 170, CA.
4 S 18(2), (3)(a): formerly in Inferior Courts Judgments Extension Act 1882, repealed by Sch 14.
5 Defined by s 50 as 'a tribunal of any description other than a court of law'.
6 S 18(2)(d), (e). It also applies to documents registered for execution in Scotland (s 18(2)(c)), to decrees in Scotland for the recovery of certain rent charges and penalties (s 18(4)(a)) and to certain orders relating to fines for contempt of court and forfeiture of recognisances in England and Wales (s 18(4)(b)).
7 S 18(3)(c).
8 S 18(6).
9 This term, culled from the Brussels Convention, art 24, applies to relief given pending trial or the outcome of an appeal: see ss 24–27.
10 S 18(5).

11 S 18(7): ie under the 1920 and 1933 schemes, under the Brussels Convention Scheme or the Maintenance Orders (Reciprocal Enforcement) Act 1972, Pt I. This precludes the possibility of 'leap-frogging' judgments into a part of the UK where they might not be registrable or otherwise receivable under the statutory scheme.

Registration

2.10 As under the previous scheme, the process to enable enforcement to be made in another part of the United Kingdom is by registration of the judgment there.[1] With the exception of arbitral awards, the judgments in one part of the United Kingdom which are within the new scheme may be enforced in another only by this process.[2] It is also provided that recognition of these judgments[3] cannot be refused solely on the grounds that the original United Kingdom court was not competent under the relevant conflict of law rules operating in the registering part of the Kingdom.[4]

In all cases, the process for enforcement requires the interested party to obtain a certificate, in the case of money provisions, or a certified copy of the original judgment in other cases, from the proper officer of the original court.[5] These documents, however, cannot be issued if the time for appeal has not expired or if any outstanding appeal is still not finally disposed of or if the enforcement is stayed or suspended or if the time for enforcement of the judgment has expired.[6] This condition must be certified to have been met when the documents are issued. Whilst this certificate and the certified copy of the original judgment suffice in relation to non-money provisions, the certificate required for money provisions must set out in prescribed forms the sum of money payable with the rate of interest, if any, and the date from which interest is payable.[7]

Thereafter registration may be applied for in the prescribed manner to the High Court in England and Wales or in Northern Ireland or the Court of Session in Scotland, as the case may be.[8] Registration in an inferior court is not permitted.[9] Application must be made within six months of issue of the relevant certificate. If the application is made in due form, with one exception it must be registered, the registering court having no power at the time of registration to look into the circumstances in which the judgment was given.[10] Exceptionally, the registration of a non-money judgment must be refused if compliance with it 'would involve a breach of the law' in the receiving part of the Kingdom.[11] This duty to refuse registration seems to be confined to cases where some legal prohibition will be broken if the defendant fulfils the judgment. It does not appear to extend to cases where the judgment requires action by the defendant which is merely not allowed for under the law. Although registration may not usually be refused, there are, in limited circumstances, powers in the registering court to set aside the registration on a subsequent application of an interested party.[12]

1 Process for judgments with money provisions is contained in Sch 6 and for those with non-money provisions in Sch 7; s 18(1).
2 S 18(8). The early scheme did not prohibit other forms of enforcement but in such cases threatened the loss of costs: JEA 1868, s 6.
3 With certain other exceptions in addition to arbitral awards, viz other tribunal awards and orders and the special categories of judgment set out in para 2.09 note 6 above: s 19(3).
4 S 19(1).
5 These are designated by Sch 6, para 2(2) and Sch 7, para 2(2).
6 Sch 6, para 3; Sch 7, para 3.
7 Sch 6, para 4; Sch 7, para 4.
8 Sch 6, para 5; Sch 7, para 5.

9 Thus it is no longer possible to register in a Sheriff Court in Scotland as was permitted under the ICJEA, 1882.
10 Sch 6, para 5(3); Sch 7, para 5(4).
11 Sch 7, para 5(5).
12 See further, para 2.12 below.

Effects of registration

2.11 The consequence of registration is that the registered documents must be given the same local force and effect as if the original judgment had been given in the registering court. The registering court has the same enforcement powers in this regard as it has in relation to its own judgments.[1] This formulation removes the uncertainty which existed in the original scheme concerning the availability of judgment summonses and bankruptcy notices.[2] Unlike the earlier legislation, these provisions do not state the date of effectiveness of the certificate or certified judgment to be that of a local judgment given at the date of registration. In consequence any limitation period for enforcement appears to run from the date of the original judgment.

The costs of obtaining the documents required for registration and of the registration itself are recoverable as if they had been costs or expenses payable under a money provision contained in the original judgment and may be included with the registered judgment.[3] Interest upon a money debt and upon sums recoverable for costs and expenses may also be included, the former at the rate and from the date stated in the certificate,[4] the latter calculated as if ordered on the date of registration.[5]

In the normal event, enforcement of the registered judgment may proceed forthwith in accordance with the practice of the registering court. But the registering court may stay proceedings for enforcement where the judgment debtor is entitled, and intends, to seek the setting aside or the quashing of the original judgment, for enough time for such an application to be dealt with.[6] If the original judgment is set aside or quashed in relation to the matter covered by the registration, the registration will presumably cease to be effective, as the basis for it has disappeared. No provision is made, however, for the case where there has been a stay of execution issued in the original jurisdiction after the registration has taken place,[7] but presumably this may be dealt with by rules of court.[8]

1 CJJA 1982, Sch 6, para 6; Sch 7, para 6, using a slightly different formulation. Rules of court may contain qualifications with respect to conditions for and manner of enforcement.
2 JEA 1868, s 4, as amended by AJA 1956, s 40.
3 Sch 6, para 7; Sch 7, para 7(1).
4 Rules of court may prescribe the manner in which the period by which interest is payable may be calculated: Sch 6, para 8(2).
5 Sch 6, para 8; Sch 7, para 7(2).
6 Sch 6, para 9; Sch 7, para 8.
7 Cf JEA 1868, s 3.
8 RSC Ord 71, rr 37–39 (SI 1983/1181) does not include such provision.

Setting aside

2.12 An application to set aside the registration itself may be made in two circumstances only. There is a duty in a registering court to set aside a registration which is shown to have been made contrary to the statutory provisions.[1] In the main, this will arise where the procedural or formal requirements of the registration process have not been complied with. The only ground of substance will be where registration of non-money provisions was allowed when it should have been refused because enforcement would involve a breach of the law.[2] It is not open to the registering court on an application to set aside to examine any of the circumstances in which the original judgment was obtained. The new scheme, as the old, requires that challenges to the original judgment shall take place in the original jurisdiction. It is quite clear that the competence of the United Kingdom courts cannot be enquired into by any other such courts under this scheme. Even the limited grounds of intervention which were allowed under the earlier scheme are not repeated—where jurisdiction of a Scottish court had been based solely upon the arrestment of property[3] or, in the case of inferior court judgments, where the defendant was not domiciled within the area of the original court.[4] Such considerations, in any case, now have to give way to the new jurisdictional bases introduced by the Act[5] which must be determined and applied by the original court and not by the receiving court.[6]

The registering court also enjoys a discretion to set aside a registration if it is satisfied that the matter in dispute which was determined by the original judgment has already been the subject of a judgment by another competent court or tribunal.[7] Presumably this discretion would not be exercised if, for example, the latter judgment had not been satisfied at the time of the application to set aside.

1 CJJA 1982, Sch 6, para 10(a); Sch 7, para 9(a).
2 See para 2.10 above.
3 JEA 1868, s 8 but not if the defendant appeared: *Re Low, Bland v Low* [1894] 1 Ch 147, 63 LJ Ch 60, CA.
4 ICJEA 1882, s 10.
5 Sch 4 and, for Scotland, Sch 8.
6 The Convention allows a receiving court under the European scheme to concern itself with certain special jurisdictional matters in relation to consumer contracts or cases of exclusive jurisdiction or where third states are involved under art 59 of the Convention: see art 28 (but excluding insurance matters—CCJA 1982, Sch 4). These considerations are not relevant to the United Kingdom scheme.
7 Sch 6, para 10(b); Sch 7, para 9(b). See paras 3.66–3.67 below in relation to the 1933 scheme.

II REGIONAL SCHEMES

2.13 There are three instances of schemes of limited application between independent states in the Commonwealth which are in fact the continuation of arrangements instituted prior to independence. All appear to follow the approach adopted by the Judgment Extension legislation and the Australian Service of Process and Execution scheme, by instituting largely administrative arrangements for judgment transfer. Such an approach is generally predicated upon the application of full faith and credit to the judgments of courts under the same sovereign and is particularly suitable where there is a shared court system. It is, therefore, unusual to find its continuance after the acquisition of independent sovereign status by each of the participating jurisdictions and a separation of the court systems.[1] For it assumes that the jurisdictional basis of the original court should be recognised without question or enquiry, no matter that the law in existence when the scheme was originally developed may have changed. It reposes full confidence in the courts and service procedures of the participating law areas and it assumes a congruence of the public policy of each of the states, even though common legal institutions have disappeared. The balance between the interests of judgment creditors and debtors may not be properly protected by reliance upon arrangements which now offer few of the safeguards which are standard in international schemes and which are normally applied under a state's conflict of law rules.

1 Thus, for example, the West African legislation (para 1.28 above) has long ceased to have effect, usually when the Commonwealth scheme of 1920 was put into operation.

(1) East African scheme

2.14 The origins of this scheme have been described earlier.[1] Legislation is still to be found in the statute books of Kenya, Tanzania and Uganda,[2] whilst the equivalent legislation for Malaŵi as it appeared in the *Laws of Nyasaland*[3] has not been reproduced subsequently, although not apparently repealed. From the terms of the legislation of the other jurisdictions, the scheme applied between the four countries[4] but Malaŵi seems now to have been excluded.[5] The legislation is as near as it can be in identical terms although terminology used is generally out-of-date, in some instances still using pre-independence names and courts. In its essentials, the scheme follows the approach of its model, the Judgment Extensions Act 1868 of the United Kingdom.

It applies to 'decrees' for any debt, damages or costs obtained or entered up in the High Courts of the countries concerned or in any court subordinate to them. If it is desired to execute that judgment on the person or property of the judgment debtor in any of the other countries, it may be transferred to the High Court or any subordinate court there. The provisions governing procedure for transfers and execution of judgments within that country are to be applied.[6] Any proceedings can be taken thereon as if the decree had been obtained locally.[7]

There is no provision in the statute for refusing to accept transfer of the decree or to set it aside or stay proceedings. Thus, as with the United Kingdom precedent, issues of jurisdiction, natural justice, fraud cannot be raised.[8] There seems no mechanism whereby the general provisions in the Civil Procedure Act intended to govern recognition of foreign judgments can be applied.[9] As one commentator concludes, 'it seems doubtful whether such a decree can be challenged . . . at all so long as the judgment is not vacated by the appropriate court of the neighbouring country which pronounced the judgment in the first place'.[10]

1 Paras 1.26 and 1.27 above.
2 Foreign Judgments Enforcement Act, Cap 43, Pt III (Kenya); Judgments Extension Ordinance, Cap 7 (Tanzania); Judgments Extension Act, Cap 46 (Uganda). Provisions are also included for execution of warrants of arrest in civil cases from the other participating states.
3 Judgments Extension Act, Cap 15, *Laws of Nyasaland* 1957.
4 The Malaŵi statute allowed extension orders to be made to other of HM dominions: s 6. Its short title included references to Northern Rhodesia (Zambia) which are not included in the operative parts.
5 Malaŵi has been the subject of a separate extension order by Kenya under the 1920 scheme which runs along-side the earlier arrangements.
6 Eg Civil Procedure Act, Cap 5, s 31 (Kenya).
7 Costs and charges of transfer and execution can be recovered as if they were part of the original decree.
8 Cf *Wotherspoon v Connolly* (1871) 9 Macph (Ct of Sess) 510; *Re Low* [1894] 1 Ch 147 at 162 on the UK legislation.
9 Civil Procedure Act, Cap 5, s 9 (Kenya).
10 S. Thanawalla, (1970) 19 ICLQ 430–446 at 441. The receiving court under the UK legislation was entitled to set aside a registration only if the certificate was not in the prescribed form: *Part v Scannell* (1875) IR 9 CL 426. Arguably similar considerations would apply in this instance too.

(2) Central African scheme

2.15 As part of the judicial arrangements in the Federation of Rhodesia and Nyasaland, legislation was enacted in 1957 for the service of process and execution of judgments modelled upon that of Australia. The legislation was maintained after the dissolution of the Federation in 1964 and was continued between Malaŵi, Zambia and Zimbabwe, despite their acquisition of independence.[1]

This scheme applies to money judgments made by any court of record, superior or inferior, (but not by traditional or native courts)[2] in civil proceedings in the other states. It extends to arbitral awards enforceable as judgments and to compensation orders made in criminal proceedings and to affiliation orders for the maintenance by a father of his illegitimate child, but not to other maintenance orders for periodical payment.[3] It is made explicit that judgments in favour of or against a government are included.[4]

The procedure involves registration of a certificate in the prescribed form granted by the proper officer of the original court in a register kept for the purpose. Leave of the court is required if registration is sought twelve months after the date of the judgment. As in the Australian legislation, the certificate is a record of the registering court and has the same force and effect as a judgment of that court. Like proceedings (including insolvency or winding-up) may be taken upon the certificate as if it were a local judgment. Costs of registration may be ordered by the registering court and become payable under the certificate.[5] Execution or other proceedings on the certificate require an affidavit from the judgment creditor or someone cognisant of the facts stating that the amount for which execution is sought is actually due and payable.[6]

The registering court is not given explicit power to set aside the registration but may grant relief as it may see fit, in addition to a power to stay proceedings.[7] The latter, in terms very similar to those in the Australian Act, may be granted on terms as to giving of security or as to the making of an application to the original court to set the judgment aside. This suggests strongly that the registering court will not, under its power to grant relief, enter into any conflict of laws considerations as they normally apply to external judgments. The validity of the judgment is seen as one for the court which handed it down. Indeed, there is an obligation imposed upon the proper officer of the court of origin to notify the registering court of any setting aside or variation or satisfaction of the original judgment.[8] It seems that, as in the Australian case, the intention was for registration to be an obligatory administrative process except perhaps where the prescribed formal requirements are not fulfilled. The court's powers are concerned with the regulation of the execution process which may be temporarily stayed if the judgment debtor can establish that there are good grounds why the judgment should not be maintained until the matter has been dealt with in the country of origin. Arguably, it may not even stay the execution permanently on the grounds that the judgment has been satisifed in whole or in part, as that appears to be also a matter to be dealt with in the country of origin.[9]

1 Service of Process and Execution of Judgments Act, Cap 4.04 (Malaŵi); Cap 90 (Zambia); Cap 153 (Zimbabwe). References in this section are to the Malaŵi Act as representative of all.

2 S 2.

3 S 10.

4 S 2.

5 S 11.
6 S 13. Provision is made for the proper officer to notify forthwith his counterpart in the original court of registration or issue of execution: s 15(1).
7 S 14.
8 S 15(2), (3). The proper officer in the receiving court is then required to cancel or replace the original certificate or enter note of its satisfaction upon it: s 15(4), (5). It is doubtful that these provisions which are drafted to have extraterritorial effect in the country of origin can be enforced.
9 S 15(3). The inability of the receiving system, since independence, to insist that appropriate action be taken in the country of origin may lead to the receiving court exercising its power to grant relief (s 14) in a case of this kind.

(3) Eastern Caribbean scheme

2.16 A direct enforcement scheme exists between the states which are subject to the Eastern Caribbean Supreme Court.[1] This court exercises an original and appellant jurisdiction as conferred upon it by the Constitutions and the legislation of the states and territories which it serves.[2] The process of the Supreme Court runs throughout the contributory states and 'any judgment of the Court shall have full force and effect and may be executed and enforced in any of the States.'[3] Accordingly, a judgment creditor may seek execution in any of the states served as if the judgment were obtained there, no matter in which of the jurisdictions the judgment was actually given. This facility however is available only in the five states in the scheme: Antigua and Barbuda, Commonwealth of Dominica, St Christopher and Nevis, St Lucia and St Vincent and the Grenadines.[4] The Order-in-Council governing the court allows extension of this facility to the dependent jurisdictions also served by the court: Anguilla, Montserrat and the Virgin Islands.[5] But the necessary legislative steps in each of these jurisdictions appear not to have been taken. At the same time, the judgments of the court from these jurisdictions appear to be enforceable in the states, although the converse is not yet authorised.

1 Similar provision was made in respect of the Federation of the West Indies, dissolved in 1962: West Indies (Federation) Order-in-Council 1957, SI 1957/1364, s 84(1): the Federal Supreme Court had a limited original jurisdiction only: ibid, ss 80–83.
2 West Indies Associated States Supreme Court Order 1967, SI 1967/223, art 9(1). The court was restyled the Eastern Caribbean Supreme Court by SI 1983/1108.
3 Ibid, art 9(3).
4 Grenada was formally deleted by SI 1983/1108, having withdrawn de facto in 1979.
5 SI 1967/223, art 10(1), extended to Anguilla: SI 1983/1107. SI 1983/1108 makes clear that the dependencies are not to be treated as 'States' for the purposes of the Order.

III INTERNATIONAL SCHEMES

2.17 Pre-eminent amongst the schemes with general Commonwealth application are the two schemes which follow closely the arrangements originally set down in the United Kingdom legislation of 1920 and 1933. Modifications have been effected in individual countries, though in most cases these are not significant. It is amongst the Canadian common law jurisdictions that most distinctive variations are to be found.[1] There are, however, other statutory forms which are intended to be used as reciprocating legislation. These are found in Bangladesh and India, New Zealand[2] and South Australia. These will be considered after the accounts of the 1920 and 1933 schemes and their principal modifications.

1 Quebec which has no legislation for direct enforcement will not be considered as the existing law based upon the Civil Code, art 1220.1 and the Code of Civil Procedure, arts 178–181 cannot be regarded as constituting reciprocal legislation or treatment for purposes of participation in the Commonwealth schemes. See W. S. Johnson, (1957) 35 Can Bar Rev 911–949; J. G. Castel *Second Commonwealth and Empire Law Conference* Ottawa, 1960, pp 137–148; E. Groffier-Atala, (1978) 38 Rev du Bar 127–160.

2 The New Zealand legislation is a remnant of the Australasian scheme developed in the mid-nineteenth century: paras 1.12–1.14 above.

(1) The 1920 scheme

2.18 The original scheme remains part of the law for a substantial number of jurisdictions within the Commonwealth, generally with little substantive amendment. Although in some cases it runs side by side with the 1933 provisions, as in the United Kingdom where it is still the main scheme for Commonwealth judgments, in a considerable number of cases it is still the only statutory scheme. The jurisdictions with this legislation are listed in Annex I. Fuller examination of the scheme is contained in Chapter 3.

Applications to register

2.19 The scheme applies to judgments or orders of any superior court of a designated jurisdiction within the Commonwealth[1] in civil proceedings whereby any sum of money is payable,[2] including arbitral awards enforceable as a judgment of the court.[3] A judgment creditor[4] may, normally within twelve months of the date of judgment,[5] apply to the prescribed superior court in the place of intended enforcement to have the judgment registered in that court.[6] Application is generally made ex parte, although the court may direct that a summons be issued.[7] It must be accompanied by an affidavit which exhibits the judgment or a verified, certified or otherwise duly authenticated copy of it.[8] In addition the affidavit must give information about the parties and state the deponent's belief that the judgment creditor is entitled to enforce the judgment, that it remains unsatisfied in whole or a stated part and that none of the statutory grounds upon which registration must be refused is present.[9] Security for costs may be ordered from the applicant[10] and will normally be ordered where the applicant is residing out of the jurisdiction and has no assets there.[11]

1 More usually 'H.M. Dominions': AJA, s 9(1).

2 AJA, s 12(1).

3 Ibid.

4 Ie the person by whom the judgment is obtained or his successor or assigns: ibid.

5 The court may extend the period: s 9(1).

6 S 9(1). Registration is usually undertaken by a Master or the Registrar.

7 RSC Ord 71, r 2 (UK). The procedural matters are contained in Rules of Court which generally follow those in the United Kingdom.

8 S 10 lays down the mechanism whereby a judgment creditor may obtain a certificate for use in another part of the Commonwealth on proof that the judgment debtor is resident in some such part to which the scheme has been extended. The residence requirement was removed for the UK in Civil Jurisdiction and Judgments Act 1982, s 35(2).

9 Ibid, r 3.

10 Ibid, r 4.

11 The position was otherwise under the ministerial and automatic arrangements of the Judgments Extension Act 1868: *Raeburn v Andrews* (1874) LR 9 QB 118, 43 LJQB 73.

Registration

2.20 The court is vested with a discretion whether to order registration which it may do 'if in all the circumstances of the case they think it is just and convenient that the judgment should be enforced'.[1] This discretion, however, may not be exercised in favour of registration in any of six circumstances:

(a) the original court acted without jurisdiction;
(b) the judgment debtor, being a person who was neither carrying on business nor ordinarily resident within the jurisdiction of the original court, did not voluntarily appear or otherwise submit or agree to submit to the jurisdiction of that court;
(c) the judgment debtor, being the defendant in the proceedings, was not duly served with the process of the original court and did not appear, notwithstanding that he was ordinarily resident or was carrying on business within the jurisdiction of that court or agreed to submit to the jurisdiction of that court;
(d) the judgment was obtained by fraud;
(e) the judgment debtor satisfies the registering court either that an appeal is pending or that he is entitled and intends to appeal against the judgment;
(f) the judgment was in respect of a cause of action which for reasons of public policy or for some other similar reason could not have been entertained by the registering court.[2]

Unlike the 1933 Act, jurisdictional requirements are not prescribed: in consequence, the registering court must apply its own conflict of law rules governing the circumstances in which the competence of foreign courts will be recognised.[3] A second point of contrast is the discretion to refuse registration even if none of the foregoing circumstances are fulfilled. This was introduced at the instance of the Sumner Committee which was concerned that applications would generally be made ex parte on 'such materials as the judgment creditor may think to produce'. 'It is not intended that leave to enforce the judgment should be given as a matter of course simply on proof that it was regularly obtained according to the procedure recognised by the forum from which it issues; nor on the other hand is it intended that on the application to enforce a judgment an examination of the merits and the cause should be obligatory'.[4]

They went on to suggest that the registering court should be particularly vigilant in cases involving ex juris service of process.[5] 'Where there has been no personal service, except in cases of deliberate evasion of it, leave to enforce a subsequent judgment should only sparingly be accorded.'[6]

Curiously, there has been little indication of the circumstances in which in practice the courts will refuse leave. Certainly, considerations of service have not been prominent in reported cases. In practice, it is unlikely that initial registration will be refused if the other statutory conditions are fulfilled, unless there is some obvious indication of misuse of the facility or an attempt is made to bring within the scheme a type of foreign money judgment not normally enforceable at common law.[7]

Once leave is given, the judgment will be entered in the appropriate register of judgments. The order for leave to register need not be served on the judgment debtor, where the proceedings are ex parte,[8] but notice of the registration itself must be served personally or by sending it to his usual place of abode or business or by other means directed by the court. If he is out of the jurisdiction, it can be served without special leave.[9] Reasonable costs relating to the registration may be recovered as if they were sums payable under the judgment.[10]

From the date of registration, the judgment has the same force and effect as if it were a judgment of the registering court.[11] But it may not be executed until the period within which an application to set aside may be made has lapsed. This period is set down in the order for leave and in the notice of registration to the debtor.[12] The court has the same control and jurisdiction over the registered judgment as over its own judgments insofar as relates to execution only.[13] Proceedings may be taken upon it as on a local judgment, including enforcement by judgment summons or the issuing of a bankruptcy notice upon it.[14] In consequence, the enforcement procedures of the registering legal system alone may be employed and any limitation therein must be observed. Enforcement can, therefore, be set aside on any grounds upon which domestic judgment enforcement can be set aside.

1 AJA, s 9(1).
2 Ibid, s 9(2). Further heads have been implicitly added for the United Kingdom by Civil Jurisdiction and Judgments Act 1982, s 31 (judgments against states when covered by state immunity) and s 32 (judgments given in proceedings in breach of agreement for settlement of disputes).
3 In large measure, the 1933 Act's statement of jurisdiction is a statement of the common law rules which will be applied by most Commonwealth jurisdictions with the 1920 statute.
4 Cmd 251, para 33.
5 Cases of actions on bills of exchange and ordinary mercantile transactions, it was suggested, stand on the same footing as cases where service had actually been effected within the jurisdiction: ibid.
6 Ibid.
7 Eg a judgment which is not final or conclusive. A judgment for taxes or fines or other penalties or even a judgment for multiple damages might be excluded in this way: see Dicey and Morris, op cit, p 1104.
8 RSC Ord 71, r 5(1).
9 Ibid, r 7(1), (2). See r 8 with respect to endorsement of service.
10 AJA, s 9(3)(c).
11 Ibid, s 9(3)(a).
12 RSC Ord 71, r 5(2), r 10.
13 AJA, s 9(3)(b).
14 This was added by the Administration of Justice Act 1956, s 40(b) for the UK. *Re a Judgment Debtor (No 2176 of 1938)* [1939] Ch 601 at 605, s 9, in its original form, was equated with similar provisions in the Judgments Extension Act 1868, s 4 which had been held not to allow of such proceedings: *Re Watson, ex p Johnston, Johnston v Watson* [1893] 1 QB 21, 62 LJQB 85, CA; *Re A Bankruptcy Notice* [1898] 1 QB 383, 67 LJQB 308.

Setting aside a registration

2.21 The judgment debtor, who must be notified of his right, may apply to have the registration set aside within the time allowed by the registering court for that purpose.[1] The matter may be dealt with on affidavit evidence but the court may direct any issue between the parties to be tried as in an action.[2] Execution will be stayed until the matter is finally determined.[3]

The court enjoys a discretion to set the registration aside, on terms, if satisfied that any of the specified prohibitions on registration in section 9 apply or that it is not just or convenient that the judgment should be enforced.[4] This is an important safeguard, for it enables the judgment debtor, who may learn of the registration only when completed, to raise any matter which might have prevented the issue of leave to register in the first place.

1 RSC Ord 71, r 9.
2 Ibid, r 9(2).

3 Ibid, r 10(2).
4 Ibid, r 9(3). As for example, because the judgment is not one within the scheme: *Platt v Platt* 1958 SC 95, 1958 SLT 94.

Relationship with other enforcement arrangements

2.22 There is no prohibition in the 1920 scheme upon the bringing of an action on the Commonwealth judgment as an alternative to registration. Given the faith in Order 14 summary judgments in the Colonial Office particularly at the time of preparation of the legislation,[1] this not surprising. On the other hand, the Act does provide that the plaintiff will not be entitled to recover any costs of any such action if the judgment is one which could have been registered, unless registration has been refused or the court orders otherwise.[2] At common law, it would also be open to a judgment creditor to sue on the original cause of action, as this has long been treated as not merging with any foreign judgment on the same matter.[3] This anomalous rule has now been abrogated in England and Wales and Northern Ireland, so that such actions can only be brought if the judgment is not enforceable or not entitled to recognition there.[4] The fact that a judgment is registrable under the 1920 scheme, therefore, precludes this course of action.

1 See para 1.25 above.
2 AJA, s 9(5).
3 *Smith v Nicolls* (1839) 5 Bing NC 208, 8 LJCP 92; *Bank of Australasia v Harding* (1850) 9 CB 661, 19 LJCP 345; *Bank of Australasia v Nias* (1851) 16 QB 717, 20 LJQB 284; *Carl-Zeiss Stiftung v Rayner & Keeler Ltd (No 2)* [1967] 1 AC 853, [1966] 2 All ER 536, HL.
4 Civil Jurisdiction and Judgments Act 1982, s 34.

(2) The 1933 scheme

2.23 The 1933 scheme, whilst designed in the first instance to accommodate foreign countries, was also intended to replace the 1920 scheme with respect to Commonwealth countries. In practice it has been employed by most Commonwealth systems mainly for the latter purpose and in many jurisdictions, it does now stand as the only arrangement in force, as the draftsman intended. Nonetheless, as we have seen, the two schemes are still to be found in a considerable number of cases. The jurisdictions with this legislation are listed in Annex I. Further examination of the scheme is contained in Chapter 3.

Applications to register

2.24 This scheme applies to judgments or orders of prescribed superior courts[1] of a designated foreign or Commonwealth jurisdiction in civil proceedings whereby a sum of money is payable or in criminal proceedings for payment of a sum of money in respect of compensation or damages to an injured party.[2] In most countries it has been extended to include arbitral awards which have become enforceable as judgments of those courts.[3] It does not apply to judgments in respect of taxes or other charges of like nature or in respect of a fine or other penalty.[4] The common law requirement that the judgment must be final and conclusive is restated.[5]

A judgment creditor[6] may apply to the prescribed superior court in the place of intended enforcement to have the judgment registered there. Such applications may be made within six years of the date of the judgment or of the final judgment in an appeal.[7]

Application is generally made ex parte, although the court may direct a summons to be issued.[8] It must be accompanied by an affidavit which exhibits the judgment or a verified or certified or otherwise duly authenticated copy.[9] The affidavit must also give information about the parties and interest due and state the deponent's belief that the judgment creditor is entitled to enforce the judgment, that it remains unsatisfied in whole or a stated part, that it can be enforced by execution in the court of origin and that it would not be, or be liable to be, set aside on the prescribed grounds.[10] If only part of a judgment is to be registered, this must be specified in the affidavit.[11] Security for costs may be ordered against the judgment creditor[12] and will normally be ordered where the applicant is residing out of the jurisdiction and has no assets there.

1 FJREA, s 1(1). Judgments on appeal from undesignated courts are excluded. By amendments in the Civil Jurisdiction and Judgments Act 1982, Sch 10, paras 1(2), 5(2), the scheme can be applied to all or designated classes of courts and tribunals. The scheme may also be limited to any designated class of judgments. Reciprocity is again a determining factor.

2 FJREA, s 11(1).

3 Following the Administration of Justice Act 1956, s 51(a) (UK). This originally applied only to jurisdictions previously under the 1920 scheme but in the UK and in many jurisdictions elsewhere, this limitation has been removed: Civil Jurisdiction and Judgments Act 1982, Sch 10, para 4, inserting a new s 10A.

4 FJREA, s 1(2)(b). Other categories of judgment may be excluded eg as under the Protection of Trading Interests Act 1980, s 5.

5 Ibid, s 1(2)(a). It is final and conclusive notwithstanding that an appeal is pending or may be taken in the country of origin: ibid, s 1(3).

6 Ie the person in whose favour the judgment was given or any person in whom the rights in the judgment have become vested by succession or assignment or otherwise: ibid, s 11(1).

7 Ibid, s 2(1).

8 RSC Ord 71, r 2. (The English rules which have been used as a model in many instances are cited as representative.)

9 Ibid, r 3(1)(a). S 10 lays down the procedure for obtaining a certificate of a judgment and its form for use in enforcement proceedings in a reciprocating country. See also RSC Ord 71, r 13, which also requires a certificate to be issued concerning details of the process, objections to jurisdiction and basis of the judgment. For the UK, see now Civil Jurisdiction and Judgments Act 1982, Sch 10, para 3, replacing s 10.

10 Ibid, r 3(1). Evidence about enforceability in the court of origin and the law under which interest is due must be given: ibid, r 3(3).

11 Ibid, r 3(2).

12 In the UK, this power may be excluded in relation to countries with which a treaty has been entered into.

Registration

2.25 The statute imposes a duty to register a judgment which meets the prescribed conditions, when the application has been made in due time and form.[1] This was a deliberate device to remove any impression of permissive treatment, as under the 1920 Act, which would have impeded the conclusion of bilateral treaty arrangements with civil law countries.[2] Certain exceptions to the duty are provided for. If the judgment is partly satisfied, the court may order registration only for the balance payable.[3] If the judgment contains different matters, some of which, if contained in separate judgments, could not be registered, the court must restrict registration to those provisions which, as separate judgments, would meet the statutory requirements.[4] Further it must refuse the registration where the judgment is not one which is within the terms of the scheme or where at the date of application it has been wholly satisfied or where at that time it cannot be enforced by execution in the country of origin[5] or, except in very limited circumstances, if the application has previously been set aside.[6] There is, however, no discretion in the registering court to refuse

registration, for example because local execution would not be just or convenient. In particular, issues as to the jurisdiction of the original court or natural justice or fraud are not tested at this stage.

The order giving leave to register need not be served upon the judgment debtor, unless made on a summons.[7] The registration itself will be entered in the register of judgments kept for the purpose.[8] Once the registration is made, notice of it must be served on the judgment debtor personally by sending it to him at his usual or last known place of abode or business or in any other manner directed by the court.[9] If he is out of the jurisdiction, service can be effected without obtaining special leave under the usual procedures available under Order 11.[10] Reasonable costs relating to the registration may be recovered as if they were sums payable under the judgment.[11]

From the date of registration, a registered judgment carries the same interest and has the same force and effect for the purposes of execution as a judgment of the registering court entered on that date. Proceedings may be taken on it in accordance with the local law and the registering court has the same control over its execution as if it has been given by the court itself.[12] Execution can, therefore, be set aside on any grounds available under the law of the enforcing forum. As with a domestic judgment, execution of a registered judgment should not be set aside because, for example, the judgment debtor has started a cross-action in the jurisdiction against the judgment creditor, especially if the same issues are involved.[13]

But execution may not issue so long as it is competent for any party to make an application to set the registration aside or until any such application has been finally determined.[14] The period for such application is set in the order for registration and is notified to the judgment debtor in the notice of registration served upon him.[15]

1 FJREA, s 2(1). The matter will normally be dealt with by a Master or the Registrar.
2 Greer Committee Report, p 61.
3 FJREA, s 2(4).
4 Ibid, s 2(5).
5 Ibid, s 2(1). These matters should be evident from the affidavit and other prescribed documentation. It makes no difference that subsequent to registration the judgment becomes unenforceable in the original country because of a pending appeal there: *Re a Debtor (No 11 of 1939)* [1939] 2 All ER 400.
6 The permitted cases are set out in ibid, s 5(2): see para 2.26, notes 4 and 7 below.
7 RSC Ord 71, r 5(2).
8 Ibid, r 6.
9 Ibid, r 7(1). The form of the notice is prescribed: r 7(3).
10 Ibid, r 7(2).
11 FJREA, s 2(6).
12 Ibid, s 2(2). Bankruptcy notices and judgment summonses may be issued: *Re A Judgment Debtor (No 2176 of 1938)* [1939] Ch 601, [1939] 1 All ER 1.
13 *Ferdinand Wagner v Laubscher Bros & Co* [1970] 2 QB 313, [1970] 2 All ER 174, CA.
14 FJREA, s 2(2), proviso.
15 RSC Ord 71, rr 5(3), 7(3), 10. The period may be extended: r 5(4).

Setting aside a registration

2.26 An application may be made by any party against whom a registered judgment may be enforced to set it aside.[1] It must be made by summons supported by affidavit. The court may order that any issue between the judgment creditor and debtor be tried as in an action.[2]

The grounds for setting aside are stated in the Act itself. Most are mandatory but two are discretionary:

(i) where the registering court is satisfied that the matter in dispute in the original proceedings previous to the judgment in those proceedings had been the subject of a final and conclusive judgment by another court of competent jurisdiction;[3]

(ii) where the registering court is satisfied that either an appeal is pending against the judgment or that the applicant intends to appeal against it.[4] In this case, as an alternative to setting aside, the court may adjourn the application until the expiry of a period in which the applicant can take the necessary steps to have the appeal disposed of.[5]

The mandatory grounds are:

(i) the judgment was not a judgment to which the scheme applies. This can arise where the judgment is:
  (a) not from a designated court in a designated jurisdiction;
  (b) not a money judgment as defined in the Act;
  (c) a judgment for taxes, fines or penalties;
  (d) not final and conclusive;

(ii) it was registered in contravention to the statutory requirements in registration. This can arise where:
  (a) registration did not follow the prescribed procedures or the prescribed proofs were not produced;
  (b) registration was not within the prescribed period from the date of the judgment;
  (c) the judgment was wholly or partly satisfied at the date of registration;[6]
  (d) it contained matters which, if in a separate judgment, could not be registered;
  (e) at the time of registration, it was unenforceable by execution in the original country;[7]

(iii) the courts of the country of the original court had no jurisdiction in the circumstances of the case;

(iv) the judgment debtor, being the defendant in the proceedings in the original court, did not (notwithstanding that process may have been duly served on him in accordance with the law of the original country) receive notice of those proceedings in sufficient time to enable him to defend the proceedings and did not appear;

(v) the judgment was obtained by fraud;

(vi) the enforcement of the judgment would be contrary to the public policy in the country of the registering court;

(vii) the rights under the judgment are not vested in the person by whom the application for registration was made.[8]

It is, therefore, only at the setting aside stage that many of the traditional defences to recognition of judgments may be introduced. If, however, no application is made by any party against whom the judgment may be enforced within the prescribed time limit, the registering court will not be required at any stage to turn its attention to these matters. Notice to the debtor of his right to apply to set aside is, therefore, an important safeguard.

1 FJREA, s 4(1).
2 RSC Ord 71, r 9.
3 FJREA, s 4(1)(b).
4 This does not prejudice a further application when the appeal has been disposed of: ibid, s 5(2).

5 Ibid, s 5(1).
6 Where partly satisfied when the whole was registered, the court may order registration of the balance outstanding: ibid, s 5(3).
7 This does not preclude further application when the judgment becomes enforceable: ibid, s 5(2).
8 Ibid, s 4(1)(a).

Jurisdictional considerations

2.27 In order to lay foundations for foreign country extensions, the 1933 Act, unlike the 1920 statute, included jurisdictional rules to be applied by the registering court in determining whether to set aside the judgment for want of competence in the original court.[1] The provisions which were included were stated to be substantially in accordance with existing common law rules.[2] In order to secure international agreements which would be likely to operate satisfactorily in practice, some small departures were made in the statute from the common law rules on in personam jurisdiction.[3] Two doubtful common law rules, relating to jurisdiction founded on nationality and upon personal service of process within the jurisdiction, were not included, partly because of their uncertain status at common law but partly because they were not found in the law of the foreign countries with which negotiations had taken place in the early 1930s.[4] The in personam provisions of the Act have been held to be exclusive.[5]

The original court is seen for the purpose of the scheme to have jurisdiction in any of the following cases:[6]

'(a) in the case of a judgment given in an action in personam—
(i) if the judgment debtor, being a defendant in the original court, submitted to the jurisdiction of that court by voluntarily appearing in the proceedings otherwise than for the purpose of protecting, or obtaining the release of, property seized, or threatened with seizure, in the proceedings or of contesting the jurisdiction of that court.[7]'

These latter provisions were thought by the Greer Committee to be slightly narrower than the existing rules in that appearance to dispute jurisdiction or protect or obtain release of property is not, as at common law, regarded as submission.[8]

'(ii) if the judgment debtor was plaintiff in, or counter-claimed in, the proceedings in the original court;
(iii) if the judgment debtor, being a defendant in the original court, had before the commencement of the proceedings agreed, in respect of the subject matter of the proceedings, to submit to the jurisdiction of that court or of the courts of the country of that court;
(iv) if the judgment debtor, being a defendant in the original court, was at the time when the proceedings were instituted resident in, or being a body corporate had its principal place of business in, the country of that court;
(v) if the judgment debtor, being a defendant in the original court, had an office or place of business in the country of that court and the proceedings in that court were in respect of a transaction effected through or at that office or place.'

'This rule, if not precisely covered by the existing Common Law Rule at any rate is at the most only a rational extension of it.'[9]

'(b) In the case of a judgment given in an action of which the subject matter was immovable property or in an action *in rem* of which the subject matter was moveable property, if the property in question was at the time of the proceedings in the original court situate in the country of that court.'

This was thought in the case of immovable property 'to go a little beyond the existing law, but the extension is not an unreasonable one'.[10]

'(c) In the case of a judgment given in an action other than any such action as is mentioned in paragraph (a) or paragraph (b) if the jurisdiction of the original court is recognised by the law of the registering court.'

Paragraph (c) is a catch-all clause under which the usual conflict of law rules of the registering court will be applied to special categories of action. These will include any matrimonial cause or any proceedings in connection with matrimonial matters, administration of the estates of deceased persons, bankruptcy, winding-up of companies, lunacy or guardianship of infants.[11] These are all cases in which specific rules of recognition are likely to be involved.

The statute also determines certain cases in which the original court cannot be deemed to have had jurisdiction:[12]

'(a) if the subject matter of the proceedings was immovable property outside the country of the original court; or

(b) except in the cases mentioned in sub-paragraphs (i), (ii) and (iii) of paragraph (a) and in paragraph (c) above, if the bringing of the proceedings in the original court was contrary to an agreement under which the dispute in question was to be settled otherwise than by proceedings in the court of the country of that court;[13] or

(c) if the judgment debtor, being a defendant in the original proceedings, was a person who under the rules of public international law was entitled to immunity from the jurisdiction of the courts of the country of the original court and did not submit to the jurisdiction of that court.'[14]

A fuller examination of these jurisdiction factors is given below in Chapter 3, paragraphs 3.34 to 3.49.

1 FJREA, s 4(2), (3).
2 Greer Committee, op cit, para 6 and pp 62–3.
3 Ibid, p 62.
4 Ibid, p 63. The doubts remain: Dicey and Morris, op cit, pp 1055–56.
5 *Société Co-opérative Sidmetal v Titan International Ltd* [1966] 1 QB 828, [1965] 3 All ER 494; *Sharps Commercials Ltd v Gas Turbines Ltd* [1956] NZLR 819.
6 FJREA, s 4(2). 'Action in personam' is defined in s 11(2), see note 11.
7 The words from 'otherwise' to 'that court' have been repealed in the UK following the enactment of Civil Jurisdiction and Judgments Act 1982, s 33 which changes the construction put upon the provision in *Henry v Geoprosco International* [1976] 2 QB 726, [1975] 2 All ER 702: para 3.38 below.
8 Greer Committee, op cit, p 63.
9 Ibid.
10 Ibid.
11 These cases are explicitly excluded from 'actions in personam' by FJREA, s 11(2).
12 Ibid, s 4(3). Said by the Greer Committee, op cit, p 63, to be 'in part a statement of the existing Common Law Rules and in part a rational interpretation of those rules on a point at present not covered by precise authority'.
13 This provision has been repealed in the UK, following the enactment of new provisions in Civil Jurisdiction and Judgments Act 1982, s 32.
14 This must be read in the light of the law of state immunity in cases where the state is involved in commercial activities. Cf Civil Jurisdiction and Judgments Act 1982, s 31.

Relationship with other enforcement arrangements

2.28 A major innovation of the 1933 Act is contained in section 6 which provides:

'No proceedings for the recovery of a sum payable under a foreign judgment being a judgment to which this Part of this Act applies, other than proceedings by way of registration of the judgment, shall be entertained by any court [in the receiving jurisdiction].'

It was designed to take away the right to bring an action upon the foreign judgment at common law, the availability of which might cause confusion in the negotiation for new bilateral arrangements with foreign countries. In any case, the only cases in which it would be used would be where the common law was wider than the Act and it would therefore apply to matters deliberately excluded from the scheme and on which there would be no reciprocity.[1] No mention was made, however, of the possibility of actions on the original cause of action which, at common law, does not merge into the foreign judgment. There is little doubt that such a course of action will be available unless the non-merger rule has been abrogated, as in the United Kingdom.[2]

The consequence of this rule, therefore, is that a judgment which is capable of being registered must be registered, if enforcement is to follow. The courts of the receiving state are required to stay any other proceedings in relation to that judgment. The implications of this have not been fully explored. In particular, it is not clear how this affects proceedings for enforcement of judgments or arbitration under other statutory schemes. If lump sum payments by way of financial relief in matrimonial proceedings are enforceable under the 1933 Act and may also be registered under a maintenance orders scheme,[3] enforcement under the former mechanism may be insisted upon.

A more serious matter: the 1933 Act now permits arbitral awards which are enforceable as judgments to be registered in most countries. Cases will arise when these may also fall within the terms of the Geneva Convention or the New York Convention, which provide their own systems of enforcement. There seems little doubt that the 1933 scheme must prevail over the former as the changes in the law to include awards were enacted subsequent to the Arbitration (Foreign Awards) Act 1930. In the case of the New York Convention, it may be argued that the 1933 Act should be read subject to the legislation implementing the Convention which is subsequent to the 1933 Act. For insistence upon compliance with the 1933 Act may lead to charges of failure by the state to carry out its international undertakings.[4] What is clear is that the provision was never intended for this purpose.

1 Greer Committee Report, p 64.
2 Civil Jurisdiction and Judgments Act 1982, s 34.
3 This will generally not be the case since the latter normally provide for periodical payments which, being capable of variation, are not final and conclusive as required by the 1933 Act.
4 See further, paras. 7.38 and 8.38 below.

Provisions for recognition of foreign judgments

2.29 In the discussions leading to the preparation of the 1933 Act, it became clear that an enforcement scheme involving non-Commonwealth countries would require a series of bilateral treaties and that these would need to deal with the question of the recognition of civil and commercial judgments generally, as well as creating a mechanism for enforcement of money judgments. For concern was expressed in a number of foreign states that disputes resolved by their judgments would be re-litigated in the United Kingdom. It quickly became apparent that rules on that matter which rested upon case law were an insufficient guarantee for those states.[1] Explicit undertakings had, therefore, to be included in the treaties but some statutorily prescribed formulation was seen as necessary to demonstrate that those undertakings had a basis in the municipal law of the United Kingdom. Section 8 was enacted for this purpose but the Greer Committee took great care to ensure that it did not alter the existing common law rules. In their view, it was 'entirely in accordance with the position at common law'.[2] Unfortunately, there seems to have been some uncertainty amongst the members of that Committee as to what that position was.[3]

1 Greer Committee Report, paras 2, 10(b). This point was established in the first Greer Committee which reported in June 1929: LCO/2, Doc No 1688.
2 Ibid, Annex V, para 13.
3 The position, as the Greer Committee saw it, was described in para 4 of their Report. See further, Chapter 4 below.

(3) The Canadian scheme

2.30 The model Act prepared, and from time to time updated, by the Conference of Commissioners on Uniformity of Legislation in Canada[1] is the basis of the legislation in force in all the common law jurisdictions in Canada,[2] although in some instances further minor modifications have been made by the enacting Legislature. The influence of both the 1920 and 1933 statutes upon the Canadian models is strong, although the legislation in force relates more closely to the earlier arrangements.

The Uniform Act was, as we have seen, designed initially for use for the enforcement of Canadian judgments. In 1958, however, it was amended to permit judgments from non-Canadian jurisdictions with reciprocal arrangements to be included. By no means all of the Canadian jurisdictions have acted upon this development[3] and, even in those cases in which the power has been taken it has been used very sparingly.[4] Indeed there is not yet full reciprocity between the provinces and the territories.[5]

1 The original model was approved in 1924, amended in 1925, revised in 1956, amended in 1957, revised in 1958 and amended again in 1962 and 1967. See (1923) 10 Proceedings of Can Bar Assoc 327, 351; Proceedings of Conference of Commissioners on Uniformity of Legislation in Canada 1956, 86; 1957, 25, 26, 111; 1958, 90; 1962, 108; 1967, 22. On the subject of enforcement in Canada, see K. H. Nadelmann, (1960) 38 Can Bar Rev 68–88; I. R. Feltham, (1959) 1 UBCL Rev 229–251; E. D. Ram, (1977) 8 Man LJ 473–520; J. Bloom, (1978) 57 Oregon LR 399–429.
2 Quebec has no comparable provisions: see para 2.17, note 1 above. Saskatchewan has a 1920 style Act, RSS 1978, J–3, under which a limited number of orders have been made.
3 New Brunswick, North West Territories, Ontario, Saskatchewan, have not adopted this addition.
4 Alberta, Nova Scotia, Prince Edward Island have no external orders.
5 See Annex III.

Applications to register

2.31 The legislation applies to judgments or orders of any court (whether superior or not) in a reciprocating jurisdiction in a civil proceedings whereby any sum of money is payable, including arbitral awards made enforceable as a judgment of a court. It does not extend to compensation orders in criminal proceedings or, by express provision in the majority of the statutes, to periodical payments of money as alimony or maintenance to a wife, former wife, reputed wife, child or other dependant.[1] In the case of Manitoba, the scheme now applies to awards by a statutory authority to the payment of money in disputes between employers and employees.[2]

A judgment creditor[3] may, within six years after the date of the judgment, apply to the appropriate local court in the place of enforcement[4] for the judgment to be registered there. The application may be made for ex parte registration in prescribed circumstances only:

'in any case in which the judgment debtor
(a) was personally served with process in the original action; or
(b) though not personally served, appeared or defended or attorned or otherwise submitted to the jurisdiction of the original court;'[5]

and, in some jurisdictions[6], if the time for appeal has expired and no appeal is pending or an appeal has been disposed of.

If these conditions are not present, reasonable notice of the *application* must be given to the judgment debtor.

These requirements are in marked contrast with both the 1920 and 1933 schemes in providing the safeguard of notice to allow the judgment debtor to protest the application for an order to register itself. The most recent form of the model Act makes clear that personal service means actual delivery to the person to be served therewith but that it does not cease to be personal service because it is effected outside the jurisdiction of the original court.[7] Where an ex parte application is made, it must be accompanied by a certificate in statutory form from the original court setting out particulars of the process, the judgment and any appeal. Security for costs, in most jurisdictions, will be ordered against a non-resident applicant.[8]

1 Except Ontario, New Brunswick and Saskatchewan.
2 SM 1977, C. 57, s 21, amending RSM R–20, s 2(1)(a).
3 The term is usually defined to include 'executors, administrators, successors and assigns'.
4 What is the appropriate court varies, in some instances being limited to the Supreme Court, in others it includes certain inferior courts.
5 In New Brunswick, ex parte proceedings are prohibited when these circumstances are *not* present. It remains in the discretion of the court whether to order registration ex parte: *Wedley v Quist* [1953] 4 DLR 620, 10 WWR (NS) 21.
6 Alberta, British Columbia, Manitoba, Newfoundland.
7 Adopted everywhere except New Brunswick, Newfoundland, Ontario, Saskatchewan.
8 See para 3.27 below.

Registration

2.32 As with the 1920 Act, the order for registration lies in the discretion of the court[1] applied to.[2] But in addition, the legislation prescribes certain circumstances which, if proved, must preclude registration. In some jurisdictions, these are matters which are expressly stated as ones to be established by the judgment debtor. In others, the statute does not make clear whether the matter may be raised and determined by the court itself.[3] In practice, however, it appears that in all cases the courts see it as their duty to refuse registration if from the judgment and accompanying facts there appears sufficient cause why the judgment should not be registered.[4] Absence of any of these defences does not give the applicant a right to registration, for the court may still decline to grant leave if not satisfied that the judgment is one which it is proper to register.[5]

The prescribed defences are in the main closely modelled upon those set out in the 1920 legislation. Indeed, all the law areas provide for absence of jurisdiction under local conflict of law rules[6] and in almost the same verbatim terms for non-submission, no due service, fraud and public policy as in that legislation.[7] In respect of three defences, differences are found. First, registration must be refused if it is shown, as in the 1920 Act, that an appeal is pending or that the time for an appeal has not elapsed. But there is no necessity, as under the 1920 Act, for the judgment debtor to show that he intends to appeal. Secondly, and more importantly, in some law areas, it is a defence to show not only that the original court acted without jurisdiction according to the conflict of law rules of the receiving court area but also that the original court acted without authority under its *own* law to adjudicate concerning the cause of action or subject matter that resulted in the alleged judgment or concerning the person of the alleged judgment debtor.[8] This represents a major divergence from the terms of the other schemes and was taken on the advice of Dr Horace Read that lack of national competence rendered the judgment a nullity which could not be recognised by a Canadian court.[9]

The third defence is an additional ground:

> 'the judgment debtor would have a good defence if an action were brought on the original judgment'.[10]

The effect of this provision is that if an action on the judgment could not have been successful, it cannot be registered.[11] Whilst it does not permit defences to be raised which might lie in relation to the original cause of action,[12] it clearly permits the judgment debtor to oppose the registration of a judgment for grounds other than those stated in the legislation. It has been invoked to challenge for want of jurisdiction,[13] manifest error in the judgment[14] and breach of natural justice.[15]

Once an order to register[16] is given, this and an exemplification or certified copy of the judgment may be filed with the proper officer of the court where the order was made. Thereupon the judgment is entered as a judgment of that court. Notice of the registration must be served upon the judgment debtor within one month[17] or such time as the court may order, if the registration was made on an ex parte order, but not otherwise. Reasonable costs of the registration are recoverable as if they were sums payable under the judgment, if duly taxed.

1 Applications are normally dealt with by a single judge.
2 *Hausman v Franchi* [1949] OWN 695.
3 New Brunswick, Ontario, Saskatchewan, Yukon, NWT, merely require that 'it be shown to the court'. Elsewhere the court must be 'satisfied'.
4 *Saskatchewan Government Insurance Office v Anderson* (1966) 57 WWR 633 (Man CA) affd (1967) 61 DLR (2d) 355 (Man).
5 As for example, because it was not a final judgment (*Cavanagh v Lisogar* (1956) 19 WWR 230 (Alta)) or has been satisfied or is for payment of tax (Cf *United States of America v Harden* (1963) 41 DLR (2d) 721).
6 The jurisdictional rules, as in the 1920 scheme, are not contained in the enforcement legislation, being in most cases governed by the common law as understood in the particular law areas, except in New Brunswick and Saskatchewan where a Foreign Judgments Act, based on another Uniform model, is in force.
7 In New Brunswick, the terms of the Foreign Judgments Act (which contains the provisions as to defences) differ, particularly with respect to 'natural justice'.
8 Not found in Ontario, Saskatchewan, Yukon, NWT.
9 Proceedings of Conference of Commissioners on Uniformity of Legislation in Canada, 1958, p 90.
10 This is found in all statutes: see para 3.70 below.
11 *Canadian Credit Men's Trust Association v Ryan* [1930] 1 DLR 280 (Alta).
12 *Re Guildhall Insurance Co and Jackson* (1968) 69 DLR (2d) 137 (Alta).
13 *Re Tangye and Smith Ltd v Pelican Carbon Co of Canada* [1935] 1 DLR 759 (Ont).
14 *Re Gacs and Maierovitz* (1968) 68 DLR (2d) 345 (BC); *Re House of Colour Ltd v Expert Decorators Ltd* (1968) 70 DLR (2d) 527 (BC).
15 *Re Reciprocal Enforcement of Judgments Act, Wigston v Chowen* (1964) 49 WWR 543.

16 In Manitoba the court may determine whether and, if so, which provisions are registrable, if the judgment contains matter which is not registrable.
17 Calculated from the date of filing: *Re Reciprocal Enforcement of Judgments Act, Wigston v Chowen*, above.

Consequences of registration

2.33 Once registered a judgment, from the date of registration, has the same force and effect as a domestic judgment entered on that date.[1] The registering court has the same control and jurisdiction over it as over its own judgments. This power is limited to questions on enforcement: there is no power to alter the terms of the judgment.[2] Proceedings may be taken upon the judgment as if it were a local judgment but, in the case of an order on an ex parte application, sale or other disposition of the judgment debtor's property can only be taken after the period for an application to set aside, with any extension by the court, has elapsed.

An application for registration may in some jurisdictions be accompanied by an ex parte application for a garnishment order.[3] The judge when ordering registration may, in his discretion, order that all debts, obligations or liabilities due to the judgment debtor from a third party be attached in accordance with the usual rules of practice.

1 *C. M. Oliver & Co Ltd v Gilroy* [1959] 18 DLR (2d) 280.
2 *Lupton v Lupton* [1946] OWN 326, [1946] 2 DLR 286.
3 These provisions are found in some of the statutes only: eg Manitoba, Newfoundland: see para 3.32 below.

Setting aside a registration

2.34 Power to apply to set aside a registration is vested in the court but it is limited to cases where the application to register was made ex parte. Those who have been given notice of that application, whether or not they make an appearance, have no power to challenge the registration once made. The judgment debtor in the case of an ex parte application is entitled to be served with notice of the registration. Any application by him to set aside must be made within one month of having that notice. It will usually be made by notice of motion supported by affidavit. The judgment debtor will be obliged to stand by the grounds which he states in his notice of motion are those on which the judgment should not be registered.[1]

The power to set aside is confined to those cases in which the court is statutorily required not to order the registration.[2] In most law areas, the decision is stated to rest in the discretion of the court but in the case of New Brunswick, the judgment debtor is expressed to be entitled to have the registration set aside on these grounds.[3] In every case, the setting aside may be on such terms as the court thinks fit.

1 *Jackson v Jackson* [1950] 1 WWR 900 (BC).
2 Para 2.32 above.
3 RNB, c.R–3, s 6(2).

Relationship with other schemes

2.35 It is usual to provide that nothing in the legislation deprives a judgment creditor of the right to bring an action for the recovery of the amount of his judgment instead of proceeding by way of registration. It is apparent that this allows both actions on judgments and actions on the original cause of action to be brought.[1] There are no provisions as to costs designed to deter litigants from such alternatives in favour of the registration procedure.

1 The non-merger rule still applies in Canada: Castel, op cit, pp 478–483, and cases cited there.

(4) India and Bangladesh

2.36 The legislation which makes least concessions to pre-existing Commonwealth models is that introduced into British India in 1937 and continued in India[1] and Bangladesh (and Pakistan[2] and Burma) as section 44A of the Code of Civil Procedure 1908. The scheme is an independent section, not controlled by other parts of the Code.[3] It applies to judgments of the superior courts of reciprocating territories. In the case of India, the latter may be any country or territory outside India notified, with the designated courts, in the Official Gazette by the central government. In the case of Bangladesh, the scheme applies to the superior courts in the United Kingdom and designated courts in any country or territory in HM dominions notified in the Official Gazette by the central government as a reciprocating territory. In neither case is there any statutory requirement that reciprocity must actually be established. Extension orders are few for India and non-existent for Bangladesh.

1 Applied to the whole of India, with limited exceptions, by Civil Procedure Code (Amendment) Act 1951, No 2.
2 It is on this basis that Pakistan has remained a reciprocating country for many Commonwealth countries. But not with India: *Punjab Co-operative Bank Ltd v Naranjan Dass Budwar* AIR 1961 Punj 369.
3 *Lakhpat Rai Sharma v Atma Singh* AIR 1962 Punj 228.

Applications

2.37 The legislation applies to decrees or judgments:

> 'under which a sum of money is payable, not being a sum of money payable in respect of taxes or other charges of a like nature or in respect of a fine or other penalty.'[1]

It is made clear that in no case is there included 'an arbitration award, even if such award is enforceable as a decree or judgment'.[2]

The procedure is the same as that for enforcing a decree of an Indian court. The application may be made to any court in India, whether or not it is to be enforced there. It may then be transmitted to the court where this execution is sought.[3] The judgment creditor files an application for execution, with a certified copy of the original judgment[4] and a certificate of the original court stating the extent, if any, to which the decree has been satisfied or adjusted.[5] The certificate is conclusive proof of the extent of the satisfaction or adjustment.[6] Notice will be directed to be issued and served upon the judgment debtor, returnable within a specified time to show cause why the judgment should not be executed.[7] Nothing more is needed to secure execution.

1 Code of Civil Procedure 1908, s 44A, Explanation 2(India) and 3(Bangladesh).
2 Ibid.
3 *Indian and General Investment Trust v Raja of Khalikote* AIR 1952 Cal 508.
4 S 44A(1). There is no limitation period in respect of applications to file: *Lakhpat Rai Sharma v Atma Singh* AIR 1971 Punj 476.
5 This is a mandatory requirement: *Uthamran v Abdul Kasim Co* AIR 1964 Mad 221.
6 S 44A(2).
7 Code of Civil Procedure 1908, Ord 21, r 22.

Consideration of applications

2.38 When the certified copy of the judgment has been duly filed, all questions relating to its execution, discharge or satisfaction must be determined by the court executing it, if necessary treating the matter as a suit.[1] In addition to the usual grounds upon which execution of a domestic judgment may be opposed under the lex fori, the court is required to refuse execution if it is shown to its satisfaction that the decree falls within one of the exceptions to the test of conclusiveness which must be applied to all foreign judgments.[2] It appears that the burden will rest upon the judgment debtor,[3] who may raise such objections at any time in the execution proceedings, to establish that the judgment falls within an exception. Whenever the objection is brought to the attention of any court concerned with execution or transmission of the judgment, that court must adjudicate on it.[4]

The grounds for objection to the judgment are stated in section 13 of the Civil Procedure Code as arising:

(a) where it has not been pronounced by a court of competent jurisdiction;
(b) where it has not been given on the merits of the case;
(c) where it appears on the face of the proceedings to be founded on an incorrect view of international law or a refusal to recognise the law of [the country of execution] in cases in which such law is applicable;
(d) where the proceedings in which the judgment was obtained are opposed to natural justice;
(e) where it has been obtained by fraud;
(f) where it sustains a claim founded on a breach of any law in force in [the country of execution].

These grounds, whilst having much in common with the common law defences to registration under the Commonwealth scheme, show some differences which have been accentuated in the considerable case law on the section.[5] The objection on grounds of want of jurisdictional competence will be determined according to the rules of private international law in the receiving state.[6] The rules applied have generally followed those observed by English courts but not in all respects, for jurisdiction founded upon nationality has also been recognised as a distinct basis for actions in personam.[7]

The objection that the original judgment was not given on its merits does not permit the executing court to sit as a court of appeal upon the original judgment to determine whether the 'right' decision was reached. The judgment will not be recognised if the original court failed to turn its mind to the facts and law raised by the cause of action or decided the matter upon a point which did not arise on the merits[8] or was given as a penalty for the conduct of the defendant and not based upon a consideration of the truth or otherwise of the plaintiff's case.[9] The fact that the decision is ex parte does not, if process has been properly served, prevent it being a decision on the merits, even though the defendant did not appear.[10] The third objection permits a judgment to be treated as inconclusive if on the face of the proceedings it appears that the original court, in the view of the executing court, failed to apply correctly the relevant conflict of law rules. Similarly, it must not be recognised if the original court failed, when the matter was drawn to their attention, to apply the substantive law of the executing state when it was applicable under the conflict of laws rules.[11] This constitutes more than a mistake of law: it requires a deliberate act of refusal to apply the correct law.[12] Natural justice is, as at common law, concerned in the main with questions of the regularity of procedure, having nothing to do with merits. It arises where it is alleged the defendant has been deprived of his opportunity properly to present his case.[13] On the other hand, fraud is construed, unlike at common law, to mean extrinsic or collateral fraud and not that which arises from matters which were subject to the original adjudication. New material facts must be adduced to show that the original judgment was obtained by fraud.[14]

The final objection will arise where the law applied in the original court was the law of the executing state but some aspect of that law was breached in so doing.[15] But it does not apply where some other law is applied which merely produces inconsistency with the law of the executing state. This ground, therefore, shows important differences from the usual objections grounded in public policy.

These grounds appear to be the sole grounds upon which execution of a foreign judgment can be rejected. Once it is found that none can be sustained, the judgment is conclusive and may be executed as if it were a local judgment.

1 Civil Procedure Code, s 47, applied by s 44A(3); Diwan, op cit, ch xxv.
2 Ibid, s 13.
3 *Abdul Rahim v Mohamed Din* AIR 1943 Cal 42.
4 *Indian and General Investment Trust Ltd v Raja of Khalikote* AIR 1952 Cal 508.
5 See Diwan, op cit, pp 607–621.
6 *Sirdar Gurdyal Singh v Raja of Faridkote* [1894] AC 670, PC; *Indian and General Investment Trust Ltd v Raja of Khalikote*, above; *Kanhaiyalal Somani v Paramsukh* AIR 1956 Nag 273.
7 Diwan, op cit, pp 617–618; *Kesar Singh v Chandulal* AIR 1955 NUC (Madh B) 3376.
8 *Mallappa Yellappa Bennur v Raghavendra Sham Rao Desphande* AIR 1938 Bom 173; *Keymer v Visvanatham* (1916) L.R. 44 Ind App 6.
9 *Vellachi v Ramanathan* AIR 1973 Mad 141.
10 *Indian and General Investment Trust v Raja of Khalikote*, above, but orse in Madras, see *Vellachi v Ramanathan*, above.
11 *Ganga Prasad v Ganeshi Lal* 1924 ILR 46 All 119.
12 *Indian and General Investment Trust v Raja of Khalikote*, above.
13 *Sankaran Govindan v Lakshmi Bharati* AIR 1974 SC 1764.
14 Ibid.
15 *Indian and General Investment Trust v Raja of Khahlikote*, above, *Kunhiman v Idrosekutty* AIR 1958 Ker 126.

Consequences of registration

2.39 Once filed and any objections adjudicated upon, the judgment may be executed in the ways provided under the Code of Civil Procedure as if it were a local judgment. Thus the whole scheme of Order 21 which deals with execution of decrees and orders is made applicable.[1] Questions of limitation will be governed thereafter by the lex fori of the executing state.[2]

1 *Morlays Ltd v Roshanlal* AIR 1961 Bom 156.
2 *Uthamran v Abdul Kasim Co* AIR 1964 Mad 221. Limitation periods begin to run when the right to execution accrues, that is, from the date of filing: *Sheik Ali v Sheik Mohamed* AIR 1967 Mad 45.

Relationship with other schemes

2.40 Nothing in s 44A precludes a judgment creditor bringing proceedings by an action on the foreign judgment[1] or on the original cause of action.[2] For, as at common law, the latter does not merge with the judgment.[3] The Indian courts have stressed that it is the choice of the judgment creditor which of the procedures he may choose to invoke.

1 *Uthamran v Abdul Kasim Co* AIR 1964 Mad 221 at 223.
2 *Verma v Gehrilal* AIR 1962 Raj 231.
3 Ibid; *Setabganj Sugar Mills v Benozir Ahmed* AIR 1952 Cal 116. The reluctance to give up this rule has been criticised: S. Malik and N. G. Mysore, (1969) 4 Alig LJ 59, at 69.

(5) The New Zealand scheme

2.41 The enforcement legislation used in the nineteenth century amongst the Australasian colonies[1] remains on the statute book in New Zealand.[2] Although the provisions were considered by one judge to have been repealed by implication by the local 1920-style statute,[3] this is not the view of the Legislature which in 1934 prescribed that thereafter the scheme could be invoked in respect of judgments which could not be enforced in New Zealand under her 1933-style legislation.[4] The continued operation of the section, however, is still in doubt, as it is stated to apply to judgments, decrees, rules and orders, whereby any sum of money is made payable, obtained in any court of any of *Her Majesty's dominions*.[5] This latter term has been the subject of judicial uncertainty in New Zealand.[6] It is only if the New Zealand courts are prepared to treat it as referring to those jurisdictions over which the Queen is Head of State, whether as Queen of the United Kingdom or otherwise, that these provisions will have any useful application.[7] It will have limited value if it is construed as applying to the Queen as Queen of New Zealand.

The scheme permits the judgment creditor to cause a memorial of his judgment, authenticated by the seal of the original court, to be filed in the Supreme Court. It thereby becomes a record of the judgment,[8] although the action of filing does not make it a local judgment on which execution may issue.[9] Execution will normally only follow after the issue and service of a summons upon the judgment debtor[10] to show cause why execution should not issue and the debtor has failed either to appear or to show cause.[11] In those circumstances, on proof of service, issue of execution can be ordered and proceedings be taken for the enforcement of the judgment by or against persons not parties to the judgment as in respect of a local judgment.[12]

Australasian courts have demanded a high standard of compliance with the statutory requirements governing the nature of the memorial and the particulars to be entered in it (name and 'additions' of parties, form and nature of the action, date of the original judgment and of any trial and the amount of verdict given).[13] Insufficient compliance renders the judgment unsuitable for execution.[14] A judgment which is duly filed is presumed to be valid and not examinable by the requested court except for defects apparent on the face of it or upon extrinsic evidence adduced to show that the foreign court had no jurisdiction or that the judgment was obtained by fraud or manifest injustice.[15] Further, any defence which a defendant may plead in an action on a foreign judgment at common law will constitute good cause for not issuing execution, such as want of due notice.[16] The New Zealand Supreme Court appears to have followed the Australian courts in seeking to be satisfied that there was some jurisdictional basis for the original judgment.[17] Domicile or residence,[18] voluntary appearance or submission[19] or perhaps presence[20] in the original country when the original proceedings were commenced is normally required.

1 Para 1.13 above. Similar legislation may still be in force in Queensland and Western Australia: see para 1.15, note 14 above.
2 Judicature Act 1908, No 89, s 56.

3 Administration of Justice Act 1922, itself repealed by the Reciprocal Enforcement Act 1934, No 11. *Corry & Co v Kelway & Son* [1925] NLZR 93. The better view is that the earlier provisions were repealed insofar as the new legislation dealt with judgments from jurisdictions covered by the terms of both statutes, in this case, the United Kingdom.

4 Reciprocal Enforcement of Judgments Act 1934, No 11, s 13. For jurisdictions within the terms of the 1934 Act, see Annex III.

5 Judicature Act 1908, No 89, s 56(1).

6 *In the Matter of the Habeas Corpus Act 1679* (SCNZ, 13 April 1976 per Wilson J, unreported): para 3.04 below.

7 Para 3.04 below.

8 S 54(1). A corporation may apply: *Ruby Extended Tin Mining Co Ltd v Woolcott* (1880) 6 VLR (L) 301. (Australian authorities are based on the equivalent statutes.)

9 Cf *Johnson v Dickson* (1870) 1 VR (L) 159; *Morrow v Bellamy* (1873) 3 QSCR 190.

10 This requires an application by the judgment creditor or his solicitor: s 56(4). The summons must be served personally or as the court directs, ibid, but may not be served out of the jurisdiction: *London Chartered Bank of Australia v McEdward* (1894) 10 WN (NSW) 195.

11 S 56(4).

12 S 56(5) and for the revival of the judgment.

13 *Gillman v Holmes* (1888) 4 WN (NSW) 190; *Heussler v Rohde* (1890) 6 WN (NSW) 129; *Higgott v Lyon* (1893) 10 WN (NSW) 130; *Splatt v Splatt* (1889) 10 LR (NSW) 227.

14 *Vacuum Oil Co Pty Ltd v Maxwell* [1926] NZLR 625.

15 *Hogan v Moore* (1884) 6 ALT 156 (Vic): on fraud, see *Ruby Extended Tin Mining Co Ltd v Woolcott*, above.

16 *Barker v Johnson* (1861) 1 QSCR 28.

17 *Wallace v Bastings* (1899) 18 NZLR 639.

18 Unless clandestinely terminated in order to avoid the debt: *Berry v Shead* (1886) 7 LR (NSW) 39.

19 *Seegner v Marks* (1895) 21 VLR 491; *Baird v Bell* (1887) 4 WN (NSW) 17 and cases referred to in para 1.13, note 3 above.

20 *Herman v Meallin* (1891) 8 WN (NSW) 38.

(6) The South Australian scheme

2.42 The Australian jurisdictions generally follow, with but minor modifications, the 1933 scheme.[1] To this there is one major exception, that of South Australia which in 1971 enacted its own distinctive legislation, the Foreign Judgments Act 1971.[2] In a number of important ways, it breaks new ground in the arrangements for direct enforcement. In particular, the Act makes general provision with respect to judgments of a court in any country or state outside Australia without the need for reciprocity in every case. Where reciprocity can be established on the grounds of the congruence of direct jurisdictional rules followed in the Supreme Court of South Australia and those relied upon by courts in another law area, the courts of that area may be proclaimed to be reciprocating and their judgments are presumed, in the absence of evidence to the contrary, to be registrable.[3] In other cases where no extension order has been made, the court must be satisfied that the judgment is registrable under the terms of the Act.

1 Cocos (Keeling) Islands still maintain the 1920 legislation, which also remains unrepealed in New South Wales and Tasmania.

2 No 72 of 1971; see 8th Report of South Australia Law Reform Committee, 1969, which rejected a Bill more closely modelled on the 1933 Act; L. Glick, (1974) 48 ALJ 538–545.

3 S 6, except where the judgment is for the enforcement of any penal or revenue law.

Applications to register

2.43 The legislation relates to judgments or orders of foreign courts in civil proceedings for the payment of a monetary sum and in criminal proceedings for monetary compensation in respect of loss or injury to a person.[1] It does not include arbitral awards. Uniquely, however, it does include judgments or orders in civil proceedings for the recovery or delivery-up of personal property[2]—a noteworthy extension of previous Commonwealth schemes. A judgment is not registrable if it is for the enforcement of any penal law or for the recovery of a non-recoverable tax.[3]

The application may be made by or on behalf of the judgment creditor[4] to a judge or Master in Chambers at any time within six years after the date of the judgment or of the final determination of any appeal.[5] It may be made ex parte in a case of urgency but direct service upon the judgment debtor can be ordered.[6] In every case the application must be accompanied by affidavits stating in particular the position concerning appeals and stay of execution in the country of origin, the extent to which the judgment has been satisfied,[7] that the application is not out of time, that the creditor is entitled to enforce the judgment and that there are no facts known upon which setting aside can be sought.[8] Security for costs may be required from the judgment creditor.[9]

1 Foreign Judgments Act 1971, s 4.
2 Ibid.
3 Ibid, s 5(2). Judgments for income tax from Papua–New Guinea alone are recoverable for this purpose: Foreign Judgments Act Amendment Act 1980, No 66, s 3.
4 Defined as the 'person against whom a judgment is enforceable in accordance with the law of the country or state in which the original court is situated': ibid, s 4.
5 Ibid, s 7(1).
6 Ibid, s 7(6), and Rules of Court (Foreign Judgments Act) 1972, r 5(1).
7 Ibid, s 7(3).
8 Rules, r 5(2).
9 Ibid, r 5(5)(b).

Registration

2.44 Where the judgment is from a court of a reciprocating jurisdiction, it is presumed to be registrable. This presumption may be rebutted by satisfying the requested court that in fact jurisdiction was wanting. In the case of judgments from other countries the requested court must be satisfied on the application than an arguable case exists that the judgment is registrable.[1] The Act prescribes that this will be the case if:

'(a) the jurisdiction of the original court in the cause of action is recognised under the rules of private international law and the judgment is final and conclusive;
(b) the circumstances in which jurisdiction was assumed by the original court justify recognition of the judgment on the basis of comity and the judgment is final and conclusive; or
(c) it is, in the opinion of the court, just and equitable that the judgment be enforced pursuant to the provisions of this Act.'[2]

If any of these conditions are fulfilled and the other matters specified by the rules of court are met, the court must register the judgment.

This represents another unique development for this type of scheme. The first of the alternative tests of registrability essentially restates the common law in requiring application of jurisdictional tests under the conflicts of law rules of the receiving law area and the evidence that the judgment was final and conclusive.[3] The second test, however, appears to carry into this field the principle developed for matrimonial causes in *Travers v Holley*[4] that recognition should be given to the assumption by foreign courts of jurisdiction in circumstances similar to those in which the receiving court will itself *assume* jurisdiction. On an application of comity, Bray CJ held that jurisdiction based upon service of the writ or notice outside the foreign jurisdiction in circumstances substantially similar to those available under the law of South Australia will suffice, always provided the judgment is final and conclusive.[5] The third test is even more adventurous, for it appears to allow a registering court to dispense with the requirement for the judgment to be final and conclusive and to recognise the assumption of jurisdiction on exorbitant grounds, as for example, nationality or the presence of assets. It appears to have been intended to cover judgments from jurisdictions applying personal law which may not completely satisfy the common law definition of judgment but are nonetheless final and conclusive.[6] It is arguable, however, that the provision does not permit any deviation from the statutory definition of judgment but is concerned solely with questions of jurisdiction or relating to finality of the judgment. To date, there is no guidance as to how the courts might exercise their broad discretion under this head. As Nygh points out,[7] there may be no hardship in recognising a judgment where the assumption of jurisdiction by the original court on exorbitant grounds has caused no injustice or inequitable consequence to the judgment debtor in the circumstances of the case. Again, the possibility that a judgment could be varied abroad, and this may not be final and conclusive, could be controlled by the imposition of conditions.

Registration of a portion of a judgment is permitted if just and equitable, when it is not registrable in all respects.[8] Interest and costs may be recovered upon the registered judgment, as well as the amount payable under the judgment.[9] Notice of the registration must be served upon the judgment debtor personally, though other modes of service may be authorised or directed, including service out of the jurisdiction.[10]

1 *Malaysia–Singapore Airlines Ltd v Parker* (1972) 3 SASR 300 (Bray CJ).
2 Foreign Judgments Act 1971, s 5(1).
3 The effect of s 7(13) is that a right of appeal or institution of an appeal does not affect the finality and conclusiveness.
4 [1953] P 246, [1953] 2 All ER 794, CA, following *Re Dulles' Settlement (No 2), Dulles v Vidler* [1951] Ch 842 at 851: see now *Re Trepca Mines Ltd* [1960] 1 WLR 1273 at 1282.
5 *Malaysia–Singapore Airlines Ltd v Parker*, above.
6 SA Law Reform Committee, 8th Rep, 1969, p 5.
7 Op cit, p 106.
8 S 7(5).
9 S 7(8).
10 S 7(6); Rules, r 7(1). Notice of service must be indorsed; otherwise execution requires leave: r 5(2).

Consequence of registration

2.45 A registered judgment has, for the purposes of execution, the same force and effect as a judgment of the Supreme Court recorded at the date of registration.[1] The court may impose conditions upon the registration as are necessary to protect the interests of the judgment debtor in the event of a successful appeal or for any other purpose.[2] Its execution is subject to the control of the Supreme Court and proceedings may be taken upon it as if it were a judgment of that court.[3] But execution must be stayed until fourteen days from the service of notice of registration on the judgment debtor or until any application to set aside is finally determined, or while any order staying execution is in force in the country of origin.[4] In addition, execution can issue within six months of registration only with leave of the court.[5]

Where the judgment of the original court is satisfied wholly or partly (otherwise than by execution upon the registered judgment), the registered judgment is deemed to be wholly or proportionally satisfied.[6] Provision is also made for the conversion of sums payable under a judgment expressed in a foreign currency or paid for in part in such a currency.[7]

1 Foreign Judgments Act 1971, s 7(7).
2 Ibid, s 7(14).
3 Ibid, s 7(7): presumably including a bankruptcy notice: cf *Re A Judgment Debtor (No 2176 of 1938)* [1939] Ch 601, [1939] 1 All ER 1.
4 Ibid, s 7(12).
5 Rules of Court (Foreign Judgments Act) 1972, r 9.
6 Foreign Judgments Act 1971, s 7(10), without prejudice to the recovery of costs.
7 Ibid, s 7(9) and (11).

Setting aside the registration

2.46 An application may be made to set aside a registration by or on behalf of a judgment debtor, who must be served with notice of registration. The application must be supported by affidavits and served upon the judgment creditor.[1] The grounds are prescribed in the statute. If the court is satisfied that any has been established, it must set the registration aside.[2] The grounds in section 8(1) are essentially those found in the 1933 Act in slightly different terms:

(i) the judgment is not registrable, (ie does not meet the tests set out in section 5[3]);
(ii) the judgment debtor did not receive notice of the proceedings in sufficient time to enable him to defend the proceedings (notwithstanding that process may have been duly served upon the judgment debtor in conformity with the law of the original court[4]);
(iii) the judgment was obtained by fraud;
(iv) the cause of action upon which the judgment was given had previously been determined by the judgment of a court having jurisdiction to adjudicate upon that cause of action;
(v) the enforcement of the judgment would be contrary to public policy;
(vi) the rights under the judgment are not vested in the person by or on behalf of whom the application for registration was made.

Nygh suggests[5] that the onus for establishing registrability continues to lie with the judgment creditor, except where the judgment is presumed to be registrable as coming from a reciprocating court.[6] In the other cases, the burden of establishing the ground for setting aside will rest with the applicant.

1 Rules of Court (Foreign Judgments) Act 1972, r 8.
2 Foreign Judgments Act 1971, s 8(3).
3 See para 2.43 above: the judgment must not be for the enforcement of any penal law or for the recovery of any non-recoverable tax: ibid, s 5(2).
4 Ibid, s 8(2).
5 Op cit, p 107.
6 Para 2.42 above.

Relationship with other schemes

2.47 This scheme, which replaced the 1920 scheme, makes no provision concerning its relationship with other methods of enforcement of foreign judgments. It must be assumed, therefore, that actions on the foreign judgment or on the original cause of action, which are permitted at common law, remain as alternative methods of enforcement.[1]

1 Cf *Hong Kong and Macao Glass Manufacturing Co Ltd v Gritton* (1886) 12 VLR 128; *Delfino v Trevis (No 2)* [1963] NSWR 194.

ANNEX I

Commonwealth Jurisdictions with Judgment Enforcement Legislation

1920 Statute[1]

- Anguilla
- Antigua and Barbuda
- Australia:
  - New South Wales
  - Northern Territory[2]
  - Tasmania[2]
- Bahamas
- Barbados
- Belize
- British Virgin Islands
- Brunei
- Canada:
  - Saskatchewan
- Christmas Island
- Cocos (Keeling) Islands
- Cyprus
- Dominica
- Falkland Islands
- Fiji
- The Gambia
- Gibraltar
- Grenada
- Guyana
- Hong Kong[2]
- Jamaica
- Kenya
- Lesotho
- Malaŵi
- Malta
- Mauritius
- Montserrat
- Nigeria
- St Christopher–Nevis
- St Helena
- St Vincent & the Grenadines
- Seychelles
- Singapore
- Solomon Islands[2]
- Sri Lanka
- Swaziland
- Trinidad and Tobago
- Uganda
- United Kingdom:
  - England & Wales
  - Scotland
  - Northern Ireland
- Zambia
- Zimbabwe

1920 Statute modified[1]

- Canada:
  - Alberta
  - British Columbia
  - Manitoba
  - New Brunswick
  - Newfoundland
  - Northwest Territories
  - Nova Scotia
  - Ontario
  - Prince Edward Island
  - Saskatchewan
  - Yukon Territory

1933 Statute

- Anguilla[1]
- Antigua and Barbuda[1,2]
- Australia:
  - Australian Capital Territory
  - Queensland[1]
  - New South Wales[1]
  - Northern Territory
  - Tasmania[1]
  - Victoria[1]
  - Western Australia[1]
- Barbados[2]
- Belize[2]
- Bermuda[1]
- Botswana[1]
- Cayman Islands[1]
- Christmas Island
- Cyprus
- Dominica[1,2]
- Fiji[1]
- The Gambia[1]
- Ghana
- Gibraltar
- Grenada[1,2]
- Guernsey
- Guyana[1,2]
- Hong Kong
- Isle of Man
- Jamaica
- Jersey
- Kenya[1,2]
- Kiribati
- Malaysia[1]
- Mauritius[2]
- Montserrat[1,2]
- New Zealand[1]
- Nigeria[1,2]
- Norfolk Island
- Papua–New Guinea
- St Christopher–Nevis[1,2]
- St Lucia[1]
- St Vincent[1]
- Seychelles[1]
- Sierra Leone[1]
- Singapore[1,2]
- Solomon Islands
- Sri Lanka[2]
- Tanzania
- Tonga[1]
- Trinidad & Tobago[1,2]
- Turks & Caicos Islands[1,2]
- Tuvalu
- Uganda[1,2]
- United Kingdom:[1]
  - England & Wales
  - Scotland
  - Northern Ireland
- Western Samoa[1]
- Zambia

Distinctive Legislation

- Bangladesh
- Cyprus (Hague Convention)
- India
- New Zealand
- South Australia
- United Kingdom (EEC)

Direct Enforcement Legislation

- Australia:
  - Australian Capital Territory
  - Queensland
  - New South Wales
  - Northern Territory
  - South Australia
  - Tasmania
  - Victoria
  - Western Australia
  - Christmas Island
  - Cocos (Keeling) Islands
  - Norfolk Island
- Central Africa:
  - Malaŵi
  - Zambia
  - Zimbabwe
- East Africa:
  - Kenya
  - [Malaŵi]
  - Tanzania
  - Uganda
- New Zealand:
  - with
  - Cook Islands
  - Niue
- United Kingdom:[1]
  - England & Wales
  - Scotland
  - Northern Ireland
- West Indies:
  - Antigua & Barbuda
  - Dominica
  - St Christopher–Nevis
  - St Lucia
  - St Vincent & the Grenadines

Notes: (1) Includes arbitral awards (2) No orders outstanding

No general enforcement legislation exists in: Cook Islands, Nauru, Niue, Quebec, Pitcairn, Tokelau, Vanuatu.

ANNEX II

Commonwealth Legislation relating to the Enforcement of Judgments

ANGUILLA:	Foreign Judgments (Reciprocal Enforcement) Act 1969, No 8.
	Reciprocal Enforcement of Judgments Act, Revised Laws, 1961, Cap 67.
ANTIGUA AND BARBUDA:	Reciprocal Enforcement of Judgments Act, Revised Laws, 1962, Cap 69.
	West Indies Associated States Supreme Court Order, 1967, SI 1967/223 (UK), Art 9(3).
	Overseas Judgments (Reciprocal Enforcement) Act 1960, Laws of the West Indies, 1962, Cap 7.
AUSTRALIA:	Foreign Antitrust Judgments (Restriction on Enforcement) Act 1979, No 13.
	Service and Execution of Process Act 1901–1974.
AUSTRALIAN CAPITAL TERRITORY:	Foreign Judgments (Reciprocal Enforcement) Ordinance 1954, No 11.
NEW SOUTH WALES:	Administration of Justice Act 1924, No 42, Part III.
	Foreign Judgments (Reciprocal Enforcement) Act 1973, No 36.
NORTHERN TERRITORY:	Foreign Judgments (Reciprocal Enforcement) Ordinance 1955, No 21.
QUEENSLAND:	Reciprocal Enforcement of Judgments Act 1959, No 37.
SOUTH AUSTRALIA:	Foreign Judgments Act 1971, No 72.
TASMANIA:	Supreme Court Civil Procedure Act 1932, No 58.
	Foreign Judgments (Reciprocal Enforcement) Act 1962, No 5 of 1963.
VICTORIA:	Foreign Judgments Act 1962, No 6916.
WESTERN AUSTRALIA:	Foreign Judgments (Reciprocal Enforcement) Act 1963, No 12.
COMMONWEALTH OF BAHAMAS:	Reciprocal Enforcement of Judgments Act, Revised Laws, Cap 44.
BANGLADESH:	Code of Civil Procedure 1908, s 44A.
BARBADOS:	Foreign and Commonwealth Judgments (Reciprocal Enforcement) Act, Revised Laws, 1971, Cap 201.

	Overseas Judgments (Reciprocal Enforcement) Act 1960, Laws of the West Indies, Cap 7.
BELIZE:	Reciprocal Enforcement of Judgments Ordinance, Revised Laws, 1958, Cap 8.
BERMUDA:	Judgments (Reciprocal Enforcement) Act 1958, Revised Laws 1972, Vol 8.71.
BOTSWANA:	Judgments (International Enforcement) Act 1981, No 16.
BRITISH VIRGIN ISLANDS:	Reciprocal Enforcement of Judgments Act, Revised Laws, 1961, Cap 65.
BRUNEI:	Reciprocal Enforcement of Judgments Enactment, 1954, No 9.
CANADA:	
ALBERTA:	Reciprocal Enforcement of Judgments Act, RSA, 1980, R-6.
BRITISH COLUMBIA:	Court Order Enforcement Act, RSBC, 1979, Cap 75, Part 2.
MANITOBA:	Reciprocal Enforcement of Judgments Act, RSM, 1970, R-20.
NEW BRUNSWICK:	Reciprocal Enforcement of Judgments Act, RSNB, 1973, R-3. Foreign Judgments Act, ibid, F-19.
NEWFOUNDLAND:	Reciprocal Enforcement of Judgments Act, RSN, 1970, Cap 327.
NORTHWEST TERRITORIES:	Reciprocal Enforcement of Judgments Ordinance, RONWT, 1974, R-1.
NOVA SCOTIA:	Reciprocal Enforcement of Judgments Act, 1973, RSNS, 1979, R-6.
ONTARIO:	Reciprocal Enforcement of Judgments Act, RSO, 1980, Cap 432.
PRINCE EDWARD ISLAND:	Reciprocal Enforcement of Judgments Act SPEI 1974, R-7.
QUEBEC:	Civil Code, Article 1220. Civil Procedure Code, Revised Laws, C-25, Articles 178–181.
SASKATCHEWAN:	Reciprocal Enforcement of Judgments Act, RSS 1978, R-3. Foreign Judgments Act, ibid, F-18. Judgments Extension Act, ibid, J-3.
YUKON TERRITORY:	Reciprocal Enforcement of Judgments Ordinance, ROYT, 1970, R-1.
CAYMAN ISLANDS:	Foreign Judgments Reciprocal Enforcement Law (Revised) (1976) Gazette, No 22 of 1976.
CHRISTMAS ISLAND:	Foreign Judgments (Reciprocal Enforcement) Ordinance 1977, No 4. Reciprocal Enforcement of Judgments Ordinance, Laws of Singapore, 1955, Cap 18.
COCOS (KEELING) ISLANDS:	Reciprocal Enforcement of Judgments Ordinance, Laws of Singapore 1955, Cap 18.

	Reciprocal Enforcement of Judgments (Amendment) Ordinance 1963, No 2.
COOK ISLANDS:	Cook Islands Act 1915, ss 142, 173, 174, Statutes of New Zealand.
CYPRUS:	Civil Procedure (Reciprocal Enforcement of Judgments) Law, Revised Laws, 1959, Cap 7. Foreign Judgments (Reciprocal Enforcement) Law, ibid, Cap 10. The Convention on the Recognition and Enforcement of Foreign Judgments in Civil and Commercial Matters and Supplementary Protocol Thereto (Ratification) Law 1976, No 11.
COMMONWEALTH OF DOMINICA:	Reciprocal Enforcement of Judgments Ordinance, Revised Laws, 1961, Cap 17. West Indies Associated States Supreme Court Order, 1967, SI 1967/223 (UK), Art 9(3). Overseas Judgments (Reciprocal Enforcement) Act, 1960, Laws of the West Indies, 1962, Cap 7.
FALKLAND ISLANDS:	Reciprocal Enforcement of Judgments, Revised Laws, 1950, Cap 56.
FIJI:	Reciprocal Enforcement of Judgments Ordinance, Revised Laws, 1967, Cap 24. Foreign Judgments (Reciprocal Enforcement), Ordinance, ibid, Cap 25.
THE GAMBIA:	Foreign Judgments (Reciprocal Enforcement) Act, Revised Laws, 1966, Cap 76. Reciprocal Enforcement of Judgments Act, ibid, Cap 162.
GHANA:	Courts Act 1971, No 372, Part V.
GIBRALTAR:	Judgments (Reciprocal Enforcement) Ordinance, Revised Laws, 1964, Cap 80.
GRENADA:	British Judgments (Enforcement) Ordinance, Revised Laws, 1958, Cap 39. Foreign Judgments (Reciprocal Enforcement) Ordinance, ibid, Cap 125. Overseas Judgments (Reciprocal Enforcement) Act 1960, Laws of the West Indies, 1962, Cap 7.
GUERNSEY:	Judgments (Reciprocal Enforcement) (Guernsey) Law 1957.
GUYANA:	Judgments Extension Ordinance, Revised Laws 1953, Cap 27. Foreign Judgments (Reciprocal Enforcement) Act, Revised Laws, 1973, Cap 7.04.
HONG KONG:	Judgments (Facilities for Enforcement) Ordinance, Revised Laws, 1964, Cap 9.

	Foreign Judgments (Reciprocal Enforcement) Ordinance, ibid, 1981, Cap 319.
INDIA:	Code of Civil Procedure 1908, s 44A.
ISLE OF MAN:	Judgments (Reciprocal Enforcement) (Isle of Man) Act 1968, No 12.
JAMAICA:	Judgments and Awards (Reciprocal Enforcement) Act, Revised Laws, 1973.
	Judgments (Foreign) (Reciprocal Enforcement) Act, Revised Laws, 1973.
	Overseas Judgments (Reciprocal Enforcement) Act 1960, Laws of the West Indies, 1962, Cap 7.
JERSEY:	Judgments (Reciprocal Enforcement) (Jersey) Law 1960.
KENYA:	Foreign Judgments Enforcement Act, Revised Laws 1967, Cap 43.
KIRIBATI:	Foreign Judgments (Reciprocal Enforcement) Ordinance, Revised Laws, 1973, Cap 5.
LESOTHO:	Reciprocal Enforcement of Judgments Proclamation 1922, No 2 Revised Laws 1960.
MALAŴI:	Judgments Extension Ordinance, Revised Laws, 1957, Cap 15.
	British and Colonial Judgments Ordinance, ibid, Cap 14.
	Service of Process and Execution of Judgments, Revised Laws, ibid, 1968, Cap 4.04.
MALAYSIA:	Reciprocal Enforcement of Judgments Act 1958, No 99.
MALTA:	British Judgments (Reciprocal Enforcement) Act, Revised Laws, 1945, Cap 86.
	Code of Organisation and Civil Procedure, ibid, Cap 15, Title V.
MAURITIUS:	Reciprocal Enforcement of Judgments Ordinance, Revised Laws, 1945, Cap 201.
	Foreign Judgments (Reciprocal Enforcement) Ordinance, 1961, No 35.
MONTSERRAT:	Reciprocal Enforcement of Judgments Act, Revised Laws, 1961, Cap 67.
	Overseas Judgments (Reciprocal Enforcement) Act 1960, Laws of the West Indies, 1962, Cap 7.
NAURU:	Civil Procedure Act 1972, ss 7, 8.
NEW ZEALAND:	Reciprocal Enforcement of Judgments Act 1934, No 11.
	Judicature Act 1908, No 89, s 56.
NIGERIA:	Reciprocal Enforcement of Judgments Ordinance, Revised Laws, 1958, Cap 175.
	Foreign Judgments (Reciprocal Enforcement) Ordinance 1960, No 31.

NORFOLK ISLAND:	Reciprocal Enforcement of Judgments Ordinance 1925–1964. Foreign Judgments (Reciprocal Enforcement) Ordinance 1978, No 8.
NIUE:	Niue Act 1966, ss 95, 126, 127, Statutes of New Zealand.
PAPUA–NEW GUINEA:	Judgments Enforcement (Reciprocal Arrangements) Act 1976, No 74 (Revised Laws, Cap 50).
ST CHRISTOPHER–NEVIS:	Reciprocal Enforcement of Judgments Act, Revised Laws, 1961, Cap 67. West Indies Associated States Supreme Court Order, 1967 SI 1967/223 (UK), Art 9(3). Overseas Judgments (Reciprocal Enforcement) Act 1960, Laws of the West Indies, 1962, Cap 7.
ST HELENA:	Reciprocal Judgments Enforcement, Revised Laws, 1950, Cap 97.
ST LUCIA:	British, Colonial and Foreign Judgments (Reciprocal Enforcement) Ordinance, Revised Laws, 1957, Cap 10. West Indies Associated States Supreme Court Order 1967, SI 1967/223 (UK), Art 9(3). Overseas Judgments (Reciprocal Enforcement) Act 1960, Laws of the West Indies, 1962, Cap 7.
ST VINCENT AND THE GRENADINES:	British Judgments (Enforcement) Act, Revised Laws, 1926, Cap 4. Foreign Judgments (Reciprocal Enforcement) Act 1958, No 18. West Indies Associated States Supreme Court Order 1967, SI 1967/223 (UK), Art 9(3). Overseas Judgments (Reciprocal Enforcement) Act 1960, Laws of the West Indies, 1962, Cap 7.
SEYCHELLES:	Foreign Judgments (Reciprocal Enforcement) Ordinance, Revised Laws, 1971, Cap 63. Reciprocal Enforcement of British Judgments Ordinance, ibid, Cap 79.
SIERRA LEONE:	Foreign Judgments (Reciprocal Enforcement) Ordinance, Revised Laws, 1960, Cap 21. Sierra Leone–Guinea Relations Act 1964, No 55.
SINGAPORE:	Reciprocal Enforcement of Commonwealth Judgments Act, Revised Laws, 1970, Cap 24. Reciprocal Enforcement of Foreign Judgments Act, ibid, Cap 25.

SOLOMON ISLANDS:	Reciprocal Enforcement of Judgments Ordinance, Revised Laws, 1969, Cap 8. Foreign Judgments (Reciprocal Enforcement) Ordinance, ibid, Cap 9.
SRI LANKA:	Reciprocal Enforcement of Judgments, Ordinance, Revised Laws, 1956, Cap 94. Reciprocal Enforcement of Foreign Judgments Ordinance, ibid, Cap 93.
SWAZILAND:	Reciprocal Enforcement of Judgments Act 1922, No 4, Revised Laws.
TANZANIA:	Judgments Extension Ordinance, Revised Laws, Cap 7. Foreign Judgments (Reciprocal Enforcement), ibid, Cap 8. Civil Procedure Code 1966, No 49, ss 11–12.
TONGA:	Reciprocal Enforcement of Judgments Act 1967, No 5
TRINIDAD AND TOBAGO:	Judgments Extension Act, Revised Laws, 1980, Cap 5:02. Overseas Judgments (Reciprocal Enforcement) Act 1960, Laws of the West Indies, 1962, Cap 7.
TURKS AND CAICOS ISLANDS:	Overseas Judgments (Reciprocal Enforcement) Act 1960, Laws of the West Indies, 1962, Cap 7.
TUVALU:	Foreign Judgments (Reciprocal Enforcement) Ordinance, Revised Laws, 1978, Cap 5.
UGANDA:	Reciprocal Enforcement of Judgments Act, Revised Laws, 1964, Cap 47. Foreign Judgments (Reciprocal Enforcement) Act, ibid, Cap 48. Judgments Extension Act, ibid, Cap 46.
UNITED KINGDOM: ENGLAND AND WALES NORTHERN IRELAND SCOTLAND	Administration of Justice Act 1920, Part II. Foreign Judgments (Reciprocal Enforcement) Act 1933. Civil Jurisdiction and Judgments Act 1982.
WESTERN SAMOA:	Reciprocal Enforcement of Judgments Act 1970, No 5. British and Colonial Judgments (Reciprocal Enforcement) Act, Revised Laws, 1959, Cap 16.
ZAMBIA:	Foreign Judgments (Reciprocal Enforcement) Act, Revised Laws, 1972, Cap 86. Service of Process and Execution of Judgments, ibid, Cap 90.
ZIMBABWE:	Reciprocal Enforcement of Judgments Act, Revised Laws, 1974, Cap 51. Service of Process and Execution of Judgments Act, ibid, Cap 53.

ANNEX III

Extension Orders under Reciprocal Enforcement Legislation

This tabulation sets out the jurisdictions to which Commonwealth countries have extended their reciprocal legislation. The reference to '1920' and '1933' indicates the scheme in question. 'Comm' and 'Non-Comm' are used to distinguish Commonwealth and Non-Commonwealth jurisdictions.

The entries have been made up from information provided by Commonwealth countries, which has been verified and amended, as far as library resources permit, to reflect recent developments. Where a jurisdiction is referred to by a former name in the original order, this has been retained.

ANGUILLA:

1920, Comm: Bahamas, Barbados, Bermuda, British Guiana [Guyana], British Honduras [Belize], England, Grenada, Jamaica, New South Wales, Nigeria, Northern Ireland, St Lucia, St Vincent, Scotland, Trinidad and Tobago.
1933, Comm & Non-Comm: None

ANTIGUA AND BARBUDA:

1920, Comm: Bahamas, Barbados, Bermuda, British Guiana [Guyana], British Honduras [Belize], England, Grenada, Jamaica, New South Wales, Nigeria, Northern Ireland, St Lucia, St Vincent, Scotland, Trinidad and Tobago.
1930, Comm & Non-Comm: None.

AUSTRALIA

Australian Capital Territory:

1933, Comm: Bahamas, Bermuda, British Columbia, British Honduras [Belize], British Virgin Islands, Cayman Islands, Cook Islands, Dominica, England, Falkland Islands, Fiji, The Gambia, Ghana, Gibraltar, Gilbert and Ellice Islands [Kiribati, Tuvalu], Grenada, Guyana, Hong Kong, India, Jamaica, Kenya, Malaŵi, Malaysia, Malta, Manitoba, Montserrat, Newfoundland and Labrador, New Zealand, Niue, Northern Ireland, St Helena, St Lucia, St Vincent, Saskatchewan, Scotland, Seychelles, Sierra Leone, Singapore, Solomon Islands, Sri Lanka, Tonga, Western Samoa.
1933, Non-Comm: France, Western Germany, Israel, Italy, Japan, Pakistan.

New South Wales:

1920, Comm: Antigua, Barbados, Basutoland [Lesotho], Bechuanaland [Botswana], British Honduras [Belize], Cyprus, Malta, Mauritius, Nigeria, Northern Rhodesia [Zambia], Southern Rhodesia [Zimbabwe], Swaziland, Tanganyika and Zanzibar [Tanzania], Trinidad and Tobago, Uganda.
1920, Non-Comm: Somaliland [in Somalia], Wei hai wei [in China].
1933, Comm: Bahamas, Bermuda, British Columbia, British Virgin Islands, Cayman Islands, Cook Islands, Dominica, England, Falkland Islands, Fiji, The Gambia, Ghana, Gibraltar, Gilbert and Ellice Islands [Kiribati, Tuvalu], Grenada, Guyana, Hong Kong, India, Jamaica, Kenya, Malaŵi, Malaysia, Manitoba, Montserrat, Newfoundland and Labrador, New Zealand, Niue, Northern Ireland, Papua–New Guinea, St Christopher–Nevis–Anguilla [St Christopher–Nevis, Anguilla], St Helena, St Lucia, St Vincent, Saskatchewan, Scotland, Seychelles, Sierra Leone, Singapore, Solomon Islands, Sri Lanka, Tonga, Tuvalu, Western Samoa.
1933, Non-Comm: France, Federal Republic of Germany, Israel, Italy, Japan, Republic of Korea, Pakistan.

Northern Territory:

1933, Comm: Bahamas, Bermuda, British Columbia, British Honduras [Belize], British Virgin Islands, Cayman Islands, Cook Islands, Dominica, England, Falkland Islands, Fiji, The Gambia, Ghana, Gibraltar, Gilbert and Ellice Islands [Kiribati, Tuvalu], Grenada, Guyana, Hong Kong, India, Jamaica, Kenya, Malaŵi, Malaysia, Malta, Manitoba, Montserrat, Newfoundland and Labrador, New Zealand, Niue, Northern Ireland, St Helena, St Lucia, St Vincent, Saskatchewan, Scotland, Seychelles, Sierra Leone, Singapore, Solomon Islands, Sri Lanka, Tonga.
1933, Non-Comm: France, Western Germany, Israel, Italy, Japan, Pakistan.

Queensland:

1933, Comm: Antigua, Bahamas, Belize, Bermuda, British Columbia, British Virgin Islands, Cayman Islands, Dominica, England, Falkland Islands, Fiji, The Gambia, Ghana, Gibraltar, Gilbert and Ellice Islands [Kiribati, Tuvalu], Grenada, Guyana, Hong Kong, India, Jamaica, Kenya, Malaŵi,

Malaysia, Malta, Manitoba, Montserrat, Newfoundland and Labrador, New Zealand, Northern Ireland, Papua–New Guinea, St Helena, St Lucia, St Vincent, Saskatchewan, Scotland, Seychelles, Sierra Leone, Singapore, Solomon Islands, Southern Rhodesia [Zimbabwe], Sri Lanka, Tonga, Trinidad and Tobago, Western Samoa.
1933, Non-Comm: Italy, Pakistan, South Africa.

Southern Australia:

Comm: Antigua, Bahamas, Belize, Bermuda, British Columbia, British Virgin Islands, Cayman Islands, Cook Islands, Dominica, Falkland Islands, Fiji, The Gambia, Ghana, Gibraltar, Grenada, Guyana, Hong Kong, India, Jamaica, Kenya, Kiribati, Malaŵi, Malaysia, Malta, Manitoba, Montserrat, Newfoundland and Labrador, New Zealand, Niue, Papua–New Guinea, St Christopher–Nevis–Anguilla [St Christopher–Nevis, Anguilla], St Helena, St Lucia, St Vincent, Saskatchewan, Seychelles, Sierra Leone, Singapore, Solomon Islands, Sri Lanka, Tonga, Tuvalu, Western Samoa.
Non-Comm: France, Federal Republic of Germany, Israel, Italy, Japan, Pakistan.

Tasmania:

1920, Comm: Malta, Trinidad and Tobago.
1933, Comm: Antigua, Bahamas, Belize, Bermuda, British Columbia, British Virgin Islands, Cayman Islands, Cook Islands, Dominica, England, Falkland Islands, Fiji, The Gambia, Ghana, Gibraltar, Gilbert Islands [Kiribati], Grenada, Guyana, Hong Kong, India, Jamaica, Kenya, Malaŵi, Malaysia, Manitoba, Montserrat, Newfoundland and Labrador, New Zealand, Niue, Northern Ireland, Papua–New Guinea, St Christopher–Nevis–Anguilla [St Christopher–Nevis, Anguilla], St Helena, St Lucia, St Vincent, Saskatchewan, Scotland, Seychelles, Sierra Leone, Singapore, Solomon Islands, Sri Lanka, Tonga, Tuvalu, Western Samoa.
1933, Non-Comm: France, Federal Republic of Germany, Israel, Italy, Japan, Pakistan.

Victoria:

1933, Comm: Antigua, Bahamas, Belize, Bermuda, British Columbia, British Virgin Islands, Cayman Islands, Cook Islands, Dominica, England, Falkland Islands, Fiji, The Gambia, Ghana, Gibraltar, Gilbert and Ellice Islands [Kiribati, Tuvalu], Grenada, Guyana, Hong Kong, India, Jamaica, Kenya, Malaŵi, Malaysia, Manitoba, Montserrat,

Newfoundland and Labrador, New Zealand, Niue, Northern Ireland, Papua–New Guinea, St Christopher–Nevis–Anguilla [St Christopher–Nevis, Anguilla], St Helena, St Lucia, St Vincent, Saskatchewan, Scotland, Seychelles, Sierra Leone, Singapore, Solomon Islands, Sri Lanka, Tonga, Tuvalu, Western Samoa.
1933, Non-Comm: France, Federal Republic of Germany, Israel, Italy, Japan, Pakistan.

Western Australia: *1933, Comm:* Antigua, Bahamas, Basutoland [Lesotho], Bechuanaland [Botswana], Bermuda, British Honduras [Belize], British Virgin Islands, Cayman Islands, Ceylon [Sri Lanka], Dominica, England, Falkland Islands, Fiji, The Gambia, Gilbert Islands [Kiribati], Grenada, Hong Kong, India, Jamaica, Kenya, Malaŵi, Malaysia, Malta, Manitoba, Newfoundland and Labrador, New Zealand, Norfolk Island, Northern Ireland, Papua–New Guinea, St Christopher–Nevis–Anguilla [St Christopher–Nevis, Anguilla], St Lucia, St Vincent, Saskatchewan, Scotland, Seychelles, Sierra Leone, Singapore, Solomon Islands, Swaziland, Tonga, Trinidad and Tobago, Western Samoa.
1933, Non-Comm: France, Federal Republic of Germany, Israel, Italy, Japan, Pakistan.

BAHAMAS: *1920, Comm:* Barbados, Bermuda, British Guiana [Guyana], British Honduras [Belize], England, Jamaica, Leeward Islands [Anguilla, Antigua, British Virgin Islands, Dominica, Montserrat, St Christopher–Nevis], Northern Ireland, St Lucia, Scotland, Trinidad [Trinidad and Tobago].

BANGLADESH: *Comm:* England, Northern Ireland, Scotland.

BARBADOS: *1920, Comm:* Bahamas, Bermuda, British Guiana [Guyana], England, Grenada, Jamaica, Leeward Islands [Anguilla, Antigua, British Virgin Islands, Dominica, Montserrat, St Christopher–Nevis], New South Wales, Nigeria, Northern Ireland, St Lucia, St Vincent, Scotland, Trinidad [Trinidad and Tobago].
1933, Comm & Non-Comm: None.

BELIZE: *1920, Comm:* Australian Capital Territory, Bahamas, Barbados, Bermuda, England, Jamaica, Leeward Islands [Anguilla, Antigua, British Virgin Islands, Dominica,

Montserrat, St Christopher–Nevis], New South Wales, Nigeria, Northern Ireland, Northern Territory, Queensland, Scotland, South Australia, Victoria, Western Australia.
1933, Comm & Non-Comm: None.

BERMUDA: *1920, Comm:* Bahamas, Barbados, British Guiana [Guyana], Dominica, England, Gibraltar, Grenada, Hong Kong, Jamaica, Leeward Islands [Anguilla, Antigua, British Virgin Islands, Montserrat, St Christopher–Nevis], Nigeria, Northern Ireland, St Lucia, St Vincent, Scotland.

BOTSWANA: *1933, Comm:* Basutoland [Lesotho], England, Ireland [Northern Ireland], Kenya, New South Wales, New Zealand, North and Central Australia [Northern Territory], Northern Rhodesia [Zambia], Nyasaland [Malaŵi], Scotland, Southern Rhodesia [Zimbabwe], Swaziland, Tanganyika and Zanzibar [Tanzania], Uganda, Victoria, Western Australia.
1933, Non-Comm: None.

BRITISH VIRGIN ISLANDS: *1920, Comm:* Bahamas, Barbados, Belize, Bermuda, England, Grenada, Guyana, Jamaica, New South Wales, Nigeria, Northern Ireland, St Lucia, St Vincent, Scotland, Trinidad [Trinidad and Tobago].

BRUNEI: *1920, Comm:* England, Hong Kong, Northern Ireland, Scotland.

CANADA

Alberta: *Comm:* British Columbia, Manitoba, Newfoundland, Northwest Territories, Nova Scotia, Ontario, Prince Edward Island, Saskatchewan, Yukon Territory.
Non-Comm: None.

British Columbia: *Comm:* Alberta, Manitoba, New Brunswick, Newfoundland, Northwest Territories, Nova Scotia, Ontario, Prince Edward Island, Saskatchewan, Victoria, Yukon Territory.
Non-Comm: Austria, Federal Republic of Germany (including Land Berlin).

Manitoba: *Comm:* Alberta, Australian Capital Territory, British Columbia, New Brunswick, Newfoundland, Northern Territory of Australia, Northwest Territories, Nova Scotia, Ontario, Prince Edward Island, Queensland, Saskatchewan, South Australia, Tasmania, Western Australia, Yukon Territory.
Non-Comm: None.

New Brunswick:	*Comm:* Alberta, British Columbia, Manitoba, Newfoundland, Nova Scotia, Ontario, Prince Edward Island, Saskatchewan. *Non-Comm:* None.
Newfoundland:	*Comm:* Alberta, Australian Capital Territory, British Columbia, Manitoba, New Brunswick, Northwest Territories, Nova Scotia, Ontario, Prince Edward Island, Queensland, Saskatchewan, Tasmania, United Kingdom [England and Wales, Northern Ireland, Scotland], Victoria, Yukon Territory. *Non-Comm:* None.
Northwest Territories:	*Comm:* Alberta, British Columbia, Manitoba, Newfoundland, Nova Scotia, Ontario, Saskatchewan, Yukon Territory. *Non-Comm:* None.
Nova Scotia:	*Comm:* Alberta, British Columbia, Manitoba, New Brunswick, Newfoundland, Northwest Territories, Ontario, Prince Edward Island, Saskatchewan, Yukon Territory. *Non-Comm:* None.
Ontario:	*Comm:* Alberta, British Columbia, Manitoba, New Brunswick, Newfoundland, Northwest Territories, Nova Scotia, Prince Edward Island, Saskatchewan, Yukon Territory. *Non-Comm:* None.
Prince Edward Island:	*Comm:* Alberta, British Columbia, Manitoba, New Brunswick, Newfoundland and Labrador, Nova Scotia, Ontario, Saskatchewan. *Non-Comm:* None.
Saskatchewan:	*Comm:* Alberta, British Columbia, Manitoba, New Brunswick, Newfoundland, Northwest Territories, Nova Scotia, Ontario, Prince Edward Island, Yukon Territory. *Non-Comm:* None. *1920, Comm:* New South Wales; Victoria, United Kingdom [England and Wales, Northern Ireland, Scotland].
Yukon Territory:	*Comm:* Alberta, British Columbia, Manitoba, Newfoundland, Nova Scotia, Northwest Territories, Ontario, Queensland, Saskatchewan, Western Australia. *Non-Comm:* None.

CAYMAN ISLANDS: *1920, Comm:* England, Northern Ireland, Queensland, Scotland, South Australia, Victoria, Western Australia.
1933, Comm & Non-Comm: None.

CHRISTMAS ISLAND: *1920, Comm:* England, Hong Kong, Malaysia, Northern Ireland, Papua–New Guinea, Scotland.
1920, Non-Comm: Pakistan.

COCOS (KEELING) ISLANDS: *1920, Comm:* England and Wales, Hong Kong, Malaysia, Northern Ireland, Scotland.
1920, Non-Comm: Pakistan.

CYPRUS: *1920, Comm:* Grenada, New South Wales.
1933, Comm: England and Wales, Northern Ireland, Scotland.
1933, Non-Comm: None.

DOMINICA: *1920, Comm:* Australian Capital Territory, Bahamas, Barbados, Bermuda, British Guiana [Guyana], British Honduras [Belize], Grenada, Jamaica, New South Wales, Nigeria, Northern Territory of Australia, Queensland, Singapore, St Lucia, St Vincent, Tasmania, Trinidad and Tobago, Victoria.
1933, Comm & Non-Comm: None.

FALKLAND ISLANDS: *1920, Comm:* England and Wales, Northern Ireland, Scotland.

FIJI: *1920, Comm:* British Solomon Islands Protectorate [Solomon Islands], England and Wales, Gilbert and Ellice Islands [Kiribati, Tuvalu], New South Wales, New Zealand, Norfolk Island, Northern Ireland, Scotland.
1920, Non-Comm: Pakistan.
1933, Comm: Australian Capital Territory, India, Northern Territory of Australia, Papua–New Guinea, Queensland, South Australia, Tasmania, Victoria, Western Australia.
1933, Non-Comm: None.

THE GAMBIA: *1920, Comm:* England and Wales, New South Wales, Northern Ireland, Scotland, Sierra Leone.
1933, Comm: Australian Capital Territory, Nigeria, Northern Territory of Australia, Tasmania.
1933, Non-Comm: None.

GHANA: *1933, Comm:* United Kingdom [England and Wales, Northern Ireland, Scotland].
1933, Non-Comm: Brazil, France, Israel, Italy, Japan, Lebanon, Senegal, Spain, United Arab Republic.

GIBRALTAR: *1933, Comm:* Australian Capital Territory, Bermuda, England and Wales, Malta, New South Wales, Nigeria, Northern Ireland, Northern Territory of Australia, Queensland, Scotland, South Australia, Tasmania, Victoria, Western Australia.

GRENADA: *1920, Comm:* Bahamas, Barbados, Bermuda, British Guiana [Guyana], British Honduras [Belize], Ceylon [Sri Lanka], Cyprus, England and Wales, Falkland Islands, Jamaica, Leeward Islands [Anguilla, Antigua, British Virgin Islands, Montserrat, St Christopher–Nevis], Mauritius, New South Wales, Nigeria, Northern Ireland, Scotland, Singapore, Trinidad [Trinidad and Tobago], Windward Islands [Dominica, St Lucia, St Vincent].
1933, Comm & Non-Comm: None.

GUERNSEY: *1933, Comm:* England and Wales, Northern Ireland, Scotland.
1933, Non-Comm: Israel, Italy, Netherlands, Netherlands Antilles, Surinam.

GUYANA: *1920, Comm:* Antigua, Bahamas, Barbados, Belize, Bermuda, British Virgin Islands, Dominica, England and Wales, Grenada, Montserrat, New South Wales, Nigeria, Northern Ireland, St Christopher–Nevis–Anguilla [Anguilla, St Christopher–Nevis], St Lucia, St Vincent, Scotland, Trinidad and Tobago.
1933: None.

HONG KONG: *1920, Comm:* United Kingdom [England and Wales, Northern Ireland, Scotland].
1933, Comm: Australia Capital Territory, Bermuda, Brunei, Ceylon [Sri Lanka], India, Malaysia, New South Wales, New Zealand, Queensland, Singapore, South Australia, Tasmania, Victoria, Western Australia.
1933, Non-Comm: Austria, Belgium, France, Federal Republic of Germany, Italy, Netherlands, Pakistan.

INDIA: *Comm:* Fiji, Hong Kong, Malaya [Malaysia], New Zealand, Sikkim, Singapore, Trinidad [Trinidad and Tobago], United Kingdom

[England and Wales, Northern Ireland, Scotland], Western Samoa.
Non-Comm: Aden [South Yemen].

ISLE OF MAN: *1933, Comm:* United Kingdom [England and Wales, Northern Ireland, Scotland].
1933, Non-Comm: Israel, Italy, Netherlands, Netherlands Antilles, Surinam.

JAMAICA: *1920, Comm:* Bahamas, Barbados, Bermuda, British Guiana [Guyana], British Honduras [Belize], Dominica, Grenada, Leeward Islands [Anguilla, Antigua and Barbuda, British Virgin Islands, Montserrat, St Christopher–Nevis], New South Wales, Nigeria, Queensland, St Lucia, St Vincent, Trinidad and Tobago.
1933, Comm: United Kingdom [England and Wales, Northern Ireland, Scotland].
1933, Non-Comm: None.

JERSEY: *1933, Comm:* England and Wales, Northern Ireland, Scotland.
1933, Non-Comm: Israel, Italy, Netherlands, Netherlands Antilles, Surinam.

KENYA: *1920, Comm:* Basutoland [Lesotho], Bechuanaland [Botswana], Malaŵi, Mauritius, New South Wales, Northern Rhodesia [Zambia], Northern Territory of Australia, Seychelles, Swaziland, Tasmania, United Kingdom [England and Wales, Northern Ireland, Scotland], Victoria.
1920, Non-Comm: British Somaliland [in Somalia].
1933, Comm & Non-Comm: None.

KIRIBATI: *1933, Comm:* Papua–New Guinea.
1933, Non-Comm: None.

LESOTHO: *1920, Comm:* Bechuanaland [Botswana], England, Ireland [Northern Ireland], Kenya, New South Wales, New Zealand, North and Central Australia [Northern Territory], Northern Rhodesia [Zambia], Nyasaland [Malaŵi], Scotland, Southern Rhodesia [Zimbabwe], Swaziland, Tanganyika and Zanzibar [Tanzania], Uganda, Victoria, Western Australia.

MALAŴI *1920, Comm:* Basutoland [Lesotho], Bechuanaland [Botswana], British Solomon Islands [Solomon Islands], Gilbert and Ellice Islands [Kiribati, Tuvalu], New South Wales, Seychelles, Swaziland, United

Kingdom [England and Wales, Northern Ireland, Scotland].
1920, Non-Comm: Somaliland [in Somalia].

MALAYSIA: *1933, Comm:* Australian Capital Territory, Hong Kong, India (except Jammu and Kashmir, Mampur, Tribal areas of Assam, Scheduled areas of Madras and Andhra), New South Wales, New Zealand, Northern Territory of Australia, Singapore, Sri Lanka, South Australia, United Kingdom [England and Wales, Northern Ireland, Scotland], Victoria, Western Australia.
1933, Non-Comm: None.

MALTA: *1920, Comm:* Bermuda, Gibraltar, New South Wales, United Kingdom [England and Wales, Northern Ireland, Scotland], Victoria, Western Australia.

MAURITIUS: *1920, Comm:* Ceylon [Sri Lanka], Grenada, Kenya, New South Wales, Seychelles, Tanganyika [Tanzania], Uganda, United Kingdom [England and Wales, Northern Ireland, Scotland], Victoria.

MONTSERRAT: *1920, Comm:* Australian Capital Territory, Australian Territories [Christmas Island, Cocos (Keeling) Islands, Norfolk Island, Papua–New Guinea], Bahamas, Barbados, Bermuda, British Guiana [Guyana], British Honduras [Belize], England, Grenada, Jamaica, Leeward Islands [Anguilla, Antigua, British Virgin Islands, Dominica, St Christopher–Nevis], New South Wales, Nigeria, Northern Ireland, Northern Territory of Australia, St Lucia, St Vincent, Scotland, Trinidad and Tobago.
1933, Comm & Non-Comm: None.

NEW ZEALAND: *1933, Comm:* Australian Capital Territory, Basutoland [Lesotho], Bechuanaland [Botswana], British Solomon Islands [Solomon Islands], Cameroons [Nigeria], Ceylon [Sri Lanka], Fiji, Gilbert and Ellice Islands [Kiribati, Tuvalu], Hong Kong, India, Federation of Malaya, North Borneo, Sarawak [Malaysia], New South Wales, Nigeria, Norfolk Island, Northern Territory of Australia, Papua–New Guinea, Queensland, Singapore, South Australia, Swaziland, Tasmania, United Kingdom [England and Wales, Northern Ireland, Scotland], Victoria, Western Australia, Western Samoa.
1933, Non-Comm: Belgium, France, Pakistan.

NIGERIA: *1920, Comm:* Barbados, Bermuda, British Guiana [Guyana], England, The Gambia, Gold Coast, including Ashanti and Northern Territories [Ghana]; Gibraltar, Grenada, Ireland [Northern Ireland], Jamaica, Leeward Islands [Anguilla, Antigua and Barbuda, British Virgin Islands, Dominica, Montserrat, St Christopher–Nevis], Newfoundland, New South Wales, St Lucia, St Vincent, Scotland, Sierra Leone, Trinidad and Tobago, Victoria.
1933, Comm & Non-Comm: None.

NORFOLK ISLAND: *1920, Comm:* England, Fiji, Ireland [Northern Ireland], New Zealand, Northern Territory of Australia, Papua New Guinea [Papua–New Guinea], Scotland, Singapore, South Australia, Strait Settlements [in Malaysia], Trinidad and Tobago, Western Australia.
1933, Comm & Non-Comm: None.

PAPUA–NEW GUINEA: *1933, Comm:* Bahamas, British Honduras [Belize], British Solomon Islands [Solomon Islands], Fiji, Gilbert and Ellice Islands [Kiribati, Tuvalu], Grenada, India, Kenya, Malaysia, Manitoba, New South Wales, New Zealand, Queensland, Sierra Leone, St Lucia, South Australia, Tasmania, Tonga, Trinidad and Tobago, United Kingdom [England and Wales, Northern Ireland, Scotland], Victoria, Virgin Islands, Western Australia.
1933, Non-Comm: New York, Pakistan.

ST CHRISTOPHER–NEVIS: *1920, Comm:* Bahamas, Barbados, Bermuda, British Guiana [Guyana], British Honduras [Belize], England, Grenada, Jamaica, New South Wales, Nigeria, St Lucia, St Vincent, Scotland, Trinidad and Tobago.
1933, Comm & Non-Comm: None.

ST HELENA (*with Ascension Island, Tristan da Cunha*): *1920, Comm:* England, New South Wales, Northern Ireland, Scotland.

ST LUCIA: *1920, Comm:* Bahamas, Barbados, British Guiana [Guyana], England, Grenada, Jamaica, Leeward Islands [Anguilla, Antigua, British Virgin Islands, Dominica, Montserrat, St Christopher–Nevis], Nigeria, Northern Ireland, St Vincent, Scotland, Singapore, Trinidad [Trinidad and Tobago].
1933, Comm & Non-Comm: None.

ST VINCENT AND THE GRENADINES:	*1920, Comm:* Bahamas, Barbados, Bermuda (or Somers Islands), England, Grenada, Guyana, Jamaica, Leeward Islands [Anguilla, Antigua, British Virgin Islands, Dominica, Montserrat, St Christopher–Nevis], New South Wales, Nigeria, Northern Ireland, Scotland, Singapore, Trinidad and Tobago. *1933, Comm:* Queensland. *1933, Non-Comm:* None.
SEYCHELLES:	*1920, Comm:* Commonwealth of Australia, British India [India], England, Mauritius, New South Wales, Northern Ireland, Nyasaland [Malaŵi], Scotland, Uganda. *1933, Comm:* Kenya. *1933, Non-Comm:* None.
SIERRA LEONE:	*1933, Comm:* The Gambia, Ghana, Nigeria. *1933, Non-Comm:* None.
SINGAPORE:	*1920, Comm:* Australian Capital Territory, Ceylon [Sri Lanka], Hong Kong, India, except Jammu and Kashmir, Malacca, Johore, Kedah, North Borneo, Brunei, Penang, Federation of Malaya, Sarawak, [Malaysia, Brunei], New South Wales, New Zealand, Norfolk Island, Northern and Central Australia [Northern Territory], Papua–New Guinea, South Australia, Tasmania, United Kingdom [England and Wales, Northern Ireland, Scotland], Victoria, Western Australia, Windward Islands [Dominica, Grenada, St Lucia, St Vincent and the Grenadines]. *1920, Non-Comm:* Pakistan. *1933, Comm & Non-Comm:* None.
SOLOMON ISLANDS:	*1920, Comm:* United Kingdom [England and Wales, Northern Ireland, Scotland]. *1933, Comm:* Papua–New Guinea. *1933, Non-Comm:* None.
SRI LANKA:	*1920, Comm:* Australian Capital Territory, Cook Islands, New Zealand, Niue, Queensland, South Australia, Tasmania, United Kingdom [England and Wales, Northern Ireland, Scotland], Western Australia, Western Samoa. *1933, Comm & Non-Comm:* None.
SWAZILAND:	*1920, Comm:* Botswana, England, Ireland [Northern Ireland], Kenya, Lesotho, Malaŵi, New Zealand, New South Wales, North and Central Australia [Northern Territory], Scotland, Southern Rhodesia [Zimbabwe], Tanzania (except Zanzibar), Uganda, Victoria, Western Australia, Zambia, Zanzibar.

TANZANIA: *1933, Comm:* Basutoland [Lesotho], Bechuanaland [Botswana], Ceylon [Sri Lanka], Mauritius, New South Wales, Northern Rhodesia [Zambia], Seychelles, Rhodesia [Zimbabwe], Swaziland, United Kingdom [England and Wales, Northern Ireland, Scotland].
1933, Non-Comm: Somaliland [in Somalia].

TONGA: *1933, Comm:* Australian Capital Territory, New South Wales, New Zealand, Northern Territory, South Australia, Victoria.
1933, Non-Comm: None.

TRINIDAD AND TOBAGO: *1920, Comm:* Bahamas, Barbados, Christmas Island, Cocos (Keeling Islands), Grenada, Guyana, India, Jamaica, Leeward Islands [Anguilla, Antigua, British Virgin Islands, Dominica, Montserrat, St Christopher–Nevis], New South Wales, Nigeria, Norfolk Island, Papua–New Guinea, Queensland, St Lucia, St Vincent, South Australia, Tasmania, United Kingdom [England and Wales, Northern Ireland, Scotland], Victoria, Western Australia.
1933, Comm & Non-Comm: None.

TURKS AND CAICOS ISLANDS: *1933, Comm & Non-Comm:* None.

TUVALU: *1933, Comm:* Papua–New Guinea.
1933, Non-Comm: None.

UGANDA: *1920, Comm:* Basutoland [Lesotho], Bechuanaland [Botswana], Ceylon [Sri Lanka], Mauritius, New South Wales, Seychelles, Swaziland, United Kingdom [England and Wales, Northern Ireland, Scotland].
1920, Non-Comm: Republic of Ireland.
1933, Comm & Non-Comm: None.

UNITED KINGDOM: *1920, Comm:* Bahamas, Barbados, Basutoland [Lesotho], Bechuanaland [Botswana], Bermuda, British Guiana [Guyana], British Honduras [Belize], British Solomon Islands [Solomon Islands], Ceylon [Sri Lanka], Cyprus, Dominica, Falkland Islands, Fiji, The Gambia, Gibraltar*, Gilbert and Ellice Islands [Kiribati, Tuvalu], Gold Coast, Ashanti, Northern Territories of Gold Coast [Ghana], Grenada, Hong Kong, Jamaica, Kenya, Leeward Islands [Anguilla, Antigua, British Virgin Islands, Montserrat, St Christopher–Nevis], Malay Federated States, Johore, Kedah, North Borneo, Strait

Settlements [Malaysia], Malta, Mauritius, Newfoundland, New South Wales, New Zealand, Nigeria, Norfolk Island, Northern Rhodesia [Zambia], Nyasaland [Malaŵi], Papua, New Guinea [Papua–New Guinea], Queensland, St Helena, St Lucia, St Vincent, Saskatchewan, Seychelles, Sierra Leone, Singapore, South Australia, Southern Rhodesia [Zimbabwe], Swaziland, Tanganyika, Zanzibar [Tanzania], Tasmania, Trinidad and Tobago, Uganda, Victoria, Western Australia.
1920, Non-Comm: Somaliland [in Somalia].
1933, Comm: Australian Capital Territory, Guernsey, India, Isle of Man, Jersey, Tonga.
1933, Non-Comm: Austria, Belgium*, France*, Germany*, Israel, Italy*, Netherlands*, Netherlands Antilles*, Norway, Pakistan, Surinam.
(Extension in respect of those marked * will be affected by the Brussels Convention on Jurisdiction and the Enforcement of Judgments in Civil and Commercial Matters by virtue of the Civil Jurisdiction and Judgments Act 1982, when brought into full force.)

WESTERN SAMOA: *1933, Comm:* New Zealand, Western Australia, Victoria.
1933, Non-Comm: None.

ZAMBIA: *1920, Comm:* Basutoland [Lesotho], Bechuanaland [Botswana], England, Ireland [Northern Ireland], Kenya, New South Wales, Nyasaland [Malaŵi], Scotland, Southern Rhodesia [Zimbabwe], Swaziland, Tanganyika [Tanzania], Victoria.
1933, Comm: British Solomon Islands [Solomon Islands], Gilbert and Ellice Islands [Kiribati, Tuvalu], Tanzania.
1933, Non-Comm: None.

ZIMBABWE: *1920, Comm:* Basutoland [Lesotho], Bechuanaland [Botswana], British Solomon Islands [Solomon Islands], Gilbert and Ellice Islands [Kiribati, Tuvalu], New South Wales, Northern Rhodesia [Zambia], Nyasaland [Malaŵi], Queensland, Swaziland, Tanganyika [in Tanzania], United Kingdom [England and Wales, Northern Ireland, Scotland], Victoria.

CHAPTER 3

The Commonwealth Money Judgment Schemes

I INTRODUCTION

3.01 The judgment enforcement schemes derived from the 1920 and 1933 United Kingdom statutes are to be found in one or other or even both forms in all parts of the Commonwealth, except the Indian Sub-Continent.[1] They remain today largely in the form in which they were originally devised[2] with very little modification to their substantive provisions. Although their operation has been the subject of judicial consideration in many jurisdictions, in general they appear to have withstood that technical examination well. Given the premises upon which they were devised, major weaknesses have not been exposed and, to a large degree, the terms of the legislation have presented remarkably few serious difficulties.

This chapter sets out to bring together, as far as that can be achieved, the Commonwealth law as it has developed around these two schemes. At many points, the analysis applied by Commonwealth judges to one scheme will be relevant to the operation of the other. The structures of the two schemes are very similar. Further the 1933 statute sets out in express terms much of what is required at common law and to which regard must be had under the less explicit provisions of the 1920 legislation. For the same reason, some reference is made to common law decisions handed down in cases where enforcement has been sought by an action on the foreign judgment.

The case law is drawn in the main, as might be expected, from the larger and older Commonwealth jurisdictions with the legislation. Cases from the new Commonwealth are less frequent, perhaps indicating the limited use of the legislation there, and in most instances they do not add significantly to the trend of the authorities from Australia, Canada, New Zealand and the United Kingdom.

1 Jurisdictions with the Commonwealth legislation are listed in Chapter 2, Annex I, the legislation in force in Annex II and the jurisdictions in respect of which extensions are in force in Annex III.

2 An outline of their provisions is set out in Chapter 2, paras 2.18–2.22 (1920 scheme); 2.30–2.35 (Canadian variant); 2.23–2.29 (1933 scheme); see A. L. Foote *Second Commonwealth and Empire Law Conference* (Ottawa, 1960) pp 149–162.

II APPLICATION OF THE SCHEMES

Relationship between the two schemes

3.02 The 1920 scheme was devised, and remains almost exclusively,[1] for use between jurisdictions within the Commonwealth or, as many statutes have it, in 'Her Majesty's dominions'. The 1933 scheme was designed primarily for non-Commonwealth states, with power to apply it to Her Majesty's dominions or, in some statutes, to the Commonwealth.[2] In fact, this scheme has been utilised more substantially for the latter purpose than for the former.

The 1933 Act makes clear that once the later scheme is made effective with respect to Her Majesty's dominions or Commonwealth generally, it must be used for extensions to any jurisdiction which is not already subject to an extension order made under the 1920 Act.[3] An extension order may also be made under the 1933 Act in respect of a jurisdiction subject to a 1920 order. In that case, the 1933 scheme applies and the 1920 Act may not be utilised again for that jurisdiction.[4] The purpose is to ensure that the later scheme is the one to be developed. In a number of countries, notably the United Kingdom,[5] this purpose has not been fulfilled, extension orders existing under both schemes in respect of Commonwealth jurisdictions, with the preponderance still under the earlier Act. In a number of other cases, either the 1933 scheme or that of 1920 exists alone, sometimes because the former has not been put into effect.[6]

The failure to replace the 1920 scheme is not easily explained. Certain differences between the two, notably with respect to arbitral awards, were dealt with in 1956 in the United Kingdom[7] and subsequently elsewhere but have not led to any significant move towards the 1933 Act. Arguably, the more detailed formulation of the latter is not seen as a sufficiently substantial improvement upon the earlier legislation to justify making new reciprocal arrangements. It may also be related to the relative lack of importance with which the schemes are viewed in many Commonwealth jurisdictions whose judgments are unlikely to be transferred to other parts of the Commonwealth.

1 Continued application to Pakistan is frequently found.
2 FJREA, s 7, under which a general order was required to make the section applicable to HM dominions, in addition to the application of the section to foreign countries. In the UK this was effected by SR & O 1933/1037; similar provision was made in other jurisdictions in which this model applies. The making of such a general order must be followed by individual extension orders in respect of particular jurisdictions within the Commonwealth: *Yukon Consolidated Gold Corpn v Clark* [1938] 2 KB 241, [1938] 1 All ER 366; *Jamieson v Northern Electricity Supply Corpn (Private) Ltd* 1970 SLT 113. For UK provisions, see a new s 1(1), (5), substituted by Civil Jurisdiction and Judgments Act 1982, Sch 10.
3 FJREA, s 7.
4 This does not preclude variation of a continuing 1920 Order: AJA, s 14(2). Apparently in the UK, an order consolidating existing lists requires legislative authority: Civil Jurisdiction and Judgments Act 1982, s 35(3), adding s 14(3).
5 See Chapter 2, Annex I for others.
6 Ibid.
7 Administration of Justice Act 1956, s 51.

The requirement of reciprocity

3.03 In contrast with domestic enforcement schemes in which full faith and credit is granted between the partner jurisdictions, there has been a constant concern in discussions on generalised enforcement schemes to protect against misuse. Governments necessarily wish to preserve to themselves the power to determine whether the privilege of their enforcement facilities should be offered to external judgments, especially those which may emanate from places in respect of which there are doubts about the quality of the judicial system and laws. The schemes allow for this by granting a discretion in relation to extension and an unfettered power of revocation of any extension order.[1] Whilst in the usual event these qualitative tests may be readily fulfilled by Commonwealth jurisdictions with their common legal traditions, the safeguard remains fundamental. In addition, governments have traditionally shown a reluctance to afford local enforcement facilities in favour of a particular jurisdiction unless there is some guarantee of similar treatment in that jurisdiction in respect of their judgments. The explicit requirement of reciprocity has therefore been insisted upon in order to secure the introduction of equivalent facilities.[2] This is most obvious in the 1920 Act which requires 'reciprocal provisions made by the legislature of the other jurisdiction'.[3] The 1933 Act, designed to meet the circumstances of non-Commonwealth states, recognises the differences inevitable in foreign legal systems by requiring only 'substantial reciprocity of treatment' for their judgments when received there.[4] In the latter case, there is no requirement for legislative provision, it being envisaged that reciprocal treatment may result from the bilateral treaty undertakings which, in United Kingdom practice at least, precede the extension order. In the practice of other Commonwealth states the guarantees of reciprocal treatment will usually be given in an exchange of notes or by similar diplomatic activity. In relation to extensions to Commonwealth jurisdictions under the 1933 Act, reciprocal treatment is usually provided by similar legislation and an undertaking to make a reciprocal extension, although the United Kingdom has recently found it necessary to employ treaty arrangements in these circumstances too.[5]

In respect of both schemes, however, the determination as to whether the legislation or the treatment accords reciprocity is that of the Executive and not the courts. Moreover, since the requirement of reciprocity must only be established when the initial order is made, its disappearance, as for example by the repeal of the reciprocal legislation in a particular jurisdiction, will not affect the validity of the extension order in favour of that jurisdiction. That is a circumstance in which the Executive would be justified in revoking the order.[6]

It is noteworthy that in a considerable number of cases reciprocity is provided by legislation which does not exactly correspond. So 1920 legislation may be reciprocated by a 1933-style statute or vice versa. More remarkably, reciprocity has been found by some jurisdictions, including the United Kingdom, in provisions in the Indian Code of Civil Procedure which, as we have seen,[7] represent a rather different approach. Reciprocity of treatment, therefore, has become in these cases a more flexible notion which allows for considerable variations in executive treatment.[8] Indeed it might be argued that the basis smacks rather of comity than reciprocity.[9]

South Australia has approached this matter in a unique way. Extension orders may be made in relation to 'courts of reciprocal jurisdiction'. This, however, is not a prerequisite of registration, for the judgments of any country will be registrable, even in the absence of an extension order, if the prescribed jurisdictional conditions are met (and the other statutory requirements fulfilled).[10] No evidence of reciprocity is required in this case and there is no limitation to the Commonwealth. An extension order, however, in favour of a named law area may be made where the Governor is satisfied that the courts of that area exercise jurisdiction on approximately the same bases as are relied upon by the Supreme Court of South Australia.[11] In such a case, the judgments of those overseas courts are presumed, in the absence of evidence to the contrary, to have fulfilled the jurisdictional requirements of the statute and, provided the judgment meets the other statutory criteria, it will be registrable without further consideration of the jurisdictional factors. It seems probable that most Commonwealth countries would be eligible under these terms.

1 AJA, s 14(2); FJREA, s 1(4). Generally, see G. D. Kennedy, (1957) Can Bar Rev 123.

2 The legislation in India and Bangladesh, whilst making no express requirement of reciprocity, refers to 'reciprocating countries': Code of Civil Procedure, s 44A. In practice, evidence of reciprocal treatment is usually sought.

3 AJA, s 14(1). Canadian statutes refer to 'reciprocal provisions'.
4 FJREA, s 1(1).
5 In relation to Tonga, SI 1980/153. Tonga is an independent Kingdom within the Commonwealth.
6 See note 1. FJREA, s 9, allows an order to be made rendering judgments from foreign countries unenforceable if substantially less favourable treatment is being granted to the legislating state's judgments. This provision does not appear to apply to HM dominions, nor is it intended to be the basis upon which extension orders under the 1933 Act are to be rendered inoperable.
7 Paras 2.36–2.40 above.
8 Dicey and Morris, op cit, p 1105, perhaps go too far in suggesting that reciprocity has ceased to obtain in these cases.
9 P. R. H. Webb, (1966) 15 ICLQ 269.
10 Foreign Judgments Act 1971, s 5, lays down the jurisdictional requirements: para 2.44 above.
11 Ibid, s 6. See *Malaysia-Singapore Airline Ltd v Parker* (1972) 3 SASR 300.

Constitutional terminology in the statutes

3.04 The terminology used in the statutes of many law areas in the Commonwealth still reflects the constitutional circumstances in the Commonwealth at the time they were enacted. Thus, for example, it is commonly provided that extension orders may be made with respect to 'any part of Her Majesty's dominions' outside the legislating jurisdiction itself.[1] This term strictly does not extend to protectorates or protected states.[2] Accordingly, in the case of the 1920 Act power to extend to such territories was expressly conferred,[3] whilst the 1933 Act gave an extended meaning to 'HM dominions' as including those cases.[4] Revised versions of the legislation have in a number of cases substituted references to 'Commonwealth' which under local legislation will be defined in a way which includes all independent members of the Commonwealth and any territory for the international relations of which such a state is responsible. Unfortunately, the earlier terminology has been retained in a number of independent Commonwealth states, including republics, raising doubts concerning the coverage of the schemes.

The term 'Her Majesty's dominions' is usually construed as a reference to those territories over which the Crown as Head of State has sovereignty. But it has been held that, as the Queen of the United Kingdom is a different legal entity from the Queen of New Zealand, a reference to 'Her Majesty's dominions' in legislation in force in New Zealand cannot be a reference to territories of both Queens.[5] On the other hand, legislative practice in the United Kingdom has consistently treated the term as extending to any state of which the Queen is Head of State and to its dependencies.[6] Given the context in which the legislation is intended to operate, it seems likely that this view would be preferred even in the republics with statutory provision of this kind.[7] What is clear, however, is that this term cannot normally extend to include a Commonwealth state for which the Queen is not Head of State. The United Kingdom legislative practice in cases where republic status is acquired is to require references to 'Her Majesty's dominions' to be construed as continuing to include the new republic.[8] This, however, applies only as far as the legislation of the United Kingdom is concerned.[9] Similar legislation in other parts of the Commonwealth does not always exist and without it, it appears clear that fresh extension orders in favour of republics cannot be made. Similar considerations apply when a state leaves the Commonwealth altogether. On the other hand, an extension order already made may not lose its validity because the place to which it refers no longer falls within the categories for which fresh orders may be made, provided the qualification existed when the order was made. It is always open to the Executive to revoke the order if it is no longer appropriate. In fact orders in favour of Pakistan, for example, no longer in the Commonwealth, are not uncommon.[10]

These considerations have their principal relevance with respect to the 1920 scheme. As the 1933 scheme provides for orders to be made in favour of foreign states, as well as HM dominions, it would be pedantic to hold that republics within the Commonwealth fall between the two categories. These shortcomings suggest that the renovation of the legislation by the introduction of appropriate references to the Commonwealth is much to be desired.[11] Inaccurate references to 'Ireland' which are often found, sometimes in revised statutes, also require attention.[12]

1 AJA, s 14; FJREA, s 7(1). Many Commonwealth statutes are expressed to apply to the United Kingdom with power to make extension orders in relation to other parts of HM dominions.

2 *Halsbury's Laws of England*, vol 6, para 803. Mandated and trusteeship territories under any Commonwealth government were also outside the term. See also Mandated and Trust Territories Act 1947.

3 AJA, s 13.

4 FJREA, s 7(3).

5 *Re Habeas Corpus Act 1679* (13 April 1976 unreported) (SCNZ), 13 per Wilson J, construing the Fugitive Offenders Act 1881, amended to extend to the Commonwealth: Act 1976, No 2, s 5(a).

6 *Halsbury*, op cit, para 803.

7 Australia has been held to be a 'British possession' for purposes of various UK Acts received into the law of Australia. That term is defined to mean 'any part of Her Majesty's dominions' (Interpretation Act 1889, s 18(2), replaced by Interpretation Act, 1978, Sch 1). *McArthur v Williams* (1936) 55 CLR 324 (Fugitive Offenders Act 1881), *McIlwraith McEacharn v Shell Co of Australia Ltd* (1945) 70 CLR 175 (Colonial Courts of Admiralty Act 1890); *R v Commissioner for Transport, ex p Cobb & Co Ltd* [1963] Qd R 547 (Merchant Shipping Act 1894); *Re Cunningham, ex p Bennett* (1967) 10 FLR 262 (Extradition Acts 1870–1933); *Southern Centre of Theosophy Inc v South Australia* (1979) 54 ALJR 43 (Judicial Committee Acts 1833–44).

8 *Halsbury*, op cit, para 803.

9 The legislation is normally given effect in the law of any territory over which the United Kingdom, at the time of enactment, had legislative authority but only as far as UK Acts and Orders-in-Council are concerned.

10 The United Kingdom made explicit saving provision: Pakistan Act 1973, s 4(5).

11 The Commonwealth Secretariat have produced a model Commonwealth Countries Act to facilitate the process of updating: *Memoranda for 1980 Meeting of Commonwealth Law Ministers*, 1980, p 276.

12 In United Kingdom law, the term must be construed as exclusive of the Republic of Ireland: SR & O 1923/405. Quaere whether this was also intended to be Imperial legislation and is applicable to all jurisdictions with the 1920 legislation?

Extensions to judgments of designated courts

3.05 An extension order under the 1920 scheme is generally effective with respect to judgments obtained in a 'superior court' of the jurisdictions concerned.[1] The Act gives no guidance to the registering court on how to establish that this condition is established.[2] To meet this shortcoming, the 1933 Act required the extension order to specify the courts which would be deemed by the requested court as superior courts for the purposes of the legislation.[3] No judgment from a court which is not so designated will fall within the registration requirements.[4] It is essential, therefore, when reciprocal arrangements are being negotiated for a full list of the courts to be within the scheme to be agreed. It is equally important that changes in the court system which affect the contents of an extension order be effected.[5]

The United Kingdom legislation has undergone an important development in this respect. For it is now possible for the extension order to be applied, on the basis of reciprocity, to inferior courts and tribunals and their judgments (howsoever called).[6] In consequence, the order must identify those courts and their judgments, or any class thereof, which are to be within the scheme.

1 AJA, s 9(1). The Canadian legislation is not normally limited to 'superior courts'.
2 Para 3.14 below.
3 FJREA, s 1(1)(b).
4 *Belmont Finance Ltd v Fitzpatrick* [1973] 2 NZLR 532.
5 Para 3.06 below.
6 FJREA, s 1(1), (5), inserted by Civil Jurisdiction and Judgments Act 1982, Sch 10.

Effect of changes in constitutional status upon extension orders

3.06 An extension order validly made at its creation will normally continue to have effect notwithstanding the change in the constitutional status of the enacting jurisdiction and/or that of the jurisdiction to which the order relates. Three particular points, however, need to be made.

First, it is not uncommon for an extant extension order to refer to a jurisdiction by a name held prior to independence. Not infrequently, the required alteration has not been the subject of legislation authorising the new name to replace the former one. It seems probable that judicial notice could be taken of the facts of history to construe the name to refer to the same jurisdiction by its present name, especially if reciprocal legislative provisions exist.[1] The second point is more difficult. A number of orders refer to separate law areas which as a result of constitutional change have been incorporated into a single jurisdiction, as for example, references to Ashanti, Gold Coast Colony, Northern Territories and Togoland, territories now comprising Ghana, or to Malaya, Johore and North Borneo, now territories making up part but not the whole of Malaysia. In the former case, there seems little difficulty in construing a reference to any part as to the whole but it remains a nice question, and certainly doubtful, whether a judgment emanating from Sarawak, part of Malaysia, could be enforced in a jurisdiction where the orders are referable only to other parts of Malaysia, which now for these purposes constitutes a single jurisdiction.[2]

References to places which have become separate jurisdictions with a different name, as a result of division of a country, present different considerations. In such a case, reference to the jurisdiction which continues under the extension name will usually not include others which have separated. So, for example, references to India cannot, without more, be construed to include Pakistan and then Bangladesh.[3] In all cases, the matter can be readily dealt with by a fresh order.[4]

The same remedy is appropriate in relation to the third shortcoming found in a number of orders under the 1933 Act, where the courts to which the scheme applies must also be listed in the extension order. Not uncommonly, references to now replaced court arrangements continue, most frequently in connection with the Supreme Court system in the Eastern Caribbean, which has undergone a number of changes of nomenclature.[5] It is questionable how far judicial notice may be taken of the changes but in any case difficulty of access in some parts of the world to instruments which have reconstituted the court systems may cause unnecessary difficulties. The refurbishment of extension orders, therefore, is a matter calling for regular consideration and would be helped if notification of constitutional changes requiring such alterations were systematically communicated by extension countries to reciprocating governments.

1 This was not the view taken in *Re Lowenthal and Air France* 1966 2 ALR Comm 301 (Kenya), where a reference to 'Northern Rhodesia' was held to be inadequate to cover independent Zambia.
2 Reciprocal Enforcement of Judgments Act 1958, s 3 (Malaysia).
3 A fortiori, Burma; *Muthiah Chettiar v Firm Shwebo* AIR 1957 Mad 25.
4 In the cases where both schemes operate, an order under the 1920 scheme can be subject to variation without bringing into effect the requirement to use the 1933 Act: AJA, s 14(2).
5 See para 2.16 above.

Coverage of the Commonwealth schemes

(a) *Extensions within the Commonwealth*

3.07 Annex III to Chapter 2 sets out, in relation to each jurisdiction, the law areas to which the scheme or schemes in force have been extended. The variation in practice will be immediately apparent. With the exception of the United Kingdom which as may be expected has been very active, the substantial majority of jurisdictions have made relative little use of their extension powers. There are remarkable lacunae involving law areas which are geographically close or with which trading arrangements might be expected to be substantial. At the same time, it is clear that the schemes have had their most prominent effect at the regional level,[1] none more so that the Canadian arrangements which have had comparatively little application to external jurisdictions. Many of the orders in the Commonwealth date from the early 1920s and it is evident that little consideration has been given to the value of additional orders in favour of those jurisdictions with which commercial connections have more recently developed. The absence of any alterations in the list suggests that, in practice, the advantages of the enforcement arrangements have not been seen as significant by those who might be thought to benefit from them.

Two other points are worthy of note. In a surprising number of cases, examples exist of 'limping' orders, that is ones for which no reciprocal arrangements can be traced. These may arise from the failure of one jurisdiction to make an original extension as agreed or from the unilateral revocation of an existing order or changes in, or even absence of, appropriate legislation. This again suggests that systematic reviews of commitments are by no means common practice.

It is also noteworthy that, though many of the statutes are designed to be used with respect to non-Commonwealth states, arrangements of that kind are relatively uncommon, notwithstanding the growth of non-Commonwealth trade in recent decades. It may be assumed that the rather more complicated assessments and negotiations which are required at the diplomatic and international level will in many cases not have been justified or may even have been beyond the technical resources of smaller Commonwealth jurisdictions.

1 Common legislation on the 1933 model was enacted for the Federation of the West Indies: Overseas Judgments (Reciprocal Enforcement) Act 1960, *Laws of the West Indies 1962*, Cap 7. No orders were made under it. On the dissolution of the Federation, the Act was adapted to become part of the law of each of the jurisdictions which had been within the Federation: Interim Commissioner (Continuation and Adaptation of Laws) Order 1962, *West Indies Gazette*, 1962, No 22. In effect this put the 1933 model in operation in respect of superior court judgments in Antigua, Barbados, Cayman Islands, Dominica, Grenada, Jamaica,

Montserrat, St Christopher–Nevis–Anguilla, St Lucia, St Vincent, Trinidad and Tobago and Turks and Caicos Islands—although in a number of these jurisdictions it was already in force: see Chapter II, Annex I. No action has been taken under the Act in any of the jurisdictions. In certain cases, the statute will have been repealed by implication.

(b) *Extensions to non-Commonwealth states*

(i) UNITED KINGDOM LEGISLATION

3.08 The greatest use of the legislation in respect of non-Commonwealth states has been by the United Kingdom,[1] principally in relation to European states.[2] The arrangements cease to have effect in relation to several of these to the extent that the Brussels Convention deals with the matter in issue.[3] In each case, clauses empowering extension in favour of dependent territories of the United Kingdom were included in the original treaty but these have not been used in every case and only with respect to Hong Kong, the Isle of Man, Guernsey and Jersey. Accordingly, the issue of extension orders under the local form of the 1933 Act has not been possible by any of the other dependencies of the United Kingdom. As we have seen, it is the practice of the United Kingdom to enter into formal treaty arrangements to constitute the basis of reciprocity. The treaty is scheduled in the extension Order-in-Council which will usually also contain additional provisions which are declared to be necessary to give effect to the treaty arrangements. These provisions may, however, not alter the substance of the 1933 Act: they are confined to the matters in respect of which the statute permits rules of court to be made.[4] The treaty, therefore, can be given domestic effect, only insofar as the judgment fulfils the requirements of the 1933 Act: the treaty itself is not given effect as part of domestic law.

The United Kingdom has made considerable use of the 1933 Act in relation to enforcement of foreign judgments under a series of multilateral conventions to which the United Kingdom is a party. As the conventions themselves require provisions for this purpose, substantial reciprocity is accorded to judgments obtained in the United Kingdom in proceedings arising under the conventions. The following are the relevant conventions:

(i) Geneva Convention on the International Carriage of Goods by Road (1956);[5]
(ii) Paris Convention on Third Party Liability in the Field of Nuclear Energy (1960);[6]
(iii) Additional Berne Convention on the Carriage of Passengers and Luggage by Rail (1966);[7]
(iv) Brussels Convention on Civil Liability for Oil Pollution Damage (1969);[8]
(v) Brussels Convention on the Establishment of an International Fund for Compensation for Oil Pollution Damage (1971);[9]
(vi) Geneva Convention on the International Carriage of Passengers and Luggage by Road (1973);[10]
(vii) Geneva Convention on a Code of Conduct for Liner Conferences (1974);[11]
(viii) Convention concerning International Carriage by Rail (1980);[12]
(ix) Brussels Multilateral Agreement relating to Route Charges (1981).[13]

The implementing legislation which makes the judgment scheme effective in relation to judgments under these conventions does not follow a completely standard pattern.[14] In most instances, however, important modifications are made to the 1933 Act, to permit judgments or determinations by the appropriate court, tribunal or administrative authority to come within the legislation, notwithstanding that it is not a 'superior court' and to displace the jurisdictional rules in section 4(2) and (3) in favour of those provided by the convention itself.[15] The 1933 legislation, has, therefore, proved to be a vehicle readily adapted for use in relation to multilateral treaties providing for transnational liability. The conventions in the main have not attracted ratifications by other Commonwealth states and extensions by the United Kingdom to her dependent territories have not been common. This development in its direct effect has, in consequence, had little impact upon intra-Commonwealth judgment enforcement.

1 Orders in favour of Pakistan are found in a number of cases, having been carried over from a time when Pakistan was in the Commonwealth.
2 France (SR & O 1936/609); Belgium (SR & O 1936/1169); Federal Republic Germany (SI 1961/1199); Norway (SI 1962/636); Austria (SI 1962/1339); Netherlands (SI 1969/1063); Israel (SI 1971/1039); Italy (SI 1973/1894); Netherlands Antilles (SI 1977/2149); Suriname (SI 1981/735).
3 France, Belgium, Germany, Netherlands, Italy, Netherland Antilles. The Brussels Convention does not entirely displace these treaties, which presumably remain available for extension to non-European dependencies of the UK: arts 55 and 56.
4 FJREA, s 3(2). These are set out in s 3(1). The matters most commonly provided for are security for costs, proof of judgment, rate of interest and translations.
5 Carriage of Goods by Road Act 1965, s 4.
6 Nuclear Installations Act 1965, s 17(4).
7 Carriage by Railway Act 1972, ss 5(1), 13.
8 Merchant Shipping (Oil Pollution) Act 1971, s 13(3).
9 Merchant Shipping Act 1974, s 6(4), (5).
10 Carriage of Passengers by Road Act 1974, s 5 (nif).
11 Merchant Shipping (Liner Conferences) Act 1982, s 5(6) (nif) preserves the 1933 scheme, notwithstanding special arrangements in the 1982 Act for proceedings under the Code.
12 International Transport Conventions Act 1983, s 6 (nif).
13 Civil Aviation (Eurocontrol) Act 1983 adding s 74A to the Civil Aviation Act 1982.
14 Saving provisions preserved the operation of the foregoing conventions following changes effected by the Civil Jurisdiction and Judgments Act 1982, s 31(3) and s 32(4)(b).
15 These are set out in Dicey and Morris, op cit, pp 1061–1066 and supplements.

(ii) AUSTRALIAN LEGISLATION

3.09 Extensions by Australian states in favour of non-Commonwealth states have been made for Federal Republic of Germany, France, Israel, Italy, Japan, Pakistan and, in one case, Korea and South Africa.[1] As extension orders are matters for state or territory governments and international relations for the Commonwealth government, the Attorney-General's Department in the latter in co-operation with the Department of Foreign Affairs is charged with ascertaining the legal status of foreign judgments in the foreign state in question and for the exchange of relevant legislation. On the basis of this information, the decision can be taken by the state or territory authority whether substantial reciprocity of treatment will exist. Generally, when such enquiries have been satisfactorily completed and an extension order made, it is common for other states or territories to follow suit without the need for extended diplomatic exchanges. The appropriate state legislation applies to relevant foreign judgments without modification.

1 Queensland has made foreign orders in favour of Pakistan and South Africa only. The other jurisdictions have all extended to all those countries listed except South Africa. New South Wales has also extended to Korea.

(iii) LEGISLATION OF OTHER COMMONWEALTH JURISDICTIONS

3.10 Uniquely amongst Commonwealth states, Ghana has employed its judgment enforcement almost exclusively for non-Commonwealth jurisdictions: of Commonwealth countries, only the United Kingdom has been favoured. Extension orders have been made for Brazil, France, Israel, Italy, Japan, Lebanon, Senegal, Spain and the United Arab Republic. There is no indication from the extending legal instrument that these arrangements are the subject of bilateral treaty arrangements.

On the other hand, bilateral treaty arrangements have been employed by Gambia with respect to Senegal and by Sierra Leone with Guinea. The former merely contains an undertaking to confer reciprocally the benefits of the respective legislations on the matter.[1] The latter imposes a duty on Sierra Leone to register civil and commercial judgments which are susceptible of execution and have become final from Guinea's 'regular courts' 'following the regular procedure', in terms compatible with the 1933 legislation, except that the judgments relating to marriage, divorce and other matters concerning civil status are also included in the category eligible for registration.[2] An appropriate extension order under the 1933 legislation has not been traced. Hong Kong which is beneficiary of treaties negotiated by the United Kingdom has a substantial list of overseas extension orders: these are Austria, Belgium, France, Germany, Italy, Israel and the Netherlands (and her Antilles dependencies). The power to modify procedural and other prescribed matters in relation to foreign states has not been used, although there is some discrepancy between the treaty undertakings and the rules of court.[3] Similarly extensions have been made by the Isle of Man, Guernsey and Jersey in relation to the latter three states.

Application to non-Commonwealth jurisdictions in other cases is uncommon. New Zealand acceded to the Anglo-French and Anglo-Belgian treaties soon after they were negotiated but no further foreign extensions have been made. New Zealand appears to be the only other jurisdiction in addition to the United Kingdom to employ the legislation to make effective multilateral treaty obligations.[4] Of the Canadian provinces with legislation capable of external application[5] only British Columbia has utilised these provisions, with respect to some European states.[6] The curious absence in the Canadian provinces of reciprocal relations with any United States jurisdictions is, perhaps, emphasised by the extension by Papua–New Guinea in favour of the United States with respect to the New York State Supreme Court of Appeal which may have been made possible by the adoption there of the Uniform Foreign Money Judgments Recognition Act.[7]

1 Agreement on closer co-operation in judicial matters, 28 April 1973, art 20.
2 Sierra Leone–Guinea Relations Act 1964, Sch, art V.
3 There is a requirement for security for costs under the Rules of Court, Order 71, r 4, which is usually dispensed with in the treaty arrangements.
4 Marine Pollution Act 1974, No 114, s 44 implementing the International Convention on Civil Liability for Oil Pollution Damage (1969).
5 The Foreign Aircraft Third Party Damages Act (Canada, RSC 1970 c.F–28) implementing the Rome Convention on Damage caused by Foreign Aircraft to Third Parties on the Surface (1952) provided for reciprocal enforcement. The legislation did not specify how this was to be made effective in Canada. Canada has now denounced the treaty.
6 Orders have been made with respect to Germany and Austria.
7 On this legislation, see B. Kulzer, (1968) 18 Buffalo LR 1–51.

III JUDGMENTS REGISTRABLE UNDER THE SCHEMES

Basic criteria

3.11 A judgment is eligible for registration only when the following conditions are present:

(a) it is a judgment or order in civil proceedings (or for compensation or damages in criminal proceedings);
(b) it is for a fixed or ascertainable sum of money;
(c) it is made by a recognised court;
(d) it is so made in a designated reciprocating jurisdiction;
(e) it is final and conclusive;
(f) it gives rise to rights in the applicant against the judgment debtor;
(g) it can be enforced by execution in the country of the original court;
(h) it was given after the relevant extension order came into effect;
(i) it has not been wholly satisfied;
(j) it is not for a sum of money in respect of taxes or a fine or penalty;
(k) it is not in a category of judgments prohibited by the lex fori from being registered.

These requirements will be examined in the following paragraphs.

(a) *Judgments in civil proceedings*[1]

3.12 Both schemes relate to judgments or orders made by a court in any civil proceedings. In determining whether a document constitutes a judgment or order[2] in civil proceedings, the requested court will not be bound either by the terms of that document or by the status claimed for it by the body from which it originated. In principle, it is for the forum court to determine, by reference to the law and practice of the place where the proceedings occurred, whether the instrument constitutes a judgment or order in civil proceedings as understood in the forum. To facilitate this process, the schemes normally provide for a judgment creditor to apply to the original court for a certified copy of the judgment.[3] Production of such a document from a Commonwealth country in which it is stated, or from which it can be determined, that the judgment meets this condition will normally conclude this matter. It will be for the judgment debtor to establish that a certified copy is irregular.

The requirement that the judgment or order must be that of a court excludes decisions by arbitrators or by tribunals which are not part of the formal judicial system. In consequence, express terms are necessary to bring these cases within 'judgments'. In respect of awards, both the 1920 and the 1933 Act (as amended) have been appropriately extended.[4] The United Kingdom Act has recently been amended to cover judgments or orders of tribunals.[5] Whether the body is a 'court' will rarely give rise to difficulty since it must be appropriately designated under the 1933 scheme or be 'a superior court' under the 1920 legislation.[6] The term 'court' will be construed as a 'court of law', that is a body exercising judicial functions as part of the system through which the state discharges its judicial power.[7]

The judgment or order must be given 'in civil proceedings', a term which is used most commonly to apply to any proceedings which are not criminal, that is, are not concerned with the conviction and punishment of a person for an offence. More positively, it is likely to be construed as including any proceedings involving a claim or application to recover money or property or to declare or to enforce a right to the advantage of the plaintiff.[8] It could extend to proceedings to recover a penalty were such judgments not excluded.[9] But it presumably applies to claims for securing a benefit under a discretionary scheme or to awards for damages made incidentally in an application for judicial review.[10] It will certainly apply to probate proceedings, bankruptcy and winding-up cases, admiralty matters, matrimonial and other domestic matters. In this respect, it does not matter whether the proceedings constitute actions in personam or actions in rem or result in judgments in personam or in rem.[11]

Generally the judgment to be enforced will be that of a court of first instance but both schemes appear to allow a judgment debtor to register a judgment or order which has been given or made on appeal when it is the source of his rights, for the Acts refer to the 'court by which the judgment was given'.[12] It will be for the requested court to determine, in the light of the law and practice of the original jurisdiction, whether the 'original court' is, in the particular case, the appeal court exercising a power to give a judgment or make an order which might have been given or made at first instance.[13] Where a judgment has been renewed in the country of origin, it is registrable, provided that the statutory conditions are fulfilled in relation to the renewed judgment.[14]

There can be no question that a default judgment granted under an Order 13 procedure will meet this condition.[15] Indeed, an extract of a bond and a disposition in security duly registered with the consent of the debtor so as to constitute a fictitious judgment has been held to be a judgment in this context, since it constituted a decree issued summarily under the lex fori.[16]

The 1933 Act includes a category of case, which though made in criminal proceedings, is analogous to those in civil cases—judgments or orders given or made by a court in such proceedings for the payment of a sum of money in respect of compensation or damages to an injured party. This is a reference to the power of certain criminal courts when dealing with crimes involving injury to person or property to make awards to the victim.[17] What is of unusual interest in these cases is that all the requirements for registration which were designed for civil matters must be fulfilled in this case too, including a jurisdictional condition.[18] Although such orders may also be enforced by action at common law,[19] the 1920 Act appears not to extend that far.

It may be asked whether an order for the registration of a foreign judgment in one jurisdiction may itself be registered under either scheme in yet another reciprocating jurisdiction. It might be argued that the original act of registration is the result of an order given or made by a court in civil proceedings, that thereby a sum of money is payable and that in consequence the original judgment has the same force and effect as if originally obtained or entered up in the first registering court.[20] Moreover a judgment obtained at common law in an action on a foreign judgment seems in principle capable of being registered in a reciprocating jurisdiction.[21] Provided that the other conditions are fulfilled, on this argument, it would be possible to leap-frog judgments for enforcement by registration in a country with which there were no reciprocal arrangements, via a third intermediary jurisdiction with which the country of origin and that finally requested have such arrangements. On principle this may be thought to be undesirable, particularly as the court finally requested would have no authority to look into any circumstances in which the original judgment was obtained. It may be suggested that the statutes in any case do not allow this construction. For the order for registration gives the *original* judgment effect in the intermediary jurisdiction and as a result a sum of money becomes payable under that judgment. The registration order itself should not be treated as an order under which a sum of money is payable.[22] Recent United Kingdom legislation has expressly excluded from registration any judgment which is:

(i) a judgment or other instrument which is regarded for the purposes of enforcement as a judgment of the court but which was given or made in another country;
(ii) a judgment given by the court in proceedings founded on a judgment of a court in another country and having as their object the enforcement of that judgment.[23]

This, it may be suggested, is no more than declaratory insofar as registered judgments are concerned but it is innovative in excluding the registration of judgments given in an action on a judgment. No cases in the Commonwealth in which this has been attempted have been traced.

Finally, it should be noted that under the 1933 Act the requested court may order registration of a judgment, which is in respect of different matters, in respect of only those parts which satisfy the statutory requirements.[24] It is arguable that, in the absence of such a power under the 1920 Act, registration of a judgment which contains matters which are not registrable must be refused, unless there is an order which, as the Act envisages, can be treated as separate from the judgment itself.[25] Manitoba courts have held that an order for costs may not be registered if the judgment to which it relates is not registrable.[26] Provision is now found in some provinces for registration of separable parts of judgments.[27]

1 AJA, ss 9(1), 12(1); FJREA, ss 1(1), 11(1).
2 'A judgment is a decision obtained in an action and every other decision is an order': *Onslow v IRC* (1890) 25 QBD 465, 59 LJQB 556, per Lord Esher MR.
3 AJA, s 10; FJREA, s 10. Note that the former has been amended in the UK to remove a requirement that the judgment creditor is resident in some part of HM dominions outside the UK: Civil Jurisdiction and Judgments Act 1982, s 35(2). On this requirement: *Bank of British West Africa, Petitioners* 1931 SLT 83.
4 See para 6.01 below.
5 Civil Jurisdiction and Judgments Act 1982, Sch 10, para 5(2).
6 See para 3.14 below.
7 Cf *A-G v BBC* [1980] 3 All ER 161, HL, especially per Lord Scarman, at 182.
8 *A-G v Radloff* (1854) 10 Exch 84 at 101–2, per Platt B.
9 *R v Hausmann* (1909) 3 Cr App Rep 3, CCA but these are excluded by express terms: para 3.21 below.
10 Eg, Supreme Court Act 1981 (UK), s 31.
11 The question of whether the original court had jurisdiction may turn upon these considerations: paras 3.37 and 3.44 below. But as to whether ancillary orders are separate judgments, see para 3.45 below.
12 Definitions of 'original court' in AJA, s 12(1); FJREA, s 11(1).
13 Cf RSC Ord 59, r 10(3). It was suggested in *Mayer Finance Co v Ross* [1929] NZLR 748 that a judgment of an inferior court removed into a superior court does not become a judgment of the latter.
14 *Skogstad v Younger and Holmes Ltd* [1972] 1 WWR 155 (NWT).
15 It may not meet the jurisdictional requirements: paras 3.37 ff. below. As to whether a default judgment is 'final and conclusive', see para 3.16 below.
16 *Taylor, Petitioner* 1931 SLT 260; cf *Berliner Industriebank AG v Jost* [1971] 2 QB 463, [1971] 2 All ER 1513, CA, where formal entry of a debt in favour of a creditor in a bankruptcy was held to constitute an unappealable judgment under the lex fori (German law).
17 Eg, Theft Act 1968 (UK), s 28(3); Criminal Justice Act 1972 (UK), s 1.
18 See paras, 3.37 ff below. Quaere whether appearance will be 'voluntary'?
19 *Raulin v Fischer* [1911] 2 KB 93, 80 LJKB 811. On forfeiture orders, see *R v Kemp* (1979) 69 Cr App Rep 330.

20 AJA, s 9(1) and (3)(a); FJREA, s 2(1), (2)(a).
21 In *Frederick A Jones Inc v Toronto General Insurance Co* [1933] 2 DLR 660, an action on a New Jersey judgment, in turn founded upon a Florida judgment, failed for want of competence of the Florida court (which could be enquired into by the New Jersey court).
22 AJA, s 12(1) is perhaps less certain since the order must be one 'whereby a sum of money is made payable'.
23 FJREA, s 2A (b) and (c) inserted by the Civil Jurisdiction and Judgments Act 1982, Sch 10, para 1.
24 Ibid, s 1(5).
25 AJA, s 12(1) 'judgment'.
26 *Paslowski v Paslowski* (1957) 11 DLR (2d) 180 (Man); *Koven v Toole* [1954] 4 DLR 856 (Man) but see orse *Cavanagh v Lisogar* (1956) 19 WWR 230 (Alta).
27 Manitoba, R–20, s 3(8); Nova Scotia, R–6, s 4(6); Yukon, R–1, s 3(5).

(b) *The judgment is for a definite sum of money*[1]

3.13 The statutes refer to judgments whereby or whereunder a sum of money is payable. If the original judgment carried no duty to pay a sum of money, it is not registrable.[2] This requirement clearly embraces cases where damages (whether the claim was for liquidated or unliquidated damages) have been ordered for a tort or breach of contract but it also extends to orders for the restitution of a sum of money belonging to another or for moneys to be paid by trustees or executors to a person entitled thereto or as a result of an action in rem in an admiralty matter, or for a balance due on the dissolution of a partnership, or for a capital sum payable by one spouse to the other, or by a parent to a child, to provide for maintenance.[3]

It should be noted that the order for payment need not have been the main purpose of the original litigation. Thus an order for payment of a sum by way of maintenance accompanying a decree granting divorce or nullity appears to be registrable in principle.[4] A sum awarded on counterclaim is also covered and there seems, in principle, no reason why a garnishee order made by a court against a third party cannot be registered, if all other conditions can be satisfied.[5] Likewise, an order for costs could be registered even though the substantive judgment did not involve a sum of money.[6] It may even be possible to register a judgment under which a party has been ordered to buy the shares of an injured shareholder and is refusing to pay a sum for them which has been determined by the court.[7]

What will be required in all cases, however, is that the sum of money is definite and ascertained or can be ascertained precisely by calculation without further reference to another body or to the same court at another time.[8] For there seems no doubt that the courts will import into the statutory phrase the meaning long accepted at common law.[9] In consequence, if it is not possible to ascertain from the judgment itself that an ascertainable sum of money is due, registration may not take place.[10] An order in matrimonial proceedings for periodical payments in respect of a wife or a child can be registered if the payments have fallen due and the arrears are no longer capable of variation,[11] although a judgment for arrears which can be altered retrospectively will not be final and conclusive.[12]

This general head is subject to two qualifications which are discussed below. The sum of money must not have been wholly paid at the time of registration and it must not constitute a tax, charge, fine or penalty.[13]

1 AJA, s 11(1); FJREA, s 1(2)(b).
2 *Platt v Platt* 1958 SC 95, 1958 SLT 94 (a New Zealand order setting aside an assignation of an interest by one spouse in an estate in favour of the other was not registrable: nor an order for account).

3 *Re Van der Kreek's Marriage* [1979] PNGLR 185. Cf *Shearn v Shearn* [1931] P1. An order to *secure* a lump sum will not meet this requirement.
4 In most Canadian jurisdictions, maintenance orders are now expressly excluded by the statutory definition of 'judgment'. For a similar Manitoba conclusion without such provision, *Re Reciprocal Enforcement of Judgments Act, Re Paslowski v Paslowski* (1957) 22 WWR 584; *Re Fleming and Fleming* (1959) 19 DLR (2d) 417. But now, Manitoba, R–20, s 3(8). For jurisdictional difficulties in relation to maintenance, see para 3.45 below.
5 Dicey and Morris, op cit, p 578, suggest that at common law the order should only be recognised if the debt is properly recoverable in the place where the order was originally made. This may be covered by statute: see para 3.18 below. There may also be jurisdictional difficulties. A garnishee order made by an administrative body for the recovery of a tax debt was not recognised in *Rossano v Manufacturers Life Insurance Co* [1963] 2 QB 352, [1962] 2 All ER 214.
6 Cf *Russell v Smyth* (1842) 9 M & W 810, 11 LJ Ex 308; *A-G for Canada v William Schutze & Co* 1901 9 SLT 4; *Platt v Platt* above. But an order for costs awarded to a defendant when the plaintiff was not successful has been treated as outside the scheme, since it was 'a mere remedy ancillary to the proceedings': *Koven v Toole* (1954) 13 WWR (NS) 444 (Man) but contra, *Cavanagh v Lisogar* (1956) 19 WWR 230 (Alta).
7 Eg Companies Act 1948 (UK), s 210.
8 *Beatty v Beatty* [1924] 1 KB 207; *Bonn v National Trust Co Ltd* [1930] 4 DLR 820 CA (Ont).
9 *Sadler v Robins* (1808) 1 Camp 253. The rule is historically explicable by the form of action, debt, which was most commonly treated as appropriate for the enforcement of foreign judgments.
10 *Taylor v Begg* [1932] NZLR 286, where the exact payments on mortgage and of interest thereon were not clear from the original judgment; cf *Perry v Perry Estate* (1983) 45 NBR (2d) 51—'half proceeds of sale of the matrimonial home'.
11 Cf *Beatty v Beatty* above; *Shearn v Shearn* above; *Splatt v Splatt* (1889) 10 NSWLR 227; *Hadden v Hadden* (1898) 6 BCR 340; *Robertson v Robertson* (1908) 16 OLR 170; *Wood v Wood* (1916) 28 DLR 367; *Patton v Reed* (1973) 30 DLR (3d) 485; *Lear v Lear* (1974) 51 DLR (3d) 56; *Upjohn v Upjohn* (1975) 7 OR (2d) 246.
12 Para 3.16 below.
13 Paras 3.20 and 3.21–23 below.

(c) *The judgment is made by a recognised court*[1]

3.14 Both schemes in their original form are confined to judgments of the superior courts of reciprocating jurisdictions although such a limitation is not normally found in the Canadian statutes. The 1933 Act goes further by permitting the extension order to specify courts of the reciprocating jurisdiction which 'shall be deemed superior courts of that country' for the purposes of the scheme.[2] It is by no means clear that this listing was intended to be an exclusive and definitive statement.[3] For the Act can be construed as applicable to any superior court whether specified or not. If this is correct, the failure to list a court will not prevent the applicant seeking to establish that it is nonetheless a superior court. The recent alteration in the United Kingdom legislation, which now refers to 'recognised courts' and which provides for only listed courts to be recognised courts does not allow this construction.[4]

In the absence of any entry in an extension order (as will be the case for the 1920 scheme), it will be for the requested court to ascertain whether a court is 'a superior court' of law within the judicial system of the reciprocating jurisdiction. In respect of most Commonwealth jurisdictions, their legislation is likely to indicate the status of the court in question. Generally a court is unlikely to be treated as superior if it is subject to the supervisory powers of another court, and if its competence is limited both to a part of the country in question and to some lesser matters within a particular category of subject matter.[5]

Without the more liberal provisions of the kind recently introduced by the United Kingdom,[6] the schemes will not extend to judgments of inferior courts or to tribunals.[7] The 1933 scheme makes it clear that the judgment of an appellate court, albeit a superior court, cannot be included if the appeal is not from a superior court.[8] The 1920 Act is silent in this respect but registration is likely to be refused in such a case since enforcement would not be just and convenient.[9]

1 AJA, s 9(1); FJREA, s 1(2).
2 FJREA, s 1(1)(b).
3 But in *Belmont Finance Ltd v Fitzpatrick* [1973] 2 NZLR 532, only designated courts were held to be superior courts.
4 Civil Jurisdiction and Judgments Act 1982, Sch 10, amending FJREA, s 1. Courts listed in existing orders are now to be deemed to be 'recognised courts': ibid, s 1(5).
5 Cf *Halsbury's Laws of England* (4th edn), vol 10, paras 710–714.
6 See note 4.
7 For arbitration tribunals, see Chapter 6 below. Cf Manitoba, R–20 extended by SM 1977, c 57, s 21(a) to awards of statutory authorities dealing with payments of money in disputes between employers and employees.
8 FJREA, s 2(2).
9 AJA, s 9(1).

(d) *The judgment is from a court in a designated reciprocating jurisdiction*[1]

3.15 Unless there is extant an extension order designating the jurisdiction in which the original court gave the judgment, registration must be refused. The fact that a fresh order cannot be validly made under the legislation in question, through a change in the constitutional status of the other jurisdiction or that the order refers to a jurisdiction which has acquired another name following independence should not prevent reliance upon an unrepealed order.[2] Where, however, a jurisdiction has been created out of one to which the order was made to apply or by combining several jurisdictions, some or all of which were referred to in the original extension orders, the position is more doubtful. For it is then difficult to hold that the court which gave the judgment in the new jurisdiction is a court of the jurisdiction designated in the extension order.

1 AJA, ss 9, 13, 14; FJREA, ss 1(1), (2), 7(1).
2 Para 3.05 above. *Fitzritsin and Wedderburn v Degayon* (1970) (unreported: WIASSC, Dominica, suit no 76/70). For the position where the legislation has been replaced by a revised statute, see *Garfin v Bird* (1960) 32 WWR 430 (BC).

(e) *The judgment is final and conclusive*

3.16 The requirement that the judgment must be final and conclusive between the parties thereto is explicit in the 1933 legislation[1] but it is undoubtedly to be read into the 1920 Act too. For it is one well established at common law.[2] It is improbable that a court would exercise its discretion to register under the earlier scheme where such a fundamental element was absent.

The locus classicus of this requirement is found in Lord Herschell's judgment in *Nouvion v Freeman*:

'it must be shown that in the Court by which [the judgment] was pronounced it conclusively, finally, and for ever established the existence of the debt . . . so as to make it *res judicata* between the parties. If it is not conclusive in the same Court which pronounced it, so that notwithstanding such a judgment the existence of the debt may between the same parties be afterwards contested in that Court, and upon proper proceedings being taken and such contest being adjudicated upon, it may be declared that there existed no obligation to pay the debt at all, then I do not think that a judgment which is of that character can be regarded as finally and conclusively evidencing the debt . . .'[3]

It follows, therefore, that a judgment which is capable of being varied or overturned by the court by which it was intitially given is not a res judicata between the parties. Similarly, a decision which requires confirmation before it has legal effect between the parties in the jurisdiction where it was made is not final.[4] The same will be the case where the sum of money has not become payable as some condition under the lex fori has yet to be met by one or other of the parties.

Whether Lord Herschell's criteria are fulfilled is determined by the requested court by reference to the law and practice of the jurisdiction in which the judgment was given.[5] The question here is not whether the judgment becomes enforceable in the original jurisdiction but whether the judgment establishes a binding liability between the parties. Thus a judgment against a partnership which, under the law of the original jurisdiction, does not bind individual partners unless further proceedings, in which defences may be put forward, are brought against them, is not final and conclusive against the partners, even though it may be binding on the partnership.[6]

Application of this rule to domestic orders for maintenance has excluded enforcement of orders for periodical payments where the sums payable are capable of retrospective variation by the same court.[7] For the original judgment does not conclusively determine the quantum of the debt. The principle applies in respect of any case in which the sum to be paid under the judgment is capable of variation by the court which made it.

One type of judgment which gives rise to difficulty in this respect is the default judgment in which, for example, judgment has been given for a fixed sum of money after the debtor has not appeared to defend. The procedure commonly followed in Commonwealth jurisdictions allows the debtor, after the judgment has been entered, to apply to the same court to set aside the judgment on a number of grounds involving procedural irregularity, fraud or a bona fide defence on the merits.[8] Similar difficulties may arise with respect to summary judgments given under an Order 14 procedure where the defendant has no defence to the claim. For this too, in many jurisdictions, is capable of being set aside by the same court if the defendant did not originally appear.[9] On one argument, these might appear to be clear cases of judgments which are not final. But as Hunter CJ convincingly argued in a British Columbia case, to so conclude would be to say that 'the clearer the plaintiff's case, the more useless his judgment will be'.[10] The 1933 Act expressly points to this conclusion, for it provides that a judgment may be final and conclusive notwithstanding that an appeal is pending or may be brought 'in the courts of the country of the original court'[11] and defines 'appeal' to include 'any proceeding by way of... setting aside the judgment'.[12] There is no suggestion here that the 'appeal' must be to another or different court.

Case law also favours this practical approach, even in respect of judgments where the time limit for setting aside is not yet past.[13] It was accepted at common law in *Boyle v Victoria Yukon Trading Co*[14] by the British Columbia Court of Appeal and has been followed in other jurisdictions too.[15] For the fact that the judgment can be set aside if certain prescribed circumstances are established by the debtor should not alter the fact that it is treated in Commonwealth jurisdictions as binding upon the parties unless and until the debtor proves his case before the original court.[16] At the same time, there have been suggestions in British Columbia decisions that registration of a default judgment should be refused if manifest error in the original judgment is evident on the face of the judgment sought to be registered, as where the judgment included sums of interest which could not be ordered under the lex fori.[17] In those cases, this conclusion has been largely based upon the Canadian special ground for resisting registration 'that the judgment debtor would have a good defence if an action were brought on the original judgment'.[18] Although it may be argued that registration of a default judgment could be refused under the 1920 scheme on the grounds that enforcement in these cases would be unjust and inconvenient, it may be doubted whether this line of authority would be widely followed.[19] But the 1933 legislation which sets out to prescribe all the grounds upon which the registration can be resisted does not allow of such an approach.[20] In many cases, however, it will not prove possible to satisfy the registering court that the jurisdictional requirements relating to submission to the court of origin have been met.[21] It is on this ground that default and summary judgments frequently fail.

A judgment which is subject to appeal in the country of origin is generally regarded at common law as final and conclusive, even where an appeal is actually pending in the country of origin, although it may be otherwise if the judgment is suspended or execution stayed until the appeal is finalised.[22] This position is expressly and similarly dealt with by the 1933 Act[23] which defines 'appeal' as including 'any proceedings by way of discharging or setting aside a judgment or an application for a new trial or a stay of execution'.[24] At the same time, the registration can be set aside or the application to set aside adjourned whilst the appeal is proceeded with.[25] Under the 1920 Act, however, registration is explicitly prohibited in a case of this kind.[26]

An important qualification to the general requirement of finality is found in a recent United Kingdom amendment.[27] It is now provided that registration will be permitted where the judgment requires the judgment debtor to make an interim payment. This envisages payments on account against a final award yet to be determined, of the kind which are possible in England where a party has already succeeded or is certain to succeed on the issue of liability.[28] As this is intended to be a limited exception to the principle of finality, the requested court may need to be assured that any power in the country of origin to reduce the interim payment will only rarely be used.

1 FJREA, s 1(2)(a).
2 In particular, see *Nouvion v Freeman* (1889) 15 App Cas 1, 59 LJ Ch 337 which concerned a 'remate' judgment from Spain, under which the defendant is entitled to have the matter relitigated in the same court in plenary proceedings. The remate judgment was not final and conclusive.
3 Ibid, at 9.
4 Thus a maintenance order accompanying a decree nisi for divorce will probably not be final until that decree is made absolute. See *Jackson v Jackson* [1950] 1 WWR 900 (BC); *Re Wilson* (1952) 7 WWR (NS) 524.
5 The effect, or lack of effect, in another jurisdiction within the same federal structure will have no relevance. The test is whether the judgment is final and conclusive in the jurisdiction in which it was pronounced: *Colt Industries Inc v Sarlie (No 2)* [1966] 3 All ER 85 at 87, per Lord Denning MR; *Overseas Food Importers and Distributors Ltd and Brandt* (1981) 126 DLR (3d) 422 (BCCA), (1981) 27 BCLR 31; *Westfal-Larsen A/S v Ikerigi Compania Naviera SA Messiniaki Bergen* [1983] 1 All ER 382.
6 *Blohn v Desser* [1962] 2 QB 116, [1961] 3 All ER 1.
7 *Harrop v Harrop* [1920] 3 KB 386, 90 LJKB 101; *Re Macartney* [1921] 1 Ch 522; *Maguire v Maguire* (1921) 64 DLR 180; *Davis v Davis* (1922) 22 SR (NSW) 185; *Ashley v Gladden* [1954] 4 DLR 848; *Smith v Smith* [1955] 1 DLR 229; *Re Paslowski and Paslowski* (1957) 11 DLR (2d) 180. See J. D. McClean *Recognition of Family Judgments in the Commonwealth* (1983).
8 Eg RSC Ord 13, especially r 9.
9 Ibid, Ord 14, especially r 11.
10 *Boyle v Victoria Yukon Trading Co* (1902) 9 BCR 213 at 223.

11 FJREA, s 1(3).
12 Ibid, s 11(1). This was deliberately included to cover the French procedure of 'opposition': Greer Committee Minutes, 10 February 1932, LCO/2, Doc No 1690.
13 Where it is past, there can be little doubt as to finality: *Jeannot v Fuerst* (1909) 100 LT 816.
14 Note 10 above. Cf *Vanquelin v Bouard* (1863) 15 CBNS 341 at 367–38.
15 There are numerous Canadian decisions: eg *Arnoldson y Serpa v Confederation Life Association* (1974) 46 DLR (3d) 641 (Ont); *MacFarlane v Briggs* (1977) 18 APR 153 (NB); *Mahon/Moore Group of Companies Ltd v Mercator Enterprises* (1978) 52 APR 372 (NS); *Hill v Bank of Montreal* (1980) 14 Alta LR (2d) 78.
16 Cf *Ainslie v Ainslie* (1927) 39 CLR 381 where a similar argument was applied by the High Court of Australia in respect of a separation order.
17 *Boyle v Victoria Yukon Trading Co*, above, at 217, applied in *Re Gacs v Maierovitz* (1968) 68 DLR (2d) 345 (BC), *Re House of Colour Ltd v Expert Decorators Ltd* (1968) 70 DLR (2d) 527 (BC); *MacFarlane v Briggs*, above.
18 See para 3.70 below.
19 *Re Hearn v Kemp and Kemp* (1969) 79 WWR 609 (Alta).
20 But the registration can be set aside whilst proceedings are taken in the original jurisdiction: FJREA, s 5(1).
21 Para 3.38 below.
22 *Colt Industries Inc v Sárlie (No 2)* [1966] 1 WLR 1287 at 1293.
23 FJREA, s 1(3).
24 Ibid, s 11(1). On stays of execution at common law, see *Colt Industries Inc v Sarlie (No 2)*, above, and *Berliner Industriebank AG v Jost* [1971] 2 QB 463 at 470–471.
25 Ibid, s 5(1).
26 AJA, s 9(2)(e). 'Appeal' is not defined in this statute but it might be expected to apply to any case in which recourse is provided under the law of the country of origin to another court to challenge the judgment on jurisdictional issues, fact or law.
27 FJREA, s 2(1)(a), inserted by the Civil Jurisdiction and Judgments Act 1982, Sch 10, para 1.
28 RSC Ord 29, Pt II.

(f) *The judgment gives rise to rights in the applicant against the judgment debtor*

3.17 A judgment cannot be registered unless the person making the application is a 'judgment creditor' within the meaning of the legislation.[1] The applicant must, therefore, be the person in whose favour the judgment was given or any person in whom the rights under the judgment have become vested by succession, assignment or otherwise.[2] It is not necessary to establish that the applicant was a party to the original proceedings if he can show that subsequent to the judgment the right to receive the payment under the judgment was transferred to him by a recognised legal act. Thus a person in whose favour a garnishee order has been made against a judgment debt owed by the debtor to the original plaintiff in principle is able to apply to register that judgment debt. Similarly, an executor or administrator or other legal representative or a trustee in bankruptcy in an appropriate case will be entitled to enforce a judgment by this mechanism.

The proceedings must be brought against a person who meets the statutory criteria for 'judgment debtor'. This is stated to cover both the person against whom the judgment was given and any person against whom the judgment is enforceable in the place where it was given.[3] The 1920 Act, however, refers, in the latter case, to persons against whom the judgment is enforceable under the law of the original court.[4] This may in theory extend to cases in which legislation expressly allows enforcement against entities outside the jurisdiction which are not accessible to local enforcement rules: eg overseas corporations. Where the obligation to pay has been transferred by some legal act in whole or in part to another who can be required to pay in the country of origin, that person may be the subject of registration proceedings. Proceedings may be brought against any corporate body subject to the jurisdiction of the requested court if the judgment was enforceable, for example, against a branch or agency of that company in the country where the judgment was given. Similarly, there seems no reason in principle why such proceedings cannot be brought against a partnership firm,[5] unless the meaning placed upon 'person' by the interpretation legislation of the requested country excludes this conclusion.[6] By the terms of the statutes, proceedings can be brought against heirs, executors, administrators, trustees or other legal representatives, if the judgment could have been enforced against them in the country of origin.

Whilst the requested court must be satisfied that the judgment debtor was amenable to the jurisdiction of the original court,[7] no such considerations apply in relation to the requested court itself. Provided that the procedural rules for registration of the requested system are complied with, it is not necessary to establish that the judgment debtor met the jurisdictional requirements for an action in that forum. Thus proceedings may be possible if the only link between the debtor and the requested jurisdiction is the presence of his assets there.[8]

1 AJA, s 9(1); FJREA, s 2(1).
2 AJA, s 12(1); FJREA, s 11(1). The former statute uses a slightly different and less clear formulation but nothing seems to turn on this.
3 FJREA, s 11(1).
4 In *Re Linley* [1951] VLR 319 an order for costs in a probate action was not registrable against an executor since he had not been a party in that capacity and thus the judgment was not enforceable against him under the law of the original court.
5 *Re Tangye & Smith Ltd v Pelican Carbon Co* [1935] 1 DLR 759 (Ont). Cf *Blohn v Desser* [1962] 2 QB 116, [1961] 3 All ER 1.
6 *Canadian Credit Men's Trust Association v Ryan* [1930] 1 DLR 280 (Alta), where 'person' could not be construed to include partnerships under the local legislation, notwithstanding that it was so construed in the country of origin. Quaere whether this is consistent with the extended terms of the legislation in general use?
7 Paras 3.37 ff below.
8 *Hunt v BP Exploration Co (Libya) Ltd* (1980) 28 ALR 145 (Qld); *Hunt v BP Exploration Co (Libya) Ltd* [1980] 1 NZLR 104.

(g) *The judgment can be enforced by execution in the country of the original court*

3.18 Only the 1933 Act carries the prohibition on registration if the judgment cannot be enforced by execution in the country of origin.[1] There is no comparable provision in the 1920 Act, although if it gives rise to issues of importance it could be imported under the registering court's discretion to refuse registration where enforcement would be unjust and inconvenient.[2]

It is not wholly apparent what circumstances are envisaged by this provision, which has no counterpart at common law. Whilst it seems certain that the condition must be present at the time of the application, it is far from clear whether enforcement by execution must be a legal or a factual possibility. It must be doubted that the latter is intended. For the inability of the creditor, for example, to find the debtor in the original jurisdiction or the absence of any assets of his there are the very reasons why registration abroad may be necessary. The prohibition on registration therefore, is intended to cover cases in which execution is not permitted in the particular case under the law of the original country. Thus it will occur where a procedure has been followed by the judgment debtor under the law which deprives the creditor of his right to execution.[3] On the other hand, it does not appear to apply merely because the debtor has obtained a stay of execution. For that is a species of appeal under the 1933 Act which recognises the power of the requested court to order registration notwithstanding the stay.[4]

Impossibility of execution of a temporary nature is also envisaged,[5] as for example, where issue of execution requires some further action in the country of origin.[6] It will also extend to a judgment which is a nullity under the laws where it is made but defects in the judgment which render it voidable only (as an omission of prescribed words) will not have this consequence until proceedings for that purpose have been initiated.[7] The provision also has clear application to cases where the debtor enjoys immunity from execution under the law as a person protected by diplomatic status[8] or as the Head of State or as the government of that or another country.[9] The purpose of the provision appears to be that of ensuring that legal restrictions on enforcement in the country of origin cannot be circumvented by registration. Treaties negotiated by the United Kingdom usually prescribe that an executory formula attached to the judgment by a foreign court will be prima facie evidence that this requirement is fulfilled, leaving it to the debtor to prove to the contrary.[10]

1 FJREA, s 2(1), proviso (b).
2 AJA, s 9(1) (not in the Canadian legislation). *Re Linley* [1951] VLR 319.
3 *Re A Debtor (No 11 of 1939)* [1939] 2 All ER 400.
4 FJREA, s 5(1) and s 11(1), 'appeal'.
5 Ibid, s 5(2) which allows a further application when execution becomes possible after registration has been set aside on this ground.
6 Eg, leave of a court: RSC Ord 46, r 2.
7 *SA Consortium General Textiles v Sun and Sand Agencies Ltd* [1978] QB 279 [1978] 2 All ER 339.
8 A privileged person who has submitted to the jurisdiction down to judgment may still assert immunity from execution: *Re Suarez, Suarez v Suarez* [1918] 1 Ch 176.
9 Eg Crown Proceedings Act 1947 (UK), s 25(4).
10 RSC Ord 71, r 11 prescribes that this may be dealt with in the relevant Order-in-Council.

(h) *The judgment was given after the relevant extension order came into effect*

3.19 This also is a requirement of the 1933 Act only. It is necessary to show that the date of the judgment was subsequent to the date on which the order extending the Act to the country where the judgment was given came into force.[1] The 1920 Act applies to judgments made before or after its passing.[2] It is, therefore, only necessary to show that the extension order is in force at the date of registration. Presumably the more restrictive provision in the later Act was thought to be necessary in a scheme designed principally for foreign countries. It gives rise to difficulties where a jurisdiction under the earlier scheme is brought within the later scheme. Unless precise provision is made, judgments given but not yet registered under the 1920 scheme will not be registrable under the 1933 legislation. Transitional legislation has been enacted to meet such cases.[3]

1 FJREA, s 1(2)(c).
2 AJA, s 12(1), 'judgment'.
3 Eg, Administration of Justice Act 1956 (UK), s 51(b).

(i) *The judgment has not been wholly satisfied*

3.20 Again this is expressed only in the 1933 Act.[1] Where the debt has been discharged, whether in the country of origin or elsewhere, the obligation under the original judgment has been met and there remains nothing under that judgment to which the scheme can apply. The 1920 Act is silent on this matter but there can be no doubt that registration can be refused in this case since enforcement would not be just and convenient.[2]

Where the debt has been partly satisfied at the date of application, its registration will be allowed under the 1933 Act in respect of the outstanding balance.[3] Registration for the whole of the sum payable is to be set aside if part of the debt has been satisfied at the date of the application[4] but in such a case there is a duty to order registration for the balance remaining payable, if the judgment debtor subsequently applies.[5] There is no equivalent provision in the 1920 Act. Whilst the requested court may have powers to permit an initial application for registration to be amended where this comes to light, rather than refuse registration altogether, it has little option but to set aside the registration of the whole judgment if this issue is raised subsequently.[6] Arguably, however, the court might order this on the terms that fresh registration of the balance may be ordered if requested.[7]

1 FJREA, s 2(1), proviso (a).
2 AJA, s 9(1). In the Canadian scheme, this would be a defence to an action on the original judgment: see para 3.70 below.
3 FJREA, s 1(4).
4 Ibid, s 4(1)(a)(i).
5 Ibid, s 5(3).
6 Eg RSC Ord 71, r 9.
7 Ibid, which allows setting aside 'on such terms as it thinks fit'.

(j) *The judgment is not for a sum of money in respect of taxes or a fine or penalty*

3.21 This condition is set out only in the 1933 Act.[1] The 1920 Act makes no explicit reference, although unlike the 1933 Act[2] this may be met under the public policy objection that registration may be refused where the cause of action was one which 'for some other similar reason could not have been entertained by the requested court'.[3] Again, the discretion to refuse registration unless enforcement would be just and convenient may be exercised to cover this case.[4] Since this represents a long-standing ground for refusing to enforce by action at common law,[5] it can readily be concluded that this will be adopted as a condition under the earlier Act.

The exclusion under the 1933 Act applies to sums payable 'in respect of taxes or other charges of a like nature or in respect of a fine or penalty'. The justification for the rule is usually found in notions of public policy which is said to preclude the giving of support to the exercise of sovereign power of another state under laws which are deemed to be essentially territorial in their scope and application.[6] The strength of this justification and the appropriateness of the rule in current practice where tax avoidance has serious economic implications is often questioned[7] but there can be no doubt of its place in both the Commonwealth schemes as at present conceived. The courts in the Commonwealth have frequently stressed that in determining whether this requirement applies, it is necessary to scrutinise the substance, and not the form, of the judgment.[8] If, therefore, the judgment will in the last analysis result in a sum being paid which was claimed in respect of a tax or like charge or of a fine or penalty, it may not be registered.

1 FJREA, s 1(2)(b).
2 Ibid, s 4(1)(a)(v).
3 AJA, s 9(2)(f).
4 Ibid, s 9(1).
5 *Re Delhi Electric Supply and Traction Co Ltd* [1954] Ch 131, [1953] 2 All ER 1452; *Government of India v Taylor* [1955] AC 491, [1955] 1 All ER 292; *Huntingdon v Attrill* [1893] AC 150, 62 LJ PC 44.

6 F. A. Mann, (1954) 3 ICLQ 465; (1955) 4 ICLQ 564; *Commrs of Taxes (Federation of Rhodesia) v McFarland* 1965 (1) SA 470.
7 Eg Castel, op cit, pp 63–91.
8 Eg *Peter Buchanan Ltd and MacHarg v McVey* [1955] AC 516n at 529; *Government of India v Taylor*, above; *Rossano v Manufacturers Life Insurance Co Ltd* [1963] 2 QB 352, [1962] 2 All ER 214; *United States v Harden* (1963) 41 DLR (2d) 721.

(i) TAX JUDGMENTS

3.22 Sums payable 'in respect of taxes or other charges of a like nature' are those which arise as result of liability under laws which result in 'non-contractual, involuntary monetary impositions in favour of the state or some department or subdivision thereof'.[1] Whether a law meets this requirement is determined in accordance with the lex fori of the requested court.[2] Thus a judgment which has as its purpose the recovery of income tax, corporation tax, capital gains tax, profit taxes, value added tax or purchase tax, municipal tax or local government rates, customs duties, estate, death or succession duties, stamp duties or of compulsory payments to a social security scheme[3] cannot be registered. Moreover, a claim which indirectly has this effect will also be caught, as for example a judgment for costs against a defendant in a case concerned with the validity of seizure of goods under customs legislation.[4] On the other hand, registration should not be refused, 'merely because enforcement of a judgement may result in reimbursement of a fund which has the blessing, or even the financial support, of a foreign state'.[5] Thus registration should be permitted of a judgment for costs in a divorce action which must be paid to a state legal aid fund by way of reimbursement[6] and for a judgment in respect of a hospital account albeit payable to a statutory hospital fund administered by a provincial commission, on behalf of a minister, out of compulsory paid premiums.[7] In neither case is the purpose of the claim directly or indirectly to enforce a statutory liability to pay a sum into public funds for the general welfare. In principle, there seems good reason for permitting public authorities to enforce judgments which are designed to recover monies paid to an individual under a statutory welfare scheme which imposes a duty to make some form of repayment or reimbursement in stated circumstances.

The case for restrictions on tax claims is particularly weak between jurisdictions which are part of the same sovereign state. Thus Canadian provinces have reciprocal enforcement arrangements in their income tax legislation.[8] The Judgment Extension scheme in the United Kingdom was never subject to it,[9] nor is the service of process and execution legislation in Australia.[10] Indeed the latter which applied to Papua–New Guinea prior to her independence, was held to allow the enforcement of tax judgments therefrom in the Australian states.[11] The departure of Papua–New Guinea from the scheme has resulted in the enactment in the Australian jurisdictions of legislation amending the 1933 statute to permit the continued enforcement of judgments for recovery of taxes on income handed down in Papua–New Guinea.[12] Penalties or interest payments thereon cannot be recovered and the governments retain the power to exclude by proclamation any categories of tax which are not found to be properly paid on income. Reciprocal provision is being made in Papua–New Guinea but it is apparent that the alteration is primarily designed to benefit the economy of a developing state from which a large percentage of Australian citizens are said to abscond without paying local income tax.

Another exceptional modification of this kind is to be found in the Isle of Man Act 1979, which allows judgments in respect of certain duties charged by the Isle of Man (in common with the United Kingdom) to be enforced in the United Kingdom by registration under the 1933 Act. The legislation may also be used to enforce judgments, civil or criminal, imposing a fine or penalty in connection with those duties.[13]

Broader exceptions to the general prohibition on this type of judgment are not likely to be secured easily since requested jurisdictions will usually wish to retain powers to refuse enforcement to tax judgments resulting from laws which are seen to be harsh, oppressive or discriminatory.[14] Although such matters might be a basis of objection to registration under the public policy ground, it may be questioned whether such a decision should be that of a court dealing with a particular set of facts rather than that of the government which is far better placed to give prior consideration to the implications of the whole of the revenue law in question. At the same time, the blanket exclusion of all tax judgments regardless of changing international practice evidenced, for example, by double taxation agreements is difficult to defend.[15]

1 Castel, op cit, p 79.
2 *Metal Industries (Salvage) Ltd v ST 'Harle' (Owners)* 1962 SLT 114, following *AG for Canada v Schulze & Co* 1901 9 SLT 4.
3 Ibid; *Connor v Connor* [1974] 1 NZLR 632.
4 *AG for Canada v Schulze & Co*, above.
5 *Connor v Connor*, above, at 637.
6 Ibid.
7 *Weir v Lohr* (1967) 65 DLR (2d) 717. The decision was influenced by a disinclination of the court to apply the doctrine to inter-provincial judgments.
8 Castel, op cit, p 89. A model Reciprocal Enforcement of Tax Judgments Act was adopted by the Conference of Commissioners on Uniformity of Legislation in Canada in 1965, *Annual Meeting*, 1966, pp 91–92. It was withdrawn in 1980.
9 Now, Civil Jurisdiction and Judgments Act 1982, s 18.
10 *Permanent Trustee Co (Canberra) Ltd v Finlayson* (1967) 9 FLR 425 (ACT); revsed on other grounds (1968) 122 CLR 338.
11 *R v White, ex p TA Field Pty Ltd* (1975) 133 CLR 113, HCA; *Chief Collector of Taxes v Bayliss* (1976) 31 FLR 490 (Vic) where such a judgment registered before independence of PNG was held to continue to have effect in Victoria after independence.
12 ACT: Ord 1982, No 36; NSW: Act 1981, No 27; NT: Act 1981, No 22; Qsld: Act 1981, No 24; SA: Act 1980, No 66; Tas: Act 1980, No 84; Vic: Act 1981, No 9621; WA: Act 1980, No 61. The matter is to be considered by the Attornies-General in Australia: (1983) Com LB 1090.
13 Isle of Man Act 1979, s 4. Certain necessary modifications are made to the scheme in connection with the registration of these judgments.
14 *Peter Buchanan Ltd and MacHarg v McVey* [1955] AC 516 at 529, where it was also noted that revenue laws may be used for the furtherance of social policies and ideals dangerous to the security of adjacent countries and for the direct furtherance of economic war.
15 J. G. Castel, (1964) 42 Can Bar Rev 277–278; Castel, op cit, pp 89–93; R. A. Dachs, (1980) 14 Jo Int Law & Econ, 281–99, discussing *R, ex rel British Columbia v Gilbertson* (1979) 597 F 2d 1161 (USCA for 9th Circuit).

(ii) JUDGMENTS IN RESPECT OF FINES AND PENALTIES

3.23 Rather different considerations are present with respect to judgments for sums payable 'in respect of a fine or penalty'. The main purpose of this prohibition is to preclude enforcement of penal laws—those under which an obligation to pay is imposed by way of punishment for some act or omission. For this would be to provide enforcement facilities for one state to enforce its sovereign power in the territory of another and to give extra-territorial effect to its criminal law. Long regarded as unacceptable in Commonwealth conflict of laws systems,[1] such a mechanism would be inconsistent with legislation concerned with the enforcement of civil judgments.

This exception is intended to deal with cases where the penalty is one imposed by an agency of the state for breach of law categorised by the requested state as of a criminal character and involving a breach of an obligation owed to the community at large rather than to a subject. It will embrace such proceedings when instituted by a state authority or official or by a common informer acting for the public benefit.[2] It cannot extend to cases where the subject is protecting his own rights, for example by invoking a contractual provision under which payments must be made for failure to perform by an agreed time.[3] On a similar argument, a judgment for additional sums ordered by way of compensation for unjustifiable opposition to the plaintiff's claim has been held to be registrable.[4] This would also be the position, it is suggested, in respect of damages awarded against a co-respondent in divorce proceedings or against directors for the issue of a false prospectus.[5] It also seems correct in principle to hold that a judgment for exemplary or even punitive damages will not fall into this category. For such sums are payable to the plaintiff for a serious invasion of some protected interest which the original court may acknowledge in this way. Although such categories of damage may no longer be ordered in some systems,[6] it is difficult to categorise them as ones which should be in conflict with this aspect of public policy, since they remain available in many Commonwealth countries.[7]

The position of treble damages which may be ordered, for example under US anti-trust legislation, is less certain at common law.[8] For although the claim is made for damages by the plaintiff, he is the beneficiary of obligations enforced essentially in the public interest, rather than because the rights or interests of the plaintiff have been interfered with in ways which call for exemplary damages. Litigants are seen as supplementing the work of the US Department of Justice (which is authorised to bring criminal proceedings in respect of the same anti-trust activities). There is much in the view that this is an indirect method of enforcing the competition policy of the United States.[9] Some United States authorities treat two thirds of a treble damages judgment as a penalty.[10] In any case, it could be argued that recognition should be refused on the grounds that enforcement would conflict with the public policy of the requested state. United Kingdom legislation has expressly prohibited registration of any external judgment for multiple damages, which is defined as 'a judgment for an amount arrived at by doubling, trebling or otherwise multiplying a sum assessed as compensation for the loss or damage sustained by the person in whose favour the judgment is given'.[11] In one jurisdiction, therefore, the matter is put beyond doubt.

1 Cf *Huntington v Attrill* [1893] AC 150.

2 Ibid, at 157–158. It has been suggested that securities exchange legislation designed to control insider training may be penal for this reason: *McIntyre Porcupine Mines Ltd v Hammond* (1975) 119 DLR (3d) 139 (Ont); *Schemmer v Property Resources Ltd* [1975] Ch 273, [1974] 3 All ER 451.

3 *Huntingdon v Attrill*, above, at 156.

4 *SA Consortium General Textiles v Sun and Sand Agencies Ltd* [1978] QB 279, [1978] 2 All ER 339.

5 *Huntingdon v Attrill*, above, at 157–158.

6 See *Rookes v Barnard* [1964] AC 1129, [1964] 1 All ER 367; *Cassell & Co Ltd v Broome* [1972] AC 1027, [1972] 1 All ER 801.

7 Per Lord Denning MR, in *SA Consortium General Textiles v Sun and Sand Agencies Ltd*, above, at 355.

8 See para 3.24 below.

9 It may be significant that the draft UK-US Civil Judgments Convention expressly excluded punitive and multiple damages (art 2(2)(b)): P. M. North, (1978) 28 NLJ 315 at p 316. On the policy issues, see memo of Government of Australia in Commonwealth Secretariat, *1980 Meeting of Commonwealth Law Ministers, Memoranda* pp 323–326.

10 Eg *Kline v Coldwell, Banker & Co* (1974) 508F 2d 226 (USCA 9th Circuit).
11 Protection of Trading Interests Act 1980, s 5. The prohibition also applies to judgments on a claim for contribution in respect of a multiple damages award: ibid, s 5(2)(c).

(k) *The judgment is not one, the registration of which is prohibited by the lex fori*

3.24 It is not the practice for the legislation governing the Commonwealth schemes to exclude particular categories of judgment from their purview. Indeed, widespread exceptions of such a kind would threaten the basis upon which reciprocity rests and, when introduced by one state, would justify a reconsideration by others of the reciprocal links.[1] Nonetheless, jurisdictions may find it expedient, when regulating international transactions by legislation, to include provisions to prevent registration of certain categories of foreign judgment. These exclusions can usually be justified under the head of public policy.

In some instances, exclusion of the judgments from registration will be an indirect consequence of general statutory provisions rendering certain entities immune from the jurisdiction of the requested court. Thus the general immunities of a foreign state or of diplomatic or consular persons may effectively preclude the registration of judgments obtained abroad, unless the judgment relates to matters covered by exceptions provided for in the legislation or unless waiver is duly given. In the past, difficult questions have arisen concerning the extent to which state corporations enjoy immunity from suit, as emanations of the state to which they belong,[2] and to which commercial transactions entered into by a state can be the subject of litigation.[3] Such considerations are of equal importance in the context of registration. Legislation of the kind enacted by the United Kingdom in 1978 now allows litigation in prescribed circumstances in both these cases[4] and, it must be presumed, will allow registration of judgments obtained elsewhere if those circumstances are met. This trend away from blanket immunities appears to be developing elsewhere in the Commonwealth.[5]

Exclusion of judgments by reason of their subject matter is only rarely found. One example may be cited from United Kingdom legislation. Registration will not be permitted of a judgment for a sum awarded in respect of injury or damage in circumstances which are covered by any international convention relating to liability in the field of nuclear energy (other than one concerned with transport), to which the United Kingdom is a party and the country of the foreign court is not.[6] The purpose is to ensure that litigation on such matters will be confined to countries within the conventions and that only the convention arrangements will be given effect in respect of nuclear damage.

Of greater significance is the legislation in Australia and the United Kingdom which is designed to prevent the enforcement of certain types of judgment arising from competition proceedings.[7] In both jurisdictions, the legislation is drafted in terms capable of applying to judgments from any country but it is apparent, both from the surrounding debates and from action taken in pursuance of them, that they are principally for use where the United States courts have assumed jurisdiction under United States legislation over the extra-territorial activities of a transnational corporation and the plaintiffs seek to enforce the judgment in the requested state in which the corporation is incorporated.

The Australian Act permits the Attorney-General to declare that particular judgments of this kind shall not be enforced or shall only be enforced to an amount specified by the Attorney-General.[8] The judgment must have been one given in proceedings instituted under any law of a kind 'commonly known as an antitrust law', a term which includes 'any law having as its purpose or as its dominant purpose the preservation of competition between manufacturing, commercial or other business enterprises or the prevention or repression of monopolies or restrictive practice in trade or commerce'.[9] An order may be made only if the original court exercised jurisdiction inconsistently with international law or comity and if the recognition or enforcement would or might be detrimental to the trade or commerce with other countries, or the trading operations of a trading or financial corporation formed in Australia, or other matters within the jurisdiction of the Commonwealth of Australia. The Attorney-General must also be satisfied that it is in the national interest that the judgment not be recognised or enforced.[10]

The United Kingdom statute approaches the matter differently from the Australian. Enforcement under the Commonwealth schemes and at common law is prohibited in respect of any judgment based upon a provision or rule of law proscribed by order of the Secretary of State.[11] Such an order may be made in respect of:

'any provision or rule of law which appears to him to be concerned with the prohibition or regulation of agreements, arrangements or practices designed to restrain, distort or restrict competition in the carrying on of business of any description or to be otherwise concerned with the promotion of such competition as aforesaid.'[12]

In contrast with Australia, therefore, prohibition relates not to particular antitrust judgments but to any judgment made pursuant to specified provisions of foreign law.[13]

The United Kingdom legislation, in addition to dealing directly with multiple damages judgments,[14] makes provision for the recovery by legal proceedings in the United Kingdom of the amount by which the award in the antitrust proceedings exceeded the part attributable to compensation. The privilege is accorded to any defendant with a specified connecting link with the United Kingdom and her dependencies (citizenship, incorporation, carrying-on of business), unless a stronger link with the overseas jurisdiction exists (ordinary residence of an individual or principal place of business of a corporation at the institution of the proceedings or carrying on of business there, the judgment being concerned with activities exclusively carried on there).[15] Provision is made for enforcement on a reciprocal basis of prescribed judgments from other jurisdictions with provisions for the recovery of multiple damages awards. The 1933 legislation may be applied to such arrangements.[16] Without such arrangements, it seems improbable that a judgment of this kind will be registrable or enforceable at common law usually for want of a jurisdictional base and also as giving rise to possible conflict with the public policy of the requested state. These latter arrangements are the model for an Australian Bill which is yet to be enacted.[17]

1 Revocation of extension orders may take place by unilateral action: AJA, s 14(2); FJREA, s 1(4).
2 Eg, *Trendtex Trading Corpn v Central Bank of Nigeria* [1977] QB 529, [1977] 1 All ER 881; *C. Czarnikow Ltd v Centrala Handlu Zagranicznego Rolimpex* [1979] AC 351, [1978] 2 All ER 1043.
3 Ibid; *I Congreso del Partido* [1978] QB 500, [1978] 1 All ER 1169.
4 State Immunity Act 1978 (UK), ss 3, 14. For UK see also CJJA 1982, s 31(1).
5 M. Sornarajah, (1982) 31 ICLQ 661 and sources cited therein.
6 Nuclear Installations Act 1965, s 17(5), (nif). See Dicey and Morris, op cit, pp 1111–1113, which sets out the conventions in issue.
7 A Foreign Proceedings and Judgments Bill on the Australian lines was considered in Canada in 1980 (Bill C–41). Legislation is also proposed for New Zealand: (1981) 7 Comm LB 800.

8 Foreign Antitrust Judgments (Restriction of Enforcement) Act 1979, No 13, s 3(2)(c) and (d).
9 Ibid, s 3(1).
10 Ibid, s 3(2).
11 Ibid, s 5. The scheme also applies to any judgment on a claim for contribution in respect of damages awarded under such a judgment.
12 Ibid, s 5(4).
13 See eg SI 1982/885. Generally D. L. Jones, (1982) 8 Comm LB 353–378.
14 Para 3.23 above.
15 Protection of Trading Interests Act 1980, s 6. The defendant in the recovery proceedings need not be within the jurisdiction of the UK court: s 6(5).
16 Ibid, s 7, as amended by Civil Jurisdiction and Judgments Act 1982, s 38.
17 Foreign Antitrust Judgments (Restriction of Enforcement) Bill 1980: (1981) 7 Comm LB 1173–1184.

Interest on the original judgment and costs of registration

3.25 The 1933 Act makes clear that a judgment may be registered for the sum payable thereunder 'including any interest which by the law of the country of the original court becomes due under the judgment up to the time of registration'.[1] It is usual for the certificate obtained in the country of origin to contain particulars of the rate of any interest payable on the judgment debt.[2] But it will always be open to the applicant at the time of registration to establish by reference to the law of original court both the entitlement to interest and the rate by which it must be calculated to that time.

That the 1920 Act is silent on this matter and that Rules of Court usually make provision only in respect of the 1933 scheme in requiring any interest due to be specified by the applicant,[3] may suggest that interest cannot be recovered under the earlier scheme. This is the view taken in Victoria.[4] A better view is that, as the Act applies to judgments 'whereby any sum of money is payable',[5] it is capable of extending to any interest which by the law of the country of the judgment is required to be paid. Moreover there seems little doubt that an action to recover interest on a judgment may be brought.

Under both schemes, registration, as of right, extends to the reasonable costs of, and incidental to, the registration of the judgment, including the costs of obtaining a certified copy of the judgment from the original court.[6]

1 FJREA, s 2(6).
2 Ibid, s 10.
3 Eg RSC Ord 71, r 3(1)(d).
4 *Re Linley* [1951] VLR 319.
5 AJA, s 12(1). Contrast the terminology of FJREA, s 11.
6 AJA, s 9(3)(c); FJREA, s 2(6).

IV REGISTRATION APPLICATIONS

Time limits

3.26 Registration of a judgment under the 1920 Act in normal cases must be applied for within twelve months of the date of the judgment.[1] The requested court may in its discretion grant an extension of this time which will usually be necessary if the judgment has been the subject of appeal.[2] This short period contrasts unfavourably with the time usually permitted under limitation statutes for bringing actions on the judgment.[3] The 1933 Act, which excludes the latter type of enforcement,[4] allows six years for the bringing of an application from the date of the judgment or any subsequent appeal.[5] The date will normally be ascertainable from the copy of the judgment which the applicant is required to furnish.[6]

1 AJA, s 9(1). This period also applies to judgments given in Commonwealth jurisdictions before the extension of the 1933 Act thereto: AJA 1956, s 51. The Canadian legislation usually provides for six years.
2 Ibid, s 9(2)(e) prohibits registration where an appeal is pending or intended.
3 *Berliner Industriebank AG v Jost* [1971] 1 QB 278, [1971] 2 All ER 117.
4 FJREA, s 6.
5 Ibid, s 2(1). See Greer Committee Report, p 60. This was very much an after-thought: LCO/2, Doc No. 1690.
6 RSC Ord 71, r 3(1)(a).

The application

3.27 Under both schemes, an application to register is to be made by the 'judgment creditor',[1] normally the person in whose favour the judgment has been given.[2] Thus any person may apply who has been a party to the original proceedings, whether as plaintiff or defendant or who has been joined to them, or has otherwise been a beneficiary of an order of the court. It will presumably extend, for example, to children to whom payments were ordered in domestic proceedings, albeit that they were not parties to them. Both Acts extend the right of application to any person to whom the rights under the judgment have been assigned or transferred or who has succeeded to them.[3]

It is a common practice for applications to be made ex parte, although the requested court is given power to direct a summons to be issued upon the judgment debtor.[4] Such a direction will be appropriate wherever there are doubts whether the judgment is one which can be registered.

Canadian practice is, in this respect, more demanding. An ex parte order may be made, albeit then in the discretion of the requested court, only where the judgment debtor:

'(a) was personally served with process in the original action, or
(b) though not personally served, appeared or defended or attorned or otherwise submitted to the jurisdiction of the original court.'[5]

It is commonly required too that the time for appeal is past and that no appeal is pending or that the appeal has been made and dismissed.[6] Where these conditions are not met, reasonable notice of the application must be given to the judgment debtor.[7] These Canadian provisions, although expressed in language similar to that used for establishing a jurisdictional basis for registration, are concerned with the separate, preliminary question.[8] In a number of cases, registrations made ex parte have been set aside because these procedural conditions have not been met.[9] Moreover, in a number of provinces the requirement of personal service has been construed to mean service within the jurisdiction of the original court and not to extend to a form of personal service ex juris.[10] This unfortunate conclusion has led some jurisdictions to make statutory modifications in order that 'service shall not be held not to be personal service merely because the service is effected outside the jurisdiction of the original court.'[11]

In most systems, when the applicant is not ordinarily resident within the jurisdiction of the country of application, the requested court will normally insist upon the provision by the plaintiff of security for the defendant's costs.[12] At the same time, this is a discretionary matter and in practice may not be required, for example, where the applicant is a reputable firm with substantial business connections within the jurisdiction, unless the costs incurred are already heavy.[13] Certain Canadian courts have suggested, by analogy with the practice under the Judgment Extension schemes,[14] that the requirement of security is not appropriate where the non-resident applicant is resident in another reciprocating jurisdiction.[15] But the better view is that since the procedure is not automatic and the defendant has a right to challenge registration and may succeed in having it set aside, security will usually be appropriate if the applicant is resident outside the registering jurisdiction.[16]

1 AJA, s 9(1); FJREA, s 2(1). An application is a civil proceeding. As to whether it is an act of bankruptcy see *Re Ley, ex p Best* (1949) 14 ABC 191.
2 AJA, s 12(1); FJREA, s 11(1). The former refers to the person 'by whom the judgment was obtained'. This may be narrower, suggesting that the person must have sought the judgment.
3 Ibid, see para 3.17 above.
4 Eg RSC Ord 71, r 1. As to who may be the subject of the application, see para 3.17 above.
5 Eg Alberta, R–6, s 2(2). The Ontario provisions are less explicit: Cap 432, s 2(2).
6 Ibid.
7 Ibid s 2(5); *Maple Leaf Lamp Co Ltd v Acme Investments Ltd* (1979) 51 APR 195 (NB).
8 *Gamble Canada Ltd v Kucherawy* [1978] 2 WWR 645 (Sask). Decisions on the meaning of terms used in relation to jurisdiction will be applicable.
9 Ibid; *G A Racicot Enterprises Ltd v Moore* (1979) 55 APR 151 (NB); *Maple Leaf Lamp Co Ltd v Acme Investments*, above.
10 *Wedlay v Quist* (1953–54) 10 WWR (NS) 21 (Alta); *Hoffman Lumber and Supply Ltd v Auld; Davies Lumber Co Ltd v Auld* (1958) 24 WWR 552 (BC); *Gamble Canada Ltd v Kucherawy*, above; *Alcor Pacific Lumber Sales Ltd v Janet Lumber Trading Co Ltd* (1978) 82 DLR (3d) 196 (Alta); *MacFarlane v Briggs* (1977) 18 APR 153 (NB); *Alberta Livestock Transplants Ltd v Pine Tree Rancho Ltd* (1978) 92 DLR (3d) 478 (Sask).
11 This follows the Model Reciprocal Enforcement of Judgments Act 1958, s 2(2) and is found in the legislation of eg Alberta, R–6, s 1(2). Cf also Statutes in British Columbia, Manitoba, Newfoundland, Nova Scotia, Prince Edward Island, Yukon.
12 *Kohn v Rinson and Stafford (Brod) Ltd* [1948] 1 KB 327, [1947] 2 All ER 839; *Sardinha v Excavations Ltd* (1977) No 793 of 1976 (Barbados). As to waiver by the defendant, see *Richardson v Macindoe* [1943] NZLR 53.
13 *Compagnie Francais de Television v Thorne Consumer Electronics* [1981] FSR 306. Cf *Aeronave SPA v Westland Charters Ltd* [1971] 3 All ER 531, [1971] 1 WLR 1445, CA. In *Landi den Hartog v Stopps* [1976] FSR 497, it was suggested that residence in the EEC was a relevant factor for a UK court.
14 Cf *Raeburn v Andrews* (1874) LR 9 QB 118, 43 LJQB 73.
15 *Henry v Henry* [1926] 3 WWR 250 (BC); *Hart v Arnold and Arnold* [1951] 2 WWR (NS) 576 (BC); *Edgar v Erickson* (1969) 69 WWR 551 (YT); *Crestwood Import and Export Ontario Ltd v Broadway Datsun Ltd and Letvad* (1977) 2 BCLR 394.
16 *Fraser v Wainwright Dome Oil Co Ltd* [1927] 1 WWR 523 (Alta); *Jorgensen v Reid* [1932] 3 WWR 250 (Sask); *Factory Tire and Rubber Co Ltd v Timac Tire Sales Ltd* (1979) 9 Alta LR (2d) 193.

Documentation required

3.28 An application to register a judgment must be supported by appropriate documentation. Under the English practice, the essentials of which are found in other Commonwealth jurisdictions, this comprises an affidavit:

(a) exhibiting the judgment (or a verified, certified or otherwise duly authenticated copy);[1]
(b) stating the name, trade or business and the usual or last known place of abode or business of the judgment creditor and debtor, so far as known to the deponent;
(c) stating to the best information or belief of the deponent:
  (i) that the judgment creditor is entitled to enforce the judgment;
  (ii) that at the date of application, the judgment has not been satisfied (or if partly satisfied, the amount outstanding);
  (iii) that none of the prescribed grounds for refusing registration is present (1920 scheme[2]);

(iv) that at the date of application the judgment can be enforced by execution in the country of the original court and that registration would not be liable to be set aside (1933 scheme[3]);

(d) specifying the amount of interest under the judgment due at the time of registration (1933 scheme[4]);

(e) identifying the parts of a judgment which are capable of being enforced, where the whole judgment cannot be registered (1933 scheme).[5]

1 Certified copies of the judgment may usually be obtained under the legislation in Commonwealth countries: AJA, s 10; FJREA, s 10. A photocopy may not be accepted: *Bougie v Timmins* (1973) No 18 of 1973 (St Vincent). Translations from foreign language judgments must be certified by a notary public or authenticated by affidavit.

2 As set out in AJA, s 9.

3 On grounds set out in FJREA, s 4. Additional evidence required by the Order in Council extending the UK Act to a foreign country must also be provided.

4 Evidence as to the law applicable may be required under the relevant Order in Council.

5 RSC Ord 71, r 3. Verification that the judgment is not proscribed under the Protection of Trading Interests 1980 is also required.

V REGISTRATION

Registration procedure

3.29 The two schemes diverge substantially in respect of the act of registration. For under the 1920 scheme, the decision to register is discretionary even when the statutory conditions are present, whereas under the 1933 Act registration is mandatory when the criteria are met. The later development was to ensure that equivalent imperative provisions were applied in foreign countries with respect to English judgments.[1] As a general rule, therefore, leave to register must be granted if the statutory requirements for registration are fulfilled.[2] At the same time, if the requested court is fully satisfied, on the basis of the affidavit or other admissions made by the applicant, that the judgment, if it were registered, would have to be set aside, it seems sensible that leave should be refused.[3]

The 1920 Act, however, except in its Canadian formulation, recognises the requested court's power to allow registration 'if in all the circumstances of the case they think that it is just and convenient that the judgment should be enforced'.[4] The limits of this discretion, which is to be judicially exercised, have not been closely examined by Commonwealth courts. For in practice, it seems rarely to have been put in issue. It remains, however, a basis for refusal of registration in cases where, for example, an action at common law to enforce a foreign judgment would fail or, perhaps, an important common law condition reproduced in the 1933 Act, not contained in the 1920, is not met. Thus where doubts existed in the mind of the judge about the extent of the liability under the judgment[5] or (in the then state of the law) about the currency of the payment when not clearly that of the requested state and the rate of exchange,[6] exercise of the discretion has been refused. Where a jurisdictional basis was technically established but shown to have arisen from an appearance entered in error, registration was refused, partly by reference to this ground.[7] Again, enforcement by registration of a Zambian judgment entered without any sort of formal proof was deemed not to be just and convenient in Kenya.[8] In all cases, as Castel suggests,[9] the courts should consider the application very carefully and exercise extreme caution requiring clear evidence before allowing registration. This is particularly the case for Canada, where the discretion is not qualified as under the 1920 Act, but where it is expressly stated that registration cannot be granted if there is any objection which would have been a good defence if an action had been brought on the judgment.[10]

When leave to register is granted, an order will be drawn up and entry made in the appropriate Register of Judgments kept for the purpose. In Canada, an exemplification or certified copy of the judgment must also be filed with the clerk of the court in which the order was made. The judgment is then entered as a judgment of that court.[11]

Under the English style practice, notice of the registration must be served upon the debtor, giving prescribed details of the registration and of the creditor (or his lawyer or agent) and notifying the right to apply to set the registration aside within the applicable time limits.[12] Unless otherwise directed, notice must be served upon the debtor personally or at his address but service out of the jurisdiction is permitted without the necessity for obtaining leave. Ex juris service has to be allowed of right. Otherwise a further condition would be added to the scheme, that of personal service in the country of registration, and any of the debtor's assets to be found there would be out of reach of the creditor, if the debtor remained abroad. If appropriate service processes are followed in the place where service is effected, personal service may be dispensed with.[13]

Canadian practice requires notice of registration to be served, in the same manner as a writ upon the debtor only in the cases where the order was made ex parte.[14] This must be done within one month of the date of filing the copy of the judgment[15] or such time as the registering court may order. Again a time limit of one month is set, by reference to the date of the notice, for the filing of any notice of application to set aside.[16]

Under all schemes an application to set aside must be made by the debtor within the time set by statute or by the court.[17] Execution under English practice will not be issued until the period for making an application to set aside has elapsed or the application determined.[18] In the Canadian variant, no sale or other disposition of the debtor's property will be valid if undertaken in the period allowed for filing for setting aside, in any case where the registration was made ex parte.[19] Where the debtor was given an opportunity to challenge the making of the registration, he may not apply to set aside and thus execution need not be delayed.

1 Greer Committee Report, p 61, where the mandatory nature of judgments resulting from actions upon foreign judgments was also relied upon.
2 FJREA, s 4.
3 *Crick v Hennessy* [1973] WAR 74: see further para 3.33 below.
4 AJA, s 9(1).
5 *Taylor v Begg* [1932] NZLR 286. See also *Lam Soon Cannery Co v Hooper & Co* [1966] 1 MLJ 198.
6 *Ibbetson* 1957 SLT (Notes) 15.
7 *Redhead v Redhead and Crothers* [1926] NZLR 131.
8 *Re Lowenthal and Air France* 1966 2 ALR Comm 301.
9 Op cit, p 541, citing *Hausman v Franchi* [1949] OWN 695.
10 Eg Alberta, R-6, s 2(6)(g): para 3.70 below.
11 Ibid, s 5.
12 See *Hunt v BP Exploration Co Ltd* (1980) 28 ALR 145 where the failure to provide rules of court dealing with notice was held insufficient to prevent registration against a debtor outside the jurisdiction. But until valid service is effected, the time to apply to set aside will not run and no execution can be issued. *BP Exploration Co (Libya) Ltd v Hunt* [1980] 1 NSWLR 496. See also, *Craig Kirke and Wright v Costello* [1982] Qd R 42, ACLD 17.8 (Qnsd).

13 RSC Ord 71, r 7, applying Ord 11, r 5 (and rr 6 and 8 which have no application to Commonwealth jurisdictions). The debtor may be held to have waived an irregularity in service if he takes steps, such as seeking extension of time for setting aside, in full knowledge of the existence and nature of the claim: *Medinelli v Malgras* 1958 SC 489.
14 Eg Alberta, R-6, s 6(1)(a).
15 *Re Reciprocal Enforcement of Judgments Act, Wigston v Chowen* (1964) 49 WWR 543 (Sask).
16 Eg Alberta, J-20, s 6(1)(b); *McCormack v Starr* [1972] 1 WWR 239 (Alta); *Alcor Pacific Lumber Sales Ltd v Janet Lumber Trading Co Ltd* (1977) 5 Alta LR (2d) 8. Failure to comply precludes a challenge to the registration.
17 Ibid; RSC Ord 71, rr 5(3), 7(3)(d) and 9(a). Failure to state the time renders the order for registration defective: *Velautham Chettyar v Sayampanathan* [1929] SSLR 98.
18 FJREA, s 9(2) proviso: RSC Ord 71, r 10.
19 Eg Alberta, R-6, s 5(a).

Currency of the registered judgment

3.30 The 1920 Act made no provision in respect of the currency in which a registered judgment should be paid, presumably leaving the matter to be regulated in accordance with the common law.[1] The 1933 statute, however, in its original version makes express provision that where the judgment is expressed in a currency other than that of the requested jurisdiction, it is to be registered as if it were a judgment for the sum due in the currency of that jurisdiction as, on the basis of the rate of exchange prevailing at the date of the original judgment, was equivalent to the sum payable.[2] This was consistent with the existing common law relating to judgments generally, which provided for conversion at the exchange prevailing on the date the cause of action arose.[3]

This may well remain the law in many jurisdictions which rely upon the original provisions of the 1933 Act. These, however, have in some cases been repealed, notably by the United Kingdom,[4] as inconsistent with the common law as restated by the House of Lords in *Miliangos v George Frank (Textiles) Ltd.*[5] In consequence of that decision, a judgment expressed in foreign currency will now be registered in that currency.[6] It will be treated as if it were a local judgment entered in a foreign currency and the debtor may, at his option, pay either in that currency or its equivalent in the local currency calculated at the date of payment[7] or, if execution is required, at the date when the particular method of enforcement is authorised.[8] This will be the position too under the 1920 Act, at least in the United Kingdom and in those jurisdictions with that Act where *Miliangos* will be followed.[9]

The position in other jurisdictions will be governed by the terms of their present legislation, including any relating to their currency. Thus a Canadian court has held that the Currency and Exchange Act of Canada prevents any court from ordering payment except in local currency.[10] Accordingly, the judgment must be converted into Canadian dollars. Most provinces follow the 1933 Act in providing for the breach-date rule.[11] This is, however, increasingly seen to be out of step with economic realities. In a series of judgments given in actions on foreign judgments, it has been held that the rate of exchange is that prevailing at the date of the Canadian judgment on the foreign judgment. Although the date of actual payment is seen as preferable, it is deemed to be impractical, as the dollar sum which would have to be paid will not be determinable at the date of the local judgment.[12] In provinces where no statutory breach-date exists, the judgment-date approach may be expected to be followed in relation to the registration of foreign judgments.

The Australian legislation too still remains with the breach-date. The difficulties of working any simple rule in present day circumstances were acknowledged in *Malaysia-Singapore Airlines Ltd v Parker*.[13] There it was also held that where several rates of exchange are effective on the same day, as for example the telegraphic and the airmail buying rates, the court should select the lowest. What is clear is that in most jurisdictions modification of existing statutory provisions is called for, unless one or other of the parties to a judgment is to be disadvantaged by swings in exchange rates between the dates of the original judgment and its registration. The solution adopted in the United Kingdom favouring conversion at the actual date of payment or at the date when the court authorises enforcement has much to commend it.[14] But this seems possible only if the judgment itself can be registered in the foreign currency.

1 But see *Ibbetson* 1957 SLT (Notes) 15. See para 3.29 note 6 above. Cp. *East India Trading Co Inc v Carmel Exporters and Importers Ltd* [1952] 2 QB 439, [1952] 1 All ER 1053.
2 FJREA, s 2(3).
3 Greer Committee Report, p 61, referring to *The Volturno* [1921] 2 AC 544. Members of the Committee would have liked to make the relevant date that of payment but this would have altered the law: Greer Committee Minutes, 7 December 1931, LCO/2, Doc No 1691.
4 Administration of Justice Act 1977, s 4(2)(b)(i), Sch 5, Part I; RSC Ord 71, as amended by SI 1977/1955.
5 [1976] AC 443, [1975] 3 All ER 801.
6 Dicey and Morris, op cit, p 1109 suggest that registration must be made in that currency. Otherwise the debtor's option is lost.
7 RSC, 71/3/1.
8 *Practice Direction* [1976] 1 All ER 669.
9 Eg *Sardinha v Excavations Ltd* (1977) No 793 of 1976 (Barbados).
10 *Batavia Times Publishing Co v Davis* (1978) 88 DLR (3d) 144 (Ont); *Farmer's National Bank v Coles* (1981) 80 APR 248 (NB), referring to Revised Statutes of Canada 1970, c-39, s 11.
11 Eg Alberta, R-6, s 3. No provisions exist in Ontario or New Brunswick.
12 *Batavia Times Publishing Co v Davis*, above; see also *AM-PAC Forest Products Inc v Phoenix Doors Ltd and Arab and Arab* (1979) 14 BCLR 63; *Martin v McNeely* (1975) 4 APR 473; *General Instruments Corpn v Maritime–Ontario Freight Lines Ltd* (1974) 8 NBR (2d) 376; *Woodpulp Inc (Canada) v Jannock Industries Ltd* (1979) 55 APR 358; *McCain Produce Co Ltd v Canadian National Railways* (1979) 25 NBR (2d) 585; *Bedford v Shaw* (1981) 33 OR (2d) 766; *Clinton v Ford* (1982) 37 OR (2d) 448.
13 (1972) 3 SASR 300.
14 This approach was supported by the English Law Commission, Law Com No 124, Cmnd 9064, (1983), para 3.15.

Control of debtor's assets

3.31 As in other civil proceedings, there is a danger for the judgment creditor that the judgment debtor may, on receipt of the notice of registration, remove his assets from the jurisdiction or in some other way dissipate them to avoid meeting his liability. The requested court, in the absence of any express authorisation, does not have power to order the debtor to make a payment into court, even as a condition of the trial of any issue which arises as a result of his application to set the registration aside.[1] There is a case for the provision of a power to order payment into court within a specified period of receipt of the notice of registration and, if payment is not made, for measures which can be used against the debtor's property to raise that sum for payment into court, pending the conclusion of any application to set aside or the expiry of the time limit for such an application.[2]

In the absence of such powers, it is probable that resort to the Mareva injunction will be increasingly made.[3] Although doubts have been expressed concerning the authority for the making of this type of interlocutory relief,[4] its general availability is now widely recognised in common law jurisdictions.[5] Its use in the context of registration of judgments has been accepted in a number of reported cases.[6]

Whilst, as in other types of civil proceedings, this jurisdiction is likely to be used with caution, the registration of the foreign judgment can readily be treated as 'a good arguable case' that the creditor will recover a certain sum from the debtor—the pre-condition of the grant of the injunction.[7] The judgment creditor must establish that there is reason to believe that there are assets of the debtor in the jurisdiction to meet the judgment but that there is a real risk that the debtor may take steps to ensure that they will not be available to meet the judgment, either by removing them from the jurisdiction or by otherwise dissipating them within the jurisdiction.[8] The grant, however, always lies in the discretion of the requested court which must consider the balance of convenience to the parties concerned[9] and must ensure adequate protection for the interests of third parties, such as any bank by which the debtor's assets are held.[10]

There seems every reason why the Mareva injunction shoud be given effect, not only until the process of registration or setting aside is complete, but also in aid of execution.[11] What is clear is that the injunction cannot be used merely to provide the applicant with security for the enforcement of the judgment. There must be a real risk that the judgment will remain unsatisfied through the dissipation by the defendant of his assets.[12]

1 *Syal v Heyward* [1948] 2 KB 443, [1948] 2 All ER 576. Note the power in certain Canadian provinces to seek a garnishment order at the time of registration: para 3.32 below.

2 See P. A. Stone, (1983) 32 ICLQ 477, at p 480, in the context of the Brussels Convention.

3 *Mareva Compania Naviera SA v International Bulk Carriers Ltd* [1975] 2 Lloyd's Rep 509, CA.

4 Authority has been found in the statutory power to grant interlocutory relief in all cases 'where it appears to the Supreme Court to be just and convenient so to do' (Supreme Court of Judicature (Consolidation) Act 1925 (UK), s 45(1)) or in the powers vesting 'all necessary jurisdiction' in the Supreme Court (Judicature Act 1908 (NZ), s 16: *Hunt v BP Exploration Co (Libya) Ltd* [1980] 1 NZLR 104; Supreme Court Act 1970 (NSW), s 23: *Riley McKay Pty Ltd v McKay* [1982] 1 NSWLR 264) and in the inherent powers of the Supreme Court, ibid. For the position in England, see now the expanded provisions in Supreme Court Act 1981, s 37: *Z Ltd v A-Z and AA-LL* [1982] QB 558, [1982] 1 All ER 556.

5 Canada: *Elesquro Inc v Ssangyong Shipping Co* (1980) 117 DLR (3d) 105 (Federal); *Liberty National Bank and Trust Co v Atkin* (1981) 121 DLR (3d) 160 (Ont); *Parmar Fisheries Ltd v Parceria Maritima Esperanca LDa* (1983) 53 NSR (2d) 338; *Feigelman v Aetna Financial Services Ltd* [1983] 2 WWR 97. See also *Buraglia v Humphreys* (1982) 39 NBR (2d) 674; *Bank of Montreal v James Main Holdings Ltd* (1982) 23 RPR 180 Ont. Australia: *Riley v McKay Pty Ltd v McKay*, above; *Hunt v BP Exploration Co (Libya) Ltd* (1980) 144 CLR 565 at 569 (Qld); *Praznovsky Sablyack* [1977] VR 114; *Sanko Steamship Co Ltd v DC Commodities (A'Asia) Pty Ltd* [1980] WAR 51 but not in *Pivovaroff v Chernabaeff* (1978) 16 SASR 329. See also C. C. Hodgekiss, (1983) 99 LQR 7–10. New Zealand: *Hunt v BP Exploration Co (Libya) Ltd* [1980] 1 NZLR 104.

6 *Perry v Zissis* [1977] 1 Lloyd's Rep 607 at 617 per Megaw LJ; *Hunt v BP Exploration Co (Libya) Ltd* [1980] 1 NZLR 104; *Hunt v BP Exploration Co (Libya) Ltd* (1980) 144 CLR 565 at 569, referring to such a grant at first instance by Queensland SC. It was refused in *Re Hunt* [1979] 2 NSWLR 406, per Powell J, overruled in *Riley McKay Pty Ltd v McKay*, CA, above.

7 *Siskina v Distos Compania Naviera SA* [1979] AC 210, [1977] 3 All ER 803. *Z Ltd v A-Z and AA-LL*, above; *Ninemia Maritime Corpn v Trave Schiffahrts gesellschaft mbH & Co KG, The Niedersachsen* [1984] 1 All ER 398; *J D Barry Pty Ltd v M and E Construction Pty Ltd* [1978] VR 185.

8 *Z Ltd v A*, above; *Ninemia Maritime Corpn v Trave Schiffahrts*, above; *PCW Ltd v Dixon* [1983] 2 All ER 158; *Prince Abdul Rahman Bin Turki Al Sudairy v Abu Taha* [1980] 3 All ER 409, [1980] 1 WLR 1268, CA

9 *Riley McKay Pty Ltd v McKay*, above.

10 *The Eleftherios* [1982] 1 All ER 796, [1982] 1 WLR 539 *The Theotokos* [1983] 2 All ER 65, [1983] 1 WLR 1294.

11 Cf *Steward Chartering Ltd v C & O Managements SA* [1980] 1 All ER 718; *Orwell Steel (Erection and Fabrication) Ltd v Asphalt and Tarmac (UK) Ltd* (1984) Times, 15 March.

12 *Ninemia Maritime Corpn v Trave Schiffahrts*, above, at 419, per Kerr LJ.

Effects of registration

3.32 Once a judgment has been registered, then, subject to any application to set aside, it will be treated under the terms of both schemes as having the same force and effect for the purposes of its execution as if it were a judgment of the requested court which had been obtained or entered upon the date of registration.[1] It does not become a judgment of the registering court. Therefore, it is quite clear that there is no power to make any modification or variation of the terms of the judgment.[2] The judgment will, from the date of registration, be subject to the same judicial supervision and control, in respect of its execution, as is exercised in relation to locally obtained judgments. Accordingly proceedings may be taken upon it and it may be executed in the same way and to the same extent as a domestic judgment.[3] It has been argued that the emphasis in the 1933 Act upon 'execution' excludes the availability of those matters of judgment enforcement which do not constitute forms of execution, such as the issue of a bankruptcy notice or a judgment summons.[4] This view has no judicial support.[5] On the other hand, the different formula in the 1920 Act which gives the courts control and jurisdiction 'only insofar as relates to execution' has been treated as having that effect.[6] Statutory removal of that limitation has been effected in some jurisdictions.[7] Execution will not, however, be permitted to issue whilst any proceedings to set aside the registration may still be instituted or, when instituted, until they have been disposed of.[8]

The Canadian legislation makes different provision in this respect by imposing restrictions upon proceedings on the registered judgment when the registration was made pursuant to an ex parte order. In that case, the debtor's property may not be sold or disposed of prior to the expiration of the one month, or such further period as the court orders, allowed for setting aside the registration.[9]

Generally, execution is not likely to be stayed merely because the judgment debtor has proceedings pending against the creditor on the same issues. Any stay of execution will be exercised on the same basis as applies to locally obtained judgments.[10] Similarly, any time limits for execution of a judgment under the lex fori will apply to the judgment as if it were locally obtained on the date of registration. Special procedures, such as the obtaining of a garnishee order, can be followed under the usual procedures, although in certain Canadian provinces, an application for a garnishment order can be made ex parte to the registering court at the same time as the application for the registration.[11] A garnishee order can be obtained against a bank deposit account in foreign currency in jurisdictions in which judgments or their registration can be made in foreign currency.[12]

A judgment, once registered, will carry interest to the same extent as a domestic judgment entered on the date of registration. This is explicit in the 1933 Act[13] and implicit in the provision of the 1920 Act which requires the judgment to have the same force and effect as a local judgment.[14] Reasonable costs of, and incidental to, registration, including those of obtaining a certified copy of the judgment are included with the registered judgment under both schemes.[15]

1 AJA, s 9(3)(a); FJREA, s 2(2)(a).

2 Cf *Lupton v Lupton* [1946] OWN 326; *Rhinhart v Rhinhart* [1973] 3 WWR 562 (NWT), *Goodchild v Onwuka* [1961] All NLR 163.

3 AJA, s 9(3)(a); FJREA, s 2(2)(b). *Oliver & Co v Gilroy* [1959] 18 DLR (2d) 280 where examination of a registered judgment debtor under the Evidence Act was held to be permissible.

4 Eg Bankruptcy Act 1914 (UK), s 1(1)(g); Debtors Act 1869 (UK), s 5.

5 *Re a Judgment Debtor (No 2176 of 1938)* [1939] Ch 601; *F Hoffman-La Roche & Co AG v Inter Continental Pharmaceuticals* [1969] 1 CLR 106 (Cyprus).
6 AJA, s 9(3)(b). Cf *Re a Bankruptcy Notice* [1898] 1 QB 383 (decided on similar words in the UK Judgment Extension Legislation); *Re Watson* [1893] 1 QB 21; *Re Bassett, ex p Farrow Bros* (1953) 16 ABC 178.
7 Cf Administration of Justice Act 1956 (UK), s 40.
8 FJREA, s 2(2), proviso; RSC Ord 71, r 10.
9 Eg Alberta, R-6, s 5(a).
10 *Ferdinand Wagner (a firm) v Laubscher Bros & Co (a firm)* [1970] 2 QB 313, [1970] 2 WLR 1019.
11 Eg Manitoba, R-20, s 9; Newfoundland, Cap 327, s 9; Prince Edward Island, R-7, s 8. A garnishment order against assets in another jurisdiction will not be allowed: registration of the judgment there is the correct procedure: *Hansen v Danstar Mines Ltd* (1978) 83 DLR (3d) 346.
12 *Choice Investments Ltd v Jeromnimon* [1981] QB 149, [1981] 1 All ER 225.
13 FJREA, s 2(2)(c).
14 AJA, s 9(3)(a). The equivalent provision in FJREA, s 2(2)(a) is limited to 'for the purposes of execution'.
15 AJA, s 9(3)(c); FJREA, s 2(6).

VI OBJECTIONS TO REGISTRATION

Grounds for refusing or setting aside a registration

3.33 The 1920 Act differs from the 1933 Act in prescribing grounds upon which the initial registration may be successfully opposed.[1] Further, even if those grounds are not established, registration may still be refused, as we have seen,[2] if local enforcement of the judgment would not be just or convenient. If on the face of the judgment and from the facts presented to it, the court, of its own motion, concludes that the registration cannot be made, it may refuse leave, even if the debtor did not establish the objection.[3]

Rules of court usually also provided for power in the debtor to apply to set aside the registration once made on the same prescribed grounds, or by reference to the just and convenient requirement or because there is some other sufficient reason.[4] Whilst an application for leave to register must be refused if the requested court is satisfied that the judgment falls within the prescribed cases, setting aside of the registration for any such a reason is not mandatory. It is open to the court, exercising a judicial decision, to refuse to set aside registration even if a ground for refusing registration appears to have existed.[5] This seems to hold good for both Canadian and English-style arrangements.

The 1933 Act is differently structured. For there is a duty to register, stated in mandatory terms, where certain conditions are fulfilled:

(a) the judgment is one within the scheme;
(b) the prescribed matters are proved;
(c) at the date of application the sum payable has not been wholly satisfied;
(d) at that date the judgment was enforceable by execution in the country where it was made.[6]

It has been suggested that registration might be refused if the requested court is of the view that the registration would have to be set aside if application were to be made.[7] But such a step will require the clearest indications from the affidavit evidence or from admissions by the applicant for the court to act in this way on its own motion. In this kind of a case, the power granted in Rules of

Court to refuse an ex parte registration but to proceed on summons may be the most appropriate procedure.[8]

Objections to registration will in the main be raised by the debtor by an application to set it aside. The grounds upon which such an application may be made are set out in the Act:[9] they constitute an exclusive list. There is no residual discretion to set aside.[10] With two exceptions,[11] all the grounds are mandatory. If any is established, the registration must be set aside. As these grounds are largely those upon which an action on a foreign judgment can be resisted, this is a more consistent approach than that in the 1920 Act.

If an application to set aside is not made within the time limit (with such extension as may be allowed), it cannot be granted.[12]

In relation to applications to set aside, the requested court usually has power to direct that the issues raised therein be tried in the same manner as an action.[13]

1 AJA, s 9(2).
2 AJA, s 9(1): see para 3.29 above. The Canadian legislation lacks this provision: see, eg Alberta, R–6, s 2(1).
3 *Saskatchewan Government Insurance Office v Anderson* (1966) 57 WWR 633; affd (1967) 61 DLR (2d) 355 (Man); *Re Gacs and Maierovitz* (1968) 68 DLR (2d) 345 (BC).
4 Eg RSC Ord 71, r 9(3). In the absence of rules of court, it may be doubted whether such a power exists. The Canadian legislation allows setting aside only where the registration was made ex parte.
5 *Bank of Montreal v HO House Ltd* (1978) 33 APR 407 (Newfd).
6 FJREA, s 1.
7 *Crick v Hennessy* [1973] WAR 74: see para 3.29 above.
8 RSC Ord 71, r 2(1).
9 FJREA, s 4(1). Additional provisions are contained in s 5.
10 Cf *Jackson v Jackson* [1950] 1 WWR 900 (BC) where setting aside on the ground that conditions in the original judgment had not been complied with was refused.
11 FJREA, s 4(1)(b) (earlier judgment in existence); s 5(1) (appeal available).
12 *Re A Debtor (No 11 of 1939)* [1939] 2 All ER 400, CA.
13 RSC Ord 71, r 9(2): *Société Coopérative Sidmetal v Titan International Ltd* [1966] 1 QB 828 at 830.

Objection 1: Absence of jurisdiction in the original court

ABSENCE OF DOMESTIC COMPETENCE

3.34 Both schemes are designed to exclude the registration of judgments given by courts which lacked competence. Thus registration may not be made or, if made, can be set aside, under the 1920 scheme where 'the original court acted without jurisdiction'.[1] Registration under the 1933 scheme must be set aside if the registering court 'is satisfied . . . that the courts of the country of the original court had no jurisdiction in the circumstances of the case.'[2] On their face, both statutes cover absence of jurisdiction under the conflicts rules of the requested state and under the domestic law of the original court. The point appears not to have arisen for decision. Even if the schemes are treated as embodying the common law,[3] it is not beyond doubt that both types of jurisdictional objection may be raised.[4] Whilst there is no unanimity amongst commentators about a requirement of local competence[5], the better view, consistent with principle and with the purpose of the legislation, is that a judgment which is a nullity for want of competence over the defendant or the cause of action under the law of the place of origin should not be enforceable under the schemes.[6] On the other hand, if the judgment is impaired by some irregularity of procedure or mistake, it should be treated as voidable, requiring further proceedings in the original jurisdiction if it is to be rendered void, and should be capable of registration until such proceedings are taken.[7] This viewpoint, strongly pressed by Read both in his writings[8] and before the Conference of Commissioners of Uniformity of Legislation in Canada,[9] was influential upon the drafting of the model Canadian Act which, in this respect, has been widely adopted in Canada. In consequence, a judgment must be refused registration there if made:

'without authority, under the law of the original court, to adjudicate concerning the cause of action or subject-matter that resulted in the judgment or concerning the person of the judgment debtor . . .'.[10]

This, it is suggested, should be the conclusion to be drawn even in absence of this declaratory provision.

1 AJA, s 9(2)(a).
2 FJREA, s 4(1)(a)(iii).
3 Eg Greer Committee Report, p 62.
4 The domestic competence requirement appears to have been thought necessary in *Castrique v Imrie* (1870) LR 4 HL 414 at 429, per Blackburn J and at 448, per Lord Chelmsford, but, semble not in *Vanquelin v Bouard* (1863) 15 CB NS 341, 33 LJCP 78 and *Pemberton v Hughes* [1899] 1 Ch 781, 68 LJ Ch 281.
5 Dicey and Morris, op cit, pp 1080–1081 suggest that this objection cannot be taken 'in general'.
6 Cf FJREA, s 1(2)(b); para 3.18 above. See Cheshire and North, op cit, pp 653–655; Castel, op cit, pp 448–452; Nygh op cit, pp 90–92.
7 Ibid. This may be the explanation of *Vanquelin v Bouard*, above, and *Pemberton v Hughes*, above.
8 H. Read, op cit, p 100.
9 *1958 Proceedings*, p 90.
10 Eg Alberta, R-6, s 2(6)(a).

ABSENCE OF INTERNATIONAL COMPETENCE

3.35 There is no question that the original court must have been competent to adjudicate under the conflict of laws rules of the requested state. Those rules are not expressly identified under the 1920 Act, leaving the matter, for the most part, to be determined by reference to the general law.[1] The 1933 Act, however, contains detailed provisions in respect of actions in personam, actions in rem and those where the subject was immovable property.[2] In other matters, the general conflict of laws of the requested state must be resorted to.[3] Although this Act provides that the original court shall be 'deemed' to have jurisdiction in the stated cases, this is probably intended to mean no more than that these rules which involve minor divergences from the common law must be given effect and not the common law. Accordingly the statute is to be treated as containing an exclusive list of grounds.[4] Efforts to extend these grounds to allow recognition of exorbitant jurisdictional bases common to both the original and requested systems on the basis of comity or reciprocity have not succeeded.[5]

Apart from the question of the jurisdictional grounds, the two schemes diverge in another major way. The 1920 Act will not permit registration where there is an absence of jurisdiction *or* where:

'the judgment debtor, being a person who was neither carrying on business nor ordinarily resident within the jurisdiction of the original court, did not voluntarily appear or otherwise submit or agree to submit to the jurisdiction of that court.'[6]

It follows, therefore, that registration must be refused, even when jurisdiction exists, if this latter condition is not met. Thus, for example, if the action is one concerning immovable property which is situated in the original jurisdiction, the debtor must also have been carrying on business or been ordinarily resident there or have voluntarily appeared, submitted or agreed to submit. Similar considerations must be applied if the matter is a matrimonial proceeding in which jurisdiction is founded upon domicile.

The 1933 Act, however, introduces appearance, submission, agreement to submit, as well as place of business and residence, only into the jurisdictional requirements for actions in personam.[7] Such considerations cannot be raised in relation to actions in rem or to those concerning immovable property or matters of personal status, where a different jurisdictional basis will suffice.

1 AJA, s 9(2)(a) contains certain implicit provisions: see below.
2 FJEA, s 4(2)(a) and (b).
3 Ibid, s 4(2)(c).
4 *Société Coopérative Sidmetal v Titan International Ltd* [1966] 1 QB 828, [1965] 3 All ER 494; *Sharps Commercials Ltd v Gas Turbines Ltd* [1956] NZLR 819; *Crick v Hennessy* [1973] WAR 74.
5 Inclusion of such grounds was initially contemplated by the Greer Committee, Minutes 7 and 17 December 1931 LCO/2, Doc No 1690. The position seems to be the same at common law. See Denning LJ, in *Re Dulles Settlement (No 2), Dulles v Vidler* [1951] Ch 842, [1951] 2 All ER 69, CA. But orse, see *Malaysia-Singapore Airlines Ltd v Parker* (1972) 3 SASR 300 in respect of the South Australian, Foreign Judgments Act 1971, s 5(1).
6 AJA, s 9(2)(b).
7 FJREA, s 4(2)(a).

TIME AT WHICH THE JURISDICTIONAL LINK MUST EXIST

3.36 Neither scheme gives comprehensive indication of the time at which the jurisdictional link must have existed. The 1920 Act is quite silent but the 1933 Act requires that residence or, in the case of a body corporate, the principal place of business must be held 'at the time when the proceedings were instituted',[1] that submission agreements must have been made 'before the commencement of the proceedings'.[2] In the case of actions in rem involving movable property and those actions involving immovable property, the property must be situate within the jurisdiction 'at the time of the proceedings'.[3] It is also apparent that appearance or submission may be only evidenced by the defendant's conduct in relation to the proceedings when commenced.[4] In the general run of events, however, it seems likely that under both Acts the required state of affairs must exist at the time when the proceedings were commenced[5] and certainly not when the cause of action arose, as has been suggested in respect of the Canadian scheme.[6] To the latter statement, there is one partial exception under the 1933 statute under which in personam jurisdiction can exist where the proceedings relate to a transaction effected through an office or place of business which was situated in the original country.[7] This transaction must have occurred before the institution of proceedings.[8]

A subsequent change of circumstances will not break the jurisdictional link. So, for example, where residence is terminated after the proceedings have been instituted, an ensuing default judgment may be registered, always provided that the required notice or service provisions have been complied with.[9]

1 FJREA, s 4(2)(a)(iv).
2 Ibid, s 4(2)(b).
3 Ibid, s 4(2)(a)(iii).
4 Ibid, s 4(2)(a)(i)–(ii).
5 Cf *Hill v Bank of Montreal* (1980) 14 Alta LR (2d) 178; *Citizen's Finance Co v O'Leary* (1979) 28 NBR (2d) 208; *Gardikiotis v Douglas Benoit Ltd* (1981) 10 Man R (2d) 361; *Re Royal Bank of*

Canada and Industmarine Ltd [1982] 3 WWR 449 (BC); *Whalen, Friesen and Friesen v Neal* (1982) 40 NBR (2d) 457; *Tunku Abaidah v Tan Boon Hoe* [1935] FMSLR 63.

6 *Wiegand v Calgary Joint Venture Ltd* [1979] 2 WWR 671 (Alta).

7 FJREA, s 4(2)(a)(v).

8 References to 'proceedings', when the term is unqualified, relate to the whole course of the litigation on the subject matter, from first instance through any appeal: *SA Consortium General Textiles v Sun and Sand Agencies Ltd* [1978] 2 All ER 339, CA at 362, per Shaw LJ.

9 AJA, s 9(2)(c); FJREA, s 4(1)(a)(iii).

Jurisdictional links

(a) ACTIONS IN PERSONAM

3·37 It is necessary for the requested court to classify the original action for the purpose of establishing jurisdiction: for it is the nature of the action and not the judgment which determines which jurisdictional rules apply.[1] In this context, an action in personam may be taken to be an action to determine questions relating to rights of parties as between themselves and to impose obligations inter partes. The 1933 Act, however, expressly excludes from this category any matrimonial cause or any proceedings in connection with matrimonial matters, the administration of estates, bankruptcy, winding-up of companies, lunacy or guardianship—matters which are usually governed by their own jurisdictional rules.[2] The great preponderance of money judgments will fall within this general head.

The 1933 Act specifies five jurisdictional bases which alone may be relied upon in respect of actions in personam.[3] No other ground may be invoked, whatever the position at common law.[4] As these are, for the most part, statements of accepted common law grounds,[5] some reliance upon them for the purpose of the 1920 Act may be thought to be appropriate, in the absence of any similar statement in that legislation. In reality, however, the treatment of jurisdictional questions under that Act, as we have seen,[6] is considerably affected by other provisions. Unless he was carrying on business or was ordinarily resident in the original country, the debtor must be shown to have voluntarily appeared or otherwise submitted to the jurisdiction or agreed to do so.[7] In the context of in personam actions, these provisions can be treated as indicating the jurisdictional grounds which may be relied upon. For the purposes of the 1920 scheme, therefore, submission, whether by appearance or otherwise, or agreement to submit must be established in every case where ordinary residence or the carrying on of business are not found. As these are all jurisdictional grounds generally accepted in the Commonwealth, there will be little point in seeking to introduce others, such as nationality[8] or presence when served[9] or availability of assets,[10] or service out of the jurisdiction[11] which have sometimes been suggested or relied upon in other types of recognition proceedings.

The common characteristic of the grounds under both statutes is a personal connection between the original debtor[12] and the original court or law area. Jurisdiction cannot be established merely by reason of the cause of action arising in that place.

1 *Re Van der Kreek's Marriage* [1979] PNGLR 185.

2 FJREA, s 11(2).

3 Ibid, s 4(2)(a).

4 *Société Coopérative Sidmetal v Titan International Ltd* [1966] 1 QB 828, [1965] 3 All ER 494; *Sharps Commercials Ltd v Gas Turbines Ltd* [1956] NZLR 819; *Coast Lines Ltd v Hudig and Veder Chartering NV* [1972] 2 QB 34 at 45.

5 Greer Committee Report, p 62.

6 Para 3.35 above.
7 AJA, s 9(2)(b).
8 *Emanuel v Symon* [1908] 1 KB 302 at 309; Castel, op cit, pp 427–429; Read, op cit, pp 151–155.
9 *Carrick v Hancock* (1895) 12 TLR 59.
10 *Becquet v McCarthy* (1831) 2 B & Ad 951, now doubted as a basis: *Sirdar Gurdyal Singh v Rajah of Faridkote* [1894] AC 670 PC, at 685.
11 *Turnbull v Walker* (1892) 67 LT 767 (refusing recognition). It makes no difference that the service rules are the same as in the requested state: *Re Trepca Mines Ltd* [1960] 1 WLR 1273, CA, at 1281–1282, per Hodson LJ; *Henry v Geoprosco International Ltd* [1976] QB 726, CA at 745.
12 FJREA, s 4(2)(a) emphasis that the original defendant must satisfy the jurisdictional links, no matter who is now 'the debtor' for the purpose of the registration process.

3.38 *(i) Voluntary appearance.* Both the Acts accept as a jurisdictional base 'voluntary appearance' in the proceedings before the original court.[1] It may be presumed that the term 'appearance' is principally used in the technical sense which prevailed in English practice until 1979, comprising the formal response by a party upon whom the original process was served, whether within or outside the jurisdiction, which both acknowledges service and indicates the defendant's answer.[2] Steps taken by the defendant under procedures permitted by the original court which have a similar result will be treated as appearances.[3] If the defendant formally notifies that he intends, or does not intend, to defend the action on its merits or otherwise makes clear that he is prepared for the court to adjudicate the merits, he will be treated as having submitted to the court's jurisdiction.[4] Actual participation in the hearing is then immaterial. Notification on his behalf by a duly authorised attorney or legal representative will have the same consequence.[5]

Appearance will also occur where the defendant challenges the judgment by an appeal on its merits, although he may not have appeared in the original proceedings.[6] On principle, the same appears to be the case where the defendant applies unsuccessfully to set aside a default judgment on a matter going to the merits.[7] For in both instances, the defendant has impliedly acknowledged the authority of the court to deal with the matter in issue. But where appearance has been withdrawn with the leave of the original court, there is no submission.[8] Generally, however, appearance once made is irrevocable and will not be affected by the defendant's subsequent decision to withdraw.[9]

In all cases, however, the appearance must be 'voluntary'. Whether it is such is a matter of fact and it is for the defendant to establish that it was not.[10] It clearly will not be so if the appearance was engendered by fraud, mistake, or compulsion through physical or similar threats to the defendant. Where, however, the defendant's decision is motivated by his concern for his assets within the jurisdiction of the original court, the position is in some respects less clear. If the defendant appears merely because he fears that, if he does not defend the action, local assets of his will be liable to seizure on a default judgment, it is perhaps excessive to treat his appearance as involuntary.[11] On the other hand, where his purpose in coming to court is either to question an existing seizure of his property, particularly if done in order to found the jurisdiction of the court or as security for satisfaction of the resulting judgment, or to prevent proceedings directed toward seizure of particular property going against him by default, different considerations arise. It is difficult to see the justification for permitting the registration of a *money judgment* arising from such proceedings. Common law has tended to treat the former of these two cases as involuntary and the latter as voluntary[12] and has been rightly criticised for the distinction.[13] On the advice of the Greer Committee, provision was introduced into the 1933 scheme under which appearance for 'the purpose of protecting, or obtaining the release of, property seized, or threatened with seizure, in the proceedings' does not constitute submission. Arguably, this should only apply to property already controlled by the court and not to any assets which might be seized after judgment.[14] The terms seem to be designed to provide, for example, for the case where the defendant in an action in rem appears to obtain release of his ship or other res, as a result of which the action becomes one in personam.

A much more controversial case relates to appearance in order to contest the jurisdiction of the original court. Again the 1933 Act explicitly treats this as involuntary appearance.[15] The 1920 Act, however, must presumably be construed by reference to the common law which on some views treats such interventions as voluntary actions, in reliance upon the much criticised cases of *Harris v Taylor*[16] and *Henry v Geoprosco International Ltd.*[17] It may be doubted whether these cases have conclusively settled the basic question; the latter case left open the question where the sole purpose of appearance was to protest the jurisdiction. At best, they are authority for the view that there is voluntary appearance where, by a conditional appearance to make application to set aside an order for service out of the jurisdiction, the defendant invites the court in its discretion not to exercise the jurisdiction which it has under its local law and the appearance becomes unconditional on the failure of the application. The defendant took his chance and must accept the consequences. How far this represents the law in other jurisdictions is unclear. A similar view was taken in New South Wales[18] but reservations have recently been expressed in the Canadian courts.[19] It is unfortunate if the issue of submission turns upon the requested court's perception of the effects of conditional appearances before the original court. As has been pertinently pointed out,[20] the purpose and safeguards which such an appearance may have where it is made may not be given the same effect elsewhere.

Since the risks of appearing at all in order to protest jurisdiction are considerable,[21] it is scarcely surprising that statutory intervention has been found to be necessary. The United Kingdom has applied the 1933 rule to all foreign judgments including those to be registered under the 1920 Act.[22] In addition, a new provision makes clear that there is no submission where there is appearance:

> 'to ask the court to dismiss or stay the proceedings on the ground that the dispute in question should be submitted to arbitration or to the determination of the courts of another country.'[23]

Even without this provision, such circumstances might properly be included amongst the cases which do not constitute voluntary appearance.[24]

1 AJA, s 9(2)(b); FJREA, s 4(2)(a)(i).

2 Replaced by 'acknowledgement of service': RSC Ord 12. Cf *Brockley Cabinet Co Ltd v Pears* (1972) 20 FLR 332 (ACT).

3 *Overseas Food Importers and Distributors Ltd and Brandt* (1981) 126 DLR (3d) 422 (BCCA) where a letter of explanation by the debtor, duly served to the Consul General, directed to the court and read there, was treated as an appearance.

4 *Bank of Bermuda Ltd v Stutz* [1965] 2 OR 121.

5 *United States of America v Cassidy* (1977) 79 DLR (3d) 635 (BC). *Re AG of British Columbia and Becker* (1978) 87 DLR (3d) 536. But semble not if the agent acts in error or without authority: *Redhead v Readhead and Crothers* [1926] NLZR 131; *MacFarlane v Briggs* (1977) 18 APR 153 (NB).

6 *SA Consortium General Textiles v Sun and Sand Agencies Ltd* [1978] QB 279, [1978] 2 All ER 339, CA.
7 Dicey and Morris, op cit p 1047, referring to *Guiard v De Clermont and Donner* [1914] 3 KB 145, 83 LJKB 1407. Criticisms are also entered upon early Canadian decisions to the contrary: eg *Esdale v Bank of Otawa* (1920) 51 DLR 485 (Alta).
8 *Macfarlane v Briggs* (1977) 18 APR 153 (NB); *Malaysia-Singapore Airlines v Parker* (1972) 3 SASR 300.
9 Ibid.
10 *Richardson v Allen* (1916) 28 DLR 134 (Alta); *Baldwin & Co v Smith* (1911) 18 WLR 207 (Sask).
11 *Voinet v Barrett* (1855) LJQB 39, CA; *De Cosse Brissac v Rathbone* (1861) 6 H & N 301, 30 LJ Ex 238; *Poissant v Poissant* [1941] 3 WWR 646. The mere fact that property of the defendant has been seized in a case which he defends on its merits will not render the appearance involuntary: *Huntingdon v Marion* (1925) 29 OWN 187.
12 *Voinet v Barrett,* above; *Henry v Geoprosco International* [1976] QB 726, CA at 746–747.
13 Cheshire and North, op cit, p 638; Castel, op cit, p 435. Commentators are not agreed which incorporates the desirable principle: P. A. Stone, (1983) 32 ICLQ 477 at p 491.
14 FJREA, s 4(2)(a)(i); Greer Committee Report, pp 62–63. See now Civil Jurisdiction and Judgments Act 1982, s 33(1)(c) (UK): P. A. Stone, loc cit, note 13 above.
15 Ibid; *Dovenmuehle v Rocca Group Ltd* (1981) 85 APR 444 (NB), applying Foreign Judgments Act, RSNB, 1973, R–19 in similar terms.
16 [1915] 2 KB 580, 84 LJKB 1839, CA questioned in *Re Dulles Settlement (No 2) Dulles v Vidler* [1951] Ch 842 at 851 per Denning LJ.
17 [1976] QB 726, [1975] 2 All ER 702. See L. Collins, (1976) 92 LQR 268.
18 *Re A Lund & Co* (1958) 2 Syd LR 580: Nygh, op cit pp 82–83.
19 *Re McCain Foods Ltd and Agricultural Publishing Co Ltd* (1980) 103 DLR (3d) 724, on appeal at 734 (Ont), where on the conditional appearance jurisdiction was not disputed, only the form of the writ. The court was asked to adjudicate on the merits. *Dovenmuehle v Rocca Group Ltd* (1981) 85 APR 444 (NB); *Clinton v Ford* (1982) 37 OR (2d) 448 where appearance to contest jurisdiction or the validity of seizure of property stated not to constitute submission (obiter).
20 J. Swan, (1981) 13 Ottawa LR 123, at p 143.
21 See *Gorthon Invest AB v Ford Motor Co Ltd,* [1976] 2 Lloyd's Rep 720, re applications to stay proceedings in favour of arbitration.
22 Civil Jurisdiction and Judgments Act 1982, s 33(1)(a). See also, RSC Ord 12, r 8(6), introduced in 1979, which states that a defendant is not to be treated as having submitted to the jurisdiction by reason of his having given notice of intention to defend followed by an application disputing jurisdiction on grounds stated in r 8(1).
23 Ibid, s 33(1)(b).
24 *Trendtex Trading Corpn v Crédit Suisse* [1981] 3 All ER 520, HL at 532, per Lord Roskill. Cf *Williams & Glyn Bank plc v Astro Dinamico Cia Naviera SA* [1984] 1 All ER 760, [1984] 1 WLR 438 HL, on the effects of an application to dispute jurisdiction and stay proceedings in domestic law.

3.39 *(ii) Appearance as plaintiff or counter-claimant.* A person who avails himself of the processes of a foreign court to bring proceedings therein must clearly be treated as having submitted to it in respect of any determination reached by that court in those proceedings. Thus successful claims against the plaintiff by a defendant whether by cross action, counterclaim or set-off will be treated by requested courts as having been made against a person who had by his own action brought himself within the original court's jurisdiction. This is explicitly provided for in the 1933 Act and is implicitly embraced in the phrase 'otherwise submit' in the 1920 Act.[1] Under the same provisions, a defendant who brings a counterclaim or a cross-action will be treated as having submitted to the jurisdiction, if the plaintiff is successful.

1 AJA, s 9(2)(b); FJREA, s 4(2)(a)(ii).

3.40 *(iii) Agreements to submit.* The 1933 Act describes this jurisdictional ground as arising where the original defendant had, before the commencement of the proceedings, agreed, in respect of the subject matter of the proceedings, to submit to the jurisdiction of the original court or of the courts of the country of that court.[1] The 1920 Act speaks only of agreeing to submit to the jurisdiction of the original court.[2] Whilst an agreement to submit generally to the jurisdiction of the courts of a foreign country confers jurisdiction on any of its courts, the converse is not the case.[3] Thus where the agreement is confined to a designated court or courts, jurisdiction will be founded only if the proceedings are commenced therein.

If this objection is raised, it will be for the applicant who relies upon it to establish that there is an agreement in existence between the parties conferring jurisdiction on the original court.[4] Where the agreement is contained in a contract, it cannot be relied upon if that contract has no validity under its proper law or no longer has legal effect at the time the proceedings were instituted.[5] A contract in which the parties stipulate that exclusive jurisdiction is vested in particular courts is a commonly found source of this type of competence.[6]

Not all agreements, however, are of this kind. In particular, a contract is not a necessity. As will be seen below, certain agreements concerning legal processes have been held to constitute agreements to submit. Although the case law is not uniform, the courts in the Commonwealth will not as a general rule imply agreements to submit: such an agreement must be explicit.[7] There seems no reason in principle why this should not be evidenced by conduct, provided that the existence of the agreement is unequivocal. Thus a choice of law clause in favour of the law of the original country as governing the contract will not constitute submission.[8] An agreement to proceed only in accordance with the law of a particular country has been held to be insufficient.[9] Similarly, it will not be enough that a contract was entered into, or was intended to be performed, in the country or that the cause of action arose there or that the defendant was in that jurisdiction at that time,[10] or that a contract allowed an action to be brought where the writ was issued, as the parties cannot have intended universal submission,[11] or that the defendant was a shareholder in a company registered in the country.[12] In any case where submission is not patently provided for in the agreement, the objection should be sustained.

Certain types of agreement, however, have been held to be unequivocal in this respect. Thus written authority by the defendant to a lawyer to appear and confess judgment in favour of the holder of a promissory note, or to the plaintiff to enter judgment where payment is not made as required, will constitute an agreement to submit to the jurisdiction of the designated court.[13] Similarly, if the defendant, or his authorised agent, agrees to accept service of process (even substituted service) at a prescribed place within a country, jurisdiction there will be conferred. In particular, the defendant by becoming a shareholder in a company will be bound by any articles of association which provide for service of process of a designated foreign court in relation to disputes on company matters.[14] This is also the case if, in accordance with those articles, the company officers elect a domicile for this purpose on behalf of a shareholder who fails to select as required.[15] On the other hand, where a director or shareholder is deemed under the law of the foreign country to have expressly submitted in respect of an action against the corporation, jurisdiction will not normally be conferred under this head, for it does not result from the defendant's actual agreement.[16]

The position of members of a partnership in this regard has been the subject of divergent decisions. It has been suggested that a sleeping partner in a foreign firm with a place of business within the jurisdiction of a foreign court thereby agrees to submit to the jurisdiction of that court with respect to transactions conducted there by the appointed agent.[17] Such a conclusion, which is difficult to reconcile with earlier authority[18] and has not been generally followed,[19] comes close to accepting the possibility of implied agreements to submit. For that reason alone, this proposition must be doubted, despite suggested reconciliation of the authorities.[20]

Agreements to arbitrate in a particular country are usually construed as agreements to submit to the jurisdiction of the courts of that country.[21] The authorities, however, are usually concerned with the courts' supervisory jurisdiction to make an order confirming the award or making it enforceable as a judgment.[22] That such an agreement involves submission to the jurisdiction of the courts to deal with the merits of the matter may be doubted, especially if such proceedings would be in breach of the agreement to arbitrate.[23]

1 FJREA, s 4(2)(a)(iii).

2 AJA, s 9(2)(b). The Canadian legislation does not contain this reference but it will be caught by 'otherwise submit'.

3 *SA Consortium General Textiles v Sun and Sand Agencies Ltd* [1978] QB 279, [1978] 2 All ER 339.

4 *Mattar and Saba v Public Trustee* [1952] 3 DLR 399 (Alta); *Re Reciprocal Enforcement of Judgments Ordinance, Traders Group Ltd v Hopkins* (1968) 1 DLR (3d) 416, affirming 69 DLR (2d) 250.

5 *Bank of Montreal v Snoxell* (1982) 143 DLR (3d) 349.

6 *EK Motors Ltd v Volkswagen Canada Ltd* [1973] 1 WWR 466. This is a rule well established at common law: *Feyerick v Hubbard* (1902) 71 LJ KB 509, 86 LT 829; *Jeannot v Fuerst* (1909) 100 LT 816, 25 TLR 424. The clause may well have been the basis of an earlier application to stay proceedings brought in the country of registration in breach of that contract: *The Eleftheria* [1970] P 94, [1969] 2 All ER 641.

7 Implied agreement was supported in *Blohn v Desser* [1962] 2 QB 116, [1961] 3 All ER 1 and *Sfeir & Co v National Insurance Co of New Zealand Ltd* [1964] 1 Lloyd's Rep 330. See also *Jamieson v Northern Electricity Supply Corpn (Private) Ltd* 1970 SLT 113 at 116: 'not lightly to be implied' but contradicts a long series of consistent dicta and decisions: *Copin v Adamson* (1874) LR 9 Ex 345, 43 LJ Ex 161; *Sirdar Gurdyal Singh v The Rajah of Faridkote* [1894] AC 670, PC; *Emanuel v Symon* [1908] 1 KB 302, 77 LJKB 180; *Vogel v R and A Kohnstamm Ltd* [1973] QB 133, [1971] 2 All ER 1428; *Traders Group Ltd v Hopkins*, above; *Mattar and Saba v Public Trustee*, above; *Gyonyor v Sanjenko* (1971) 23 DLR (3d) 695 (Alta).

8 *Sirdar Gurdyal Singh v The Rajah of Faridkote*, above; *Dunbee Ltd v Gilman & Co (Australia) Pty Ltd* [1968] 2 Lloyd's Rep 394 (NSW).

9 *Keenco v South Australia and Territory Air Service Ltd* (1974) 8 SA SR 216.

10 *Traders Group Ltd v Hopkins*, above; *Sirdar Gurdyal Singh v The Rajah of Faridkote*, above; *Gifford v Calkin* (1911) 45 NSR 277; *Gyonyor v Sanjenko*, above.

11 *Traders Group Ltd v Hopkins*, above.

12 *Copin v Adamson*, above.

13 *Ritter v Fairfield* (1900) 32 OR 350, CA; *Metropolitan Trust and Savings Co v Osborne* (1910) 16 OWR 226; *Re Hughes and Sharpe* (1968) 70 DLR (2d) 298 (BC); *Batavia Times Publishing Co v Davis* (1978) 82 DLR (3d) 247; affd (1980) 105 DLR (3d) 192.

14 *Copin v Adamson*, above; *Bank of Australasia v Harding* (1850) 9 CB 661, 19 LJCP 345; *Bank of Australia v Nias* (1851) 16 QB 717, 20 LJQB 284.

15 *Copin v Adamson*, above. Cf *Carveth v Railway Asbestos Packing Co* (1913) 4 OWN 872, on election of domicile.

16 *Veco Drilling Inc v Armstrong* [1982] 1 WWR 177 (BC).

17 *Blohn v Desser* [1962] 2 QB 116, [1961] 3 All ER 1.

18 *Emanuel v Symon* (1908] 1 KB 302, 77 LJKB 180, CA.

19 *Vogel v R and A Kohnstamm Ltd* [1973] QB 133, [1971] 2 All ER 1428.

20 Dicey and Morris, op cit, p 1052, suggesting that *Emanuel v Symons* could be read as concerned with the relationship of the partners, whilst *Blohn v Desser* concerns third parties. The latter decision had been widely criticised: P. S. C. Lewis, (1961) 10 ICLQ 910; I. H. Jacobs, (1961) Camb LJ 184; E. J. Cohn, (1962) 11 ICLQ 583; P. R. H. Webb, (1962) 25 MLR 96.

21 *Tracomin SA v Sudan Oil Seeds Co Ltd (No 2)* [1983] 3 All ER 140, [1983] 1 WLR 1026, CA.

22 *International Alltex Corpn v Lawler Creations Ltd* [1965] IR 264.

23 Para 3.48 below.

3.41 *(iv) Residence.* The 1920 Act by implication recognises jurisdiction where the defendant was 'ordinarily resident'.[1] The 1933 Act is more explicit, not only providing for 'residence' of the defendant at the time of the institution of proceedings but in making clear, in the case of corporate bodies, that the equivalent is to be its principal place of business.[2]

Does the use of 'ordinarily' in the earlier statute constitute a more demanding test? There are authorities which suggest that, in the case of individuals, 'residence' simpliciter may involve little more than actual presence in the jurisdiction when the proceedings began.[3] If that is the case, 'ordinarily resident' which requires some continuing connection will be more stringent. On the other hand, the distinction is drawn elsewhere, for example between presence and residence for purposes of service out of the jurisdiction,[4] and, given the criticism of founding jurisdiction on the basis of a mere transitory connection with a country,[5] there must be doubt that presence alone is intended by this explicit reference to 'residence' in the legislation, whatever the position at common law.[6] In that case, it will be unnecessary to distinguish 'residence' from 'ordinary residence'.

The term is generally used to connote physical presence in a country with some intention, and some element, of continuity or regularity, unaffected by occasional temporary absences. It arises where the defendant has his usual place of living, that more regularly used than other places.[7] Yet there is little doubt that residence of this kind can be established in more than one place.[8]

In the case of an individual, the connection can only be made by that individual through his personal presence. Residence cannot be acquired via an agent or through a partner carrying on business on the individual's behalf.[9] It will end if he leaves in circumstances which indicate he is unlikely to return.[10]

In the case of corporations, the 1920 Act will presumably be construed by reference to the common law. There, a corporation is generally held to be resident or ordinarily resident where its central management and control are exercised.[11] Difficulties in cases where control is divided between countries[12] are unlikely to affect this scheme. For in practice, jurisdiction may more readily be founded on the carrying on of business.[13]

The 1933 scheme requires that the corporation must have its 'principal place of business' in the country. By its terms, this suggests that there can only be one such place. Presumably that is the place where the central management and control are actually carried out, rather than the place of incorporation or even that of a nominal 'head' office. But as with residence, it is possible, though exceptional, for this to take place to an equal extent in more than one country. In such a case, there seems no escaping from the conclusion that a company has more than one principal place of residence.[14]

1 AJA, s 9(2)(b).
2 FJREA, s 4(2)(a)(iv).
3 Eg *Herman v Meallin* (1891) 8 WN (NSW) 38; *Carrick v Hancock* (1895) 12 TLR 59; *Forbes v Simmons* (1914) 20 DLR 100; Castel, op cit, p 430.
4 RSC Ord 11, r 1(1)(c) which requires ordinary residence in contrast when Ord 10, r 1 which implicitly allows personal service on a transient defendant. See also, *Colt Industries Inc v Sarlie* [1966] 1 All ER 673, [1966] 1 WLR 440, CA; *Maharanee of Baroda v Wildenstein* [1972] 2 QB 283, [1972] 2 All ER 689, CA.
5 Eg Dicey and Morris, op cit, p 1053. See now the position under the EEC Convention on Jurisdiction and the Enforcement of Judgments on Civil and Commercial Matters, art 2 which treats this as exorbitant jurisdiction which may no longer be applied: Civil Jurisdiction and Judgments Act 1982, s 2.

6 *Marshall v Houghton* [1923] 2 WWR 553 (Man) treated 'residence' in this way.
7 *Re Reciprocal Enforcement of Judgments Act, Re Duncan and Hirsch* [1952] 3 DLR 850; J. D. McClean, (1962) 11 ICLQ 1153 at pp 1161–1166.
8 *Canton Trust and Commercial Bank Ltd v Wong* (1968) 89 WN (Pt 1) NSW 189. Dicey and Morris, op cit, p 1053 refer to cases where the defendant has come into a country either as a result of force or fraud against him. Even if jurisdiction on the basis of presence was taken by the original court, it may be doubted whether 'residence' in the sense here suggested will have been established.
9 *Seegner v Marks* (1895) 21 VLR 491.
10 *Re Duncan and Hirsch*, above.
11 Cf *De Beers Consolidated Mines Ltd v Howe* [1906] AC 455, 75 LJKB 858, HL; *Sfeir & Co v National Insurance Co of New Zealand Ltd* [1964] 1 Lloyd's Rep 330.
12 *Swedish Central Rly Co Ltd v Thompson* [1925] AC 495, 94 LJKB 527, HL; *Egyptian Delta Land and Investment Co v Todd* [1929] AC 1, 98 LJKB 1, HL.
13 *Sfeir & Co v National Insurance Co of New Zealand Ltd*, above; *Littauer Glove Corpn v F. W. Millington (1920) Ltd* (1928) 44 TLR 746: para 3.42 below.
14 Dicey and Morris, op cit, pp 728–729.

3.42 *(v) Carrying on business (1920 scheme only).* Referred to only in the 1920 Act,[1] this head, unlike at common law, is applicable not only to corporations but to individuals and to partnerships.[2] The link must be present at the time the proceedings are instituted.[3]

In construing these provisions, it has been suggested that the authorities relating to the assumption of jurisdiction over foreign corporations can be relied upon.[4] But there must be consistency with the application of the requirement to individuals. What is clear from these cases is that this link may be established without the debtor himself being physically present in the jurisdiction at the time. For his business can be carried on by others undertaking business activities there on his behalf. It is also apparent that the phrase 'carrying on' implies some element of regularity in the activities. As far as corporations are concerned, it has been held that this calls for 'a definite and to some reasonable extent permanent place' within the jurisdiction.[5] In the case of individuals normally resident outside the jurisdiction, periodic visits to seek orders to be fulfilled outside the jurisdiction for delivery in the jurisdiction will probably not be enough.[6] The connection must be of a more substantial nature. In all cases there must be evidence of activities of a business nature in the country in question. This will usually involve the making of contracts there which will be performed there or which at least give rise to liabilities on the defendant there. Accordingly, the soliciting of orders by agents will constitute carrying on of business, if, for example, they have an exclusive sales agency and a local office through which they promote the defendant's interests[7] but not if they lack authority to make contracts.[8] Mere presence of a representative will be insufficient if no local business is actually transacted through him. The ownership of a factory for which rents are received and the conduct of business correspondence through a box number in the jurisdiction have been treated as sufficient.[9]

In the context of the enforcement legislation, recent Canadian decisions have usefully suggested that three elements should normally be looked for. There must be activities in the country which occupy the time, attention and labour of the defendant or his servants or employees, they must involve the incurring of liabilities on the defendant's behalf to other persons there, and they must be undertaken for profit or for the purpose of a livelihood by the defendant.[10] This approach is consistent with the only English authority on the Act in which jurisdiction over an externally-based corporation was held not to be established by the activities of a local firm in settling insurance claims which involve the exercise by them of a limited authority to bind the defendant. For the activities were undertaken for their own business purposes and not those of the defendant.[11] In a decision of liberal application in Canada, the requirements were met by activities of an external trading firm, with no agent, office, place of business or employees in the law area, which used on hire a local trading firm 'as needed as called' to perform services in the law area for customers there, on average once a month over the previous year.[12] It may be suggested that a more substantial link between the debtor or his servants or employees and the law area is called for than is implied in this decision.

1 AJA, s 9(2)(b), doubted as a distinct jurisdictional head: *Canadian Credit Men's Trust Association Ltd v Ryan* [1930] 1 DLR 280 (Alta).
2 *Re Tangye and Smith Ltd v Pelican Carbon Co* [1935] 1 DLR 759 (Ont); *Miller v BC Turf Ltd* (1969) 8 DLR (3d) 383 (BC). Common law appears to confine this head to corporations: ibid.
3 *Re Royal Bank of Canada and Industmarine Ltd* [1982] 3 WWR 449 (BC).
4 *Littauer Glove Corpn v F. W. Millington (1920) Ltd* (1928) 44 TLR 746; *Vogel v R. and A. Kohnstamm Ltd* [1973] QB 133, [1971] 2 All ER 1428.
5 Ibid.
6 *Re Tangye and Smith Ltd v Pelican Carbon Co*, above.
7 *Moore v Mercator Enterprises Ltd* (1978) 90 DLR (3d) 590.
8 *Vogel v R. and A. Kohnstamm Ltd*, above.
9 *Canton Trust and Commercial Bank Ltd v Wong* (1968) 89 WN (Pt 1) NSW 189.
10 *Miller v BC Turf Ltd*, above, applying *Re Pszon* [1946] 2 DLR 506 (Ont); *Moore v Mercator Enterprises Ltd*, above.
11 *Sfeir & Co v National Insurance Co of New Zealand Ltd* [1964] 1 Lloyd's Rep 330.
12 *McLellan v Elwood's Ltd* (1980) 70 APR 358 (NB).

3·43 *(vi) Office or place of business (1933 scheme only).* Jurisdiction will be founded under the 1933 legislation if the debtor had an office or place of business in the country of the original court and the proceedings in that court were in respect of a transaction effected through or at that office or place.[1] This is not a common law link, although the Greer Committee believed that at the most the provision was only a rational extension, presumably, of the carrying on of business link, which the Act does not allow.[2]

No authority in which this provision has been examined has been traced. The existence of an office or place of business of the debtor at the time of the transaction should give rise to few problems. But, Dicey and Morris point out,[3] there is an element of imprecision concerning the circumstances in which a transaction should be held to be effected through or at an office or place of business. If, as implied above, this condition is an extension of the carrying on of business factor, it should only be fulfilled where the transaction relates to the business activities of the defendant and is one undertaken in that connection by the defendant or by his agents, servants or employees. It should not be enough that the defendant entered into a purely personal transaction whilst at his office on an overseas visit.

1 FJREA, s 4(2)(a)(v).
2 Greer Committee Report, p 63.
3 Op cit, pp 1054–55.

(b) ACTIONS INVOLVING IMMOVABLES AND ACTIONS IN REM INVOLVING MOVABLES

3·44 The 1933 Act specifies a different jurisdictional link for cases where the original proceedings were concerned with an action the subject matter of which was immovables or with an action in rem of which the subject matter was movable.[1] Such a link will also be required in similar cases when arising under the 1920 Act in so far as it represents the common law but, as indicated earlier,[2] that Act demands in addition the fulfilment of certain requirements which are normally associated with in personam actions.

It should be again stressed that the registering court, which is required to classify the original proceedings for purposes of jurisdiction, is concerned with the nature of the original *action* and not of the resulting judgment.[3] Although the Commonwealth schemes are concerned with the enforcement of money judgments which give rise to obligations which are classically in personam, the legislation accepts that these may derive from actions which were not in personam or which were brought to settle claims over immovables. The jurisdictional requirements under the schemes must relate to the circumstances when the original court assumed jurisdiction over the matter and be consistent with the common law in that regard.

The 1933 Act states the jurisdictional link as requiring the property in question in either case to be situate in the country[4] of the original court 'at the time of the proceedings'. Where the property is movable, it seems probable that it must be situate in the country at the commencement of proceedings and not throughout,[5] especially where the debtor has provided security for its release. The Greer Committee was of the view that the statutory provision represented the common law in respect of actions in rem but went beyond existing law with respect to actions over immovable property, though not unreasonably in the light of its direct jurisdictional rules on the matter.[6] This extension now seems to be accepted by commentators and judiciary,[7] and will doubtless apply similarly to such matters when arising under the 1920 Act.

The application of these provisions is not without problems. Thus, for example, service ex juris is often permitted in respect of 'a claim or contract affecting land' situate in the country from which service was issued.[8] If these cases fall within the category of 'actions of which the subject matter was immovable property', jurisdiction will be established and an ensuing money judgment will be registrable. This is surely not the correct construction. The provision is concerned, it may be suggested, with claims which are specifically directed to immovables, as for example, to determine claims to title or possession of the land in question, especially to secure a judgment or order in rem, or which seek specifically the settlement of the whole or any part of it.[9] It is only in such cases that it seems correct to speak of the immovables as being 'the subject matter' of the action. Accordingly, the provisions do not extend to cases where the proceedings are concerned with claims for damages arising from trespass or other torts affecting land not involving such issues or where the court has power to order settlement of land as an order ancillary to the central claim of the proceedings.[10] In the former case, the proceedings will be treated as in personam proceedings and, unless there has been submission, the ensuing judgment will not be registrable.[11] In the latter case, the jurisdictional link will depend upon the nature of the original action.[12] One consequence of this view is that actions with respect to torts affecting land *outside* the original jurisdiction are not governed by these jurisdictional requirements but will be treated in the same way as other in personam judgments.[13]

Actions in rem the subject of which is movable property will arise in Admiralty where a claim is made against a ship, aircraft, hovercraft or any cargo or freight. Such proceedings may result in the sale of the res and the application of the proceeds to the satisfaction of the claim.[14] To found jurisdiction, the res must be in the country of the original court at the time of the proceedings, which may, of course, be occasioned by the arrest of the res itself.

It is, however, usually open to the defendant, in order to avoid the arrest or to obtain release of the res, to make a payment into court to provide security from which any judgment or order can be met. Under English law, if the defendant submits to the jurisdiction by appearance, the action proceeds no longer as an action in rem but as one in personam.[15] As we have seen, however, appearance to obtain the release of property threatened with seizure is not treated as submission to the jurisdiction for in personam actions, at least under the 1933 scheme.[16] If this appearance is to be treated as inadequate by the requested court for purpose of in personam jurisdiction, it may be difficult for that court to accept the reclassification of the action by the original court. On such an argument, provided the res was in the original country at the time of the proceedings but not otherwise,[17] jurisdiction will exist under this provision. On the other hand, if the reclassification of the action is accepted on the basis of the appearance, it seems a little illogical for the requested court to treat the appearance as involuntary and require another in personam jurisdictional link. Yet the Act would require this conclusion. But if the movables are not within the jurisdiction when the proceedings are undertaken because they have been released or were not arrested, there are good arguments for the requested court to accept the original court's reclassification of the action as in personam and, as in any such case, to require an appropriate link, other than the appearance to obtain the release or to prevent the arrest. This seems the stronger view.

In the case of the 1920 Act, if the action is treated as one in rem, the defendant must be shown also to have voluntarily appeared or agreed to submit, unless he was ordinarily resident or carrying on business in the jurisdiction.[18]

1 FJREA, s 4(2)(b).
2 Para 3.35 above.
3 *Re Van der Kreek's Marriage* [1979] PNGLR 185; *Re A Judgment, McCormac v Gardner* [1937] NZLR 517 at 519.
4 'Country', in a federal context, is limited to the area having its distinct conflict of laws system.
5 Cf *Brockley Cabinet Co Ltd v Pears* (1972) 20 FLR 333, on 'proceedings'.
6 Greer Committee Report, p 63.
7 Dicey and Morris, op cit, p 1068; Cheshire and North, op cit, p 645; Nygh, op cit, pp 84–85: *Re Trepca Mines Ltd* [1960] 3 All ER 304n, [1960] 1 WLR 1273
8 RSC Ord 11, r 1(1)(b). But cf r 1(1)(c) which allows ex juris service where the whole subject matter is land.
9 *Re Van der Kreek's Marriage*, above.
10 Ibid.
11 *Re A Judgment, McCormac v Gardner*, above.
12 Para 3.45 below.
13 Subject to FJREA, s 4(3)(a); para 3.46 below. Jurisdiction to hear such matters, which was doubted in *British South Africa Co v Companhia de Moçambique* [1893] AC 602, 63 LJQB 70 and *Hesperides Hotels v Muftizade* [1979] AC 508, [1978] 2 All ER 1168, HL has now been conferred upon English courts: Civil Jurisdiction and Judgments Act 1982, s 30.
14 Castel, op cit, ch 10. Cf RSC Ord 75.
15 *The August 8* [1983] 2 AC 450, [1983] 2 WLR 419, PC, following *The Gemma* [1899] P 285 at 292.
16 Para 3.38 above.
17 Para 3.36 above.
18 AJA, s 9(2)(b); para 3.35 above.

(c) OTHER CATEGORIES OF ACTIONS

3.45 In respect of actions, other than the actions designated as in personam, those of which the subject matter is immovables or actions in rem the subject matter of which is movable property, the original court will be deemed to have had jurisdiction if its jurisdiction 'is recognised by the law of the registering court'.[1] Attempts have been made to found jurisdiction under this provision in respect of in personam actions on grounds not set out in the statute but alleged to exist under the general law of the requested state. The view correctly taken has been that actions which fall within the earlier categories are governed exclusively by those provisions. Actions falling outside those provisions even though they lead to judgments in personam will be governed by this requirement.[2] Some guidance as to the kinds of matter which may be brought under this head is given by the proceedings excluded by the 1933 Act from actions in personam—matrimonial causes, proceedings in connection with matrimonial matters, administration of the estates of deceased persons, bankruptcy, winding up of companies, lunacy or guardianship of infants.[3] In addition, proceedings involving movables, which are not strictly actions in rem or in personam and those concerned with personal status, not covered by the cases mentioned in the earlier provision, will be subject to this rule. In most instances, the ensuing judgment will not be within the schemes as sums of money will not be payable. But payments may be ordered as ancillary to these judgments, for example, by way of costs or as maintenance or even damages in domestic proceedings. Such orders will be judgments or orders in personam, although the actions from which they ensued were not in personam. In the questionable decision of Scrutton L. J. in *Phillips v Batho*,[4] an award of damages against a co-respondent in divorce proceedings in India was held to be a judgment enforceable by action in England. Jurisdiction was founded, in respect of the matrimonial cause, on the basis of the domicile of the husband and wife. This led to an order dissolving the marriage which was a judgment in rem conclusive everywhere. In the court's opinion, the order for damages being ancillary to that should also be recognised. This conclusion has been criticised by the judiciary and commentators alike[5] who assert that the order being in personam required the fulfilment of the appropriate jurisdictional rules by the defendant, in this case by submission, which had not occurred.

The 1933 Act, however, may well approach the matter in a different way.[6] For whatever the status of the resulting judgment, for the purposes of jurisdiction it is the status of the original proceedings which is in point. An order made in matrimonial proceedings, by the terms of the statute, is not an action in personam. Under section 4(2)(c), therefore, the requested court must determine whether the jurisdiction exercised by the original court in the type of proceedings in question is recognised by the law of the requested state. Where the party against whom the order to pay was made is also a party to the substantive judgment in the case, that order should be enforceable if the original court is recognised to have jurisdiction to decide the original matrimonial cause.[7]

A different case may arise, however, where the order is made, as in *Phillips v Batho*, against a third party who is not the subject of the substantive judgment. Whilst it is clear that the original court must have jurisdiction over the main suit,[8] is it necessary to show that there is distinct jurisdiction over the third party who is required to pay? On principle, there is a strong case for the requested court to insist upon a jurisdictional base for the order against the actual debtor and that the jurisdictional link be that which is required in actions in personam, although this is not under the statute an action in personam.[9] As the judgment debtor, the defendant should have the full protection of the statute in his own right.

No attempt will be made here to examine the jurisdictional rules applicable to the various categories of actions covered by this head. These must be ascertained by reference to the general conflict rules on recognition binding on the particular court. It should, however, be noted that in respect of certain categories of judgment, other Commonwealth enforcement schemes may have application. This is true of maintenance orders and other domestic proceedings,[10] of probates,[11] bankruptcy,[12] and winding up.[13]

1 FJREA, s 4(2)(c). The position under the 1920 Act should be similar.
2 *Société Coopérative Sidmetal v Titan International Ltd* [1966] 1 QB 828, [1965] 3 All ER 494; *Sharps Commercials Ltd v Gas Turbines Ltd* [1956] NZLR 819; *Re Van der Kreek's Marriage* [1979] PNGLR 185 but see *Sfeir & Co v National Insurance Co of New Zealand Ltd* [1964] 1 Lloyd's Rep 330 at 336, per Mocatta J.
3 FJREA, s 10(2).
4 [1913] 3 KB 25, 82 LJKB 882.
5 *Redhead v Redhead and Crothers* [1926] NZLR 131; *Patterson v D'Agostino* (1975) 58 DLR (3d) 63; *Re Van der Kreek's Marriage*, above. Cf *Jacobs v Jacobs and Ceen* [1950] P 146, [1950] 1 All ER 96. Dicey and Morris, op cit, p 1058; Cheshire and North, op cit, p 649; Read, op cit, pp 264–267.
6 *Sharps Commercials Ltd v Gas Turbines Ltd*, above, at 823, per McGregor J; *Re Van der Kreek's Marriage*, above.
7 *Re Van der Kreek's Marriage*, above. Cf *Simons v Simons* [1939] 1 KB 490.
8 By terms of FJREA, s 4(2)(c). Cf *Simons v Simons*, above, at 499.
9 *Redhead v Redhead and Crothers*, above; *Ruta v Ruta and Samuliak* [1929] 1 WWR 744. Under FJREA, s 4(2)(a), the in personam jurisdiction rules only apply in respect of debtors who were defendants in the original proceedings.
10 J. D. McClean *Recognition of Family Judgments in the Commonwealth* (1983).
11 On the Colonial Probates scheme, see J. D. McClean and K. W. Patchett *The Recognition and Enforcement of Judgments and Orders and the Service of Process in the Commonwealth* (1977) ch 7.
12 Ibid, ch 5.
13 Ibid, ch 6.

Cases in which jurisdiction must not be recognised

3.46 The 1933 Act sets out three circumstances in which the jurisdiction of the original court, whatever the basis of its assumption of jurisdiction or whether an acceptable basis for recognition of its jurisdiction otherwise exists, cannot be recognised for the purposes of the legislation.[1] These were said by the Greer Committee to be in part a statement of existing rules of common law and in part a rational interpretation of these rules.[2] They have been supplemented or affected in the United Kingdom by additional statutory rules which will apply also to cases arising under the 1920 Act. Where they go beyond the common law or such rules are not applicable, these exceptions can only be made effective under the 1920 Act by the requested court holding that they constitute reasons why local enforcement is not 'just and convenient'.[3]

1 FJREA, s 4(3). Additional exceptions of a specific nature are found in the UK to give effect to certain treaty obligations which set out special regimes for the settlement of disputes arising thereunder: Dicey and Morris, op cit, pp 1061–1066. For the schemes, see para 3.08 above.
2 Greer Committee Report, p 63.
3 AJA, s 9(1). This course of action is not available under the Canadian legislation.

(a) IMMOVABLES OUTSIDE THE COUNTRY OF THE ORIGINAL COURT

3.47 Where the subject matter of the proceedings was immovable property outside the country[1] of the original court, the jurisdiction of that court must not be recognised under the 1933 Act.[2] Dicey and Morris question whether this does not go beyond the common law which, in any case, is far from clear.[3] The provision should not be seen as applicable to cases merely because the judgment affects such property. As we have seen earlier,[4] there is a trend towards allowing assumption of jurisdiction to deal with torts affecting external property which may in due course be recognised by other courts under their conflict of laws. If this exception is construed as confined to cases involving questions of title and the right to possession and claims specifically directed at specified land, it will prevent recognition of ensuing money judgments only where such issues arise. It is in this respect particularly that the statutory exception may be found to be too wide, if indeed common law recognition of such judgments in tort claims may be given.[5]

1 'Country' means the area to which a distinct conflict of laws system applies.
2 FJREA, s 4(3)(a).
3 Op cit, pp 1070–1072; *Re Trepca Mines Ltd* [1960] 2 All ER 304 n, [1960] 1 WLR 1273.
4 Para 3.44 above.
5 Dicey and Morris, op cit, p 1072. But see *Duke v Andler* [1932] SCR 734, 4 DLR 529 which suggests the wider exception is applicable.

(b) CONFLICT WITH A JURISDICTION AGREEMENT

3.48 The 1933 Act holds that jurisdiction will not be recognised 'if the bringing of the proceedings in the original court was contrary to an agreement under which the dispute in question was to be settled otherwise than by proceedings in the courts of the country of that court'.[1] This is applicable only where the jurisdictional bases relied upon are residence or the presence of the principal place of business or a transaction through a local office or place of business, in the case of actions in personam, or the situs of the property in the case of immovables and actions in rem involving movables.[2] In these cases, therefore, refusal of the foreign court to decline jurisdiction in favour of another system's courts or an arbitral tribunal in accordance with the agreement will prevent the ensuing judgment from being registered. In the other actions in personam, however, any submission to the original court or any provision in the same or another valid agreement giving jurisdiction to the courts of that country will suffice, notwithstanding the agreement. The agreement to be effective must be exclusive in the sense of vesting the jurisdiction elsewhere than in the courts of the original country. Where an application to stay the original proceedings to make the agreement effective (and to protect the defendant's assets) is in fact unsuccessful, it will not constitute submission.[3]

The position under the 1920 Act is less certain in the absence of any provision or indeed of any clear rule at common law. It has been doubted whether recognition can yet be refused on this ground.[4] The possibility that prorogation and arbitration agreements are capable of divesting a court of jurisdiction in favour of another tribunal has been only slowly and reluctantly conceded. In any case, refusal of a stay of proceedings usually involves the exercise of a discretion.[5] Refusal therefore to enforce the resulting judgment would involve the application by the requested court of a mandatory rule contrary to the discretionary decision of the original court not to stay the action. Further, there is authority, albeit controversial, for the view that an unsuccessful application to the original court for the exercise of that discretion by reason of a pre-existing arbitration agreement constitutes submission to its jurisdiction.[6] In the present state of the common law, a judgment is likely to be registrable under the 1920 Act where the debtor was carrying on business in the original area and took no steps to invoke the agreement or where he took the steps and failed to obtain a stay.

This unhappy consequence has been resolved in the United Kingdom by a general statutory extension of the 1933 rule,[7] slightly modified. The substance of the rule is unchanged but it now applies to all types of action provided that the proceedings were not brought by, or with the agreement of, the person against whom the judgment was given or that person did not counterclaim or otherwise submit. In these cases, the debtor can be treated as having accepted the authority of the court to deal with the matter.

The provision makes explicit what is likely to be the case also at common law in providing that the agreement must not be:

'illegal, void or unenforceable or . . . incapable of being performed for reasons not attributable to the fault of the party bringing the proceedings . . .'[8]

The requested court is not bound by the decision of the overseas court on any of these issues.[9]

1 FJREA, s 4(3)(b).
2 Ibid, s 4(2)(a)(iv), (v); s 4(2)(b). Paras 3.41, 3.43 and 3.44 above.
3 Para 3.38 above.
4 Dicey and Morris, op cit, p 1061; O. Kahn-Freund, (1977) 26 ICLQ 825 at 855.
5 But not where an arbitration under the Geneva or New York schemes is involved: paras 7.17–7.18 and 8.14–8.15 below. Generally on these agreements, see M. Pryles, (1976) 25 ICLQ 543–582.
6 *Henry v Geoprosco International Ltd* [1976] QB 726, para 3.38 above. See Civil Jurisdiction and Judgments Act 1982, s 33 (UK).
7 Civil Jurisdiction and Judgments Act 1982, s 32. It does not apply to judgments arising from certain convention regimes to which the UK is party, including the Brussels Convention: ibid, s 32(4). It does apply to judgments given before that Act came into force, except where already registered: *Tracomin SA v Sudan Seeds* [1983] 3 All ER 137, [1983] 1 WLR 1026.
8 Ibid, s 32(2). This is modelled upon the New York Convention scheme and the Arbitration Act 1975, s 1. See paras 8.17–8.19 below for a discussion of the law which should be referred to to determine these matters.
9 Ibid, s 32(3).

(c) IMMUNITY OF THE DEBTOR UNDER INTERNATIONAL LAW

3.49 The 1933 Act deals specifically with persons who under the rules of public international law are entitled to immunity from the jurisdiction of the courts of the country from which the judgment came.[1] The sole circumstance where jurisdiction can be recognised is if the person submitted to that jurisdiction. There is no equivalent statement in the 1920 Act but there is little doubt that a requested court would find it not 'just and convenient' to enforce[2] a judgment against such a person if he had not submitted. In this context too, an appearance by or on behalf of such a person to protest the exercise of the jurisdiction should not be construed as an appearance.[3]

This provision will be applicable to states and those of their agencies enjoying state immunity and to those who enjoy diplomatic and consular privileges, under the rules of public international law. It will be for the requested court to determine what these rules are in any particular case but it may be expected that it will take into account relevant international treaties[4] as well as its own legislation and that of the original country for that purpose.[5] There is no suggestion that the requested court is *bound* to apply one or other of these sources. Difficulties may be experienced with respect to the developing theory of restrictive state immunity which is increasingly seen as excluding state agencies engaged upon commercial transactions from those who enjoy immunity.[6] For there is as yet no common position amongst Commonwealth countries.

The United Kingdom has supplemented this rule in respect of overseas judgments given against other states. These include judgments against the government or any department of government or the sovereign or Head of State in his public capacity or any entity, distinct from the executive organs of government, in proceedings related to actions taken by that entity in exercise of the sovereign authority of the state.[7] Such a judgment may only be recognised and thus registered if, had it not been given against the state, it could have been registered and provided that the original court would have had jurisdiction if it had applied the United Kingdom rules determining the limits of state immunity.[8] It is improbable that any Commonwealth country will in fact assume jurisdiction in matters in which the courts of the United Kingdom will not. The converse is perhaps more likely and may require a requested Commonwealth court to determine under the 1933 provisions how far the United Kingdom rules constitute public international law.

1 FJREA, s 4(3)(c).
2 AJA, s 9(1).
3 Para 3.38 above.
4 Eg Vienna Convention on Diplomatic Intercourse and Immunities 1961; Vienna Convention on Consular Relations 1963.
5 In the United Kingdom, for example, the Diplomatic Privileges Act 1964, the Consular Relations Act 1968, the International Organisations Act 1968, the State Immunity Act 1978.
6 Eg *Trendtex Trading Corpn v Central Bank of Nigeria* [1977] QB 529, [1977] 1 All ER 881.
7 Civil Jurisdiction and Judgments Act 1982, s 31(2). It does not extend to judgments given under certain convention schemes to which the UK is party: ibid, s 31(3).
8 Ibid, s 31(1). The rules are contained in the State Immunity Act 1978, ss 2–11.

Objection 2: The judgment is not a judgment to which the scheme applies

3.50 The 1933 Act requires registration to be set aside in this case.[1] The Act identifies the conditions which must be fulfilled in this respect.[2] These have been examined in paragraphs 3.11 to 3.16 and 3.19, 3.21 to 3.24. Conditions set out in paras 3.17, 3.18 and 3.20 are the subject of separate provisions.[3] The 1920 Act does not explicitly refer to this case but registration is possible only if the basic characteristics of judgments within that scheme are present.[4] Thus, in the same kinds of circumstances as under the 1933 Act, registration should be refused or set aside.

1 FJREA, s 4(1)(a)(i).
2 Ibid, s 1(2) and the definition of 'judgment' in s 11(1).
3 Para 3.51 below.
4 AJA, s 9(1) and the definition of 'judgment' in s 12(1).

Objection 3: The judgment was registered in contravention of the statute

3.51 The 1933 Act makes explicit provision for this case:[1] it must also be available under the 1920 scheme too as a 'sufficient reason' for setting aside the registration.[2] This will clearly apply under the former where the judgment has been wholly or partly satisfied[3] or where it cannot be enforced by execution in the country of origin.[4] But it also seems to cover cases in which the judgment was registered in a currency other than that permitted[5] or with an incorrect statement of the judgment debt[6] or where it contains matters which cannot be registered.[7] It may be assumed that all these cases can be dealt with similarly under the 1920 Act, on the grounds that the court in granting the initial registration had failed to exercise its discretion to order registration correctly.[8]

In addition, it will be possible to challenge under this head for non-compliance with any procedural prerequisites of either scheme which are preliminary to registration and which can be considered as central to its validity or effectiveness. Thus setting aside of a registration should be possible when the application has been made out of time[9] and no extension given, or in favour of a person not entitled to apply[10] or there was a substantial defect in the supporting documentation.[11]

1 FJREA, s 4(2)(a)(i).
2 RSC Ord 71, r 9(3).
3 FJREA, s 2(1), proviso (a). An outstanding balance may, however, be registered: s 2(4). Where an application is set aside on the ground that the judgment for the whole sum had been partly satisfied at the time of registration, the judgment creditor may apply for the registration of the outstanding balance: ibid s 5(3). There is no equivalent under the 1920 Act but see para 3.20 above.
4 Ibid, s 2(1), proviso (b). A further application may be made, if the registration is set aside, when the judgment has become so enforceable: ibid, s 5(2).
5 Ibid, s 2(3): para 3.30 above.
6 Ibid, s 2(4) allows registration of an outstanding balance: para 3.20 above.
7 Ibid, s 2(5) allows registration of parts of judgments: para 3.12 above.
8 AJA, s 9(1) which allows registration where enforcement would be 'just and convenient'.
9 Para 3.26 above.
10 Para 3.27 above.
11 Para 3.28 above. This may be useful if there has been fraud or deliberate misleading in the documents.

Objection 4: The judgment debtor had inadequate notice of the original proceedings

3.52 Common law places relatively little emphasis upon the question of whether the debtor was adequately notified of the original proceedings. He is deemed to have been subject to the procedures of the original court, once it is seen that the court was jurisdictionally competent under the conflicts rules of the requested state. The requested court will not normally enquire whether the exercise of that jurisdiction followed upon adequate notice.[1] Compliance with the procedural rules of the foreign system in this respect, even if it dispenses with notice, will suffice.[2]

The 1920 Act, however, treats this question separately from the jurisdictional considerations. Under this scheme, a judgment is not registrable where:

'the judgment debtor, being the defendant in the proceedings, was not duly served with the process of the original court and did not appear, notwithstanding that he was ordinarily resident or was carrying on business within the jurisdiction of that court or agreed to submit to the jurisdiction of that court'.[3]

This formulation emphasises that the defendant may have satisfied one of the jurisdictional requirements but usually a further requirement relating to service must also be met.

The 1933 scheme adopts a similar approach but with significant differences:

'the judgment debtor, being the defendant in the proceedings in the original court, did not (notwithstanding that process may have been duly served on him in accordance with the law of the country of the original court) receive notice of those proceedings in sufficient time to enable him to defend the proceedings and did not appear.'[4]

In this case, therefore, the receiving court must concern itself with the adequacy of the notice of the actual proceedings rather than with the question of whether the initiating process was duly served. There seems little doubt that this was a deliberate change in the law to overcome limitations and uncertainties in the earlier requirements.[5]

But both schemes are concerned that the original defendant[6] received notification which would afford him an opportunity to defend himself in the proceedings. Accordingly under both schemes, no objection can be brought under this ground if the judgment debtor appeared in the original proceedings. Appearance negatives the absence of due service or notice. On the other hand, if there is due service or notice, it matters not for *this* purpose that the defendant fails to appear. It may be assumed that 'appearance' is used in much the same sense as applied in respect of jurisdiction.[7] It will occur where, through some action under the procedures of the original court, the defendant has communicated to the court to indicate an awareness that proceedings have been initiated against him and that he intends to take some part in those proceedings. In neither statute, however, is the appearance required to be 'voluntary'. This, it is thought, is deliberate. For the reason for participating in the proceedings is irrelevant. That steps have been taken, for example, to contest the jurisdiction or to protect property[8] is evidence that the defendant was aware of the proceedings, which is what the provision seeks to ensure.

A general point applies in relation to the defence under both schemes. It is not open to the plaintiff to argue that the defendant has waived the requirement of actual notice or due service by an agreement to submit to the jurisdiction of a foreign court or to accept specific forms of substituted service. Waiver of this kind has long been recognised at common law.[9] The express terms of the statutory schemes cut across this rule and thus the defences will remain available, notwithstanding the fact that the defendant has agreed to submit to the particular jurisdiction.

The defences that there has been no due service of process (1920 Act) or insufficient service (1933 Act) are not necessarily the same, as the 1933 provision by its terms makes apparent. Under the latter Act, the requested court must make a judgment whether any notice given, whether through due service of process or otherwise, was in sufficient time for the defendant to defend the proceedings. Both statutory provisions, however, lack complete clarity.

1 Dicey and Morris, op cit, pp 1088–1090.
2 *Jeannot v Fuerst* (1909) 100 LT 816, 25 TLR 424.
3 AJA, s 9(2)(c). The jurisdictional requirements stated apply whether the action is in personam or not: para 3.35 above.
4 FJREA, s 4(1)(a)(iii).
5 Cf Greer Committee Report, para 6.
6 This applies in respect of any person joined with the original defendant. Where the judgment debtor was the plaintiff in the original proceedings, the fact of his having initiated the proceedings makes this requirement inapplicable.
7 Para 3.38 above.
8 Although this may not constitute 'voluntary appearance' for the purposes of grounding jurisdiction, jurisdiction may be proved upon other grounds.
9 *Vallée v Dumergue* (1849) 4 Exch 290, 18 LJ Ex 398; *Jamieson v Robb* (1881) 7 VLR (L) 170; *Copin v Adamson* (1875) 1 Ex D 17, 45 LJQB 15, CA; *Ritter v Fairfield* (1900) 32 OR 350; *Re Hughes and Sharp* (1968) 70 DLR (2d) 298; *Batavia Times Publishing Co v Davis*, above.

(a) *Due service under the 1920 scheme*

3·53 The 1920 scheme is concerned exclusively with the question of service of process. If the service was good it is irrelevant that the defendant had no actual knowledge or that it gave inadequate notice.

What is due service of process under the 1920 scheme? On one view, it will be enough if the rules on service of process prevailing in the country of the original court have been duly complied with.[1] Some strength may perhaps be given to this view by the express reference to that law in the 1933 provisions. On the other hand, what if the rules of service provide only a limited chance that the defendant will actually learn of the process? As Dicey and Morris point out,[2] it is not to be expected that substituted service on an absent defendant in the form of a writ nailed to a court-house door in a foreign jurisdiction, valid according to the law of that jurisdiction,[3] will be treated as 'due service'. Yet it is then difficult to determine where the line will be drawn. A requested court must not refuse recognition to procedural arrangements for service in other systems merely because they are not used in its own. There are likely to be methods of service which, though they do not normally involve the kinds of personal service used by common law systems, are equally effective for the purpose of commencing legal proceedings. In consequence, it is a little difficult to go along with the suggestion of Dicey and Morris that 'due service' must involve personal service.[4] This has certainly not been the position at common law which must have been in the minds of those who drafted the 1920 Act.[5] A defendant who resides in a foreign jurisdiction is subject to the procedural laws of that country[6] and if, for example, process may be commenced there by attachment of property or a notice exhibited on the property of the defendant in the jurisdiction, should a receiving court be able to refuse registration when that process has been duly carried out? Thus in *Becquet v MacCarthy*,[7] service was effected upon a public officer in Mauritius rather than upon the defendant (or his attorney) who, though formerly resident there, was absent at the time proceedings were commenced. Lord Tenterden, accepting that Mauritius law permitted such service and that the officer might be expected to perform a public duty in communicating with the defendant, held that this method of service was not so contrary to natural justice as to render the judgment unrecognisable.

Cases on the statutory provisions are few and of limited guidance. In *Gacs and Maierovitz*[8] the Supreme Court of British Columbia held that the term 'duly served' was not limited to cases of personal service but that substituted service at the defendant's address in the jurisdiction was good. In reaching this conclusion, McIntyre J was influenced by the use elsewhere in the statute of 'personal service'.[9] The same conclusion, however, was reached on similar facts in New South Wales where no such alternative phraseology is used.[10] In *Hoffman Lumber and Supply Ltd v Auld*,[11] however, it was suggested that 'duly served' may require service within the jurisdiction of the foreign court and could not extend to service ex juris under the law of that country. This proposition seems unduly restrictive.

In attempting to determine what should be treated as 'due service', regard must be had to the context of the usage. The aim is to ensure that the defendant is adequately informed of impending proceedings which he may wish to defend. Accordingly, the receiving court may wish to exclude modes of service which carry a real risk that this will not be achieved.[12] This is not likely to be the case where the defendant was present in the foreign jurisdiction at the time the initiating process was commenced, and one of the standard modes of service available under the law of that country was complied with. A defendant cannot expect any privileged treatment in this respect whilst he is immediately subject to the jurisdiction. In such a case, it should not matter whether the service was personal or not, if it was a usual form of local service.

It is where the defendant is not present in the issuing jurisdiction that a serious possibility of ignorance of the procedings may arise. This cannot be said to occur where the defendant, though absent, has agreed that someone designated by him can receive the service or there is a local legal practitioner or public official with the necessary authority.[13] On the other hand, substituted service in the form of an advertisement or published notice or posting to an address in the original jurisdiction is less easy to support when the defendant is actually out of that jurisdiction. As common law systems are unlikely to allow substituted service to found jurisdiction in their courts in such circumstances,[14] arguably these are the kinds of case in which it would be proper to hold that there had not been due service.

Where the method of service involves issue of process to another country where the defendant is to be found, other considerations are relevant. It will surely be enough if the process has been issued in accordance with the law of the originating state and has actually been delivered to the defendant by a method which satisfies the law of the state where it is effected. Thus due service appears to have occurred where notice of a writ has been authorised for ex juris service under an Order 11 procedure and has then been served to the person of the defendant abroad under a locally approved method, even if it does not fulfil the requirements of personal service in the issuing state. It should not matter that this has been achieved by use of Letters of Request or by diplomatic or consular means. Similarly, there seems a case for accepting as due service delivery of the process to the defendant's residence or places of business, provided that use of such methods is acceptable under the law of the issuing state and of the state of service.

On the other hand, substituted service in the form of an advertisement or by post (without evidence of delivery at the defendant's residence or place of business) is less easy to support. In common law practice, such arrangements are only likely to be ordered if there is a strong probability that they will be effective to give notice of impending proceedings. A case can be made for saying that these forms will be inadequate unless the documents were in fact received.

These conclusions draw some strength from the Hague Convention on the Service Abroad of Judicial and Extra-judicial Documents in Civil or Commercial Matters. Under this convention, it is required that judgments should not be given until it is established that the originating process was:

'(a) ... served by a method prescribed by the internal law of the state addressed for the service of documents in domestic actions upon persons who are within its territory; or

(b) ... actually delivered to the defendant or his residence by another method provided by this Convention ...'[15]

Where the judgment has been given in a state party to the convention against a defendant who was served in another such state in a way which satisfies this requirement, it is hard to resist the conclusion that the courts of the third state should be satisfied that there has been due service. Indeed there is much to be said for adopting the principles embodied in this article to determine whether there has been due service of process under the 1920 legislation in respect of an absentee defendant.

1 *Sfeir & Co v National Insurance Co of New Zealand* [1964] 1 Lloyd's Rep 330 at 341; *McLellan v Elwood's Ltd* (1980) 70 APR 358 (NB).

2 Op cit, pp 1090–1091.

3 *Buchanan v Rucker* (1808) 9 East 192.

4 Op cit, p 1091.
5 Cf *Shearer v McLean* (1903) 36 NBR 284 at 291.
6 *Romano v Maggiora (No 3)* [1937] 1 WWR 490.
7 (1831) 2 B & Ad 951.
8 (1968) 68 DLR (2d) 345 (BC).
9 At 347. See also *Re Reciprocal Enforcement of Judgments Act, Re Hearn v Kemp and Kemp* (1969) 70 WWR 609 (Alta). The term is used in relation to ex parte orders for registration: para 3.27 above.
10 *British Motor Trade Association v Godden* (1950) 67 WN (NSW) 135.
11 (1958) 24 WWR 552 (BC).
12 But negligence of the defendants, eg in notifying a change of address from that given for service, will negative this defence: *Re Hearn v Kemp and Kemp*, above.
13 *Batavia Times Publishing Co v Davis* (1978) 82 DLR (3d) 247; affd (1980) 105 DLR (3d) 192.
14 *Porter v Freudenberg* [1915] 1 KB 857, 84 LJKB 1001.
15 Art 15.

(b) *Notice under the 1933 scheme*

3.54 The 1933 scheme is less concerned with the question of service than with the question of sufficiency of notice. The Act makes quite clear that there may be good service and yet the notice may be insufficient. This provision appears to put its essential emphasis upon the requirement of actual knowledge by the defendant of the initiation of the proceedings against him.[1] The defendant, therefore, must be able to show either that he has not received any notice at all that an action has been initiated or that it has not come in sufficient time. He cannot invoke the defence on the grounds of not having received notice of subsequent steps in the proceedings, such as interlocutory proceedings.[2]

The section ('notwithstanding that process *may* have been duly served . . .') does not entitle the receiving court to enter into the question of whether there was due service per se.[3] It will be concerned with service solely to determine whether it conveyed sufficient notice to the defendant. Where the process was not duly served, it still seems possible to counter the defence by showing that the defendant received notice through some other means in sufficient time.

If actual notice, therefore, is required, certain forms of substituted service may not be enough, unless it can be shown that in the end the defendant personally received the process or information of what it contained. So for example, proof of advertisement or of postal service or delivery at a known address may well be inadequate. A more difficult problem arises where the defendant has designated an agent or has a lawyer authorised to receive process. As these are arrangements made by the defendant for his own purposes, it seems appropriate that notice to an agent should be treated as actual notice to the defendant.[4] But the same cannot be said if a court has ordered substituted service upon someone other than the defendant or his authorised agent, in the absence of evidence that notice has been conveyed to the defendant.

Presumably, though the section does not say so in express words, the notification to the defendant will need to be in sufficient detail to put the defendant on notice as to where, in which court, by whom and in relation to what cause of action the initiating process was obtained. For without such information, the defendant will not be able to take steps to defend the proceedings as the provision intends. Moreover, it must surely come from an authoritative source upon which the defendant can rely, though perhaps it need not be in an official form or even in a written form, if the source is unimpeachable (eg a lawyer).[5] So, it is suggested, information received by the defendant merely that a writ has been issued against him in a foreign jurisdiction should not be treated as 'notice' for the purposes of this defence. The obligation is to ensure that the defendant *receives* notice: this surely cannot be fulfilled where the defendant must seek out further information before he knows what proceedings he has to defend.

The requirement of receipt 'in sufficient time to enable him to defend the proceedings' is not without uncertainty. Can the defendant argue that he should have been given adequate time to prepare his case for presentation in proceedings by way of defence? Or must it be merely in sufficient time for notice of intention to defend to be entered in the original court within its usual time limits? Or is the defendant to be allowed time to determine whether he wishes to defend or not, to notify his intention and, if he decides to defend, to serve his defence in due time?

The provision in this aspect is principally aimed at those cases where a default judgment has been entered against the defendant usually when he has failed to indicate his intention to participate in the original proceedings. Accordingly, it may be suggested that what is required is that he had sufficient time to take the necessary steps to prevent such a judgment being entered. What is important is that he must have adequate time to take professional advice about the claim and to notify the original court, if he decides to defend.

As we have seen if the defendant does notify the original court, he should be treated for this provision as having appeared. If he fails to notify having had adequate time to do so, the defence will not be available. On the other hand, if notice of the proceedings is received too late to prevent the initial entry of the judgment, it will make no difference that the defendant still had time to apply to set the default judgment aside. In such a case he is entitled to have the registration set aside.[6]

In determining what is adequate time, the requested court is likely to apply a standard based upon its own requirements for notification of a defence in response to its own process when issued out of the jurisdiction.[7]

1 *Ramus v Donaldson* (1959) 3 Jo African Law 201 (Tanz); *Brockley Cabinet Co Ltd v Pears* (1972) 20 FLR 333 (ACT).
2 *Brockley Cabinet Co Ltd v Pears*, above.
3 The Hague Convention requires both due service and adequacy of notice.
4 In the case of a corporate body, actual notice probably requires notification to a lawyer or other person authorised by the corporation to act on its behalf in matters of litigation.
5 *Reynolds v Fenton* (1846) 3 CB 187, 16 LJCP 15.
6 *Barclays Bank Ltd v Piacun* (1983) ACLD 35.475 (Qsld).
7 Cf RSC Ord 11, r 4(4) and Extra-Jurisdiction Tables, Part 4B.

Objection 5: The judgment was obtained by fraud

(a) *Fraud by or upon the original court*

3·55 Both enforcement schemes permit the registration of a judgment to be resisted before a requested court on the ground that 'the judgment was obtained by fraud'.[1] In this respect they exhibit a characteristic commonly found in enforcement schemes and one which has long been recognised in some form at common law as a defence to actions on foreign judgments.[2] Whilst common law practice has generally been followed in relation to the statutory schemes, there is some difference of opinion between Commonwealth courts on what must be proved in order to establish fraud. For there has been a growing trend to doubt, and in some cases reject, the basis of the English courts' approach in those cases in which the matter in issue in the original court involved fraud by the judgment creditor upon the debtor.

It is, however apparent from their terms that the enforcement schemes are not confined to those cases. Whilst direct precedents are absent (presumably because the incidence of these cases is low), there can be no doubt that registration could be defeated, as can actions on a judgment, by showing that the court itself had committed fraud through the malpractice of the judge or other officials, as for example where they are interested parties[3] or by being in receipt of bribes, especially from the judgment creditor, or where the judgment has been prepared prior to the hearing.[4]

This defence may also extend to cases where the foreign court deliberately made an error, as for example, by knowingly and wilfully refusing to apply a crucially relevant legal provision, including applicable foreign law.[5] Such an allegation will be difficult to prove, especially between Commonwealth courts which are traditionally reluctant to question each other's probity. A general assertion of corruption or venality in the courts of a particular country will carry no weight.[6] Fraud must be alleged in precise terms and proved conclusively. It is also unquestioned that registration should not take place of a judgment of a foreign court which has been induced, by the fraud of one or even both of the parties, to assume jurisdiction when, if the true facts were known, it would have been obliged to refuse so to do. Thus where the court has been deliberately deceived concerning relevant facts relating to the jurisdictional criteria, registration should be denied.[7]

1 AJA, s 9(2)(d); FJREA, s 4(1)(a)(iv).
2 Dicey and Morris, op cit, pp 1082–1085.
3 *Price v Dewhurst* (1837) 8 Sim 279, 6 LJ Ch 226.
4 *Abdul Wazid v Viswanathan* AIR 1953 Mad 261.
5 Castel, op cit, p 499, referring to Piggott's discussion (op cit, p 113, fn 258) of *Cammell v Sewell* (1858) 27 LJ Ex 447. Such matter may be more appropriately raised as a failure of natural justice: para 3.63 below.
6 *Price v Dewhurst*, above; *Abouloff v Oppenheimer* (1882) 10 QBD 295, 52 LJQB, CA.
7 Ibid. Cf *Biggar v Biggar* [1930] 2 DLR 940.

(b) *Fraud upon the debtor*

3.56 There is general agreement that fraud practised upon the debtor by the other party to the suit can be successfully relied upon if the facts upon which it is based have only become known subsequent to the original judgment and the issue, therefore, was not capable of being put to the court in the original hearing.[1] It is at this point, however, that Commonwealth jurisprudence diverges. For in certain jurisdictions, especially the Canadian provinces, allegations of fraud *only* succeed if they are the consequence of new evidence of a decisive nature which has been discovered since the original judgment was given. In other systems, however, which follow English precedents, the courts have been prepared to examine allegations of fraud which are intrinsic—that is, relate to matters which were in issue and were decided upon by the foreign court or which are based upon matters which could have been put in issue but were not.

The English approach was adopted in full awareness of its inconsistency with the principle that foreign judgments are conclusive on the merits. But the English courts have put emphasis upon their unwillingness to allow parties to take advantage of frauds which they themselves have perpetrated. The requested court may need to enter upon issues that were or could have been the subject of determination by the original court in order to determine whether deception was successfully practised by the party.[2] This approach has been consistently followed even where the evidence of fraud adduced before the requested court is exactly the same as that which led the original court to find against an identical allegation.[3] This approach has prevailed in respect of the enforcement schemes. Thus in *Syal v Heyward*,[4] the Court of Appeal ruled that if the defendant opposing registration shows a prima facie case that the original court was deceived, he is entitled to have the issues tried even though the court may have to go into matters which were or could have been raised at the trial. Thus, fraud can be raised whether or not the party alleging it knew at the time of the original hearing of the facts which he must rely on to establish it. Such an approach has been widely questioned by academic writers[5] as flying in the face of the principle of res judicata which is a central feature of recognition. For it requires matters to be re-tried on their merits (including, perhaps, the veracity of parties) and makes the requested court the final arbiter of what constitutes fraud. Moreover, it may permit a party to avoid raising the issues in the original court, either by not introducing them or by absenting himself from the hearing,[6] with the intention of introducing the matter if action is taken to enforce the resulting decision as a foreign judgment. As one text notes, this is an indulgence that has nothing to commend it.[7] If a defendant wishes to challenge the original decision for such fraud, it is argued, it should be before the courts of the original jurisdiction either on appeal or by action to set aside. Ironically in the latter case in respect of *domestic* judgments English common law requires new evidence of a decisive character subsequently discovered.[8] Thus the English approach to foreign judgments permits a court asked to register a judgment to apply to it closer powers of investigation than will be applied at common law in respect of a fraud in domestic judgments.

These considerations throw doubts upon the acceptability of the English doctrine. Canadian courts, after a flirtation with the English approach,[9] have favoured the requirement of extrinsic fraud, thereby confining the challenge to cases where the party alleging fraud seeks to rely upon facts which came to his knowledge after the original hearing and which are material to the original decision.[10] Similar reservations to the English approach have been expressed by the Indian courts which have tended towards the Canadian approach.[11] Although Australian academic opinion favours the Canadian view,[12] judicial authority supports the English approach.[13] In New Zealand the Court of Appeal, whilst following English authorities on the nature of the defence, has suggested that other considerations may arise under the enforcement legislation.[14] As evidence of fraud will rarely be evident from the affidavits, it will usually be necessary for the requested court to order the issue of fraud to be tried, before any decision to set aside or refuse registration can be reached. Whether to make such an order lies within the discretion of the court. In exercising that discretion, the court should take into account whether the issues could have been raised in the original hearing, whether the defendant had deliberately refrained from participating in the original proceedings and, if so, what he foresaw as the probable consequences. If the defendant had notice of the evidence and took no steps to contradict it, especially, the court implied, if this was to provide an opportunity to invoke fraud as an objection to any subsequent registration, it might prove difficult to persuade a registering court to grant a trial of the issue of fraud.[15] In so deciding, the court declined to follow its English counterpart[16] on the powers of a registering court on the question of directing a trial on the issue, at least where the defendant deliberately refrained from raising it in the original proceedings. This is welcome, though limited, recognition that issues of this kind should be heard by the original court.

1 Cf *Ochsenbein v Papelier* (1873) 8 Ch App 695, 42 LJ Ch 861; *Woodruff v McLennan* (1887) 14 OAR 242.
2 *Abouloff v Oppenheimer* (1882) 10 QBD 295 at 302, per Lord Coleridge, and at 308, per Brett LJ.
3 *Vadala v Lawes* (1890) 25 QBD 310, 63 LT 128, CA; *Ellerman Lines Ltd v Read* [1928] 2 KB 144, 97 LJKB 366.
4 [1948] 2 KB 443, [1948] 2 All ER 576. The requested court has no power to impose a condition that the defendant bring the money in issue into the court by which the question of deceit is to be resolved.
5 See in particular, Read, op cit, pp 377–81; R. H. Graveson, (1949) 12 MLR 105. The approach on fraud contrasts sharply with that taken in respect of public policy in *Israel Discount Bank of New York v Hadjipateras* [1983] 3 All ER 129, [1984] 1 WLR 137: para 3.57 below.
6 As in *Syal v Heyward,* above.
7 Cheshire and North, op cit, p 661.
8 D. M. Gordon, (1961) 77 LQR 358, 533.
9 *Hollender v Ffoulkes* (1894) 26 OR 61; dicta in *Johnston v Barkley* (1905) 10 OLR 724, CA; *Anderson Produce Co v Nesbitt* (1903) 2 OWR 430, affg 1 OWR 818.
10 *Woodruff v McLennan* (1887), above; *Jacobs v Beaver Silver Cobalt Mining Co* (1908) 17 OLR 496, CA; *Johnson v Occidental Syndicate Ltd* (1911) 20 OWR 67; affd 4 DLR 727, CA; dicta in *MacDonald v Pier* [1923] SCR 107 at 120–121 (Ont); *Manolopoulos v Pnaiffe* [1930] 2 DLR 169 (NS); *Mahon/Moore Group of Companies Ltd v Mercator Enterprises Ltd* (1978) 52 APR 327 (NS). Where the alleged fraud relates to matters which would not have been admissible in the original hearing, it cannot be relied upon: *Patton v Reed* (1972) 30 DLR (3d) 494 (BC). Generally, see Castel, op cit, pp 488–499.
11 *Popat Virji v Damodar* AIR 1934 Bom 390; *Sundaram Pillai v Kandaswami Pillai* AIR 1941 Mad 387; *Abdul Wazid v Vishwanathan,* AIR 1953 Mad 261; *Sankaram Govindan v Lakshmi* AIR 1974 SC 1764.
12 Eg Nygh, op cit, pp 93–94.
13 *Norman v Norman (No 2)* (1968) 12 FLR 39 at 47, per Fox J.
14 *Svirskis v Gibson* [1977] 2 NZLR 4.
15 The issue of fraud was directed for trial in this case.
16 *Syal v Heyward,* above.

Objection 6: The judgment offends against the public policy of the requested system

3.57 The assertion that a foreign judgment will not be enforced if contrary to the public policy of the forum is commonplace in conflict of laws. It is the ultimate safeguard open to domestic courts to decline to give their assistance to foreign judgments which are seen to be objectionable or against some recognised domestic interest. There are surprisingly few reported decisions in the Commonwealth on the question of public policy in relation to the enforcement of judgments, making it difficult to indicate with any accuracy the kinds of circumstances in which the issue might properly arise. What is clear is that public policy must always be seen as a question for the receiving court to examine in the context of its current domestic law. Accordingly, precedents from other jurisdictions, as indeed older precedents from the same jurisdiction, must be taken with care.

The relevant provisions of the principal statutory schemes are not identical. The 1920 legislation provides that no judgment can be registered thereunder if:

'the judgment was in respect of a cause of action which for reasons of public policy or for some other similar reason could not have been entertained by the registering court'.[1]

The 1933 Act has a significantly different formulation. Registration must be set aside if the registering court is satisfied that:

'the enforcement of the judgment would be contrary to public policy in the country of the registering court.'[2]

This objection seems capable of dealing with the circumstances referred to under the earlier Act, for the enforcement of a judgment in respect of a cause of action objectionable on public policy grounds is likely to be contrary to a country's public policy. But the 1933 ground is capable of wider application, since, consistent with the general purpose of the legislation, it is concerned with the effects of *enforcement* in the requested jurisdiction.[3] In practice, little may turn upon the difference, for the 1920 Act requires registration to be granted where the requested court 'in all the circumstances of the case... thinks it just and convenient that the judgment be enforced' locally.[4] Where such conditions are not present, registration should be refused or, if made, set aside.[5] The combined effect of the 1920 provisions, therefore, allows a requested court powers of control analogous to those contained in the public policy provisions of the 1933 Act.

The underlying aim of the public policy objection is to deny to a successful foreign litigant access to the legal facilities of the requested state in cases in which it will offend against the juristic values of that state to lend assistance. As the Court of Appeal in England has recently stressed,[6] the basis of the objection arises out of differences between the law and practice of the original jurisdiction and in the requested state, differences which the latter finds in conflict with its basic values. Where the law and practice are essentially the same in both systems this objection cannot be raised in the requested state. For it is to be assumed that any such objections will have been taken in the original proceedings. If the judgment goes against the debtor there on those issues or if he omitted to raise them, he may not reopen them in the recognition proceedings.[7] In consequence, the judgment is to be treated as conclusive in this respect on the issues which are common to both systems. It may be expected, therefore, that successful objections on this ground to the registration of Commonwealth judgments will be rare, since there is still much law and practice in common through a common legal tradition. Indeed in a reciprocal enforcement scheme in which shared values will have been a factor in the making of extension orders, public policy will be an effective objection only in exceptional circumstances.

1 AJA, s 9(2)(f).
2 FJREA, s 4(1)(a)(v).
3 Dicey and Morris, op cit, p 1087.
4 AJA, s 9(1). In the Canadian case, reliance could be made on the 'good defence' objection: para 3.70 below.
5 Eg RSC Ord 71, r 9(3).
6 *Israel Discount Bank v Hadjipateras* [1983] 3 All ER 129, [1984] 1 WLR 137.
7 Following *Ellis v M'Henry* (1871) LR 6 CP 228 at 238, per Bovill CJ and *Tracomin SA v Sudan Oil Seeds Co Ltd (No 2)* [1983] 2 All ER 129 (not reversed on this point by [1983] 3 All ER 140, [1983] 1 WLR 1026, CA).

(a) *Judgments in respect of a cause of action which could not be entertained by the requested court*

3.58 The formulation used by the 1920 Act is not completely clear. Is it necessary to show that the actual cause of action arising where and how it did could not have been litigated in the requested jurisdiction, for example, because it was prohibited or was unknown, or because it arose from a contract regarded as tainted under its law? Or does the requested state have to enquire whether the cause of action is of a *type* which could not be litigated in the requested jurisdiction, had the events taken place there?[1] The former view seems preferable. For proceedings may be brought in most systems in respect of causes of action with a foreign element which, if that element were absent, could not have been brought.[2] The provision is designed to prevent enforcement of a judgment in respect of the particular cause of action because *that* cause of action could not have been entertained for public policy reasons.

1 J. Bloom, (1978) 57 Oregon Law Review 399 at p 423.
2 Eg certain contracts void, but not illegal, under the lex fori but valid according to the proper law: eg wagering contracts: *Saxby v Fulton* [1909] 2 KB 208, 78 LJKB 781, CA.

(i) JUDGMENTS IN RESPECT OF TAXES OR CHARGES OR ENFORCING FINES OR PENALTIES

3.59 These are expressly excluded from the scheme under the 1933 legislation[1] but, in the absence of explicit provisions under the 1920 statute, their registration could be challenged on this ground. For they are judgments in respect of causes of action which for 'some other similar reason' to public policy (ie matters limited to the territorial authority of another system) could not have been entertained by the registering court. These have been examined elsewhere.[2]

1 FJREA, s 1(2)(b).
2 Para 3.21 above.

(ii) JUDGMENTS BASED UPON A CAUSE OF ACTION PROHIBITED OR CONTRAVENING THE LAW OF THE REQUESTED STATE

3.60 Where the lex fori explicitly prohibits proceedings on certain causes of action, registration of a foreign judgment in respect of any such cause of action would permit the circumvention of that prohibition. Registration in such a case is likely to be treated as contrary to public policy. Thus a judgment for damages for breach of promise of marriage should not be registrable in England, as statute expressly prohibits actions of that kind in English courts.[1] Similarly, a judgment to enforce a wager rendered in a country where winnings are recoverable by action is not likely to be registrable in a country where suits to recover wagers are prohibited.[2] Again registration of a judgment for damages for breach of a contract which was entered into in contravention of a statute, such as the Unfair Contract Terms Act 1977 should be refused. For that Act has explicit provisions to prevent its evasion.[3]

Similarly, registration is likely to be refused where the transaction which is the subject of the cause of action involves a contravention of requirements in the lex fori. So, for example, a judgment for the repayment by the defendant of a loan taken in breach of the exchange control legislation of the requested country is unlikely to be registrable.[4] Equally, enforcement of payments in respect of transactions which involve the export of prohibited items from the requested state is unlikely to be permitted.[5] But this head should extend only to cases where there is some imperative requirement of the lex fori which applies to the transaction or cause of action. Where, for example, the judgment relates to a transaction valid under the law which governs it, it will not be contrary to public policy to enforce it merely because it would be void if the lex fori had applied.[6] Thus a judgment for the recovery of money lent in a foreign country for the purposes of gaming when the transaction is governed by law under which loans for gaining are lawful is registrable, notwithstanding that such transactions would be void under the lex fori.[7] There is no principle that judgments in respect of contracts valid according to the proper law but which involve consideration which under the lex fori would have been illegal should be treated as unenforceable.[8]

1 Law Reform (Miscellaneous Provisions) Act 1970, s 1(1).
2 *Moulis v Owen* [1907] 1 KB 746, 76 LJKB 396, CA. The Gaming Act 1845, s 18 (UK) expressly prohibits actions to recover winnings.
3 S 27(2).
4 Cf *Boissevain v Weil* [1950] AC 327, [1950] 1 All ER 728, HL.
5 Cf *Regazzoni v K. C. Sethia Ltd* [1958] AC 301, [1957] 3 All ER 286, HL.
6 See *Mackender v Feldia AG* [1967] 2 QB 590, [1966] 3 All ER 847.
7 Cf *Saxby v Fulton* [1909] 2 KB 208, 78 LJKB 781; *Bank of Montreal v Snoxell* (1982) 143 DLR (3d) 349 (Alta).
8 Cf *Re Bonacina, Le Brasseur v Bonacina* [1912] 2 Ch 394, 81 LJ Ch 674 but orse, *Ling v Yip* (1975) 54 DLR (3d) 317 but see J. Swan, (1981) 13 Ottawa L Rev 123 at pp 151–152. This conclusion may be otherwise if the statute rendering the consideration illegal is construed as applicable to all contracts whatever their proper law.

(iii) JUDGMENTS BASED UPON A CONTRACT WHICH IS CONTRARY TO THE PUBLIC POLICY OF THE REQUESTED STATE

3.61 Just as a court will not enforce a contract which is inconsistent with its public policy, so it is unlikely to allow a foreign judgment based upon such a contract to be registered.[1] Thus, for example, a contract which imposed unreasonable restraint on trade,[2] is champertous,[3] is obtained by duress or coercion[4] or induced by undue influence[5] or which adversely interferes with the forum state's relations with other states[6] will not give rise to a registrable judgment. This is the case whether or not the contract is valid according to the proper law. As we have seen,[7] however, the defects must be present in the distinctive public policy of the requested state and not capable of being raised in similar circumstances in the original proceedings.

1 *Re Macartney, Macfarlane v Macartney* [1921] 1 Ch 522 at 528, per Astbury J, referring to *Rousillon v Rousillon* (1880) 14 Ch D 351 at 369, per Fry J.
2 Cf *Rousillon v Rousillon*, above.
3 *Re Trepca Mines Ltd (No 2)* [1963] Ch 199 at 218; *Trendtex Trading Corpn v Crédit Suisse* [1982] AC 679, [1981] 3 All ER 520.
4 Cf *Kaufman v Gerson* [1904] 1 KB 591, 73 LJKB 320, CA.
5 Cf *Foster v Driscoll* [1929] 1 KB 470, 98 LJKB 282, CA.
6 *Israel Discount Bank v Hadjipateras* [1983] 3 All ER 129, [1984] 1 WLR 137.
7 Ibid, para 3.57 above.

(iv) JUDGMENTS BASED UPON A CAUSE OF ACTION CONTRARY TO THE FUNDAMENTAL VALUES OF MORALITY OF THE REQUESTED STATE

3.62 Although this is a generally recognised feature of public policy its limits are the least easy to determine. For prevailing value systems, even when restricted by precedent, will vary from time to time and place to place. It is not fulfilled merely by adducing evidence of differences in the values of the two systems. The objection is likely to be successful only if the original cause of action is viewed as thoroughly objectionable according to the prevailing values of the forum. It exists for 'the protection of social institutions or the advancement of moral principles'.[1] So, for example, a judgment for damages arising from the application of blatently discriminatory law or of oppressive and confiscatory legislation which interfered with private rights may fall under this head. In *Mayo-Perrott v Mayo-Perrott*[2] the Supreme Court of the Republic of Ireland refused to enforce in the Republic a judgment for costs comprised in a decree for divorce granted in England. For to do so would be to give aid to the recovery of costs for an action which in Ireland is repugnant to the distinctive policy which neither permits divorce nor recognises foreign divorces.

But cases are rarely as clear cut as this. In *Re Macartney*,[3] a Maltese judgment which ordered the personal representatives of a deceased putative father to pay perpetual maintenance for the benefit of his illegitimate daughter was not enforced in England. The general grant of permanent rights against putative fathers and their estates under Maltese law was thought to be against English public policy, largely, it appears, because the child would continue to benefit after reaching her majority.

Doubts have been expressed concerning the basis of this decision, not least because it was made unnecessary when Astbury J went on to hold that the judgment was in any case not final and conclusive. The judge did not find the action directly contrary to general morality: his objection seems to have been directed against the 'general recognition of the permanent rights of illegitimate children and their spinster mothers'.[4] It is arguable that in many countries of the Commonwealth where greater recognition has been given in recent years to claims against the estates of putative fathers, this argument would now be difficult to sustain.

Similarly, it is possible that difficulties might also be experienced in relation to judgments arising out of contracts which, though good where they were made, were questionable according to the morality of the requested country. In *Pope v Pope*,[5] an Ontario judgment granted on an agreement to pay alimony under a separation agreement between a wife on the one part and the husband and his fiancée on the other was held to be enforceable in British Columbia. Because cohabitation had ceased when the agreement was entered, the judgment could not be treated as contrary to public policy. It made no difference that the fiancée was a party to it. The Supreme Court stressed that to succeed it would be necessary to show that refusal to register would be 'in the interest of the safety of the State or the economic or social well-being of the State and the people as a whole'.[6] Merely because a cause of action is unknown to the requested state or has been abolished there[7] does not contradict the fundamental values of the receiving society. Because a foreign legal system provides a remedy in certain circumstances, when the receiving court does not, cannot, in principle, be a very compelling reason for refusing assistance in the requested court.

There are, it must be acknowledged, decisions to the contrary. Thus in *Re Macartney*,[8] a second ground for refusing enforcement, again unnecessary to support the decision, was that the right to a posthumous affiliation order was unknown to English law. Astbury J, whilst he may also have been influenced by the supporting view then expressed by Dicey, relied upon an early New York decision to that effect.[9] The Irish Supreme Court also adopted this approach in refusing the enforcement of the judgment on divorce costs, because divorce is unknown to Irish law.[10] But this view has been criticised, correctly it is suggested, in other decisions. Thus in *Burchell v Burchell*,[11] a judgment of an Ohio court in divorce proceedings against a wife, requiring her to make a lump sum payment to her husband representing his equitable interest in a property in Ontario was enforced in Ontario, even though proceedings against a wife for alimony could not be brought there. There are dicta to the same effect in the English Queen's Bench Division,[12] where Parker CJ cited Cardozo J in his usual perceptiveness:

'If aid is to be withheld here, it must be because the cause of action in its nature offends our sense of justice or menaces the public welfare. We may even have no legislation on the subject. That is not enough to show that public policy forbids us to enforce the foreign right. A right of action is property. If a foreign statute gives the right, the mere fact that we do not give a like right is no reason for refusing to help the plaintiff in getting what belongs to him. We are not so provincial as to say that every solution of a problem is money because we deal with it otherwise at home.'[13]

This, it is thought, neatly encapsulates the correct principle. Despite the suggestion of Dicey and Morris[14] that the 1920 scheme formulation comes close to saying that, if the cause of action is unknown to the lex fori, the judgment cannot be registered, the words appear not to prevent the preferred construction being applied. A fortiori, it will be difficult for a requested court to refuse registration where the cause of action, though known to it, was dealt with in ways unknown to the requested state. Thus a judgment for alimony will not be refused registration because the divorce was granted on grounds unrecognised by the lex fori.[15] Again, a judgment providing for payment of money in circumstances which are beyond the jurisdiction of the requested court will not, for that reason, offend the value system of the requested state. Accordingly a requested court which has no powers of its own to order payment of arrears of maintenance more than a year old may still enforce a final and conclusive judgment for consolidated arrears including those over a year old.[16] Indeed, it can be argued that it may enforce any final judgment, however long-standing the maintenance arrears,[17] even when this local rule against hoarding is based upon public policy considerations.[18] The reasons for local public policy may not be strong enough to require them to be universally applied.

1 *United States of America v Cassidy* (1977) 79 DLR (3d) 635 at 637 (BC), where 'lifting the corporate veil' in order to permit proceedings against the defendant personally was held not to be contrary to public policy.
2 [1958] IR 336. Cf *Vervaeke v Smith* [1983] 1 AC 145, [1982] 2 All ER 144, where the House of Lords refused to recognise a foreign decree holding a marriage to be a nullity as sham, as this was inconsistent with an earlier English decision that the marriage was valid. Both decisions were based upon public policy grounds.
3 [1921] 1 Ch 522.
4 Ibid, at 527.
5 [1940] 2 DLR 661 (BC).
6 Ibid, at 667.
7 Cf *Neporany v Kir* 5 AD (2d) 438 (1958) where a Canadian judgment for seduction and criminal conversation was successfully sued upon in New York, despite the abolition of the cause of action there.
8 Above.
9 *De Brimone v Penniman* (1873) 10 Blatchford Circuit Court Reports 436.
10 *Mayo-Perrott v Mayo-Perrott*, above.
11 [1926] 2 DLR 595. (The husband was domiciled in Ohio.)
12 *Phrantzes v Argenti* [1960] 1 All ER 778 at 782–783.
13 *Loucks v Standard Oil Co of New York* (1919) 224 New York Reports 99 at 110.
14 Op cit, p 1087.
15 Cf *Burpee v Burpee* [1929] 3 DLR 18 (BC); *Meyers v Meyers* [1935] OWN 547.
16 *Patton v Reed* (1972) 30 DLR (3d) 494 (BC).
17 *Stark v Stark* (1978) 94 DLR (3d) 556 (Alta); *Beatty v Beatty* [1924] 1 KB 807, 93 LJKB 750, CA; *Re Reciprocal Enforcement of Judgments Act, Mackowey v Mackowey* (1954) 14 WWR (NS) 190 (BC). But see dicta to the contrary in *Patton v Reed*, above, at 499, where it seems to have been argued that, for public policy reasons, the judgment should not be regarded as final and conclusive.
18 This prohibition is to prevent a party being crippled by the burden of arrears to meet maintenance already provided by other means: *Patton v Reed*, above, at 499.

(b) *Judgments obtained in breach of natural justice*

3.63 Neither scheme makes reference to cases where the original judgment was obtained without due process, although both encompass certain features under the heads of want of due service or adequate notice[1] and fraud.[2] Any objections to enforcement on grounds of other defects of this nature must be dealt with as matters of public policy (1933 scheme) or as 'unjust or inconvenient' (1920 scheme). There seems little doubt that the propriety of the original proceedings may be investigated if they offend against the forum's views of substantial justice.[3] But, as a rule, participants in foreign cases are expected to take procedural requirements and court processes as they find them. If there has been non-compliance, participants are expected to seek their remedy before the appropriate appellate or reviewing court in the original jurisdiction. Allegations about the procedural injustice of the original court will not be readily admitted in registration processes. Indeed, Dicey and Morris claim that they have not encountered a single reported judgment in which a foreign judgment in personam has been successfully impeached on this ground.[4] The unlikelihood of this in the context of the registration schemes needs little elaboration. It is improbable that extensions will be made in favour of jurisdictions about whose legal processes any doubts are entertained on this ground.

That said, it is still possible to envisage circumstances in which a judgment has been obtained in a country within the scheme which has undergone serious political changes and where the courts are no longer able to provide adequate protection for foreign parties. It surely cannot be questioned, despite the paucity of case law, that this objection is open to a litigant who has been denied a fair opportunity to defend himself in circumstances which are an affront to the standards required by the receiving state;[5] for example, failure by lawyers instructed from abroad to present a defence or refusal by the original court to hear the lawyers briefed on the defendant's behalf.[6] Equally, this objection should be available if there is evidence of judicial bias or corruption which cannot be corrected for want of recourse to effective local procedures.[7] This should be so, it may be argued, even though an objection was taken in the original court or could have been taken and was not. On the other hand, the failure to take such an objection or the overruling of the objection before a court in a system which provides proper safeguards for the interests of litigants will be fatal to an argument under this head.[8] Similarly if the want of opportunity to be heard is the consequence of the defendant's own failure to take appropriate action, the objection must fail.[9]

It is unlikely that any receiving court would refuse registration on this ground unless there had been forensic irregularities of a very serious nature which precluded the possibility of a fair and impartial trial.[10] Differences in procedure, as for example, the admission of hearsay evidence or the want of the chance to cross-examine or payment into court as a condition of leave to defend a summary judgment will not, in themselves, be enough.[11] It is also clear that the courts will not permit this ground to be used as a device to examine the merits of the original judgment. It is not contrary to natural justice that the judgment was patently erroneous or involved an incorrect application of the relevant law or was based on inadequate evidence.[12] This may, however, be subject to one qualification. The requested court, it can be argued, is entitled to look at the merits of a judgment if it is alleged that the law applied in that case was itself fundamentally repugnant to the standards of morality of the receiving state[13] or was 'an instrument of oppression and discrimination'.[14]

It has also been suggested in older accounts[15] that the requested court may examine the original decision if it is alleged that the foreign court had perversely reached a wrong decision on the matter of the foreign law to be applied. This was in effect the basis of the decision in *Simpson v Fogo*[16] but it is inconsistent with the approach adopted in *Godard v Gray*[17] and has been questioned in the House of Lords.[18] It would also be inconsistent with the principles underlying recognition of judgments if receiving courts were able to review the application by other states of their conflicts rules, anymore than to question the way in which they applied their other domestic law. Yet what if the foreign court 'though directed by its own law to apply the law of country X obstinately refused to do so'?[19] Or again, what if the original decision involved 'obstinately or dishonestly shutting one's eyes to what one knows to be right'[20] on the question of what law to apply or deliberately applying domestic law which is at variance with generally accepted doctrines of private international law?[21] Such issues would normally be seen by a receiving court as suitable for remedy by the appellate bodies of the original jurisdiction. Yet a public policy argument in favour of non-recognition is strong in the exceptional case where all the courts of a particular country have blatantly and perversely refused to apply the law of another system which should be applied under the prevailing conflicts rules there or under generally accepted doctrines.[22]

1 Paras 3.52–3.54 above.
2 Paras 3.55–3.56 above.
3 Cf *Pemberton v Hughes* [1899] 1 Ch 781, CA at 790, per Lord Linley.
4 Op cit, p 1089.
5 *Lissack v Duarte* 1974 (4) SA 560: failure to apprise the defendant of the correct procedure was fatal.
6 Cf *Newmarch v Newmarch* [1978] Fam 79, [1978] 1 All ER 1 (divorce); *Re House of Colour Ltd v Expert Decorators Ltd* (1968) 70 DLR (2d) 527.
7 Cf *Price v Dewhurst* (1837) 8 Sim 279, 6 LJ Ch 226.
8 *Jacobson v Franchon* (1927) 138 LT 386, CA.
9 *Re Reciprocal Enforcement of Judgments Act, Wigston v Chowen* (1964) 49 WWR 543 (Sask); *Pilavachi & Co Ltd v International Chemical Co Ltd* [1965] 1 CLR 97 (Cyprus), where the defendant's inability to finance his defence from abroad was held not to deprive him of his opportunity to present his case.
10 Cf *Hilton v Guyot* 159 US 113 (1895).
11 Ibid, *De Cosse Brissac v Rathbone* (1861) 6 H & N 301, 30 LJ Ex 238; *Scarpetta v Lowenfeld* (1911) 27 TLR 509; *Robinson v Fenner* [1913] 3 KB 835, 83 LJKB 81; *May v Shell Co of Hong Kong Ltd* [1981] 1 WWR 193 (BC).
12 *Godard v Grey* (1870) LR 6 QB 139, 40 LJQB 62; *Robinson v Fenner*, above; *SRL Rolimex v McMormack Zatman Ltd* (1979) 78 APR 436 (NB).
13 *Burchell v Burchell* [1926] 2 DLR 595 at 602–3 (Ont). See para 3.62 above.
14 This phrase, used in relation to the question of public policy as relating to the application of exchange control legislation to contracts, appears to have equal relevance in this context: *Re Helbert Wagg & Co Ltd* [1956] Ch 323 at 352.
15 Piggott, op cit, p 380.
16 (1863) 1 Hem & M 195, 32 LJ Ch 249.
17 (1870) LR 6 QB 139, 40 LJQB 62.
18 *Carl-Zeiss Stiftung v Rayner and Keeler Ltd (No 2)* [1966] 2 All ER 536 at 555 and 592; *Tracomin SA v Sudan Oil Seeds Co Ltd* [1983] 1 All ER 404 at 415, per Staughton J.
19 Nygh, op cit, pp 95–96.
20 Lord Reid, in *Carl-Zeiss Stiftung v Rayner and Keeler Ltd (No 2)* above, at 555.
21 Ibid.
22 Cf *Castrique v Imrie* (1870) LR 4 HL 414 at 445, per Lord Hatherley LC.

(c) *The enforcement itself offends public policy*

3.64 There are likely to be few circumstances when objection can be taken on public policy grounds to enforcement as such, rather than to the cause of action or the original proceedings. It should make no difference to whom the payment will actually be made, as for example that it may be used to reimburse public funds of another state, if the judgment is of a kind which can be recognised.[1] It should make no difference that the moneys paid may be subject to local exchange controls.

But there are cases where the lex fori refuses to allow its process to be used against particular categories of defendant. In such cases, though the judgment itself was capable of being recognised, it may be proper to prevent the registration because it is not consistent with the interests of the state that local process be made available against the defendant.

The foreign diplomat, for example, generally has immunity from local process, unless explicitly waived. Thus registration of a judgment given, for example, before the diplomatic appointment to the receiving state could be resisted by him on this ground. There seems a good case for saying that the protection of diplomatic and related types of immunity is grounded in public policy.

Similarly, the property of a foreign sovereign is generally immune from process to enforce any judgments, whether obtained within or without the jurisdiction. Even where the judgment is obtained in another country in circumstances which permit the receiving court to recognise it, it will normally not be registrable unless the sovereign expressly consents or unless, in jurisdictions with modern legislation on sovereign immunity, the property against which it will be enforced is in use, or is intended for use, for commercial purposes.[2] Again, respect for sovereign immunity is part of the public policy of a state and should preclude the registration of judgments just as it prevents the commencement of local legal proceedings. Similar considerations will apply with respect to international organisations and their members to the extent that they are given immunity from process under the lex fori.

1 *Connor v Connor* [1974] 1 NZLR 632.

2 Cf State Immunity Act 1978 (UK), s 13(2), (3); see *Alcom Ltd v Republic of Colombia* [1984] 2 All ER 6 HL establishing that moneys in the current bank account of a diplomatic mission may not be immune if the balance in the account is solely to meet liabilities incurred in commercial transactions.

Objection 7: The applicant was not the person in whom the rights under the judgment were vested

3.65 The 1933 scheme requires a registering court to set aside a registration if it is satisfied:

> 'that the rights under the judgment are not vested in the person by whom the application for registration was made'.[1]

The statute permits an application to be made only by 'a judgment creditor',[2] a term defined as:

> 'the person in whose favour the judgment was given and includes any person in whom the rights under the judgment have become vested by succession or assignment or otherwise.'[3]

The main purpose of this provision is to meet the case where the original judgment creditor has lost his rights in the judgment as, for example, on bankruptcy when they may have become vested in the trustee in bankruptcy.[4] This ground permits the debtor to resist registration should the original creditor attempt to claim an entitlement which he no longer enjoys. This is not a case in which the registration was in fact made in contravention of the Act,[5] as the applicant fulfilled the statutory criteria as the person in whose favour the judgment was given. It is, of course, only the judgment debtor who may resist on this ground,[6] not the person in whom the rights under the judgment are actually vested,[7] whatever his powers may be under other general procedures.[8] The provision will allow an objection where the rights in the judgment have been transferred subsequent to the registration itself, provided that the application to set aside is made within the permitted time.

The 1920 scheme has no equivalent provision but arguably the requested court should exercise its discretion not to allow registration in equivalent circumstances which, given a similar definition of 'judgment creditor',[9] could equally well arise under that scheme. It is surely 'not just or convenient' to allow a person to enforce a judgment the rights in which he has lost to another person.[10]

1 FJREA, s 4(2)(a)(vi).
2 Ibid, s 2(1).
3 Ibid, s 11(1): see para 3.17, above.
4 Greer Committee; Minutes of Meeting, 25 April 1932, LCO/2, Doc No 1690.
5 FJREA, s 4(2)(a)(i): paras 3.50 and 3.51 above.
6 FJREA, s 4(1).
7 The person actually entitled to the payment will also be a 'judgment creditor' able to seek registration in his own right.
8 Eg by invoking the courts' inherent power to stay proceedings which are an abuse of process.
9 AJA, s 12(1).
10 AJA, s 9(1); RSC Ord 71, r 9(3) (UK). Similarly under the Canadian legislation, it could be argued that this would constitute a good defence if the case was an action on the judgment: para 3.70 below.

Objection 8: The existence of a prior judgment on the same matter

(a) *Nature of the discretion*

3.66 The 1933 scheme permits the setting aside of a registered judgment where it is shown that 'the matter in dispute... had previously to the date of the judgment... been the subject of a final and conclusive judgment by a court having jurisdiction in the matter'.[1] The 1920 scheme does not deal explicitly with this case but the discretion which permits registration to be refused or set aside on the grounds that local enforcement would be unjust or inconvenient allows similar considerations to be invoked.[2] Both statutes, therefore, involve the exercise of a discretion by the registering court in this respect. There is, however, little guidance from case law as to its exercise. The origins of this section are to be found in a proposal that the requested court should refuse registration where the judgment was in respect of a matter which had already formed the subject matter of a decision of a court of competent jurisdiction situated in any part of HM dominions and was inconsistent with it. This was thought a desirable innovation to protect against the enforcement of foreign judgments which had failed to recognise an earlier judgment from the Commonwealth.[3] This was subsequently made discretionary and extended to judgments of foreign courts, it being noted that, although there was no reported authority, the courts at common law, without doubt, had the power to deal with this circumstance either by recognising one judgment as a defence to an action on the other if they conflicted or by staying proceedings to enforce the later foreign judgment.[4]

The purpose of the section, therefore, was to remove any obligation to register a judgment which was inconsistent with an earlier judgment between the parties dealing with the same matter. Almost certainly it was intended to be used in cases where, had the proceedings which led to the second judgment occurred in the requested state, the early judgment would have had to be recognised as a defence to those proceedings. Although doubts existed in 1933 as to application of estoppel in respect of foreign judgments, it was well established at common law that further proceedings should not be brought on the same cause of action by an unsuccessful plaintiff or by a successful plaintiff where an earlier judgment on the matter had been satisfied.[5] The 1933 provision, however, is expressed in terms which are capable of applying more broadly, especially following the development of estoppel per rem judicatam. Recent judicial pronouncements have treated this provision as reflecting the doctrine of res judicata[6] and allowing the requested court thereby to apply that doctrine as part of the lex fori.[7]

The 1933 Act stipulates three pre-requisites for all cases.

(i) *Both judgments must have been concerned with the same matter in dispute.* The provision does not require identity of cause of action or of parties, unlike the recognition provisions in section 8.[8] The omission may have been to ensure that it is irrelevant that the parties were plaintiff in one case and defendant in the other, so long as the same matter was involved, and that judgments in rem which are binding on all parties are within the scope of the provision. The omission of any reference to causes of action allows application of the provision to judgments creating an issue estoppel as well as those effecting cause of action estoppel. Although the former doctrine in its application to foreign judgments is of recent origin,[9] there are suggestions that the provision extends this far.[10] It seems improbable, however, that registration will be refused unless the issue which has been decided differently in the later proceedings was one which went to the roots of the requested judgment. It is much more likely that this provision will be invoked where the same cause of action or claim arising from the same facts is involved between the same parties. The requested court is unlikely to enter upon the question of whether the second court applied or should have applied an estoppel.[11] In essence, this ground seems to be a species of public policy which it is for the requested court to decide.

Where the scheme is expressed to apply to arbitral awards which have become enforceable in the same manner as a judgment in the country of origin, the registering court must consider whether to set aside if there is in existence an award on the same matter which has become so enforceable before the later judgment was entered.

(ii) *The earlier judgment must have been final and conclusive on the matter in dispute.* The reference to 'final and conclusive' will have the same construction as is applied in respect of the requested judgment itself.[12] The earlier judgment must have so determined the matter in dispute as to make it res judicata in the original jurisdiction and thus not capable of being re-opened before the court giving that judgment.

(iii) *The earlier judgment must have been handed down by a court having jurisdiction in the matter.* It is not clear whether the reference is to jurisdiction under the law of the original state or under the conflicts rules of the requested state or both. The 1933 Act requires its jurisdictional rules to be applied only in respect of the requested judgment.[13] Moreover, the phrase 'jurisdiction in the matter' could be construed as a reference to the internal law of the original state.[14] Despite the differences in language, it seems logical that the same requirements will be sought as are applied to the requested judgment.[15] Thus both domestic and international jurisdiction will be required. Where the first judgment was a nullity by the law of the original state or would not be recognised under the conflict rules if presented for enforcement in the requested state, it must be ignored and this rule will have no application.

1 FJREA, s 4(1)(b).
2 AJA, s 9(1) and RSC Ord 71, r 9(3).
3 Rough draft of the statute prepared by W. E. Beckett in 1929: LCO/2, Doc No 1688.
4 A further 'rough draft' was appended to the confidential Gwyer–Beckett Report on Treaty Negotiations, July 1931, Annex I, II, LCO/2, Doc No 1688.
5 See para 4.02 below.
6 *Vervaeke v Smith* [1982] 2 All ER 144, HL at 151, per Lord Hailsham LC, at 154, per Lord Diplock, and at 156, per Lord Simon.
7 For the view that estoppel per rem judicatam is adjectival law, see ibid, per Lord Simon at 156; Dicey and Morris, op cit, p 1190.
8 Para 4.04 below.
9 *Carl-Zeiss Stiftung v Rayner and Keeler Ltd (No 2)* [1967] 1 AC 853, [1966] 2 All ER 536.
10 *Vervaeke v Smith*, above, per Lord Hailsham LC at 151 and Lord Simon at 156 and in the Court of Appeal [1981] 1 All ER 55 at 90, per Arnold P.
11 *Godard v Grey* (1870) LR 6 QB 139, 40 LJQB 62. See note 7.
12 Para 3.16 above.
13 FJREA, s 4(1)(a)(ii) and s 4(2).
14 Cf 'jurisdiction in the circumstances of the case' in FJREA, s 4(1)(a)(ii).
15 Paras 3.34 and 3.35 above.

(b) *Exercise of the discretion*

3.67 There are three sets of circumstances in which the discretion to set aside registration on this ground may need to be considered.

(i) *Where the earlier judgment is a judgment of a court in the registering state.* It may be expected that the requested court will invariably give preference to a judgment handed down in its own jurisdiction which has already become enforceable. As one English judge suggested, it is only if recognition is statutorily required that a foreign judgment will be recognised in preference to an earlier English judgment on the same matter.[1] Registration of a foreign judgment which is to the same effect as that of a local court would in any case be superfluous, whilst registration of a judgment which is to a different effect would be to contradict the authority of the local courts whose decision must be treated as rendering the matter res judicata. The suggestion of Arnold P in *Vervaeke v Smith*[2] that setting aside might depend upon whether the foreign court was applying the law of the requested state which was also applied in the earlier judgment of the requested state should be treated with caution. For even if a foreign law were applied by both, the local and earlier judgment will surely be given priority. Similar considerations should apply where the first judgment is a foreign judgment which has been registered in the requested state or has been the subject of a successful common law action upon it. For in both cases, enforcement of that judgment has been authorised by the requested state.

(ii) *Where both judgments are to the same effect and both are foreign.* This may arise where the plaintiff obtains a money judgment in subsequent proceedings in the same matter in respect of which the defendant was unsuccessful in earlier litigation. Again, the plaintiff may have pursued his claim before the courts of different states and succeeded in both, though the sum payable may not be the same in both. Where the sum is the same, there seems no reason why the applicant should not have the second registered, so long as the debt has not been satisfied at the time of application.[3] The principle of estoppel has no application in such a case. On the other hand, if the first judgment is satisfied before payment is made under the registered judgment, registration of the latter should be set aside.

The case for permitting the registration of the later judgment is strengthened where, for any reason, the first cannot be enforced, for example, for want of assets in the country where it was made or its enforcement in the original state is complicated or expensive. More difficult issues arise when the earlier judgment is for a greater sum than the later judgment. As the creditor will be foregoing part of his entitlement by seeking to enforce a smaller sum, the registering court should not prevent registration. Such a course of action is likely in any case to be sought only where there are difficulties in obtaining the sum due under the earlier judgment. Most Commonwealth jurisdictions are likely to treat the satisfaction of a registered judgment elsewhere as full satisfaction of another judgment on the same dispute between the same parties, should the plaintiff seek to enforce the latter.[4]

Where the later judgment involves a larger sum than was awarded under the earlier judgment, there seems no reason in principle why the judgment creditor should not have advantage of it, so long as the former is not satisfied.[5] There is one possible qualification. On one view,[6] the first judgment may qualify as one to which recognition must be granted by virtue of section 8 of the 1933 Act as a judgment from a scheme jurisdiction which is registrable, or would have been registrable if a sum of money had been ordered. If this view is accepted, then registration of the later judgment should be set aside. This, it is suggested elsewhere,[7] is not the true effect of section 8.

(iii) *Where the earlier judgment is in conflict with the later judgment and both are foreign.* This case can only arise where registration is sought for a money judgment handed down against the judgment debtor who had been successful in his defence in earlier proceedings between the same parties on the same claim.[8] It is in this case that the discretion to set aside will usually be exercised.[9] For in the eyes of the requested court, the matter was conclusively decided by the first judgment. This, however, is subject to one qualification. If the judgment creditor can establish that the earlier judgment, despite being final and conclusive and given by a competent court, has been refused recognition in the requested state or that it fails to meet the criteria for recognition either at common law or under section 8,[10] then the registration of the later judgment should be allowed to stand. It is only where both judgments qualify for recognition in the requested state that the later one should be refused registration.

1 *Vervaeke v Smith* [1981] 1 All ER 55 at 90, per Everleigh LJ. The Court of Appeal gave fuller consideration to this provision than the House of Lords. It may be noted that the Brussels Convention on Jurisdiction and Enforcement of Judgments in Civil and Commercial Matters, 1968, gives absolute priority to domestic judgments of the requested state: art 27(3).

2 Ibid, at 90.

3 FJREA, s 2(1), proviso (b).

4 Cf. *Taylor v Hollard* [1902] 1 KB 676, 71 LJKB 278; *Kohnke v Karger* [1951] 2 KB 670, [1951] 2 All ER 179; *Clinton v Ford* (1982) 37 OR (2d) 448.
5 *Barber v Lamb* (1860) 8 CBNS 95, 29 LJCP 234.
6 *Black-Clawson International Ltd v Papierwerke Waldhof-Aschaffenburg AG* [1975] 1 All ER 810 at 817, per Lord Reid.
7 Para 4.05 below.
8 For this purpose, the 'debtor' may have been the plaintiff in the original proceedings who successfully met a counterclaim by the original defendant who, as the judgment creditor, obtained judgment in the later proceedings.
9 Wolff, op cit, p 270, has argued that neither judgment has stronger claims to be recognised and thus neither should be. The Brussels Convention, art 27(5), prohibits recognition of judgments irreconcilable with earlier judgments given in non-contracting states.
10 See Chapter 4 below.

Objection 9: An appeal has been successful or the judgment has been set aside in the country of origin

3.68 Where an appeal on a requested judgment has been successful or the judgment has been set aside in the country of origin *before* the application to register, it cannot be registered under either scheme. It is, of course, not enforceable by execution in the original country at the date of application (1933 Act)[1] and its enforcement would not be just and convenient (1920 Act).[2] Where, however, such proceedings are completed after the registration, the picture is less clear. Under the 1920 Act, the initial registration almost certainly should not have been made since the appeal would have been pending:[3] registration should be set aside for that reason.[4] Under the 1933 Act, however, objection will be taken for the first time on an application to set aside. The sole ground for setting aside which seems available will be that the judgment was registered in contravention of the requirement that it be enforceable in the country of origin.[5] But the relevant time in that respect is the date of the application for registration, not that for setting aside. In the event that the judgment was enforceable in the country of origin at that time, notwithstanding a pending appeal, there is no obvious ground to set aside unless the judgment is treated as having been extinguished and is not therefore one to which the scheme applies.[6] Some of the Australian statutes, therefore, make specific provision requiring setting aside in that case.[7]

1 FJREA, s 2(1)(b).
2 AJA, s 9(1).
3 AJA, s 9(2)(e).
4 Eg RSC Ord 71, r 9(3).
5 FJREA, s 4(1)(a); *Re A Debtor (No 11 of 1939)* [1939] 2 All ER 400, CA.
6 Ibid.
7 ACT, Ord 1954, No 11, s 8(1)(a)(v); cf NT, Ord 1955, No 21, s 8(1)(a)(v).

Objection 10: An appeal is pending or intended[1]

3.69 The 1920 Act requires an application for registration to be refused where 'the judgment debtor satisfies the registering court either that an appeal is pending or that he is entitled and intends to appeal against the judgment'.[2] Under the 1933 scheme, the matter can only be raised by the debtor on an application to be set aside:[3] this may be raised at the same stage under the 1920 scheme too.[4] Presumably in both schemes the date at which the appeal must be pending or intended will be that on which the debtor applies to set aside. In both instances, the decision to set aside rests in the discretion of the registering court which, in granting an application, may impose such terms as it thinks just. As an alternative to setting aside, the 1933 Act permits an application to set aside on this ground to be adjourned, on such terms as the court thinks just, until the expiration of such period as appears to the court to be reasonably sufficient to enable the applicant to take the necessary steps to have the appeal disposed of by the competent tribunal.[5] This is not possible under the 1920 scheme.

The 1933 Act has a further apparent difference in its extended definition of 'appeal' which 'includes any proceeding by way of discharging or setting aside a judgment or an application for a new trial or a stay of execution'.[6] It is arguable that a court in the 1920 scheme could adopt a similar extensive construction by treating these cases as within its power to set aside 'for sufficient reason'.[7]

Under what circumstances can the registering court refuse to exercise its discretion to set aside or adjourn, and allow the original judgment to be enforced? The English Court of Appeal has suggested that registration should normally be ordered even where there are arguable grounds for disputing the judgment on appeal. 'Full faith and credit' should be given to a judgment which in other respects meets the requirements for registration, notwithstanding the availability of appeal.[8] This is consistent with the common law approach under which a judgment is final and conclusive, notwithstanding an appeal,[9] and thus enforceable. There will usually be imposed a stay of execution or at least conditions on execution which will protect the interests of those with the right to appeal.[10] Such an approach is particularly sensible where the appeal is unlikely to affect the outcome and where the debtor is using the procedure as a deliberate delaying tactic.[11]

Elsewhere in the Commonwealth, however, the width of the statutory discretion and a reluctance to see it glossed as in England have been stressed. It has been suggested that a bona fide appeal on difficult issues where the outcome is far from clear at least justifies an adjournment of the application, if not setting aside, with a liberty to come back to seek setting aside, if the matter is to be the subject of a lengthy delay through appeal to the highest court in the country of origin.[12] Similarly, it has been suggested that an application to set aside should be adjourned where the appeal is imminent and where immediate execution involving a forced sale of local assets might lead to losses to the debtor which cannot be covered by conditions imposed on the execution.[13] In both instances, imposition of terms in adjourning the application is likely to be necessary.

One draw-back of setting aside a registration on this ground under the 1920 Act should be noted. Unless the court, when setting aside, has authority to permit a new application to be made if the appeal against the judgment is unsuccessful, setting aside would remove the creditor's ability to utilise these procedures altogether. For there is no explicit power to renew an application for registration when the appeal is disposed of, as under the 1933 Act.[14] The 1920 Act, of course, is based upon the premise that no initial registration should be made where an appeal was pending or intended. The absence of an equivalent provision to the 1933 subsection is a weakness. In cases where registration has in fact occurred, it may be necessary to allow it to stand but with a stay of execution pending the outcome of the appeal.

1 As to the effects of the availability of appeals on the finality of judgments, see para 3.16 above.
2 AJA, s 9(2)(e). The Canadian legislation is more precise by requiring that the appeal be pending or the time within which it may be brought has not expired.
3 FJREA, s 5(1).
4 Cf RSC Ord 71, r 9(3).

5 FJREA, s 5(1).
6 Ibid, s 11(1).
7 See note 4.
8 *SA Consortium General Textiles v Sun and Sand Agencies* [1978] QB 279, [1978] 2 All ER 339. A fortiori, if the defendant is seeking stay in order to pursue a counterclaim in a foreign action.
9 Para 3.16 above.
10 *Nouvion v Freeman* (1889) 15 App Cas 1, 59 LJ Ch 337; *Colt Industries Inc v Sarlie (No 2)* [1966] 3 All ER 85, [1966] 1 WLR 1287.
11 As in *Re A Debtor (No 11 of 1939)* [1939] 2 All ER 400.
12 *Hunt v BP Exploration Co (Libya) Ltd* [1980] 1 NZLR 104.
13 *BP Exploration Co (Libya) Ltd v Hunt* [1980] 1 NSWLR 496.
14 FJREA, s 5(2). On renewed applications, see para 3.71 below.

Objection 11: There would be a good defence if the proceedings were by action on the judgment (Canada only)

3.70 The Canadian legislation does not contain any discretion to refuse or to set aside registration where the enforcement would be unjust or inconvenient. The discretion to register, however, may not be exercised where the judgment debtor shows that he 'would have a good defence if an action were brought on the original judgment'.[1] The purpose of the provision is to ensure that registration cannot occur in cases where an action on the judgment would fail in the requested jurisdiction.[2] It is not a mechanism to permit the debtor to raise defences which might be raised in that jurisdiction in proceedings to try the original cause of action.[3]

In consequence, the debtor may invoke in aid the rules, whether common law or statutory, in force in the requested jurisdiction on the question of recognition of foreign judgments. These may include defences which are evident also from the terms of the enforcement legislation itself, as, for example, want of jurisdiction in the original court or of finality of the original judgment.[4] But the provision also allows resort to be made to unique or unusual rules which have been adopted by the legislature or developed by the courts in particular Canadian jurisdictions. The proposal of the Commissioners on Uniformity of Legislation in Canada that a model Act on defences should be adopted to eliminate differences has been taken up in only two provinces.[5]

Reliance upon this provision, however, requires the debtor to establish that there is a high probability of success and that the defence is patent from the material already before the requested court or which is capable of being presented in a Chambers application. For the defence to be asserted must be 'good'.[6]

The provision has been relied upon to set aside the ex parte registration of default judgments on the grounds of absence of jurisdiction of the original court at common law.[7] It has been invoked to challenge the original proceedings as allegedly having been obtained contrary to natural justice,[8] where the judgment was not of a kind upon which an action could be brought in the province[9] or where the judgment was of a kind not enforceable in the requested jurisdiction,[10] or because the defence of set-off could have been raised in an action.[11]

This ground also operates in certain provinces to allow the defendant to reopen the merits of external judgments under unusual statutory provisions which have been long in force in those juridictions.[12] Although the Uniformity Commissioners were of the view that such a defence should not be applied under the enforcement legislation, whatever the position in relation to actions on the judgment,[13] in a number of cases the statutes have been invoked. The requested court, however, is unlikely to allow a defence on the original merits to be raised if it calls for a trial de novo by the requested court which would involve the credibility of witnesses or put in question matters of arguable law. To permit a full re-trial would completely undermine the scheme.[14] It is, however, apparent that the defence will operate if the error is patent from the material available for the application for registration. A similar position obtains in British Columbia where, even without statutory provision, registration has been set aside for manifest error in the original judgment[15] in application of a general common law defence in that province.[16]

Although the point has not been explicitly taken, there seems no reason why courts outside Canada employing the 1920 Act should not use their discretionary powers to refuse registration where an action on the judgment would fail under the law of the requested state.[17] The 1933 Act, however, contains an exhaustive statement of the grounds for setting aside.[18]

1 Eg Alberta, R–6, s 2(6)(g). The provision is derived from the Model Uniform Act, prepared by the Conference of Commissioners on Uniformity of Legislation in Canada, in 1924.
2 *Canadian Credit Men's Trust Association Ltd v Ryan* [1930] 1 DLR 280 (Alta). See K. H. Nadleman, (1960) 38 Can Bar Rev 68 at pp 72–3.
3 *Re Guildhall Insurance Co and Jackson* (1968) 69 DLR (2d) 137 (Alta) *Hill v Bank of Montreal* (1980) 14 Alta LR (2d) 78; *Eggleton v Broadway Agencies* (1982) 32 AR 61. Insofar as *Ling v Yip* (1975) 54 DLR (3d) 317 (Alta) suggests otherwise, it must be doubted: J. Swan, (1981) 13 Ottawa L Rev 123 at pp 151–2.
4 *Re Guildhall Insurance Co and Jackson,* above.
5 The model Foreign Judgments Act has been adopted, with some modifications, in New Brunswick: F–19, and in Saskatchewan, F–18. The model was finalised in *Proceedings of Conference of Commissioners on Uniformity of Legislation in Canada* 1933, p 35 and further revised, ibid 1964, p 107. Further revisions are in hand.
6 *Re Aero Trades Western Ltd and Ben Hocum & Son Ltd* (1974) 51 DLR (3d) 617 (Man).
7 *Canadian Credit Men's Trust Association Ltd v Ryan,* above; *Re Tangye and Smith Ltd v Pelican Carbon Co of Canada* [1935] 1 DLR 759 (Ont); *Eggleton v Broadways Agencies,* above; *Rafferty's Restaurants Ltd v Sawchuck* (1983) 20 MR (2d) 440.
8 *Re Reciprocal Enforcement of Judgments Act, Wigston v Chowen* (1964) 49 WWR 543 (Sask).
9 *Koven v Toole* (1954) 13 WWR (NS) 444 (Man); but see para 3.12 above.
10 Para 3.12 above.
11 *Ling v Yip,* above; *Alberta Livestock Transplants Ltd v Pine Tree Rancho Ltd* (1978) 92 DLR (3d) 478 (Sask). But the fact that the defendant had a credit note in his favour prior to the *original* judgment does not constitute a good defence: *Re a Reciprocal Enforcement of Judgments Act, Re An Ontario Judgment, Gagnon v Safety Freight Ltd* (1959) 27 WWR 678 (Man).
12 Castel, op cit, pp 471–478. Ontario (in relation to Quebec judgments), Judicature Act, RSO, cap 223, ss 54–56; Manitoba, Queens Bench Act, RSM, C–280, s 83; Nova Scotia, Rules of Practice, Order XXV, r 38; Prince Edward Island, Rules of Court, O.35. See Law Reform Commission of Manitoba, Report No 21, 1976 which recommended the retention of the Manitoba provisions as a necessary safeguard for Manitoba debtors.
13 (1925) 10 Proceedings Can Bar Ass 387. Also of this view: *Re Hearn v Kemp and Kemp* (1969) 70 WWR 609 (Alta).
14 *Re Aero Trades Western Ltd and Ben Hocum & Son Ltd,* above. Whilst the Manitoba provisions are made 'subject to the Reciprocal Enforcement of Judgments Act', the latter does not explicitly override the former in this respect.
15 *Re Gacs and Maierovitz* (1968) 68 DLR (2d) 345; *Re House of Colour Ltd v Expert Decorators Ltd* (1968) 70 DLR (2d) 527.
16 *Boyle v Victoria Yukon Trading Co* (1902) 9 BCR 213, CA: see para 3.16 above.
17 Cf RSC Ord 71, r 9(3): 'there is some other sufficient reason for setting aside'.
18 Para 3.33 above.

Further applications for registration after setting aside

3.71 The 1933 Act explicitly allows a further application for registration to be made where the registration was set aside because an appeal was pending or intended and where the judgment was not at the date of the application enforceable by execution in the country of origin.[1] In both instances, a further application is possible when the obstacle has disappeared. Where the registration is set aside because it has been partly satisfied, a further application is permitted in relation to the outstanding balance.[2] The implication is that, in other cases of setting aside under the 1933 Act, no further application will be allowed. As the grounds for setting aside are in the main concerned with irreversible defects in the judgment, this must be the case. The one possible exception may be where the application was made by a person not entitled under the judgment.[3] Such a condition should not preclude an application by the appropriate person, on the argument that this may be treated as a first, not a renewed, application.

The 1920 Act is silent on this matter. Arguably, it would be open to the court when setting aside the application to impose a term, if it thinks fit, allowing a further application when a particular condition has been met.[4] Following the comment given above, such authorisation will be needed only if the registration is set aside because the judgment had been partly satisfied.[5]

1 FJREA, s 5(2).
2 Ibid, s 5(3).
3 Ibid, s 4(1)(a)(vi).
4 Cf RSC Ord 71, r 9(3).
5 For the position where registration was made when an appeal was pending, see para 3.69 above.

VII RELATIONSHIP WITH OTHER ENFORCEMENT SCHEMES

3.72 The 1920 scheme stands as an alternative to any other form of enforcement procedure locally available. There is only one limitation. Where proceedings are brought by way of an action on the judgment, whether by trial or under the summary judgment procedure,[1] the plaintiff is not normally entitled to recover any costs in that action if the judgment might have been registered under the scheme. This restriction does not apply where an application to register has been refused (which, it may be suggested, includes cases in which registration has been set aside) or unless the court otherwise orders.[2] Nor does it apply where the proceedings are brought upon the original cause of action.[3] The 1933 Act is more demanding:

> 'No proceedings for the recovery of a sum payable under a foreign judgment, being a judgment to which this Part of this Act applies, other than proceedings by way of registration of the judgment, shall be entertained by any court . . .'[4]

The purpose of this section is to take away the right to bring an action on the judgment at common law. The Greer Committee thought that the existence of an alternative procedure might lead to confusion amongst civil law countries within the scheme. Moreover, the provision would preclude the possibility of actions on those money judgments which were deliberately excluded from the scheme or which were brought because of perceived differences between jurisdictional rules under the statute and at common law.[5]

Two points need to be made, however. The restriction applies to those judgments to which the 1933 Act applies—viz, a judgment, as defined in the Act,[6] given by a designated court in a country covered by an extension order, which is final and conclusive, is for a sum of money, other than for a tax, fine or penalty, and is given after the scheme is extended to the country in question.[7] If a judgment meets these requirements, not only may the creditor not seek initial enforcement through an action on the judgment, but if registration is refused or the registration is set aside, no action may be brought subsequently at common law on the judgment. As the conditions for refusal or setting aside are close to those which will cause an action to fail, this conclusion produces little hardship.

Secondly, on its face, the provision does not appear to preclude an action on the original cause of action. At common law, the original cause of action is not treated as having merged into the foreign judgment, as is the case with domestic judgments. Thus, an action on the original cause of action in theory remains at common law one of the alternative courses of action.[8] Accordingly, a successful plaintiff may sue notwithstanding the judgment in his favour.[9] Where, however, judgment is against him, the plaintiff can be met with the argument that the original judgment must be treated as conclusive between the parties, if it satisfies the recognition requirements of section 8 of the 1933 Act or of the common law.[10] The Greer Committee in its discussions saw one purpose of section 8 was to provide a good defence against a second action on the same cause of action by the same litigant,[11] where a judgment already existed which met the statutory recognition conditions.

The non-merger rule, much criticised by commentators, has been abrogated for England and Wales and Northern Ireland by the Civil Jurisdiction and Judgments Act 1982.[12] No proceedings may now be brought there by any person on a cause of action in respect of which a judgment has been given in his favour in proceedings between the same parties, or their privies, in a court whether in the United Kingdom or outside, unless the judgment is not enforceable or entitled to recognition. Subject to the latter qualification, therefore, the 1933 Act has become the sole method of proceeding for enforcing a money claim which is the subject of a Commonwealth judgment to which the 1933 scheme applies.

1 RSC Ord 14. *Grant v Easton* (1883) 13 QBD 302, 53 LJQB 68, CA
2 AJA, s 9(5). Canadian statutes preserve the right to sue on the judgment or the original cause of action: eg Manitoba, R–20, s 13.
3 See below.
4 FJREA, s 6.
5 Greer Committee Report, p 64; Minutes of Meeting of 10 February 1932, LCO/2, Doc No 1690.
6 FJREA, s 11(1). See para 3.12 above.
7 Ibid, s 1(1), (2): see paras 3.13 to 3.19 above.
8 Dicey and Morris op cit, p 1110.
9 *Hall v Odber* (1809) 11 East 118; *Smith v Nicolls* (1839) 5 Bing NC 208, 8 LJCP 92; *Bank of Australasia v Harding* (1850) 9 CB 661, 19 LJCP 345; *Bank of Australasia v Nias* (1851) 16 QB 717, 20 LJQB 284; *Carl-Zeiss Stiftung v Rayner and Keeler (No 2)* [1967] 1 AC 853, [1966] 2 All ER 536; *Delfino v Trevis (No 2)* [1963] NSWR 194; *Dent v Hutton* [1924] 1 DLR 401. For other Canadian authorities, see Castel, op cit, p 479, n 255. Generally, see Read, op cit, pp 114–21 who argues that the foreign judgment should be treated as rendering the issue res judicata. For the argument that subsequent litigation may in a proper case be struck out as oppressive and vexatious, see J. Bloom, (1978) 57 Oregon Law Review 399 at p 406.
10 See Chapter 4 below. The section does not extend to plaintiff's judgments: para 4.05 below.
11 Minutes of Meeting of 18 February 1932, per Lord Justice Greer and of 5 April 1932, per H. C. Gutteridge, LRO/2, Doc No 1690.
12 S 34. P. A. Stone, (1983) 32 ICLQ 477 at 491 argues that the provision should not prevent actions on the same cause of action to enforce a money claim where the original judgment was for non-monetary relief and the plaintiff seeks to found estoppel thereon as to the matters decided.

CHAPTER 4

Recognition of Judgments under the Commonwealth Schemes

Introduction

4.01 Whilst the 1920 Act is concerned solely with questions of enforcement, the 1933 statute contains a provision dealing with the 'general effect of certain foreign judgments' which is concerned with the question of recognition.[1] In jurisdictions in which the former legislation applies, the general common law will normally apply in relation to recognition, and in particular on questions of estoppel per rem judicatam.[2] Further, as a registered judgment is to have the same force and effect as a judgment of the registering court, it may be argued that for all purposes relating to estoppel, whether cause of action or issue estoppel, such a judgment will not be distinguished from a locally obtained judgment.[3]

Where provisions modelled on section 8 of the 1933 Act operate, the position is less clear. The provisions are intended to operate only in respect of judgments from jurisdictions to which the scheme is extended but their exact effect, and especially their relationship with the common law, have been matters of some uncertainty amongst both judiciary and commentators. The circumstances which led to its inclusion in the legislation make evident that the section was deliberately drafted to confine its operation to what was then thought to be the common law on questions of recognition. Unfortunately, these objectives have been obscured by the convoluted form of the section and by the subsequent willingness of the courts to allow greater play to estoppel per rem judicatam in relation to foreign judgments.

1 FJREA, s 8.

2 Cheshire and North, op cit, pp 651–658; Dicey and Morris, op cit, pp 1072–1077; Castel, op cit, pp 463–478; Nygh, op cit, pp 87–90; *Tracomin SA v Sudan Oil Seeds Co Ltd* [1983] 1 All ER 404, [1983] 1 WLR 662; affd [1983] 3 All ER 137, [1983] 1 WLR 1026, CA. The Uniform Foreign Judgments Act devised in Canada is designed for this purpose: see the *Proceedings of the Conference of Commissioners on Uniformity of Legislation*, 1963, pp 95–103 and 1964, pp 26 and 107 ff for the Revised Model. An earlier version has been adopted by New Brunswick, RSNB, 1973, F-19: *Dovenmuehle v Rocca Group Ltd* (1981) 34 NBR (2d) 444 and Saskatchewan, RSS, 1978, F-18: see *Bobovec v Mesaric* (1981) 7 Sask R 175. A further revision is currently under discussion. See also Code of Civil Procedure 1908 (India), s 13, adopted in Kenya (Civil Procedure Act 1936, No 5, s 9); Tanzania (Civil Procedure Code 1966, No 49, s 11) and Uganda (Civil Procedure Act, Cap 65, s 9): S. Thanawalla, (1970) 19 ICLQ 430–446. Cf also Civil Procedure Act 1972 (Nauru), ss 7–8.

3 AJA, s 9(3)(a). Dicey and Morris, op cit, pp 1117–1120.

The Greer Committee proposals

4.02 The first draft appears in the confidential Gwyer-Beckett Report of July 1931 to the Foreign Office concerning the exploratory treaty negotiations conducted in Belgium, France and Germany.[1] In addition to suggested draft conventions, a rough draft of 'the future statute' was put forward.[2] This stated that

'A valid foreign judgment shall be recognised as conclusive of the matters of law and fact dealt with therein to the same extent and in the same manner as a judgment of a court of the United Kingdom given in the same matter and in similar circumstances.'[3]

This was explained as requiring a judgment to be recognised as 'conclusive on the matter adjudicated therein and operative as a valid defence to an action on the same matter if either (1) it was in favour of the defendant, or (2) it has been satisfied.'[4] This was the basis of the first and second drafts of the Bill produced for the consideration of the Greer Committee, with the addition of the proviso that 'in the case of an action in personam, a judgment shall only be recognised as conclusive and unimpeachable as between the parties thereto and their privies'.[5]

Beckett, who was progenitor of these formulations, justified them by asserting that a foreign judgment was just as much res judicata as an English judgment in the same circumstances and that the law did not limit recognition to those foreign judgments which were for sums of money.[6] The first proposition was strongly contested by the Chairman who doubted that it correctly stated the common law. He 'could not find that the doctrine of estoppel had ever been recognised as applying to foreign judgments'. The adoption of the proposed formula would produce the result that 'an estoppel applies not merely to the fact that the amount mentioned is due but also covers the essential grounds which are involved in the decision'.[7] By way of illustration he gave a case determining a husband's responsibility for the debts of his wife in which the fact that the lady was not his wife was put in issue by the pleadings and established. 'That finding as a ground for decision would be an estoppel between the parties in any subsequent litigation, although not the actual subject of the judgment.' In relation to a foreign judgment this would give rise to 'difficulties in determining when a question was merely cognisable by the way and when it was really an essential part of the judgment'. In so far as Dicey appeared to state the position otherwise,[8] he thought Dicey was wrong.

Professor H. C. Gutteridge supported this latter view, making particular point of the fact that there is no merger of a cause of action in a foreign judgment. It was inappropriate to introduce notions of estoppel when the plaintiff can sue on the original cause of action and prove the same facts again.[9]

The Committee accepted the Chairman's conclusion:

'... if it was desired to state that a foreign judgment in personam was a good defence against a new action on the same facts, he agreed that English law recognises them [sic] as being conclusive but if it was meant to state that a foreign judgment was to be conclusive as to everything decided on the pleadings and included in the record of the judgment, then he considered such a statement revolutionary and could not agree to its inclusion in the Bill.'[10]

His concern was also expressed in relation to similar formulations used in the draft conventions, which he feared 'might be construed as involving the recognition, not merely of the actual decision, but of the preliminary points which had been raised in the course of the judgment in order to arrive at the decision'.[11] It was agreed, therefore, to make clear that:

'recognition of a judgment means that such a judgment shall be treated as conclusive in any further action between the parties as to the matter thereby adjudicated upon and shall constitute a defence as to such matter in any further action between them in respect of the same cause of action.'[12]

Still not satisfied, Greer subsequently put forward a draft of the form of words which is now found in the Act, ironically 'to prevent a future argument that the words of the statute had the effect of giving a wider area to the binding quality of a foreign judgment than it has at common law.' At the same time, Beckett proposed that what is now section 8(3) be included to make that point absolutely clear.[13]

1 This printed Report, never published, was prepared by Sir Maurice Gwyer (Treasury Solicitor) and W. E. Beckett (Legal Adviser to the Foreign Office): LCO/2, Doc No 1688. A draft Bill, prepared by Beckett in 1929, did not deal with recognition: LCO/2, Doc No 1687 (T7404/661/371), nor was it considered by the first Greer Committee.
2 Ibid, Appendix I.
3 Ibid, cl 5(1). Foreign judgments were deemed to be valid unless absence of jurisdiction, fraud, insufficient notice where the judgment was obtained in default, or conflict with public policy were shown: ibid, cl 5(2). The jurisdictional rules were set out in cl 5(2) in terms wider than those accepted at common law.
4 Ibid, Appendix II, p 26.
5 Contained in LCO/2, Doc No 1690; 1st draft (1931), cl 7. This referred for the first time to judgments which could and were registered and those which could not be but if they were, would not be set aside. The second draft, now cl 9, included a fuller reference to the grounds for setting aside.
6 Minutes of Meeting of 10 February 1932: LCO/2, Doc No 1690.
7 Ibid, 18 February 1932.
8 Dicey *Conflict of Laws* (4th edn) rule 112, p 449 from which the words used in the clause were drawn. The same formula is found in the original Canadian Model Foreign Judgments Act, cl 4.
9 Minutes of Meeting of 18 February 1932. Gutteridge developed his position in (1932) 13 BYBIL 49 at pp 60–64.
10 Ibid.
11 Minutes of Meeting of 5 April 1932.
12 Minutes of Meeting of 11 April 1932. This precise terminology was entered into the conventions then under discussion.
13 Minutes of Meeting of 18 April 1932. The latter may well have been seen by him as allowing a wider construction if s 8(1) proved to be too narrow: see Greer Committee Report, p 7, footnote. See para 4.04 below for the text.

The Greer Committee conclusions

4.03 This account of the preparatory discussion suggests that section 8 was designed:

(i) to restate the common law on recognition of foreign judgments without amendment;[1]
(ii) to ensure that a foreign judgment will be recognised as binding upon the person against whom it was given, unless he can establish certain objections, so as to preclude re-litigation on the same cause of action;[2]
(iii) to provide that a judgment on the merits is a complete answer to an identical action brought by an unsuccessful plaintiff on the same subject matter and claiming the same relief;[3]
(iv) to confirm that the foreign judgment is not examinable on its merits and is impeachable only on prescribed grounds;[4]
(v) to preclude arguments that the principle of estoppel per rem judicatam was being introduced with respect to foreign judgments.[5]

As the Supreme Court of India has suggested in relation to the not dissimilar section 11 of the Indian Code of Civil Procedure 1908, the provision seems to have been concerned rather more with public policy considerations than with estoppel. Its purpose seems to have been to ensure that there was an end to litigation and that no-one should be put at risk twice on the same matter.[6]

Although discussions initially embraced judgments in rem it is probable that the Committee was only concerned to make detailed provision with respect to judgments in personam.[7] There is no evidence that the Committee gave any particular attention to the extent to which the section applies to judgments of a successful plaintiff: it was discussed throughout in relation to defensive objections by a successful defendant.[8] Lord Reid's contrary conclusion[9] is not borne out by the Minutes of the Committee. No discussion was entered upon whether a judgment decided otherwise than on the merits was to be recognised as rendering a matter in any way res judicata.[10] Whether the final version of the section fulfilled the Committee's objectives may be doubted in the light of its subsequent treatment.

1 In holding otherwise, the English Court of Appeal and Lord Diplock (dissenting) in *Black-Clawson International Ltd v Papierwerke Waldhof-Aschaffenburg AG* [1974] QB 660, [1974] 2 All ER 611; [1975] AC 591, [1975] 1 All ER 810 were in error.

2 Cf H. C. Gutteridge, (1932) 13 BYBIL 49 at 61.

3 Ibid; *Callandar v Dittrich* (1842) 4 Man & G 68, 1 Dowl NS 730.

4 Ibid.

5 The Greer Committee Report states at p 7 that the judgment will be recognised as conclusive between the original parties 'as regards the question therein adjudicated upon'. This phrase was explained as referring to 'the actual decision (the operative parts of the judgments) as opposed to the grounds or reasoning upon which it was based in the course of which other points of law or fact may have been incidentally decided as preliminaries (necessary or otherwise) to the final conclusion'. Cf Gutteridge, loc cit, note 2, at p 63: 'it would appear advisable to treat the foreign judgment as merely conclusive of the immediate and direct object of the litigation.'

6 *NP Venkateswara Prabhu v NP Krishna Prabhu* AIR 1977 SC 1268 at 1272, per Beg J.

7 Ibid, where the explanation given by the Committee in terms comparable with s 8(1) is said to apply to judgments in ordinary proceedings in personam.

8 But the published explanation states that a recognised judgment can be relied upon by any of the original parties or their privies 'if further proceedings are brought in England by any other such party or his privy in respect of the same cause of action': ibid.

9 *Black-Clawson International Ltd v Papierwerke Waldhof-Aschaffenburg AG* [1975] 1 All ER 810 at 815–817.

10 References to *Harris v Quine* (1869) LR 4 QB 653, 38 LJQB 331 are made in the context that any foreign judgment *on the merits* may be relied upon. Cf Gutteridge, loc cit, note 2, p 61.

Judgments within section 8

4.04 Section 8 reads as follows:

'(1) Subject to the provisions of this section, a judgment to which Part I of this Act applies or would have applied if a sum of money had been payable thereunder, whether it can be registered or not, shall be recognised . . . as conclusive between the parties thereto in all proceedings founded on the same cause of action and may be relied upon by way of defence or counterclaim in any such proceedings.

(2) This section shall not apply in the case of any judgment—

(a) where the judgment has been registered and the registration thereof has been set aside on some ground other than—

(i) that the sum of money was not payable under the judgment; or

(ii) that the judgment had been wholly or partly satisfied or;

(iii) that at the date of the application the judgment could not be enforced by execution in the country of the original court; or

(b) where the judgment has not been registered, it is shown (whether it could have been registered or not) that if it had been registered the registration thereof would have been set aside on an application for that purpose on some ground other than one of the grounds specified in paragraph (a) of this subsection.

(3) Nothing in this section shall be taken to prevent any court recognising any judgment as conclusive of any matter of law or fact decided therein if that judgment would have been so recognised before the passing of this Act.'

As Arnold P has commented, this is not drafted so as to yield up its meaning easily or quickly.[1] The section in prescribing the judgments to which the section applies lays down positive and negative requirements, both of which draw heavily upon the provisions used for the purposes of registration under Part I of the statute. The exact nature of that connection requires analysis.

1 *Vervaeke v Smith* [1981] 1 All ER 55 at 89. Lord Reid, however, commended the skills of the Act's draftsmen: *Black-Clawson International Ltd v Papierwerke Waldhof-Aschaffenburg AG* [1975] 1 All ER 810 at 816.

Plaintiff's or defendant's judgments?

4.05 Section 8 deals with judgments 'to which Part I' applies. Such judgments according to section 1(2) are required to fulfil the following requirements:

- (i) it must be a judgment or order given or made by a court in any civil proceedings or a judgment or order given or made by a court in any criminal proceedings for the payment of a sum of money in respect of compensation or damages to an injured party;[1]
- (ii) the judgment must be that of a superior court of a foreign country to which the Act has been extended (other than a judgment on appeal from a court which is not a superior court);[2]
- (iii) the judgment must be final and conclusive between the parties thereto;
- (iv) there must be a sum of money payable thereunder;
- (v) the judgment must have been given after the relevant extension order came into force.[3]

Section 8, however, is also concerned with any judgments to which Part I 'would have applied if a sum of money had been payable'. This has been the cause of some judicial uncertainty. Thus Lord Reid concluded from these words that a foreign judgment in favour of a defendant was not included.[4] For where a defendant succeeds in his defence there is no liability upon him to make any payment. Thus, no sum of money could have been payable in that case. In his view, the purpose of the section was to preclude further actions by a successful plaintiff to get an even more favourable judgment and to prevent a successful plaintiff from counterclaiming on a satisfied judgment, should the defendant sue him on some other cause of action. This view was not shared by the majority of the House of Lords who put greater stress upon the references to '*all* proceedings founded on the same cause of action' and to 'by way of defence or counterclaim', as referring to judgments given in favour of the defendant.[5] As we have seen, this accords with the common law and with the intentions of the Greer Committee.[6]

Can this section also apply to the judgments in favour of the original plaintiff too, as Lord Reid envisaged? To allow this would produce conflict with the non-merger rule which permits a successful plaintiff a second action on the same cause of action. This possibility was certainly part of the common law in 1933.[7] The suggested interpretation would involve an alteration in the common law, which was not intended. The only exception known to the non-merger rule is where the judgment in favour of the plaintiff has been satisfied.[8] Recognition in that case is allowed for by section 8(2)(a)(ii). Recognition of the plaintiff's judgment is implicit where enforcement proceedings are based upon it.

1 FJREA, s 11(1).

2 Ibid, s 2(1).
3 Ibid, s 2(2).
4 *Black-Clawson International Ltd v Papierwerke* [1975] 1 All ER 810 at 816.
5 Ibid, per Viscount Dilhorne, at 820; per Lord Diplock, at 833; per Lord Simon, at 848. Lord Wilberforce reserved his opinion, at 832.
6 Greer Committee Report, para 4. The point is put beyond doubt in the Canadian Uniform Foreign Judgments Act (revised 1964), cl 4, which is modelled on s 8.
7 *Hall v Odber* (1809) 11 East 118; *Smith v Nicolls* (1839) 5 Bing NC 208, 8 LJCP 92.
8 *Barber v Lamb* (1860) 8 CBNS 95, 29 LJCP 234; *Taylor v Hollard* [1902] 1 KB 676, 71 LJKB 278.

Judgments in rem

4.06 A second difficulty highlighted by Lord Reid, when references to money payments are omitted, was the possible inclusion within section 8(1) of all kinds of judgment including those on status, family matters and in rem. 'No one suggests that section 8 was meant to deal with them.'[1] The evidence, however, is equivocal. There is little doubt that in their later discussions the Greer Committee were concentrating on judgments in personam.

The terminology of section 8(1) which makes a judgment conclusive between the same bodies on the same cause of action is not obviously consistent with any treatment of judgments in rem which are conclusive for the whole world.[2] Indeed it may be argued that Part I of the Act in effect only applies to judgments or orders in personam, albeit that these may derive from actions in rem or actions in personam or orders, such as those for costs, which are ancillary to judgments in rem.[3] On this view, it would be appropriate to conclude that section 8 applies to judgments in personam whether involving the payment of money or not and not to any other categories of judgments. The evidence of the conventions which were negotiated during the preparation of section 8 tends to the opposite conclusion.[4] These conventions impose a duty of recognition upon the United Kingdom in respect of judgments of civil and commercial matters generally, subject in some conventions to certain specific exceptions.[5] Thus the convention with France does not apply to judgments on matters of family law or status, succession or administration of estates or bankruptcy or winding-up of companies.[6] Only the latter two are excluded in respect of Germany.[7] There are no exceptions of this kind in the case of Belgium or in most of the conventions subsequently negotiated.[8] The Greer Committee pointed out the exceptional exclusion of certain categories of non-money judgments from the Anglo-French convention, whilst stating that the provisions relating to recognition in the conventions were in accord with section 8.[9] The implication is that the duty of recognition imposed by that section was not intended to be confined to judgments in personam.[10]

This, it may be suggested, is the better view. The terminology employed in section 8(1) is explained by the fact that the Greer Committee was seeking to protect a successful defendant from further litigation by the unsuccessful plaintiff on the same cause of action. It was, therefore, a statement which can apply to all such foreign judgments whether in personam or in rem, when they meet the appropriate criteria for recognition.[11] On this view, the section extends to judgments in matrimonial causes and on matters of status to preclude re-litigation of a cause of action by an unsuccessful petitioner or applicant.

1 *Black-Clawson International Ltd v Papierwerke*, above, at 817, a view with which Everleigh LJ and Cumming-Bruce LJ were inclined to agree: *Vervaeke v Smith* [1981] 1 All ER 55 at 90. This point was not examined in the House of Lords, [1982] 2 All ER 144. The revised Uniform Foreign Judgments Act of Canada is limited to actions in personam, cl 4.

2 Greer Committee Report, para 4. Application to judgments in rem was initially intended: Notes on Revised Draft (2nd Draft) of the Bill, LCO/2, Doc No 1689.
3 Cf FJREA, s 4(2) and s 11(2): see paras 3.12 and 3.45 above.
4 This is the conclusion of Arnold P in *Vervaeke v Smith* [1981] 1 All ER 55 at 89.
5 In later conventions, different formulations were used, eg 'judgments in civil matters' (Norway), 'judgments in civil proceedings' (Israel and Netherlands).
6 Convention of 18 January 1934, SR & O 1936/1169, art 2, para 3(b). See similarly, UK–Netherlands Convention, 17 November 1967, SI 1969/1063, art II(2). Norway excludes 'matters of family law or status, including judgments in matrimonial causes or concerning pecuniary relations between spouses': UK–Norway Convention, 12 June 1961, SI 1962/636, art II(2).
7 Convention of 14 July 1960, SI 1961/1199, art II(2).
8 Convention of 2 May 1934, SR & O 1936/1169, art 4.3. This is also the case with respect to UK–Austria Convention, 14 July 1961, SI 1962/1339, art 2(2); UK–Israel Convention, 28 October 1970, SI 1971/1039, art 2; UK–Italy Convention, 16 January 1974, SI 1973/1894, art II. UK–Tonga Convention, 28 June 1979, SI 1980/153 is in terms following s 8.
9 Greer Committee Report, p 68.
10 The exceptions to the duty to recognise set out on the convention relate to the contracting parties' international responsibility. The possibility that municipal law may also allow recognition in additional cases is explicitly provided for: eg UK–France Convention, above, art 2, para 4.
11 See further para 4.08 below.

Judgments in criminal proceedings and arbitral awards

4.07 Two further considerations arise which have not been adverted to in any decision. First the definition of 'judgment' in the Act extends to 'any judgment or order given by a court in any criminal proceedings for the payment of a sum of money in respect of compensation or damages to an injured party'.[1] Does it follow that when the reference to money payment is omitted, as section 8(1) allows, that other kinds of judgments or orders in criminal proceedings are caught by section 8? The conventions clearly confine recognition to judgments awarding compensation payments.[2] That case is covered by section 8, as it is by the common law[3] but there are obvious arguments against any wider application to other types of criminal judgments. First, the words in the definition are likely to be construed strictly, so that the provision applies only to those judgments in criminal proceedings which, at common law, are given recognition. Secondly, the requested court will apply the well settled common law rule that the effect should not be given, directly or indirectly, to a penal law of a foreign system.[4]

The second consideration relates to the extension of the definition of 'judgment' in many jurisdictions to embrace arbitration awards which have become enforceable in the same manner as a judgment.[5] The effect of this, it appears, is to make an arbitration award of that kind, in respect of which the other criteria in the section are also fulfilled, a defence to any legal proceedings, whether by a subsequent arbitration or more importantly in a court, brought by an unsuccessful plaintiff on the same cause of action.[6]

It may be concluded, therefore, that section 8 applies to any judgment:

(i) whether in personam or in rem or relating to status given in any civil proceedings[7] or in any criminal proceedings ordering payment of compensation or an arbitral award which has become enforceable in the same manner as a judgment;
(ii) when in favour of the plaintiff and has been satisfied or when in favour of the defendant;
(iii) by a designated court of a jurisdiction to which the scheme extends;
(iv) given after the date of the extension;

(v) whether or not money is in fact payable thereunder;
(vi) whether or not the judgment is registered or capable of being registered;
(vii) and is final and conclusive in the original jurisdiction between the parties thereto.[8]

1 FJREA, s 11(1).
2 Eg UK–France Convention, above, art 2, para 2.
3 *Raulin v Fischer* [1911] 2 KB 93, 80 LJKB 811.
4 *Huntingdon v Attrill* [1893] AC 150, 62 LJPC 44.
5 FJREA, s 11(1) as extended: for UK, see now Civil Jurisdiction and Judgments Act 1982, Sch 12.
6 See para 6.30 below.
7 Other than an appeal from a court which is not designated.
8 See para 3.16 above.

Negativing factors

4.08 Section 8(2) in effect sets out the circumstances in which a foreign judgment cannot be granted recognition. Its rather obscure form seems designed to avoid statutory repetition of the similar conditions under which a foreign judgment is to be refused enforcement. Accordingly, the latter conditions, which must be invoked in an application to set aside, are utilised in the context of recognition.[1] But three of the circumstances in which a registration may be set aside are not relevant in relation to recognition, as they are not concerned with the judgment itself. As a consequence the obligation to give recognition is not affected by the fact that no sum of money is payable under the judgment, that the judgment has been wholly or partly satisfied, or that the judgment cannot be enforced by execution in the country of origin.[2]

A judgment the registration of which has been set aside on any of the other prescribed grounds cannot be recognised. Recognition must also be refused both where a judgment was registrable but registration would have been set aside on any of those grounds and where a judgment was not registrable but if it had been, the registration would have been similarly set aside. This leaves unmentioned judgments which have been registered and where the registration is capable of being set aside but has not been. It may be assumed that the party resisting recognition must apply for the registration to be set aside within the time limit which is fixed or extended.[3] If he fails to do so, the judgment must be recognised under the terms of section 8(1).[4]

The grounds for setting aside are not listed in section 8.[5] They are to be found in sections 4 and 5 and may be summarised as:

(a) the judgment is not a judgment to which the Act applies;[6]
(b) the judgment was registered in contravention of the Act;[7]
  (i) the application was made out of time;[8]
  (ii) the judgment contains matters which cannot be registered;[9]
  (iii) the judgment is in favour of a person not entitled to apply;[10]
  (iv) the judgment is not registered in the correct currency;[11]
  (v) the judgment incorrectly states the quantum of the judgment debt;[12]
  (vi) there is a substantial defect in the supporting documentation;[13]
(c) absence of jurisdiction in the original court;[14]
(d) inadequate notice was received by the debtor who did not appear;[15]
(e) the judgment was obtained by fraud;[16]
(f) its enforcement would be contrary to public policy;[17]
(g) the rights under the judgment were not vested in the applicant for registration;[18]

(h) there is an earlier conclusive judgment from a competent court on the matter in dispute;[19]
(i) an appeal is pending or intended.[20]

Certain of these grounds, however, are related to those which are expressly excluded and presumably will not be applicable in this context, viz those in (b)(ii), (iv) and (v), and, in the case of a judgment which has not been registered, (b)(vi). There is no obligation to produce for the purposes of recognition the documentation required for registration.[21]

With respect to judgments which have not been registered, the requested court must decide whether the judgment 'would have been set aside' in an application for registration. Two of the grounds, (h), the existence of an earlier judgment, and (i), pending or intended appeals, are discretionary. The requested court must, therefore, decide in these cases that the discretion to set aside *would* have been exercised in a registration case.[22] Thus, if the court concludes that an application to set aside for a pending appeal would have been adjourned,[23] this condition will not be met and the judgment could be recognised. In all other cases where a ground is established, refusal to apply section 8 is mandatory.[24]

1 Principally, FJREA, s 4.
2 Ibid, s 1(2)(b); s 2(1) proviso, see paras 3.18–3.20 above.
3 An application to extend the time to apply to set aside cannot be made after the expiry of the permitted time under English-style rules: Ord 71, r 5(4).
4 Except where 'judgment is not a judgment to which the Act applies' (s 4(1)(a)(i)) which is one of the positive characteristics in s 8(1).
5 The Greer Committee made reference only to grounds in (a), (c), (d), (e) and (f): Report, pp 64–65.
6 FJREA, s 4(1)(a)(i).
7 Ibid, para 3.51 above.
8 Ibid, s 1(1); para 3.26 above.
9 Ibid, s 2(5); para 3.12 above.
10 Para 3.27 above.
11 Ibid, s 2(3); para 3.30 above.
12 Ibid, s 2(4); para 3.20 above.
13 Para 3.28 above.
14 Ibid, s 4(1)(a)(ii); paras 3.34ff above.
15 Ibid, s 4(1)(a)(iii); paras 3.52–3.54 above.
16 Ibid, s 4(1)(a)(iv); paras 3.55–3.56 above.
17 Ibid, s 4(1)(a)(v); para 3.57 above. Is 'recognition' to be substituted for 'enforcement'?
18 Ibid, s 4(1)(a)(vi); para 3.65 above.
19 Ibid, s 4(1)(b); paras 3.66–3.67 above.
20 Ibid, s 5(1); para 3.68 above.
21 A certificate may be obtained under s 10 for purposes of enforcement only.
22 See *Vervaeke v Smith* [1981] 1 All ER 55 at 90, per Arnold P, CA.
23 FJREA, s 5(2).
24 *Vervaeke v Smith* [1982] 2 All ER 144 at 154, per Lord Diplock, HL.

The intended effect of section 8

4.09 Although section 8 was intended to be a restatement of the common law at the time it was enacted, it is to the section, rather than to the common law, that reference should first be made when questions arise as to the recognition of judgments from jurisdictions to which the scheme has been extended. The difficulty is to determine its exact effect.

Section 8 imposes upon the requested court a duty to recognise a judgment, to which it applies:

'as conclusive between the parties thereto in all proceedings founded on the same cause of action'.

In consequence of this, the judgment 'may be relied upon by way of defence or counterclaim in any such proceedings'.[1] The section does not make apparent in what respects the judgment must be treated as conclusive. It is this point which has been the source of most judicial uncertainty. The Greer Committee explained, in respect of proceedings in personam, that the judgment is conclusive 'as regards the question therein adjudicated upon'.[2] This, they further explained, as referring to 'the actual decision (the operative parts of the judgment)'. This they saw as 'opposed to the grounds or reasoning upon which it may be based, in the course of which other points of law or fact may have been incidentally decided as preliminaries (necessary or otherwise) to the final conclusion'.[3] It is apparent from their Minutes that the Greer Committee introduced the latter part of the explanation deliberately to meet any argument that what is now called 'issue estoppel' was included.[4] It does not seem to have been intended that the judgment would be treated as conclusive of issues relating to the cause of action which should have been raised in the original court but were not; rather that the matter cannot be re-litigated on the ground that those matters were not raised.[5] The conclusion of some Law Lords that issue estoppel was not in the minds of the Greer Committee is erroneous.[6] The suggestion in the Court of Appeal that section 8(1) is concerned with cause of action estoppel is only a little nearer the Committee's intention.[7] For the section was not designed to provide for estoppel per rem judicatam as it applies with respect to domestic judgments.[8] Its purpose was to preclude re-litigation of a matter which had already been the subject of a recognisable foreign judgment, insofar as this was consistent with the doctrine that the foreign judgment does not merge with the original cause of action.[9] Although a plaintiff is permitted to sue on the original cause of action if he chooses, instead of enforcing the judgment itself, he cannot be permitted to rely upon the judgment previously obtained in his favour as res judicata. The defendant in such a case must be permitted to raise any relevant defences whether put before the original court or not.[10] Accordingly, it was not thought appropriate to treat the common law as creating a general estoppel in relation to foreign judgments. The section was intended to have the lesser effect of providing the successful defendant in the original proceedings with an effective defence or counterclaim if he were sued again or an unsuccessful defendant with an effective defence if the plaintiff sought to bring a further action when the original judgment had been satisfied.

For this reason, section 8(1) was intended to apply where the original judgment constituted a final determination of the rights of the parties[11] concerning the disputed claim. The existence of a judgment was to provide a defence in any subsequent litigation designed to produce a further such determination in relation to the same claim except where a successful plaintiff is suing again on his original cause of action.[12] This is surely narrower than cause of action estoppel which is designed to preclude any original party (or his privy) who was unsuccessful in the original proceedings disputing or questioning the decision on the merits in subsequent proceedings.[13]

1 FJREA, s 8(1).

2 Greer Committee Report, para 4. This was the terminology in use at the time: Dicey *Conflict of Laws* (4th edn) p 449, but see Read, op cit, pp 87ff. It is also employed in the preponderance of the conventions. See eg UK–France Convention, SR & O 1936/609, art 3, para 3.

3 Ibid, footnote. The Committee wondered whether this statement, in contrast with the common law, might be 'slightly too narrow': see para 4.13 below.

4 Minutes of Meeting of 18 February 1931, LCO/2, Doc No 1690: see para 4.02. As to issue estoppel, see *Carl-Zeiss Stiftung v Rayner and Keeler (No 2)* [1967] 1 AC 853, [1966] 2 All ER 536, HL, a case to which s 8 appears to have applied but was not referred to.

5 *Henderson v Henderson* (1843) 3 Hare 100 at 114–115, per Wigram VC, cited with approval in *Vervaeke v Smith* [1982] 2 All ER 144 at 156, per Lord Simon.

6 *Black-Clawson International Ltd v Papierwerke Waldhof-Aschaffenburg AG* [1975] 1 All ER 810 at 820–821, per Lord Dilhorne; at 841, per Lord Simon.

7 Ibid [1974] 1 All ER 611 at 615, per Lord Denning MR. The suggestion, ibid, that s 8(3) dealt with issue estoppel also has foundation, though it was possibly not confined to such matters: para 4.13 below. See Lord Wilberforce to this effect: [1975] 1 All ER 810 at 831.

8 Para 4.02 above.

9 See *Carl-Zeiss Stiftung v Rayner and Keeler (No 2)*, above, per Lord Reid, at 555 and Lord Hodson, at 561.

10 Ibid, per Lord Guest, at 567.

11 The definitions of 'judgment' in almost all the conventions (e.g. UK–France Convention, above, art 1, para 4) use these words.

12 *Jacobson v Franchon* (1929) 44 TLR 103 at 104, per Atkin LJ: see para 4.03 note 6 above.

13 *Carl-Zeiss Stiftung v Rayner and Keeler (No 2)*, above, per Lord Guest at 364 citing Spencer Bower on *The Doctrine of Res Judicata* p 3. Cf Lord Dilhorne, in *Black-Clawson International Ltd v Papierwerke*, above, at 820: cause of action estoppel 'prevents a party to an action from asserting or denying, as against the other party, the existence of a particular cause of action, the non-existence or existence of which has been determined by a court of competent jurisdiction in previous litigation between the same parties'.

The effect of section 8 as judicially interpreted

4.10 The tortuous language of the section has presented difficulties in the only case in which this section has been fully examined. Even reference to the Greer Committee Report by the House of Lords (itself a controversial issue) failed to eliminate judicial uncertainties.

In *Black-Clawson International Ltd v Papierwerke Waldhof-Aschaffenburg AG*,[1] the original West German court had dismissed proceedings on certain bills of exchange on the grounds that the three-year limitation period for bringing proceedings in Germany had expired. Subsequent English proceedings between the same parties on the bills were brought within the longer English limitation period. The defendants argued that the original judgment in refusing a remedy was conclusive and that no further proceedings could be brought. The House of Lords, by a majority,[2] in essence concluded that the original judgment was not one on the merits but merely barred the grant of a remedy.[3] The English action could proceed, as the plaintiff's rights in respect of the matter in dispute had not been adjudicated upon.

There is little doubt that this conclusion is consistent with the intentions of those who prepared the legislation. Unfortunately the four Law Lords considering the question did not show complete agreement when examining the notion of conclusiveness.[4] Lord Wilberforce was of the view that the courts must examine the judgment to 'see what it decided and hold it conclusive as a judgment and for what it adjudicates'. It is not the dispositive part of the judgment or formal order—'the suit is dismissed'—which is conclusive: it is conclusive in respect of the matter adjudicated upon. A judgment is, therefore, conclusive 'for what was decided and nothing more'. If it was not decided on the merits, it could not be conclusive on the merits.[5] Similarly, Lord Dilhorne asserted that a foreign judgment is conclusive as to the matter therein adjudicated, of 'what it decides and not of what it does not decide'. Accordingly, as the judgment was decided on the question of the application of the limitation rules, it could not be conclusive of the merits.[6] Lord Simon agreed that it is not the dispositive part of the judgment which is conclusive. For him, it is the whole judgment including the grounds of the decision, in this case that the claim was time barred.[7] So far as this approach suggests that a judgment is conclusive with respect to matters of law or fact which were necessary to the decision,[8] it must be questioned. If, on the other hand, Lord Simon means that the judgment cannot be conclusive on the rights of parties, if they have never been adjudicated upon, this is consistent both with Lord Wilberforce and Lord Dilhorne and with the Greer Committee.

Lord Diplock's analysis is more questionable. For him, what is conclusive is the dispositive part of the judgment which 'embodies a decision on the ultimate question of whether the plaintiff is entitled to the remedy he claimed that the court ought to grant him against the defendant as redress for the facts he relied on as constituting his cause of action'. This view derives from the fact that the judgment is 'conclusive of that of which the foreign judgment is conclusive in the country of the foreign court'.[9] With respect, this is to make the equation between the use of the word 'conclusive' in respect of a judgment which is 'final and conclusive'[10] in the original court and its use in respect of its status before the requested court. Moreover, to treat the judgment as conclusive as to an entitlement to a remedy could result, as in the type of case in point, in making the judgment conclusive 'as to more than it actually decided'.[11] This approach, therefore, is difficult to defend.[12]

For the majority, therefore, the section, as the common law, does not prevent the re-litigation of the original cause of action where the judgment is classified, under the law of the requested state, as not on its merits.[13] In this instance, the section follows the common law in treating the question of limitation as procedural, to be governed by the lex fori, and not substantive and concerned with the merits of the claim. *Harris v Quine*[14] was not displaced, for section 8 does not establish that the mere existence of a judgment between the same parties on the same cause of action, whatever the basis for the decision, constitutes an effective defence.

1 [1975] 1 All ER 810.
2 Lord Diplock dissented.
3 Applying *Harris v Quine* (1869) LR 4 QB 453, 38 LJQB 331. Cf *Re Low, Bland v Low* [1894] 1 Ch 147 at 162. See also H. C. Gutteridge, (1932) 13 BYBIL 49, at p 61, n 5.
4 Lord Reid decided the matter on the ground that section 8 had no application to defendants' judgments: see para 4.03 above. If wrong on this, however, he was inclined to agree with the conclusions of the other Law Lords: [1975] 1 All ER 810 at 817–818.
5 Ibid, at 831 and 832.
6 Ibid, at 825 and 826.
7 Ibid, at 846.
8 There is this implication in ibid, at 847.
9 Ibid, at 834 and 838.
10 Para 3.16 above.
11 [1975] 1 All ER 810 at 845, per Lord Simon.
12 Lord Diplock also held, as had the Court of Appeal, that the section which was 'plain and unambiguous' had replaced pre-existing common law to achieve this result. Not only was this not the purpose of the Greer Committee, but it is patent that the references to 'conclusiveness' are ambiguous and should be resolved by reference to common law usage.
13 The burden is upon the defendant to show that the judgment was on the merits: *Quickstad v McNeill* [1932] 4 DLR 427 (BC); *Tracomin SA v Sudan Oil Seeds Co Ltd* [1983] 1 All ER 404 at 413.
14 (1869) LR 4 QB 653, 38 LJQB 331.

The limits of *Black-Clawson*

4.11 The limits of this decision should be noted. Issues of limitation are not invariably treated as matters of procedure under the law of the original court.

In certain circumstances, the expiry of a prescribed period extinguishes the plaintiff's rights, rather than merely barring his remedy. In such a case, a requested court should treat the judgment as one on the merits, since it constitutes a final determination of the rights of the parties and the judgment should be recognised. This position is accepted at common law.[1] The English Law Commission has gone further in its recent proposal that all foreign judgments decided on a limitation point should be treated under the English rules of private international law as conclusive on the merits, giving rise to an estoppel per rem judicatam.[2] The consequence would be that a judgment reached upon the question of limitation would be treated as a defence to further litigation before the English courts. There is much to be said in logic for this position.

Lord Diplock was of the view that following *Harris v Quine* produced illogicalities under the 1933 Act. For there are, he suggested, other circumstances in which the original judgment may be given on the ground of non-compliance with a procedural rule of the original court, as for example, judgments given by default.[3] Yet such judgments were clearly envisaged as within the 1933 Act,[4] although they can no more be treated as on the merits than a decision that the remedy is time barred. Again, it is submitted, the analysis is defective. For default judgments are an example of a case where non-compliance by a defendant with procedural opportunities is treated by the original court as confirming the rights of the plaintiff under his claim, although it has not in fact been the subject of an adjudication. Moreover, recognition is required under section 8 in this case only if the plaintiff's judgment has been satisfied when the subsequent proceedings are brought. The limitation cases were concerned with the recognition of *defendants'* judgments.

A final point on the question of limitation. There is the implication from the analysis of Viscount Dilhorne and Lord Wilberforce[5] that a foreign judgment deciding that a remedy is time barred should be recognised under the section as conclusive on that matter. This may be questioned.[6] At the best, this seems more properly connected with issue estoppel[7] with which section 8(1) is not concerned. It would be more accurate to treat decisions of this kind as incapable of recognition in any respect under this provision.[8]

1 *Harris v Quine* (1869) LR 4 QB 653 at 658. Cf per Lord Wilberforce in *Black-Clawson International Ltd v Papierwerke,* above, at 829. But the rule may be altered by statute, see eg British Columbia: Limitation of Actions Act, RSBC 1979, Cap 236, s 9 (recovery of debts, damages or other monies): Castel, op cit pp 614–615. Cf also Uniform Limitations of Actions Act, s 44 which extinguishes rights to recover moneys charged on land when the limitation period expires.

2 Law Com No 114 (1982), paras 4.58–4.71. The recommendation applies whether the foreign court applied its own law or that of any other country on the question of limitation.

3 [1975] 1 All ER 810 at 833–834. A procedural decision of an interlocutory nature will not be conclusive: *Tracomin SA v Sudan Oil Seeds Co Ltd* [1983] 1 All ER 404 at 413.

4 FJREA, s 4(1)(a)(iii): see paras 3.12 and 3.16 above.

5 [1975] 1 All ER 810 at 825–826, 831, 832.

6 See A. J. F. Jaffey, (1975) 38 MLR 585–588.

7 Cf *Carl-Zeiss Stiftung v Rayner and Keeler (No 2)* [1967] 1 AC 853, [1966] 2 All ER 536, where the issue was: had the respondents established want of authority on the part of the appellant's solicitors to issue the writ?

8 In this matter, the section seems inconsistent with the requirement of the Brussels Convention, Title III. See Report of P. Schlosser, OJ 1979, C 59/71, para 191.

Other judicial uncertainties

4.12 There are other uncertainties about the meaning of section 8(1) amongst the Law Lords. Recognition is only required if the later proceedings are 'founded on the same cause of action'. It is not clear what this phrase embraces in this context. Lord Reid suggested that the term 'cause of action' usually refers to 'a right alleged to flow from the facts pleaded'.[1] On this view, both proceedings would need to be concerned with asserting the same right flowing from the same facts. Lord Reid rejected this analysis on the grounds that it did not allow for a case where the subsequent action was being brought by the original defendant. For technically he would be asserting *his* right, albeit from the same facts. For this reason, he argued that the term was intended as a reference to the facts themselves which must be the same in both proceedings.[2] As already indicated,[3] Lord Reid's inclusion of judgments in favour of the original plaintiff within section 8 is incorrect and in consequence his own objection lacks merit. A mere identity in the factual circumstances cannot be enough since the same facts can give rise to different causes of action. The essential purpose of the section is to ensure that a subsequent court may not re-examine the claims already decided in respect of a particular set of facts. The term should not be treated in any technical sense employed by the common law, since it was intended originally to apply more with respect to foreign than to Commonwealth legal systems.[4] It may be more appropriate to require that both actions are concerned to determine the rights of the same parties in connection with the same grievances arising from a particular set of factual circumstances. In this sense, the provision may be consistent with the common law requirement that the proceedings are concerned to secure the same relief.[5] It is for the requested court, of course, to determine whether this condition is fulfilled.

A further uncertainty in the *Black-Clawson* judgment relates to the provision that the judgment 'may be relied upon by way of defence or counterclaim' in subsequent proceedings on the same cause of action. Viscount Dilhorne found this somewhat obscure.[6] Whilst a judgment is readily seen as being capable of being relied upon by way of defence in such proceedings, it is less obvious how it may be relied upon there by way of counterclaim. The usual case will be for a defendant to wish to rely upon it where the defendant is being sued by the same plaintiff on a different cause of action.[7] The case intended is surely where an unsuccessful plaintiff seeks to re-litigate a cause of action. The defendant not only may rely upon the original judgment as a defence but, if he acquired rights under it, may rely upon it as a counterclaim if it has not been satisfied. A counterclaim on a foreign judgment by the defendant where the plaintiff's cause of action is not the same is a different case. That may be introduced only if the defendant has, by registration or action, acquired judgment rights within the requested jurisdiction.

A last point of difficulty concerns the operation of this section in respect of judgments relating to status or otherwise in rem, to which, it has been argued earlier,[8] the section applies. If this is the case, section 8(1) makes such judgments conclusive only between the original parties or their privies, whereas at common law, such judgments are treated as binding in the world at large.[9] This wider rule, it is suggested, is not in question. The purpose of section 8(1) is merely to prevent the same parties re-litigating the same matter in dispute[10] and that may be as necessary in the case of a judgment in rem as one in personam. In this context, the conditions for recognition are contained in section 8(1) and (2). If a judgment in rem is to be relied upon by anyone, other than the original parties or their privies, or in proceedings on a different cause of action, the criteria for recognition are to be found in the common law.[11]

1 [1975] 1 All ER 810 at 817.
2 In *Quickstad v McNeill* [1932] 4 DLR 427, the requirement was held to be identity of subject matter: cf FJREA, s 4(1)(b). See *Letang v Cooper* [1964] 2 All ER 929 at 934, per Lord Diplock LJ: 'simply a factual situation the existence of which entitles one person to obtain from the court a remedy against another person.'
3 Para 4.05 above.
4 UK–Belgium Convention, SR & O 1936/1169, art 3.3 in the French language version refers to 'toute nouvelle action intentée pour le même motif'.
5 *Callander v Dittrich* (1842) 4 Man & G 68, 1 Dowl NS 730. 'Relief' is not intended to refer to the same remedy: it appears to mean settlement of the same grievance in favour of the same party.
6 [1975] 1 All ER 810 at 826. This had also troubled the Court of Appeal, [1974] 2 All ER 611.
7 Ibid, at 817, per Lord Reid.
8 Para 4.02 above.
9 Cf Greer Committee Report, para 4.
10 Always provided that the jurisdictional requirements are fulfilled in the subsequent proceedings.
11 *Castrique v Imrie* (1870) LR 4 HL 414, 39 LJCP 350; Piggott, op cit, Book IV; Read, op cit, pp 133–144.

Saving of the common law on recognition

4.13 Section 8(3) authorises the recognition of a judgment 'as conclusive of any matter of law or fact decided therein' if the judgment would have been so recognised before the passing of the 1933 Act. The provision may, in part, have been included to confirm the long-standing common law rule in *Godard v Gray*[1] that a judgment by a competent foreign court cannot be challenged for errors of law or fact made by that court. Accordingly, any party relying upon a foreign judgment may be confident that such issues cannot be reopened by way of objection to its recognition.[2] Its stated purpose, however, was to save the common law rules in any cases where the rule laid down by the Act may be narrower in operation than the common law.[3] As we have seen,[4] the members of the Greer Committee were doubtful concerning the application of estoppel to foreign judgments, but that position does not seem to have been shared by Beckett who proposed the inclusion of this subsection. It is possible that he saw this as a device for allowing the application of the doctrine to the full extent to which the law may prove to allow. If this is the case, he was remarkably prescient, for, though the subject was hardly explored until the 1960s, application of estoppel has now been judicially acknowledged.[5] Gutteridge also seems to have been uncertain about the extent to which foreign judgments might be treated as conclusive, particularly as regards matters which could have been raised in the original proceedings but were not.[6] This provision may have provided some reassurance.

It is quite probable, therefore, that this provision was prepared with considerations of estoppel, including issue estoppel, in mind. Although the latter phrase had only just been coined,[7] the Greer Committee was made aware of the difficulties in its application in the context of foreign judgments.[8] As we have seen,[9] the section as a whole was drafted to avoid the impression that estoppel was being introduced into the law by the section. The saving clause was inserted ex abundanti cautela.[10] Yet it must remain a matter of speculation whether, and if so to what extent, estoppel would have been applied before the passing of the Act. There seems to be nothing in this section which prevents its application under the common law as subsequently developed.[11]

1 (1870) LR 6 QB 139; Cf *Bank of Australasia v Nias* (1851) 16 QB 717, 20 LJQB 284; *Ellis v*

M'Henry (1871) LR 6 CP 228, 40 LJCP 109; *Castrique v Imrie* (1870) LR 4 HL 414, 39 LJCP 350.

2 The words used appear to be modelled on Dicey *Conflict of Laws* (4th edn) r 112, where these points were examined: Notes on 2nd Draft of 1933 Bill, LCO/2, Doc No 1689.

3 Greer Committee Report, p 64.

4 Para 4.02 above.

5 *Carl-Zeiss Stiftung v Rayner and Keeler (No 2)* [1967] 1 AC 853, [1966] 2 All ER 536, HL, Lord Guest dissenting on the question.

6 (1932) 13 BYBIL 49 at 62.

7 The term was coined by Higgins J (dissenting) in *Hoystead v Taxation Commrs* (1921) 29 CLR 537 at 561, affd [1926] AC 155, PC. But the concept is found in relation to domestic judgments from *Duchess of Kingston's Case* (1776) 1 East PC 468, 20 State Tr 355.

8 Minutes of Meeting of 18 February 1932, LCO/2, Doc No 1690: para 4.02 above.

9 Para 4.03 above.

10 Cf per Lord Dilhorne, *Black-Clawson International Ltd v Papierwerke* [1975] 1 All ER 810 at 821.

11 The essentials of issue estoppel—that the identical issue in proceedings between the same parties or their privies had been the subject of a final and conclusive judgment by a competent court—were examined by the House of Lords in *Carl-Zeiss Stiftung v Rayner and Keeler (No 2)*, above. The possibility that the requirements will require further elaboration is apparent, per Lord Reid at 555, Lord Upjohn at 573 and Lord Wilberforce at 585–6. See also *Vervaeke v Smith* [1982] 2 All ER 144, [1981] 2 WLR 855, HL; *Tracomin SA v Sudan Oil Seeds Co Ltd* [1983] 1 All ER 404, [1983] 1 WLR 662; affd [1983] 3 All ER 137, [1983] 1 WLR 1026.

Effect of abolition of the non-merger rule

4.14 Section 34 of the Civil Jurisdiction and Judgments Act 1982 of the United Kingdom provides that:

'No proceedings may be brought by a person in England, Wales and Northern Ireland on a cause of action in respect of which a judgment has been given in his favour in proceedings between the same parties, or their privies ... in a court of an overseas country, unless that judgment is not enforceable or entitled to recognition ...'

This removal of the much criticised non-merger rule will modify the effect of section 8 by preventing a successful plaintiff from suing again on the same cause of action.[1] This, however, appears not always to be the case, for such actions may be still brought if the judgment is not enforceable as a money judgment or is not entitled to recognition.[2] As we have seen earlier,[3] section 8 does not require recognition of the successful plaintiff's judgment unless it has been satisfied. It appears, therefore, that the abrogation of the non-merger rule has altered the duty of recognition in relation to only those plaintiff's judgments which are registrable as money judgments.[4]

1 Presumably he may rely upon estoppels in respect of issues decided by the judgment, where the requisite conditions for issue estoppel are present: see para 4.13 above, note 11.

2 *Tracomin SA v Sudan Oil Seeds Co Ltd* [1983] 3 All ER 137, [1983] 1 WLR 1026.

3 Para 4.05 above.

4 Para 3.72 above; P. A. Stone, (1983) 32 ICLQ 477, at pp 491–2.

PART II

Arbitral Awards

CHAPTER 5

Enforcement Schemes: Origins and Development

Introduction

5.01 Although the development of schemes for enforcement of arbitral awards involving Commonwealth jurisdictions had links and largely coincided with the development of the judgment schemes, different forces were at play. Concern for the extension of international arbitration as a device well suited to the mercantile community was growing in the early years of this century in the commercial world which found its centre in the City of London. United Kingdom commercial interests, therefore, predominated. These were particularly concerned to foster the effectiveness of arbitration conducted in the United Kingdom and therefore to ensure that agreements to arbitrate there were implemented and that awards made there were enforceable abroad. Although this necessarily had implications for the British jurisdictions abroad with which substantial trading took place, it was of greater importance to the United Kingdom that foreign jurisdictions, particularly competing European nations which might have reservations about English arbitrations when affecting their commerce, should be involved. In the evolution of schemes for arbitral awards, therefore, these considerations have favoured multilateral treaty arrangements in which other nation states will participate. There is little evidence of a distinctive Commonwealth dimension or that other parts of the Commonwealth actively pressed for schemes as beneficial to their trading needs.

Common law relating to foreign arbitrations

5.02 As commercial arbitrations with an international element became more common at the turn of the century, the English courts began to work out the common law approach to agreements for such arbitrations and the consequential awards. Thus, they applied section 11 of the Common Law Procedure Act 1854 to agreements to arbitrate abroad, thereby allowing a party to seek a stay of legal proceedings initiated in the English courts.[1] Conversely, a party could be required to desist from foreign legal proceedings in breach of an undertaking to arbitrate in England.[2] Although actions to enforce foreign awards appear to have been brought, considerable uncertainty existed at this period as to their position at common law. The actions were based upon the award, not on the original cause of action but it was initially unclear whether this was on the basis that the submission to arbitration implied a contract to give effect to the award or that the award was a foreign judgment. In one of the earliest cases, recognition was refused because the foreign award was not enforceable as a judgment in the jurisdiction in which it was made.[3] It was only at a later date that the action was acknowledged to be based upon the arbitration contract:[4] the conditions for recognition were not prescribed until 1927 when international agreement was on the point of being reached.[5] The circumstances in which a court may decline to recognise the foreign award at common law were, and indeed to some extent remain, unclear.[6]

1 *Law v Garrett* (1878) 8 Ch D 26, 38 LT 3, CA.
2 *Pena Copper Mines Ltd v Rio Tinto Co Ltd* (1911) 105 LT 846, CA.
3 *Merrifield, Ziegler & Co v Liverpool Cotton Association Ltd* (1911) 105 LT 97, a decision now thought to turn on its particular facts: *Dalmia Dairy Industries Ltd v National Bank of Pakistan* [1978] 2 Lloyd's Rep 223 at 250. It was not until *Norske Atlas Insurance Co Ltd v London General Insurance Co Ltd* (1927) 43 TLR 541 (Mackinnon J) that a successful common law action to enforce a foreign award was reported.
4 *Bremer Oeltransport GmbH v Drewry* [1933] 1 KB 753, 102 LJKB 360, CA: the view expressed to the Imperial Conference of 1911 was that enforcement depended upon the award being made a judgment or being enforceable on a court order (citing *Henley v Soper* (1828) 8 B & C 16, 6 LJOSKB 210; *Alivon v Furnival* (1834) 40 RR 561: Cd 5746 I, p 137). See now *The St Anna* [1983] 2 All ER 691, [1983] 1 WLR 895 and *Agromet Motoimport v Maulden Engineering Company (Beds) Ltd* (1984) Times, 17 April.
5 *Norske Atlas*, above, at 542, stating three conditions: submission, conduct of the arbitration according to the submission and an award final and valid according to the lex fori.
6 Many of the clarifying decisions are of relatively recent origin: Dicey and Morris, op cit, pp 1123–1140.

Arbitration awards and the 1920 judgments scheme

5.03 The need for international action in this area had long been pressed upon the British Government by national trade associations and Chambers of Commerce in the United Kingdom concerned about the inability of their members to enforce arbitral awards in their favour against foreign traders in their home jurisdiction.[1] Various international bodies took an active interest in the matter, often in the context of judgment enforcement generally, culminating in 1910 in a resolution of the International Chamber of Commerce, asking the British Government to institute an enquiry into the conditions under which awards were made in different countries.[2] The matter was referred to the Board of Trade which through the Colonial Office and the Foreign Office sought information concerning both Empire and foreign country experience.[3] The enquiry was Anglo-centric, being confined to the questions of the validity of agreements for United Kingdom arbitration and the enforcement of United Kingdom awards. The returns revealed a considerable divergence of opinion and practice, even amongst dominions and especially with respect to the mechanism for the local enforcement of United Kingdom awards.[4] The value, particularly to the British interests, of developing common arrangements was evident. Accordingly, on the Board of Trade's initiative, the matter was put on the agenda of the Imperial Conference, 1911, where it was studied by a committee under the chairmanship of Sir Rufus Isaacs.[5] The Committee supported the principle of introducing arrangements for enforcement of awards, finding merit in the Chairman's suggestion that an award, confirmed by a court order in the place of arbitration, should be capable of being registered elsewhere under legislation following the lines of the Judgments Extension Act.[6] As we have seen,[7] this led the Imperial Conference to express support for a judgments extension scheme which could deal with judgments or orders for the reinforcement of arbitration awards.[8] There was strong support in the evidence submitted to the Dominions Royal Commission in the course of hearings in the dominions in the next five years.[8] The draft Judgment Extensions Bill 1916 reflected Conference discussions in this respect, making the proposed money judgments scheme applicable to 'any award in proceedings in an arbitration which may be enforced in the same manner as a judgment or order of a court to the same effect', provided that the court was a Superior Court of any part of His Majesty's dominions within the scheme.[9] The Sumner Committee in 1919 took a similar view that the Act should apply only where an order had been made, under the law of the country of the arbitration, giving effect to the award as if it were a judgment.[10] They were unable to support any international scheme for enforcing foreign awards as such, whilst 'the preliminary work of preparing an international accord by voluntary effort is far from complete'.[11] Much experience of a system on a smaller scale or between particular countries was first needed. A first step might, in the light of some experience in the British Empire, be to establish a reciprocal scheme with the United States.[11] International action was premature. The immediate development, therefore, was confined to the inclusion of provision in the Administration of Justice Act 1920 of any

'award in proceedings on an arbitration if the award has, in pursuance of the law in force in the place where it was made, become enforceable in the same manner as a judgment given by a court in that place.'[12]

Equivalent provision is a feature of all the legislation based upon this model.

1 See para 1.30 above.
2 At the Fourth Congress in London: see Cd 6517, p 79. The British Imperial Council of Commerce appears to have taken the major initiative, ibid, pp 86–87. The Sumner Committee in 1919 implied that the question of enforcement had not been a pressing one until 1910; Report, p 9. This was probably true as far as the dominions were concerned.
3 Replies were published in 1911; Cd 6126.
4 A summary of dominion replies was put before the Imperial Conference, 1911: Cd 5746—I, pp 130–137. Many referred to their legislation adopting the Common Law Procedure Act 1854 (UK), s 11, allowing stay of proceedings where an agreement to arbitrate had been entered into.
5 Then Attorney-General, Cd 5745, pp 160–162, 326–332.
6 Ibid, p 328. Many jurisdictions already had some legislation for enforcement of awards by leave of a Judge of the High Court, based upon Arbitration Act 1889 (UK), s 12 (now Arbitration Act 1950, s 26). Doubts were widespread that this could be used for foreign awards which were not stilled until *Dalmia Cement Ltd v National Bank of Pakistan* [1975] QB 9, [1974] 3 All ER 189.
7 Para 1.30 above, Cd 5745, p 424.
8 Para 1.31 above.
9 The Bill is printed in Cmd 251, Appendix A.
10 Ibid, p 11.
11 Ibid, p 13.
12 S 12(1).

League of Nations: the Geneva Protocol of 1923

5.04 This parochial view was not universally shared. The matter had continued to excite the interest of international bodies, such as the International Law Association and the International Congress of Chambers of Commerce and a number of bilateral conventions began to be negotiated amongst European nations in the immediate aftermath of World War I.[1] The matter was also raised in the League of Nations as one likely to facilitate the desired security and development of international commercial relations. The British Empire representative pressed the matter before the Economic Committee in March 1922[2] leading to the establishment of a Committee of Experts, sitting under the Chairmanship of Mr Mackinnon, later to be an English High Court Judge, to consider the effects of agreements to submit commercial contract disputes to arbitration. The Committee reported in July that there was great diversity in law both on the status of foreign arbitration clauses and on enforcing foreign awards.[3] It argued strongly that a clause compromissoire should be recognised as having legal effect and that court proceedings on the same matter be required to be stayed if the arbitration, to which parties of different nationalities had agreed, could be effectively carried out under the law of the country designated as the place of arbitration. 'People who have agreed to an arbitration clause [should] be made to respect and comply with the bargain they have made.' But, like the Sumner Committee whose report was made available, they felt that action on enforcement of awards would be premature. The vast majority of awards were in any case complied with and, in the absence of any consensus on enforcement of judgments, it was unlikely that the more difficult question of awards could be resolved.[4] Accordingly, their proposals to secure general recognition of arbitration clauses were as far as they were able to go which 'may not amount to much . . . but might not be difficult to secure'. This cautious approach was endorsed by the Economic Committee and in September 1922 by the Council of the League, the question of enforcement being passed for study to the Legal Section of the Secretariat.[5] The Assembly of the League endorsed the recommendation that countries should put into effect legislation to give effect to agreements if they did not already have it.[6] The Report of the Committee of Experts was circulated to all member states in October 1922 with this purpose in mind. More positive action, however, was needed. Accordingly in the first part of 1923, the Economic Committee, in consultation with a drafting committee of legal experts, produced a draft Protocol the substance of which had already received the approval of the Council. The final version was circulated to member states for their comments in May 1923.[7] The matter came before the Second Committee of the Assembly in September when considering the work of the Economic Committee. A subcommittee, with the assistance of legal experts, revised the circulated text in the light of comments received, making no changes of substance.[8] The Second Committee approved of the redrafted version,[9] which was accepted by the Assembly with little discussion[10] a few days later. The Protocol, dated September 24 1923, was immediately opened for signature, 'having aroused great interest in the commercial circles of every country'[11] and having been formulated with remarkable, perhaps too great, speed and good will.

1 France–Belgium Convention, 8 July 1899, was one of the earliest. In the post-war period, Austria–Italy Convention, 6 April 1922; Italy–Yugoslavia–Czechoslovakia Convention, 26 April 1922; Czechoslovakia–Yugoslavia Convention, 19 March 1923; see also Treaty of Lausanne, 24 July 1923.

2 Sir Hubert Llewellyn Smith, LNOJ, 1922, p 616.

3 LNOJ, 1922, pp 1410–1414.

4 The British League of Nations Union had pressed for this, as well as for the question of judgments to be tackled: LNOJ, 1922, pp 993–994, 1413. The latter question was deferred as outside the competence of the Economic Committee but referred to other competent authorities (the Secretariat): ibid, pp 1404–1405.

5 LNOJ, 1922, pp 1396–1397, 1404.

6 Third Assembly Records, Plenary Meeting, p 317. The Economic Commission of the Genoa Conference, 1922, Resolutions, art 14, urged action on this matter to be continued.

7 Circular Letter, No 56, 26 May 1923; LNOJ, 1923, pp 206, 835–836.

8 The subcommittee included Sir Hubert Llewellyn Smith (British Empire) and Sir Henry Strakosh (South Africa). This Report is in Fourth Assembly Records, Second Committee Minutes, pp 60–61.

9 Ibid, pp 27–30. Some unease was expressed about the extent to which the law of the country of arbitration was to apply.

10 Fourth Assembly Records, Plenary Session, pp 71–73. It was made clear that the Protocol did not apply to arbitration between states, although under national legislation, it might apply where a state which operated a commercial activity became a party to a dispute.

11 Report of Economic Committee, LNOJ, 1923, p 948.

The Protocol arrangements

5.05 The Protocol had four principal purposes:

(i) to oblige contracting states to recognise the validity of agreements to arbitrate disputes, particularly in commercial matters,[1] between parties who were subject to the jurisdiction of different contracting states, wherever the arbitration was to take place;[2]

(ii) to require contracting states to ensure that such awards as were made within their jurisdiction would be executed there according to national law;[3]

(iii) to put tribunals in contracting states, on an application by any party to an agreement, under a duty to refer disputes covered by the arbitration agreements to the agreed arbitrators, rather than themselves proceeding with the matter,[4]

(iv) to provide by what rules the arbitral procedure would be recognised as being regulated and to oblige contracting parties to facilitate arbitral proceedings in their country.[5]

The Protocol was applicable from the outset to dependent and mandated territories of contracting parties unless excluded by express declaration, without prejudice to later declarations adhering any such jurisdictions separately.[6] HM Government's initial declaration was limited to Great Britain and Northern Ireland: extensions were made separately for other jurisdictions within the Empire.

Unhappily, the Protocol is not without difficulties in interpretation, compounded by discrepancies between the English and French texts, both of which are authentic.[7] This latter aspect had caused problems in Commonwealth jurisdictions, as only the English, and the less accurate, text was appended to the legislation giving it force.[8] Some of the uncertainties subsequently perceived in both versions of the Protocol were deliberately left on one side by the draftsmen who saw themselves creating a minimum regime of obligation, leaving other issues to be determined by national law. Thus whether the scheme applied to verbal arbitration agreements, whether a matter was a commercial one or one capable of being settled by arbitration, whether a commercial agreement to which one party was a state was included were to be determined by the law of the state required to give effect to the Protocol.

One matter which has presented serious uncertainty, however, is the requirement that the parties to the agreement must be 'subject respectively to the jurisdiction of different Contracting States'.[9] Although this may have been a reference to links of nationality,[10] there are suggestions that it was intended to refer to persons living in different contracting states.[11] The lack of clarity weakened the scheme.[12]

1 Contracting states could limit the obligation to disputes from commercial contracts.
2 Art 1.
3 Art 3.
4 Art 4.
5 Art 2.
6 Art 8.

7 The main differences are set out in Russell, op cit, (18th edn, 1970) pp 453–454.
8 See para 7.12 below.
9 Art 1. In the French text, 'parties soumises respectivement à la jurisdiction d'Etats contractant différents'.
10 See Subcommittee on Arbitration Clauses, LNOJ, 1922, at p 1413. Nationality may not have been referred to because of the special difficulties of that concept in the British Empire, to the individual parts of which the Protocol would apply.
11 See Report of Rapporteur, Fourth Assembly Records, Minutes of Second Committee, p 340. See now *Brazendale & Co Ltd v Saint Frères SA* [1970] 2 Lloyd's Rep 34; para 7.13 below.
12 P. Contini, (1959) 8 Am J Comp L 283 at p 289; A. Nussbaum, (1942) 56 Harv LR 219 at p 235.

Implementation of the Protocol within the Empire

5.06 For some jurisdictions, the substance of the Protocol involved a radical departure from past practice.[1] For the United Kingdom, however, and the jurisdictions within the Empire, much of what was required was already considered to be provided for. The only requirement needed was to put the courts under a duty to refuse to continue legal proceedings in relation to matters covered by the agreement to arbitrate. Accordingly the Arbitration Clauses (Protocol) Act 1924 was enacted in the United Kingdom, obliging a stay of proceedings to be granted by a court on an application by a party.[2] It was this legislation which became the model for the 37 jurisdictions in the British Empire in which the Protocol initially took effect.[3] Although this represents a very substantial part of the jurisdictions within the scheme at that time (some 71 in all), the effect was not to establish as a by-product a scheme for the British Empire. As we have seen, a condition of the arrangement was that the agreement must be between parties subject to the jurisdiction of different contracting states. The United Kingdom, in the capacity of a contracting state, adhered on behalf of most parts of the Empire. Only New Zealand and India also had the status of contracting parties ratifying in their own right.[4] Accordingly only the latter cases can be constituted as 'different Contracting States'. This was likely to cause little hardship as under existing arbitration legislation courts were likely to exercise their discretion in favour of staying legal proceedings in cases of this nature.

1 Private International Law Committee Report, p 4.
2 S 1, re-enacted, as amended by the Arbitration (Foreign Awards) Act 1930, s 8, in Arbitration Act 1950, s 4(2). This amendment was the consequence of proposals by the Committee on the Law of Arbitration in 1927, Cmd 2817. This is discussed below, para 5.07.
3 Almost all were in the period 1925–1926. See Chapter 7, Annex I, below.
4 New Zealand, 9 June 1926, TS 32/1926; India, 23 October 1937, TS 56/1937.

League of Nations: the Geneva Convention of 1927

5.07 The question of enforcement of foreign awards remained. In the United Kingdom this was contained within the terms of reference of the Committee on the Law of Arbitration.[1] The Committee reported in 1927 that they saw little or no reason to consider the matter 'since an action on the foreign award is perfectly feasible'.[2] It was enough to suggest that it should be made clear that service out of the jurisdiction and the summary judgment procedure under Order XIV would generally be available.[3] This parochial, rather complacent, view was not shared by traders and jurists particularly in other parts of Europe.

The success of the Protocol scheme had rapidly given rise to complaints about the absence of any international agreement on this aspect of arbitration. Indeed, the Protocol may well have aggravated the position. For, recourse to the courts having been excluded where an agreement to arbitrate existed, a party might find himself with an award he could not enforce abroad as readily as he might have been able to enforce a judgment—which he could not obtain. This was pointed out by contrast with the draft convention produced in 1925 by the Hague Conference on Private International Law under which arbitral awards would be required to be given effect as judgments in the place they were made. Thereby they became enforceable under the proposed judgment scheme. The Economic Committee reported to the Council of the League of Nations in 1926 that adhesions to the Protocol might have been inhibited by this shortcoming.[4] The Council agreed to the establishment of an Expert Committee to examine the matter, taking as its starting point a French text prepared by some members of the Economic Committee, drawing upon the Hague Conference draft.[5] The Expert Committee reported in April 1927, producing a draft Protocol on Awards,[6] since a multilateral scheme was seen to be an urgent practical need which bilateral arrangements would not satisfy. They were agreed that the new scheme must be limited to awards arising from Protocol agreements: application to all awards would give rise to too great complexity. Even so, it should only extend to those awards which had been made in a state party to the new agreement, thereby reflecting the underlying considerations of reciprocity which normally exist in this field. The scheme should be able to co-exist with bilateral treaties which were generally more precisely suited to the particular circumstances of the countries involved. The draft Protocol, as it was then called, was approved by the Economic Committee and sent around to member states, having been placed on the agenda of the coming Assembly. A generally favourable response was obtained, the World Economic Conference in 1927 in particular strongly supporting adhesion.[7] Government comments were considered by the Second Committee to which the draft was referred,[8] on the report of a Committee of Jurists which had produced a revised draft.[9] The form of this instrument had been reconsidered on the request of the British Government, at the behest of the Imperial Conference of 1926 which had agreed that fuller acknowledgment of dominion status should be given in treaty negotiations. Accordingly, a convention format was adopted.[10] The new version followed a new draft produced by the British Government to take account of these matters.[11]

The Second Committee endorsed the report and draft convention. In particular, it rejected the suggestion that closer adherence to the Hague Conference approach would have been more desirable. As awards derived from private agreements, it was desirable that the enforcing jurisdiction should have a wider control than that advocated by the Conference in respect of judgments.[12] The Assembly itself, accepting the Second Committee's recommendations, resolved on 26 September 1927 to open the Convention on the Execution of Foreign Arbitral Awards to all states which were contracting parties to the 1923 Protocol.[13] Again the enterprise had been completed with considerable speed.

1 Chairman, Mackinnon J.
2 Cmd 2817, para 31. The *Norske Atlas* case (para 5.02, note 3 above) was decided about this time.
3 Ibid, para 32.
4 LNOJ, 1926, p 1242.
5 Ibid, pp 1382–1383. It was recognised that alterations would be necessary to take account of

the Anglo-Saxon approach: the findings of a 'Special Committee' to which the British Government had referred the matter were to be taken into account (the Mackinnon Committee): ibid, pp 1359–1362.

6 LNOJ, 1927, pp 890–899. An interim report had indicated that the Committee was seeking 'a few formulae which would be wide and elastic enough to fit all cases': ibid, pp 582–583. The Chairman was Professor M. D. Anzilotti: the British Empire expert was H. Claughton Scott KC.

7 LNOJ, 1927, p 77.

8 Eighth Assembly Records, Minutes of Second Committee (Technical Organisations), p 180.

9 The Committee included H. Claughton Scott KC (British Empire) and Sir Edward Chaimer, legal adviser to the Secretary of State for India.

10 This was not the first; see Convention establishing the International Relief Union, 12 July 1927.

11 Report of the Committee of Jurists, Eighth Assembly Records, Minutes of Second Committee, pp 71–88, which contains a detailed discussion of comments received and a report on the final draft by Dr Leitmaier (Austria).

12 Report of Second Committee to Eighth Assembly, ibid, pp 457–460.

13 LNOJ, 1928, pp 134–135.

The Convention arrangements

5.08 The principal purpose of the Convention was to oblige contracting parties to recognise and enforce in accordance with local law arbitral awards made, in pursuance of agreements covered by the Protocol, in the territory of a contracting party and between persons 'subject to the jurisdiction of one of the Contracting Parties'.[1] The Convention laid down the conditions which must be satisfied,[2] the circumstances in which recognition and enforcement can be refused[3] and the minimum documentation which must be produced.[4] The Convention did not apply to dependencies, protectorates or mandated territories unless specifically mentioned: separate declarations might be made by a contracting party in respect of such jurisdictions if the 1923 Protocol applied to them.[5] Although not as marred by language infelicities as the Protocol, the Convention is not without its difficulties in interpretation.[6] Nonetheless it was regarded as a considerable achievement; indeed according to one commentator, the scheme was 'probably the foremost original contribution of the League to international legislation'.[7] Unhappily, in practice, it has not lived up to these expectations. The burden of substantiating his entitlement imposed by the Convention upon a party seeking to enforce his award and the opportunities afforded to the debtor to obstruct the enforcement process greatly weakened its effectiveness.

1 Art 1.

2 Ibid.

3 Arts 2 and 3. These laid down circumstances in which a state is not bound to grant recognition: local law or treaty agreement could permit recognition even in these circumstances: Report of Second Committee, para 5.07, note 12, above, p 459.

4 Art 4. These provisions were said to be 'descriptive and not exhaustive': ibid.

5 Art 10.

6 See A. Nussbaum, (1942) 56 Harv LR 219, passim; E. G. Lorenzen, (1935–36) 45 Yale LJ 39, passim. See para 7.21 below.

7 Nussbaum, loc cit, at p 222.

Implementation of the Convention within the Empire

5.09 Changes were required, as a result of the Convention, in common law practice. The Arbitration (Foreign Awards) Act 1930 was enacted by the United Kingdom Parliament, having been delayed by a general election. Legislation modelled upon this statute was adopted in many jurisdictions, enabling His Majesty's Government to ratify the Convention and to make declarations with respect to some 27 jurisdictions.[1] Ratifications were also entered by India and New Zealand (and extended by her to Western Samoa). Again this represented a substantial part of the total of jurisdictions in the scheme at that period (54)[2] but again it is doubtful that the legislation was capable of being used for the enforcement of awards between persons in different parts of the Empire. For the parties to the award must be subject to the jurisdiction of different Powers[3] but, at least in the law of the United Kingdom, the same Power, His Majesty the King of Great Britain, Ireland and the British Dominions beyond the seas, Emperor of India, was involved in respect of the dependent jurisdictions.[4] At the best, the scheme would be applicable between the United Kingdom (and dependencies) and India and New Zealand, each of which entered separate ratifications.[5]

The implementing legislation did not follow the exact language of the Convention. This, coupled with certain inherent shortcomings in the language of the Convention itself, weakened the scheme by introducing an element of uncertainty and undesirable variations in practice.[6] In operation, it seems not to have been as successful as its protagonists had hoped,[7] although a number of states in the post-World War II period have joined the scheme, including five from the Commonwealth.[8]

1 These are set out in SRO and SI Revised 1948, Vol II at pp 749–760. They were mainly made 1930–1931.

2 There have been a small number of adhesions subsequent to World War II: see Chapter 7, Annex I, below.

3 Arbitration (Foreign Awards) Act 1930, s 1. These provisions were altered following an intervention by Lord Atkin, 75 HL Official Report (1929–1930) cols 99–107, in an attempt to make clear that the scheme depended on reciprocity and did not apply to wholly national arbitrations, ie those between GB citizens in Great Britain.

4 See Orders-in-Council, referred to in note 1. The Power is named as His Britannic Majesty in the case of both the United Kingdom and New Zealand.

5 See SR & O 1930/674 (New Zealand); SR & O 1939/137 (India).

6 See paras 7.21–7.22 below.

7 A. Nussbaum, (1942) 56 Harv LR 219 at p 236. The Private International Law Committee attributed the paucity of use to the fact that most awards are complied with: op cit, p 5.

8 See Chapter 7, Annex I, below. A revised Order-in-Council of reciprocating jurisdictions was published by the UK: SI 1978/186, added to by SI 1979/304 (which does not include all the states notified to the UN).

Arbitration awards and the 1933 scheme

5.10 The existence of the new Convention caused the Greer Committee when considering the money judgments scheme in 1932 not to propose inclusion of any provision for arbitral awards, as these were 'sufficiently provided for' by the 1930 Act.[1] The discrepancy between the proposed statute and the 1920 Act in this respect was doubtless of little importance so long as the former was to be used in respect of foreign states party to the Convention. But it was relevant when the inclusion of Commonwealth jurisdictions under the 1933 scheme came into question. The want of provision of a kind found in the earlier scheme seems to have represented an obstacle which was only removed in 1956 for the United Kingdom. Provision analogous to that used in the 1920 Act was introduced in respect of those jurisdictions to which the 1920 Act had been extended.[2] Not all jurisdictions with this legislation have followed suit, whereas others have now extended the scheme to apply to arbitral awards enforceable as judgments in any jurisdiction with which reciprocal arrangements may be concluded.[3] The inadequacy of these schemes, as well as the

Geneva scheme, may be the explanation of the continued use of actions at common law upon a foreign award and the development of section 26 of the Arbitration Act 1950 for use in relation to foreign awards.[4]

1 Cmd 4213, p 55.
2 Administration of Justice Act 1956, s 51.
3 See Chapter 2, Annex I, above, for list. This now includes the United Kingdom: Civil Jurisdicition and Judgments Act 1982, Sch 10.
4 *Dalmia Cement Ltd v National Bank of Pakistan* [1974] 2 Lloyd's Rep 98 at 106; *Re John Helmsing Schiffahrtsgesellschaft MbH and Marechart Ltd* (1981) 121 DLR (3d) 486 (Fed Ct of Canada). But see *Mauritius Steam Navigation Co Ltd v International Shipping Lines Ltd* 1969 (3) ALR Comm 34 (Nigeria); *M Hamburger & Sons Ltd v Nyanza Impex Ltd* 1975 (1) ALR Comm 90 (Kenya).

United Nations: the New York Convention

5.11 Revival of world commerce and the revitalisation of international commercial arbitration after World War II brought the issue once more to the fore. With it came a growing demand for the replacement of the Geneva arrangements which were increasingly seen to have shortcomings. The result was the New York Convention on the Recognition and Enforcement of Foreign Arbitral Awards, 10 June 1958. The formulation of this Convention seems not to have excited as much interest as its predecessor. British businessmen were said to have neither strong opposition nor much enthusiasm.[1] There was no major identifiable Commonwealth input, although the United Kingdom, especially through its Private International Law Committee, made a substantial contribution. It was, of course, negotiated at a time when the Commonwealth comprised but a small proportion of its present membership[2] but, as far as can be judged from the public responses of the governments of the time, the preparation of a new treaty in this field occasioned relatively little positive concern, the United Kingdom in particular doubting whether there was any practical urgency in replacing the existing Geneva scheme.[3] India, Sri Lanka (then Ceylon) and to a lesser extent, Australia and Pakistan did indicate their support for updating international arrangements.[4]

1 Cmnd 1515, para 5.
2 Ten in 1958 (including South Africa and newly independent Ghana and Malaya).
3 UN Doc E/2822, Add 4.
4 UN Doc E/CONF 2/SR 3, 5 and 6.

Negotiation of the New York Convention

5.12 The initiative for the Convention came in 1953 from the International Chamber of Commerce which asked the Economic and Social Council of the United Nations to take action to consider improved enforcement facilities for arbitral awards, providing a report and draft Convention to that end.[1] In 1954 the Council established an ad hoc Committee, of whose eight government representatives, three were from Commonwealth states.[2] This Committee, which saw itself acting essentially as technical experts more than as representatives, reported in 1955[3] producing a modified draft Convention of their own.[4] On a number of important issues relating to those substantive parts of the draft on which the Committee members were divided, the Commonwealth states took similar positions.[5]

The draft Convention was submitted to member and non-member states and a number of non-governmental organisations for their comments. Of those replying, only three, India, New Zealand and the United Kingdom, were from the Commonwealth.[6] In 1958, a Conference was convened to conclude the Convention.[7] Of the 45 states represented at the Conference, five were from the Commonwealth: Australia, India, Pakistan, Sri Lanka and the United Kingdom, with the Federation of Malaya, newly independent, as an observer. Seventeen states submitted formal amendments to the draft Convention. Of the three from the Commonwealth, the United Kingdom proposed numerous changes, whilst Pakistan and Sri Lanka made a small number of less substantial suggestions.[8] During the Conference itself, both in the Working Parties and at the Plenary Sessions, the United Kingdom appears to have taken the most active role of Commonwealth states with India and Sri Lanka making influential contributions from time to time.[9]

1 UN Doc E/C 2/373: for government responses thereto see UN Doc E/AC 42/1. The Draft was examined by the Private International Law Committee (UK), having been circulated for comments to trade associations. It did not receive the Committee's support: op cit, paras 3 and 4.
2 Australia (A. H. Loomes); India (M. B. Mehta (alt S. Krishnamurti)); UK (B. A. Wortley (alt W. V. J. Evans)): UNESCO Res 520 (xvii) of 6 April 1954.
3 UN Doc E/2704.
4 UN Doc E/AC 42/SR10/3. The Private International Law Committee, whose views had been the basis of instructions to the UK representative, found the new draft free of the objections made to the ICC draft. Cmnd 1515, para 5.
5 Eg Report UN Doc E/2704, paras 19, 44, 49.
6 UN Doc E/2822 Add 1, 4 and 6. The most substantial set of comments were from the UK, based upon the comments of the Private International Law Committee, 3rd Report (not published).
7 Following UNESCO Res 604 (xxi) of 3 May 1956.
8 UN Doc E/CONF 26/7 and 26/L 7–35.
9 B. A. Wortley (UK); Sir Claude Corea (Sri Lanka) and C. K. Daphtary (India—Chairman of Working Party No 1) were prominent.

Ratifications by Commonwealth states

5.13 The Convention finally agreed upon was signed by India, of those ten states signing immediately, and later in 1958 by Pakistan[1] and Sri Lanka. No other Commonwealth state signed during the period available for signatures.[2] In the ensuing 25 years, some 11 Commonwealth states have become contracting parties, in the case of India and Sri Lanka by ratification and in the others by accession.[3] In addition, Australia and the United Kingdom have extended the Convention to certain of the territories for whose international relations they are or were then responsible.[4]

There are, therefore, to date, some 21 jurisdictions in the Commonwealth which are within the ambit of the Convention.[5] All but five have enacted implementing legislation. Although treaties are not self-executing in their law, Nigeria, Sri Lanka, Tanzania and Trinidad and Tobago have no domestic legislation.[6] It must be doubted whether, in the absence of municipal law, the Convention can be given effect in any of those contracting states.

1 Pakistan has not ratified.
2 The United Kingdom, having reservations about art II, did not sign at that time.
3 See Chapter 8, Annex I below.
4 Under art X. Belize, now independent, has not notified adhesion to the Convention in her own right: see para 8.02 below. See Chapter 8, Annex II below, for a list of the dependencies.
5 In addition, Alderney, Barbados, British Virgin Islands and Guernsey have enacted the necessary legislation.

6 Cyprus, where treaties are largely self-executing, has enacted a Law to ratify the Convention (Law No 84 of 1979). Dependencies of the UK have legislated in terms virtually identical to the Arbitration Act 1975 of the UK. For a list of implementing legislation, see Chapter 8, Annex III, below.

Implementation of the Convention within the Commonwealth

5.14 In relation to the Geneva scheme, implementing legislation in the Commonwealth followed a standard pattern set by the English Acts. This has not been the case in relation to the New York Convention, no doubt in part because the United Kingdom was not the first Commonwealth state in the field on this occasion. Australia in particular legislated in 1974.[1] This was perhaps unexpected as the Private International Law Committee had supported the adhesion by the United Kingdom in 1961,[2] with certain reservations, the main ones of which could be resolved in the implementing legislation on lines they proposed. The Committee concluded that the Convention appeared to be acceptable to the business community and to go as far towards facilitating the enforcement of foreign awards as was reasonable in a multilateral convention.[3] But it was not until 1975 that the required legislation was enacted,[4] by which time the new scheme had become established among a number of the United Kingdom's trading partners. Subsequent legislation in other parts of the Commonwealth, notably in dependent jurisdictions of the United Kingdom, has drawn heavily upon this model.

1 The federal legislation, enacted in 1974, replaced state legislation which had been passed in eg New South Wales (Act 1973–36), Queensland (Act 1973–34, Part VIII); Tasmania (Act 1972–59) but not brought into force.
2 Cmnd 1515.
3 Paras 20–21. A number of defects and obscurities in the text were noted (ibid, Appendix 3) but these did not justify rejection of the Convention.
4 Curiously, Gibraltar enacted legislation in 1974 closely modelled upon the UK legislation which was passed in the following year.

Application of the Convention among Commonwealth states

5.15 Given the doubts which have been adverted to earlier concerning the Geneva scheme, it is perhaps surprising that many of the Commonwealth states or jurisdictions once within that scheme have not taken steps to adopt its replacement. At the same time, ten jurisdictions which are parties to the New York Convention were never within the scope of its predecessor—Australia and its four dependencies, Bermuda, Botswana, Cyprus, Nigeria and Trinidad and Tobago. This Convention, therefore, may come to be recognised in the Commonwealth as much as an opportunity to introduce an international enforcement scheme for the first time as that of replacing an outmoded system. Arguably, the incidence of litigation involving arbitral awards in most of the states within the Geneva scheme has been so low that its deficiencies have not become evident there and thus no significant commercial pressures have developed for its supersession. There is little evidence that the New York Convention has been viewed as providing particularly for inter-Commonwealth needs in this matter and such uniformity of approach as there is between those Commonwealth jurisdictions which have legislated on the Convention is traceable principally to the Convention and to a lesser extent to the United Kingdom model legislation used for the Geneva scheme and more recently to the 1975 Act. The Convention is to be seen as a multilateral scheme for independent states which, as a result of the negotiating activities of a handful of Commonwealth representatives, is appropriate for Commonwealth states. The Convention is effective between one independent Commonwealth state, party to it, or any of its declared dependencies on the one hand and any other such state or any of its declared dependencies on the other. But as an international instrument, it does not apply between a contracting state and its declared dependencies. To that extent its usefulness for Commonwealth purposes is limited.

Standing of the Convention

5.16 It seems generally acknowledged that 'the Convention has satisfactorily met the general purpose for which it was adopted'.[1] Such problems as have been identified in its operation are not seen as substantial enough to justify any amendment to its provisions.[2] In consequence, its wider adoption and application within the Commonwealth would be justified and has been commended to the Commonwealth Law Ministers.[3]

1 United Nations Commission on International Trade Law, *Study on the Application and Interpretation of the Convention on Recognition and Enforcement of Foreign Arbitral Awards (New York, 1958): Report of the Secretary General,* UN Doc A/CN/168 1979, para 50 ('UNCITRAL Report').

2 Ibid.

3 By the Commonwealth Secretariat in 1977, *Meeting of Commonwealth Law Ministers: Minutes of Meeting and Memoranda*, p 286, following J. D. McClean and K. W. Patchett *A further Report* 1977, paras 454–455. Explanatory Documentation prepared for this purpose is contained in Commonwealth Secretariat, *The New York Convention on the Recognition and Enforcement of Foreign Arbitral Awards* (1981).

General structure of the Convention

5.17 Whilst the Convention is principally concerned with the recognition and enforcement of arbitral awards, provision is also made for the recognition of certain arbitration agreements.[1] The Geneva scheme had dealt with the latter matter in the Protocol and early discussions for the New York Convention favoured a similar approach.[2] But the separation of the recognition of awards and agreements into two distinct instruments carried with it the possibility that, by adhesion to the awards treaty only, a state could escape its obligations by refusing to recognise the agreement from which the award derived. Accordingly, persuaded by the arguments of the United Kingdom delegate, a single convention was accepted as desirable.[3] A primary object of the Convention is to replace the Geneva scheme and thus, as between contracting parties to the former, the latter ceases to operate.[4] On the other hand, the New York Convention is permitted to coexist with multilateral or bilateral arrangements on the matter of awards and does not deprive any party of any other right he may have to avail himself of an award.[5]

1 Art II.

2 The ad hoc Committee confined its proposals to awards, notwithstanding the contrary views of the three Commonwealth members: UN Doc E/2704, para 19. For Conference discussions on the place of the agreements clause, see UN Docs E/CONF 26/R 9 and E/CONF 26/SR 21.

3 L. V. Quigley (1961) 70 Yale LJ 1049, at p 1063.

4 Art VII.2.

5 Art VII.1.

Purposes of the Convention

5.18 In outline, the Convention seeks to achieve two central purposes:

(a) to require contracting states to recognise relevant arbitration agreements and thus to refuse access to their courts by those who have agreed to submit relevant disputes to arbitration;[1]

(b) to require contracting states to recognise relevant arbitral awards and, if requested so to do, to make available domestic enforcement facilities without discriminating against those awards.[2]

In the matter of awards, the Convention introduced a number of improvements over the Geneva scheme, amongst which the most notable are:

(i) removal of the major restrictions upon the range of awards which were within the scheme;[3]

(ii) clarification of the burden of proving the award and in particular the imposition upon the award debtor of the obligation to raise the more substantial grounds for refusing enforcement of awards;[4]

(iii) clarification of certain of the grounds for refusing recognition and enforcement, in particular those concerning finality of awards subject to appeal and those which may be in conflict with the lex fori.[5]

The Convention for all its improvements leaves a number of issues unclear, not least the law which must be applied by the enforcing court to determine some of the issues which may arise before it.[6] In addition, it gives little guidance as to the kinds of arbitration agreements which, because of their overriding connection with the country of enforcement, might be excluded from an international scheme as domestic.[7] Further, though the Convention allows a contracting party to exclude itself altogether from any obligations in respect of awards from non-contracting states,[8] it fails to make clear the extent to which a contracting state can, if at all, impose conditions upon the recognition of non-contracting state awards. These issues have in a number of cases been the subject of domestic provision in the legislation of the Commonwealth and are examined in Chapter 8.[9]

1 Art II.
2 Art III.
3 Art I.
4 Art IV and V.
5 Art V.
6 Eg, Art II.1 and .3; Art V (a), (b), (d).
7 Art II.
8 Art I.3.
9 For a general review, see P. Sanders, (1979) 13 International Lawyer 269–287.

International investment disputes

5.19 One last international development, with wide Commonwealth application, should be noted in the matter of arbitration. It relates to awards made by Arbitral Tribunals under the auspices of the International Centre for Settlement of Investment Disputes in the resolution of legal disputes arising directly out of investments between states and nationals of other states. The Centre and the arrangements for conciliation and arbitration of such disputes were established pursuant to the Washington Convention on the Settlement of Investment Disputes between States and Nationals of other States, 18 March 1965. This Convention has been widely adhered to, with ratifications by some 25 Commonwealth states.[1] In addition, the United Kingdom adhered on behalf of 23 other jurisdictions, as dependencies.[2] Of these, 12 have since achieved independence[3] and have provisionally accepted to continue their obligations until a final decision is taken on the question of succession. In relation to this group, the United Kingdom statute, which was extended by Order-in-Council[4] to these jurisdictions as part of their law, continues to provide the legal framework for the domestic enforcement and arrangements in respect of awards handed down under the Convention. Similar legislation is found in other Commonwealth countries.

1 Botswana, Cyprus, Fiji, The Gambia, Guyana, Jamaica, Kenya, Lesotho, Malaŵi, Malaysia, Mauritius, New Zealand (but not Cook Islands, Niue or Tokelau), Nigeria, Papua-New Guinea, Seychelles, Sierra Leone, Singapore, Solomon Islands, Sri Lanka, Swaziland, Trinidad and Tobago, Uganda, United Kingdom, Western Samoa, Zambia. In addition Australia and Barbados have signed but not ratified.
2 Anguilla, British Virgin Islands, Cayman Islands, Falkland Islands, Gibraltar, Guernsey, Hong Kong, Jersey, Montserrat, St Helena, Turks and Caicos Islands are the remaining dependencies.
3 Antigua and Barbuda, Commonwealth of the Bahamas, Belize, Commonwealth of Dominica, Grenada, Kiribati, Mauritius, St Christopher and Nevis, St Lucia, St Vincent and the Grenadines, Tonga and Tuvalu.
4 Arbitration (International Investment Disputes) Act 1966, s 6; SI 1967/159; SI 1967/585; SI 1968/1199; SI 1979/572.

Arbitration arrangements

5.20 The Convention authorises any contracting party or any national[1] of another contracting party wishing to institute arbitration proceedings on a legal dispute relating to an investment between them[2] to make a request to the Secretary-General of the Centre.[3] Unless the request is manifestly outside the jurisdiction of the Centre,[4] the request will be registered and an Arbitral Tribunal drawn up from the Panel of Arbitrators.[5] The Tribunal must decide the dispute in accordance with any rules of law agreed by the parties or, in the absence of agreement, with the law of the contracting state party to the dispute.[6] The award must deal with every question submitted and state the reasons.[7]

Disputes as to interpretation and requests for revision may be made to the Centre, usually for decision of the original Tribunal.[8] Annulment may also be sought which must be considered by an ad hoc Committee drawn from the Panel.[9] In all cases, enforcement will be stayed pending decision.[10] An award may be annulled on the grounds that the Tribunal was not properly constituted or had manifestly exceeded its powers or that there was corruption on the part of a member or a serious departure from a fundamental rule of procedure or that the award failed to state the reasons.[11] If the award is invalidated, the matter may be re-submitted to a new Tribunal.[12]

The award is binding on the parties and 'shall not be subject to appeal or any other remedy' except those provided for in the Convention.[13] Each contracting state is required to recognise any award and to enforce the pecuniary obligations within its territories as if it were a final judgment.[14] Execution of the award is governed by the law of the state in which the execution is sought.[15]

1 Art 25(2) sets out the dates at which nationality is to be determined.
2 Art 25(1): the parties to the dispute must consent in writing to submit to the Centre.
3 Art 36(1) and (2).
4 Contracting states may notify the Centre of any class of disputes which it will or will not consider submitting to the Centre: art 25(4).
5 Art 37. Panels are made up of persons of high moral character and recognised competence designated by each contracting state and by the Chairman: arts 12–16.

6 Art 42. Parties may agree the procedural rules but in the absence thereof the Arbitration Rules of the Centre apply: art 45.
7 Art 48.
8 Arts 50 and 51.
9 Art 52.
10 Arts 50(2), 51(4), 52(5).
11 Art 52(1).
12 Art 52(6).
13 Art 53.
14 Art 54(1).
15 Art 54(3).

Enforcement of investment dispute awards

5.21 The Arbitration (International Investment Disputes) Act 1966[1] regulates the mechanism for the enforcement of the award in the United Kingdom and a considerable number of Commonwealth jurisdictions to which it has been extended.[2] It will be taken as representative. The person[3] seeking recognition or enforcement of the award in England is entitled to have it registered in the High Court on proof of prescribed matters in the form of an affidavit exhibiting a copy of the award certified by the Secretary-General of the Centre. This affidavit must state information very similar to that required for registering a foreign judgment under the 1920 scheme.[4] In particular, the applicant must state his belief that the grounds upon which a judgment cannot be registered under that Act are not present in relation to the award.[5]

Where pecuniary obligations are involved, the award is to be registered in the currency in which it is expressed[6] and for the reasonable costs of and incidental to the registration.[7] Registration may not take place if pecuniary obligations have been wholly satisfied and, if partly satisfied, it is permitted only for the balance.[8] A registered award involving pecuniary obligations has the same force and effect, for purposes of execution, as a local judgment and proceedings may be taken on the award, the sum is to carry the same interest and the court is to have the same control over execution, as if it had been a local judgment.[9] Here too there is a close resemblance to the judgments scheme.[10]

1 Ch 41.
2 Listed in para 5.19, notes 2 and 3 above.
3 The statute is binding upon the Crown: s 1(8).
4 RSC Ord 73, r 9(4), applying Order 71, r 3. For the requirements under the judgments scheme, see para 3.28 above.
5 AJA, s 9(2); these are set out in para 2.20 above. For the implications of this requirement, see para 5.22 below.
6 The requirement to register in the forum currency (s 1(3)) was repealed by the Administration of Justice Act 1977. If converted in local currency, it will be at the rate of exchange at the date of payment.
7 S 1(4).
8 S 1(5).
9 S 2(1).
10 Para 3.32 above.

Obligations in relation to the recognition and enforcement of awards

5.22 Notice of the registration must be served upon the debtor.[1] No provision, however, is made for him to apply to set the registration aside.[2] He may, however, seek a provisional stay of execution on the ground that a stay has been granted under the Convention (which must be granted) or on the ground that an application has been made to the Centre which may result in a stay (which the court may grant if it is appropriate).[3] The intention is clear that it is not for the requested court to enter into questions relating to the interpretation, revision or validity of the awards: the Convention requires these to be settled under the Convention arrangements.[4] The requirement that the applicant's affidavit must state that the 1920 grounds for setting aside are not present[5] may suggest that those considerations can be raised by the debtor if he questions the veracity of the affidavit in this respect.[6] It must be doubted whether this would be consistent with the Convention. The New Zealand Act is more explicit in authorising the requested court to refuse enforcement to an award which is contrary to the law of New Zealand.[7] This public policy safeguard, which may only be intended to apply where the execution of the award would contradict some explicit prohibition of the lex fori,[8] could be construed as allowing the requested court to establish that New Zealand law has been correctly applied in cases where this applies to the resolution of the dispute.[9] This is so clearly against the Convention[10] that it is unlikely to be adopted. The suggested construction may be justified by the requirement that the forum law governing the execution is to be followed.[11]

1 RSC Ord 71, r (1), applied by Ord 73, r 9(2). The notice must usually be served personally but this can be done ex juris, without leave.
2 RSC Ord 73, r 9(2) does not incorporate Ord 71, r 9, which deals with setting aside.
3 Ibid, r 9(6): for stays under the Convention, see para 5.20, note 10 above.
4 Convention, art 50–52; para 5.20 above.
5 Ord 73, r 9(4), applying Ord 71, r 3(1)(c)(iii).
6 *Halsbury's Laws of England*, Vol 2, para 651, note 12.
7 Arbitration (International Investment Disputes) Act 1979, No 39, s 5(2)(c).
8 See paras 3.36 and 3.64 above.
9 Convention, art 42; para 5.20 above.
10 Ibid, art 54(1).
11 Ibid, art 54(3).

CHAPTER 6

Awards under the Commonwealth Money Judgments Schemes

I INTRODUCTION

6.01 Enforcement of arbitral awards by registration is possible under both Commonwealth schemes, although in the case of the 1933 legislation only if that has been appropriately amended.[1] The schemes extend to two cases:

(a) where the arbitral award has been the subject of legal proceedings in a reciprocating Commonwealth country and a judgment has been handed down upon it, the judgment may be registered in the same circumstances as any other judgment for a fixed sum of money;

(b) where the award has 'in pursuance of the law in force in the place where it was made, become enforceable in the same manner as a judgment given by a court in that place'.[2]

The former case will not be considered here as the registration proceedings will relate to the judgment, rather than the award. If the award has been successfully sued upon at common law or if a judgment has been entered in respect of an award, for the summary enforcement of which leave had been previously granted,[3] it will be necessary to establish that the judicial proceedings and the ensuing judgment, rather than the arbitration proceedings and the ensuing award fulfil the criteria for registration.[4] These have already been considered.[5]

In relation to the second case, rather different and difficult considerations arise since the registration process must be concerned with the award and the arbitration from which it derived. There is very little case law on this matter, probably indicating little use of the schemes in this context. This may not be surprising as the special characteristics of arbitration and awards are not clearly reflected in the statutes, which deal with the matter merely by including awards within the definition of 'judgments'. In consequence the terminology of the schemes which are drafted throughout as applying to judgments stricto sensu fits on occasions uncomfortably with awards. It must be assumed, however, that the term 'award' as used in the Acts must be substituted for 'judgment' wherever that term appears, however awkwardly that may read. So for example, the statutes refer to 'judgments given in superior courts' of reciprocating countries.[6] In the context of awards, should this be read as a reference to awards made by an arbitral body in a reciprocating country which have, under the law of that country, become enforceable in the same manner as a judgment which has been given by any court of that country or only by a superior court of that country or only by a recognised court of that country?[7] Presumably the first is intended. It cannot have been intended that arbitral bodies had to be designated under the 1933 Act.

There seems little doubt that the criteria in the statutes must be fulfilled mutatis mutandis in respect of the award before registration can be finalised. If it had been intended that the proceedings to make the award enforceable as a judgment were to be those to which the criteria are to be applied, rather different provision would have been made.

1 The Foreign Judgments (Reciprocal Enforcement) Act 1933 was amended in the United Kingdom by the Administration of Justice Act 1956, s 51(a) with application to those jurisdictions to which the 1920 Act had been extended. Few Commonwealth countries so restricted the application. The restriction has now been lifted in the United Kingdom; see Civil Jurisdiction and Judgments Act 1982, Sch 10, inserting a new s 10A into FJREA.
2 AJA, s 12(1); FJREA, s 11(1), as extended (see note 1).
3 Pursuant to legislation equivalent to the Arbitration Act 1950 (UK), s 26: see Russell, op cit, pp 369–377.
4 *Union Nationale des Coopératives Agricoles de Céréales v Robert Catterall & Co Ltd* [1959] 2 QB 44 at 54.
5 Chapter 3.
6 AJA, s 9(1); FJREA, s 1(1) and (2).
7 Dicey and Morris, op cit, p 1156.

Application of the schemes within the Commonwealth

6.02 Every Commonwealth jurisdiction which still applies the 1920 legislation thereby makes provision for the enforcement of awards from those jurisdictions in respect of which extension orders have been made.[1] Where the 1933 scheme runs, most jurisdictions now allow enforcement of awards from all designated reciprocating jurisdictions. On the other hand, some have failed altogether to include awards within the terms of their legislation, whilst others followed United Kingdom legislation, now repealed, which limits application to those designated Commonwealth areas which were formerly dealt with by extension orders under the 1920 statute but to which the 1933 had subsequently been applied.[2] The consequence of these latter shortcomings is that this mechanism for enforcement of awards is not co-extensive with the judgment enforcement arrangements.

It should be stressed that the absence of reciprocity in this respect does not appear to have caused difficulty in making or continuing particular extension orders, although it has been said to have militated against the replacement of the 1920 scheme by the 1933 scheme.[3] The Indian scheme, in particular, does not extend to arbitration awards, even if enforceable as a decree or judgment.[4]

1 AJA, s 11.
2 See para 6.01, note 1 and for application of the schemes, Chapter 3, Part II. These jurisdictions are indicated in Chapter 2, Annex I, above.
3 Dicey and Morris, op cit, pp 1154–1155.
4 Code of Civil Procedure 1908, s 44A.

II ARBITRAL AWARDS REGISTRABLE UNDER THE SCHEME

6.03 In order to be registered, an arbitral award must fulfil the following conditions. It must be:

(i) one which has been made in a designated reciprocating Commonwealth jurisdiction;
(ii) one whereby a sum of money is payable which has not been wholly satisfied;
(iii) one which, in pursuance of the law of the reciprocating jurisdiction, has become enforceable in the same manner as a judgment of a local superior court;
(iv) one which can be enforced by execution in the country where it was made;[1]

(v) one which is final and conclusive as between the parties;
(vi) one which is made after the relevant extension order has come into effect.

The extent to which these conditions are all applicable will be considered in the following paragraphs.

1 Applicable to the 1933 scheme only? See para 6.07 below.

(a) The award must have been made in a designated reciprocating jurisdiction[1]

6.04 It must be established that the place in which the award was made is one designated by an appropriate extension order under one or other of the statutes which makes provision for the enforcement of awards.[2] As a general rule, the award will be deemed to be made in the place where the arbitration was carried out. This will normally be determined in or under the terms of the arbitration agreement. If the agreement provides for an appeal to another entity in another country, it is arguable that in some cases it is the place where the award of the latter is made to which reference must be made.[3] It is clear that the scheme does not extend to awards made elsewhere which may have been subjected to summary enforcement procedures in a particular Commonwealth jurisdiction.[4] The fact that enforcement facilities have been made available there cannot make up for the fact that the award itself was not made in that jurisdiction.

1 AJA, s 9(1); FJREA, s 1(2).
2 Paras 3.06–3.10, 3.14 and 3.15 above.
3 The actual effect of an appeal would have to be determined, presumably, by the law governing the arbitration. In English law, an appeal award is treated as if it were the award of the arbitrator: *E E and Brian Smith (1928) Ltd v Wheatsheaf Mills Ltd* [1939] 2 KB 302, [1939] 2 All ER 251; *N V Arnold Otto Meyer v Aune* [1939] 3 All ER 168.
4 Under the equivalent of Arbitration Act 1950 (UK), s 26. *Dalmia Cement Ltd v National Bank of Pakistan* [1975] QB 9, [1974] 3 All ER 189.

(b) The award must be one whereby a sum of money is payable[1] which has not been wholly satisfied

6.05 The statutes governing both schemes make explicit that the award must be for a fixed sum of money. Both seem capable of covering awards which merely establish and measure the extent of liability under a contract as well as those under which a sum is determined by way of damages for breach of contract.[2] On the other hand, an award which is not for a definite or calculable sum of money will not be caught.[3] Presumably, if the arbitrator by agreement or by the law governing the arbitration has power to award costs of the reference,[4] including those of the award, these too may be recovered.

No registration is permitted under the 1933 scheme if the award has been wholly satisfied.[5] Although not explicitly stated, it would presumably be a ground for refusal to exercise the court's power to register under the 1920 statute.[6] Although unlikely to be common subjects of awards, any tax, charge of a like nature, fine or other penalty ordered by the award cannot be recovered.[7] Any award which is for multiple damages cannot be enforced in the United Kingdom,[8] a requirement which will override any provision in the agreement or in the law governing the arbitration.

1 AJA, s 12(1); FJREA, s 1(2)(b).
2 For this distinction, see eg *F J Bloemen Pty Ltd v Gold Coast City Council* [1973] AC 115, [1972] 3 All ER 357, PC.

3 See para 3.13 above.
4 As under Arbitration Act 1950 (UK), s 18(1): *Bank Mellat v Helliniki Techniki SA* [1984] QB 291, [1983] 3 All ER 428, CA. For interest, see below, para 6.10.
5 FJREA, s 2(1), proviso (b).
6 AJA, s 9(1). RSC Ord 71, r 3(1)(c)(ii) requires that the affidavit by the applicant must state that this condition is met.
7 FJREA, s 1(2)(b). The usual common law rule will be attracted to the 1920 Act.
8 Protection of Trading Interests Act 1980, s 5.

(c) The award must be one which, in pursuance of the law of the reciprocating country, has become enforceable in the same manner as a judgment given by a court of that country[1]

6.06 It must be shown that in the designated Commonwealth jurisdiction there is provision under the law for the award to become enforceable as a judgment of a local court[2] and that that law has been utilised. In most instances, Commonwealth jurisdictions have a provision, modelled upon a United Kingdom power, for awards to become enforceable in the same manner as a judgment to the same effect, by leave of the High or Supreme Court or a judge thereof.[3] It appears, therefore, that this or some such similar process is envisaged by this requirement. Arbitral awards cannot become enforceable in the same manner as a judgment without some judicial intervention, even though the award may create a legally recognised obligation between the parties.

The applicant must produce an affidavit stating that to the best information and belief of the deponent this condition is fulfilled.[4] The requested court will not look behind the grant of leave in the country of origin. It will be for the courts of that country to determine, under its law, whether the conditions for the grant are present.[5]

This requirement of judicial endorsement in the country of origin contrasts with the common law, the Geneva and the New York schemes under which the foreign award is enforceable on proof of its finality without the need for judicial action in the place of its making.[6] It might appear that this factor is an unnecessary additional requirement for registration in other jurisdictions. When choosing a particular place for the arbitration (which may well be conducted under a different system of law), the parties may not be concerned to enforce the award in that place.[7] Yet as a prerequisite of registration, there must be judicial intercession there, in which questions relating to the validity of the award ought to be put in issue.[8] But on registration the requested court is not expected to enquire into questions relating to the validity of the award, other than those specifically identified in the enforcement statutes. Thus questions of whether the arbitral body has correctly dealt with the procedures according to the law governing the arbitration proceedings[9] probably cannot be raised in registration proceedings, even though at common law and under the international schemes they are central to recognition and enforcement. On the other hand questions of jurisdiction are issues for the requested court.[10]

1 AJA, s 12(1); FJREA, s 10.
2 There is probably no need to show it to be a recognised court.
3 Arbitration Act 1950, s 26.
4 Eg, RSC Ord 73, r 8(b).
5 For English law, see Russell, op cit, pp 371–374.
6 Paras 6.08, 7.27 and 8.35 below.
7 For example in *Dalmia Cement Ltd v National Bank of Pakistan* [1975] QB 9, [1974] 3 All ER 189, the arbitration was held in Switzerland at the arbitrator's choice, under the law of India and the award was payable in India.

8 *Middlemiss and Gould (a firm) v Hartlepool Corpn* [1973] 1 All ER 172, [1972] 1 WLR 1643, CA.
9 *Norske Atlas Insurance Co Ltd v London General Insurance Co Ltd* (1927) 28 Ll L Rep 104; paras 7.26 and 8.34 below.
10 Dicey and Morris, op cit, p 1138; paras 6.19–6.20 below.

(d) The award must be one which can be enforced by execution in the country where it was made[1]

6.07 This is an express requirement only in the 1933 scheme. If it applies in relation to the 1920 scheme, it will be the consequence of the general discretion to refuse registrations, for example in circumstances which at common law would be a ground for refusing recognition. This does not appear to be the case. Moreover, evidence of this is not required when application is made to register the award under that Act.[2]

It is a nice question whether this requirement, in the context of the awards, adds anything to the immediately previous condition. In the normal event, an award which has been the subject of the summary procedure can be enforced. On the other hand, it seems probable that the court of registration may require to be satisfied that there are no impediments to execution in the country of origin. Thus evidence that the award was obtained against a person protected by state or diplomatic immunity or against whom the award could not be enforced until the termination of his bankruptcy[3] should preclude registration. Further, if the execution of the award has been suspended or prohibited pending further proceedings in the place of origin,[4] the condition appears not to be met; similarly, where the period within which execution must be brought has expired or where failure to take some formal step has rendered the award a nullity[5] or unenforceable.

It is not obvious that this condition is useful in its application to awards, particularly where the law governing the agreement under which the award was made or that governing the arbitration was not that of the country where the award was made. The place where the award is made may have little relevance in connection with its enforcement in another jurisdiction, especially if the parties have chosen a different law to govern the arbitration. Moreover, it seems inconsistent with the common law rule that how a foreign award can be made enforceable under the law governing the arbitration proceedings is not a matter which should concern the requested court.[6]

1 FJREA, s 2(1), proviso (b).
2 RSC Ord 71, r 3.
3 Cf *Berliner Industriebank AG v Jost* [1971] 2 QB 463, [1971] 2 All ER 1513, CA.
4 Ibid.
5 Cf *SA Consortium General Textiles v Sun and Sand Agencies Ltd* [1978] QB 279, [1978] 2 All ER 339, CA.
6 This rule is generally taken to have been established by *Union Nationale des Coopératives Agricoles des Céréales v Robert Catterall & Co Ltd* [1959] 2 QB 44, [1959] 1 All ER 721 (under the Geneva scheme), displacing *Merrifield Ziegler & Co v Liverpool Cotton Association Ltd* (1911) 105 LT 97 which had appeared to establish that the award must be actually enforceable in the country of origin: Dicey and Morris, op cit, p 1135.

(e) The award must be final and conclusive as between the parties[1]

6.08 This is the subject of explicit provision in the 1933 scheme and as a central common law requirement must be implicit under the earlier scheme. In consequence, an award should not be registered under either statute unless the court is satisfied that what was determined by the arbitrator produced a result under the law which governed the arbitration proceedings which, in the requested court's view, constituted a res judicata between parties.[2] This will normally be the case where there remains no matter within the reference to the arbitrator which can be reopened or further considered by him. Thus the requirement under the law of the place where the award is made that it must be confirmed by court order will not affect the finality of the award, so long as the court is concerned only with questions of formal validity and not with merits.[3] On the other hand, a term of the agreement that the award is to have temporary effect or to be interim only will take it outside this condition. The position where appeals to a court of law are pending or possible is clear. The 1933 Act explicitly provides that this condition is met, notwithstanding any appeal.[4] By contrast, the 1920 Act prohibits registration in those circumstances,[5] whatever the status of the award at common law. This prohibition appears also to be a requirement in cases under the 1920 scheme where an appeal to another arbitral tribunal is pending or intended. The position in respect to such appeals under the 1933 Act is not explicit. For an award is 'deemed' final under the Act only where an appeal to a *court* is involved. The gap would probably be filled by reference to the general common law rule, in relation to judgments, to the same effect.[6] At the same time, a court order granting a general stay of execution pending an appeal will prevent the award from being treated as final by a requested court.[7]

There remains the question whether an award is final which is liable to be set aside by the courts in the country of origin or to be remitted to the arbitrator or to be declared not to be binding or where the award has been stated as a special case, as is provided for in many Commonwealth Arbitration statutes.[8] Some of these, however, appear clearly to be equated with an appeal proper for the purposes of the 1933 scheme. For 'appeal' is defined as including—

'any proceedings by way of discharge or setting aside a judgment or an application for a new trial or a stay of execution.'[9]

Applying this provision to the case of awards, it appears clear that proceedings to set aside, as a species of appeal, will not affect finality but will be a basis for setting aside the registration until the matter is resolved. But an application for a declaration that an award is not binding or to remit the award presents different problems. On the one hand, the registering court might be influenced by the provision commonly found in arbitration legislation that an award is not to be deemed final if any proceedings for the purpose of contesting the validity of the award are pending in the country in which it was made.[10] Certainly, an application to remit can lead to the making of a fresh award by the same arbitrator[11], a fact which has been considered at common law to raise doubts about finality. A declaration that an award is not binding will obviously prevent the award having finality. Yet it is not obvious that the mere pendency of such proceedings or an intention to initiate them should permit the registering court to treat the award as, in some way, provisional and not final as to its findings.[12] There is a case, surely, for equating these processes with appeals proper by a less than literal construction of the definition of 'appeal' set out above in its application to awards. As a result, the registration should be made but it would be open to be set aside where any such proceedings were intended or commenced. The position is, however, different where the arbitrator has stated a case to the High Court, for until the matters so referred are resolved the award lacks completion.

In relation to the 1920 scheme, no statutory guidance is given in the relevant statute. For no extended meaning is given to the word 'appeal'. It may, however, be suggested that a similar approach should be adopted to that postulated in respect of the 1933 Act. For there seems no convincing argument at common law why, in the absence of clear indication under the law governing the arbitration, the possibility or initiation of procedures for the review of an award render the determination of the arbitrator in some way interim. The situation, of course, alters once the court decides to interfere with the award.[13]

In any case, it seems likely that the registering court under its general discretion to refuse registration[14] would be likely to refuse registration where such proceedings are pending or intended as in the case of appeals.[15]

1 FJREA, s 1(2)(a). As amended in the UK, this now allows for interim payments: Civil Jurisdiction and Judgments Act 1982, Sch 10.
2 This test is suggested by the approach of the Court of Appeal in *Union Nationale des Coopératives Agricoles des Céréales v Robert Catterall & Co Ltd* [1959] 2 QB 44, [1959] 1 All ER 721. Although stated in relation to the Geneva scheme, it appears to have general application.
3 Ibid. References to 'conclusiveness' are unusual in the context of awards.
4 FJREA, s 1(3). Power is given to set aside a registration where an appeal is pending or intended: ibid, s 5(1).
5 AJA, s 9(2)(e).
6 *Nouvion v Freeman* (1889) 15 App Cas 1, 59 LJ Ch 337, HL; *Colt Industries Inc v Sarlie (No 2)* [1966] 3 All ER 685, [1966] 1 WLR 1287, CA.
7 Cf *Berliner Industriebank AG v Jost* [1971] 2 QB 463, [1971] 2 All ER 1513.
8 Cf Arbitration Act 1950 (UK), ss 21, 22 and 23(2); RSC Ord 73, r 2(3).
9 FJREA, s 11(1).
10 Arbitration Act 1950 (UK), s 39, though this is, in strict law, applicable to Geneva scheme awards: *Union Nationale des Coopératives Agricoles des Céréales v Robert Catterall & Co Ltd*, above.
11 The power to remit under the Arbitration Act 1950, s 22 is limited to remitting the whole award: *Exormisis Shipping SA v Oonsoo* [1975] 1 Lloyd's Rep 432.
12 Dicey and Morris, op cit, p 1131, contra but no arguments are developed.
13 In *Berliner Industriebank AG v Jost* [1971] 2 All ER 1513 at 1518, Salmon LJ suggested that a stay of execution pending an appeal might render a judgment no longer final. The same argument seems applicable to awards.
14 AJA, s 9(1).
15 Ibid, s 9(2)(e).

(f) The award must be handed down after the relevant extension order has come into effect[1]

6.09 The 1933 legislation makes clear that the scheme applies only in respect of awards given after the order designating the reciprocating jurisdiction has been put into operation. It does not exclude awards because the arbitration agreements or references to arbitration were made prior to that date or arbitration proceedings were commenced before that date. The 1920 Act is silent on this particular issue, although on construction it applies to awards as it applies to judgments 'made before or after the passing of the Act'.[2] It appears, therefore, probable that awards pre-existing particular extension orders are within the scheme.

1 FJREA, s 1(2)(c).
2 AJA, s 12(1). See *Kuwait Minister of Public Works v Sir Frederick Snow & Partners* [1983] 2 All ER 754, CA at 761 on the policy arguments favouring a broad construction in respect of the New York Convention awards: affd [1984] 1 All ER 733, [1984] 2 WLR 340, HL.

Interest on the original award[1]

6.10 Most awards made in Commonwealth countries are likely to be governed by a provision equivalent to Arbitration Act 1950, section 20 of the

United Kingdom, under which a sum directed to be paid by an award, unless the award otherwise directs, carries interest from the date of the award at the same rate as a judgment debt.

The 1933 Act, in relation to judgments, makes clear that any interest due up to the time of registration is to be added to the sum payable under the judgment itself.[2] The equivalent rule will apply to awards in respect of interest payable under the terms of the agreement or under the law of the country of the award, unless the arbitrator has vetoed the payment of any interest.[3] It is not open to the registering court to alter the rate of interest duly applied by the arbitrator.[4]

As suggested earlier in relation to judgments,[5] a similar position exists under the 1920 Act, although there is no express provision to that effect. For the Act applies to awards 'whereby any sum of money is payable'.[6] Moreover, since interest can be sued for by an action on a judgment, by analogy, it seems appropriate that interest can be included as part of the registered award where it has been awarded by the arbitrator or it has become payable thereon by the terms of the agreement or pursuant to an applicable statute. In all these cases, there is an ascertainable sum of money which is payable to the creditor in consequence of the award.

1 Cost of registration may also be included: AJA, s 9(3)(c); FJREA, s 2(6).
2 Ibid.
3 *Timber Shipping Co SA v London and Overseas Freighters Ltd* [1972] AC 1, [1971] 2 All ER 599, HL. Under the Arbitration Act 1950, s 26, the arbitrator may not adopt another rate of interest.
4 By analogy with *Dalmia Dairy Industries Ltd v National Bank of Pakistan* [1978] 2 Lloyd's Rep 223, CA at 272–275, 301–303.
5 Para 3.25 above.
6 AJA, s 12(1).

III REGISTRATION APPLICATIONS

Time limits

6.11 Registration may be applied for, in the case of the 1920 scheme, only within twelve months after the date of the award, unless the court allows an extension, as it generally will, for example in the case of an award under appeal.[1] Under the 1933 statute, the period is six years from the date of the award or of any subsequent appeal.[2]

The date of the award, it might be thought, is the date on which the arbitrator finally determines the matter referred to him and thereby divests himself of any power to alter his determination. But it is arguable that, at common law, it will in fact be the date on which the arbitrator notifies the parties that he has completed the reference.[3] In the absence of evidence to the contrary, the date on the award itself will normally be relied upon.

These provisions preclude the need to determine from what point of time the statutory limitation period[4] runs in relation to the initiation of enforcement proceedings.[5] It is, however, apparent in the case of the 1920 Act that the time allowed for registration is short, given that it may be necessary to make the award enforceable as a judgment in the place of the award before registration can be commenced.

1 AJA, s 9(1).
2 FJREA, s 2(1).
3 *Brooke v Mitchell* (1840) 6 M & W 473, 9 LJ Ex 269.

4 As determined by the lex fori: *British Linen Co v Drummond* (1830) 10 B & C 903, 9 LJOSKB 213.
5 It is unclear whether this runs from the accrual of the original cause of action or from the date of the award: see Russell, op cit, pp 6–7. For the UK, Limitation Act 1980, s 7 and *Kuwait Minister of Public Works v Sir Frederick Snow Partners* [1983] 2 All ER 754, CA at 757, per Kerr LJ.

The application

6.12 Under both schemes, the application must be made by the 'judgment creditor',[1] the party to the arbitration in whose favour the award has ordered payment of a sum of money and thus in whom rights under the award are initially vested. The arbitrator has no jurisdiction to make a binding order in respect of anyone who was not a party to the agreement and the ensuing arbitration. An application may, however, also be made by any person to whom the rights under the award have been subsequently assigned or transferred or who has succeeded to them.[2]

Under English practice, which is widely followed, the application will normally be made ex parte;[3] security for costs will usually be required if the applicant is not resident within the jurisdiction.[4] But a summons may be issued at the discretion of the court to 'the judgment debtor'[5] who, in the context of awards, will usually be the party to the award against whom the award was made. Proceedings for registration may also be brought against any person against whom the award is enforceable in the place where the award was made (1920 scheme[6]) or under 'the law of the original court' (1933 scheme[7]). The latter phrase, when applied to an award, will no doubt be given the same effect as in the 1920 provision, by the substitution of 'the law of the place where the award was made'.[8]

1 AJA, s 9(1); FJREA, s 2(1).
2 AJA, s 12(1) (confined to assignment and succession); FJREA, s 11(1).
3 RSC Ord 71, r 2, as applied by Ord 73, r 8.
4 Ibid, Ord 71, r 4 (as applied): *Kohn v Rinson and Stafford (Brod) Ltd* [1948] 1 KB 327, [1947] 2 All ER 839: see para 3.27 above.
5 Ibid, Ord 71, r 2 (as applied).
6 AJA, s 12(1): presumably to be determined by the law of that place.
7 FJREA, s 11(1).
8 Cf RSC Ord 73, r 8(b) which makes this adaptation in relation to Ord 71. It should be noted that an Act cannot be construed by direct reference to subordinate legislation made under it: *Jackson v Hall* [1980] AC 854, [1980] 1 All ER 177, HL. This uncertainty illustrates again the artificiality of the inclusion of awards in the legislation.

Documentation required

6.13 Under English practice, which is widely followed in the Commonwealth, the applicant for registration must support his application by an affidavit. This is required to:

(a) exhibit the award (or a verified, certified or duly authenticated copy of it), if necessary with a translation;
(b) so far as known to the deponent, state the name, trade or business and usual or last known place of abode or business of the applicant and of the person against whom enforcement is sought;
(c) state that:
  (i) the applicant is entitled to enforce the award;
  (ii) the award has not been satisfied (or the extent to which it has not been satisfied);
  (iii) none of the prescribed grounds for refusing registration is present (1920 scheme[1]);

(iv) the award can be enforced by execution in the place where the award was made and registration is not liable to be set aside (1933 scheme[2]);

(v) the award has become enforceable in the same manner as a judgment, in pursuance of the law in the place where it was made;

(d) set out the amount of interest which has come due, up to the time of registration, under the law of the country where the award was made (1933 scheme).[3]

It will be noted that copies of the arbitration agreement are not expressly required, although this is the practice under the international schemes[4] and where an application for leave to enforce as a judgment is made.[5]

1 AJA, s 9.
2 FJREA, s 4.
3 RSC Ord 71, r 3, as applied and added to by Ord 73, r 8. See also the requirement in English law that the affidavit verifies that the award is not one to which the Protection of Trading Interests Act 1980 applies.
4 Paras 7.23 and 8.27 below.
5 RSC Ord 73, r 10. Additional evidence may be required in particular extension Orders in Council: ibid, Ord 71, r 3.

IV REGISTRATION

Registration procedure

6.14 If leave to register is given an order will be drawn up and entry made in the Register of Judgments.[1] Under the 1920 Act, the court may refuse to register where it is not just or convenient to enforce the judgment and in particular will do so if any of the prescribed grounds for refusing registration appears to be present.[2] Under the 1933 Act, provided that the award is one within the scheme, leave must be granted.[3]

Notice of the registration must be served upon the debtor, giving details of the registration, of the creditor (or his lawyer or agent) and the right to apply for setting aside and the time limits applicable.[4] The notice must normally be served personally or at his address[5] but provision is made for service out of the jurisdiction without the necessity for leave to be obtained. In such a case, the usual rules apply which dispense with the need for personal service if appropriate forum service processes are followed.[6]

In no case may execution be issued until the period for making an application to set aside has elapsed or until such an application has been determined.[7] An application to set aside must be made by the person against whom the award is to be enforced by summons within the time limit set by the court under either scheme.[8]

1 RSC Ord 71, rr 5 and 6, as applied by Ord 73, r 8. No order giving leave to register need be served upon the other party, unless it has been made on a summons: ibid, r 5(2).
2 AJA, s 9(2).
3 FJREA, s 4.
4 RSC, Ord 71, r 7 (as applied). See further, para 3.29 above.
5 Ibid, r 7(1) but the court may order otherwise.
6 Ibid, applying Ord 11, r 5.
7 Ibid, r 10 (as applied).
8 Ibid, and r 5(3), r 7(3)(d). The period may be extended by the court, r 5(4).

Currency of the registered award

6.15 Under the original provisions of the 1933 Act, awards could only be registered in the forum currency, any conversion of the sum of the award to be made at the rate of exchange prevailing at the date of the award.[1] The 1920 Act, again silent on the matter, appears to have been subject to the common law rule to the same effect.[2] Under the pressure of rapidly changing exchange rates, the common law was restated in the United Kingdom[3] and the statutory rule was repealed.[4] But the 1933 provisions remain in force in a number of jurisdictions.

It now seems clear that under the common law where an award has been expressed in a foreign currency,[5] it may now be paid in that currency and that if conversion is needed, the date of conversion will be the date of the award.[6] If enforcement is necessary in the place of the award, and an action to enforce the award has been successful there or leave to enforce an award under the summary procedures has been granted, it will be granted in the foreign currency of the award. Any conversion into local currency will be made at the rate of exchange prevailing at the date when the enforcement procedure is initiated.[7]

Where enforcement by registration is sought in a jurisdiction now following the current United Kingdom law, the position is straightforward. An application to register an award rendered in a foreign currency may be granted. Indeed, it has been suggested that it must be so registered.[8] The date at which the rate of exchange for conversion into the local currency is determined will be the date of actual payment[9] or if execution is required, the date when the particular method of enforcement is authorised.[10]

1 FJREA, s 2(3): cf RSC (1965) Ord 71, r 3(2).
2 See para 3.30 above. See *Universal Transport Co Ltd v Tzortzis* 1973 (2) ALR Comm 323 (Kenya).
3 *Miliangos v George Frank (Textiles) Ltd* [1976] AC 443, [1975] 3 All ER 801, HL.
4 Administration of Justice Act 1977, s 4; RSC Ord 71, as amended by SI 1977/1955.
5 Awards may now be made in foreign currencies: *Jugoslavenska Oceanska Plovidba v Castle Investment Co Inc* [1974] QB 292; *The Despina R* [1979] 1 All ER 421, HL.
6 Ibid, at 300, 302, 305, 306; *Miliangos*, above, at 469.
7 *Miliangos*, above, at 469, per Lord Wilberforce; Law Commission, Law Com No 124, Cmnd 9064, para 2.43.
8 Dicey and Morris, op cit, p 1109.
9 RSC, 71/3/1.
10 *Practice Direction* [1976] 1 All ER 669, [1976] 1 WLR 83.

Control of the debtor's assets

6.16 It has already been suggested in relation to judgments that the *Mareva* injunction promises to be a useful device in preventing a judgment debtor from removing assets against which the registered judgment may be enforced.[1] No judgments have been reported where this device has been employed in respect of arbitral awards pending registration[2] but it appears an equally appropriate device in this respect.

1 Para 3.31 above.
2 But see *The Rena K* [1979] QB 377, [1979] 1 All ER 397 in relation to the commencement of an arbitration. In *Sanko SS Co Ltd v DC Commodities (A'Asia) Pty Ltd* [1980] WAR 51, the injunction was used to freeze assets of a local company pending a foreign arbitration.

Effects of registration

6.17 The registration of an award under either scheme ensures that the award will be treated, and proceedings may be taken upon it, as if it were a judgment of the requested court entered on the date of registration and that it may be executed in the same way and to the same extent.[1] It will carry interest in the same way as a domestic judgment entered at the date of registration.[2] It is thereafter subject to the same judicial supervision as a judgment entered locally. As a consequence, any restrictions which may exist under the lex fori concerning the enforcement of arbitral awards will not apply once the award has been registered as a judgment.

There is, however, one possible qualification. The 1933 Act requires a registered award to be given the same force and effect as a judgment 'for the purposes of execution'. This, it might be argued, precludes the use of means of enforcement which do not constitute modes of execution, such as the issue of a bankruptcy notice or a judgment summons.[3] This is not the view of the English courts.[4] By contrast, the 1920 Act which allows the registering court control and jurisdiction over the award 'only insofar as relates to execution'[5] clearly prevents such non-execution processes from being available.[6] Statutory amendment is required to overcome this.[7]

Execution will, however, not issue whilst any proceedings to set aside the registration may be instituted or, if instituted, until they are disposed of.[8] But a stay of execution will not normally be granted merely because the debtor is pursuing another action against the creditor.[9] A garnishee order can be applied for on the basis of the award when registered in the usual way.[10] In some Canadian jurisdictions, however, it may be applied for simultaneously with the application to have the award registered.[11]

1 AJA, s 9(3); FJREA, s 2(2). Again there is not an exact fit in respect of 'awards' in provisions drafted in terms of 'judgments'. But it does not appear likely that a registered award would be held to have the same effect as an award given in a domestic arbitration, since the latter cannot be enforced until, at least, leave to enforce in the same manner as a judgment is given.
2 FJREA, s 2(2)(c); AJA, s 9(3)(a).
3 Cf the position in respect of the Arbitration Act 1950, s 26 in which it was held that a bankruptcy notice cannot be served until a judgment is entered: *Re A Bankruptcy Notice, Re A Judgment Debtor* [1907] 1 KB 478, 76 LJKB 171, CA.
4 *Re A Judgment Debtor (No 2176 of 1938)* [1939] Ch 601, [1939] 1 All ER 1, CA.
5 AJA, s 9(3)(b). See Bankruptcy Act 1914 (UK), s 1(1)(g); Debtors Act 1869 (UK), s 5.
6 Cf *Re A Bankruptcy Notice* [1898] 1 QB 383, 67 LJQB 308, CA (decided on similar words in the United Kingdom Judgment Extension scheme); *Re A Judgment Debtor*, above, following *Re Watson* [1893] 1 QB 21, 62 LJQB 85.
7 As for example in the Administration of Justice Act 1956 (UK), s 40.
8 FJREA, s 2(2) proviso; RSC Ord 71, r 10, as applied, Ord 73, r 8.
9 *Ferdinand Wagner (a firm) v Laubscher Bros & Co (a firm)* [1970] 2 QB 313, [1970] 2 All ER 174, CA.
10 For English practice, see RSC Ord 49.
11 Castel, op cit, p 553 and para 3.32 above.

V OBJECTIONS TO REGISTRATION

Grounds for refusing or setting aside registration

6.18 The 1920 Act prescribes grounds upon which registration can be opposed and which, if established, preclude registration.[1] In addition the court has a discretion to refuse registration where, in their view, local enforcement of the award would not be just or convenient.[2] If the award is registered, a subsequent application may be made to set the registration aside on the prescribed grounds or by reference to the just and convenience test or where there is some other sufficient reason.[3] Thus, registration is discretionary in all cases except where it must be refused. Setting aside of the registration is entirely discretionary even where the grounds are those upon which registration could not have been made.

The 1933 scheme, however, demands automatic registration where certain conditions are fulfilled:

(a) the award is one within the scheme;
(b) the prescribed matters are proved;
(c) at the date of application the sum payable is not wholly satisfied;
(d) at that date the award was enforceable by execution in the country where it was made.[4]

Proceedings may, however, be subsequently brought to set the registration aside on grounds specified in the statute.[5] The majority of grounds are mandatory. It seems clear that these are intended to be exclusive of other grounds, since no residual discretion is vested in the registering court under the 1933 scheme.

It is open to the court asked to set the registration aside to direct that the issues thereby raised be tried in the same way as an action.[6]

1 AJA, s 9(2).
2 AJA, s 9(1).
3 RSC Ord 71, r 9(3), as applied by Ord 73, r 8. See para 3.33 above.
4 FJREA, s 2(1): the terminology is that contained in Ord 73, r 8. See further para 3.33 above.
5 FJREA, s 4(1).
6 RSC Ord 71, r 9(2), as applied.

Objection 1: Absence of jurisdiction

6.19 Both statutes specify absence of jurisdiction as a ground for challenging registration.[1] It has been suggested in relation to judgments that this provision allows a requested court to have regard to questions of jurisdiction under the conflicts rules of the requested court and under the law of the country of origin.[2] This distinction is difficult to maintain in the context of awards. For as a rule, it may be suggested, very similar criteria are likely to be applied, since the competence of the arbitrator derives from the arbitration agreement, giving rise to the same kinds of questions in both contexts.[3]

The legislation gives no guidance as to how jurisdictional issues come before the registering court. There is no obligation upon the applicant to provide a copy of the agreement, only a copy of the award, or to make reference to it in the accompanying affidavit.[4] The burden at common law is upon the applicant to establish compliance but it will generally be enough to produce a copy of an award which on its face appears to fulfil these requirements. It will then fall to the other party to establish, by way of objection, that the award was not after all regular in any of these respects, by producing the agreement.[5] The legislation in making this a ground of challenge suggests a similar approach.

It must, however, be noted that the court in the country of the award which gave leave for summary enforcement will usually have thereby provided the debtor with an opportunity to raise jurisdictional questions relating to the validity of the award.[6] In allowing a challenge on these issues, therefore, the requested court will be re-examining matters which have already been before a competent court or could have been raised there by the debtor. In this respect the decision of the foreign court to make the award enforceable as a judgment may be capable of being recognised as creating an estoppel per rem judicatam on these issues.[7] On the other hand, there is a trend,[8] which may be applied in this context, that the requested court is not bound by any decision of a foreign court on matters of a kind which relate to questions of international competence.

1 AJA, s 9(2)(a); FJREA, s 4(1)(a)(ii) which states that 'the courts of the country of the original court had no jurisdiction, for which a direct substitution in respect of "award" is not possible, reference being made to the particular arbitration in every instance'.
2 Para 3.34 above.
3 Para 6.20 below.
4 RSC Ord 71, r 3, as applied by Ord 73, r 8.
5 *Kianta Osakeyhtio v Britain and Overseas Trading Co Ltd* [1954] 1 Lloyd's Rep 247, CA at 250–251 and see ibid, [1953] 2 Lloyd's Rep 569 at 573, QBD.
6 Russell, op cit, pp 371–373, makes clear that leave should not be granted if there is a real ground for doubting the validity of the award: *Middlemiss and Gould v Hartlepool Corpn* [1973] 1 All ER 172, [1972] 1 WLR 1643, CA.
7 Cf *Carl-Zeiss Stiftung v Rayner and Keeler (No 2)* [1967] 1 AC 853, [1966] 2 All ER 536; para 4.11 above.
8 Eg Civil Jurisdiction and Judgments Act 1982, s 32(3).

Absence of international jurisdiction in the arbitral body

6.20 Jurisdictional rules are prescribed for the purposes of the 1933 scheme:[1] the 1920 statute is silent leaving the matter to be determined under the conflict of laws rules of the requested state. The 1933 rules are, of course, referrable to judgments, dealing with them differently according to the requested court's classification of the types of action leading to the judgments.[2] It is by no means clear how this approach can be applied in the context of awards. With some effort, an award can usually be equated with a judgment in personam[3] but is less easy to determine whether the claim referred to arbitration is equivalent to an action in personam or an action in rem concerning movables, for example. Where for example, the arbitration concerns a claim for injuries received from a ship,[4] will this be treated as an action in rem involving a movable so that the property must be situated in the place where the arbitration occurred? Given that arbitrations often take place where it suits the convenience of those affected and that place is often the subject of particular agreement, it may be suggested that the specific jurisdictional rules in the 1933 Act should have no application. Rather, reference should be made to the third general basis of jurisdiction in the statute—that which is recognised by the law of the requested court.[5]

In a common law jurisdiction, therefore, both schemes will require reference to the rules developed in relation to actions upon awards.[6] Similar conditions are prescribed under the Geneva and New York Convention schemes.[7] Jurisdiction will be recognised at common law where there has been a valid submission to the arbitrators, in pursuance of an agreement between the parties which is valid according to the proper law of the contract.[8] This may require reference to their agreement to refer future disputes and to the actual reference to the arbitrators. In consequence, if the submission is not within the scope of the agreement or if the agreement itself is not valid or has no legal effect under the proper law, at the time of the submission, or if the arbitrator exceeds the terms of the authority vested in him under the agreement or is incompetent under the law governing the agreement, the basis of the arbitration disappears.[9] In such cases, the jurisdiction is not capable of being recognised. There is strong similarity in the effect of this conclusion with that achieved by applying the essence of the ground for in personam jurisdiction under the 1933 Act relating to agreements to submit.[10] Further, this approach ensures that the case does not fall within the prohibition against registration under the 1920 Act where the award debtor did not voluntarily appear, or otherwise submit or agree to submit to the jurisdiction of the arbitrator.[11]

The legislation, however, contains prohibitions of a jurisdictional nature.[12] Thus in relation to judgments, the original court is deemed not to have jurisdiction if the subject matter of the proceedings was immovable property outside the country of that court.[13] There is a not dissimilar rule at common law.[14] Application with respect to arbitration produces the rather unexpected results that an award concerning a dispute as to immovables will not be registrable if the parties have selected a venue for the arbitration other than the place of the immovables, even if the law of the latter is to govern the arbitration.[15] The other statutory limitation in respect of awards against persons with immunity under international law[16] will not normally apply, as the exception, where there has been submission to the arbitrator's jurisdiction, will usually be met.[17]

1 FJREA, s 4(2) and (3).
2 FJREA, s 4(2)(c): see para 3.37 above.
3 An award is binding on the parties only or those claiming through them: *Martin v Boulanger* (1883) 8 App Cas 296, 52 LJPC 31. Cf *The Beldis* [1936] P 51, 106 LJP 22, CA.
4 Cf *The Sylph* (1867) LR 2 A & E 24, 37 LJ Adm 14.
5 FJREA, s 4(2)(c).
6 Dicey and Morris, op cit, p 1156.
7 Paras 7.24–7.26, 8.31, 8.33–8.34 below.
8 *Dalmia Dairy Industries Ltd v National Bank of Pakistan* [1978] 2 Lloyd's Rep 223, CA. In English law there is a strong, but rebuttable, presumption that the proper law is the law of the country in which the arbitration is held: *Compagnie d'Armement Maritime SA v Compagnie Tunisienne de Navigation SA* [1971] AC 572, [1970] 3 All ER 71, HL; Dicey and Morris, op cit, p 1127.
9 *Dalmia Dairy Industries Ltd v National Bank of Pakistan,* above; *Kianta Osakeyhtio v Britain and Overseas Trading Co Ltd* [1954] 1 Lloyd's Rep 247, CA; cf *Benidai Trading Co Ltd v Gouws and Gouws Pty Ltd* 1977 (3) SALR 1020 (South Africa).
10 FJREA, s 4(2)(a)(iii) but this only applies if the judgment debtor was 'a defendant in the original court', a term which further suggests that those grounds are unsuited to arbitration. For agreements to submit, see para 3.40 above.
11 AJA, s 9(2)(b). The debtor must be 'a person who was neither carrying on business nor ordinarily resident within the jurisdiction of the original court'—a term which again seems unsuited to the circumstances of awards.
12 The exception relating to cases brought contrary to agreement to settle the matter otherwise than by proceedings in the courts of the country of origin, is stated to have no application: FJREA, s 4(3)(b). In the UK see now Civil Jurisdiction and Judgments Act 1982, s 32 which does not appear to apply to arbitral awards, though the introduction of 'tribunal' in the definition of 'court' in s 50 leaves the matter uncertain.
13 FJREA, s 4(3)(a).
14 Para 3.47 above.
15 FJREA, s 4(3)(c).
16 In many commercial matters, immunity of state agencies from jurisdiction may not be claimable: see eg State Immunity Act 1978 (UK), s 3(1)(a); cf s 9(1) excepting also written submission of disputes to arbitration; Diplomatic Privileges Act 1964 (UK), Sch 1, art 31.
17 This may be the position also at common law: Russell, op cit, p 297, citing *Petrol Shipping Corpn v Kingdom of Greece, Ministry of Commerce Purchase Directorate* [1966] 2 Lloyd's Rep 431 (USA).

Objection 2: The award is not an award to which the scheme applies

6.21 The 1933 Act requires registration to be set aside in this case.[1] The statute itself identifies the conditions which make an award one to which the Act applies:[2] these are set out in paragraphs 6.04–6.06 and 6.08–6.09.[3] The 1920 Act does not explicitly refer to this as a ground of challenge but it is evident that the registration should be refused if the basic characteristics of an enforceable award are not present.[4] These appear to be the same as for the later scheme.

1 FJREA, s 4(1)(a)(i).
2 Ibid, s 1(2) and the definitions of 'judgment' in s 11(1) and of 'award' in s 10(A) in the UK Act.
3 Except in respect of the requirement that the award must not be wholly satisfied: see para 3.20 above.
4 AJA, s 9(1) and the definition of 'judgment' in s 12(1).

Objection 3: The award was registered in contravention of the statute

6.22 Explicitly stated in the 1933 Act,[1] this will also be a ground for setting aside, as a 'sufficient reason', under the 1920 Act.[2] The grounds for this under the 1933 Act are that the award has been satisfied or that it cannot be enforced in the country of origin.[3] It would presumably also extend to cases where the judgment is registered in an incorrect currency (where explicit provision exists),[4] for the incorrect sum of money outstanding,[5] or if it contains matters which cannot be registered.[6] In the case of the 1920 scheme, similar considerations may be raised. In addition, non compliance with procedural requirements of either scheme could be raised under this head.[7]

1 FJREA, s 4(2)(a)(i).
2 RSC Ord 71, r 9(3), as applied by Ord 73, r 8.
3 FJREA, s 2(1) proviso: paras 6.05 and 6.07 above. Where the application is set aside on the ground that it is not enforceable by execution in the country where it was made, a further application may be made, when that condition is subsequently met: FJREA, s 5(2). Where a judgment for the whole sum has been partly satisfied, registration in respect of the balance is permitted: FJREA, s 5(3).
4 Ibid, s 2(3).
5 Ibid, s 2(4).
6 Ibid, s 2(5).
7 Para 3.51 above; these might be grounded in procedures referred to in paras 6.11 to 6.13 above.

Objection 4: The award debtor had inadequate notice of the arbitration proceedings

6.23 Both statutes allow challenge for an absence of due notice, although in rather different terms.[1] Thus the 1920 Act requires that the debtor, 'being the defendant' was not duly served with the process of the original court and that he did not appear 'notwithstanding that he ... agreed to submit to the jurisdiction of that court'. The 1933 Act stipulates that the debtor, 'being the defendant' notwithstanding that process may have been duly served on him in accordance with the law of the country of the original court, did not receive notice in sufficient time to enable him to defend and did not appear. These provisions also are awkward in the context of awards. Presumably the challenge on this ground can only be made where the award debtor was not the party to invoke the arbitration agreement and set the arbitration into motion. Secondly, it will be necessary to determine in both schemes what is the equivalent of 'service with the process of the original court' or 'process in accordance with the law of the country of that court'. Under the 1920 scheme, the law which determines what steps may be lawfully taken to commence an arbitration is not identified. This may be designated in the arbitration agreement but in other cases, until the arbitration has actually been commenced, it may not be possible to identify that law. Indeed, in some instances until an arbitrator has been appointed, the place of arbitration may not be identified and in consequence the law of that place, which so often governs these matters, will not be established.[2] There seems little alternative in such a case to referring to the law governing the agreement.[3] The 1933 Act clearly identifies the relevant law, in its implicit reference to the place of arbitration. Fortunately, the provision is so phrased that failure to comply with that law because another law was relied upon would not be fatal, provided adequate notice is given.

Under the law of most Commonwealth states, it is probable that the notification procedures used to commence an arbitration will be treated as equivalent to service of process. This normally occurs when there is notification served by one party upon the other requiring appointment of an arbitrator or requiring submission of a dispute to an agreed arbitrator.[4] If this is the case, the very process of bringing an arbitration in being will constitute notice of the proceedings. In practice, the arbitrator will determine and notify the time and place of the hearing taking into consideration the convenience of the parties. It seems in practice unlikely, therefore, that the institution of the arbitration will occur without the debtor having been notified. Whether, under the 1920 scheme, that notice is 'due' is a question for the requested court but in principle it seems open to it to examine the adequacy of the notice, as well as actual compliance with the permitted procedures.[5] Similarly under the 1933 Act, whatever the notification procedures actually used, the requested court can determine whether they provided sufficient time to 'defend' the case—in this context, presumably to prepare his side of the dispute. It should be noted that neither scheme requires that notification of the hearing, as distinct from the commencement of the arbitration, must be given. These rules, however, only apply when the debtor does not 'appear'.[6] The term 'appearance', in the context of judgments, may be given a technical meaning, related to the formal steps which must be taken to respond to the original process. There is no exact equivalent in relation to arbitrations. There is no requirement to notify an intention to respond since there is a contractual obligation to accept arbitration. The mere fact that the party is involved in the choice of arbitrator may not be enough, since until that is done, it may be said that there is no arbitration in which to appear.[7] It is clear that 'appear' involves something more than being a party to an agreement to accept the arbitrator's jurisdiction.[8] In this context, 'appear' may mean to participate in the arbitration proceedings. A party cannot claim inadequate notice, if in fact he takes steps to be involved in the arbitration. If this is correct, the requested court may have to determine whether the party has taken a sufficient part in those proceedings, especially where he has deliberately absented himself from any preliminary stages and has not been represented.[9] Taking part in a preliminary meeting or submitting documentation to the arbitrator should be treated as adequate for this purpose. The unsuitability of these statutory provisions for awards, therefore, is evident. It seems sensible to conclude that the debtor will never find it easy to invoke this ground.

1 AJA, s 9(2)(c); FJREA, s 4(1)(a)(iii).

2 *James Miller and Partners v Whitworth Street Estates (Manchester)* [1970] AC 583, [1970] 1 All ER 796, HL.

3 Cf *International Tank and Pipe SAK v Kuwait Aviation Fueling Co KSC* [1975] QB 224, [1975] 1 All ER 242, CA.

4 Cf *The Agios Lazaros* [1976] 2 Lloyd's Rep 47 at 51, per Lord Denning MR.

5 Dicey and Morris, op cit, pp 1091–2. But contra, *Sfeir & Co v National Insurance Co of New Zealand* [1964] 1 Lloyd's Rep 330 at 341.

6 AJA, s 9(2)(c) continues 'notwithstanding that he was ordinarily resident or was carrying on business within the jurisdiction of that court or agreed to submit to the jurisdiction of that court'. Much of this has little place in the context of arbitration.

7 *Tradax Export SA v Volkswagenwerk AG* [1970] 1 QB 537, [1970] 1 All ER 420, CA; *Toepfer v Cremer* [1975] 2 Lloyd's Rep 118, CA.

8 See note 6.

9 On power of arbitrators to proceed ex parte in such cases, see Russell, op cit, pp 262–264.

Objection 5: The award was obtained by fraud

6.24 This ground is prescribed in respect of both schemes.[1] It is available to challenge the award whether the fraud is that of another party to the arbitration or it has been perpetuated by the arbitrator. It has already been suggested,[2] in the case of judgments, that on principle this ground should only be available when the allegation of fraud was not made or was not capable of being asserted in the original proceedings. On the other hand, there is authority on the 1933 Act which permits the question to be raised for the purpose of setting aside the registration even when it could have been raised in the original court.[3] It can be argued that the latter construction would be useful in the context of awards. For an arbitrator may be regarded as an unsuitable agent to enquire into issues of fraud. It is commonly provided that the courts in the place of arbitration have power to revoke the requirement to arbitrate insofar as the dispute involves a question whether a party to it is guilty of fraud.[4] Issues of fraud, therefore, are rarely referred to arbitration, presumably because it is felt that arbitrators are not the best tribunal for the resolution of such matters. Nonetheless allegations of fraud may be made or be relevant in an arbitration. The trend to limit judicial review of awards on grounds of error of fact or law on the face of the record[5] may ensure that the arbitrator's treatment of matters to which fraud is relevant is immune from judicial control. This may strengthen the case for the refusal to register an award in which it is shown that the arbitrator failed to take proper account of an allegation of fraud. There is, however, no escape from the fact that this may involve the judicial reconsideration of the merits of the matter in dispute, which is contradictory to the generally accepted purpose of arbitration. These matters in any case may be raised when the award is made enforceable as a judgment in the place where it was made.

It is more appropriate that this ground be invoked in cases equivalent to misconduct resulting from fraud by the arbitrator or another party in which setting aside of an award may usually be made by a court.[6] Thus where an arbitrator is shown to be corrupt or to have furthered his own interest in the result of the arbitration or where the other party had deliberately misled the arbitrator or the objecting party through false evidence or concealing facts,[7] the registration should not be permitted.

1 AJA, s 9(2)(d); FJREA, s 4(1)(a)(iv). Any questions of law will be determined by reference to the law governing the arbitration.

2 Para 3.56 above.

3 *Syal v Heyward* [1948] 2 KB 443, [1948] 2 All ER 576, CA; *Svirskis v Gibson* [1977] 2 NZLR 4.

4 Cf Arbitration Act 1950 (UK), s 24(2) but this power may, in the law of the United Kingdom, be excluded by agreement: Arbitration Act 1979, s 3(5). On s 24(2), see Russell, op cit, pp 148–149 and 186–188.

5 Eg Arbitration Act 1979 (UK), s 1.

6 Cf Arbitration Act 1950 (UK), s 23(2) in relation to misconduct by arbitrator or proceedings where the arbitration or award has been improperly procured.

7 See, for various examples of misconduct of these kinds, Russell, op cit, pp 411–413.

Objection 6: The award offends against public policy

(a) *The claim or the enforcement of that award contravenes public policy*

6.25 This again is provided for by both schemes but in rather different terms. Under the 1920 Act, judgments cannot be registered if 'in respect of a cause of action which for reasons of public policy . . . could not have been entertained in the registering court'.[1] By contrast, the 1933 statute refers to 'enforcement of the judgment [which] would be contrary to the public policy of the registering court'.[2] There is no doubt that in both cases it is the public policy of the forum which must be applied.[3] Again these terms do not exactly fit with arbitral awards. It is suggested that the 1920 Act requires the requested court to establish whether the subject matter in dispute which was referred to the arbitrator was one which could not for this reason have been the subject of arbitration proceedings under the lex fori. This seems a more appropriate test than that which might be applied on a strict construction—ie that the matter could not have been a cause of action in the forum courts. For it enables the court to apply the same standards to foreign awards as it would apply to awards made in the forum.

In consequence, the courts should refuse awards where the subject matter would have been illegal or criminal or void under statute or where the contract which was the subject of the arbitration would have been contrary to public policy, eg in restraint of trade, or contrary to public morality.[4]

For all that the 1933 Act appears to be concerned with the question of whether *enforcement* of the award would be contrary to public policy, the same types of case will be covered. For enforcement will normally be refused if the subject matter could not have been referred to arbitration under the lex fori on public policy grounds. It is suggested in para 6.26 below that refusal would be possible on this ground where there is evidence of non-compliance with the principles of natural justice. The provision will also extend to cases where enforcement proceedings could not be brought in the forum. It might be argued, for example, that an award which required payment to be affected in some third jurisdiction, or otherwise required specific performance in respect of the payment, over which the forum courts could exercise no supervision should be refused registration.[5] Again refusal might be justified if the forum country is in hostilities with the country of which the beneficiary is a national and a resident or where enforcement must involve the deliberate contravention of the laws of a friendly state or where enforcement would be in conflict with the requirements of the law of the forum on questions of sovereign or diplomatic immunity.[6] As similar terminology is found under both the Geneva and New York schemes, consistency with the approaches followed there should be sought.[7] It may also be suggested that these considerations would justify refusal of registration under the 1920 scheme as cases where it is not just and convenient for local enforcement to be permitted.[8]

1 AJA, s 9(2)(f).
2 FJREA, s 4(1)(a)(vi).
3 The public policy of the place of arbitration may be put in issue in that place when the leave for summary enforcement there is sought: *Dalmia Dairy Industries Ltd v National Bank of Pakistan* [1978] 2 Lloyd's Rep 223.
4 Russell, op cit, ch 3.
5 Cf *Dalmia Dairy Industries Ltd v National Bank of Pakistan*, above.
6 Waiver of immunity may be obtained. Quaere whether the requested court should require waiver before registration?
7 Paras 7.28 and 8.36 below.
8 AJA, s 9(1).

(b) *The arbitration proceedings were contrary to natural justice*

6.26 Neither statute expressly allows a challenge to registration on account of a breach of natural justice, although both deal with one aspect, that of giving adequate notice.[1] It is, however, a common law ground for refusing to enforce a foreign award.[2] It may be expected, therefore, that a requested court would be prepared to allow an objection on this ground either as an element of its public policy or, in the 1920 scheme, because enforcement would not be 'just and convenient'.[3] It is well recognised that arbitrations are to be conducted by arbitrators who are honest, impartial and disinterested and who act fairly to both parties.[4] In principle, therefore, a serious divergence from these standards by the arbitrator should justify a requested court in refusing registration.

There is little guidance from the case law whether the courts may be more or less ready to intervene in respect of awards than in respect of judgments, or how serious the divergence from procedural standards will be required. In the *Dalmia Dairy Industries* case,[5] Kerr J accepted that due compliance with the procedural rules, which the parties had agreed would govern the arbitration, would preclude a challenge on the ground that an oral hearing was not permitted. There may be other circumstances in which the parties can agree to accept lower standards than might be normal in a court of law. Thus Russell assets that 'parties who are free to choose their own tribunal may, provided that they act with full knowledge, choose dishonest, partial or interested arbitrators'.[6] Whilst it is common for parties to be allowed to go back upon such an agreement and to prevent the arbitration taking place,[7] it must be doubted that a court should refuse to register an award if the parties have in fact declined to take such a step. Indeed, one English judge has suggested in respect of a domestic arbitration that the parties can dispense with the rules of natural justice if they choose.[8] Since agreement is at the heart of arbitration, a requested court may well conclude that it is not contrary to local public policy to enforce a foreign award where the parties with full knowledge have allowed the arbitrator to proceed in breach of the audi alteram partem principle.[9]

Where the breach is not with the full knowledge of the party, different considerations apply. At common law, it has long been recognised that it is no defence to an action on an award to plead misconduct by the arbitrator which results in insufficiency or want of hearing.[10] The proper course of action is to have the award set aside by the appropriate court.[11] It could well be argued, therefore, that in any case where it is open to the party to institute proceedings in the country of award to set it aside on grounds of the arbitrator's misconduct, registration should be refused or set aside until such steps have been taken.[12] Nonetheless, Dicey and Morris, in discussing the common law defences to enforcement of foreign awards, argue that this ground should be available as there is a greater risk of a miscarriage of justice in an arbitration than in a court.[13] Where there is evidence of manifest and prejudicial bias upon the part of an arbitrator or a flagrant refusal to permit one party to adduce essential evidence or arguments, it does seem improbable that a requested court would not refuse the registration of the award. At the same time, account must be taken of the fact that the award will have been made enforceable as a judgment by court processes in the place in which it was made.

1 Para 6.23 above.

2 *Dalmia Dairy Industries Ltd v National Bank of Pakistan* [1978] 2 Lloyd's Rep 223, CA at 269, per Kerr J.
3 Para 6.25 above; AJA, s 9(1).
4 Russell, op cit, pp 110, 213–218.
5 Note 2.
6 Russell, op cit, p 110.
7 Eg Arbitration Act 1950 (UK), s 24(1). For relevant grounds, see Russell, op cit, pp 411–421.
8 *Norman Hughes & Co Ltd v Ruthin BC* (1971) 222 Estates Gazette 163.
9 In *Israel Discount Bank of New York v Hadjipateras* [1983] 3 All ER 129, [1984] 1 WLR 137, the Court of Appeal stressed that public policy could not be invoked where the law and practice of the forum are the same as those followed in the original court.
10 The rule in *Thorburn v Barnes* (1867) LR 2 CP 384 at 402, approved in *Oppenheim v Mahomed Haneef* [1922] 1 AC 482 PC at 487; *Scrimaglio v Thornett and Fehr* (1921) 18 Ll L Rep 148.
11 Eg Arbitration Act 1950 (UK), s 23(2).
12 Para 6.29 below.
13 Op cit, pp 1138–139.

Objection 7: The applicant was not the person in whom the rights under the award are vested.

6.27 The 1933 Act contains explicit provision for this ground;[1] the 1920 Act is silent. There seems little doubt, in the latter case, that registration would also be refused since enforcement would not be just and convenient.[2] Both statutes provide extended meanings which would be applied to 'award creditors'.[3] Unless at the time of the application, the applicant can bring himself within the category of those entitled to receive the payment ordered by the arbitration, registration should be refused or set aside, as the case may be.

1 FJREA, s 4(1)(a)(vi).
2 AJA, s 9(1).
3 Para 6.12 above.

Objection 8: The existence of a prior judgment or award on the same matter

6.28 The 1933 Act, by implication, gives the registering court a discretion to set aside where the matter in dispute in the arbitration had, previously to the date of the award in the arbitration, been the subject of a final and conclusive judgment by a court of competent jurisdiction or a binding award by an earlier arbitration.[1] The 1920 Act is again silent but it is open to the registering court to refuse to register on this ground as not being 'just and convenient'.[2]

Although the statute does not say so, it may be expected that this power will only be used where the dispute is on the same subject matter and between the same parties in both proceedings.

Presumably the objection would be effective where, for example, there has been a judicial decision in country A dismissing the disputed issue on its merits but a subsequent arbitration has been conducted in country B which has been favourable to the original plaintiff.[3] On the other hand, the discretion to set aside might not be exercised where, for example, both decisions were favourable to the applicant, provided that a sum of money is still payable in order to settle the matter in dispute. It should be open to a creditor to enforce his award, if that is procedurally easier than enforcing the previous judgment, so long as he is not receiving payment twice for the same matter.

1 FJREA, s 4(1)(b).
2 AJA, s 9(1).
3 See further paras 3.66–3.67 above.

Objection 9: An appeal is pending or is intended[1]

6.29 The 1920 legislation requires an application for registration to be refused where the award debtor establishes that he has an appeal pending or that he intends to institute an appeal to which he is entitled.[2] Under both schemes a registration once made can be set aside on this ground, again in both cases in the discretion of the court.[3] If the registration is set aside under the 1933 Act a further application may be made when the appeal is disposed of.[4] The 1933 scheme, as an alternative, permits an application to set aside on this ground to be adjourned for such period as appears to the court to be reasonably sufficient to enable the applicant to take the necessary steps to have the appeal disposed of by the competent tribunal.[5]

The 1933 Act gives an extended meaning to 'appeal' which is of particular relevance in the context of awards. The term is stated to include 'any proceeding by way of discharging or setting aside [an award] or an application for a new [arbitration] or a stay of execution.'[6] It is apparent, therefore, that procedures of the kind found in many Arbitration statutes in the Commonwealth for judicial review of awards will fall within this description.[7] The 1920 Act contains no such definition but it may be suggested that it would be open to a court to treat such procedures in the same way as an appeal proper when exercising its discretion whether to register as just and convenient or to set aside as not being just and convenient or for a sufficient reason.[8]

Both Acts are capable of covering appeals to a second tier arbitral body or to a court. Registration may take place even though the time for appeals or judicial review has not yet expired under the law of the place of the award, if there is no evidence of the debtor's intention to appeal. For the award is final.[9] The English courts have stressed the desirability of registration of a foreign *judgment* and their reluctance to set aside, pending the taking of an appeal.[10] But whether the same reticence would be shown in respect of arbitral awards may be doubted given the greater possibility of error or miscarriages of justice to which arbitral proceedings can give rise.

1 See also earlier discussion in relation to finality of awards, para 6.08 above. For where an appeal has been successful or the award set aside, see para 3.68 above.
2 AJA, s 9(2)(e).
3 FJREA, s 5(1). For the 1920 scheme, see RSC Ord 71, r 9(3), applied by Ord 73, r 8. The court may impose such terms as it thinks just.
4 FJREA, s 5(2). It is doubtful whether, in the absence of a similar provision in AJA, that a further application can be made under that scheme, unless the court has set aside on those terms: RSC Ord 71, r 9(3), as applied.
5 Ibid, s 5(1). This is not possible under the 1920 Act.
6 Ibid, s 11(1), with adaptations.
7 Eg Arbitration Act 1950 (UK), s 23; Arbitration Act 1979 (UK), s 1. For common law powers to set aside for errors of law or fact (now repealed in the United Kingdom): Russell, op cit, (19th edn) pp 437 ff.
8 AJA, s 9(1); RSC Ord 71, r 9(3), as applied.
9 Para 6.08 above.
10 *SA Consortium General Textiles v Sun and Sand Agencies Ltd* [1978] 2 All ER 339, CA at 353, per Lord Denning MR. See further para 3.69 above.

VI RECOGNITION OF ARBITRAL AWARDS

6.30 The two statutes are principally concerned with questions relating to enforcement. They do not clearly set out to deal with the question of the effect of a registered award other than as the basis for enforcement of the debt implicit in the award. The 1920 Act, however, states that the award, from the date of registration, is to have the same force and effect as a judgment of the registering court.[1] This may be appropriate to permit a registered award to be invoked by way of defence or set-off or counterclaim and as constituting a res judicata on the issues which it decides between the parties, in the same way as a domestic judgment.[2] The 1933 Act, however, merely gives the same force and effect to the registered award 'for the purposes of execution',[3] precluding a similar argument. In respect of judgments, it is apparent that section 8 deals with certain questions of recognition but its application to awards in some jurisdictions is a matter of conjecture. The original extension of the United Kingdom Act to awards had effect in respect of Part I only, whereas section 8 appears in Part II.[4] The recent replacement of that extension provision has no such limitation.[5] Similarly, most other jurisdictions which include awards in their 1933 scheme have not explicitly limited its effect to questions of enforcement. The consequence, therefore, in these cases is that unless set aside on certain grounds[6] an award which has been registered must be recognised as conclusive between the parties thereto in all proceedings founded on the same cause of action and may be relied on by way of defence or counterclaim in any such proceedings. Of greater moment perhaps, the requirement also applies to awards within the scheme or which would have been within the scheme had a sum of money been payable even if not registered or not capable of being registered,[7] unless, if it had been registered, it would have been set aside on the specified grounds.[8] This complex provision has caused some difficulties in respect of judgments but its application in respect of certain arbitral awards has escaped notice.[9] The uncertain state of the common law on the question of recognition of arbitral awards[10] may be relieved by the availability of these statutory provisions which are discussed in Chapter 4. The common law is preserved in respect of recognition of awards as conclusive of any matter of law or fact decided thereon.[11]

1 AJA, s 9(2)(a).
2 Dicey and Morris, op cit, pp 1117–1120.
3 FJREA, s 2(2)(a).
4 Administration of Justice Act 1956, s 51. It can be argued that as section 8 applies to 'judgments' under Part I, it also applies to awards.
5 FJREA, s 10A, inserted by Civil Jursdiction and Judgments Act 1982, Sch 10.
6 FJREA, s 8(2)(a).
7 Ibid, s 8(1). For awards within the scheme, see para 6.21 above.
8 Ibid, s 8(2)(b).
9 Para 4.07 above.
10 Dicey and Morris, op cit, p 1132.
11 FJREA, s 8(3): see para 4.13 above.

VII RELATIONSHIP WITH OTHER ENFORCEMENT ARRANGEMENTS

Awards upon which a foreign judgment has been obtained

6.31 The drafting of the two statutes obscures the extent of their application to cases where the award has been subjected to legal proceedings and a judgment obtained in the country where it was made. Does the beneficiary of the award have freedom to choose whether to seek registration of the award or to apply for registration of the judgment? Where a judgment has been obtained, there is no question that enforcement may be secured by registration if the scheme's criteria are met.[1] But must the application be restricted to the latter case? This may be important in cases where, for example, it may be difficult to establish that the court had jurisdiction to enter a judgment under the rules of private international law of the requested court.[2]

The central issue in these cases will be whether the foreign award has merged into the foreign judgment under the conflict of laws rules of the requested state. At common law, the position is far from clear. It is recognised, with full acknowledgment of the illogicality of the rule in comparison with domestic litigation,[3] that there is no merger of the cause of action and a foreign judgment upon it. The matter has never been conclusively decided in relation to arbitral awards.[4] The argument of illogicality may have less force in relation to awards for which independent methods of enforcement have been provided under various schemes which would be lost if only the judgment may be relied upon.

The matter seems now to have been resolved in the opposite way under the law of England and Wales and Northern Ireland. For in respect of judgments no proceedings may be brought there by any person on a cause of action in respect of which a judgment has been given in his favour in proceedings between the same parties or their privies in a court of an overseas country, unless that judgment is not enforceable or entitled to recognition in the requested jurisdiction.[5] As the original award is generally accepted as constituting a cause of action, there seems little doubt that so long as the foreign judgment on the award is registrable or otherwise capable of being enforced, the original award may not be registered. If, however, the judgment is not registrable or will not be recognised at common law, as for example for want of jurisdiction, the award can be registered. To that extent non-merger is retained. It may be expected that other common law jurisdictions will follow this lead, even as a proposition of common law. On the other hand, it is by no means clear that this section also precludes action upon the original cause of action when an award, rather than a judgment, has been obtained.[6]

1 *East India Trading Co Inc v Carmel Exporters and Importers Ltd* [1952] 2 QB 439, [1952] 1 All ER 1053; *International Alltex Corpn v Lawler Creations Ltd* [1965] IR 264.

2 Where, for example, the proceedings were brought against a defendant who had neither submitted or agreed to submit to the court's jurisdiction nor was resident or had any links with the country of that court.

3 See *Carl-Zeiss Stiftung v Rayner and Keeler Ltd (No 2)* [1967] 1 AC 853 at 917, 927, 938.

4 On the English position, see Dicey and Morris, op cit, p 1129. Non-merger was supported in *Badat & Co v East India Trading Co* AIR 1964 SC 538, a case which has been much criticised mainly on other grounds: K. P. Hariani, (1967) 7 Ind Jo Int Law 21 at pp 38–43; V. C. Govindaraj, (1964) 13 ICLQ 1465 at p 1467; A. B. Shroff, (1979) 21 Jo Ind L Inst 31, pp 33–35; U. Baxi, (1968) 10 Jo Ind Law Inst 149, pp 157–170.

5 Civil Jurisdiction and Judgments Act 1982, s 34.

6 The references in the section to 'court' which is defined as including 'tribunal of any description' and to 'judgment' which is defined as meaning 'any judgment or order (by whatever name called) given or made by a court in any civil proceedings' may be wide enough to cover this case: s 50. See para 6.32 below.

Relationship of schemes with other methods of enforcement

6.32 The 1920 scheme procedures are clearly an alternative to any other enforcement process which might be available, whether by an action on the award at common law, or by seeking leave under the equivalent of section 26 of the Arbitration Act 1950[1] or by enforcing as a foreign award under the Geneva Scheme[2] or as a convention award under the New York Convention scheme.[3] Only one limiting factor exists. If the alternative chosen is to bring a common law action on the award when the award could be registered under the Act, the plaintiff will be denied his costs of that action, unless he has already failed in an application for registration or unless the court orders otherwise.[4] This constraint does not appear to be applicable to applications for leave to enforce in the same manner as a judgment, which is likely to be used in respect of the Geneva and New York schemes.

The position under the 1933 Act is more complex. For that Act provides, when adapted to arbitral awards, that:

'No proceedings for the recovery of a sum payable under a foreign [award] being an [award] to which this Part of this Act applies, other than proceedings by way of registration of the [award], shall be entertained by any court in the [forum].'[5]

This mandatory requirement applies in respect of any arbitral award made in a reciprocating Commonwealth jurisdiction when that award is one which is capable of being registered under the Act. If any of the basic conditions implicit in the definition of 'award' are not fulfilled,[6] alternative procedures appear to be available in relation to that award. Thus, an award which is not enforceable in the same manner as a judgment in the country where it was made[7] will fall outside the prohibition. Given that an award will not usually become so enforceable without further proceedings in the country of the award, it may be expected that the section 6 prohibition can often be circumvented, leaving the applicant with the choice of alternative remedies,[8] such as suing on the award or seeking leave under the summary procedure.

Does section 6 preclude other proceedings where registration under the 1933 Act has been attempted and has failed or has been set aside? Since it appears that further applications under the Act cannot normally be made,[9] section 6 may well be given such a construction.

Again it may be questioned whether the section effectively prevents all alternative modes of award enforcement. It will certainly preclude application for leave to enforce under the equivalent of section 26 of the Arbitration Act 1950 or a common law action on the award. Less certain is its application to foreign awards within the Geneva Convention scheme. There are indications that such awards were deliberately excluded from the 1933 Act because the international arrangements were thought to be adequate.[10] Thus when section 6 was first drafted, enforcement of awards was not dealt with. Yet when the 1956 amendments introduced awards into the scheme, it must surely have been apparent that if section 6 was applicable to foreign awards, the Geneva scheme would be excluded. The non-application of section 6 has only recently been put beyond doubt in the United Kingdom: it remains a difficulty in most other jurisdictions with the two schemes.[11]

The New York Convention presents even more troublesome concerns. For the legislation implementing that particular convention must be taken to have been enacted in the full knowledge of the restriction in section 6 and of the provision in the Convention which explicitly permits a multiplicity of enforcement schemes.[12] Again, the conflict has only recently been removed as far as the United Kingdom is concerned. It remains in a number of other jurisdictions.[13]

There remain two other possibilities. First, an action at common law on the original cause of action may be considered. Such an action could hardly be said to constitute proceedings for the recovery of a sum payable under a foreign award within section 6. This assumes, however, that such an action can be brought. Whether this is so will depend upon whether the original cause of action has merged into the foreign award. If it has, then it cannot thereafter be the basis of further proceedings anywhere. It is generally agreed that this will be determined by the law governing the arbitration proceedings.[14]

The second possibility is that of bringing an action at common law on the award where the award has been the subject of a judgment in the court of origin. For it might be argued that section 6 can only be applied with difficulty to such cases. It would then be necessary to read the section as prohibiting proceedings for the recovery of a sum payable under the *award* other than by way of registration of the *judgment* obtained on that award. It has been suggested in the previous paragraph that it is unlikely that an action will be permitted if the judgment is capable of registration or will otherwise be recognised in the requested jurisdiction. If it is not, then section 6 will in any case not apply. For it will not surely be construed to require proceedings for registration to be brought if they are doomed to failure.

1 This may now be possible in countries following English decisions: see *Dalmia Cement Ltd v National Bank of Pakistan* [1975] QB 9 at 19–23, provided that the agreement is one which fulfils the requirements of s 32 of the Arbitration Act 1950 (UK).
2 See para 7.38 below.
3 See para 8.38 below.
4 AJA, s 9(5).
5 FJREA, s 6.
6 FJREA, s 1(2) and s 11(1): see para 6.21 above.
7 For the UK, see FJREA, s 10A.
8 The fact that an award is not enforceable in the country of origin is not a prohibition to other proceedings: see *Dalmia Dairy Industries Ltd v National Bank of Pakistan* [1978] 2 Lloyd's Rep 223, CA at 250, per Kerr J.
9 Further applications may be made after a setting aside, only if the latter was on the grounds of a pending appeal or because the award was not enforceable by execution in the place it was made: FJREA, s 5(2).
10 Sumner Committee Report, Annex V.
11 Civil Jurisdiction and Judgments Act 1982, Sch 10, in the new FJREA, s 10A. See further para 7.38 below.
12 New York Convention, art VII.1.
13 See further para 8.38, below.
14 Dicey and Morris, op cit, p 1129. Russell, op cit, p 89, suggests that in English law the matter may turn upon the nature of the award: *F J Bloemen Pty Ltd v Gold Coast City Council* [1973] AC 115, [1972] 3 All ER 357, PC. For merger under United Kingdom law, see Civil Jurisdiction and Judgments Act 1982, s 34; para 3.72 above.

CHAPTER 7

The Geneva Scheme

I COMMONWEALTH APPLICATION

Background

7.01 The Geneva Protocol on Arbitration Clauses of 1923 and the Geneva Convention on the Execution of Foreign Arbitral Awards of 1927 are regarded as being amongst the more successful achievements of the League of Nations.[1] As one of the principal proponents of these arrangements, the United Kingdom used its Imperial authority to cause the Geneva scheme to become widely accepted in the dominions and British dependencies and protectorates. Moreover the legislation incorporating the scheme continues on the statute books of the preponderance of Commonwealth jurisdictions. As will be suggested, it is questionable how far those provisions remain effective in the changed Commonwealth.[2] It is equally doubtful whether they still have much value. In practice, they appear not to have been invoked as widely as may have been expected[3] and they have been shown to suffer from a number of serious weaknesses which have militated against their usefulness.[4]

The purpose of the Geneva treaties was twofold. Under the Protocol, contracting states were required to recognise international arbitral agreements in commercial matters. For some states, though not those following English law, this involved a radical change in the law,[5] as did the Protocol's consequential requirement that disputes under such agreements must be dealt with by the agreed arbitral body and not by the courts of any contracting state. The second purpose was to impose upon parties to the Convention the obligation to recognise and enforce the awards which may be made under those agreements. By designating a common set of provisions which, if fulfilled, would permit the award to be enforced in any contracting state, it was intended to introduce greater uniformity amongst states and eliminate the numerous differences in existing practice which presented serious obstacles to the easy enforcement of awards.

1 A. Nussbaum, (1942) 56 Harv LR 219 at p 222. See paras 5.04–5.09 above.
2 See paras 7.07–7.10 below.
3 The Private International Law Committee, op cit, p 5, attributed this to the fact that most awards are complied with.
4 Nussbaum, loc cit, note 1 above, at pp 236–240.
5 Private International Law Committee, op cit, p 4.

Continued application of the Geneva scheme within the Commonwealth

7.02 In the great majority of cases, the Geneva scheme became applicable to jurisdictions within the present Commonwealth by action taken in respect of the 'British Empire', by the Crown as a metropolitan Power. Only the India and New Zealand Governments ratified the treaties by their own action. In all cases, implementing legislation, modelled upon that enacted in the United Kingdom, gave domestic effect to the agreements.[1] The continuance of these treaties in jurisdictions which have subsequently achieved independence is a matter of conjecture which is complicated by the terminology of the implementing legislation.

1 Arbitration Clauses (Protocol) Act 1924; Arbitration (Foreign Awards) Act 1930.

The scope of the Protocol

7.03 Acceptance of the Protocol's obligations by a contracting Power did not 'include' any dependencies of that Power if a declaration to that effect was made.[1] Such a declaration was made initially by the 'British Empire' effectively limiting application to Great Britain and Northern Ireland and by India excluding 'territories in India of any Prince or Chief under the sovereignty of His Majesty'. New Zealand, on the other hand, ratified without so declaring, the Protocol thereby becoming effective in respect of Western Samoa, then under its mandate, and probably her dependencies. The United Kingdom subsequently notified the Secretary of the League that it had adhered to the Protocol on behalf of some 37 of its dependent jurisdictions.[2] Further such inclusions were made, as late as in 1965 in the case of Hong Kong.

The Protocol remains open to adherence by any independent state[3] by deposit of ratification with the United Nations Secretary-General or, in the case of independence of a dependency already included, by notification of a decision to succeed to the original adhesion. In the Commonwealth, the former course of action was taken by Bangladesh in 1979 and the latter by the Bahamas (1979), Malta (1966) and Mauritius (1969). Uganda (1965) has signed but not ratified.

There are, therefore, only eight independent Commonwealth states formally listed by the UN Secretary-General as parties. Moreover, the Protocol now 'includes' only nine dependencies of the United Kingdom and, probably, three of New Zealand, those previously included having achieved independence. Whether the latter have succeeded to the Protocol, a matter of considerable uncertainty, will be discussed in paragraph 7.05 below.

In addition to these limiting factors, it should be noted that the Protocol has no effect between parties (and included dependencies) which are within the New York Convention.[4]

1 Protocol, art 8. 'Dependencies' is here used to refer to colonies, overseas possessions or territories, protectorates or territories over which a mandate was exercised.
2 Listed in the UN List of Signatories, Ratifications, etc as at 31 December 1982, ST/LEG/SER.E/2.
3 Protocol, art 5.
4 New York Convention, art VII. 2.

The scope of the Convention

7.04 The Convention is open to any state on whose behalf the Protocol has been ratified.[1] It does not apply to any dependency[2] of any high contracting party unless 'specially mentioned' but it may be applied by a declaration to any dependency to which the Protocol has been applied.[3] As with the Protocol, the Convention was initially ratified by India, New Zealand and Great Britain and Northern Ireland. It was applied by New Zealand to Western Samoa[4] and in the immediately subsequent years by the United Kingdom in respect of 31 dependent jurisdictions, six less than those within the Protocol ments.[5] The power to make further extensions was used by the United Kingdom in respect of Hong Kong as recently as 1965.

As with the Protocol the Convention has been ratified by Bangladesh (1979), and the Bahamas (1979), Malta (1966), Mauritius (1969) notified their succession. Uganda (1965) has signed but not ratified. Accordingly, the same eight Commonwealth states are listed by the UN Secretary-General as contracting parties, as for the Protocol. The Convention only applies in respect of dependencies of the United Kingdom, some eight in total. The question of succession by former dependencies to the Convention is examined in the following paragraph. The Convention, as the Protocol, cannot be invoked between those states which are parties to the New York Convention.

1 Convention, art 7.
2 The Convention refers to 'colonies, protectorates or territories under sovereignty or mandate of any High Contracting Party': Ibid, art 10.
3 Ibid.
4 Her dependencies, though perhaps within the Protocol, were not within the Convention.
5 Ceylon, Gambia (Colony and Protectorate), St Helena, S Rhodesia, Trans-Jordan were not included.

The problem of treaty succession

7.05 There is increasing support for the view that on independence a state will start with a clean slate as far as treaty obligations are concerned.[1] Practice in the Commonwealth may have modified this position to an extent as a result principally of any devolution agreement entered into between the former sovereign and the newly independent state or of a unilateral declaration made by the latter.[2] The former, the less common of the two devices, is generally conceived of as constituting a treaty between the original sovereign and the new state.[3] The International Law Commission concludes that they constitute in essence an indication of the general willingness of the new state to continue past treaty arrangements made on its behalf and a formal declaration of its responsibility in future for its own treaty relations. Though practice in this respect is variable, third states may rely upon these agreements and this may well lead to continuity where such states assent expressly or tacitly. But generally, it must be doubted whether, without evidence of this assent or some act of novation to the specific treaty by the new state, such agreements are likely to be considered as effectual to achieve succession.[4] In the context of the Protocol and Convention, for which implementing domestic legislation has been continued after independence, it is arguable that continued use of that legislation might be treated as evidence of the new state's intentions towards the treaties.[5]

The most common device, increasingly used in the Commonwealth, is the unilateral declaration under which the new state declares that it will continue existing treaties made on its behalf, usually stated to be on the basis of reciprocity, pending the determination of a final decision on individual treaties. A time limit for such an exercise is sometimes imposed. Such a unilateral act cannot bind other states which must in law be free to accept or reject what may be seen as a proposed course of action. At the most, they provide a 'basis for a collateral agreement in simplified form between the newly independent state and the individual parties to its predecessor's treaties for the provisional application of the treaties after independence'.[6] The agreement may be express or more commonly provided by conduct in treating the treaty as continuing.

Such declarations have been made by a considerable number of states, although in some cases the elected time limit may have expired, without notification to the UN Secretary-General of an intention to succeed to particular treaties.[7] How far such a declaration may be relied upon by any particular Commonwealth state will depend upon the extent to which that state agrees to the new state's proposition contained in the declaration. Notwithstanding the Privy Council advice in *Molefi v Principal Legal Adviser*[8] in which the courts were recognised as having power to give effect to such a unilateral declaration, the better view is that the acceptance of that declaration is for decision by the Executive. Again it may be argued that the maintenance of the implementing legislation is an indication of the new state's intention to stand for the time being by the former obligations.

It is apparent, therefore, that in a considerable number of cases uncertainties surround the question whether a particular Commonwealth state will be treated as a contracting party by others. In many instances, intricacies of state succession in the practice of different states will make it difficult for any party to an arbitration agreement to determine with any degree of security whether he is likely to be within the scope of the obligations under the Protocol or Convention. Resolution of the matter may be achieved in particular jurisdictions by the existence of an Executive order listing the contracting parties. Thus, in respect of the Convention, the United Kingdom issued in 1978 a revised list of 'Geneva Convention States'.[9] Of the new Commonwealth states this list includes only Grenada, Kenya, Mauritius and Tanzania.[10] This list sets out such Powers as 'Her Majesty, being satisfied that reciprocal provisions have been made', declares to be parties to the Convention.

Similar provisions authorising the issue of such lists are found in almost all Commonwealth countries with this legislation. Regrettably, most jurisdictions appear to rely upon the Orders-in-Council made by the United Kingdom whilst they were still dependent. Although contained as part of local law after independence, these orders have not usually been updated. Accordingly, whatever the standing of particular Commonwealth countries in international law with respect to the Convention, in most instances, the relevant executive order may well not have been amended to give domestic effect to an international succession to the Convention. The overall effect is to create grave uncertainty as to the availability of the Geneva scheme where one of the countries involved in a particular case is a new Commonwealth country.

1 See eg, I. Brownlie *Principles of Public International Law* (3rd ed 1979) p 666 and the commentary on arts 8 and 9 of the Draft Convention on Succession of States in respect of Treaties *Yearbook of International Law Commission* 1974 Vol II PE. 1 (Doc A/9610/Rev. 1).

2 For the exceptional cases of India and Pakistan (then a member of the Commonwealth), see para 7.10 below.

3 See International Law Commission op cit, p 185. They are normally registered with the UN Secretary-General under UN Charter, art 102.

4 Ibid, pp 184–186.

5 They were entered into, for example, by Ghana, Jamaica and Western Samoa. For Western Samoa, see para 7.09, note 2 below. Ghana, however, has repealed its legislation, which suggests that succession has not occurred: Arbitration Act 1961, s 43. Uganda, having signed the treaties after independence has not ratified them, again suggesting that succession has not taken place.

6 Ibid, p 192.

7 Several states have notified their succession: Bahamas (1979), Mauritius (1969) and Malta (1966).

8 [1971] AC 182, [1970] 3 All ER 724.

9 SI 1978/186 and SI 1979/304: the previous instruments have not been revoked, suggesting that uncertainties in the status of the originally designated jurisdictions not included in the revised list have not been resolved.
10 Only Mauritius appears on the UN listing: see Annex I to this chapter.

Domestic status of the Protocol

7.06 The statutory provisions introduced to give effect to the Protocol obligation relate to agreements to which the Protocol applies.[1] The Protocol is stated to apply to agreements 'between parties subject respectively to the jurisdiction of different Contracting States'.[2] It is necessary, therefore, in any litigation in which the provisions are invoked to establish that the states to the jurisdiction of which the parties are subject[3] are in each case distinct contracting states. This status is not in practice designated by any domestic order in respect of the Protocol. It will normally be established in accordance with the lex fori rules for establishing facts of state: as, for example, by obtaining an Executive certificate. It has been suggested[4] in Scotland that the United Kingdom Order-in-Council setting out the contracting parties to the Convention may be used as evidence that the Protocol applies, since a state cannot be a party to the former unless having first ratified the latter.[5] On the other hand, omission from the Order-in-Council, which is prepared for use in respect of enforcement of awards, cannot be conclusive of the question of participation in the Protocol scheme. It follows, therefore, that the international law questions discussed earlier may well arise, creating considerable uncertainty, prior to litigation, whether one of the parties to an agreement is subject to the jurisdiction of one of the new Commonwealth states which has not expressly indicated adherence to the Protocol. A further consequence of the requirement that the parties must be subject to the jurisdiction of different contracting states is that, for the purposes of the statute, dependencies cannot be treated as distinct from their metropolitan power. For the latter is the contracting party. Thus the Protocol scheme cannot be put into effect between two dependencies of the same contracting state nor between a dependency and the contracting state. The Protocol requirements, therefore, do not extend to arbitration agreements, for example, between parties connected[6] with the United Kingdom, on the one hand, and Hong Kong on the other.

1 Eg Arbitration Act 1950 (UK), s 4(2).
2 Art 1.
3 This matter is adverted to in para 7.13 below.
4 *Masinimport v Scottish Mechanical Light Industries Ltd* 1976 SC 102 at 107.
5 Convention, art 7.
6 What is required in this respect is discussed in para 7.13 below.

Legislation giving effect to the Protocol

7.07 In the preponderance of cases, Commonwealth jurisdictions have enacted provisions requiring the stay of legal proceedings in respect of matters required by agreement to be arbitrated, in almost common form modelled upon the Arbitration Clauses (Protocol) Act 1924[1] of the United Kingdom. In a number of jurisdictions, however, which the United Kingdom included amongst the dependencies within the Protocol, local legislation appears never to have been enacted—Cayman Islands, Ceylon, Gambia Colony and Protectorate, St Helena, Southern Rhodesia and Turks and Caicos Islands. If the independent states of the Gambia, Sri Lanka and Zimbabwe have succeeded to the Protocol, there appears no appropriate legislation to give it local effect.

In a number of other cases, the original legislation duly enacted by a dependency has been repealed without replacing provisions, as for example in Anguilla, British Virgin Islands, Ghana, Grenada and St Christopher-Nevis.

The most anomalous case is that of states, like Malaŵi, which have enacted the relevant legislation[2] although they have not, in their own right, adhered to the Protocol nor as a dependency been the subject of any declaration of inclusion by the United Kingdom. There seems no reason why the provisions of the legislation may not be invoked as part of the municipal law of Malaŵi, notwithstanding that that country is not within the Protocol ambit. Indeed the same conclusion seems to be applicable with respect to any Commonwealth jurisdiction with the implementing legislation if its terms are fulfilled, whether or not the jurisdiction is itself subject to the Protocol's obligations.[3] The latter question will be relevant in determining whether the conditions of the legislation are fulfilled but it does not affect the application of the legislation itself. This, it is suggested, will be the case, for example, in respect of Jersey,[4] in respect of which no declaration appears to have been made by the United Kingdom.

1 Replaced by Arbitration Act 1950, s 4(2), itself repealed in the United Kingdom by Arbitration Act 1975, s 8(2)(a) and replaced by, ibid, s 1, under the New York Convention.
2 Cap 6:03, s 6(2).
3 *Kassamali Gulamhusein Co (Kenya) Ltd v Kyrtatas Bros Ltd* 1968 (2) ALR Comm 350 (Kenya).
4 Jersey, Law of 11 February 1926 which applied the 1924 Act was confirmed by Order-in-Council. The position was the same in the Isle of Man and Guernsey until the replacement of the staying provisions by New York Convention provision: Arbitration Act 1976, Ch 24, s 5; Arbitration (Guernsey) Law 1982 (confirmed by Order in Council), s 5. See also Arbitration (Alderney) Law 1983, s 5.

Domestic status of the Convention

7.08 As we have seen in paragraph 7.06, it is common practice for the legislation implementing the Convention to require the Executive to make orders designating, on the basis of reciprocity, both the Powers which are parties to the Convention and the territories to which the Convention applies.[1] Such instruments will have full effect in municipal law and will govern the extent to which the Convention, as given effect by the legislation, can be relied upon in a particular jurisdiction. For the definition of 'foreign award' requires that the award must be between parties subject to the jurisdiction of a *listed* contracting party and must have been made in a *listed* territory.

In the usual case, the implementing legislation enacted by countries when dependent makes clear that the lists in the Orders-in-Council issued by the United Kingdom are effective for the purpose of the dependency's legislation. On achieving independence, the terminology has not always been altered to vest the power to make orders in an appropriate local executive authority. Whilst there is no doubt that the Orders-in-Council preceding independence will continue to have their effect as part of the municipal law, it must be questioned whether subsequent Orders-in-Council made in the United Kingdom can be relied upon. In other cases, the terminology has been altered with appropriate terms, but implementing instruments have not always been made by the designated authority. Although prima facie the original United Kingdom Orders-in-Council would continue as part of municipal law, they do not always fulfil the terms in which the instruments are now described by the amended legislation and probably cannot be relied upon.

Not only does the consequential absence of effective instruments prevent applications to invoke the legislation of a particular jurisdiction, it also means that the condition of reciprocity is absent, thereby justifying the exclusion or removal of that jurisdiction from the list of contracting states in another country's executive listing. This may well explain the omission of certain states, such as Malta, from the United Kingdom statutory instruments, notwithstanding their inclusion in the UN Secretary-General's list of contracting parties.

The unsatisfactory and uncertain nature of dependence upon United Kingdom Orders-in-Council, many of which will be inaccessible in the countries concerned, presents serious difficulties for the litigant. For those which gained independence prior to 1978, the antiquated Orders-in-Council issued under the original United Kingdom Act must be referred to.[2] For those still dependent or gaining independence after 1978, a substantially revised Order-in-Council has effect,[3] although this does not include a considerable number of the independent Commonwealth states originally included in the scheme as dependencies. Few Commonwealth countries have systematically faced up to this difficulty, by producing modern up-to-date lists of contracting parties and territories.[4] The need to meet the requirement of reciprocity makes such a task a demanding responsibility. The lists which have been produced do not reflect the international position as to participation in the Convention.[5]

There is one further difficulty posed for those jurisdictions still relying upon pre-1978 Orders-in-Council. If the legislation is to be invoked in relation to a person subject to the jurisdiction of the country in question, that country must be a 'Power' declared to be a party to the Convention. The early Orders-in-Council designated Heads of State as the Powers, not the states themselves. The designation used in each Order-in-Council in this respect was 'His Britannic Majesty' or 'His Majesty the King of Great Britain, Ireland and the British Dominions beyond the seas, Emperor of India'. Individual parts of the Empire were separately listed as territories to which the Convention applied. O'Connell has suggested[6] that this had the effect of making the Crown a distinct Power with regard to each of the listed territories, thereby permitting colonial awards to be enforced in the United Kingdom and vice-versa. It may be questioned whether this is correct, particularly as the revised form of the Order-in-Council makes clear that the United Kingdom alone is the contracting party. The earlier Orders-in-Council, it is suggested, give effect to the prevailing practice that treaties negotiated by the Crown on behalf of the Empire normally have no operation as conventions between the countries under the Crown. New Zealand and India, in this case, participated in the negotiations in their own right as dominions and in these cases the Crown was treated as a distinct 'Power'. The consequence of this conclusion is that those Commonwealth countries still listed in the older Orders-in-Council as dependencies will be excluded from designation as contracting parties and persons subject to their jurisdiction will fall outside the legislation. It is also apparent that the designations used are wholly inappropriate for the Heads of State of countries which have achieved their independence. This is particularly so for the republics. In these cases, the orders can have no effect. It is clear that, for this reason, modern local instruments are needed. At the same time, it must be questioned whether the Kenya solution is acceptable. For this requires that in every case one of the parties to an award must be subject to Kenya's jurisdiction, the other being subject to the jurisdiction of another contracting state.[7] This restriction appears to conflict with the Convention.[8]

1 This process was introduced at the instance of Lord Atkin to ensure the presence of reciprocal treatment: 75 HL Official Report (1930) cols 103, 170. See Arbitration Act 1950 (UK), s 35(1) for present provision.
2 This may be part of the explanation for the decision not to revoke pre-1978 Orders-in-Council, when the revised United Kingdom Order-in-Council was issued.
3 SI 1978/186, added to by SI 1979/304.
4 New Zealand expressly enacted in 1957 that UK Orders-in-Council up to 1957 were to be in force in New Zealand: Act 1933, No 4, s 4(2), amended Act 1957, No 44. These were subsequently replaced by a local order in 1977.
5 For example, the Kenya list comprises six non-Commonwealth states and Malta, Mauritius, New Zealand, Uganda, United Kingdom and Zambia.
6 D. P. O'Connell *State Succession in Municipal International Law* (1967) Vol II, p 357.
7 Cap 49, s 31(1)(b).
8 Convention, art 1.

Legislation giving effect to the Convention

7.09 The legislation to give effect to the Convention has largely followed the model provided by the United Kingdom Act 1930. A number of the territories to which the Convention applies have never enacted the legislation[1] or have subsequently repealed it.[2] In consequence, no enforcement proceedings can be brought in those places, although enforcement remains possible in any country, with the appropriate statute, in respect of any awards made in those territories.

Legislation exists in Malaŵi, although that country is not a party to the Convention. As with the Protocol, there seems no reason why enforcement provisions cannot be brought there, if the terms of the legislation are otherwise fulfilled. But it appears that no ministerial order designating Powers or territories can be validly made since the condition of reciprocity cannot be fulfilled.[3]

A similar difficulty arises with respect to the Isle of Man, Jersey and Guernsey.[4] In each the relevant legislation has been enacted there by the local Legislature although the United Kingdom appears never to have issued an Order-in-Council designating these as territories to which the Convention applies. The effect of this appears to be that awards made in any of these territories fall outside the scheme. Nonetheless, enforcement proceedings may be brought in those jurisdictions under their legislation in respect of any foreign award. In these cases, it is clear that the Orders-in-Council made by the United Kingdom apply to determine which are contracting parties and Convention territories for the purposes of the legislation.

1 Eg Cayman Islands and Turks and Caicos Islands.
2 Anguilla, British Virgin Islands, Ghana, St Christopher–Nevis. Grenada, which has repealed the Protocol provisions, continues the Convention statute. Presumably the latter's references to the Protocol are unaffected by the repeal of the former legislation. Western Samoa has repealed the Geneva legislation and replaced it by very similar provisions which are made applicable to all foreign awards without reference to the Geneva Convention: Arbitration Act 1976, No 9, Part II.
3 Cap 6:03, s 36: to this effect see *Kassamali Gulamhusein Co (Kenya) Ltd v Kyrtatas Bros Ltd* 1968 (2) ALR Comm 350 (Kenya).
4 Isle of Man, Arbitration Act 1976, c 24, Pt II; Arbitration (Guernsey) Law 1982, Pt II; Jersey: Law of 9 April 1931 applying the 1930 Act and confirmed by Order-in-Council: see also Arbitration (Alderney) Law 1983, Pt II.

India–Pakistan illustration

7.10 Some of the difficulties described in the foregoing paragraphs are graphically illustrated by a series of cases involving India, Pakistan and the United Kingdom, each of which has legislation in similar form.[1]

In *Francesco Corsi v Gorakhram Gokalchand*,[2] the Bombay High Court was asked to enforce an arbitral award obtained in London against an Indian exporter. It was argued that the Convention had not been entered into by the Government of independent India and that the declaration of the Central Government in 1938 that His Britannic Majesty was the Power whereby the Convention applied to British India[3] was inadequate. The court held that India was an original party to the Convention and continued as such by virtue of independence arrangements,[4] although no attention was given to the question whether the agreement of other parties to the Convention was first required. The deficiencies of the terminology of the 1938 Order were not closely examined: the general provisions of the law effecting the change from the monarchy to the Republic were sufficient.

The same considerations, however, did not apply to Pakistan. In *Yangtze (London) Ltd v Barlas Bros (Karachi) & Co*,[5] the Supreme Court of Pakistan, although prepared to accept that Pakistan may have succeeded to the Convention in international law, held that, for the purposes of the legislation, Pakistan was not a designated contracting party. Pakistan had not been designated as a Power by an order under the legislation in force in Pakistan and the original designation in favour of India, whatever its effect under Indian law, could not be relied upon as a reference to Pakistan. Accordingly an award made in London was not enforceable against a Pakistani exporter. Retrospective legislation was required to reverse the effects of this decision.[6]

In *Dalmia Cement Ltd v National Bank of Pakistan*,[7] Kerr J concluded that neither Pakistan nor India had been properly designated for the purposes of the United Kingdom legislation under the Orders-in-Council then operating. The designation of 'His Britannic Majesty' had not been replaced by references to the Presidents of these independent Republics and the courts could not construe the orders as having that effect. This matter was rectified by the United Kingdom in the revised Order-in-Council of 1978.[8] But similar alterations do not seem always to have been made by other jurisdictions which rely upon the earlier Orders-in-Council.

These cases suggest that the Geneva scheme may have been weakened in its application among Commonwealth countries by the failure to reflect in implementing legislation and instruments the prevailing position in international and constitutional law of particular jurisdictions. There is little doubt that the cumbersome designation arrangements, which were introduced to ensure reciprocity, are quite unsuited for use in an international scheme. Until those Commonwealth countries which accept obligations under the Convention modernise their instruments of application, serious problems in relying upon the local legislation are likely to occur.

1 The Arbitration (Protocol and Convention) Act 1937 of British India has continued in force in both India and Pakistan: see K. Hossain, (1960) 36 BYBIL 370–375.
2 AIR 1960 Bom 91.
3 Gazette of India, 1938, Pt I, p 24.
4 Indian Independence (International Arrangements) Order 1947.
5 PLD 1961 SC 573.
6 Pakistan Foreign Awards and Maintenance Orders Enforcement (Amendment) Order 1962.
7 [1975] QB 9, [1974] 3 All ER 189.
8 SI 1978/186.

II ARBITRATION AGREEMENTS WITHIN THE SCHEME

The Protocol in Commonwealth law

7.11 The legislation implementing the Protocol was confined to the matter of staying legal proceedings in respect of matters which parties had agreed to refer to arbitration. The legislation, therefore, does not directly relate to the recognition and enforcement of arbitral awards. Nonetheless, it has generally been seen as an integral part of the Geneva scheme for giving effect to arbitration awards and justifies some study. The treatment in that respect, however, will be short. For the trend in the Commonwealth has been to replace the original legislation by new provisions based upon the New York Convention which remove a number of legal uncertainties. As there is considerable similarity in the procedures of the old and new legislation it is the latter which will receive fuller treatment.[1] There is, however, one important respect in which the scope of the Protocol must be covered in connection with the enforcement arrangements. An award can only be enforced under those arrangements if made 'in pursuance of an agreement for arbitration to which the Protocol applies'.[2] It is necessary, therefore, to determine the conditions which must be fulfilled in this respect.

1 See Chapter 8, Part III below.
2 Arbitration Act 1950 (UK), s 35(1)(a).

Agreements to which the Protocol applies

7.12 The Protocol, in the English language text, applies to agreements:

'whether relating to existing or future differences between parties, subject respectively to the jurisdiction of different Contracting States, by which the parties to a contract agree to submit to arbitration all or any differences that may arise in connection with such contract relating to commercial matters or to any other matter capable of settlement by arbitration, whether or not the arbitration is to take place in a country to which jurisdiction none of the parties is subject.'[1]

Contracting parties were given the option to limit their obligations to contracts considered as commercial under their national laws.[2]

In essence, this rather involved provision establishes four requirements:

(i) an agreement to submit to arbitration all or any differences between parties to a contract, arising in connection with that contract, whether the differences are existing or future;
(ii) those parties must be subject respectively to the jurisdiction of different contracting states;
(iii) the differences may relate to commercial matters or to any other matter capable of settlement by arbitration (unless restricted to the former);
(iv) the place of arbitration is not to have any materiality.

These requirements are not without difficulties of interpretation, compounded by discrepancies between the English and French texts, both of which are authentic. Thus the French text makes clear that condition (i) embraces both submissions to arbitration and agreements to refer;[3] the English text is misleading in this respect. The French text is more explicit in respect of condition (iv), although the difference is not material.[4]

In other respects, both versions of the text are obscure. Thus it was not made clear whether the scheme was confined to agreements or contracts made or evidenced in writing, although this may have been the intention. More importantly, the requirement in condition (ii) that parties must be 'subject to the jurisdiction'[5] of a contracting state is not self-evident. It is capable of referring to links of nationality, domicile, residence, place of business or even to the law governing the contract or arbitration.[6] The travaux préparatoires suggest that a deliberately vague term was adopted to accommodate a number of different positions.[7] The Protocol is also silent as to the system of law by reference to which answers may be reached to the questions of whether differences relate to commercial matters or to matters capable of settlement by arbitration. It seems that the courts asked to give effect to the Protocol definition were intended to apply their national law to these questions.[8] Finally, the Protocol does not indicate whether it applies to agreements to which a government is a party, although again this appears not to have been the intention of those who prepared it.[9]

1 Art 1.
2 Ibid. This option was exercised by Bangladesh, India: see Act 1937, No 6, s 3.
3 The text reads 'compromis ainsi que . . . la clause compromissoire'.
4 The text reads 'même si le dit arbitrage doit avoir lieu dans un pays autre que celui à la jurisdiction duquel est soumise chacune des parties au contract'.
5 The French text reads 'soumis à la jurisdiction'.
6 P. Contini, (1959) 8 AJIL 283 at 289; A. Nussbaum, (1942) 56 Harv LR 219 at pp 234–235.
7 Report of Sub-Committee on Arbitration Clauses, LNOJ 1922, 1410, at p 1413; Rapporteur's Report, Fourth Assembly Records, pp 339–340.
8 Second Committee discussions on Draft Protocol, Fourth Assembly Records, C.II, pp 27–30. Article 1 makes clear that national law defines what are commercial contracts where the scheme has been so confined.
9 Report to Fourth Assembly, 24 September 1923, Fourth Assembly Records, p 12 and Report of Second Committee, C.II, pp 28ff.

Agreements to which the legislation applies

7.13 The shortcomings of the Protocol have unfortunately been reflected in the treatment by courts in the Commonwealth of the statutory provisions which, as we have seen, give no better guidance on this question. The principal difficulty has arisen with reference to the staying of legal proceedings in favour of arbitration and concerns the question whether the requirement is limited to cases where an actual submission to arbitration has taken place or whether it also applies where any agreement to arbitrate exists. As this difficulty derives from the particular terminology of the Protocol legislation, it will be considered in the context of the staying of proceedings.[1] It has no relevance where awards have actually been made.

A further difficulty which has arisen in the context of staying does have application to the enforcement of awards: it concerns the requirement that the parties must be subject respectively to the jurisdiction of different contracting states. Curiously, this difficult phrase[2] does not appear to have been the subject of direct judicial decision until 1970. In *Brazendale & Co Ltd v Saint Frères SA*,[3] Mocatta J rejected the link of nationality which he concluded could lead to absurd results,[4] not least in cases of dual nationality. Instead, he held that the Protocol requirements would be satisfied if the parties to the contract have places of residence or carry on business in two different contracting states and if the contract in question results from business so conducted. This construction satisfactorily ensures that 'international contracts' are caught, as the Protocol clearly intends, and that contracts between parties who have their business residences in the same country where they do business will be subject to municipal regulation. As the judge emphasised,[5] this approach has the virtue of bringing within the Protocol contracts of parties who, though having their business operations in the same country and in other contracting states too, have conducted the dealings in question through the latter countries. It was also suggested that the date at which subjection to jurisdiction is to be determined is that of the agreement to refer contractual disputes to arbitration. For the Protocol applies the qualifying phrase to the contract containing or comprising the agreement to arbitrate.[6]

The applicability of the Protocol to oral arbitration agreements has not been resolved. The legislation is generally silent in this respect, although a written agreement is common requirement in domestic legislation.[7] Where such a requirement governs the making of a particular agreement, the award will not be enforceable under other provisions of the legislation[8] but it can be argued that there is nothing in the Protocol itself or the legislation referring to it which requires that conclusion.[9]

It remains for decision whether the Protocol applies to agreements one party to which is a government or the state itself. Whilst it is often made clear that for the purposes of staying proceedings, agreements involving the government of the forum are not included,[10] other cases are not dealt with. There seems little reason in principle why agreements to which a state or state entity engaging in commercial or trading activities should be excluded from the Protocol. Whether an ensuing award will be enforceable is a different issue.[11]

The agreement must relate to commercial matters or to any other matters capable of settlement by arbitration.[12] In the case of Bangladesh and India, the scheme is confined to the former category as determined by the relevant national law.[13] The term 'commercial' has presented some difficulties. In particular, it has been held not to apply to technical assistance or know-how agreements, as these were of a 'professional character', not involving business or commerce or participation in profits, since they only required payment of fees.[14]

Just as the place of the arbitration is of no relevance in this context, the fact that the parties have chosen to govern the arbitration proceedings by a particular national system of law does not take the agreement outside the scope of the Protocol. This is a matter which may be determined by 'the will of the parties' in the agreement to refer future disputes to arbitration.[15] It should be noted that the validity of any agreement to which the Protocol applies may be put in issue in any proceedings to give effect to the agreement[16] or to an award made in pursuance of that agreement.[17]

An agreement to which the Protocol applies under the terms of the Commonwealth legislation may be summarised as arising where:

(a) the agreement is either to refer existing or future differences to arbitration or to submit an existing difference to named arbitrators;[18]
(b) the parties, at the time of making the agreement, were resident and carrying on business in the territory of two different contracting parties to the Protocol and their contract resulted from business so conducted;
(c) the agreement was written or oral, unless the latter is prohibited by the law governing the agreement;
(d) the differences relate to commercial matters or to any other matters capable of settlement by arbitration, unless restricted to the former by the legislation of the state in which the provision is invoked;
(e) the differences arise from a contract between the parties to the agreement who may include the state acting in a commercial or trading capacity.

1 Para 7.15 below.
2 The Private International Law Committee, op cit, p6, termed it 'unduly restrictive and difficult to construe'.
3 [1970] 2 Lloyd's Rep 34.
4 Eg, where the agreement was made in England between a United Kingdom company and a foreign national long resident and carrying on business in England.
5 [1970] 2 Lloyd's Rep 34 at 41. This emphasis on residence is consistent with dicta in *Union Nationale des Coopératives Agricoles de Céréales v Robert Catterall & Co Ltd* [1959] 2 QB 44 at 50, CA.
6 Ibid, at 40 and 42.
7 Eg, Arbitration Act 1950 (UK), s 32.
8 Ibid, s 37(1)(a): see para 7.24 below.
9 Dicey and Morris (8th edn) p 1074.
10 Eg, Arbitration Act 1950 (UK), s 30.
11 Para 7.29 below.
12 Arbitration Act 1950 (UK), s 37(1)(a). Cf similarly, para 8.05 below.
13 Arbitration Protocol and Convention Act 1937, No 6, s 3. This section has been replaced in India by the Foreign Awards (Recognition and Enforcement) Act 1961, No 45, s 10 but the limitation appears still to apply in respect of awards enforced under the earlier Act: *Ramji Dayawala & Sons P Ltd v Invest Import* AIR 1981 SC 2085.
14 *Société de Traction et d'Electricité SA v Kamani Engineering Co Ltd* 1964 AIR SC 558 but see Report of Committee on Commercial Arbitration, 1964, pp 28–31 which recommends that a broader interpretation should be provided for.
15 *Francesco Corsi v Gorakhram Gokalchand* AIR 1960 Bom 91, correctly criticising *W Wood & Sons Ltd v Bengal Corpn* AIR 1956 Cal 238 and *Bajrang Electric Steel Co Private Ltd v Commrs for the Port of Calcutta* AIR 1957 Cal 240, contra.
16 Para 7.18(i) below.
17 Para 7.24 below.
18 Para 7.16 below.

III RECOGNITION OF ARBITRATION AGREEMENTS

The Protocol obligations

7.14 The purpose of the Protocol was to ensure that arbitration agreements would be given full force in national systems. Most of its particular obligations were already given effect by the existing law of arbitration in Commonwealth countries. Thus it was not necessary to make fresh provision to 'recognise the validity of agreements'[1] or to provide for the will of the parties and the law of the place of arbitration to govern arbitral procedure[2] or to facilitate procedural steps applicable to settlement by arbitration.[3] Similarly the duty to ensure the execution of local awards made under Protocol agreements was already provided for.[4]

The central obligation which was new in Commonwealth practice was contained in article 4 which provided that:

> 'the tribunals of the Contracting Parties, on being seized of a dispute regarding a contract between persons to whom Article I applies and including an arbitration agreement whether referring to present or future differences which is valid in virtue of the said article and capable of being carried into effect, shall refer the parties on the application of either of them to the decision of the arbitrators.'

The article makes clear that the tribunals retain their competence 'in case the agreement or the arbitration cannot proceed or becomes inoperative'.

There are again unfortunate differences between the two language versions. The French version makes clear that the obligation extends both to agreements and to actual submissions to arbitration.[5] More seriously, the term 'dispute' has been used as the equivalent of the French term 'litige' which is used to refer to a law suit, and thus wider than a dispute in the sense of disputation or opposite reasoning.[6] The apparent intention was that courts would be obliged to stay legal proceedings whenever a law suit was commenced on a matter within the arbitration agreement, whether or not the defendant could be proceeded against on default.[7]

Apart from these discrepancies, there are a number of obscurities. Thus, for example, the Protocol in using the phrase 'seized of a dispute' gave no indication of when that event occurred or, more importantly, whether and, if so, when, a request to stay proceedings can be made too late. Again, it is not made clear by which law it will be decided whether an agreement is 'capable of being carried into effect' or whether an agreement or the arbitration 'cannot proceed' or became 'inoperative'.

1 Art 1.

2 Art 2. The reference to 'will of the parties' is taken as indicating that the parties may choose the applicable law. In the absence of such a choice, the law of the place of arbitration will normally apply: *James Miller v Whitworth Street Estates (Manchester) Ltd* [1970] AC 583, [1970] 1 All ER 796. The will of the parties may be expressed in the instrument whereby the parties agree to refer their dispute to arbitration: *Francesco Corsi v Gorakhram Gokalchand* AIR 1960 Bom 91.

3 Art 2. The English version, in referring to 'arbitral procedure applicable to existing differences', inexpertly renders the French 'la procedure d'arbitrage par compromis', a reference to the procedure following actual submission to arbitration.

4 Art 5.

5 '... comportant un compromis ou une clause compromissoire...'. The use of 'including' in the English text obscures the implications of 'comportant' which indicates that the arbitration agreement must arise from the contract: Russell, op cit, (18th edn) p 453.

6 A. Nussbaum, (1942) 56 Harv LR 219 at p 225.

7 Ibid.

Article 4 of the Protocol in Commonwealth legislation

7.15 The Commonwealth legislation generally followed the model developed in the United Kingdom Act of 1924, as amended in 1930.[1] These provisions may be summarised as follows:

- (i) where legal proceedings have been commenced by or on behalf of a party to a submission to arbitration made in pursuance of an agreement to which the Protocol applies against another such party;
- (ii) and the proceedings are in respect of any matter agreed to be referred to arbitration;
- (iii) any party to the proceedings may apply for the stay of the proceedings;
- (iv) the application may be made at any time after appearance and before delivering any pleadings or taking any other steps in the proceedings;[2]
- (v) the court *must* stay the proceedings;
- (vi) unless it is satisfied that
  - (i) the agreement or arbitration has become inoperative;
  - (ii) the agreement or arbitration cannot proceed;
  - (iii) there is not in fact any dispute between the parties with regard to the matter agreed to be referred.

The legislation diverged from the terms of the Protocol in three important respects. First, it required that the parties must be parties to a submission to arbitration made in pursuance of a Protocol agreement. Secondly, it went further in indicating at what time applications may or may not be made. Thirdly, it introduced an additional ground for refusing a stay of proceedings, as the result of an amendment following the recommendations of the United Kingdom Committee on the Law of Arbitration in 1927.[3] Each of these variations has been the subject of controversy and litigation.

1 Arbitration Clauses (Protocol) Act 1924, s 1, as amended by Arbitration (Foreign Awards) Act 1930, s 8, consolidated in Arbitration Act 1950, s 4(2) and replaced by Arbitration Act 1975, s 8(2).
2 This formulation shows minor variations as a result of differences in procedures in particular Commonwealth jurisdictions. See para 7.17 below.
3 Cmd 2817, chaired by Mackinnon J, see para 5.07 above. For discussion, see para 7.18 (iii) below.

Meaning of 'submission to arbitration'

7.16 Whilst the French language version makes clear that the staying process is to apply to cases where an actual submission of an existing dispute has taken place or where there is an agreement to refer, which has not yet been followed by a submission, the English language version and the additional language of the legislation were far from clear. Dicta in an early English decision[1] and commentators tended to favour the narrower construction.[2] Decisions of the Indian courts firmly supported the interpretation that an actual submission to arbitrators must be made by all the parties to the agreement.[3]

Such a conclusion leads to the possibility that a party to an agreement, finding arbitration inconvenient and preferring instead to litigate, could achieve this end merely by refusing to be a party to the submission.[4] Since this results in the failure to give effect to the arbitration agreement it clearly runs contrary to the aims of the Protocol.[5]

This consequence was recognised by Scarman J in *The Merak*.[6] By deciding that the term 'submission' carried the same meaning as that formerly attached to the word as used in section 27 of the Arbitration Act 1889, he held that it included agreements to refer as well as an actual submission to designated arbitrators.[7] The qualifying reference in the section to agreements to which the Protocol applies was merely 'to establish the link that there must be between the agreement to submit present or future differences to arbitration and the agreement of a commercial or business character between the parties of a certain class to which the Protocol applies'.[8] On this basis, a bare submission which does not link with the contract between the parties to which the arbitration agreement relates would not be within the legislation. This too seems consistent with the purposes of the Protocol and in particular its French text.

1 *Radio Publicity (Universal) Ltd v Compagnie Luxembourgeoise de Radiodifusion* [1936] 2 All ER 721 at 726.
2 Eg Russell, op cit, (18th edn) p 453.
3 *Bajrang Electric Steel Co v Commrs for Port of Calcutta* AIR 1957 Cal 240; *Wood & Son Ltd v Bengal Corpn* AIR 1959 Cal 8; *Société de Traction et d'Electricité SA v Kamani Engineering Co Ltd* (1963) 66 Bom LR 558, AIR 1965 Bom 114; *Ramji Dayawala & Sons P Ltd v Invest Import* AIR 1981 SC 2085.
4 K. P. Hariani, (1967) 7 Ind Jo IL 31 at p 37.
5 The Report of the Committee on Commercial Arbitration (1964) of India accordingly proposed an amendment to obviate this consequence.
6 [1965] P 223 esp at 235–239. This part of the judgment was not contested in the Court of Appeal, [1965] 1 All ER 230. It was followed in *Unipat AG v Dowty Hydraulic Units Ltd* [1967] RPC 401 and *Brazendale & Co Ltd v Saint Frères SA* [1970] 2 Lloyd's Rep 34; *Kassamali Gulamhusein Co (Kenya) Ltd v Kytatas Bros Ltd* 1968 (2) ALR Comm 350 (Kenya).
7 These latter circumstances had been present in *Radio Publicity (Universal) Ltd v Compagnie Luxembourgeoise de Radiodifusion*, above.
8 [1965] P 223 at 239, per Scarman J.

Applications for stay of legal proceedings

7.17 The power to seek a stay rests with any party to the legal proceedings in question. The burden of proving that the requirements of the section are met, in particular that there is an agreement to arbitrate and that it is one to which the Protocol applies[1] rests upon the applicant. The failure of such a party to establish the requirements of the section will not prevent a successful application by another party who can.[2]

The legal proceedings must have been commenced between parties to the arbitration agreement or the submission or persons claiming through or under them.[3] There seems no reason why the stay cannot be sought by persons who have been joined to the proceedings but who were not concerned in the agreement or submission.[4]

Moreover, the proceedings must be in respect of a matter agreed to be referred to arbitration[5] and must relate to a subject which, according to the terms of the agreement construed according to the law governing it, is within those agreed to be arbitrable. Disputes on these issues will be determined by the court unless it concludes that the parties have expressly agreed to refer those questions to arbitration too. In such a case, the conditions for granting a stay are automatically fulfilled.[6]

The application to stay may be made at any time after appearance[7] and before delivery of any pleadings or the taking of any other steps in the proceedings. The purpose of these provisions is to preclude the grant of a stay where the applicant has become so concerned with the litigation that he may be said to have waived his right to arbitration. Thus if a defendant in a case has taken some positive procedural steps,[8] such as delivering pleadings, issuing a summons for discovery, making a counterclaim,[9] obtaining a summons for direction, he will not be permitted to stay the course of the litigation. On the other hand, he is entitled to take procedural steps which are essentially defensive of his rights, to 'parry a blow' of the plaintiff,[10] as for example to defend an application for an interlocutory injunction or to make a demand for a statement of claim.[11]

1 On this, see para 7.13 above.
2 Cf *Eastern Counties Farmers v J J Cunningham Ltd* [1962] 1 Lloyd's Rep 261, CA.
3 Where the matter is raised in legal proceedings for the first time by a counterclaim, the delivery of the counterclaim constitutes the commencement: *Radio Publicity (Universal) Ltd v Compagnie Luxembourgeoise de Radiodifusion* [1936] 2 All ER 721.
4 But contra, *Bajrang Electric Steel Co v Commrs for Port of Calcutta* AIR 1957 Cal 240. It is irrelevant that the parties are both already subject to the jurisdiction of the court: *Unipat A G v Dowty Hydraulic Units Ltd* [1967] RPC 401.
5 There must be an unequivocal agreement for arbitration: *Bajrang Electric Steel Co v Commrs for Port of Calcutta,* above.
6 Cf *Heyman v Darwins Ltd* [1942] AC 356, [1942] 1 All ER 337.
7 Presumably under RSC Ord 12 (revised) acknowledgment of service and notice of intention to defend constitute appearance for this purpose.
8 *Roussel-Uclaf v G D Searle & Co Ltd* [1978] 1 Lloyd's Rep 225.
9 *Kamani Engineering Corpn Ltd v Société de Traction et d'Electricité SA* AIR 1965 Bom 114 at 119.
10 *Roussel-Uclaf v G D Searle & Co Ltd* above, at 231, per Graham J.
11 Similar terminology is found in the Arbitration Act 1950, s 4(1) and in the Arbitration Act 1975, s 1(1). For the additional case law in these cases, see Russell, op cit, pp 173–175, 180; and para 8.15 below.

The duty to stay legal proceedings

7.18 Where the applicant satisfies the court that the case is one falling within the terms of the section, there is a mandatory duty on the court to grant a stay of the proceedings in favour of the arbitration, unless the party seeking to determine the matter by litigation satisfies the court that one of the three grounds of objection is met.

(i) The agreement or arbitration has become inoperative

The most obvious circumstances will arise where the agreement (or the submission to arbitrators or the contract[1] to which they relate) is invalid or has been repudiated by the parties or has otherwise come to an end. The section does not indicate the law by which such questions should be determined. The better view is that reference should be made to the law governing the arbitration agreement,[2] although in a number of cases, the lex fori appears to have been considered appropriate.[3] Where the question is one of the validity of the agreement, only cases where it is void ab initio will fall within the defence. Agreements which are voidable, ie only void when so determined by decision, must be put to the arbitrator for that decision.[4]

An agreement will not be inoperative merely because the claim in favour of arbitration is out of time. For this would be an incentive to a party wishing to litigate to delay reference to an arbitral tribunal until the time for doing so has expired.[5]

What law governs the question whether the arbitration itself has become inoperative is also uncertain. The better view, it may be suggested, is that it should be resolved by reference to the law governing the arbitration proceedings. This seems the most appropriate to deal with such questions as whether the chosen arbitrator is disqualified or whether he or his authority has been removed and no provision exists for a replacement.

(ii) The agreement or arbitration cannot proceed

These words may have been intended to supplement the previous objection by bringing in cases of physical rather than legal impossibility. If so, it would be more likely to be invoked in respect of the arbitration than the agreement. It will extend to cases where the arbitration cannot take place in the selected country by reason of hostilities or pestilence and to cases in which the parties have declined to appoint an arbitrator or cannot reach agreement upon one.[6] It clearly does not apply merely because one of the parties is unable to pay his costs of arbitration.[7]

(iii) There is not in fact any dispute between the parties with regard to the matter agreed to be referred

This additional ground was introduced to prevent the development of an incipient practice of a party demanding arbitration although he could offer no reason for refusing to satisfy a contractual debt. There is little doubt, however, that the Protocol was intended to apply wherever relevant litigation had been commenced, as the French text indicates.[8] The provision in operation has probably done little damage to the Protocol's aim. Certainly there is no evidence of Commonwealth courts weighing defences raised by a party to establish whether a dispute exists or not, thereby introducing an oblique discretionary element into the grant of stay or protracting the legal processes, as one commentator feared.[9] The mandatory nature of the duty in the Protocol has been recognised, if sometimes grudgingly, in almost every jurisdiction.[10] The ground enables an undisputed case to be dealt with by summary court processes applicable where no defence is possible. It appears not to have led to legal difficulty in its original form but identical wording in the Arbitration Act, 1975[11] has given rise to a series of decisions which have application in this context, and will be discussed there.[12]

1 The fact that the original contract has ended will not necessarily prevent disputes which have arisen under it being subject to the arbitration agreement: *Radio Publicity Ltd v Compagnie Luxembourgeoise de Radiodifusion* [1936] 2 All ER 721 at 728.
2 Dicey and Morris, op cit, (8th edn) p 1076.
3 *Radio Publicity Ltd v Compagnie Luxembourgeoise de Radiodifusion*, above, at 728; *The Tradesman* [1961] 3 All ER 661 [1962] 1 WLR 61; *Société de Traction et d'Electricité SA v Kamani Engineering Co Ltd* 1964 AIR SC 558.
4 *The Tradesman*, above.
5 *The Merak* [1965] P 223 at 229.
6 Dicey and Morris, op cit, p 1162, unless under the relevant law, a court has power to appoint a replacement.
7 Cf *The Rena K* [1979] QB 377 [1979] 1 All ER 397.
8 Para 7.14 above.
9 A. Nussbaum, (1942) 56 Harv LR 219, at p 227, note 49.
10 See dicta in *Kamani Engineering Corpn v Société de Traction* AIR 1965 Bom 114 (Desai J) to the contrary but the correct view is emphasised in *W Wood & Son Ltd v Bengal Corpn* AIR 1959 Cal 8.
11 S 1(1).
12 See para 8.13 below.

Terms and conditions of staying

7.19 The Protocol is silent upon the question whether the order staying the legal proceedings may be subject to terms and conditions. This may be important where the action is an action in rem against a ship or other property or where it seems possible that subsequent events will occur under which the agreement, or more probably the arbitration, could become inoperative or incapable of proceeding. It seems that such a power does not exist. Indeed where the provision is contained in consolidating legislation based upon the Arbitration Act 1950 (UK), the imposition of terms will be forbidden.[1] Moreover, in the case where the subject matter is a ship, it appears that the court has no choice on granting a stay but to release the ship and in consequence not to take any alternative security.[2] On the other hand if there is a strong possibility that the stay will be removed for some good cause, the court might be justified in refusing the release altogether or at least adding to the order for release a term requiring alternative security against the judgment or settlement of the action.[3] But these are not conditions attached to the order for stay itself. It may also be open to a party to seek a Mareva injunction.[4]

A stay on legal proceedings once imposed under this section will remain effective unless either of the first two objections subsequently materialises. Then it is open to a party to have the stay removed. But there must be evidence to show that one or other of the events is likely to happen.[5]

1 Arbitration Act 1950, s 18: see *The Golden Trader* [1974] 2 All ER 686 at 695.
2 Ibid at 696, applying *The Cap Bon* [1967] 1 Lloyd's Rep 543.
3 *The Rena K* [1979] 1 All ER 397 at 415.
4 *Rasu Maritima SA v Pertamina* [1977] 2 Lloyd's Rep 397: see para 3.31 above.
5 *The Golden Trader*, above.

IV ENFORCEMENT OF ARBITRAL AWARDS

Enforcement under the Protocol and the Convention

7.20 The Geneva Protocol made passing reference to the enforcement of awards. Each contracting party undertook

> 'to ensure the execution by its authorities and in accordance with the provisions of its national law of arbitral awards made in its own territory under the preceding articles.'[1]

But such an undertaking did nothing to ensure that awards made in other states were as equally readily enforced. As Lorenzen pointed out,[2] the staying provisions in the Protocol made arrangements for those cases an absolute necessity. For if the award was not enforceable when litigation had been stayed, the creditor would be without a remedy. The Geneva Convention, therefore, set out to remedy this shortcoming by requiring specified categories of foreign awards to be recognised as binding and to be enforced by the forum procedures in all contracting states. It specifies the essential procedures for proving the award before the courts of those countries and it itemises the grounds upon which recognition and enforcement may be resisted and refused.

1 Art 3.
2 E. G. Lorenzen, (1935–36) 45 Yale LJ 39 at pp 63–64.

Awards within the Convention scheme

7.21 The Convention lays down in outline terms the characteristics which an award must be shown to have in order to be within the scheme.[1] These are:

(a) the award must be made in pursuance of an agreement whether relating to existing or future differences[2] covered by the Protocol;
(b) it must have been made between persons who are 'subject to the jurisdiction of one of the high contracting parties';
(c) it must have been made in a territory of one of the contracting parties to which the Convention applies.

As with the Protocol, the Convention is inelegantly drafted. The French language version, but not the English, makes it clear that the agreement may be an agreement to refer to arbitration or an actual submission. In consequence, if the enforcing state does not recognise the agreement or the submission as one to which the Protocol applies, any award thereunder will be outside the Convention. The conditions examined earlier must, therefore, be fulfilled.[3] The jurisdictional link in (b) was almost certainly intended to require that the parties must be subject to the jurisdiction of different contracting parties. The same difficulties concerning the application of this obscure phrase exist here as under the Protocol.[4] It presumably must be determined in this instance at the date of the award, the same test also having been applied in respect of the parties to the agreement at the time that was made.[5]

1 Art 1.
2 Referred to in subsequent provisions of the Convention as 'a submission to arbitration': art 1.
3 See paras 7.11–7.13 above. Any limitation to commercial contracts must be given effect.
4 Ibid. A. Nussbaum, (1942) 56 Harv LR 219 at p 235.
5 See para 7.13 above.

Awards within the Geneva scheme legislation

7.22 The implementing legislation in the Commonwealth although repeating the essentials of the three Convention characteristics shows differences from the text of the Convention. Thus, it requires that the award (designated for the purposes of the legislation as a 'foreign award') must be made in pursuance of 'an agreement for arbitration' to which the Protocol applies, thereby avoiding use of the term 'submission' and the connected problems of interpretation.[1] The effect, however, appears that it will be enough to show that either the original arbitration agreement or a subsequent submission to arbitrators was within the terms of the Protocol but not necessarily both, where both are present.

A second difference is that it is made quite clear that the award must be between persons 'subject to the jurisdiction' of different Powers which are parties to the Convention as identified in some form of legislative instrument.[2] As with the Protocol provisions, the legislation gives no guidance on the meaning of 'subject to the jurisdiction'. It must be assumed that the construction in *Brazendale & Co Ltd v Saint Frères SA*[3] will have equal force in this context. The effect will be that the party to the award must have been resident or carrying on business in the territory of a contracting party, including any of its designated dependencies. Thus a person carrying on business in, for example, Hong Kong will be 'subject to the jurisdiction' of the United Kingdom, one of the contracting parties, for the purposes of the legislation. Thirdly, the award must have been made in one of the territories which have been declared by a legislative instrument to be territories to which the Convention applies.[4] It is clearly immaterial that the parties have no connection by nationality, residence or otherwise with that territory. Fourthly, the legislation adds a condition which is not contained in the Convention. The scheme is stated not to apply to any award made on an arbitration agreement governed by the law of the forum.[5] The purpose is to exclude from the scheme those awards thought to have a significant forum or domestic link, with which the Convention should not be concerned. Fifthly, the implementing legislation normally indicates that only those awards which have been made subsequent to the coming into force of that legislation can be enforced.[6] It is probable, however, that it can be used in relation to such awards if made prior to accession and listing of a contracting state provided that this condition is fulfilled by the time the enforcement proceedings are commenced.[7] Lastly, this scheme seems capable of applying to an award, although, by reason of proceedings taken elsewhere, it has become enforceable there as a judgment. To disentitle a party succeeding in an arbitration from using the Convention procedures in a case where enforcement proceedings taken in the place of the award have not secured implementation of the award seems contrary to the aims of the agreement. On the other hand, the enforcing court may feel constrained, if under the lex fori foreign awards are deemed to merge into foreign judgment so that they cannot be sued upon as an original cause of action.[8]

In sum, the legislation relates to 'foreign awards' which occur where:

(a) the award is made in pursuance of an agreement for arbitration to which the Protocol applies;[9]
(b) the agreement is not one governed by the lex fori;
(c) the award is between persons who were resident or carrying on business, at the time of the award, in different listed contracting states;
(d) the award was made in one of the listed territories.

1 The explicit reference to 'agreement for arbitration' in the Arbitration Act 1950 (UK), s 35(1)(a) allows a different construction from the rather strained construction used by Scarman J in *The Merak* [1965] P 223 in respect of the Protocol legislation: see para 7.16 above.

2 Arbitration Act 1950 (UK), s 35(1)(b): for the difficulties in respect of the listing, see para 7.08 above.

3 [1970] 2 Lloyd's Rep 34; see para 7.13 above.

4 Arbitration Act 1950 (UK), s 35(1)(c).

5 Ibid, s 40(b), re-enacting the Arbitration (Foreign Awards) Act 1930, s 6.

6 The Convention merely requires that it applies to awards made after the Protocol was put into force: art 6. Some Commonwealth legislation does not restrict to post-legislation awards: eg, Arbitration Act, 1975, No 12 (Antigua).

7 Cf *Kuwait Minister of Public Works v Sir Frederick Snow & Partners* [1984] 1 All ER 733, [1984] 2 WLR 340, under the New York Convention.

8 The common law is not settled on this matter: *L Oppenheim & Co v Mahomed Haneef* [1922] 1 AC 482 at 488. The better view is that the anomalous rule which applies to non-merger of foreign judgments (now abolished in the UK by Civil Jurisdiction and Judgments Act 1982, s 34) does not apply to awards: Dicey and Morris, op cit, p 1129.

9 The conditions in this respect are set out in para 7.13 above.

V ENFORCEMENT PROCEEDINGS

Enforcement requirements

7.23 The Convention requires that the party seeking to enforce an award must supply the following:[1]

(i) the original award or a copy duly authenticated according to the requirements of the law of the country in which it was made;
(ii) documentary or other evidence to prove that the award has 'become final'[2] in the country in which it was made;
(iii) when necessary, documentary or other evidence to prove that the award is one within the scheme and that certain conditions of enforceability prescribed by article 1[3] have been fulfilled.

Translations can be required by the receiving state. These must be certified as correct by a diplomatic or consular agent of the country to which the applicant 'belongs' or by a sworn translator in the receiving country.[4]

Implementing legislation generally follows these provisions with all their blemishes.[5] It is usually left to rules of court to amplify concerning the evidence which has to be supplied but the power appears to have been little used.[6] It must be doubted whether a requirement of *additional* evidence is consistent with the Convention.

It is not enough for the applicant merely to produce evidence of the award and that it is a foreign award within the terms of the legislation. It also falls to the applicant to establish, by producing such evidence as may be necessary, that the award was regular in having fulfilled certain prescribed conditions of enforceability.[7] There are in effect four such conditions.[8] In addition, there are two other conditions of enforceability prescribed upon which the applicant is not required to produce any supporting evidence.[9] Unless the documentation provided, on its face, gives evidence of irregularity in either respect, the award may be presumed to be valid in that regard. It is open to the party resisting enforcement and, it may be assumed, the court proprio motu to raise these latter issues. As they are conditions of enforceability, the burden may lie with the applicant to prove that they are met.[10] On the other hand, there is much in the view that at least when raised by the defendant the burden should fall on him.[11] Proof that an award does not conflict with public policy would impose a heavy burden on the applicant.

1 Art 4.

2 As defined in art 1, para 2(d): see para 7.27 below.

3 Art 1, para 1 and para 2(a) and (c): see paras 7.24 to 7.27 below.

4 Art 4, para 2.

5 Eg Arbitration Act 1950 (UK), s 38. An example of a blemish is the reference to 'the country to which that party belongs' used in the legislation. It is by no means clear whether this is a

reference to nationality or a reference back to the country to whose jurisdiction he is subject (see para 7.22 above). It is probably the latter.

6 Arbitration Act 1950, s 38(3). But if enforcement is by the summary procedure (Arbitration Act 1950, s 26), the agreement or a copy thereof must be produced: RSC Ord 73, r 10.

7 Ibid, s 38(1)(c).

8 Paras 7.24–7.27 below.

9 Paras 7.28–7.29 below.

10 *Se Se Oil v Gorakhram Gokalchand* (1962) 64 Bom LR 113.

11 *Kianta Osakeyhtio v Britain and Overseas Trading Co Ltd* [1954] 1 Lloyd's Rep 247 at 250–251, per Somervell LJ.

Conditions of enforceability to be established by the applicant

(a) *The award was made in pursuance of an agreement for arbitration which was valid under the law by which it was governed*[1]

7.24 The Convention applies the condition to a submission to arbitration which is defined to cover an original agreement to arbitrate and a reference to the arbitrators. It is not apparent whether both must be valid, where both exist. The statute is ambiguous in its application of the condition to the 'agreement for arbitration'. It may be suggested that this term should be given the wider construction to cover awards made by pursuance of original agreements or of references, and further that the requested court should be concerned with the validity of both sources of the award.

Neither Convention nor implementing legislation gives any indication of the law which is to govern validity. It was no doubt intended that such matters would be resolved according to the conflict of laws rules of the enforcing state.[2] No decisions on the legislation appear to exist but the general view of commentators favours this construction, so that in systems applying English based conflict of laws the proper law will apply, leaving the matter to be determined by reference to the choice of the parties or, in the absence of choice, as ascertained by the courts.[3] Similar considerations apply, it may be suggested to questions of formal validity. This is not governed by the Convention itself which, unlike the New York Convention,[4] contains no rules on the matter. Such questions may, therefore, under English law be determined by reference to the lex loci contractus or to the proper law[5] but not the lex fori.[6] Where the law governing the agreement is that of the enforcing state the ensuing award is outside the scheme.[7]

In effect, this condition excludes from the scheme cases where the arbitrators lacked jurisdiction through the invalidity of the instrument upon which their jurisdiction depended or because the award cannot be connected with a valid agreement to arbitrate.

If the award does not relate to the contract to which the arbitration agreement applies, this condition is not present. This may arise where there has been substituted a new contract, to which no arbitration clause was attached, which constituted an accord and satisfaction under the proper law.[8]

1 Art 1, para 2(1) (using slightly different wording); Arbitration Act 1950 (UK), ss 37(1)(a) and 38(1)(c).

2 A. Nussbaum, (1942) 56 Harv LR 219 at p 235.

3 Russell, op cit, p 337; Private International Law Committee, op cit, p 30, which pointed out that in English law the choice of the country of arbitration is very strong evidence of an intention that the contract is to be governed by the law of that country.

4 See para 8.23 below.

5 Dicey and Morris, op cit, r 148.

6 *Offshore International SA v Banco Central SA* [1976] 2 Lloyds LR 402 at 405, per Ackner J.

7 Arbitration Act 1950 (UK), s 40: see para 7.22 above.

8 *Kianta Osakeyhtio v Britain and Overseas Trading Co* [1954] 1 Lloyd's Rep 247, CA.

(b) *The award was made by the tribunal provided for in the agreement or constituted in the manner agreed upon by the parties*[1]

7.25 The arbitration must have been carried out by the arbitral body originally designated by the parties in their arbitration agreement or in their submission. If the arbitrators were not precisely defined there, arbitrators subsequently selected by the parties must make the award, always provided that the selection was made in accordance with the processes agreed by the parties. The essence of arbitration being decision by an agreed arbitral body, an award made otherwise than by that process cannot be enforced.

1 Art 1, para 2(c); Arbitration Act 1950 (UK), s 37(1)(b), and s 38(1)(c).

(c) *The award was made in conformity with the law governing the arbitration procedure*[1]

7.26 The English text of the Convention differs from the French which makes clear that it is not the award which must conform with the law governing the arbitration procedure but the tribunal making the award.[2] The English text and the legislation treat compliance of the award with the law governing procedure as a distinct requirement. The difference is of some significance, for the English text permits an enforcing court to take account of procedural deviations by the arbitrators, whereas, under the French, only questions of the constitution of the tribunal may be considered under this head. This latter approach is consistent with the fact that separate provision is made for questions of invalidity for non-compliance with the law governing arbitral procedure, which may be raised by the debtor to challenge enforcement.[3] The legislative requirement, if not in conformity with the Convention, is nonetheless inescapable. Not surprisingly, the statute gives no guidance as to the law which should be held to govern the arbitration procedure, in particular whether the parties may select a law to prevail over the law of the place of arbitration, as the Protocol permits.[4] In *Union Nationale de Coopératives Agricoles de Céréales v Robert Catterall & Co Ltd*,[5] the English Court of Appeal gave effect to the rules adopted by the Arbitration Chamber of Copenhagen which had been selected by the parties, there being no disagreement that Danish law was the law applicable as a consequence. It may, however, be doubted that a system of rules to govern procedure may be chosen by the parties to the exclusion of any system of national law. In that case and in absence of any choice at all, the law of the place of arbitration is generally considered to be the most appropriate in this respect.[6]

Indian courts have held that this ground is not limited to statutory provisions regulating arbitration procedure but extends to relevant judicial decisions requiring compliance with the principles of natural justice as part of the law governing the proceedings. In consequence an award will not be enforced if the arbitrators do not function together or there has been a failure to give any hearing at all or the hearing has been ex parte or if the award was not made on the evidence submitted.[7]

These latter issues, which might also have been dealt with by the public policy requirements,[8] indicate how unfortunate it is that the Convention requirement was inexpertly rendered. It is by no means apparent how an applicant can *prove*, as is required,[9] that this condition is satisfied or what evidence will establish that this requirement, especially so broadly interpreted, has been met. In practice, it is probably enough to produce an award which is regular on its face, in the absence of evidence to the contrary.

1 Art 1, para 2(c); Arbitration Act 1950 (UK), s 37(1)(c) and s 38(1)(c).
2 '...la sentence ait été prononcée par le tribunal arbitral...constitué conformement a l'accord des parties et aux règles applicables à la procedure d'arbitrage'.
3 Art 3.
4 Protocol, art 2: see para 7.14 above. Arbitration Act 1950 (UK), s 37(3) makes no reference to the law governing arbitration procedure.
5 [1959] 2 QB 44, [1959] 1 All ER 721: see similarly *Mury Expo-tation v Khaitan & Sons* AIR 1956 Cal 644 at 647.
6 Russell, op cit, pp 243–244; *James Miller v Whitworth Street (Manchester) Estates* [1970] AC 583, [1970] 1 All ER 796.
7 *S Mohammed Naim v Rouraffic and Far Eastern Ltd* AIR 1960 Cal 146; *S Anonmina Lucchesse Olii E Vini Lucca v Gorakharam* AIR 1964 Mad 532 where the failures of the arbitration were found to be so fundamental that there was in reality no arbitration. Arguably, this challenge could also be made by reference to the condition in para 7.25 above.
8 Below, para 7.29.
9 Arbitration Act 1950 (UK), s 38(1)(c); para 7.23 above.

(d) *The award has become final in the country in which it was made*[1]

7.27 The Convention, in amplification of this requirement of finality, indicated two circumstances in which an award should not be considered as final: 'if it is open to *opposition, appel* or *pourvoi en cassation* (in the countries where such forms of procedure exist) or if it is proved that any proceedings for the purpose of contesting the validity of the award are pending'.[2] Clearly then, the Convention envisages that an award cannot be enforced if some further legal process has been initiated to examine the validity of the award or where there is still the possibility of challenge by some formal procedure. This gives a different connotation from that entailed in the common law term 'final and conclusive' in respect of judgments.[3] It is possible that this provision was intended to provide a definition for the purpose of the Convention.[4]

The implementing legislation, whilst restating the essentials of the requirement, does not contain the explanatory provisions. Instead, it states that:

> 'an award shall not be deemed final if any proceedings for the purpose of contesting the validity of the award are pending in the country in which it is made.'[5]

The English Court of Appeal has insisted that this must not be used as a definition of finality, although the marginal note implies otherwise, nor indeed as indicating that an award will necessarily be final if no such proceedings are pending.[6] Rather, it was suggested the term 'final' should be given the meaning attached at common law to the phrase 'final and conclusive'. Whether an award has become final must be established by reference to the law of the country where the award was made, but that law would be utilised to show whether the award was final in the common law sense used by the legislation. This, in the view of the English Court of Appeal, means that the disputed matter has been determined as between the parties according to their bargain, notwithstanding that an appeal or further legal process may be brought or is pending. In the latter instance, however, for the purposes of the enforcement legislation, the award shall not be *deemed* to be final.[7] In the instant case, the fact that, under the law of the place where the award was made, a requirement that a local judgment must be obtained before the award could become enforceable there did not prevent the award becoming final.[8]

Dicey and Morris must be correct in their comment that the English approach does not accord with the Convention and that section 39, instead of reflecting the explanation given by the Convention, has been given a construction which finds no correspondence in the Convention.[9]

The English Court of Appeal has suggested that in practice if there is no challenge to the award, there will be little difficulty in persuading the enforcing court that the award should be treated as final.[10] But this was not the aim of the Convention. On the other hand, it must be noted that the Convention, by imposing the burden of establishing finality and producing the necessary evidence of it upon the applicant, creates an intolerable burden on those occasions where the losing party takes every legal opportunity open to him to contest the validity of the award, especially in systems in which generous time limits for initiating proceedings to set aside the award are allowed.[11]

1 Art 1, para 2(d); Arbitration Act 1950 (UK), s 37(1)(d) and s 38(1)(b).
2 Art 1, para 2(d).
3 See para 3.16 above.
4 Cf art 4(2) which refers to 'final in the sense defined in Article 1(d)'. *Colt Industries Inc v Sarlie (No 2)* [1966] 3 All ER 85, [1966] 1 WLR 1287.
5 Arbitration Act 1950 (UK), s 39.
6 *Union Nationale de Coopératives Agricoles de Céréales v Robert Catterall & Co Ltd* [1959] 2 QB 44 at 51, per Lord Evershed MR.
7 Ibid.
8 Similarly, *Se Se Oil v Gorakhram Gokalchand* (1962) 64 Bom LR 113 but orse, *Badat & Co v East India Trading Co* AIR 1964 SC 538 (not a case upon the Geneva Convention).
9 Op cit, p 1145.
10 *Union Nationale de Coopératives Agricoles de Céréales v Robert Catterall & Co Ltd*, above, at 51. Cf *Se Se Oil v Gorakhram Gokalchand*, above, similarly in cases where the time for setting aside is long past.
11 Private International Law Committee, op cit, p 6.

(e) *The award was made in respect of a matter which may lawfully be referred to arbitration under the law of the enforcing jurisdiction*[1]

7.28 Although using slightly different language, the terms of the Convention and the implementing legislation appear to have no difference in effect. The purpose is clear—to ensure that the enforcing state will only enforce awards on matters which could be arbitrated there under its domestic law.[2] There is much in the view that this requirement is of little practical value. Insofar as it prevents conflicts with the public policy of the enforcing state, it is repetitive of other provisions of the Convention.[3] Insofar as it introduces other considerations of a domestic nature, it can be said to be dealing with issues which have little relevance to the enforcement of foreign awards.[4] Nonetheless, if this condition is not met by the applicant, the court may not enforce the award under the terms of the Geneva scheme.[5]

1 Art 1, para 2(b); Arbitration Act 1950 (UK), s 37(1)(e).
2 The statute in referring to matters to be referred to arbitration used a formulation used elsewhere in the Arbitration legislation, see Russell, op cit, ch 3, for these matters under English law.
3 See para 7.29 below.
4 J. D. M. Lew, (1976) 10 International Lawyer 425 at p 432.
5 The matter is dealt with differently under the New York Convention, see para 8.36 below.

(f) *Enforcement of the award must not be contrary to the public policy or the law of the enforcing state*[1]

7.29 The inclusion of the reference to public policy is consistent with the usual practice in schemes of this kind. In the absence of any reference to other safeguards such as those relating to fraud, it appears that a broad construction of the term may have been intended. In its other respects the condition is unusual, especially as the terms of the Convention, particularly in the French version, and those of the implementing statute do not exactly match. For the statute refers to 'the law' of the enforcing state whilst the Convention speaks of 'the principles of the law' and more distinctively in the French text 'principes du droit public'. It seems probable that the purpose of the Convention in this respect was to allow enforcement to be refused where it would conflict with basic prohibitions imposed in the law of the enforcing state to protect state interests.[2] Such an interpretation gives the phrase the characteristics of the public policy safeguard. It can be doubted that it was ever intended to give the enforcing court a virtual power to retry the dispute for determination whether the same result as that of the award would have resulted, for example, under the local commercial laws.

The English language version may have led some courts in this latter direction.[3] Thus certain Indian decisions, for example, appear to have held, in effect, that an award should not be enforced if it gave rise to effects which would be illegal under the law governing contracts.[4] The better view, it is suggested is that the provision should be concerned solely with legal rules of a mandatory nature which are directed towards the question of the effects of the enforcement, rather than the content, of the award.[5] The purpose is to preclude the plaintiff from taking steps in reliance upon his award which are prohibited by the lex fori. Thus prohibition of enforcement which would lead to a breach of local revenue or exchange control regulations or of import or export laws appears to be the kind of case intended. Again, enforcement against an entity which enjoys sovereign immunity under the lex fori seems to be covered. This seems to be the position taken by the Scottish High Court.[6]

Insofar as the public policy provision is concerned, it is probable that a broad construction must be given to this to cover circumstances which in common law are usually separately designated. There is little doubt, for example, that an award obtained by fraud or as a result of evidence acquired by blackmail, extortion or deceit could be refused enforcement. It is probable, however, that a common law court would permit such considerations to be invoked only if they were unknown to the party relying upon them at the time of arbitration and not raised then by him.[7] Similarly, it would be appropriate under this head to challenge enforcement on the grounds of a fundamental breach of the duty to act fairly by the arbitrators, as for example in failing to allow one of the parties to present his case, taking evidence in the absence of a party, or demonstrating bias in favour of one of the parties. It should, however, be pointed out that most systems of law make provision for the award to be set aside in the place in which it was made on grounds such as these. It may have been the intention of the Convention that such matters should be so challenged and until the opportunity for challenge had been exhausted the award was not to be final.[8] The construction given to 'finality' in the legislation makes it probable that issues of this kind would be raised when enforcement was sought.

It is probably under this head that a court may refuse to enforce an award which requires enforcement of some foreign revenue law (should such a case arise) or which requires effect to be given to an agreement which infringes some basic moral principle of the forum. It has also been suggested that it extends to cases where the enforcement could give effect to a contract which would be illegal under the lex fori.[9] It is probable that such cases are better embraced within the condition which requires the matter of the award to be such as can lawfully be referred to arbitration under the lex fori.[10]

1 Art 1, para 2(e); Arbitration Act 1950 (UK), s 37(1).
2 Cf Dicey and Morris, op cit, p 1146.
3 Private International Law Committee, op cit, p 7.
4 *Shiva Jute Baling Ltd v Hindley & Co Ltd* AIR 1959 SC 1357 (but the award in question was not held to be illegal); *S Anonmina Lucchesse Olii E Vini Lucca v Gorakharam* AIR 1964 Mad 532 (where the issue was not fully distinguished from the public policy objection). It does not extend to the laws of limitation in the lex fori: *Mury Exploitation v Khaitan & Sons* AIR 1956 Cal 644.
5 Dicey and Morris, op cit p 1146.
6 *Masinimport v Scottish Mechanical Light Industries Ltd* 1976 SC 102.
7 Ibid, at 109, per Lord Keith.
8 Para 7.27 above.
9 *S Anonmina Lucchesse Olii E Vini Lucca v Gorakharam*, above.
10 Para 7.28 above.

Proceedings in respect of enforceable awards

7.30 It is common for the implementing statutes to provide for the mechanism of enforcement of those foreign awards which satisfy the conditions of enforceability described earlier. Although there is a Convention obligation to provide rules of enforcement, these need not be those utilised for domestic awards. Nonetheless the United Kingdom statute is representative in providing, as for domestic awards, that the method of enforcement may be either by a common law action or, by leave of the High Court or a judge thereof, in the same manner as a judgment or order to the same effect, in which case, the judgment may be entered in terms of the award.[1] The latter course may not always be necessary since, once leave is given, the award can be enforced by the ordinary means of execution.[2] In English practice, the courts may insist upon an action, rather than summary enforcement, if there are real grounds for doubting the validity of the award or presumably the fulfilment of the criteria under the conditions described.[3]

Summary enforcement is no longer confined to 'reasonably clear cases' as once was thought to be the case,[4] but it will presumably be less easy to satisfy the requirements in respect of a foreign award. Certainly the summary procedure will not be permitted if the judgment which is entered will not be to the same effect as the award, for example, where the award requires payment in a particular country abroad.[5] On the other hand, unless the lex fori prohibits, the court may order entry of the judgment for payment in a foreign currency in which the award was made or by conversion into local currency at the rate prevailing at the date of the award.[6] For the order will be to the 'same effect' as the award. Entry of the summary judgment does not render a foreign award into a local award, although it is enforceable as such. Thus an Indian court has held that the limitation statute does not apply to the filing of a foreign award in the court in accordance with the Indian legislation.[7] Under English practice, however, the processes to enforce a foreign award must be initiated within six years of the accrual of the cause of action. This has been held to occur when the defendant fails to fulfil the implied term in his agreement to honour the award.[8]

A foreign award which is enforceable under this scheme is to be treated as binding for all purposes on the persons between whom it was made. The courts must, therefore, recognise it when relied upon by way of defence, set off or other local legal proceedings.[9] What needs to be stressed is that in this case, as with enforcement, the conditions of enforceability have to be established by the person relying upon the award.

1 Arbitration Act 1950 (UK), s 36(1), applying s 26 in the latter respect. See generally, Russell, op cit, ch 20, in respect of particular procedural requirements.
2 Entry as a judgment (which was introduced by the Arbitration Act 1934 (UK), s 10) would be needed in order, for example, to issue a bankruptcy notice: *Re A Bankruptcy Notice* [1907] 1 KB 478, 76 LJKB 171. Report of Committee on the Law of Arbitration, 1927, Cmd 2817, para 17.
3 *Middlemiss and Gould v Hartlepool Corpn* [1972] 1 WLR 1643 at 1647, CA.
4 *Union Nationale de Coopératives Agricoles de Céréales v Robert Catterall & Co Ltd* [1959] 1 All ER 721 at 725, per Scrutton LJ.
5 *Dalmia Cement v National Bank of Pakistan* [1975] QB 9, [1974] 3 All ER 189.
6 *Jugoslavenska Oceanska Providba v Castle Investment Co Inc* [1974] QB 292.
7 *Francesco Corsi v Gorakhram Gokalchand* AIR 1960 Bom 91.
8 *Agromet Motoimport v Maulden Engineering Company (Beds) Ltd* (1984) Times, 17 April, applying the Limitation Act 1980, s 7.
9 Arbitration Act 1950 (UK), s 36(2).

VI GROUNDS OF OBJECTION

7.31 Once the conditions of enforceability are established by the applicant, the requested court is expected to recognise and enforce the award. There are available, however, under the Convention, five grounds upon which the award-debtor may object to enforcement. The first four of these are stated by the Convention to be mandatory grounds for refusal of recognition:[1] the fifth is stated to rest in the requested court's discretion.[2] The implementing legislation follows this pattern. Although neither Convention nor statutes so state, it is evident that the onus for raising these issues lies with the person resisting enforcement or recognition who must satisfy the court that the objection is proved.

1 Paras 7.32–7.35 below.
2 Para 7.36 below.

Objection 1: The award has been annulled in the country in which it was made[1]

7.32 The Convention assumed that proceedings for enforcement of an award would not normally be permitted if the possibility of a challenge to the validity of the award was still open. Not only would the award not be final[2] but the court could be asked to adjourn the proceedings to allow such a challenge to be mounted.[3] The legislation achieves a similar effect by providing that an award is not deemed final if proceedings to challenge the award in the place where it was made are pending.[4] Where such proceedings have been successfully completed, the basis of the enforcement action has been removed and enforcement must be refused.

It should be noted that this ground applies only in respect of proceedings in the country where the award was made. Invalidation by a court assuming jurisdiction on the basis that the arbitration agreement or the arbitration itself was governed by the law of that jurisdiction is not caught under this provision.[5]

The grounds upon which the award was invalidated are determined by the competent authority in, and by the law of, the country where the award was made (including where relevant its conflict of laws rules). The enforcing court may, it is suggested, only concern itself with the question of whether a finding of invalidity has been made by the tribunal competent under the law of the country of the award.

1 Art 2(a); Arbitration Act 1950 (UK), s 37(2)(a).
2 Para 7.27 above.
3 Para 7.36 below. The court is also empowered merely to refuse to enforce the award.
4 Arbitration Act 1950 (UK), s 39: para 7.27 above.
5 See para 7.36 below.

Objection 2: The party against whom it is sought to enforce the award was not given notice of the arbitration proceedings in sufficient time to enable him to present his case or was under some legal incapacity and was not properly represented[1]

7.33 This objection relates to certain features of the rules of natural justice. They clearly do not exhaust all the objections which might be made on the basis of procedural fairness. For example, the ground does not extend to circumstances in which a party, though given notice, was denied an opportunity to present his case. Challenge on other such grounds must be made by reference to failure to respect the law governing the arbitration procedure,[2] to the public policy ground[3] or under the discretion head.[4] There are scarcely any indications from case law on the legislation of the judicial approach to these matters.[5]

In relation to the matter of notice, the terminology used is close to that found in the 1933 judgments scheme. It may be expected, therefore, that an approach consistent with that used under that scheme will be followed.[6]

Questions of incapacity of the objecting party will be determined in relation to the time of commencement of the arbitration and by reference to the law governing the arbitration. Whether a party was properly represented seems to be a question of fact, although it will be necessary for the enforcing court to abide by any restrictions upon representation of those under incapacity imposed by the law governing the arbitration. Where the law denies any representation, the issue becomes one for the public policy of the enforcing state. The ground does not concern itself with questions of representation generally.

1 Art 2(b); Arbitration Act 1950 (UK), s 37(2)(b).
2 Para 7.26 above.
3 Para 7.29 above.
4 Para 7.36 below.
5 *S Anonmina Lucchesse Olii E Vini Lucca v Gorakharam Gokalchand* AIR 1964 Mad 532, holding that defects in the process of giving notice of the proceedings rendered the award unenforceable. It is not clear that the court was relying upon this ground.
6 FJREA, s 4(1)(a)(iii), discussed at para 3.54 above.

Objection 3: The award does not deal with all the questions referred[1]

7.34 It is probable that this legislative provision is narrower than that intended by the Convention. For the latter speaks of 'differences contemplated by or falling within the terms of the submission to arbitration', the latter term, in the French text, clearly referring to both the original arbitration agreement and the particular submission.[2] It seems very probable that the Convention was designed to prevent the enforcement of an award where the dispute decided was not one envisaged by the original agreement or was not that which was referred to the arbitrators. The statute has a rather different emphasis because it appears to be concerned merely to ensure that the arbitrators have dealt with all the issues referred to them. That particular matter is the subject of a separate provision in the Convention, under which the enforcing tribunal is given a discretion to deal with such cases either by postponing recognition or enforcement or granting it subject to receiving such guarantees as the tribunal sees fit.[3] The legislation, however, relates this power specifically to this ground of objection, so that the court's discretion arises whenever the objection is fulfilled.

The effect of the legislation, therefore, is that the enforcing court may concern itself solely with the question of whether all the matters which were referred to the arbitrators have been dealt with in the award. In such a case, the court may postpone the enforcement until the matters are subject to a further award on the outstanding matters or permit enforcement where the terms of the award are unlikely to be affected by any subsequent supplementary award, but if necessary requiring security to be given by the applicant against the outcome of further proceedings.

This makes nonsense of the Convention provision which was surely intended to contain grounds for refusing enforcement altogether. It leaves the important contention that the award did not deal with a matter covered by the agreement or did not resolve the issue actually referred to the arbitrator unprovided for by explicit provision. It is necessary to bring these within other provisions designed for other cases.[4]

1 Art 2(c); Arbitration Act 1950 (UK), s 37(2)(c).
2 '...le différend visé dans le compromis ou rentrant dans les prévisions de la clause compromissoire'.
3 Art 2, 2nd para. The French text again makes this clear.
4 Para 7.24 above and 7.35 below. *Kianta Osakeyhtio v Britain and Overseas Trading Co Ltd* [1953] 2 Lloyds Rep 569 at 573, per Devlin J.

Objection 4: The award contains decisions on matters beyond the scope of the agreement for arbitration[1]

7.35 The French text of the Convention makes clear that this was intended to cover cases of excess of authority by the arbitrators both in respect of the original arbitration agreement and the actual submission. It is not totally clear that the legislation permits this construction in respect of the term 'agreement for arbitration'. But it may be submitted that the term should carry this broader meaning.[2]

Accordingly, the courts must refuse enforcement of an award which contains decisions on matters in dealing with which the arbitrators have gone beyond the jurisdiction as defined by the original agreement and the reference. Thus where they deal with a dispute which arises out of a different agreement from that upon which their jurisdiction rests, the ensuing award cannot be enforced.[3] Cases in which the arbitrators, whilst acting on matters within their jurisdiction, have rendered a decision on matters outside their prescribed area of competence will also be covered by this ground.[4] There is no power to sever any parts of an award to permit the remainder to be enforced.

1 Art 2(c); Arbitration Act 1950 (UK), s 37(2)(c).
2 Ibid, s 32 defines 'arbitration agreement' in this way for the purposes of the other Parts of the Consolidating Arbitration Act.
3 *Kianta Osakeyhtio v Britain and Overseas Trading Co Ltd* [1954] 1 Lloyd's Rep 247, CA.
4 Ibid, [1953] 2 Lloyd's Rep 569 at 573, per Devlin J; [1954] 1 Lloyds Rep 247 at 251, per Somervell LJ. The outcome may be different if under the law governing the arbitration the arbitrators have power to decide disputes as to their jurisdiction.

Objection 5: Invalidity of the award[1]

7.36 The Convention permits a party resisting enforcement to prove that there is some ground upon which he is entitled to contest the validity of the award in a court of law. The ground does not deal with matters already covered by particular provisions of the Convention. The enforcing court may either refuse enforcement or adjourn it allowing a reasonable time for the award to be annulled by the competent tribunal. The grounds which may be alleged are not prescribed but they must be ones prescribed by the law governing the arbitration procedure.[2]

The provision identifies six grounds relating to invalidity which cannot be subjected to this discretionary power. These are the invalidity of the original agreement,[3] an incorrect tribunal or improperly constituted tribunal,[4] non-conformity with the law governing arbitration procedure,[5] insufficient notice or representation,[6] failure to deal with all referred questions[7] and decisions in excess of the agreement.[8]

The implementing legislation generally follows the Convention, but does not include any reference to the law under which the invalidity may be claimed to exist. As the English text of the Convention is invariably annexed to the statute, it would be open to a court to refer to that text for the purpose of construing the section and apply the law governing the arbitration procedure. On the other hand, it seems probable that the enforcing court may wish to permit a party to challenge an award in the country where it was made on the grounds that it was invalid under the law of that country, although it was not necessarily invalid under the law chosen by the parties to govern the arbitration. Where the law governing the arbitration happens to be the law of the enforcing state, it would be open to the enforcing court to decide the issue and, if the ground of invalidity were established, to refuse enforcement without allowing reference to another court.

The effects of this provision are potentially damaging to the Convention's operation. For it enables a debtor to raise allegations concerning the validity of the award as a stalling device. If there is any apparent basis for the claim, the enforcing court will be unlikely to order enforcement. It is unlikely that the proof required by the section can be more than a prima facie case. As time limits for proceedings to challenge awards are in some jurisdictions very generous, the adjournment of the enforcement provides scope for extensive obstructive tactics by a defendant.[9]

1 Art 3; Arbitration Act 1950 (UK), s 37(3).
2 In the French text, 'd'après les règles de droit applicables à la procedure d'arbitrage'. The law is not identified by the Convention: see para 7.26 above.
3 Arbitration Act 1950, s 37(1)(a): para 7.24 above.
4 Ibid, s 37(1)(b): para 7.25 above.
5 Ibid, s 37(1)(c): para 7.26 above.
6 Ibid, s 37(2)(b): para 7.33 above.
7 Ibid, para 7.34 above.
8 Ibid, para 7.35 above.
9 Private International Law Committee, op cit, pp 14 and 33.

VII RELATIONSHIP WITH OTHER SCHEMES

7.38 It is commonly provided that the Geneva scheme for enforcement of awards is not to prejudice the rights of persons seeking to enforce their awards by other means.[1] Accordingly, actions upon the foreign award at common law[2] and proceedings for leave to enforce under the summary enforcement provisions[3] and, where applicable, under the judgments schemes[4] are available alternatives. Although there are few reported decisions on these matters and the conditions which must be fulfilled are not completely certain, there is a case for saying that few of the peculiar features of the Geneva legislation are mirrored in common law practice. It seems probable that in the absence of any obligation to proceed under the Geneva provisions, the common law mechanisms may be more attractive. If the award has become the subject of a judgment in the country in which it was made, it can be enforced as a foreign judgment by action at common law[5] or under the Commonwealth schemes if applicable.[6] Indeed, it is arguable that the award may be treated as having merged into the foreign judgment and only the latter may be enforced.[7]

Where the award has become enforceable in the same manner as a judgment in the place where it was made, it might appear that it can only be enforced by registration in any jurisdiction where the 1933 scheme requirements would be met.[8] This is probably an oversight, as awards were included in the 1933 Act as an afterthought. Any restrictions upon the availability of the Convention should be resisted.[9] Indeed, the choice of alternatives is now allowed in the United Kingdom as a result of recent amendment.[10]

Where the award would be both a foreign award under the Geneva Scheme and a Convention award under the New York scheme, proceedings may be brought only under the latter.[11]

1 Arbitration Act 1950 (UK), s 40(a).
2 *Norske Atlas Insurance Co Ltd v London General Insurance Co* (1927) 28 LL L Rep 104; *Bremer Oeltransport GmbH v Drewry* [1933] 1 KB 753; Dicey and Morris, op cit, pp 1125 ff.
3 *Dalmia Cement Ltd v National Bank of Pakistan* [1975] QB 9, [1974] 3 All ER 189; Dicey and Morris, op cit, pp 1131–1132.
4 Chapter 6 above.
5 *East India Trading Co Inc v Carmel Exporters and Importers Ltd* [1952] 2 QB 439, [1952] 1 All ER 1053; *International Alltex Corpn v Lawler Creations Ltd* [1965] IR 264. As to whether the award can be enforced by suing on the original cause of action, see para 8.38, below, in relation to the New York scheme where similar considerations apply.
6 Para 6.32 above.
7 Ibid, for a fuller discussion see para 7.22, note 8 above.
8 FJREA, s 6.
9 See discussion at para 6.32 above and 8.38 below.
10 Civil Jurisdiction and Judgments Act 1982, Sch 10, inserting FJREA, s 10A.
11 Para 8.38 below.

ANNEX I

Geneva Protocol and Convention

List of Parties

Principal Source: Multilateral Treaties Deposited with the Secretary-General, Status as at 31 December, 1982. ST/LEG/SER.E/2.

†Albania (Protocol only)
Austria
†**Bahamas* (1979)
†*Bangladesh* (1979)
Belgium
†Brazil (Protocol only)
Czechoslovakia
Denmark
[Estonia]
Finland
France
Federal Republic of Germany
German Democratic Republic
Greece
†§*Grenada*
†Iraq (Protocol only)
Ireland
Israel
Italy
Japan
†§*Kenya*
†Luxembourg
†**Malta* (1966)
†**Mauritius* (1969)
Monaco (Protocol only)
Netherlands and certain dependencies
New Zealand and *Western Samoa* (1926, 1929)
Norway (Protocol only)
Poland (Protocol only)
†Portugal
Romania
Spain
Sweden
Switzerland
§*Tanzania*
Thailand
Uganda (1965) (signed only)
United Kingdom (1924, 1930) and certain dependencies
Yugoslavia

Commonwealth States in italics, with date of adhesion.
*By succession, notified to UN.
§By succession (see para 7.05 above).
†Not parties to the New York Convention.

Present dependencies in Commonwealth in respect of which Protocol and Convention may apply

United Kingdom: Alderney[1]
Anguilla[2]
British Virgin Islands[2]
Cayman Islands[2]
Falkland Islands
Guernsey[1]
Gibraltar
Hong Kong
Isle of Man[1]
Jersey[1]
Montserrat
St Helena (Protocol only)[2]
Turks and Caicos Islands[2]

New Zealand: Cook Islands
Niue
Tokelau (Protocol only)[2]

1 No declarations extant; but legislation in force.
2 No local legislation allowing Geneva scheme to be invoked in these territories.

ANNEX II

Commonwealth Legislation

ALDERNEY:	Arbitration (Alderney) Law 1983, No XIII.
ANTIGUA:	Arbitration Act 1975, No 12, s 5(2) and Part IX.
BAHAMAS:	Arbitration Clauses (Protocol) Act, Revised Laws, 1965, Cap 178. Arbitration (Foreign Awards) Act, ibid, Cap 179.
BANGLADESH:	Arbitration (Protocol and Convention) Act 1937, No 6 (of India).
BELIZE:	Arbitration Ordinance, Revised Laws, 1958, Cap 13, Part II.
DOMINICA:	Arbitration (Foreign Awards) Ordinance, Revised Laws, 1961, Cap 3.
FALKLAND ISLANDS:	Arbitration (Foreign Awards) Ordinance, Revised Laws, 1950, Cap 5.
GIBRALTAR:	Arbitration Ordinance, Revised Laws, 1964, Cap 6, Part III (to be repealed, see Act 1983, No 12).
GUERNSEY:	Arbitration (Guernsey) Law 1982, Part II.
GRENADA:	Arbitration (Foreign Awards) Ordinance, Revised Laws, 1958, Cap 21.
GUYANA:	Arbitration Act, Cap 7.03, Revised Laws, 1973, Part II and Part III.
HONG KONG:	Arbitration Ordinance, Cap 341, Revised Laws, 1982, Part III.
ISLE OF MAN:	Arbitration Act 1976, c 24, Part II.
INDIA:	Arbitration (Protocol and Convention) Act 1937, No 6.
JAMAICA:	Arbitration Clauses (Protocol) Act, Revised Laws, 1973. Arbitration (Foreign Awards) Act, ibid.
JERSEY:	Loi (1926) rendant applicable . . . Arbitration Clauses (Protocol) Act 1924. Loi (1931) rendant applicable . . . Arbitration (Foreign Awards) Act 1930.
KENYA:	Arbitration Act, Cap 49, Revised Laws, 1962, s 6(2) and Part III.
MALAŴI:	Arbitration Act, Cap 6:03, Revised Laws, 1968, s 6(2) and Part III.
MALTA:	Arbitration Clauses (Protocol) Ordinance, Revised Laws, 1942, Cap 126. Arbitration (Foreign Awards) Ordinance, ibid, Cap 127.

MAURITIUS:	Arbitration Clauses (Protocol) Ordinance, Revised Laws, 1945, Cap 164. Arbitration (Foreign Awards) Ordinance, ibid, Cap 165.
MONTSERRAT:	Arbitration (Foreign Awards) Act, Revised Laws, 1961, Cap 7.
NEWFOUNDLAND:	Arbitration (Foreign Awards) Act 1931, 22 Geo V, C 2.
NEW ZEALAND:	Arbitration Clauses (Protocol) and the Arbitration (Foreign Awards) Act 1933, No 4.
ST LUCIA:	Arbitration (Foreign Awards) Ordinance, Revised Laws, 1957, Cap 15. Arbitration Clauses (Protocol) Ordinance, ibid, Cap 16.
ST VINCENT:	Arbitration Clauses (Foreign Awards) Act 1931, No 15. Arbitration Clauses (Protocol) Act 1932, No 25.
TANZANIA:	Arbitration Ordinance, Revised Laws, Cap 15, Supp 66–74, Parts II and IV.
UGANDA:	Arbitration Act, Revised Laws, 1964, Cap 55, Parts II and III.
UNITED KINGDOM:	Arbitration Act 1950, s 4(2) and Part II.
WESTERN SAMOA:	Arbitration Act 1976, No 9, Part II: see para 7.09, note 2 above.
ZAMBIA:	Arbitration Act, Revised Laws, 1972, Cap 180, Parts III and IV.

CHAPTER 8

The New York Scheme

I APPLICATION OF THE SCHEME

Background

8.01 The New York Convention on the Recognition and Enforcement of Foreign Arbitral Awards is intended to replace the Geneva scheme, though preserving its main features, and at the same time to remove some of the shortcomings of the earlier scheme, particularly in respect of the enforcement of arbitral awards.[1] The UNCITRAL Report to the UN Secretary General in 1979 on the working of the Convention concluded that the Convention 'has satisfactorily met the general purpose for which it was adopted'.[2]

As with its predecessor, the aims of the Convention were two fold, first to oblige contracting states to recognise arbitration agreements and to ensure that parties stand by their agreement to arbitrate and secondly to provide a scheme for the recognition and enforcement of resultant arbitral awards to which contracting states are required to give effect.

1 For the background see paras 5.11 to 5.18 above: Private International Law Committee, 5th Report, (1961), Cmnd 1515; G. Gaja *International Commercial Arbitration: New York Convention* (1980).

2 A/CN.9/168 in *Yearbook of UN Commission on International Trade Law* 1979, vol X, 100–108 at p 108. Certain shortcomings were, however, identified.

Application in the Commonwealth

8.02 The changed nature of the Commonwealth since World War II has eliminated the possibility of many of the constitutional and succession issues which now beset the continued application of the Geneva scheme. Provision is made in the Convention for states to become contracting parties by signature and ratification (prior to 31 December 1958) or accession, provided only that they are a member of the United Nations or any of its specialised agencies or party to the Statute of the International Court of Justice or otherwise if invited by the General Assembly.[1] All the independent members of the Commonwealth are eligible and to date eleven of these have availed themselves of their right.[2] In addition, any state may declare that the Convention is to extend to all or any of the territories for the international relations of which it is responsible.[3] Such declarations have been made by Australia and the United Kingdom in respect of a number of such territories.[4] In only one instance has such a declaration been made with respect to a territory which has subsequently become independent. That state, Belize, has notified that it will continue to be bound, provisionally and on the basis of reciprocity, by multilateral treaties entered into by the United Kingdom on its behalf. Full succession will be decided upon, in this case, during the course of the post-independence review of treaty commitments.

The Convention does not contemplate the possibility of its operation between a metropolitan state and any of its territories or between those territories. The contracting party is solely under an obligation to ensure that the Convention is given effect vis-à-vis other contracting parties in the territories named in the declarations. The New York Convention, therefore, remains in its formative stage as a scheme for the enforcement of awards within the Commonwealth. Without the stimulus of the United Kingdom with its developed interest in arbitration, the scheme has but slowly attracted the interest of the Commonwealth states. It should be noted, however, that in many such jurisdictions commercial arbitrations are relatively uncommon and the adhesion of those jurisdictions to the scheme is unlikely to provide significant or obvious immediate benefits for their commercial sector.

1 Arts VIII and IX.
2 See Annex I below.
3 Art X. Art XI sets down particular obligations where the contracting state is a federal or non-unitary state.
4 See Annex II below. Malaysia, though not a party, permits certain types of arbitration awards (those under the Convention on the Settlement of Investment Disputes (1965), under UNCITRAL Arbitration Rules or the Kuala Lumpur Regional Centre for Arbitration Rules) to be enforced in accordance with the Convention in Malaysia: Act 1980, No A478.

Commonwealth legislation giving effect to the Convention

8.03 Legislation giving effect to the Convention has been enacted in most but not all of the Commonwealth states which are parties to the Convention and in or in respect of the dependent territories declared to be within the scheme. It has also been enacted in certain jurisdictions not yet within the scheme. Presumably, if all the statutory provisions can be fulfilled, such legislation may nonetheless be invoked in those jurisidictions. In four cases, Nigeria,[1] Sri Lanka, Trinidad and Tobago and Tanzania, there appears to be no legislation to give effect to the Convention, although the states have completed the international steps to become parties.[2]

The legislation usually makes detailed provisions for the local requirements, in terms usually close to those of the Convention. For this reason, the Commonwealth legislation exhibits many similarities in content and, through similar legislative drafting practices, in style. Unlike the Geneva legislation, however, there is no one model predominating amongst these contracting states.[3] Cyprus merely ratified the Convention itself, the exact terms of which are self-executing and which the Cyprus courts are required to apply. Botswana and Ghana, in a little more detail, give the central provisions of the Convention force of law in their countries.[4]

The majority of statutes make some provision for the government to issue a legislative instrument identifying the contracting states. In the case of Ghana and India, these lists are the sole source of this information. This puts a serious onus upon the states to keep such lists up to date, which does not appear always to be the case.[5] In the United Kingdom model and the New Zealand statute, however, the Orders-in-Council[6] are stated to be conclusive evidence of the fact that a state is a contracting party.[7] The implication in the former legislation is that other evidence may be adduced to prove the fact.[8] This is expressly provided for in New Zealand, where the proof may be provided through a certificate from the Foreign Affairs Ministry.[9] A similar mechanism is used in Australia.[10] This appears to preclude the need to show a fully up-to-date list in any proceedings.

In none of these arrangements is there any requirement before listing or certifying a state to show the existence of reciprocal arrangements to give effect to the Convention in favour of the legislating state. The New Zealand Act, however, does permit the issue of an Order-in-Council rendering unenforceable any Convention awards from a particular country which offer substantially less favourable treatment to awards made in New Zealand arbitrations.[11] Botswana prohibits enforcement of awards there if a 'similar award made in Botswana' is not enforceable in the other contracting state.[12] This provision, which would be implemented by the Botswana court asked to enforce the Convention award, could be used in relation to awards from contracting states without reciprocal arrangements. Given that certain contracting states have not enacted what appears to be necessary domestic legislation, the protection afforded by the New Zealand provision is attractive.

1 On Nigeria, see I. Achebe, (1974) 8 J World Trade Law 420 *Murmansk State Steamship Line v Kano Oil Millers Ltd* 1974 (1) ALR Comm 1 held that in the absence of local legislation effect could not be given to the Convention in Nigeria.
2 See Annex III below for legislation in force. Note New South Wales: Act 1973, No 36; Queensland: Act 1973, No 34 (Part VIII); Tasmania: Act 1972, No 59 have been displaced by the Commonwealth: Act 1974, No 136, s 12.
3 The Arbitration Act 1975 (UK) provides the model for all dependent jurisdictions of the United Kingdom.
4 Convention on the Recognition and Enforcement of Foreign Arbitral Awards (Ratification) Law, 1979, No 84 (Cyprus); Recognition and Enforcement of Foreign Arbitral Awards Act, cap 06:2 (Botswana); Arbitration Act 1961, No 38, Part III (Ghana).
5 Ghana allows the legislation to be applied to non-Convention states on the basis of reciprocity: ibid, s 36(2). Cf, Foreign Awards (Recognition and Enforcement) Act 1961, No 45 (India), s 2(b).
6 The Orders-in-Council made by Her Majesty are effective in the territories, usually after a local notice has been officially published stating that fact.
7 Arbitration Act 1975 (UK), s 7(3); Arbitration (Foreign Agreements and Awards) Act 1982, No 21 (NZ), s 12(1).
8 *Kuwait State Government v Sir Frederick Snow & Partners* [1981] 1 Lloyd's Rep 656 at 666 per Mocatta J (revsd on other grounds: [1984] 1 All ER 733, [1984] 2 WLR 340, HL).
9 Act 1982, No 21.
10 Arbitration (Foreign Awards and Agreements) Act 1974, No 136, s 10(1).
11 Act 1982, No 21, s 13.
12 Cap 06:2, s 3(3).

II ARBITRATION AGREEMENTS WITHIN THE SCHEME

Agreements to which the Convention applies

8.04 In dealing with arbitration agreements, the Convention is concerned in the main with the circumstances in which recognition must be given to them, particularly for the purpose of preventing legal proceedings where arbitration was accepted by the agreement.[1] Unlike the Geneva scheme,[2] it is not made absolutely clear whether the types of agreements contemplated by these provisions are meant to be linked with the types of award which are enforceable in the later parts of the Convention. This, however, appears to have been the intention, for the applicant seeking to enforce an award is required to supply 'the original agreement referred to in Article II'.[3] In the Commonwealth legislation, Botswana and Cyprus by following the terms of the Convention achieve the same effect. The Australian, Indian and New Zealand statutes define arbitration agreements by reference to the terms of the Convention.[4] Ghana[5] and the United Kingdom,[6] whilst adopting the language of the Convention in its essentials, do not overtly connect the agreements which must be recognised with the awards which must be enforced.

Indeed, it does not necessarily follow that the award which ensues from an arbitration in favour of which legal proceedings have been stayed under the scheme will be of a kind which is enforceable under the Convention.[7] Moreover, the duty to stay proceedings may not arise under some of the legislation even though the award from the arbitration would be of the kind which is enforceable under the scheme. For as we shall see,[8] conditions additional to those in the Convention have been introduced in certain states which must be fulfilled before a duty to stay arises.

It follows, therefore, that different considerations may be relevant to determine the agreements which are within the scheme dependent upon whether the issue is related to the staying of legal proceedings[9] or to the enforcement of the award. There is, however, a common core of requirements which are present in both instances and these will be described in the following paragraph.

1 Art II.
2 Para 7.11 above.
3 Art IV.1(b): see also art V.1(a).
4 Act 1974, No 136, s 3(1) and s 8(5) (Australia); Act 1961, No 45, s 2 (India); Act 1982, No 21, s 2 (NZ).
5 Act 1961, No 38, s 5 and s 36.
6 Act 1975, s 7(1).
7 Para 8.05 below.
8 Para 8.06 below.
9 Other legislation may exclude certain types of agreement from the power to stay: eg Merchant Shipping (Liner Conferences) Act 1982 (UK), s 7 which makes similar provisions of its own.

Essentials of agreements within the scheme

8.05 Article II of the Convention imposes upon contracting parties the obligation to recognise any agreement in writing under which the parties undertake to submit to arbitration:

> 'all or any differences which have arisen or which may arise between them in respect of a defined legal relationship, whether contractual or not, concerning a subject matter capable of settlement by arbitration'.[1]

Whilst the Convention is explicitly confined to agreements in writing, it is made clear that 'agreement' embraces an arbitral clause in a contract or an arbitration agreement signed by the parties or contained in an exchange of letters or telegrams.[2] The Commonwealth statutes, by adopting these terms by reference or by restatement, all give effect to the obligation.[3] These provisions are not intended to be an exhaustive statement. For they are capable of extending to a contract referring to standard or general conditions which include an arbitration clause, provided that the contract is written or signed by the parties or is contained in letters or telegrams between them. Similarly a bill of lading incorporating terms of a charter-party containing an arbitration clause will be within the provision.[4] On the other hand, an arbitration clause in a sales confirmation agreement sent by one party but not returned by the other should not be recognised.

It is evident that the provisions cover not only agreements to submit an existing dispute (a submission) but also agreements to submit disputes that may arise at some future time (sometimes known as promissory clauses).[5]

The matters which may be the subject of arbitration under the scheme are 'differences between the parties in respect of a defined legal relationship, whether contractual or not'. In addition to matters of contract, these will include tortious wrongs, disputes concerning the quantum of damages, and claims arising out of a collision at sea or in relation to immovables. All that is necessary is to establish that there has been a relationship between the parties created by or under some system of law and that a difference has arisen in connection therewith. For some legal systems, however, where arbitration is normally used only in relation to commercial disputes, this may seem too wide. Accordingly, the Convention permits any contracting party to enter a reservation linking the Convention's application to differences considered as commercial under the law of the declarant state.[6] Such a reservation is of primary value for those states whose legal system draws a clear distinction, for example in the form of separate codes, between civil and commercial matters. Reservations of this kind have been entered by Botswana, Cyprus, India, Nigeria and Trinidad and Tobago but in neither of the states with municipal legislation has this restriction been expressly applied to arbitration agreements[7] and it may be doubted for that reason whether it can be invoked to resist recognition of an agreement under the legislation.[8]

A further requirement is that the differences must concern 'a subject matter capable of settlement by arbitration'. This provision appears to take account of the fact that many jurisdictions forbid the submission of certain questions to arbitration. The Convention does not prescribe by which legal system this question is to be resolved, although it will be for the requested court to determine the issue. Article V.2(a) does, however, lay down that the lex fori applies when a similar question is to be determined in the context of recognition and enforcement of awards. It can be argued that the lex fori should be applied to agreements too, on the public policy ground that the requested court should not lend its support in cases where the use of arbitration would not be permitted locally. But it is equally arguable that the requested state should apply its conflict of laws rules and that reference be made to the law chosen by the parties to govern their agreement or, in the absence thereof, under the proper law as determined by the court.[9] For these are questions which touch upon matters of substance. The analogy with article V.2(a) is not exact, for that provision was inserted to give the requested court power to prevent improper use of its enforcement facilities, but leaving it to the person challenging the enforcement of the award to raise any questions of the validity of the agreement under article V.1(a). But, the argument goes, it should be possible for *either* party to resist recognition of the agreement as such on grounds related to validity. Against this, it should be pointed out that questions of nullity and the like may be raised explicitly in relation to agreements under article II.3 and therefore it seems unnecessary to bring them up in this context.

None of the Commonwealth statutes deals with this matter. Indeed, most merely make cross-reference to the Convention terminology itself, whilst the United Kingdom reproduces the essentials of that terminology.[10] In principle, the requested court may be prepared to consider both the lex fori and the law governing that agreement.

A further question which the Convention does not conclusively settle is whether the agreement must be one which will lead to an award enforceable under the Convention. There is no doubt that article II was introduced to ensure that the enforcement of awards would not be hampered by the requested state deciding that the agreement underlying the award should not be recognised. The converse, however, does not seem to have been given close consideration.[11] Adopting a broad construction of article II, it would not seem open to a contracting party to refuse recognition to an arbitration agreement, on the ground, for example, that the award would be made in a non-contracting state, even though such awards would not be recognised by the requested state under the Convention.[12] This interpretation may have been intended in all the Commonwealth statutes as no limitations are applied in this respect. An Indian court, however, has ruled that the agreement can only be recognised if it gives rise to an award within the meaning of the scheme.[13] This view has merit. For it enables staying proceedings to be used to facilitate the making of only those awards which can be enforced under the Convention.[14] Moreover, it enables the requested court to give effect to any 'commercial reservation' in relation to agreements even if it is applied in the legislation explicitly only in respect of awards. Finally, it has the effect of excluding certain agreements, for example those which will give rise to awards in the requested state itself. This effectively restricts the Convention to agreements which have some foreign element. Yet if this interpretation were to be followed some difficulties may arise in determining whether the agreement would give rise to a Convention award. Will it be possible prior to the submission to determine conclusively where the award will be made? For there would need to be a clear indication that the award would be made in another state before recognition of the agreement could be accorded.[15] In the absence of clear legislative provision, it may be questioned whether this construction of the statutes was intended, however sensible this view of the Convention seems.[16]

1 Art II.1.
2 Art II.2.
3 For references, see para 8.04, notes 4, 5 and 6 above.
4 Eg, *The Rena K* [1979] QB 377, [1979] 1 All ER 397. For discussion of some of the problems which have arisen in non-Commonwealth jurisdictions, see UNCITRAL Report, paras 19–26.
5 Generally, see Gaja, op cit, I.B.3.
6 Art I.3.
7 Botswana: Cap 06:02 (indeed art II.1 is not given force of law); India: Foreign Awards (Recognition and Enforcement) Act 1961, s 2 applies to awards.
8 But in *Indian Organic Chemicals Ltd v Chemtext Fibres Inc* AIR 1978 Bom 106, the High Court of Bombay appears to have limited agreements to those concerned with commercial matters by applying the limitation as it applies to awards to the agreement upon which the awards depend: see below and also para 8.23 below.
9 Generally on this provision, see L. V. Quigley, (1961) 70 Yale LJ 1049–1082 at p 1064.
10 For references, see para 8.04, notes 4, 5 and 6.
11 A proposal to this end was not adopted by the UN Conference, see UN Doc E/CONF.26/L.52; E/CONF.26/SR.21.
12 This is the view taken by the Private International Law Committee Report, at p 27.
13 *Indian Organic Chemicals Ltd v Chemtex Fibres Inc*, above.
14 See generally Gaga, op cit, I.A.2, in favour of this view which is given widespread support: see authorities cited in note 6 to that commentary. Cf Quigley, loc cit, note 9, above, at p 1064.
15 Private International Law Committee Report, para 18.
16 It should be noted that the Geneva provisions in respect of staying agreements have usually been replaced by the new legislation. If the suggested interpretation were to be employed, many agreements caught by that earlier legislation would now be outside the purview of the new Act. Act 1961 No 45 (India), s 10 does not repeal the earlier staying provisions, lending weight to the interpretation in the *Indian Organic Chemicals Case*, above.

The foreign element in agreements within the scheme

8.06 One further difficulty which arises from the drafting of article II is the apparent absence of any limitation of the scheme to those agreements with some foreign element. Had the connection with awards been effected, it would have been clear that, for example, agreements for arbitration in the requested state would usually have fallen outside the scheme. As drafted, however, no such restrictions appear. It seems probable that those who negotiated the Convention had no intention of applying its provisions to agreements in which other contracting states could have no conceivable interest.

This issue arises principally in connection with the staying provisions, as those relating to enforcement of awards contain a foreign connection requirement.[1] The statutes of Botswana, Cyprus, Ghana and India are silent on the question. On the face of it, therefore, the recognition provisions should apply to *any* written arbitration agreement. Yet these provisions usually co-exist with other statutory powers of a similar kind which are intended for use with respect to domestic agreements.[2] Implicitly, therefore, some limitation upon the Convention legislation's applicability must be found. Two possibilities exist. First, the Convention could be restricted to those agreements which will give rise to Convention awards. But doubts have already been expressed on this. Secondly, the scope of the alternative legislation can be determined and the Convention excluded from application to agreements within the former. The Ghana legislation lends itself to this approach: it expressly applies the alternative procedure to agreements governed by the law of Ghana.[3] By a less obvious route, a similar conclusion may be suggested for India, the legislation of which excludes recognition of awards made in respect of an agreement governed by the law of India,[4] thereby suggesting that this is the criterion for determining the domestic link. If this is correct, then the Convention requirement will govern all arbitration agreements other than those governed by the law of the requested state. Whether an agreement is so governed will be determined in accordance with the conflict of laws rules of that state.

In other Commonwealth states, the legislation as it applies to staying legal proceedings has grappled with this problem. But Australia, New Zealand and those jurisdictions adopting the United Kingdom model have taken rather different approaches in determining which agreements are 'domestic' and which 'foreign'. The Australian statute sets out to prescribe in positive terms the agreements which are within the Convention scheme. Such an agreement is one where:

(a) the arbitration prodecure is governed by the law[5] of another contracting state; or
(b) the arbitration procedure is governed by the law[5] of a non-contracting state, provided that a party to the agreement was the Commonwealth of Australia or a state of Australia or a person domiciled or ordinarily resident in Australia at the time of the agreement; or
(c) a party to the agreement was a government in another contracting state;[6] or
(d) a party to the agreement was domiciled or ordinarily resident in another contracting state, at the time of the agreement.[7]

This emphasis upon connecting links with countries which are parties to the Convention has been justified as putting the onus upon non-contracting states to join the Convention.[8] Thus, certain foreign agreements are excluded where the arbitration procedure is to be governed by the law of a non-contracting state and the parties are domiciled or ordinarily resident or a government in any such state. But the purpose is also to identify those agreements which are essentially Australian as distinct from those which may take place in Australia but have no Australian connections. In consequence there are excluded from the scope of the staying duty those 'domestic' agreements where the arbitration procedure is governed by Australian law and the parties are domiciled or ordinarily resident or a government in Australia or in a non-contracting state. It is, however, possible to conceive of certain agreements which could give rise to a Convention award being caught by these exclusions, for example, where the parties unconnected with any Convention country have agreed to arbitration in a Convention country following a procedure which is governed by the law of a non-contracting state. To that extent, the Australian approach may not wholly fulfil a purpose of the Convention. New Zealand has adopted a simpler formulation, also prescribing in positive terms the types of agreement which are covered by the staying duty:

'every arbitration agreement which provides expressly or by implication for arbitration in another country than New Zealand'.[9]

There is no intention in this case to limit the scheme to agreements which require arbitration in another contracting state. But it does exclude all cases of agreements for arbitration in New Zealand even when involving parties whose legal connections are entirely with other states. The United Kingdom takes a very liberal approach to the matter. Although it seeks to exclude agreements wholly connected with the United Kingdom, like the New Zealand Act it draws no distinction between contracting and non-contracting states in its treatment of 'foreign' agreements. But this has resulted in remarkably convoluted provision. The Convention legislation is made applicable to those agreements which are 'not domestic':[10] it then defines what is a 'domestic' agreement, but using essentially negative terminology.[11] Such an agreement is one—

'which does not provide, expressly or by implication for arbitration in a State other than the United Kingdom and to which neither—

(a) an individual who is a national of, or habitually resident in, any State other than the United Kingdom; and

(b) a body corporate which is incorporated in, or whose central management and control is exercised in, any State other than the United Kingdom,

is a party at the time the proceedings are commenced.'[12]

This definition is wider in effect than the Australian, bringing within the scheme, it appears, any agreement for arbitration in the United Kingdom itself, if one party is connected by a nationality or habitual residence with another foreign state, whether a contracting state or not.[13] In both cases, the agreement will give rise to an award which will not be enforceable in the United Kingdom under the Convention.[14] The provision is also unusual in introducing considerations of nationality, a connecting factor which generally has little acceptance in the private international law of most common law jurisdictions in the Commonwealth. Indeed it has been suggested that this kind of provision is inconsistent with the Convention.[15]

The differences in approach between the Australian, New Zealand and United Kingdom legislation may produce different results. Thus an arbitration in the forum to be governed by, say, the law of Singapore (a non-contracting state) between parties to an agreement who are nationals and habitually resident in Singapore will be a foreign agreement under United Kingdom law (as a party is a national or habitually resident in another state), a domestic agreement under New Zealand law (as arbitration is in the forum) and outside the Australian legislation (as neither party is domiciled or ordinarily resident in a contracting state or in the forum, though the arbitration is under the law of a non-contracting state). It may be questioned whether those who negotiated the Convention intended this degree of variation in practice.

1 Para 8.24 below.
2 These are normally contained in the general arbitration legislation. Eg Arbitration Act 1950 (UK), s 4(1).
3 Act 1961, No 38, s 35.
4 Act 1961, No 45, s 9(b). This follows the 1930 Act, s 6.
5 Whether determined by virtue of express terms of the agreement or otherwise. The relevant time is the time the agreement was made.
6 Or in a territory of such country to which the Convention has been extended.
7 1974 Act, s 7(1).
8 A. M. D'Aloiso (1977) Aus Bus LR 296 at p 299.
9 Act 1982, No 21, s 4(4).
10 Act 1975, s 1(2).
11 Although in other respects following the UK Act, the Bermuda legislation uses a positive formulation which appears to have the same effect: Act 1975, No 1, s 2(2).
12 Act 1975, s 1(4). It follows in part the recommendations of the Private International Law Committee Report, para 19. A further requirement was also suggested, as an alternative to (a) and (b), viz, the agreement to arbitration was not governed by the law of a part of the United Kingdom.
13 The drafting suggests that the time at which the connecting link becomes relevant is when the question of recognition arises in proceedings.
14 S 7(1) requires that the award be made in a contracting state other than the UK.
15 Gaja, op cit, I.A.3 and note 19 thereto.

Application to pre-Convention agreements

8.07 A last point of uncertainty is whether the Convention applies to arbitration agreements already concluded when it comes into effect. Again the Convention is silent. One argument in favour of retroactivity is that otherwise hardship would be caused for those cases which were within the Geneva Protocol but which are no longer covered by it since it is displaced by the Convention.[1] The Commonwealth legislation is not always clear. Whilst the Australian and New Zealand statutes expressly apply the scheme to agreements made prior to that Act,[2] the statutes of Botswana, Cyprus, Ghana and India and the United Kingdom model are silent. In the case of Ghana and India, it is made clear that the scheme does not apply to awards pre-existing the statute[3] implying that it might also be the case with agreements. Moreover, the Indian Protocol legislation has not been replaced with respect to agreements.[4] In the case of Ghana and the United Kingdom, however, the provisions implementing the Protocol have been repealed[5] and thus agreements can only be brought within the Convention-based provisions. The United Kingdom Act was taken to have retrospective effect in two cases[6] and a similar conclusion has been reached in relation to awards.[7] The initial argument set out above, when coupled with the benefits from giving effect to pre-existing agreements, seems strong enough to justify such a presumption of retroactivity in the case of agreements.

1 Art VII.2: see Gaja, op cit, at I.A.5.
2 Australia: Act 1974, No 136, s 14: New Zealand: Act 1982, No 21, s 11.

3 Act 1961, No 38, s 36 (Ghana); Act 1961, No 45, s 2 (India). Note that the question of whether the other state was a contracting party at that time was treated as irrelevant in *Strojexport v Edward Nasser & Co (Motors) Ltd* 1965 ALR Comm 493 (Ghana).

4 Act 1961, No 45, s 10: see Arbitration (Protocol and Convention) Act 1937, s 3.

5 Act 1961, No 38, s 43 (Ghana); Act 1975, s 8 (UK); *Murmansk State Steamship Line v Kano Oil Miller Ltd* 1974 (1) ALR Comm 1 (Nigeria) suggests that the Act does not apply retrospectively but no arguments are given.

6 *Nova (Jersey) Knit Ltd v Kammgarn Spinnerei GmbH* [1977] 2 All ER 463, [1977] 1 WLR 713, HL; *The Jocelyne* [1977] 2 Lloyd's Rep 121 at 128: the matter was left open in *Dalmia Dairy Industries Ltd v National Bank of Pakistan* [1978] 2 Lloyd's Rep 223 at 238.

7 *Kuwait Minister of Public Works v Sir Frederick Snow & Partners* [1984] 1 All ER 733, HL, esp at 739, per Lord Brandon.

III RECOGNITION OF ARBITRATION AGREEMENTS

Extent to which recognition of agreements is required

8.08 Article II.1 requires contracting states to 'recognise' the arbitration agreements within the scheme, contrasting with the obligation to 'recognise and enforce' awards under article III. This difference is explained by the fact that the purpose of article II was to protect awards by requiring states to recognise the agreements from which they derived. A move to include the Geneva Protocol provision which requires recognition of the *validity* of agreements failed, for fear that states might be obliged to treat as valid an agreement which would result in an award unenforceable under article V.[1] There seems little doubt from its history that article II was not intended to create any *general* obligation on states to ensure that effect is given to all arbitration agreements. Nor, it is suggested, was it intended to impose a uniform rule on the form of agreements which would apply to, and facilitate the enforcement of, domestic arbitration.[2] For this would preclude any power to question the formal validity of an agreement when it satisfied the Convention definition.

The Commonwealth statutes have generally confined this duty to recognise to the terms of the more specific obligation set out in article II.3, that is, to stay judicial proceedings on matters which are within the arbitration agreement so that the arbitration can take place.[3] This seems consistent with the purpose for which the article was introduced.

1 Art V.1(a) itself deals with certain questions of validity: UN Doc E/CONF. 26/SR.21.

2 Gaja, op cit, I.B.1 and notes 36–38 thereto.

3 Botswana achieves this by giving legal effect to the actual paragraph of the art: Cap 06:02, s 4(a). Cyprus, where the Convention is self-executing, makes no provision in domestic terms.

The duty to stay legal proceedings

8.09 The central requirement of this article, therefore, is that the courts of any contracting state, when requested to do so, must refer the parties to an agreement to arbitration in accordance with their agreement, if the court is 'seized of an action in a matter in respect of which the parties have made [such] an agreement'. The court may disregard this obligation only if it finds the agreement to be null and void, inoperative or incapable of being performed[1] or, implicitly, if the action is found not to concern matters covered by the agreement or if in fact there is no relevant agreement in existence or there is a dispute whether a relevant agreement exists.[2]

The staying provisions in the most of the Commonwealth legislation owe much to the equivalent provisions evolved by the United Kingdom to give effect to the Geneva Protocol.[3]

Indeed the Indian statute implementing the New York Convention reproduced the previous (and questionable) restriction of the staying provisions to cases in which there was 'a submission made in pursuance to an agreement'[4] This required legislative amendment to bring the statute into line with the Convention's wider application.[5]

1 Art II.3.
2 Cf *Willcock v Pickfords Removals Ltd* [1979] 1 Lloyd's Rep 24 (a case relating to a domestic arbitration agreement).
3 Arbitration Clauses (Protocol) Act 1924, s 1, as amended by the Arbitration (Foreign Awards) Act 1930, s 8, consolidated in the Arbitration Act 1950, s 4(2) and repealed by the Arbitration Act 1975, s 8.
4 Act 1968, No 45, s 3.
5 Foreign Awards (Recognition and Enforcement) Amendment Act 1973 No 47, reversing *V/O Tractoro-export, Moscow v Tarapore & Co, Madras* AIR 1971 SC 1 (where it was also suggested that an injunction to stay *foreign* legal proceedings might be available). The amendment had prospective effect only: *Food Corpn of India v Mardestine Compcnia Naviera* AIR 1977 Ker 108.

Conditions necessary for the order to stay

8.10 The Commonwealth legislation imposes a duty upon domestic courts to stay legal proceedings before them when certain conditions are fulfilled. There is no discretion of the kind usually found in respect of domestic agreements.[1] The conditions are:

(a) the agreement is one within the scheme;
(b) commencement of legal proceedings by any party to the agreement or any person claiming through or under him against any other party or such person;
(c) the legal proceedings are in respect of a matter agreed to be referred to arbitration;
(d) the application to stay is made by any party to the proceedings;
(e) the application is made at the prescribed time.

These conditions are examined in the following paragraphs.

1 Eg Arbitration Act 1950 (UK), s 4(1) in respect of domestic agreements. Semble an application may be made under this provision in respect of any agreement which fails to meet the criteria set by the New York Convention: *Dalmia Cement v National Bank of Pakistan* [1974] 3 All ER 189 at 200. Where a party to a domestic agreement is also a party, with a third party, to a non-domestic agreement under which liability to indemnify in respect of breaches of the former may be passed, an application to stay proceedings in favour of the domestic agreement will require consideration of the possibility of an application to stay in respect of the latter: *The Jemrix* [1981] 2 Lloyd's Rep 544.

(a) *The agreement is one within the scheme*

8.11 The requirements in this respect have already been examined[1] It needs, however, to be emphasised that it is in this context that most of the legislation insists upon a foreign element in the agreement.[2]

1 Para 8.05 above.
2 Para 8.06 above.

(b) *Commmencement of legal proceedings*[1]

8.12 Legal proceedings in this context may be commenced not only by writ or other originating process but also by delivery of a counterclaim which for the first time introduces matters covered by the arbitration agreement.[2] They may be commenced by an original party to the agreement against any other such party or in either instance, by or against one who is claiming 'through or under such a party'. This extension will apply to persons who have been substituted for the original party as a result, for example, of inheritance, assignment or the appointment of a trustee in bankruptcy.[3] But it may also include a wholly owned subsidiary company which is so closely related to the parent company which was a party to the agreement that it can be said to be within the purview of the arbitration clause.[4] Arguably, the courts may be prepared to hold in an appropriate case that such a parent company may be a person claiming through a subsidiary which was the party to the original agreement.

1 Australia: Act 1974, No 136, s 7(2) and (4); Ghana: Act 1961, No 38, s 40; India: Act 1961, No 45, s 3 (as substituted Act 1973, No 47); New Zealand: Act 1982, No 21, s 4(1); United Kingdom: Act 1975, s 1(1).

2 Cf *Radio Publicity (Universal) Ltd v Compagnie Luxembourgeoise de Radiodifusion* [1936] 2 All ER 721 (Geneva scheme).

3 This terminology is found both in the Geneva legislation (para 7.17 above) and in domestic legislation. For the latter, see Russell, op cit, pp 169–170.

4 *Roussel-Uclaf v G. D. Searle & Co Ltd* [1978] 1 Lloyd's Rep 225.

(c) *The legal proceedings are in respect of a matter agreed to be referred to arbitration*[1]

8.13 Patently, the court may not stay legal proceedings under this provision unless the matter to which they relate is one within the arbitration agreement and for that reason is subject to settlement by arbitration. A matter which is found by the court to be independent of those which have been agreed to be referred to arbitration cannot be stayed under these provisions.[2] There must be a clear, explicit intention to incorporate the terms of an agreement into the instrument which is the subject of the legal proceedings.[3] The burden of satisfying the court that the matter should be referred to arbitration appears to rest with the party applying for the stay.[4]

It is perhaps not too substantial a step to exclude also those cases in which 'there is not in fact any dispute between the parties with regard to the matter agreed to be referred'. For though a matter may strictly be within the competence of the arbitrator there seems little justification for requiring him to act where there is nothing for him to settle. Compulsory reference of matters over which there is no dispute, it can be argued, rather than speeding a settlement, would allow of deliberate delays designed to prevent the issue of legal processes which would bring the matter to an early conclusion.[5] Accordingly both the Indian statute and United Kingdom model[6] include the quoted words, culled from the Geneva scheme legislation,[7] despite some doubts concerning their consistency with the more general wording of the Convention itself.[8] The New Zealand Act arrives at much the same result by limiting the power to 'any matter *in dispute* between the parties which the parties have agreed to refer to arbitration'.[9]

The burden of satisfying the court that this exception is fulfilled lies with the plaintiff in the legal proceedings sought to be stayed.[10] The shift of onus in this respect is likely to ensure that arbitration rather than litigation will be resorted to, as agreed, where there is any uncertainty about the subject matter covered by the agreement.[11] It is only where the plaintiff produces clear evidence that by operation of law a sum of money is indisputably due or that the applicant for the stay has agreed or admitted that liability is due and money is payable by him that arbitration cannot be insisted upon.[12] Thus a claim for a liquidated sum of money under a bill of exchange in respect of which no recognised defence can be put forward is unlikely to be stayed.[13] Again, freight which has been prima facie earned by completion of a voyage in accordance with the terms of the charterparty has been held recoverable in the courts without deduction, any counterclaims or disputes as to the performance of the charterparty being treated as distinct issues for the arbitration.[14]

But even if the defendant has admitted liability, any question of the quantum of damage which has not been agreed must be referred to arbitration.[15] For agreement or admission have been treated as essential by the English courts, if the matter is not to be stayed. The fact that the applicant has not responded to the claim under the agreement does not constitute an admission[16] nor is the fact that parties have proceeded as if their contract was effective when they could have treated it as frustrated decisive.[17] Issues which are arguable in relation to the subject matter of the agreement or contract must be dealt with by the agreed arbitrator, rather than a judge. It is apparent, therefore, that this legislative gloss upon the Convention provisions will not be allowed to defeat the parties' agreed preference for arbitration.

> 'If on analysis what the plaintiff is asking or demanding involves a matter on which agreement has not been reached and which falls fairly and squarely within the terms of the arbitration agreement, then the applicant is entitled to insist on arbitration rather than litigation.[18]

The Australian legislation has adopted a different approach. The court will grant a stay only if the legal proceedings 'involve the determination of a matter that, in pursuance of the agreement, is capable of settlement by arbitration'.[19] This has been construed not to extend to every issue which would or might arise for decision in the course of determining a claim: it is intended to refer to claims for relief of kinds which are proper for determination in a court but which, because of the agreement, are capable of settlement by arbitration. Accordingly, arbitration will be required, even though the plaintiff seeks to raise issues by legal proceedings which are not within the agreement, if those issues are independent of the matter upon which the arbitration can give relief.[20] The burden of proving this lies, it is submitted, on the plaintiff in the legal proceedings. If this approach is pursued consistently, it seems probable that a matter should be referred to arbitration even if there is no dispute to be settled, where it is possible for the arbitrator to give the relief claimed. On the other hand, it may be open to the court to refuse a stay on the grounds that, in the absence of a dispute, the claim does not fall for 'determination' and thus the court can give a remedy at once. In the context of the Australian statute, this position seems less convincing.

1 Australia: Act 1974, No 136, s 7(2); Ghana: Act 1961, No 38, s 40; India: Act 1961, No 45, s 3 (as substituted, 1973, No 47); New Zealand: Act 1982, No 21, s 4(1); United Kingdom: Act 1975, s 1(1). The variations are noted below.

2 *Nova (Jersey) Knit Ltd v Kammgarn Spinnerei GmbH* [1977] 2 All ER 463, [1977] 1 WLR 713 where the House of Lords held that actions on bills of exchange were not in respect of a matter agreed to be referred. See also *The Jocelyne* [1977] 2 Lloyd's Rep 121; *OTM Ltd v Hydranautics* [1981] 2 Lloyd's Rep 211.

3 *Skips A/S Nordheim v Syrian Petroleum Co Ltd, The Varenna* [1983] 3 All ER 645, [1984] 2 WLR 156, where the dispute related to a bill of lading which did not incorporate an arbitration clause contained in the charterparty.

4 *Nova (Jersey) Knit Ltd*, above, at 479, per Lord Russell. Order for service out of the jurisdiction to commence legal proceedings has been refused where a stay would be granted because the plaintiff's claim lay within the arbitration agreement: *A & B v C & D* [1982] 1 Lloyd's Rep 166.
5 This was the view taken by the Private International Law Committee Report, p 27.
6 India: Act 1961, No 45, s 3 (as substituted); UK: Act 1975, s 1(1).
7 See para 7.18(iii) above.
8 Dicey and Morris, op cit, p 1163 but orse, Gaja, op cit, I.B.1. Given the broad obligation in art II.1 to recognise agreements concerning 'subject matter' capable of settlement by arbitration, there is some point in this objection.
9 Act 1982, No 21, s 4(1) (italics supplied).
10 *Nova (Jersey) Knit Ltd*, above, at 467, per Lord Wilberforce.
11 F. A. Mann, (1982) 98 LQR 530–532, argues that the onus should be upon the applicant for the stay to establish that there is in fact a dispute, thereby ensuring that he cannot rely upon his own inactivity or silence with respect to the plaintiff's demand, in order to avoid summary legal process. This view seems inconsistent with the Convention objectives.
12 See *Tradax Internacional SA v Cerrahogullari TAS, The M Eregli* [1981] 3 All ER 344 at 350, per Kerr J (not a case under the New York Convention).
13 *Nova (Jersey) Knit Ltd*, above, Lord Salmon dissenting. The decision rests heavily upon the commercial nature of the bill of exchange.
14 *Cleobulos Shipping Co Ltd v Intertanker Ltd, The Cleon* [1982] Com LR 146. The decision turns upon the particular rules relating to payment of freight.
15 *Associated Bulk Carriers Ltd v Koch Shipping Inc, The Fuohsan Maru* [1978] 2 All ER 254, CA, Lord Denning MR dissenting.
16 *Ellerine Bros (Pty) Ltd v Klinger* [1982] 2 All ER 737, [1982] 1 WLR 1375, CA.
17 *Kissavos Shipping Co SA v Empresa Cubana de Fletes, The Agathon* [1982] 2 Lloyd's Rep 211, CA.
18 *Ellerine Bros (Pty) Ltd v Klinger*, above, at 741, per Templeman LJ.
19 Act 1974, No 136, s 7(2)(b).
20 *Flakt Australia Ltd v Wilkins and Davies Construction Co Ltd* [1979] 2 NSWLR 243.

(d) *The application to be made by a party to the proceedings*[1]

8.14 In most of the legislation the application to stay can be made by any party to the legal proceedings. Thus any of the defendants may apply: it is not necessary for all to join in the application. Nothing in the section requires the applicant to be a party to the original agreement. In the Australian Act, however, the application may only be made by a party to the agreement or a person claiming through or under that party.[2]

1 Australia: Act 1974, No 136, s 7(2); Ghana: Act 1961, No 38, s 40; India: Act 1961, No 45, s 3 (as substituted, Act 1973, No 47); New Zealand: Act 1982, No 21, s 4(1); United Kingdom: Act 1975, s 1(1).
2 Act 1974, No 136, s 7(4).

(e) *The application to be made at the prescribed time*[1]

8.15 The Convention allows the request to be made when the court is 'seized of an action'. With the exception of the New Zealand Act, Commonwealth statutes have seen fit to give particularity to this phrase in terms relevant to their legal system.[2] In doing so, it has been necessary to deal with the question of the earliest point of time when such a request may be made and the point of time after legal proceedings have been commenced at which the right to apply is lost. For it is clear that the parties may, if they agree, waive their agreement to arbitrate, allowing the matter to be settled by a court. Accordingly, if a party, in full awareness of the arbitration clause, participates in a legal action, he cannot subsequently fall back upon his right to arbitrate. There must come a point at which a party by acquiescing in the other's institution of the court process is deemed to have waived his right to arbitrate. The New Zealand Act merely allows the application to be made 'at any time' after the legal proceedings have been commenced.[3] It remains to be seen whether the courts will hold that the right to apply is lost by participation in the court proceedings. In the other cases, limits are prescribed. Thus a request cannot be made before 'the service of the writ of summons' (Ghana) or 'appearance' (India, United Kingdom[4]) or before the proceedings are 'pending' (Australia), presumably meaning after service of the writ but before the pleadings are closed.[5] A request for stay cannot be made after 'the date fixed for hearing' (Ghana), 'the filing of a written statement' (India) or 'delivery of any pleadings' (UK) or after 'taking any other steps in the proceedings' (India, UK), or, presumably, when proceedings are no longer pending (Australia).[6]

The phrase 'taking any steps in the proceedings'[7] has been held to involve more than seeking an interlocutory injunction or other interim relief, since this may be necessary whether a stay is given or not.[8] It must involve, it has been suggested, 'a positive act by way of offence on the part of the defendant (ie he who now seeks the stay in order to arbitrate) rather than merely parrying a blow by the plaintiff'.[9] It must be an act 'which implicitly affirms the correctness of the proceedings and the willingness of the defendant to go along with the determination by the courts of law instead of arbitration'.[10] Accordingly, an application to strike out a defective statement of claim may not be such a step.[11] Equally, an application for a statement of claim[12] or for particulars[13] will not constitute such a step, whilst an affidavit claiming a defence to a summons for summary judgment,[14] or a summons for extension of time to deliver a defence[15] or an order for discovery of documents will be.[16] In all cases, the defendant must demonstrate unequivocally by his conduct his intention to abide by the court proceedings and to forego his right to arbitrate.[17] It seems clear, therefore, that an application by a defendant for a Mareva injunction to restrain the plaintiff from removing assets from the jurisdiction pending the settlement of a counterclaim or other interim relief to provide security will not necessarily constitute a step in the legal proceedings. For such an injunction may be obtained as a preliminary to an arbitration which the defendant, it is suggested, would still be able to demand.[18]

1 Australia: Act 1974, No 136, s 7(2); Ghana: Act 1961, No 38, s 40; India: Act 1961, No 45, s 3 (as substituted, Act 1973, No 47); New Zealand: Act 1982, No 21, s 4(1); United Kingdom: Act 1975, s 1(1).
2 In respect of Botswana and Cyprus, the Convention language itself will require judicial interpretation.
3 Act 1982, No 21, s 4(1).
4 Under RSC Ord 12, r 10, acknowledgment of service is now treated as entry of appearance.
5 *Flakt Australia Ltd v Wilkins and Davies Construction Co Ltd* [1979] 2 NSWLR 243.
6 This may be after pleadings have closed (ibid) but arguably before the setting down for trial.
7 Already replete with precedents under domestic law, see Russell, op cit, pp 173–175.
8 *Roussel-Uclaf v G. D. Searle & Co Ltd* [1978] 1 Lloyd's Rep 225; cf *Food Corpn of India v Yadav Engineering and Contractor* AIR 1982 SC 1302 (under domestic legislation).
9 Ibid, per Graham J, at 231.
10 *Eagle Star Insurance Co Ltd v Yuval Insurance Co Ltd* [1978] 1 Lloyd's Rep 357 at 361, per Lord Denning MR.
11 Ibid, though Goff LJ and Shaw LJ were not prepared to treat this as always the case.
12 *Ives and Barker v Willans* [1894] 2 Ch 478, 63 LJ Ch 521, CA. The cases in footnotes 12–16 are not on the New York Convention legislation.
13 *Parker, Gaines & Co Ltd v Turpin* [1918] 1 KB 358 at 361.
14 *Pitchers Ltd v Plaza (Queensbury) Ltd* [1940] 1 All ER 151, 162 LT 213, CA.
15 *Fords Hotel Co Ltd v Bartlett* [1896] AC 1, 65 LJQB 166, HL.
16 *Parker, Gaines & Co Ltd v Turpin*, above.
17 *Eagle Star Insurance Co Ltd v Yuval Insurance Co Ltd*, above, at 361.
18 *The Rena K* [1979] 1 All ER 397 at 418, per Brandon J; *Roussel-Uclaf v G. D. Searle & Co Ltd*, above.

Grounds for resisting the stay of proceedings

8.16 Where the foregoing conditions are satisfied, the court must grant the stay of the legal proceedings and refer the parties to their arbitration, unless one of the prescribed exceptions can be established by the party seeking to continue the legal proceedings. If the plaintiff can discharge this burden, the stay must be refused: if he cannot, it must be granted.[1] The three exceptions in the Convention are that the agreement is 'null and void, inoperative or incapable of being performed'. All are included in the implementing legislation which also, in the case of India and the United Kingdom, adds the additional exception relating to non-existing disputes.[2] Unfortunately, they give rise to problems of interpretation which have not been clarified in any of the implementing legislation. In particular, it is far from clear what choice of law rules should be adopted by a court in establishing that these conditions are fulfilled.[3]

One explanation for this lacuna is that these provisions were introduced to facilitate the recognition of awards, and thus the choice of law rules as they refer to agreements in that context should be followed in this. There was, therefore, no necessity to introduce alternative or merely replicating choice of law rules.[4] In following this line of argument in relation to the validity and the operative character of an agreement, it has been argued that 'all that needs ascertaining is that there may be a law which will give effect to an award made on the basis of the agreement'.[5]

To discover this requires references to the choice of law rules set out in article V.1(a) which control the question of the validity of agreements in the context of awards. (None of the other choice of law rules, relating to awards in article V would have relevance prior to the inception of the arbitration.) Accordingly, if there is validity by the law actually chosen by the parties or, failing such a choice, by the law of any jurisdiction in which the award could be made, this condition will be satisfied.

There are, however, difficulties in this argument, not least because the requested court will normally wish to apply its own law, regardless of the choice of law, where the agreement appears to be in breach of local public policy rules.[6] This may not be allowed for, if article V.1(a) contains the only criteria.[7] In any case, it may be doubted whether this line of argument can be employed in respect of any of those Commonwealth statutes which do not confine the staying rules to agreements giving rise to Convention awards. The Australian, New Zealand and the United Kingdom statutes in particular certainly apply to other agreements.[8] In that case, the choice of law will presumably have to be determined in accordance with the conflict of laws rules of the forum state. At the same time, it must be acknowledged that difficulties also arise from this interpretation. For there is always the possibility that a different choice of law will be made to determine validity in the case of staying from that which would be applied under article V.1(a) in the context of the recognition of awards.[9]

It seems probable, however, that the requested state, if applying the English conflict of laws, will normally give priority, in determining the choice of law, to the law selected by the parties themselves, consistently with article V.1(a). In the absence of such a choice, the proper law may well be that of the place of the arbitration—again consistently with article V.1(a)—although any presumption in favour of that law may be displaced by other factors.[10] The requested state may also refuse to recognise the agreement if it conflicts with local public policy.

Question of formal validity may, of course, be determined by the lex loci contractus or the proper law[11]—and these may again be inconsistent with the choice of law required by article V.1(a). What seems clear is that in the absence of the incorporation of article II.1 into municipal law, there is no room for the argument that that provision contains the requirements relating to formal validity.[12] Insofar as the exceptions relate to questions of law connected with the arbitration process, the law governing that process will apply.[13] As will be apparent from the following paragraphs, limited assistance only can be obtained on these points from Commonwealth case law to date.

1 *Nova (Jersey) Knit Ltd v Kammgarn Spinnerei GmbH* [1977] 2 All ER 463 at 467, per Lord Wilberforce. Though the Arbitration Act 1975 (UK), s 7(5) follows the Convention, art II.3, in specifying that the court 'find' the exceptions, the burden appears to lie upon the plaintiff. The court should not refuse a stay on the ground that an issue of fraud more suited for judicial decision is involved, for example, under Arbitration Act 1950 (UK), s 24(2)): *Paczy v Haendler and Natermann GmbH* [1979] FSR 420, per Whitford J.

2 Para 8.13 above.

3 The question whether an agreement is 'incapable of being performed' seems unlikely often to give rise to choice of law questions. If it is to be given distinct meaning from questions of invalidity and inoperativeness, it seems to be essentially a question of fact.

4 Gaja, op cit, I.B.4. An alternative explanation for the absence is the relative late adoption of this article: see para 5.17 above.

5 Ibid.

6 In relation to recognition of awards, public policy is a distinct ground for refusal: art V.2(b).

7 Ibid, Dicey and Morris, op cit, p 1162: D. R. Thomas, [1981] 1 LMCLQ 17 at 25.

8 Para 8.05 above.

9 Gaja, op cit, I.B.4.

10 The presumption in favour of the lex loci arbitri is strong, not least when the agreement comprises a submission of an existing dispute (*Hamlyn & Co v Talisker Distillery* [1894] AC 202, 71 LT 1, HL) but it may be rebutted when the place of arbitration will be only one of the factors indicating the proper law: *James Miller & Partners Ltd v Whitworth Street Estates (Manchester) Ltd* [1970] AC 583, [1970] 1 All ER 796, HL; *Compagnie d'Armement Maritime SA v Compagnie Tunisienne de Navigation SA* [1971] AC 572, [1970] 3 All ER 71, HL.

11 Dicey and Morris, op cit, pp 784 ff.

12 See Gaja, op cit, I.C.2. for this argument and para 8.08 above.

13 Under English conflict rules, in the absence of any choice of law by the parties themselves, this will be the lex loci arbitri: *James Miller & Partners Ltd v Whitworth Street Estates (Manchester) Ltd*, above.

1. *The agreement is null and void*[1]

8.17 The question of validity has been touched upon in two decisions. In one[2], an arbitration clause was held to be null and void as derogating from a mandatory requirement of the CMR Convention governing arbitration thereunder which was part of the enacted law to be applied by the court hearing the application to stay. This requirement, although also applicable under the proper law,[3] appears to have been applied as part of the lex fori, presumably in accordance with English public policy. In the other case, *The Hollandia,*[4] Lord Diplock held that a choice of forum clause in favour of a foreign *court,* despite being in accord with the proper law,[5] would not be enforced in the face of the contrary requirements of the Hague-Visby rules which were enacted law of the lex fori, binding on the requested court. Nonetheless he appears to have had doubts that a similar conclusion would be applied to a clause prescribing non-domestic arbitration.[6] Arguably, this was for the narrow reason that the Hague-Visby rules were not seen as affecting the agreement for foreign *arbitrations*. Certainly Lord Diplock seemed to favour the view that the question of validity of the contract in this instance might be one for the arbitrator, applying the law chosen by the parties or, in the absence thereof, the proper law of the contract.[7] This suggests that the requested court should only refuse to grant a stay where it is clear that the arbitrator has no alternative but to apply a law which contradicts the lex fori of the requested court.[8] The issue remains whether the question of validity is confined to cases of void ab initio, or whether, as seems more probable, it extends to cases in which it can be shown that the arbitral clause has become null and void by the time proceedings are brought.[9] The matter must surely turn upon whether supervening events have rendered the jurisdictional basis of the arbitration void, not the contract of which it may be part.[10]

1 Australia: Act, No 136, s 7(5); Ghana: Act 1961, No 38, s 40; India: Act 1961, No 45, s 3 (as substituted Act 1973, No 47); New Zealand: Act 1982, No 21, s 4(1); United Kingdom, Act 1975, s 1(1).
2 *AB Bofors-Uva CAV Ltd v AB Skandia Transport* [1982] 1 Lloyd's Rep 410.
3 Swedish law.
4 [1983] 1 AC 565, [1982] 3 All ER 1141, HL.
5 Dutch law. The choice of the particular forum would lead to the application of the law of the forum which was contrary to the Hague-Visby rules which the English courts were required by Parliament to apply to the bills of lading in question.
6 At 1147.
7 If the arbitrator does in fact apply such a law in making an award, the issue would arise if steps are taken to enforce that award: see para 8.31 below.
8 At 1147.
9 See D. R. Thomas, [1981] 1 LMCLQ 17 at p 23.
10 Cf *Prodexport State Company for Foreign Trade v E D & F Mann Ltd* [1973] 1 QB 389, [1973] 1 All ER 355.

2. *The agreement is inoperative*[1]

8.18 It seems probable that the term 'inoperative' will be treated as covering cases different from those caught by the phrase 'null and void'. Thus, if it can be shown that the agreement to arbitrate, though initially valid, has been discharged, replaced or frustrated or has been put into suspense through the fulfilment of some contractual provision or by agreement,[2] the agreement is inoperative. One test suggested is whether the arbitration would have no practical operation or serve no useful purpose.[3] But the mere fact that the arbitration may duplicate related legal proceedings and lead to inconsistent findings of law and fact is not enough to render the agreement inoperative.[4] Further, the termination of the contract in which the agreement appears will not be caught by the term so long as there are disputes thereunder to be settled,[5] nor will a failure to abide by the agreement which has been waived.[6] Moreover, it is no ground for refusing the stay that the time limit for arbitrating the matter will have expired: for the parties have chosen their forum and the time constraints which go with it.[7]

1 Australia: Act 1974, No 136, s 7(5); Ghana: Act 1961, No 38, s 40; India: Act 1961, No 45, s 3 (as substituted by Act 1973, No 47); New Zealand: Act 1982, No 21, s 4(1); United Kingdom: Act 1975, s 1(1).
2 Cf *The El Amria (No 2)* [1980] 2 Lloyd's Rep 166.
3 *Lonrho v Shell Petroleum* (1978) Times, 1 February. This case was affd on appeal by both the CA and HL, [1980] QB 358, [1980] 2 WLR 367, CA; affd [1980] 1 WLR 627, HL.
4 Ibid.
5 *Radio Publicity (Universal) Ltd v Compagnie Luxembourgeoise de Radiodifusion* [1936] 2 All ER 721 (under the Geneva scheme legislation).
6 Ibid.
7 See *The Merak* [1965] P 223, [1965] 1 All ER 230, CA under domestic legislation.

3. *The agreement is incapable of being performed*[1]

8.19 The term 'incapable of being performed' appears likely to give rise in the main to questions of fact. The question, however, is whether the arbitration *agreement* can be performed, not whether the parties to it can perform their parts of the agreement. The condition is fulfilled only 'if the circumstances are such that it [the agreement] can no longer be performed, even if both parties were ready, able and willing to perform it'.[2] Accordingly, the fact that one of the parties may lack financial resources to take the matter to arbitration[3] or to satisfy the award, if made,[4] will have no effect.

More positively, it seems the condition will be met if the arbitration is in practical terms impossible, for reasons outside the control of the parties, eg the named arbitrator has died or he refuses to act and there is no provision for an alternate. If the incapacity arises from the activities of one of the parties (eg refusal to appoint an arbitrator or to take part in the arbitral process), the remedy lies under the law governing the arbitration to make the arbitration effective, and not by-passing the arbitration.

1 Australia: Act 1974, No 136, s 7(5); Ghana: Act 1961, No 38, s 40; India: Act 1961, No 45, s 3 (as substituted by Act 1973, No 47); New Zealand: Act 1982, No 21, s 4(1); United Kingdom, Act 1975, s 1(1).
2 *Paczy v Haendler and Natermann GmbH* [1981] 1 Lloyd's Rep 302, CA at 307, per Buckley LJ.
3 Ibid.
4 *The Rena K* [1979] QB 377, [1979] 1 All ER 397.

4. *There is no dispute between the parties with regard to the matter agreed to be referred*[1]

8.20 As we have seen[2] this is an additional ground which may be invoked by the plaintiff in the legal proceedings to resist their stay in India or those jurisdictions adopting the United Kingdom model.

1 India: Act 1961, No 45, s 3 (as substituted by Act 1973, No 47); United Kingdom: Act 1975, s 1(1).
2 Para 8.13 above.

Imposition of conditions or terms on the stay

8.20 The Convention does not provide for the requested court to grant the stay of legal proceedings subject to conditions or terms. Indeed, certain commentators take the view that this is quite inconsistent with the purpose of the Convention.[1] This view may have carried weight with the draftsmen of most of the Commonwealth statutes, since only the Australian and New Zealand Acts contain provisions of this kind. The others are silent in this respect which has led the English courts to conclude that the statute does not authorise the court expressly or impliedly to attach terms to the order staying the action[2] or to make any order for interim payment of any sum when liability is admitted.[3] At the same time, the interest which the plaintiff is seeking to protect by bringing legal proceedings may, on occasion, appear to justify some intervention by the court even when requiring him to proceed to arbitration. Accordingly, the Australian statute contains provisions permitting the requested court to order the stay 'upon such conditions (if any) as it thinks fit'[4] and to make interim or supplementary orders in relation to any property that is the subject matter to which the stay relates, 'for the purpose of preserving the rights of the parties'.[5] The New Zealand statute has provisions of a similar nature.[6] The former power has been used in Australia to impose conditions designed to expedite the arbitration with the threat of termination of the stay if a condition is broken.[7] It is probable that this may be the most common use of the power. It may be doubted whether conditions can be imposed which interfere with the agreed arbitral process or with the obligation to arbitrate since these would be inconsistent with the Convention scheme but, arguably, it may be open to the court where liability is not disputed to require the making of interim payment on account of a sum, the quantum of which it is for the arbitrator to settle.

The power to make interim or supplementary orders may only be used against property which is the subject matter of the arbitration: it cannot be used to freeze a party's assets pending an award of general damages.[8] It seems probable that the power will be useful where the subject matter is a vessel or an aircraft and the court wishes to order the retention of the security or to order its release subject to the provision of an alternative security for the satisfaction of any future award.

The need for powers of this latter kind has been experienced by the English courts which have filled the gap in the legislation from other sources. Although the staying of an action in rem is normally followed by the release of any arrested security,[9] Brandon J has been prepared to find that the order for release of arrested property lies in the judge's discretion and as part of the discretion the release may be made conditional. In his view the release should be conditional, if the stay may not be final[10] but if it will be final, release should be unconditional.[11] Thus if there is a real likelihood that the stay will be removed, for example because the arbitration cannot be carried out, or even because the award may not be satisfied and the action in rem is not merged in the award,[12] the court may make an order which retains the security or requires alternative security pending the outcome of the revitalised legal proceedings.

Brandon J has also accepted that a Mareva injunction could be issued in a proper case to a plaintiff in stayed legal proceedings which would incidentally provide him with security against any subsequent award. Moreover, it could be issued by the court subject to a term that the arbitration be commenced within a specific time 'together with such other terms, if any, as it thinks fit'.[13]

More recently, English courts have manifested their concern to protect a party pending the outcome of arbitration by granting interim relief in the form of an interlocutory mandatory order to execute a contractual obligation to activate a letter of credit, the proceeds of which were then secured pending the result of the arbitration.[14] Whilst this was a exceptional case involving the court's general power to order interim relief in the case of a contract governed by English law,[15] it furnishes further evidence that a stay under the Arbitration Act 1975 may be coupled with orders designed to prevent the dissipation of the defendant's assets which otherwise may not be available to satisfy an award. It appears, therefore, that these ancillary developments bring the powers of the courts under the United Kingdom style legislation close to those under the Antipodean legislation, particularly where the action stayed is one in rem. This trend is to be welcomed as one designed to make arbitral awards meaningful.

New statutory provisions will allow an English court, on staying Admiralty proceedings, to order that property arrested be retained as security for the satisfaction of any subsequent award on the matter in dispute if the award is enforceable in England—whether under the Convention or the judgment schemes or otherwise.[16] Alternatively the court may order that the stay be conditional on the provision of equivalent security for the satisfaction of the award.

1 Eg A. S. Holmes, (1981) 21 Virginia Jo of International Law, 785–804; UNCITRAL Report, para 29.
2 *The Rena K* [1979] 1 All ER 397 at 412, per Brandon J.
3 *The Fuohson Maru* [1978] 1 Lloyd's Rep 24; *The Agrabele* [1979] 2 Lloyd's Rep 117. For powers derived from other sources, see below.
4 Act 1974, No 136, s 7(2).
5 Ibid, s 7(3).
6 Act 1982, No 21, ss 4(2) and 4(3). The property orders are not expressly limited to 'interim or supplementary orders', although in practice this is likely to be the case. Nor are they stated to be for the purpose of 'preserving rights of the parties'. Further, they may be used in respect of property which 'may be the subject-matter of the dispute between the parties to the arbitration agreement'.
7 *Flakt Australia Ltd v Wilkins and Davies Construction Co Ltd* [1979] 2 NSWLR 243.
8 A Mareva injunction may be available in this respect, insofar as the Australian courts follow English authorities: *The Rena K* [1979] 1 All ER 397 at 419: see below.
9 *The Rena K,* above.
10 Ibid, at 415: The relevant power is contained in RSC Ord 75, r 13(4).
11 *The Golden Trader* [1974] 1 Lloyd's Rep 378.
12 *The Rena K,* above, at 417: but see doubts of Brandon J on this point in the earlier case of *The Golden Trader,* above, at 385. See also *The Vasso* [1984] 1 All ER 1126, [1984] 2 WLR 570; *The Tuyuti* (1984) Times, 12 April.
13 *The Rena K,* above, at 417–8. Brandon J believed the power to be implicit in the power to issue interlocutory injunctions but proffered in aid the more specific provisions of the domestic arbitration legislation: Arbitration Act 1950, s 12(6). See also *Third Chandris Shipping Corpn v Unimarine SA* [1979] QB 645, [1979] 2 All ER 972, CA (injunction sought prior to an application to stay). Generally on Mareva injunctions, see para 3.31 above.
14 *Astro Exito Navegacion SA v Southland Enterprise Co Ltd (No 2)* [1983] 2 AC 787, [1983] 2 All ER 725 HL.
15 Under the earlier equivalent of Supreme Court Act 1981, s 37.
16 Civil Jurisdiction and Judgments Act 1982, s 26, applying also to Northern Ireland (not in force). Conditions may be attached, particularly in respect of the institution or prosecution of the arbitration: ibid, s 26(2).

IV ENFORCEMENT OF ARBITRAL AWARDS

Enforcement under the Convention[1]

8.21 The central purpose of the Convention is to impose upon contracting states the obligation to recognise all arbitral awards within the scheme as binding and to secure their enforcement, if requested so to do, under the lex fori. Whilst the actual process which may be used for enforcement is to be determined by the forum state, there is an obligation not to discriminate by imposing substantially more onerous conditions or higher fees or charges than are applied in respect of domestic arbitral awards.[2]

In contrast with the Geneva scheme, the Convention sets out to facilitate the enforcement of awards by requiring the applicant merely to produce the prescribed formal evidence of an award which is within the scheme.[3] Unless another party establishes that the award should not be recognised on one of the prescribed grounds,[4] the applicant must be permitted to proceed to enforce the award in accordance with the appropriate local processes.

1 Generally, see the UNCITRAL Report.
2 Art III.
3 Art IV.
4 Arts V and VI.

Awards within the Convention scheme

8.22 The Convention determines the characteristics of awards within the Convention scheme in outline terms only. The essential qualities which are required may be stated as:

(a) the award must arise 'out of differences between persons, whether physical or legal';[1]
(b) it may be made by arbitrators appointed ad hoc or by a permanent body to which the parties have submitted;[2]
(c) the award must be one made pursuant to a written agreement capable of recognition under the Convention and thus must deal with a difference in respect of a defined legal relationship, whether contractual or not, concerning a subject matter capable of settlement by arbitration;[3]
(d) awards may be limited to those which settle differences 'arising out of legal relationships, whether contractual or not, which are considered as commercial under the national law of the relevant Contracting State';[4]
(e) the award must have been made in:
    (i) the territory of any state, other than the state where enforcement is requested;[5] or
    (ii) (if the state of enforcement has so declared when adhering to the Convention), the territory of another contracting state only;[6] or
    (iii) (unless excluded by the state of enforcement when adhering to the Convention), the territory of that state itself, if the award is not considered by that state to be a domestic award.[7]

It is an important feature of the Convention that it does not include in its requirement any further connecting factors, such as nationality, domicile, residence or place of business, which the parties to the award must fulfil before the duty to recognise and enforce arises. It is clear that the Convention does not permit contracting states to add such provisions into its implementing legislation.

These provisions have given rise to rather less uncertainty than the equivalent criteria in the Geneva scheme.[8]

1 Art I.1.
2 Art I.2.
3 Art II.1. See para 8.05 above. The relationship between awards and agreements is apparent in arts IV.1(b) and V.1(a).
4 Art I.3.
5 Art I.1.
6 Art I.3. The restriction may be made 'on the basis of reciprocity'.
7 Ibid, but no reference is made to reciprocity.
8 UNCITRAL Report, paras 4–11.

Awards within the New York Convention legislation

(a) *Types of award*

8.23 The implementing legislation in the Commonwealth largely follows the terminology used in the Convention,[1] but some important variations do exist. Certain difficulties of interpretation may also be adverted to. It is uncommon for the legislation to deal explicitly with factors (a) and (b) above, although Australia, Botswana, Cyprus and New Zealand require reference to the Convention for the definition of 'award',[1] whilst the Indian statute uses similar terminology.[2] Neither Ghana nor the United Kingdom statute directly or indirectly refers to these elements: it may be assumed that these characteristics are carried over from other provisions of the law.[3]

The requirement that the award must deal with differences between persons, whether physical or legal, is clearly capable of applying to awards involving public authorities or the state or its agencies. The mere fact that a state has become a party to the Convention does not constitute waiver of an immunity which may be claimed before a foreign court.[4] But issues of state immunity, particularly in respect of non-commercial transactions of a state organ, are capable of being raised in a challenge to the enforcement of individual awards.[5]

The link between enforceable awards and arbitration agreements which must be recognised under the Convention is also explicit in all but the Ghana and United Kingdom statutes.[6] In the latter case, however, the definitions, by using terminology equivalent to that of the Convention, almost certainly produce the same result.[7] In the case of Ghana, the application of the general law definitions probably leads to the same effect.[8]

In two instances, the scheme has been confined to awards which settle differences which arise out of legal relationships which are considered to be commercial under the law of the state concerned. The states so providing are Botswana and India.[9] This provision may be enacted only if a reservation to that effect has been entered at the time of acceding to the Convention.[10] This reservation was provided principally for those states which preserve, usually through separate codes of law, a distinction between civil law and commercial law. The effect is that, for example, awards arising out of non-commercial contracts[11] or general delictual claims will be excluded. The distinction is less easy to work where the principles of law are derived from statutes and common law and serious difficulties can ensue in those cases in determining whether a particular relationship is 'commercial' or not. Thus an Indian court has held that a plant construction contract, though having commercial implications, was not 'commercial' as there was no legal rule in Indian law conferring such character upon the contract.[12]

A consequence of this reservation is that other jurisdictions may avail themselves of article XIV which in effect enables a state to refuse to apply the Convention in respect of another state to the extent that that other is not bound by the Convention. Only Botswana in the Commonwealth has enacted authority to its courts which would enable this reciprocal restriction to be applied.[13] In the absence of such provision in, for example, the United Kingdom, non-commercial awards made in India are enforceable under the United Kingdom law, although such awards made in the United Kingdom fall outside the Indian scheme of enforcement.

1 Australia: Act 1961, No 136, s 3(1); New Zealand: Act 1982, No 21, s 2. Botswana and Cyprus give effect to the exact terms of the Convention.
2 Act 1961, No 45, s 2.
3 Eg Ghana: Act 1961, No 38, s 4.
4 Private International Law Committee Report, p 23; New Zealand: Act 1982, No 21, s 3.
5 UNCITRAL Report, para 9 and para 8.37 below. *Petrol Shipping Corpn v Kingdom of Greece* [1966] 2 Lloyd's Rep 431 (US DC).
6 For references, see notes 1 and 2 above. Awards made in pursuance of agreements in which the duty to stay does not arise may be Convention awards: para 8.03 above.
7 Act 1975, s 7(1).
8 Act 1961, No 38, s 5.
9 Botswana: Cap 06:02, s 3(2); India: Act 1961, No 45, s 2. Cyprus, Nigeria and Trinidad and Tobago have entered a reservation to this effect but have no domestic legislation.
10 Art I.3.

11 *Kamani Engineering Corpn Ltd v Société de Traction et d'Electricité SA* AIR 1965 Bom 114 (technical assistance contract not a commercial contract).
12 *Indian Organic Chemicals Ltd v Chemtex Fibres Inc* AIR 1978 Bom 106. A. B. Schroff, (1979) 21 Jo Ind Law Inst 31 at p 40, suggests that employment issues, licence agreements and know-how contracts might also be treated as non-commercial.
13 Cap 06:02, s 3(3).

(b) *Locus of the award*

8.24 The Convention applies to awards made outside the state in which enforcement is requested, whether they are made in another contracting state or not. It was clear, however, from the early stages of negotiation that most states would wish to enter the scheme only if they could be assured of reciprocal treatment for awards made in their own territory. Accordingly, the Convention allows states on adhering to the Convention, to confine the scheme 'on the basis of reciprocity'[1] to only such awards as are made in other contracting states. Such reservations have been made and are reflected in the legislation of Botswana, Cyprus, India, New Zealand and the United Kingdom model.[2]

Unfortunately this mechanism fails to provide for a half-way house which would permit a Convention state to extend the scheme to awards made in specified non-contracting states. As the Convention, in the absence of any reservation, requires enforcement of awards made in *any* state other than the requested state, it seems that extension to selected non-contracting states by municipal legislation will be inconsistent with the Convention, however sensible this may be.[3] If this view is correct, doubts must be expressed concerning the approaches of the Australian and Ghanaian legislation,[4] neither state having entered a reservation. The Australian statute requires a non-contracting state award to be enforced only where the person seeking enforcement is, at the time of application, domiciled or ordinarily resident in Australia or another Convention country.[5] The benefits, therefore, accrue only to those who have a recognised connection with a Convention country. It may be conceded that this is consistent with the spirit of the Convention.

The Ghana Act allows the scheme to be applied by legislative instrument to any non-contracting state on the basis of reciprocity.[6] This appears to stand the Convention article on its head, for reciprocity is the basis of any *limitation* to contracting state awards. The Indian Act could be construed to permit similar orders to be made, though the intention appears to be to use gazetting to notify only Convention territories.[7]

The Convention also applies to arbitral awards not considered as domestic awards by the state where enforcement is sought and by implication covers such awards even when made in that state.[8] A reservation restricting the application of the Convention to awards made in other contracting states will in effect exclude these awards too. These cases are expressly withheld from the scheme in Australia, India, New Zealand and the United Kingdom[9] and, on construction, under the Botswana statute.[10] Awards made in dependencies would qualify for enforcement in the metropolitan state, were this exclusion not made.

Ghana, which has no reservation under article I.3, allows enforcement of those awards made in Ghana which are made in pursuance of an arbitration agreement not governed by the law of Ghana.[11] This is a rather unusual definition of a non-domestic award but it is open to a Convention country to adopt its own definition for this purpose.[12] The Indian statute, on the other hand, purports to exclude from the Convention scheme any award 'made on an arbitration agreement governed by the law of India'.[13] This follows the format of the Geneva scheme.[14] Insofar as this requires the Indian courts to refuse enforcement to an award made in another contracting state (as designated under the statute),[15] this appears to be contrary to the Convention. For it is not open to a state to designate as domestic any award made in another state.[16] Article XIV justifies other contracting states refusing enforcement to corresponding awards made in the territory of India, although only the courts in Botswana in the Commonwealth have an appropriate statutory power.[17]

1 This phrase may have been inserted to make clear that the purpose of art I.3 was to secure reciprocal treatment. Alternatively, it may have been introduced to re-emphasise that a contracting state should not obtain benefits from the Convention in excess of its own commitment: art XIV.

2 Botswana: Cap 06:02, s 3(1); India: Act 1961, No 45, s 2(b); New Zealand: Act 1982, No 21, s 2; United Kingdom: Act 1975, s 1(1). Reservations are also contained in instruments of accession in respect of UK dependencies. The UK reservation was entered some five years after accession, when notifying extension to certain other territories (art X). This seems inconsistent with art I.3.

3 A. M. D'Aloiso, (1977) Aus Bus LR 295 at p 305, to the contrary.

4 The Indian legislation is equivocal on this: see below.

5 Act 1974, No 136, s 8(4).

6 Act 1961, No 38, s 36(2). See Legislative Instrument No 261 of 1963 and *Strojexport v Edward Nasser & Co (Motors) Ltd* 1965 ALR Comm 493.

7 Act 1961, No 45, s 2(b).

8 On the history of this provision, see Private International Law Committee Report, pp 22–23. For discussion of awards not considered by the lex fori as domestic because of insufficient connection with the forum, see I. Szasy, (1966) 14 Am Jo Comp Law 658–672; J. D. W. Lew *Applicable Law in International Commercial Arbitration* pp 13–14.

9 Australia: Act 1961, No 136, s 3(1): 'foreign award'; India: Act 1961, No 45, s 2; New Zealand: Act 1982, No 21, s 2: 'Convention award'; United Kingdom: Act 1975, s 7(1): 'Convention award'. Australia has not entered a reservation under art I.3.

10 Cap 06:02, s 3(1): Botswana has entered a reservation.

11 Act 1961, No 38, s 36(1): 'foreign award'. S 35 makes clear that domestic awards are those made pursuant to an agreement governed by the law of Ghana.

12 Art I.1. The distinction drawn in United Kingdom practice is between those made in the United Kingdom and those outside. Private International Law Committee Report, p 21.

13 Act 1961, No 45, s 9(b).

14 Para 7.22 above.

15 Act 1961, No 45, s 2(b) requires notification of the territories to which the Convention applies.

16 Art I.1. Private International Law Committee Report, p 22; Gaja, op cit, I.A.3.

17 Cap 06:02, s 3(3).

(c) *Pre-existing awards*

8.25 The Convention is silent on the question of its application to arbitral awards made before its entry into force in any particular contracting state. The UNCITRAL Report supports the desirability of retroactive application of the Convention as it is essentially of a procedural nature but suggests that the matter should be dealt with in the implementing legislation.[1] The Australian and New Zealand statutes are explicitly applied to pre-existing awards.[2] The Botswana and Ghana legislation applies only in respect of awards made after the commencement of that legislation[3] and the Indian in respect of awards made after the date of her ratification.[4] There is no limitation that the country of the award must have been a Convention or reciprocating country (in cases where that is a requirement) at the time the award was made.

The United Kingdom model, like the Convention, is silent on these matters. After some hesitation, the statute has now been held to apply to awards irrespective of whether published before or after the date when the foreign state in which they were made became a contracting party. It is enough that that state is a contracting party when the enforcement proceedings are commenced in the requested court.[5] It has also been accepted that a pre-existing award which in other respects satisfies the statutory criteria becomes enforceable on the accession to the Convention of the state in which enforcement is requested.[6] This construction is surely consistent with the aims of the Convention which was designed to improve enforcement facilities. It also ensures that an award initially enforceable under the Geneva scheme will continue to be enforceable, if all conditions are fulfilled under the New York Convention, despite the displacement of the former by the latter scheme.[7]

1 UNCITRAL Report, paras 12–14.
2 Australia: Act 1974, No 136, s 14; New Zealand: Act 1982, No 21, s 11.
3 Botswana: Cap 06:02, s 3(1); Ghana: Act 1961, No 38, s 36 and *Strojexport v Edward Nasser & Co Motors Ltd* 1965 ALR Comm 493.
4 Act 1961, No 45, s 2.
5 *Kuwait Minister of Public Works v Sir Frederick Snow & Partners* [1984] 1 All ER 733, [1984] 2 WLR 340, HL.
6 Ibid, [1983] 2 All ER 754, CA at 760, per Kerr LJ.
7 Ibid, [1984] 1 All ER 733, HL at 739, per Lord Brandon. Cf art VII.2; Act 1975, s 2.

(d) *Awards which have become enforceable as a judgment*

8.26 An award may be subjected to legal proceedings in the place where it was made. For example, it may be made enforceable by entry as a judgment after leave has been given, or an action on the award may be successfully brought. It has been argued that the Convention should apply to these awards, notwithstanding the existence of the judgment.[1] To hold otherwise would be to deprive the beneficiary of the relatively clear and straightforward arrangements in the Convention scheme and require him instead to follow the available procedures for judgment enforcement (which in some instances may require an action on the judgment). The Convention was designed to run side by side with other enforcement facilities[2] and in principle it should remain open to the beneficiary to choose whichever course appears best to suit his interest.

There is little doubt that this is the case where the legal proceedings in the country of origin are designed to give the award domestic enforceability[3] in the law of that jurisdiction. But where those legal proceedings are taken upon the award as a cause of action and a judgment is obtained thereon, the award may be treated as merged into the judgment not only in domestic law[4] but by the private international law of the requested state. It has already been suggested that the trend of the common law may be in the direction set by the recent Civil Jurisdiction and Judgments Act 1982, s 34, and that proceedings in relation to the award itself may be contemplated only if the judgment upon it cannot be registered or otherwise recognised.[5]

Moreover, in cases where the award has become enforceable in the same manner as a judgment, as by the leave of a judge, jurisdictions with the 1933 Act may face the proposition that, by virtue of section 6 of that Act, registration must be used, rather than enforcement under the Convention. This is further discussed in paragraph 8.38 below.

1 Gaja, op cit, I.C.4; C. E. Costa and J. J. Limmerer, (1976) 8 Law, Policy and International Business 737 at pp 757ff.

2 Art VII.1.
3 *Union Nationale des Coopératives Agricoles de Céréales v Robert Catterall & Co Ltd* [1959] 2 QB 44, [1959] 1 All ER 721.
4 At common law, a domestic award which is subject to a local judgment is treated as merged into that judgment: Russell, op cit, p 368, referring to *L Oppenheim & Co v Mohomed Haneef* [1922] 1 AC 482 at 488 where the Privy Council appears to have acknowledged this point.
5 Para 6.31 above.

V ENFORCEMENT PROCEEDINGS

Requirements for enforcement

8.27 The party seeking to enforce an award has the burden of proving it before the court to which he applies. This he must do by supplying, at the time of making his application, formal evidence of the award, as prescribed in the Convention:

(a) the duly authenticated original award or a duly certified copy of it; and
(b) the original arbitration agreement or a duly certified copy of it.[1]

If any of the documents is not in the official language of the enforcing state, the applicant must produce a certified translation.[2]

The implementing legislation reproduces these requirements in most cases without significant deviation.[3] The Ghana Act, however, requires authentication in the manner required by the law of the place of the award.[4] This appears to have been carried over from the Geneva scheme and is not what was intended.[5] The Australian Act specifically lays down local requirements for what constitutes due authentication and certification[6] and makes provision, as does the New Zealand Act, for documents to be received as prima facie evidence of the matters to which they relate.[7] The latter provisions are in line with the aim of the Convention in reducing the onus of proof which is placed upon the applicant. In the other jurisdictions, it will be for the enforcing court to determine that the documents are duly authenticated or certified. The court may, it is suggested, apply the lex fori for that purpose. It is not necessary to produce documentary evidence that the conditions of enforceability have been met, as was the case under the Geneva scheme.[8]

It may also be suggested that the applicant can be required to establish that the award is 'a Convention award' if the matter is put in issue or, where such a restriction is imposed, that the award is of a commercial nature.

Once the applicant has fulfilled these formal requirements, the obligation under the Convention is to recognise the award as binding and to enforce it in accordance with the rules of the forum,[9] unless the party against whom the award will be enforced or the court itself raises an effective objection. In such circumstances, the court has a discretion to treat the award as unenforceable. The grounds upon which an objection can be sustained are those prescribed by the Convention.[10]

The implementing legislation closely follows the Convention in these matters too, although some modifications have been enacted.[11] The New Zealand Act declares that an award *shall* not be enforceable if the party against whom it is sought to enforce the award establishes one of his grounds of objection but, in practice, the discretion in other statutes is more apparent than real. The United Kingdom model is alone in providing what was always intended, that the grounds for refusal stated in the Convention constitute an exclusive list.[12]

1 Art IV.1.
2 Art IV.2. Certification may be by 'an official or sworn translator or by a diplomatic or consular agent'. The Australian Act (1974, No 136, s 9(4)) and the New Zealand Act (1982, No 21, s 6(2)) require the diplomatic or consular agent of the country where the award is made. In other cases, it will be open to the enforcing court to recognise other diplomatic or consular agents who may be competent.
3 Australia: Act 1974, No 136, s 9(1) and (3); Ghana: Act 1961, No 38, s 38; India: Act 1961, No 45, s 8; New Zealand: Act 1982, No 21, s 6(1) and (2); United Kingdom: Act 1975, s 4.
4 Act 1961, No 38, s 38: the agreement may also be authenticated in such other manner as may be sufficient according to the law of Ghana.
5 The Geneva scheme requires authentication according to the lex loci arbitri.
6 Act 1974, No 136, s 9(2). The requirement is satisfied if the authentication or certification purports to have been done by the arbitrator or officer of the tribunal, unless the contrary is shown. Other forms may be accepted by the court when satisfied by them.
7 Ibid, s 9(5); New Zealand: Act 1982, No 21, s 6(3).
8 Para 7.23 above.
9 Art III.
10 Arts IV and V.
11 Australia: Act 1974, No 136, s 8; Ghana: Act 1961, No 38, ss 37 and 39 (adopting arts IV and V); India: Act 1961, No 45, ss 6 and 7; New Zealand: Act 1982, No 21, ss 5 and 7; United Kingdom: Act 1975, ss 3 and 5. Botswana and Cyprus rely upon the Convention itself.
12 Act 1975, s 5(1).

Proceedings in respect of enforceable awards

8.28 The Convention imposes an obligation to recognise awards and to enforce them in accordance with the rules of procedure of the forum. No standard mechanism is required, although there is a duty in every case not to impose discriminatory conditions, fees or charges.[1]

The implementing statutes provide a little differently in this respect but to the same effect. Thus Australia and Botswana merely provide that such proceedings may be taken as are available in respect of a locally made award.[2] Ghana, New Zealand and the United Kingdom specifically provide for enforcement by action which, presumably, allows Order 14 summary judgments to be sought, or by the method provided for the Arbitration legislation, that is by leave of the court in the same manner as a judgment or order to the same effect.[3] In the latter case, judgment may be then entered in terms of the award.[4] India, after providing that awards will be enforceable as if made on a matter referred to arbitration in India, requires all proceedings to be commenced by an application to file the award, which the court may order if satisfied that the award is enforceable. A judgment will then be pronounced according to the award and a decree, providing for the method of enforcement, follows.[5] As was discussed in the context of the Geneva scheme,[6] a requested court in which leave may be granted for summary enforcement may insist upon proceedings by way of an action if there are real grounds for doubting the validity of the award or that the conditions for enforcement are fulfilled or if the entry of a judgment would not be to the same effect as the award.[7]

It may be expected that parties resident abroad without assets in the jurisdiction will be required to give security for costs when initiating proceedings.[8] Unless the lex fori prohibits, the court may order payment in a foreign currency in which the award was made or by conversion into local currency at the rate prevailing at the date of the award.[9] The award does not become a domestic award as a result of these procedures. Enforcement processes, however, must be initiated within the time limits prescribed by the lex fori. Under English law, for example, an application for leave to enforce an award as if it were a judgment must be made within six years of the failure of the defendant to honour the award, as, impliedly, he is required to do by the terms of his agreement.[10]

Explicit provision is usually made to require enforceable awards to be treated as binding upon the parties and that such an award may be relied upon by way of defence, set off or otherwise in any legal proceedings in the forum.[11] In such a case, the conditions of enforceability will have to be established by the party seeking to rely upon the award and the grounds of objection may be raised by any party wishing to dispute its recognition.

1 Art III.
2 Australia: Act 1974, No 136, s 8(2); Botswana: Cap 06:02, s 3(1). Cyprus makes no provision in Law 1979, No 84.
3 Ghana: Act 1961, No 38, s 37(1); New Zealand: Act 1982, No 21, s 5(1). United Kingdom: Act 1975, s 3(2). Some variations may be found amongst those systems adopting the UK model.
4 Judgments may not always be necessary since once given the award can be enforced by ordinary means of execution. It may be needed to issue a bankruptcy notice: *Re A Bankruptcy Notice* [1907] 1 KB 478; *Re Hayek* (1957) 19 ABC 1. Costs ordered by the arbitrator and comprised in the award will be enforceable: *Bank Meilat v Helliniki Techniki SA* [1984] QB 291, [1983] 3 All ER 428.
5 Act 1961, No 45, ss 4–6. *Satish Kumar v Surinder Kumar* AIR 1970 SC 833.
6 Para 7.31 above.
7 Cf *Hudson Strumpffabrik GmbH v Bentley Engineering Co Ltd* [1962] 2 QB 587, [1962] 3 All ER 460.
8 *Dalmia Cement v National Bank of Pakistan* [1975] 1 QB 9, [1974] 3 All ER 689.
9 *Jugoslavenska Oceanska Providba v Castle Investment Co Inc* [1974] QB 292, [1973] 3 All ER 498; *SEAS of Paris v Stockholms Rederiaktiebolag SVEA of Stockholm* [1979] AC 685; *Oil and Natural Gas Commission, Dehradun UP v Forasol* AIR 1982 Delhi 184.
10 *Agromet Motimport v Maulden Engineering Company (Beds) Ltd* (1984) Times, 17 April, applying the Limitation Act 1980, s 7. Cf for India, para 7.30, note 7, above.
11 Australia: Act 1974, No 136, s 8(1); Ghana: Act 1961, No 38, s 37(2); India: Act 1961, No 45, s 4(2); New Zealand: Act 1982, No 21, s 5(2); United Kingdom: Act 1975, s 3(2).

VI GROUNDS OF OBJECTION TO ENFORCEMENT

8.29 The Convention identifies eight grounds upon which the person against whom the award was made may resist enforcement. These are substantially reproduced in the Commonwealth statutes. When raised by the award debtor, the burden of proving that the ground is fulfilled will rest upon him. In addition, however, the last two grounds may be raised by the requested court of its own motion.[1] In such a case, the applicant is likely to be called upon to satisfy the court that the award is one to which enforcement should be granted.[2]

Although the grounds are expressed in discretionary terms, in practice enforcement is almost certain to be refused when the terms are fulfilled.

1 Art V.1 and 2.
2 This is particularly the case where the court needs to be satisfied that the award was in respect of a matter capable of settlement by arbitration, as this is one of the elements intrinsic to an award within the scheme, which the applicant has to establish: paras 8.22 above and 8.36 below.

Objection 1: A party to the arbitration agreement was (under the law applicable to him) under some incapacity[1]

8.30 Although the Convention and the Indian statute speak of the incapacity of the parties, it is clear that, as the Australian, New Zealand and United Kingdom legislation has it, that incapacity of any party suffices. The Australian and New Zealand provisions usefully make clear what must have been intended that the date at which incapacity is relevant is the date at which the agreement was made, rather than when the award was made or the enforcement sought.

The clear purpose of this objection, as of the next, is that an award which derives from a defective agreement should not be enforced. This is determined under 'the law applicable' to the incapacitated party, which it is suggested will be determined in accordance with the conflict of laws rules of the state where enforcement is sought.[2]

1 Art V.1(a) which is applied by reference in Botswana, Cyprus and Ghana. Australia: Act 1974, No 136, s 8(5)(a); India: Act 1961, No 45, s 7(1)(a)(i); New Zealand: Act 1982, No 21, s 7(1)(a); United Kingdom: Act 1975, s 5(2)(a).

2 Private International Law Committee Report, p 30. The English law on the matter can hardly be said to be settled: Cheshire, op cit, pp 221–223; Dicey and Morris, op cit, pp 778–783. Semble the law of the country with which the contract is most substantially connected applies.

Objection 2: The agreement under which the award was made is not valid[1]

8.31 The choice of law rules to determine questions of validity are pointed to in the Convention. The law to be applied is that to which the parties have subjected the agreement or, failing any indication on the matter, the law of the country where the award was made. The compromise is said to have affirmed 'the principle that the agreement was subject to law and that the choice should be determined by applying the conflict rules of the enforcing country'.[2]

The Convention terminology is varied by legislation in two instances. The Australian and New Zealand statutes require reference to 'the law expressed in the agreement to be applicable to it'. If there is none so expressed, then the lex loci arbitri, as in other statutes, applies. This might be thought to deviate from the original Convention language which appears to permit the courts to *infer* the choice of law from the terms of the contract. The subsidiary Convention rule is clearly intended to apply where the parties' intentions are not capable of being determined. In that respect, the requirement in favour of the law of the place of arbitration is consistent with common law practice.[3]

The requirement to apply the clear choice of the parties appears to be categoric, leaving no room to the enforcing court to apply another law, even where their choice appears capricious and lacks any genuine basis or is designed to avoid some mandatory provision of law which would otherwise apply.[4] It is probable that refusal of enforcement could be justified in these circumstances under the public policy head.[5] It should perhaps be re-emphasised that the agreement must also meet the formal Convention requirements set in article II. Thus an agreement which is not a written agreement in the eyes of the enforcing court does not pass the first hurdle.[6]

1 Art V(1)(a), which is applied by reference in Botswana, Cyprus and Ghana. Australia: Act 1974, No 136, s 8(5)(b); India: Act 1961, No 45, s 7(1)(a)(i); New Zealand: Act 1982, No 21, s 7(1)(b); United Kingdom: Act 1975, s 5(2)(b).

2 Private International Law Committee Report, p 30.

3 Ibid; Dicey and Morris, op cit, pp 761–762. See *Compagnie d'Armement Maritime SA v Compagnie Tunisienne de Navigation SA* [1971] AC 572 which makes clear that the choice of place of arbitration is a strong indicator, not an invariable choice, of the law of that place.

4 Under the common law, the courts are unlikely to give effect to such a choice: Dicey and Morris, op cit, pp 755–756.

5 Para 8.37 below.

6 Para 8.05, above. UNCITRAL Report, paras 19–26, examines a series of non-Commonwealth decisions in which this requirement has been discussed.

Objection 3: The party was not given proper notice of the appointment of the arbitrator or of the arbitration proceedings or was otherwise unable to present his case[1]

8.32 As other schemes, the Convention seeks to prevent enforcement of an award made in violation of the principles of due process. The implementing statutes follow its terms without significant variation. Both are silent upon the law to be applied to determine whether a violation has occurred. This lacuna, it has been argued, was deliberate in order that an international standard in very general terms was created leaving the enforcing court a wide discretion to decide on the particular factual circumstances.[2] It seems probable, however, that where occasion to apply legal factors arises, Commonwealth courts will apply the lex fori which generally governs public policy matters such as this.

Procedural questions relating to notice, however, are likely to be determined by reference to the agreed arbitration processes. What is 'proper' may well be the subject of explicit provision.[3] Where the processes have not been agreed, reference will presumably be made to the law governing the arbitration.[4] If those legal requirements are also fulfilled in respect of notifying the appointment of the arbitrator or the proceedings to the party in question, it seems unlikely that want of 'proper notice' will be readily established. Moreover, it is unlikely that Commonwealth courts will be easily persuaded that a procedure freely agreed to or chosen by the parties will be improper in this respect. The fault will normally be one of failure to comply with the agreed processes.

Whether the defendant was unable to present his case will normally be a question of fact. Only those obstructions experienced by a party which prevent the arbitrator determining the nature of the case which the party wishes to advance are likely to be caught. There is little doubt, however, that this ground allows a party to assert that he has not had an adequate opportunity to be heard, particularly if the arbitrator has shown partiality in his treatment of that party. On the other hand, compliance with processes for the hearing resulting from the deliberate choice of the parties of a set of rules will normally be enough. It seems also that this objection may be invoked to cover cases where participation was prevented by force majeure and the like.[5]

1 Art V.1(b) which is applied by reference in Botswana, Cyprus and Ghana. Australia: Act 1974, No 136, s 8(5)(c); India: Act 1961, No 45, s 7(1)(a)(ii); New Zealand: Act 1982, No 21, s 7(1)(c); United Kingdom: Act 1975, s 5(2)(c).
2 Gaja, op cit, I.C.4.
3 D. R. Thomas, [1981] 1 LMCLQ 17 at p 35.
4 Ibid. The law governing the arbitration is likely to be the law chosen by the parties or, if no choice can be discovered, the law of the place of arbitration para 8.34 below.
5 L. V. Quigley, (1961) 70 Yale LJ 1049 at p 1067.

Objection 4: The award deals with a difference not contemplated by, or not falling within the terms of, the submission to arbitration or contains decisions on matters beyond the scope of the submission[1]

8.33 The implementing statutes follow the Convention with no variation of substance, with the exception of the Indian Act. This restates the ground as related to any award which 'deals with questions not required or contains decisions on matters beyond the scope of the *agreement*'.[2] In using 'agreement' rather than 'submission', the draftsman of the Act appears to have been aware that the Convention is not using 'submission' in the limited, practical sense of the actual reference of a particular dispute to a particular arbitral body which it has acquired in common law jurisdictions. It is clearly intended to deal also with cases in which the arbitrators exceed their jurisdiction as defined by the original agreement. This distinction is not universally made and, in the case of the Geneva Convention, similar terminology has given rise to confusion.[3] There seems little doubt that the term 'submission' is used in the New York Convention in the same way as under the Arbitration Act 1889[4] to cover both circumstances.[5] If this is the case, the Indian re-wording in excluding actual references to arbitrators is altogether too narrow to fulfil the Convention requirements.

The purpose of the ground, therefore, is to prevent enforcement of awards where (a) the arbitrators dealt with a difference which was not covered by the terms of the original agreement or, if it was, was not covered by the terms of the actual reference; and (b) the arbitrators have included in the award a decision on a matter which was not within the scope of the original agreement or if it was, was not within the scope of the actual reference. It may be necessary under this ground to determine, by construction, the intended limits of the agreement or reference or indeed the extent to which the arbitrators may determine their own jurisdiction.[6] No guidance is given as to determining the choice of law for this purpose. Presumably, the court will apply its conflict of laws rules governing questions of construction which, at common law, will be the proper law.[7]

The Convention takes account of the possibility that the award may not be wholly defective by allowing decisions on matters which are within the arbitrator's authority to stand where they can be separated from those which are in excess of that authority. The implementing legislation provides similarly.[8]

1 Art V.1(c) which is applied by reference in Botswana, Cyprus and Ghana. Australia: Act 1974, No 136, s 8(5)(d) and 8(6); New Zealand: Act 1982, No 21, s 7(1)(d) and 7(4); United Kingdom: Act 1975, s 5(2)(d) and 5(4).
2 Act 1961, No 45, s 7(a)(iii), italics supplied.
3 Para 7.16 above.
4 S 27. By contrast, the more recent legislation uses 'arbitration agreement' instead of 'submission': Arbitration Act 1950 (UK), s 32. Russell, op cit, p 44.
5 See *The Merak* [1965] P 223 at 235–239, per Scarman J (in the context of the Geneva Scheme).
6 See *Dalmia Dairy Industries Ltd v National Bank of Pakistan* [1978] 2 Lloyd's Rep 223.
7 Dicey and Morris, op cit, pp 808–810, rule 150.
8 See notes 1 and 2 above. This is not the case at common law: Russell, op cit, pp 427–430.

Objection 5: The composition of the arbitral authority or the arbitral procedure was not in accordance with the agreement of the parties or, failing such agreement, was not in accordance with the law of the country where the arbitration took place[1]

8.34 The implementing legislation adopts the exact language of this ground of objection. It is an important purpose of this ground to give recognition, to a high degree, to party autonomy in determining the way in which the arbitration will be conducted. Indeed, this is said to be a considerable advance upon the equivalent provisions in the Geneva scheme.[2] It is only where the parties fail to agree upon the make-up of the arbitral body or the procedure to be followed that the applicable law is indicated. What is not completely clear, however, is whether the parties have complete autonomy in their choice of procedural rules. Some commentators draw support for complete autonomy both from a literal view of the paragraph itself and from the travaux préparatoires.[3] On this view, the parties may agree to the making of awards by procedures completely independent of national laws.[4] A more convincing case, however, can be made that, since the agreement must be valid under some system of law,[5] the arbitration procedures also are intended to be subject to law.[6] Thus the party automony lies in the freedom to choose any system of law and, if the parties wish, in the selection of procedural rules insofar as they are consistent with that law.[7]

It is only if the parties do not choose a law to govern arbitral procedure that the law of the place of arbitration will apply against which any procedural rules selected must be measured. A requested court retains a safeguard in its power to refuse enforcement which would be contrary to public policy on account of a substantial deviation from natural justice in the procedures adopted.[8]

The further problem may arise in some situations in determining the country where the arbitration took place for the purpose of determining the applicable law. It seems likely that, where proceedings have been conducted in several countries, only one system of law should be relevant to determine questions of procedural conformity.[9] In such cases, the law of the country where the award was in the end made seems to be the most appropriate. This is consistent with explicit reference to that law elsewhere in this article.[10]

1 Art V.1(d), which is applied by references in Botswana, Cyprus and Ghana. Australia: Act 1974, No 136, s 8(5)(e); India: Act 1961, No 45, s 7(a)(iv); New Zealand: Act 1982, No 21, s 7(1)(e); United Kingdom: Act 1975, s 5(2)(e).
2 M. Quilling, (1981) 11 Georgia J Int & Comp Law 635 at p 647. For Geneva provisions, see para 7.26 above.
3 Gaja, op cit, I.C.3 for discussion of competing views. The UNCITRAL Report states that reported cases (outside the Commonwealth) indicate that the parties' wishes are limited only by the public policy ground: para 8.37 below.
4 An 'international award', said to be a conception of the International Chamber of Commerce: Private International Law Committee Report, p 31.
5 Para 8.31 above.
6 *Report of 60th Conference of the International Law Association,* 1982, pp 281–282 for a discussion of delocalised arbitrations in this context. *Amin Rasheed Shipping Corpn v Kuwait Insurance Co* [1984] AC 50, [1983] 2 All ER 884, HL.
7 Private International Law Committee Report, above: Gaja, loc cit, above. L. V. Quigley, (1961) 70 Yale LJ 1049 at pp 1068–1069.
8 Ibid. See para 8.37 below.
9 Gaja, op cit, I.C.3.
10 Art V.1(a) and V.1(e). *Compagnie St Gobain Pont à Mousson v Fertilizer Corpn of India Ltd* (High Court of Delhi, 1970) (1977) II YB Comm Arb 245.

Objection 6: The award has not yet become binding on the parties or has been set aside or suspended by a competent authority of the country in which, or under the law of which, it was made[1]

8.35 Again the implementing legislation closely follows the terms of the Convention.[2] It avoids any reference to notions of 'finality' of the award found in other schemes: the use of the term 'binding' seems to have been deliberate. It was adopted principally to make clear that the award could be treated as having effect without the need to comply with local enforcement requirements in the country of origin.[3] The term has been stated to mean that 'the award is no longer open to ordinary means of recourse, such as appeals to a court or to a second arbitration instance; extraordinary means of recourse which may lead to setting aside, annulment or suspension are relevant as grounds for refusal only after they have been successful'.[4] In an examination of this provision prior to its enactment in the United Kingdom, the Private International Law Committee took 'binding' to mean much the same as 'final and conclusive' in the judgment enforcement legislation, that is that the matter had become res judicata between the parties.[5] In consequence, an award would not be binding if further recourse may be had to another arbitral tribunal, as on appeal: but 'the fact that recourse may be had to a court of law does not prevent the award from being binding'.[6] Thus as at common law an award will be binding notwithstanding that an appeal to a court is pending or that such an appeal may be intended. The Private International Law Committee were rightly concerned lest the loser should be able to obstruct enforcement by taking any kind of legal proceedings. Such a consideration may persuade Commonwealth courts to apply the common law approach in this context.[7] But this approach is in marked contrast with that favoured by UNCITRAL and it may be questioned whether such a construction is consistent with the Convention. No provision is made for adjourning a case where an appeal is under way, although such a power exists where an application to set aside or suspend has been entered.[8] This suggests that the availability of an appeal was intended to prevent an award being binding.

The court asked to enforce the award will presumably determine whether this condition exists by reference to the law of the state in which it was made or, if different, under the law under which the award was made.[9] If, under either system, the award is subject to an appeal which has not been concluded or the time for its taking has not elapsed, the enforcement should be refused. Arguably, if some further procedure which is mandatory under that law to render the award *effective* between the parties (as distinct from being *enforceable* in a particular jurisdiction) has not been complied with, the award may not be binding.[9]

A second purpose of this objection is to maintain the authority of the courts of a state over arbitral processes which take place in that state or under its law. Accordingly, if any award has been set aside or suspended by a competent court,[10] it should not be enforced in any contracting state. The Convention leaves it to the law of the state where the application for these processes is made to determine the grounds upon which setting aside or suspension can be ordered.

This provision envisages that awards may be set aside by a court of a country under the law of which the award was given. It has been argued that this should arise only in respect of awards made in the requested state itself under a foreign law, where under article I.1, that state has agreed to enforce such awards.[11] Only Ghana in the Commonwealth allows such awards to be enforced. In any case, it may be doubted whether Commonwealth courts are usually vested with these kinds of power over awards made in another jurisdiction, notwithstanding that their law was applied in the making of the award.

Where the proceedings to set aside or to suspend are pending in another state, the receiving court may, in its discretion, adjourn the proceedings.[12] In such a case, the party against whom the award is made may be required to give security until the outcome of the proceedings. There is, however, no duty to adjourn in cases of this kind. Given the restrictions upon the receiving court's power to examine failures in the original arbitration, it seems better practice to adjourn where serious irregularities in the arbitration, such as patent error of law, are to be put in issue and the foreign court applied to has competence to deal with them.

1 Art V.1(e) which is applied by reference in Botswana, Cyprus and Ghana. Australia: Act 1974, No 136, s 8(5)(f) and (8); India: Act 1961, No 45, s 7(1)(a)(v) and (2); New Zealand: Act 1982, No 21, s 7(1)(e) and (3); United Kingdom: Act 1975, s 5(2)(f) and (5).
2 The Australian statute refers to 'the parties to the agreement', words not found in the other legislation.
3 E/CONF 26/SR 17 and 23 (in which some differences of approach are identifiable); Gaja, op cit, I.C.4. There was agreement that a double exequatur (one where the award was made and one where it was to be enforced) should not be necessary for enforcement.
4 UNCITRAL Report, para 41. In relation to setting aside etc, see below.
5 Report, pp 31–32.
6 Ibid, para 14. See also HC Official Report (5th series) cols 629–631 and HC Official Report SCB, 28 January 1975, col 5. On 'two tier' arbitrations, and effect of second tier appeal on the finality of the original award, see *Amalgamated Metal Corpn Ltd v Khoon Seng Co* [1977] 2 Lloyd's Rep 310, HL.
7 Ibid.
8 Art V.1, which is implemented in similar terms by the Commonwealth legislation: see note 1.
9 Private International Law Committee Report, p 32; T. V. Firth, (1970) Arb Jo 1–22. But see below, text to note 11 for a possible limitation in respect of the law under which the award was made.
10 The legislation refers to 'competent tribunal'. It will be for the law in the place of the award or under which the award was made to determine which bodies are competent tribunals.
11 Gaja, op cit, I.C.4.
12 Art VI and references in note 1.

Objection 7: The subject matter of the difference is not capable of arbitration under the law of the country where enforcement is sought.[1]

8.36 This ground appears in the Commonwealth legislation with minor variations. The United Kingdom model, for example, omits any reference to the law to be referred to but there can be little doubt that the lex fori would be applied, as the matter is clearly provided for in the Convention.[2]

The purpose of this ground is to preclude the requested court from having to enforce an award in relation to a matter which could not have been dealt with by arbitration in its jurisdiction. The analogies with the public policy objection are clear.[3] It appears that there is a recognisable trend to interpret this ground narrowly,[4] although no Commonwealth cases have been discovered to bear this out. Arguably, the discretion in respect of this ground which the court enjoys will allow it to recognise certain awards which were quite properly dealt with under the governing law, even though domestic transactions of a similar kind would not occur.[5] It is, however, difficult to advance illustrations of when that is likely to ensue. The court may insist upon proof that the equivalent domestic arbitration is of a kind prohibited by the lex fori or that the subject matter would involve an illegality under that law, rather than that an equivalent arbitration could not have been brought in the forum.[6] In this respect, its practical effect may be even more limited than the equivalent provisions in the Geneva scheme.[7]

1 Art V.2(a) which is applied by reference in Botswana, Cyprus and Ghana. Australia: Act 1974, No 136, s 8(7)(a); India: Act 1961, No 45, 7(1)(b)(i); New Zealand: Act 1982, No 21, s 7(2)(a); United Kingdom: Act 1975, s 5(3).
2 Dicey and Morris, op cit, p 1152; Russell, op cit, p 384, with hesitation: see paras 8.05 and 8.22 above in relation to a similar requirement in respect of the agreement.
3 L. V. Quigley, (1961) 70 Yale LJ 1049 at p 1070; UNCITRAL Report, para 44.
4 UNCITRAL Report, para 45.
5 For the matters which may or may not be referred under English law, see Russell, op cit, ch 3.
6 Russell, op cit, p 384.
7 Para 7.28 above.

Objection 8: The enforcement of the award would be contrary to the public policy of the country where enforcement is sought[1]

8.37 This ground for refusal is found in similar terms in all the Commonwealth legislation. Although no explicit reference is made to the law which regulates the matter, there can be no doubt that it is the lex fori in every case, consistently with universal conflict of laws practice.

A tendency to restraint in applying this head has been noted in international practice.[2] This would be consistent with Commonwealth practice on other enforcement schemes. There is no evidence from any decided cases that this ground is likely to be used in ways which will diminish the effectiveness of the scheme. There is, of course, a countervailing policy in holding parties to their agreements and thus to the outcome of the arbitration.[3]

It is noteworthy that the ground requires the *enforcement* of the award to contravene public policy. Thus, enforcement which would require contravention of local currency or exchange laws or other such controls would be refused. It might be expected also that deliberate attempts to circumvent mandatory provisions of the lex fori would be resisted. Again, enforcement of an award might be refused because it contravened domestic requirements on the matter of sovereign immunity. It would be under this head that any conflict between the award or the way in which the award was obtained and basic standards of morality and justice prevailing under the lex fori would be resolved. Arguably, fraud, bias or corruption on the part of the arbitral tribunal—matters not explicitly dealt with by the Convention—could be asserted under this head notably where the facts have become known only after the award has been made.[4] But it seems probable that only serious procedural shortcomings in the arbitral process constituting breaches of natural justice will be recognised as vitiating enforcement. Minor divergences from the practice prevailing in the country of enforcement should not, it is suggested, be treated as issues involving public policy particularly when the procedure agreed between the parties has been followed.[5] In such matters, it may be appropriate for the party opposing enforcement to be permitted to challenge the award before the courts in the place it was made under the governing law.[6] In this context, an issue recently raised in the United Kingdom may be mentioned.[7] If the arbitration has taken place only after a long delay occasioned by one of the parties in whose favour the award was finally made, may the courts of the country where the award is sought to be relied upon refuse to enforce it, on the grounds that natural justice, which requires a fair process, has been breached? Arguably, if the party challenging the award has failed to take appropriate steps to prevent the arbitration proceeding in the country where it was to take place,[8] this objection should not be sustained. On the other hand, if such facilities were not open to him, the requested court may be prepared to refuse recognition or enforcement if the party's interests had been fundamentally impaired by the delay.

The fact that parties to the award may be nationals of countries at war with each other will not require the conclusion that its enforcement in a third country friendly to both countries would be contrary to the public policy of the third country.[9] The position might be different if the country of enforcement were itself involved in the hostilities or if the enforcement of the award there would confirm a deliberate contravention of the laws of a friendly state.[10]

In general, however, the courts of the Commonwealth appear to have subscribed to the view that it is part of their public policy to ensure as far as possible that arbitration awards are made effective.

1 Art V.2(b) which is applied by reference in Botswana, Cyprus and Ghana. Australia: Act 1974, No 136, s 8(7)(b); India: Act 1961, No 45, s 7(1)(b)(ii); New Zealand: Act 1982, No 21, s 7(2)(b); United Kingdom, Act 1975, s 5(3).
2 UNCITRAL Report, paras 46–47.
3 J. Goldring, (1976) 15 Col Jo Transnational Law 216 at p 243.
4 Cf *Masinimport v Scottish Mechanical Light Industries Ltd* 1976 SLT 245 at 249, per Lord Keith. Gaja, op cit, I.C.5; Dicey and Morris, op cit, pp 1138–1139.
5 *Dalmia Dairy Industries v National Bank of Pakistan* [1978] 2 Lloyd's Rep 223, CA at 269–270, per Kerr J. In this case refusal to hear oral evidence, in accordance with the ICC rules which applied, was not contrary to natural justice. Cf *Societa Anonmina Lucchesse Olii e Vini Lucca v Gorakharam Gokalchand* AIR 1964 Mad 532.
6 *L Oppenheim & Co v Mahomed Haneef* [1922] 1 AC 482, 91 LJPC 205, PC.
7 *Black-Clawson International Ltd v Papierwerke Waldhof-Aschaffenburg A–G* [1981] 2 Lloyd's Rep 446 at 458, per Mustill J.
8 As under *Bremer Vulkan Schiffbau Und Maschinenfabrik v South India Shipping Corpn* [1981] AC 909, [1981] 1 All ER 289, HL. The same should be the case if an application can be made to review or set aside the award in the country of origin on this ground.
9 *Dalmia Dairy Industries Ltd v National Bank of Pakistan* [1978] 2 Lloyd's Rep 223, CA at 299–301, per Megaw LJ.
10 Cf *Regazzoni v K C Sethia (1944) Ltd* [1958] AC 301, [1957] 3 All ER 286, HL.

VII RELATIONSHIP WITH OTHER SCHEMES

8.38 The Convention makes clear that, with one exception, other schemes of enforcement of awards were not to be affected by its introduction. No one was to be deprived of any right to avail himself of an arbitral award in the manner and to the extent allowed by the law or treaties of any country where enforcement may be sought.[1] The exception required that the Geneva scheme cease to have effect between contracting states on their becoming bound, and to the extent to which they became bound, by the New York Convention.[2]

Those Commonwealth states associated with the Geneva scheme have accordingly provided that the earlier legislation does not apply or is repealed in respect of Convention awards.[3] Ghana has gone further by repealing the earlier legislation altogether.[4] In addition, the statutes normally preserve any rights which may exist under other parts of the lex fori for enforcing foreign awards.[5] As a result, actions upon foreign awards at common law,[6] or upon a foreign judgment based upon the award,[7] proceedings for leave to enforce under the summary enforcement provisions, where such are allowed,[8] and, where applicable, applications under the judgments schemes where the award has become enforceable as a judgment or where it has been the subject of a judgment[9] are available alternatives. Few reported decisions are to be found in relation to enforcement of foreign awards under these procedures. The conditions which must be fulfilled are therefore somewhat uncertain. It is arguable, however, that the New York scheme offers a more straightforward process of enforcement, with less inherent uncertainty as to the extent to which objections to enforcement may succeed.[10]

In almost all the countries or territories with the Convention legislation, there is also in force a statute modelled upon the United Kingdom Foreign Judgments (Reciprocal Enforcement) Act 1933.[11] Section 6 of that Act provides that registration thereunder is the only enforcement proceeding which may be brought in the courts for the recovery of a sum payable under a foreign judgment capable of registration under that Act. Thus it appears that any award which has become enforceable in the same manner as a judgment or which has been made the subject of a judgment in a reciprocating country must be enforced under that Act. There is a clear possibility that a Convention award in respect of which the appropriate steps have been taken in the courts of the country where it was made will also satisfy the criteria under the 1933 Act. Does this mean that enforcement under the Convention scheme will be refused? The New Zealand Convention statute puts the question beyond doubt by providing that proceedings under the Convention legislation may be brought notwithstanding the former restriction.[12] In the United Kingdom, the Foreign Judgments (Reciprocal Enforcement) Act 1933 has been amended to exclude awards from the requirement.[13] In other cases, the point has not yet been taken. It can be argued, however, that the courts should give priority to the international obligations to which the legislation is intended to give domestic effect. In so far as the later Act is inconsistent with an earlier statute as a result of those obligations (which are contained in the Convention often scheduled to it), it should prevail. If, however, the award has not become enforceable as a judgment, the Convention scheme is unaffected by the judgment legislation. Neither requirement precludes an action upon the original cause of action if it has not become merged in the foreign award under the law governing the arbitration.[14]

1 Art VII.1.
2 Art VII.2.
3 India: Act 1961, No 45, s 10; New Zealand: Act 1982, No 21, s 10; United Kingdom: Act 1975, s 2.
4 Act 1961, No 38, s 43.
5 Australia: Act 1974, No 136, s 12(2); Ghana: Act 1961, No 38, s 41; India: Act 1961, No 45, s 9(1); New Zealand: Act 1982, No 21, s 8; United Kingdom: Act 1975, s 6.
6 *Bremer Oeltransport GmbH v Drewry* [1933] 1 KB 753, 102 LJKB 753; *Badat & Co Bombay v East India Trading Co* 1964 AIR SC 538. This is the more usual procedure: Russell, op cit, p 377.
7 *East India Trading Co Inc v Carmel Exporters and Importers Ltd* [1952] 2 QB 439, [1952] 1 All ER 1053; *International Alltex Corpn v Lawler Creations Ltd* [1965] IR 264.
8 *Dalmia Cement Ltd v National Bank of Pakistan* [1974] QB 9, [1974] 3 All ER 189; but see contra, *Mauritius Steam Navigation Co Ltd v International Shipping Lines Ltd* 1969 (3) ALR Comm 34 (Nigeria).
9 Chapter 6 above.
10 Russell, op cit, p 385.
11 In respect of Commonwealth jurisdictions to which the New York scheme has been applied, exclusive provisions of this kind are found in the legislation of all the Australian states and territories, except South Australia and Cocos (Keeling) Islands, of Barbados, Belize, Botswana, Cyprus, Ghana and the United Kingdom and of the following UK dependencies: Bermuda, Cayman Islands, Gibraltar, Hong Kong, Isle of Man, Guernsey and Jersey. For legislation, see Annex III to Chapter 2 above.
12 Act 1982, No 21, s 9.
13 S 10A inserted by Civil Jurisdiction and Judgments Act 1982, Sch 10.
14 Paras 6.32 and 8.26 above.

ANNEX I

States Party to the New York Convention

Principal source: United Nation multilateral treaties deposited with the Secretary-General as at 31 December 1982 ST/LEG/SER.E.2.

*Australia** (1975)
Austria
Belgium
Benin
Botswana (1971)
Bulgaria
Byelorussian SSR
Central African Republic
Chile
Colombia
Cuba
Cyprus (1980)
Czechoslovakia
Denmark
Djibouti
Ecuador
Egypt
Finland
France*
Federal Republic of Germany
German Democratic Republic
Ghana (1968)
Greece
Holy See
Hungary
India (1960)
Indonesia
Ireland
Israel
Italy
Japan
Jordan
Democratic Kampuchea
Republic of Korea
Kuwait
Madagascar
Mexico
Monaco
Morocco
Netherlands*
New Zealand (1983)
Niger
Nigeria (1970)
Norway
Philippines
Poland
Romania
San Marino
South Africa
Spain
Sri Lanka (1962)
Sweden
Switzerland
Syrian Arab Republic
Thailand
Trinidad and Tobago (1966)
Tunisia
Ukrainian SSR
Union of Soviet Socialist Republics
*United Kingdom** (1975)
United Republic of Tanzania (1964)
United States of America*
Uruguay
Yugoslavia

* Extended to certain dependencies. Commonwealth states are in italics with date of accession. Barbados, although having legislation in force, has not yet formally acceded.

ANNEX II

Extensions to Dependencies of Commonwealth States

The following jurisdictions were brought within the Convention by Australia and the United Kingdom.

Australia

Australian Antarctic Territory (1975)
Christmas Island (1975)
Cocos (Keeling) Islands (1975)
Norfolk Island (1975)

United Kingdom

Alderney[2]
Belize (1981)[1]
Bermuda (1980)
British Virgin Islands[2]
Cayman Islands (1981)
Gibraltar (1980)
Guernsey[2]
Hong Kong (1980)
Isle of Man (1980)

1 Now independent.
2 No extension order has been made, though local legislation exists.

ANNEX III

Commonwealth Legislation

Alderney:	Arbitration (Alderney) Law, 1983, No XIII, Part III.
Australia:	Arbitration (Foreign Awards and Agreements) Act 1974, No 136.
Barbados:	Foreign Arbitral Awards Act 1980, No 19.
Belize:	Arbitration (Amendment) Ordinance 1980, No 21.
Bermuda:	Arbitration (Foreign Awards) Act 1976, No 1.
Botswana:	Recognition and Enforcement of Foreign Arbitral Awards Act, Revised Laws, 1965, cap 06:02.
British Virgin Islands:	Arbitration Ordinance 1976, No 7, s 62 and Part IX (ss 33–37).
Cayman Islands:	Foreign Arbitral Awards Enforcement Law 1975, No 30.
Cyprus:	Convention on the Recognition and Enforcement of Foreign Arbitral Awards (Ratification) Law 1979, No 84.
Ghana:	Arbitration Act 1961, No 38, Part III.
Gibraltar:	Arbitration (1958 New York Convention) Ordinance 1974, No 17.
Guernsey:	Arbitration (Guernsey) Law 1982, Part III.
Hong Kong:	Arbitration Ordinance, Revised Laws, 1982, Cap 341, s 6A and Part IV (ss 41–46).
India:	Foreign Awards (Recognition and Enforcement) Act 1961, No 45 (amended Act 1973, No 47).
Isle of Man:	Arbitration Act 1976, s 5 and Part III (ss 37–40).
New Zealand:	Arbitration (Foreign Agreements and Awards) Act 1982, No 21.
United Kingdom:	Arbitration Act 1975, c 3.

Although Nigeria, Sri Lanka and Trinidad and Tobago and the United Republic of Tanzania are parties to the Convention no implementing legislation has been enacted.

Index

References are to chapter and paragraph numbers. 'A' references (e.g. 2.AII) are to chapter and annex.